The magnificent lady of a war-torn sea

THE BIG 'E'

Here is the whole incredible story, from her beginnings in a troubled time of peace to her courageous exploits in battle—told by a man who knows naval warfare firsthand and who brings to his exciting account the skills of a researcher and the passion of a natural-born yarn spinner.

THE BIG E

The Story of the
USS Enterprise

Commander
Edward P. Stafford, U.S.N.

Foreword by
Admiral Arthur W. Radford, U.S.N.
(Ret.)

BALLANTINE BOOKS • NEW YORK

Library of Congress Catalog Card Number: 62-17168

ISBN 0-345-31504-9

This edition published by arrangement with Random House, Inc.

Manufactured in the United States of America

First Ballantine Books Edition: January 1974
Fourth Printing: February 1984

CONTENTS

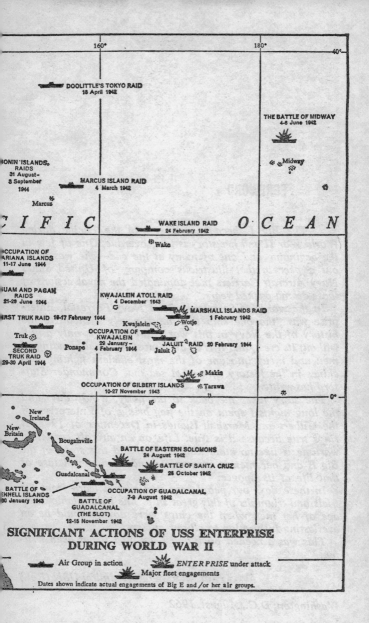

160°   180°   40°

DOOLITTLE'S TOKYO RAID
18 April 1942

THE BATTLE OF MIDWAY
4–6 June 1942

BONIN ISLANDS
RAIDS
31 August–
3 September
1944

Midway

MARCUS ISLAND RAID
4 March 1942

Marcus

C I F I C   O C E A N

WAKE ISLAND RAID
24 February 1942

Wake

OCCUPATION OF
MARIANA ISLANDS
11–17 June 1944

GUAM AND PAGAN
RAIDS
21–29 June 1944

KWAJALEIN ATOLL RAID
4 December 1943

FIRST TRUK RAID 16–17 February 1944

MARSHALL ISLANDS RAID
1 February 1942

Wotje

Kwajalein

Truk

OCCUPATION OF
KWAJALEIN
29 January–
4 February 1944

Ponape

JALUIT RAID 20 February 1944

SECOND
TRUK RAID
29–30 April 1944

Jaluit

Makin

OCCUPATION OF GILBERT ISLANDS
10–27 November 1943

Tarawa

0°

New
Ireland

New
Britain

Bougainville

BATTLE OF EASTERN SOLOMONS
24 August 1942

BATTLE OF SANTA CRUZ
26 October 1942

Guadalcanal

BATTLE OF
RENNELL ISLANDS
30 January 1943

OCCUPATION OF GUADALCANAL
7–9 August 1942

BATTLE OF
GUADALCANAL
(THE SLOT)
12–15 November 1942

SIGNIFICANT ACTIONS OF USS ENTERPRISE
DURING WORLD WAR II

Air Group in action   *ENTERPRISE* under attack

Major fleet engagements

Dates shown indicate actual engagements of Big E and /or her air groups.

FOREWORD

The Big E became a legend in the Pacific during World War II and her story is long overdue. One of few in the beginning and one of many at the end—she was without a peer in that illustrious company of United States Navy Aircraft Carriers that dominated the naval actions of those drama-packed years.

In the words of Secretary of the Navy Forrestal, Enterprise was "the one ship that most nearly symbolizes the history of the Navy in this war." But a ship is only a hull without its crew, and it is of an almost mystical blending of men and metal into one of the most efficient fighting machines in the history of war at sea that Commander Stafford has written.

The story takes me back to the noisy, windy days and the long nights I spent on the flag bridge of Enterprise off the Gilbert and Marshall Islands in December of 1943. It rings true because it is true. Life on an aircraft carrier in wartime is like no other kind of life, and this story of the Big E and her men is a complete and dramatic picture of that life at its apogee.

In these days our people can and should learn from the trials and triumphs of this great ship. The indomitable courage of her men when the chips were down should be an everlasting inspiration to all our citizens.

This was a needed book and I am glad it has been written.

ARTHUR W. RADFORD, *Admiral USN (Ret.)*

Washington, D.C., August, 1962

BOOK ONE

1 PEACE

In Europe the Second World War was in its third year, but two oceans and a continent to the westward, on the sunny tips of the mid-Pacific mountains, the long habit of peace remained unbroken. The islands lay scattered in the sea as if some boastful Titan had braced his feet at Vladivostok, balled earth and rock together, and hurled at Patagonia. It was a long throw, even for a Titan, yet he might have made it had the missile stayed together. But in the thin air high over the 30th parallel it came apart and fell, the small pieces striking first and the heavy ones carrying farther toward the target. So they lay in the days of the Titans when the earth was new—Midway, Laysan, Maro Reef, the Gardner Pinnacles, French Frigate Shoals, Necker, Nihoa, Kauai, Oahu, Molokai, Maui and Hawaii—in a broken chain from northwest to southeast, dreaming greenly in the sun.

And so they still lay in November of 1941. Over all the islands the trade wind blew white puffs of cumulus and the surf hammered patiently at the black rocks and white beaches. During the afternoons the cumulus built up and darkened, and in the high places the warm rain fell, rattling on the leaves, and the wind blew in sudden violent gusts.

On the leeward side of Oahu, protected by the green ridge of Koolau, forever topped with banks of clouds, Honolulu faced southwest to seaward. To its left was Diamond Head, which looks from the sea like a narrow cape but which is really a round volcanic crater on the shore. Then, nearer, was Waikiki where, with Europe closed, business was better than ever and the big outriggers and the surfboards crowded the breakers and the Kanaka beach boys pretty much took their choice of the lush young flesh that covered the sand in front of the Royal Hawaiian. Then there was the city itself and the Aloha Tower, where the cruise ships still arrived and departed regularly to the ukeleles and the leis, and the factories which process the pineapples can be smelled for miles when the wind is right.

West of the city was the U. S. Army air base at Hickam Field, where the B-18s and the P-40s and a few new B-17s stood in neat rows ringed with sentries; then Pearl Harbor, loaded with gray ships, awnings rigged over the holystoned wood and the young Officers of the Deck erect and military on their quarter-decks with gloves and glass. In the middle of Pearl Harbor, Ford Island lay flat under the concrete of the Naval Air Station; traveling cranes towered at the docksides. A few miles away, in the cane fields beyond Pearl, was the Marine Corps Air Station at Ewa (approximately rhymes with "nevah").

Toward the end of November, 1941, two big ships, among others, got under way from Honolulu.

The *Lurline* sailed from the Aloha Tower for the Coast. Her passengers were necklaced with fragrant leis. On the pier the ukuleles plunked and strummed and a line of hula girls with gardenias at their temples motioned with their graceful hands and swung their grass skirts and dark hair in farewell. Decks and dock were bright with flowered shirts and dresses. From ship and shore the waving and the shouting continued even after the long, hoarse, deafening whistle swamped them as she backed away.

Just a week later the second ship departed. No music, no hula girls, no party. Strictly business. The only colors except gray were in the ensign at her gaff. Nor did she sail from the Aloha Tower, but slipped quietly out of Pearl Harbor, passed Hickam and Fort Kamehameha and through the torpedo nets to sea. There she turned her sharp bow west. This was the United States ship, *Enterprise,* an aircraft carrier, destined in a few terrible years to hold as proud a combat record as any ship of any nation in any war, but now, like her people, young and well trained, but untried.

Eight hundred and twenty-seven feet long, 114 feet wide and displacing 20,000 tons when empty and unarmed, the *Enterprise* was both a warship and an airfield. Steam turbines turning four big bronze propellers gave her better than thirty knots of speed and behind the propellers a single rudder as big as the side of a house swung at a touch from the bridge to provide the maneuverability she needed. Captain and mess cook, pilot and fireman, more than two thousand men lived, and would fight, in her. Like any warship she had guns; long five-inch, dual-purpose rifles to reach out across the surface or far up into the sky, and dozens of smaller caliber automatic weapons for infighting. And she had a new and secret device called radar, whereby, according to those who understood and believed in it, planes, ships and coastal areas could be made out, ranges and bearings accurately measured to them and the enemy found in the blackest darkness or the thickest fog.

Millions of gallons of fuel oil sloshed in her storage tanks and nearly two hundred thousand gallons of high-octane gasoline were ready for her planes. Her magazines were stacked with ammunition for her own guns and bombs, torpedoes and machine-gun cartridges for the aircraft. In her storerooms were all the rags, potatoes, cotter pins, engines, toothpaste and Spam, all the shoes, wrenches, paper and soap to keep her at sea for many weeks. Her generators could light a city, her galleys feed it. On the hangar deck each Sunday the congregations met, and every evening a first-run movie entertained the crew.

But the reason the *Enterprise* existed was the flight deck that covered her from stem to stern and the eighty-odd aircraft which operated from it. The deck was broken only by the "island" amidships on the starboard side, which housed the control centers of the ship. On both bows were catapults, across the after third stretched the cables of the arresting gear, and forward, aft, and amidships a heavy-duty elevator took planes from the flight deck to the cavernous hangar deck below it, crammed with parked aircraft and lined with shops for storage, repair or rearming.

Without her aircraft *Enterprise* was nothing. With them she was a fast, self-sufficient, elusive nest of death and destruction. She could, if the war games had proved anything, slam her load of bombs and torpedoes and machine-gun bullets into an enemy base or fleet at dawn from a couple of hundred miles at sea and by the next dawn do the same thing to another enemy force a thousand miles away. And in the meantime let them try to find her in all that ocean. And if they found her, let them try to get at her through her fighters and her guns. Already, at the age of three, *Enterprise* had a reputation, earned in the strict sweat of peacetime training where the discipline is harsh and quick and the old proven traditions insisted upon. She was known in the fleet as an effective, efficient ship, where somehow things always "clicked," where everyone got along with everyone else, and the job got done and well done. Because "E" stands for *Enterprise* and excellence and the coveted Efficiency award, for which all ships of the fleet compete each year, and because she was young and big-muscled and her crew loved her, they came to call her the Big E, and that is the only nickname that ever really stuck.

As she swung west from Oahu that November morning, the long flight deck, which looked anything but long from the air, was empty. Then in midmorning the sound of planes came from astern and in a few minutes they were circling overhead. It is a sight one never tires of seeing even if it is seen every day, sometimes with the sweat of fear running down the back and sometimes with the old-brass taste of absolute fatigue in the mouth. And this day the neat wedge-shaped formations, blue wings flashing down across the sky and the solid roar of scores of engines could stop the breath with pride and touch the heart.

The planes circled a long time. They had plenty of fuel and Vice Admiral William F. Halsey was interested in getting his task force well under way before taking the air group aboard. They swung in wide left turns at a comfortable altitude and in loose formation to ease the pilots. The eight-inch guns of three heavy cruisers protected *Enterprise* from surface attack and six destroyers fanned out ahead and on both flanks searching for submarines. There were no slow ships.

Shortly before noon brightly colored signal flags streamed out of the flag bags of the *Enterprise* and soared up her halyards. When they had snapped in the wind for a minute or two, they dove smartly out of sight and the long wakes all curved at once until the wind blew straight down the Big E's flight deck.

The circling air group saw the signal and the turn. It descended in tight formations, preparing to land. On a small platform on the portside of the flight deck at the stern, the landing signal officer stood ready to bring them in. He was Hubert B. Harden, a lieutenant, junior grade, and a pilot, and this day he had extra work to do. In addition to the 18 TBD Devastator torpedo bombers of Torpedo Six, the 36 SBD Dauntless dive bombers of Scouting and Bombing Six, and the 18 F4F-3 Wildcats of Fighting Six, there were an extra dozen fighters with Marine markings.

The fighters came in first, stubby Grumman Wildcats with squared-off wing tips. They swept straight up the starboard side in right echelons of four, hooks down, and opposite the bow they began to break. Each plane in its turn banked sharply left and away until it was flying in the opposite direction down the portside of the carrier. As each was well clear, the next blue wing swung abruptly up against the sky and followed until all four were strung out at equal intervals on the reverse of the ship's course. Each pilot, as he broke, dropped his wheels and his landing flaps, and the swift, sleek birds became slow and droning insects with dangling feet.

Bert Harden picked up the planes as they turned left again toward the ship and with positive movements of the paddles in his hands he told the pilots how the approach was progressing. Bert could tell at once (and his paddles instantly relayed the information) whether the plane was too fast or too slow, too high or too low, wings level or not, and finally he decided with either a slash or a flurry of paddles whether the pilot could "cut" and land or be "waved off" to try again.

He waved off only a few this day. One by one the Wildcats plumped down. Their extended hooks engaged arresting cables and they stopped abruptly, throwing the pilot forward against his belt. But another plane was always turning into the groove, coached by the educated paddles of the LSO, and sailors in bright green jerseys sprang out of the catwalks at the edges of the deck to disengage the hook while another in a yellow jersey vigorously signaled each pilot to taxi forward out of the way.

The Dauntless dive bombers and scouting planes came next with their gunners riding backward, canopies open and the twin machine guns angling up and aft; then the ungainly and obsolescent Devastators, each with its crew of three, and its wheels which, even when retracted, protruded well out of the bottom of the wing.

While the last torpedo plane was lumbering up the Big E's wake, the bright flags fluttered again; as it hit the deck they rattled down, and carrier, cruisers and destroyers, as though a single hand controlled all helms, swung back to westward.

To their surprise, the airmen were ordered directly from their planes to their squadron ready rooms. The *Enterprise* air group had come out for a couple of days of exercises. The Marines were to shoot a few refresher landings and return that evening to Ewa. But in their ready rooms, in various stages of sweat-stained flight gear, with helmet pushed up or to the side or hand-held or dangling from some part of the flight suit, with the yellow Mae West life jackets on or off or in between, and carrying plotting boards, toilet kits and light baggage of various kinds, they reunited, back at work after the pleasant but not quite normal time ashore. To most of them it secretly felt good.

Slowly they quieted and sat down until each long room with its rows of deep chairs looked like the interior of a loaded bus.

Each pilot was handed one of the mimeographed sheets. As he read and reread the terse order, the crowded rooms of sweaty young airmen became as still as a convent chapel during retreat. It said:

1. The *Enterprise* is now operating under war conditions.
2. At any time, day or night, we must be ready for instant action.
3. Hostile submarines may be encountered.

It said further, simply: "Steady nerves and stout hearts are needed now."

The order was signed by Captain George D. Murray of *Enterprise,* and on the bottom left it carried the words:

> Approved: November 28, 1941
> W. F. Halsey
> Vice Admiral, U. S. Navy
> Commander Aircraft, Battle Force

The ready rooms suddenly hummed with talk, words or phrases of conjecture and query spoken in a low voice to the man in the next seat, bodies bent forward or to the side, or leaned backward to bring mouths closer to ears.

Briefing officers informed the air group that the task force was headed for Wake with Marine fighters for island defense.

Admiral Halsey had directed that any Japanese or unidentified ship or aircraft approaching the force was to be destroyed. Guns were to be manned and ready continuously. Regular searches were to be conducted ahead and on both flanks, and each search aircraft would carry a 500-pound bomb.

On the twenty-eight of November, 1941, the USS *Enterprise* was at war.

After twenty-three years of peace it is not easy to go to

war. Even for a warship. And it is hard to believe. Admiral Halsey's staff operations officer, Commander William H. Buracker, was incredulous. He doubted the admiral's authority in time of peace to order his pilots and gunners to destroy ships and planes of another nation. He took the order to Halsey in his cabin and asked, "Do you realize that this means war?"

"Yes."

"Now, goddammit, Admiral, you can't start a private war of your own! Who's going to take the responsibility?"

"I'll take it!" said Bill Halsey. "And if anything gets in my way we'll shoot first and argue afterwards."

During the long decades of peace and practice the war heads of torpedoes remain stowed in their magazines and the "fish" carry substitute heads filled with water to simulate the weight of explosive. Aircraft machine guns carry ammunition only on scheduled gunnery training flights and then, in the interest of economy, just a few rounds per gun. Gunnery training is conducted at comfortable altitudes in tropical or semitropical climates to take advantage of the high percentage of flyable weather. Planes are painted for easy identification by friendly eyes. Ships are furnished for comfort over the long pull, with stuffed furniture and carpets and curtains in wardroom areas and chief's quarters, even an occasional piano, lots of convenient wooden tables, lockers and shelves in the crew's quarters.

Enterprise had been stripped of most of her inflammables a few weeks earlier in Pearl Harbor—except for the piano in the wardroom which the officers had unanimously requested to be allowed to keep. But otherwise the back-breaking transition from peace to war had to be accomplished at once. The sailors of the Big E who broke out and secured the warheads to the torpedoes and fixed the 500-pound bombs under the wings of the Dauntlesses did not realize that their task was far from being a new one, that men had been doing the same kind of thing for all the centuries that swords had been painfully hammered into plowshares and back again. And if they had realized, it would have made no difference. There were still the thousands of rounds of machine-gun ammunition to be belted and installed in the planes which had only recently been repainted in wartime colors—blue-gray on top to blend with the sea, light gray beneath to blend with the sky, and red and white bars on the vertical stabilizer for positive identification.

Some things needed doing that could not be done. There was no armor in the fighters to protect the pilot, and self-sealing fuel tanks were not yet on board—a single bullet in a vulnerable spot could wipe out a plane in blood or fire. The venerable TBD Devastator torpedo bombers, on which the force depended to inflict the most serious damage on opposing surface ships, were slow and clumsy. The Grumman TBF Avengers scheduled to replace them were still in the late stages of design and far from available to fleet squadrons.

But when war comes, it is fought initially with what exists, not what is desired or is scheduled soon to be delivered, and the Big E, as ready as she could make herself, steamed steadily westward for Wake.

While the scouts droned out on their long triangular courses and the lookouts methodically swept their sectors with binoculars—slowly from aft to forward—checking the sky for planes, the horizon for smoke or the nearly invisible lump that could mean a ship, the near and middle distance for periscopes or torpedo wakes—and while crews stood wartime watches at the ready guns, the Marines and their aircraft also prepared to fight.

On the big gymnasiumlike hangar deck, smelling of engine oil, gasoline and sweat, mechanics worked over the Marine fighters. Engines, guns, control cables, landing gear, radios were overhauled and tested, any defective parts replaced or repaired. There were no machine shops and few maintenance facilities of any kind on Wake and everyone knew it.

In Fighting Six's slightly steamy ready room in the carrier's island, Wildcat school was in progress. Major Paul Putnam, commanding Marine Fighting Squadron 211, had asked the skipper of the Big E's fighters, Lieutenant Commander Wade McClusky, to furnish his pilots with all available information on flying and fighting the Grumman F4F Wildcat. The Marine pilots had only recently received their planes and had been able to get no more than fifteen or twenty hours of flight time in them with no instruction in bombing, gunnery or carrier operations.

Wade McClusky turned his squadron into an accelerated academy of aerial warfare. Every department "checked out" its Marine opposite numbers. Lieutenant (junior grade) James F. Gray lectured at length on the guns and gunnery tactics. Other pilots covered flight characteristics, systems, carrier landing techniques, engines and cruise control, navigation and bombing methods. Lieutenant (j.g.) J. C. Kelley instructed them in recognition with silhouettes of Japanese aircraft. He was doubtful of the value of his teaching, however, since his latest pictures showed nonretractable landing gear on all types and he thought this unrealistic. He was not sure what insignia the Japanese painted on their planes.

The Marine squadron was an alert and intelligent outfit and their questions were numerous, practical and direct. Their "motivation" was the ultimate. They were well aware that a few days or weeks after leaving their classes the knowledge gained there might be tested in combat.

Thus the bright midocean days went by. The long wakes stretched across the sea and every night the sun set dead ahead.

Aboard the *Enterprise* there was no December 1. On that day she crossed the International Date Line and time skipped from November 30 to December 2. Some of the men wondered. If the ship were never to cross back but always stayed west of the date line, what would happen to that day? By simply traveling westward had they shortened life one precious day?

It was a lovely moonlit night on this particular second of December which had arrived out of eternity ahead of schedule, and on the blacked-out flight deck the men stood in their hundreds and let it blow over their bodies and into their minds on the tropic wind. It seemed a pause in the stream of events. The men came up out of the ship as though in response to a command. They stood in silent or softly talking groups or alone—young sailors from the hangar deck and firerooms and galley; salty old chiefs on whose years of experience and toughness in the face of danger and difficulties the ship finally depended; pilots and ship's officers not long out of college or the Naval Academy, groping for a meaning out of their youth, the incredible signs and rumors of war, and the pouring moonlight; thoughtful, professionally remote senior officers, forgetting for the moment the incredible weight of responsibility under which they were living, responsibility to the service, which was their life and the nation which lay beyond it, to this ship and this deckload of humanity still moving westward at 20 knots.

No cloud obscured the moon. No sudden wind blew chill

But a moment came when it was over. Slowly the deck emptied until only the silent aircraft were left waiting with folded wings for the morning launch.

At daylight the Marines took off for Wake. The men of the Big E watched them go in silence. One after the other the chunky Wildcats roared down the deck and hopped into the air. The mechs and ordnancemen and radiomen and all the people who worked on them stopped to watch; the carrier pilots, who had tried in the few days available to make a gift of all the technical knowledge they possessed, looked and were proud and sad at once. Lieutenant Commander Frank Corbin, the executive officer of Fighting Six, remarked that the Marines were good but he thought a dozen of them were "kind of light to take on the whole Jap air force."

Commander Howard L. "Brigham" Young, who commanded the *Enterprise* air group, provided a navigational escort for the Marines with some of his scout bombers. When he was close enough to see in the distance the white sand and dark brush of the atoll, pointing like a broken arrowhead at the southeast, Young and his scouts waved and headed back under threatening skies. They found *Enterprise* and her accompanying ships already en route for Pearl.

That day Ensign John H. L. Vogt reported sighting a large fleet through the haze and between the low clouds at the limit of his search leg. No nation except Japan and the United States had fleets in the central Pacific. This one, if it existed, could only have been Japanese. Suppose it had been closer and Vogt had attacked? Who, then, would have started the war? Not until years after that war was over and Japanese naval records could be checked was it found that the visibility had played tricks on Vogt. No Japanese ships had been within hundreds of miles of the reported sighting on that date.

As the ships crossed the 180th meridian again, eastbound, there were two December 5s—and the men were even with time again.

On the second fifth, many of the Big E's men thought of their families who were that day being evacuated to the States because of the increasing tension with Japan. They remembered that, because of operations, they had not been on the dock by the Aloha Tower to meet them when they had arrived, and here they were at sea again when they departed. But they were comforted by the thought that in two weeks they were due to rejoin their families on the Coast and they happily planned what they would do with the golden stateside days and nights.

December 6 was rough and rainy and the crew was tiring of the morning and evening call to battle stations and the long ready watches between. The task force slowed to ease the destroyers that sliced and rolled in the heavy seas. This meant no Saturday night in Honolulu and no luxurious sleep or Sunday morning on the golf course. There was some griping in the big ships, but on the *Enterprise, Sergeant York* was showing and the hangar-deck movie audience forgot their troubles as Gary Cooper wet his big thumb and touched up his front sight.

On the flight deck, planes were positioned aft for the dawn launch on December 7.

2 WAR

The first plane off the Enterprise *the day the war began* was the air group commander's. He and his wingman were air-borne in two SBDs at 6:15 A.M. headed for Ford Island in the middle of Pearl Harbor.

Twelve minutes later the rest of Scouting Six was launched to search ahead of the ships and then follow in. Lucky aviators. They would be home in two hours with the ship still eight hours at sea.

In the rear seat of Commander Brigham Young's Dauntless was a lieutenant commander on Admiral Halsey's staff with a report of the Wake delivery too highly classified for radio transmission.

By 8:20, Young was close enough to notice planes circling the Marine Corps Air Station at Ewa. He assumed they were Army aircraft. Then he saw scattered black puffs of antiaircraft bursts over Pearl and was surprised to find what seemed to be target practice taking place on Sunday morning. While he was wondering how he was going to get into Ford Island through the flak, and thinking that, if this were target practice, every safety precaution he knew was being violated, one of the Army planes he had noticed broke away from the others and swept down on him. Lieutenant Commander Bromfield B. Nichol in the rear seat saw what looked like a lot of burning cigarette butts flash past him. Where they struck the wing, pieces of aluminum shredded off. When the "Army" plane pulled up, Brig Young was at war. On wings and fuselage was the red disk of the Rising Sun.

Both SBDs dived violently for the Ford Island runway, with Young longing for the trained gunner who normally sat at his back, and Nichol tried to unlimber the .30-calibers. Both planes managed to shake off the Japanese and effect a landing despite the ships' gunners who now trusted no one and were firing at everything that flew. There was no chance in the desperate seconds between surprise attack and touch-down to warn the rest of the air group already approaching the island.

As Young rode the brakes and his Dauntless slowed, a sailor on the field leveled a machine gun at it. During the last shattering, bloody hour he had forgotten there could be any planes at Pearl Harbor not actively seeking his death. He was stopped from opening fire by a nearby pilot who advanced on him wielding a rock the size of his head.

It seemed to Brig Young that a week had passed since the dawn launch, but it was just 8:35 A.M.

Ten minutes later Lieutenant Commander Hallsted Hopping, the skipper of Scouting Six, brought his squadron in. Or most of it. No one is certain what happened to Ensign Manuel Gonzales. His last words were the first to alert the *Enterprise*. Out of the Sunday silence west of Oahu they came crackling from her speakers, pleading, urgent: "Please don't shoot! Don't shoot! This is an American plane." Then in a moment, evidently to his rear-seatman, "We're on fire. Bail out!" and the speakers were quiet again. He did not return and no trace was ever found. Ensign John H. L. Vogt, who had reported the fleet off Wake, never made it to Ford Island. The Marines at Ewa saw a Dauntless which was probably his, in a twisting, swirling, low altitude mix-up with two or three Zeros, fixed and free guns all firing at once. They watched it get on the tail of an enemy fighter and grimly stay there as though the pouring tracers were a towline, until the Japanese suddenly lost speed and pulled up so sharply that the Dauntless plowed into him. They didn't see anything after that because they were dodging the pieces of flaming metal that scattered for a square mile over the cane fields and the air station.

Lieutenant (j.g.) C. E. Dickinson and Ensign J. R. McCarthy came in together at 1,500 feet from their routine morning search. They too saw the smoke rising from Pearl Harbor while still far at sea and at first thought it was from the usual burning of the cane fields before harvest. But when they noticed the AA fire they guessed the truth, readied their guns and bored in after what looked to them like an enemy patrol plane. They lost it in the smoke of the burning battleships and a moment later half a dozen Japanese fighters found them.

It was not much of a fight. The Dauntless was designed to be a dive bomber. And it was an excellent one. But it was not a match for the Zeros that swarmed over Oahu that December morning. Nevertheless Dickinson's gunner, Roger Miller, shot one down before he died under the guns of the others. Both pilots had their planes riddled and were forced to bail out at low altitude.

McCarthy's leg was broken by the tail of the spinning SBD and he spent several months in the hospital. His gunner, unable to extricate himself in time, died in the crash of his plane. Dickinson landed unhurt near Ewa Field and made his way toward Ford Island. En route he watched Marines standing in the open road, professionally firing their rifles at the strafing Japs, saw the USS *Nevada* make its fighting sortie from Battleship Row, noted that the enemy dive bombers did not attack at the steep angle he had been trained to use, and finally was knocked flat on the concrete of Ford Island when a bomb detonated the magazine of the destroyer *Shaw* a few hundred yards away.

Ensign E. T. Deacon used up all his ammunition in another hopeless dogfight with the murderous Zeros and then, with a wounded leg and a shot-up aircraft, glided for Hickam Field. It was just a little too far, and he landed in the water just short of the runway, unpacked and inflated his rubber boat, lifted his wounded gunner aboard and paddled ashore. When he was certain the gunner was in good hands, he too somehow got through the burning madhouse of Pearl and across to Ford Island.

Thus did the lucky aviators of Scouting Six, who had hoped to have the precious extra hours on Oahu, come to their destination that incredible Sunday.

In the *Enterprise,* steaming steadily into the low morning sun for Pearl, awareness came slowly in small capsules of garbled phrases from her radios. It was as though the ship were a person to whom the bitter news could not be told in one dose.

In his flag quarters Admiral Halsey had showered and shaved and put on a clean uniform after watching the early SBDs out of sight. He breakfasted with his flag secretary, Lieutenant H. Douglas Moulton, and was on his second cup of coffee when Moulton answered the phone from Radio Central and reported an air raid on Pearl Harbor.

Halsey sprang to his feet in dismay. He was certain the Pearl gunners were firing at Lieutenant Commander Hallsted Hopping's Dauntlesses due to arrive at just that moment.

The ship's supply officer, Commander Charles Fox, was in charge of the watch in the code room. There he had just heard Gonzales' eloquent few words and seen the men on watch sit up straight "with what-the-hell expressions on their faces," and in the next few moments recognized the voice of Lieutenant Earl Gallaher, the executive officer of Scouting Six, an old hand and steady under pressure. His voice was natural and calm as he made his report:

"Pearl Harbor is under attack by Japanese aircraft."

He was too calm. The men in the code room were certain now this was all a drill. The thought of an actual Japanese attack on the Oahu they knew so well was simply unacceptable.

Routinely Gallaher's message was relayed to the bridge where it corroborated the message received by Halsey and resulted immediately in the insistent, repeated clanging of the general alarm, the call to battle stations.

In the code room the radios kept talking. The voices were strained, the words fantastic, impossible.

"Two enemy carriers thirty miles bearing 085 from Barber's Point."

"Enemy landing party headed for the ammunition depot."

"Japanese paratroops and gliders landing at Kaneohe."

"Eight enemy transports rounding Barber's Point."

But the admiral knew it was no drill. He had a message in his hand by eight o'clock which told him so:

AIR RAID PEARL HARBOR X THIS IS NO DRILL

At 8:23 he received another:

ALERT X JAPANESE PLANES ATTACKING PEARL AND

AIRFIELDS ON OAHU

Halsey kept no secrets from the men of *Enterprise* that day. The word was passed over the public address system. Hardly anyone believed it. The habit of peace was hard to break.

But in the code room they intercepted a message ordering all medical officers in the Pearl area to rush all available anesthetics to the Naval Hospital. Realization began to come.

The admiral appeared on his bridge. His was not a drill face.

Snap hooks clicked in the hands of the signalmen and their multicolored flags soared to the yardarm. The message:

PREPARE FOR BATTLE

The flags stayed up much longer than usual. When at last they plumped like well-shot birds to the deck of the signal bridge, simultaneously from foremast and mainmast of each two-masted ship in the force, the stars and stripes broke clean and bright into the morning sun. The challenge was accepted. It seemed that the ships surged forward under the defiant battle colors.

The Big E was busy all day launching and recovering her aircraft as Halsey groped for the enemy. With her scouts either at Ford Island or down on its approaches, and her remaining planes needed for strikes once the enemy was found, *Enterprise* was nearly blind, but a combat air patrol (CAP) of four fighters went up at once and searched the area around the force.

At 10:15 three more Wildcats took off on an inner air patrol. Their mission was close-in defense of the task force, especially the carrier.

Thirty minutes past noon, skipper Wade McClusky's division was launched to relieve the first four planes on CAP. They in turn were relieved at three o'clock by three two-plane sections under Gray, Mehle and Heisel.

Between launches there were the air-borne patrols to re-

cover and all the time the persistent radios delivered the
news of the new war.

The men worked hard and stood their watches well. In
the heat of the fire- and engine rooms, amidst the gleaming
metal and the humming machinery with its hot oil smell,
they worked sweating in T shirts, colored rags dangling
from their hip pockets. Carefully they watched the needles
of their gauges and swung the big throttle wheels in answer
to jingled orders from the bridge. Knowing palms felt bearing housings for temperature and vibration. Meticulous en-
tries were made in logs and bell books and machinery records.

In the galley the tattooed cooks, in their white aprons
and spotless hats, moved along the steam tables piled with
fried chicken. The bakers finished a batch of apple pies and
started on cookies for the evening meal. There were two
thousand young men to be fed three meals a day.

Mechs and ordnancemen in the shops and on the hangar
deck went painstakingly about their special jobs. Each detail of clearance and adjustment, each measurement of
spark and torque and voltage, received its proportionate attention.

The flight deck was like a sea-borne athletic field where
half a dozen teams in bright, contrasting jerseys surged forward and aft, mingling and separating, organized and intent, in the constant aromatic odor of high-octane gasoline
and to the roar of aircraft engines under the noon sun and
the steady trades. The entire deck activity was organized by
Lieutenant Commander William "Slim" Townsend, long-
legged and fast. Flight Deck Chief V. A. Prather kept it
moving. Townsend covered the deck a hundred times a day,
seeing for himself, and no matter how fast the blue-jerseyed
plane handlers pushed, or the green arresting-gear men disengaged their hooks, Prather was behind them with his
spraddle legged walk and his scratchy voice to speed them
up.

"Bear a hand there!" "Shake it up, you guys!" "You, sail-
or, get the lead out!"

Even in 1940, when the Big E had set a fleet record for
the rapid launching and recovery of aircraft, it had not
been good enough for the flight deck chief. He knew a
dozen places where seconds could have been shaved off if
his men had just moved a little faster.

Above the flight deck in the storied island, the captain

supervised all operations and the officer of the deck, the skipper's direct representative, kept his watch. Heavy black binoculars swung from the strap around his neck and rode his lower chest at the level of his elbows. He was all over the bridge, checking the bearings and distances of the other ships with bearing ring and statimeter, peering over the helmsman's shoulder at the steering compass, noting wind direction and velocity, observing the planes in the pattern and orbiting overhead. All the nerve fibers of the ship came together in his hands.

High over the force each pair of Wildcats was beautifully alone. In loose formation the pilots swung out on various headings and then back. Their eyes searched the blue sea and the sky, returning most often to the eastward where the islands were now and then a smudge on the horizon. They looked across the short wings at each other and saw sweat-stained khaki or white helmets with gray goggles, and yellow Mae West life jackets over khaki shirts. Left hands held throttle knobs or, with the throttle correctly set for the moment, rested forward on the cockpit edge. Right hands lightly held the sticks. They checked altitude and air speed, fuel consumption and position in formation, and again searched the wide sea and the sky.

Of course there was plenty of loud talk aboard, and a lot of it was in earnest. Much was not. But it all helped.

"So the yellow bastards started it . . . let's finish it! Yipee! We'll show 'em how to go to town!"

"So they asked for it, and we sure are going to give it to 'em."

Little Benny Sablan, a twenty-year-old Chamorro officer's cook from Guam, was more conservative.

"I know Japanese," he said, "he is very bad. And tricky. But we Americans too smart. We catch him and give him hell."

While the fighters circled overhead and watched for a possible attack, Admiral Halsey readied his torpedo planes and bombers for action and waited for some indication of the enemy's position.

Hal Hopping's Scouts at Ford Island tried to get it for him. They managed to get nine planes out on a search sector from northwest to northeast, but they found nothing.

Earl Gallaher, on his own initiative, flew out 175 miles to the northwest, the direction he had seen taken by the retiring Japanese pilots. He likewise found nothing.

Hopping himself took off through a storm of "friendly" AA fire, as soon as his plane was gassed, to check on two enemy carriers reported off Barber's Point. He found the United States heavy cruiser *Minneapolis* at sea on maneuvers that Sunday.

Ensign Richard "Bucky" Walters, running down a shore-based radio direction finder bearing on a Japanese carrier late in the afternoon, reported an enemy formation to the south of Oahu.

This was what Admiral Halsey was waiting for.

The Big E shot up into the wind and off roared the carefully hoarded strike group, every plane that Torpedo Six could get in the air plus six SBDs of Bombing Six with smoke tanks to screen the torpedo attack and six fighters to cover. A long search found only a force of friendly cruisers and destroyers that had fought their way out of Pearl and were trying to join up with Halsey. It turned out that the bearing given Walters was a reciprocal, the exact opposite of the correct one. The enemy signals had come from the north.

The sun set, but the long day was not over.

Torpedo Six under Lieutenant Eugene Lindsey and the six "smokers" from the bombing squadron began the long flight back to the ship. It was a black moonless night. The majority of the twenty-odd pilots groping back through the tropic darkness were partially trained in night operations, but many had never before even been air-borne in a TBD after sunset. All carried precious 2,000-pound torpedoes which might be needed at any hour.

Lindsey's navigation was good but when "many bogies" appeared on the Big E's radars, the director swung around to track, and the loaded ready guns trained out and followed the torpedo planes and dive bombers as they approached the ship in the darkness. Eager, nervous fingers were on the firing keys that first night of the war and only at a dangerously late moment did Gunnery Control receive word that the approaching planes were friendly.

One by one the heavy Devastators, with their three-man crews and their long torpedoes, lumbered down wind abeam the carrier, swung ponderously crosswind and picked up the illuminated green wands of an invisible Bert Harden.

When the first one thumped down on the deck and engaged the arresting gear, it was the first airplane ever to land aboard a carrier with a live torpedo. They all made it, but there was a bad moment.

One TBD came down too hard and the metal strap supporting the torpedo parted. The long, deadly "fish," smoking, with its propellers turning, with TNT enough in its nose to sink a battleship, skidded down the flight deck. Forward of the light wire barrier were the planes just recovered. Slightly to starboard was the island structure which housed the control center of the ship. And on the darkened bridge were Admiral Halsey and Captain Murray.

As the torpedo began to lose momentum, a pair of long legs flashed out of the shadows and a figure leaped astride it. Steered and slowed with violent pressures of hands, feet, legs and buttocks, it was kept straight ahead until it stopped short of the barrier and was then held from rolling with the deck until it could be secured. The legs belonged to Slim Townsend, the flight deck officer.

The strike group was safely back aboard, but its escorting fighters, without sufficient fuel for return to the ship, had been ordered into Pearl.

At 8:45 P.M. Lieutenant Hebel called Ford Island tower, reported his flight of six off Diamond Head and requested landing instructions. He was cleared over the field with navigation lights on, preparatory to landing.

The planes approached with the dim surf lines of the Oahu coast under their left wings. The new blackout was not tight and points and cracks of light showed here and there along the beach.

Pearl Harbor was dark and still. At irregular intervals red spots glowed along what had been Battleship Row and traces of black smoke still fouled the night air over the air station.

The day had been a long, fantastic dream divided between ready room and cockpit. This last flight had already lasted four hours. Now, with the field in sight through their prop disks and their wings sweeping in across the darkened coastline, the pilots began to relax.

At an even thousand feet, in a neat right echelon, red and green port and starboard wing-tip lights bright and friendly, Hebel gave the signal and six sets of wheels dropped down into the air stream. The formation slowed to the increased drag as Drydock Channel passed below. In a few seconds the first plane would be touching down.

From the cluster of blacked-out but still burning ships in

the Navy Yard, just across the narrow channel from Ford Island, a single string of tracers sprang up at the homing Wildcats. A second later another joined, converging. In half a minute Hebel's pilots were laced with fire from every gun that would bear. Red lines of heavy machine-gun bullets swept the lighted formation and the black puffs of fused projectiles jarred and staggered the dazzled aviators. On a score of decks the big guns flashed yellow and the small ones winked redly with steady mechanical precision. The guns ashore joined in.

Herb Menge's plane went in a long, shallow glide straight across Ford Island and into Pearl City, where it exploded in an orange fireball and then burned fiercely for several minutes. Herb died instantly.

Hebel banked sharply right but failed to evade the eager gunners. His Wildcat crash-landed and burned in a cane field north of Aeia. Fritz survived the crash but died the following day.

When the ships opened fire, Dave Flynn, Jimmy Daniels and Gayle Herman all immediately flicked out their lights. Herman dove, spiraling, for the runway and landed. He was under fire even when on the ground. At daylight he counted eighteen holes in his F4F.

Flynn and Daniels cranked up their wheels and separately headed out to sea "with everything in the cockpit as far forward as it would go."

After the shooting stopped, Daniels came back in, low, fast and dark, and landed safely despite a burst of gunfire at the last minute.

Flynn had the same thing in mind, but on the return trip his damaged engine stopped and he parachuted into a cane field at Barber's Point.

Still it was not over.

Ensigns Bucky Walters and Ben Troemel of Scouting Six had seen enough of Pearl Harbor flak for one day. When they returned after dark from an afternoon search, they elected to land at Kaneohe, across the mountains.

The field and runways were dark and there was no response from the tower but they were tired and low on gas and in they came. Walters was first. He swung carefully onto final approach, wheels hanging, flaps down, power on, settling slowly for the landing mat. Peering down past the nose, he thought he could see some objects on the field but guessed there was some construction in progress. He chopped his throttle back and stalled the SBD into a solid three-point landing. Just ahead and to the right the night sprouted a parked truck. The Dauntless was still rolling at sixty or seventy miles an hour. He stomped left brake and rudder. The plane swerved and a wrecked sedan appeared immediately dead ahead. Walters' right leg went stiff and his toe ground in the brake. The tortured dive bomber skidded around to starboard and stopped under the loom of a mobile crane directly in its path.

Troemel had the same experience, except that he had an additional obstruction to concern him—Walters' SBD. At the end of a violently crooked double stripe of smoking rubber he brought his aircraft to a halt nose to nose with a concrete mixer. Neither Dauntless had a scratch.

The commanding officer of the U. S. Naval Air Station at Kaneohe was displeased. He had ordered the field blocked to make a Jap landing impossible. Every available vehicle and movable piece of machinery had been driven or towed into position accordingly. Then, after dark, two dive bombers had landed unscathed. Walters and Troemel said later that they would not have dared try it in daylight.

It was 9:30 P.M. and the first day of the war was over for *Enterprise*. The Big E, untouched, cruised with her supporting ships off Kauai. Bombing Six and Torpedo Six were aboard intact. The remnants of Scouting Six were ashore at Ford Island, Ewa and Kaneohe. Fighting Six was hurt, Menges was dead, Hebel and Allen dying. Four Wildcats and at least five Dauntlesses were lost, others badly damaged.

A few hundred miles to the northwest was the Japanese Air Attack Force. In two darkened parallel columns steamed the carriers *Akagi, Kaga, Soryu, Hiryu, Shokaku* and *Zuikaku*. At the end of each column was a battleship, on either flank a heavy cruiser, ahead a line of destroyers. Aboard the carriers were Japan's best air groups, with only negligible losses after launching 360 planes against Oahu.

At dawn on the eighth of December *Enterprise* launched her combat air patrol. During breakfast the planes of Scouting Six returned from Oahu.

And now, for the first time, the crew knew how bad it was in Pearl. In the wardroom Brig Young and Brom Nichol told a silent table lined with khaki shirts and serious faces how they came to Ford Island. The scout pilots, with eloquently maneuvering hands, described what they had seen of the terrible seventh. Below, in mess halls and living spaces the gunners told their stories. Like batons in a relay race, the words passed through the ship until in shops and shaft alleys, boiler rooms and bilges, from bridge to fireroom fo'c'sle to fantail, every man had an impression of the situation in which the Big E found herself that day.

It was specifically this. The battle force, the heart of the fleet, had been destroyed. Somewhere to the south was the carrier *Lexington* with her supporting ships, a force roughly similar to that commanded by Admiral Halsey. *Saratoga* was four days away in San Diego. *Lexington* and *Enterprise* were the only two operational carriers in the central Pacific, and with their cruisers and destroyers the only effective combatant units of the U. S. Navy.

It took no War College graduate to conclude from the hundreds of carrier aircraft that had leveled Pearl Harbor that the Japanese had far stronger forces in the area. No one knew where they were, when or if they would strike again, or whether or not that strike would accompany an attempt to occupy the Hawaiian Islands. After the seventh, anything seemed possible. And if the Japanese were able to capture Pearl, or by a second assault destroy oil storage and pumping facilities missed the first time, the *Enterprise*, without sufficient fuel to reach the West Coast would, in a few days, be drifting helplessly on the high seas.

Captain Murray had the figures. *Enterprise* had only 50 per cent of her fuel oil left. The cruisers were down to 30 per cent, the destroyers 20.

At 11:00 A.M. on the eighth, Admiral Halsey ordered his ships to Pearl.

In the afternoon, all that could fly of Fighting Six was launched for the Army's Wheeler Field on Oahu to augment the Army fighters in the air defense of the Islands.

The sun had just set as the Big E nosed into the channel. No one could remember when a carrier had attempted that channel after sunset. From her bow, black oil from the tanks of broken ships turned back on itself and oozed away. Flight deck and catwalks, bridge, fo'c'sle and fantail were crowded with men, and every port and hatch was jammed with faces. On both sides the shore was lined with hastily erected, fully manned antiaircraft guns of all sizes and calibers. A soldier at Hickam yelled across the water.

"You'd better get the hell out of here or the Japs will nail you too."

They passed the battleship *Nevada,* heavily aground to port on Hospital Point, the only ship to get under way from Battleship Row that awful morning. Coming around Ford Island, the carrier had to swing wide to avoid the old battleship *Utah,* ripped to pieces and lying on the mud of the harbor bottom. For years she had been used as a target ship. But she had been moored in the carrier *Saratoga's* usual berth and her heavily timbered topsides slightly resembled a flight deck from the air.

The place smelled bad. Instead of the lush, flowery smell of tropical forests which usually came down off the hills on the land breeze, there was the sick-sweet odor of fuel oil, seared flesh and the charred wood and fabric smell of a half-burned house after the fire. Black smoke was layered in the sky from the still-burning *Arizona.*

The feeling aboard *Enterprise* was anger and unease. The crew began to feel the treachery of the Sunday morning murders. Subconsciously they compared the harbor they had left on November 28, proud and shipshape, with the oil-soaked mess before them. On the bridge, the admiral was heard to mutter, "Before we're through with 'em, the Japanese language will be spoken only in Hell!"

The nervousness of the professional seaman in confined waters took hold of them all. It was a form of claustrophobia. In here among the wrecks the Big E was trapped and vulnerable. If this was what happened to battlewagons with their sixteen inches of armor, the case of the carrier was hopeless. They felt the need of sea room to wheel and launch, to run free and fire, circle and recover. For the first time, they were eager to get out of Pearl Harbor.

At six o'clock the *Enterprise* tied up in the darkness and the job of fueling and provisioning began. Commander Charles Fox was in charge. His was the responsibility for the logistic readiness of the ship. Under him fell the functions that in civilian life would be accomplished by grocer, baker, restaurateur, clothier, hardware merchant, warehouseman, treasurer, auditor and banker for a community of two thousand. His preparations had been made as a matter of routine. Records had been checked to determine what supplies were necessary to fill the storerooms to capacity and requisitions had been neatly typed accordingly. All storage spaces had been cleaned and made ready for restocking. Refrigerated areas had been defrosted in rotation, washed and dried. Working parties totaling over three hundred men were organized and standing by, each under a petty officer; each had a specific part of the task to do.

A tanker came alongside at once, hoses were rigged and immediately stiffened to the rush of oil. Outboard of the tanker a tug secured a line of deep-draft target rafts to take any torpedoes intended for the Big E. Then loaded lighters began arriving from the Navy Yard. Working in total darkness, except for a flickering red light from the burning *Arizona* which partially illuminated the wrong side of the ship, *Enterprise* working parties hoisted the heavy, bulky stores aboard. From hand to hand along the passage-ways and down the ladders went crates, cans, bales and boxes to their proper stowage. Bosun's mates shouted, storekeepers read labels and kept count, instructions were passed up and down the long lines of sweating sailors.

It was a job which, in daylight and with the convenience of loading from the dock, normally takes twelve hours of hard work. On this December night under the blackout, and despite the jittery sentries who regularly fired on the boats between the ship and the Navy Yard, it was completed in eight hours.

Charlie Fox went to the bridge to make his report in person to Captain Murray who had hardly left it for a day and a half. The two men had been friends since they had served in the same destroyer five years before the First World War.

"Very well, Charlie," replied the captain. "A good job well done. We'll soon be ready to go." And shortly after three o'clock in the morning, tugs towed away the target rafts and eased the high bow out into the stream. Once again, in total darkness now, the big carrier negotiated the tricky, wreck-filled channel, and by 4:00 A.M. the Big E was back at sea where she belonged.

3 GUARDING THE ISLANDS

The sea to which Enterprise *returned from the ruins* of Pearl Harbor seemed different from any she had sailed before. The Pacific had become an unknown ocean hiding an invisible enemy.

The seventh of December in a single stroke had blotted from the charts the arching great-circle routes plied by the world's shipping; it had extinguished the lighthouses, subverted the buoys and threatened the shallows with mines. Each white puff of cumulus was suspect of aiding a snooper. The silver path of the moon placed a ship in silhouette for torpedoes. Morning and evening twilight, the time for celestial observations when both the stars and the horizon are visible, became a time of tension for the unarmed merchant crewman as well as the man-o'-warsman, for then a ship could be sighted from a cockpit or a periscope it could not see.

The whole incredible Pacific, which could receive every acre of land on earth and still retain respectable dimensions, crackled and sparkled with war wherever the grasping Japanese tentacles encountered resistance in its vastness. Out of this now mysterious ocean had come the planes that smashed Pearl Harbor. No American knew where they had gone or when they would be back.

Halsey took the Big E out to the northwest on patrol.

After daylight, Fighting Six landed aboard having spent the night at Wheeler Field as a unit (with the official call sign of "Sailor") in the Army air defense system. All of Wheeler's regular mess halls had been destroyed and the squadron had eaten in blacked-out emergency dining areas and slept in vacant private quarters whose only advantage was a plentiful liquor supply. But even with that advantage sleep had been nearly impossible with the repeated night-long rattle of small-arms fire from nervous sentries, and in the early dawn they had returned on foot to their planes armed with the proper password and personally escorted by the brigadier general commanding the field.

From the mess in Pearl Harbor, still sickeningly smoking, the fighter pilots brought back several stories about the tragic seventh. At Wheeler, they said, the Army had a bulldozer push all the aircraft wreckage into a single pile and out of the pile they had built three flyable planes. They had learned that *Enterprise* gunners, left ashore at Ewa to attend a Marine course in the maintenance and operation of machine guns, had taken such good advantage of their instruction that they had been given credit for the destruction of three enemy aircraft and a possible fourth, shot down with guns issued only for training.

One story was that the incoming Japanese attack force had been detected on radar far at sea "but no one would listen to the guy." Another concerned the air station at Kaneohe. A Japanese egg peddler had tried to deliver his produce to the officers' quarters early on that Sunday morning and the Marine gate sentry had discovered a radio transmitter under the eggs.

Before lunch on the tenth, Admiral Halsey came into the wardroom and delivered a short, emphatic talk to the pilots. The tenor of this speech can be summed up in a single prophetic remark entered in a Fighting Six diary, "Those Japs had better look out for that man."

On that same day, *Enterprise* pilots sighted three enemy submarines in widely separated areas, all running on the surface. One crash-dived and escaped. A Bombing Six Dauntless made a direct hit on a second as it was attempting to submerge. Dickinson of Scouting Six flew through several minutes of antiaircraft fire when the third chose to fight it out on the surface, then climbed to attack altitude and carefully placed his bomb right alongside amidships. He saw the sub stop and, dead in the water, settle out of sight on an even keel, leaving a spreading patch of oil and debris. The Big E was credited with the first combatant ship sunk by U. S. Forces in World War II.

When the crew learned of these encounters, the men were delighted that even such light return blows were at last being struck, but they became overly sensitive to the presence of other subs. In the warm waters of the central Pacific, ruffled by the trade winds and inhabited by a hundred varieties of whale and porpoise, marlin and dolphin, an uneasy lookout with a sharp but inexperienced eye could see a periscope or a torpedo almost at will. Many an innocent deck swab, lost overboard long ago by some negligent sailor and floating vertically, handle up, has caused a task force to turn away at high speed, expending hundreds of barrels of fuel oil, and 10,000 men to leave their normal tasks and rush to battle stations. A playful porpoise just below the surface, coming straight and fast for the bow of a ship at night, with luminous phosphorescent bubbles sliding from his nose and stretching out behind him, can make the mouth of the saltiest destroyer skipper go dry for a moment; and to the searching sonar of a destroyer, a whale returns nearly as good an echo as a submarine and shows about the same speed and depth. The way a certain white-cap breaks exactly simulates the feather thrown up by a moving periscope, and a man must be taught to look for the 'scope itself and to be seriously alarmed only by those whitecaps which are going in a different direction from their fellows.

Thus it was no wonder that in those first weeks of guarding the islands, the green and eager sailors and young officers of *Enterprise* reported a dozen submarines a day where there were none or very few. And it was the same throughout the force. The destroyers fired hundreds of depth charges; casualties were heavy among the whales and blackfish off Oahu. But it was far better to drop and question later than chance a Japanese 24-inch torpedo in the thin side of a scarce and invaluable United States aircraft carrier.

Finally the admiral sent a message comforting his commanders with the thought that if all the reported torpedo wakes were real, the enemy submarines were now out of torpedoes and must return to base and reload. He added that too many depth charges were being expended against neutral fish.

It was a good thing for the men of the Big E that they had their sub kills to think about. All the other news that dribbled eastward out of the suddenly unknown Pacific was bad.

To these men who knew from their history books that the United States of America had never lost a war and was invincible, it seemed that the impossible was happening, that a war in these December days was being very rapidly lost. They had seen for themselves the mighty battleships which they had believed were the backbone of the fleet, holed and helpless in the Pearl Harbor mud. And after the survivors of those ships had been distributed among undamaged vessels, the men of *Enterprise* had been startled awake by their nightmare screams in their own berthing compartments. In the wardroom and ready rooms, empty chairs and lockers reminded the young pilots of their dead friends.

The Big E's tour of sentry duty lasted a month.

In the ship's newspaper, the men learned that Wake was under attack, and they remembered the faces and voices of the Marines they had delivered there. On the single day of December 10, Guam, which Congress had decided not to fortify, was invaded by the Japanese; Cavite Navy Yard at Manila was bombed out of existence and the enemy had landed in the Philippines; the big, new British battleship, *Prince of Wales,* pride of the Royal Navy, which had beaten off the pilots of the German Luftwaffe in the Mediterranean and had helped sink the great *Bismarck* in the Atlantic, and aboard which Winston Churchill and Franklin Roosevelt had signed the Atlantic Charter in a bay in Newfoundland, was lost, with the battleship *Repulse,* to enemy air action off Malaya.

From Shanghai came word that the little gunboat, USS *Wake,* had been captured intact and recommissioned in the Japanese Navy. The enemy was moving rapidly on Manila, Hong Kong, Singapore.

And *Enterprise* steamed back and forth, north and west of Oahu.

Her pilots flew routine searches and patrols, slept, played cribbage, wondered why the Russians had not yet bombed Tokyo, griped at the inaction and asked each other, "What the hell kind of a war is this?"

The spirits of the crew rose when the task force turned west and fell when it swung back eastward again. The men exulted when they heard that the Wake Marine pilots had sunk an enemy destroyer and damaged a cruiser. "Apparently," a VF-6 pilot said, "those soldiers were paying attention to our lectures."

During the short periods back in Pearl to refuel and reprovision, the men were depressed by the broken port, and when on the twenty-third of December, after a relief expedition had turned back, Wake Island fell, many a profane and tatooed sailor found a private place in which to weep. But twice more, submarines were sighted, attacked and damaged if not destroyed.

There were some anxious moments when, on separate occasions, Lieutenant Jack Blitch, of Bombing Six, and Lieutenant (j.g.) Carleton Fogg, of Scouting Six, were long overdue on their patrols. For an hour or two it was thought they were lost and the ship was tense and silent, the tiny radar room with its single indispensable scope and its diagrams of the search sectors was crowded with pilots listening for news. Their two squadron commanders watched the clock and grimly figured fuel reserves remaining in the two planes. Neither pilot broke radio silence to save his skin, and both returned at last to the ship, Blitch long after dark.

Then the tension relaxed, the needling began and it all became a joke on the "lost" pilots. But it had been no joke while they were unreported.

Crossing and recrossing the International Date Line west of Midway, *Enterprise* had two Christmases. Neither was very merry, although the admiral made the "Merry Christmas" signal by flag hoist on the first day and hoisted it again on the second with the "first repeater" pennant. Charlie Fox served roast turkey with all the trimmings, and Fighting Six sent out mimeographed Christmas cards to the other squadrons and the ship's company carrying a drawing of Santa Claus in full armor and a verse:

> *'Twas Christmas Day in the ready room*
> *Not a single pilot there.*
> *And we a-sail in the Pacific,*
> *Only God and Knox knows where.*
> *But they've even got that censored,*
> *And so it comes to pass,*
> *To all hands a Happy New Year,*
> *And a joyous and Merry Christmas.*

On the repeat Christmas, the force steamed through a daylong rain. All flights were canceled and the bored pilots spent the day in their bunks remembering other Christmases and dreaming vaguely of future ones.

New Year's Eve was just another night of fueling and loading stores in Pearl.

Once more she went out to cover the island approaches. And then, on January 9, 1942, *Enterprise* was ordered into real offensive action against the enemy.

4 INTO THE SOUTH SEAS

All day and well into the night of the tenth of January the Big E took on stores. It was obvious to the crew that something different was planned. The "black gang" reported more fuel aboard than ever before. The gunner's mates opened unused magazines and crammed them with explosives of a hundred kinds. Charlie Fox's storekeepers filled their meat lockers and storerooms to the overhead. In a diary of a Fighting Six pilot was the succinct entry: "Are loading for bear."

When she sailed at noon on the eleventh, *Enterprise* was in good company. With her were the heavy cruisers *Chester*, *Northampton* and *Salt Lake City*, and the fleet tanker *Platte;* the destroyers *Dunlap*, *Balch*, *Maury*, *Ralph Talbot*, *Blue* and *McCall* fanned out ahead. Admiral Halsey and Captain Murray walked the bridge and their steps had a spring, their eyes a glint that had been lacking in the long covering patrols to the northwestward.

The high command, watching the enemy spread out over the Pacific, had guessed he would next move southeastward from bases in the Marshall and Gilbert Islands to take Samoa and cut the vital sea route between the United States and Australia. Marine reinforcements were already outbound from San Diego under the protection of another task group built around the Big E's sister ship *Yorktown*, just arrived from the Atlantic. The two forces were to assure the unmolested landing of the Marines and their equipment at Pago Pago, Samoa, join up and . . . aboard the *Enterprise* only the skipper and Bill Halsey knew what came next.

In those first days of her initial combat cruise the Big E's luck was all bad.

Early on the twelfth came news that a deep-running enemy torpedo had found the carrier *Saratoga,* and hurt her so badly that she was bound for Pearl and a stateside navy yard. This left only *Enterprise*, *Yorktown* and *Lexington* to face the Japanese Navy that had been able to throw six big carriers into the one strike against Pearl.

On the thirteenth a Scouting Six pilot lost his head in an emergency and broke radio silence, endangering the entire operation. On the same day Bert Harden miraculously escaped serious injury when he was hit by a target sleeve as it was being snatched off the deck at 90 knots by the tow plane.

On the fourteenth a man was washed overboard and lost from the destroyer *Blue.*

The sixteenth was the worst day. A seaman aboard the *Salt Lake* was killed in a turret accident. A landing Dauntless tore loose an arresting wire and plunged off the deck edge onto the catwalk. The plane's left wheel struck a chief petty officer in the head and he died later in the day. The chief was G. F. Lawhon, an aviation machinist's mate who had put the ship in commission in 1938, one of the solid, experienced key men who hold a ship together and make it work. Lawhon had devised the first system for recovering the tow strap from a catapulted plane as it becomes airborne and had helped perfect the precisely stressed shearing pins in the flight-deck barriers which hold up the barrier until the shock of the plane has been absorbed. Lawhon's death was the first of the war on *Enterprise* attributable to the risks inherent in carrier operations, and having nothing directly to do with enemy action.

On the afternoon the chief was killed, a Torpedo Six Devastator failed to return from its search mission. Lost and low on fuel, this pilot also broke radio silence, first to ask for a bearing back to the ship and then to report that he was making a water landing. A search was launched at daylight but the lost Torpedo Plane was not found. With the heartless logic of wartime operations which cannot risk a ship or a task force to help a three-man plane crew, the Big E continued on her course. But Chief Harold Dixon, the TBD pilot, Tony Pastula, the bombardier, and Gene Aldrich, the gunner, were unhurt in a smooth ditching. For thirty-four days they rowed, drifted, sailed and paddled in their eight-by-four-foot rubber raft, burned raw by the equatorial sun, beaten by the pounding seas, surviving somehow on an occasional fish, bird, drifting coconut or the marine growth on floating stumps, drinking what rain water they could catch and save. When they landed, starved and horribly weak, through the vicious surf on Puka Puka Island, 750 miles from where they went down, they had actually traveled a thousand miles and were just one day ahead of a typhoon which would have been their certain death.

The eleven carefully assorted ships slid down over the bulge of an earth which seemed to their crews a planet made of water. In the low latitudes the heat was a living force. The faces of the Big E's men gleamed and their clothing was dark and sodden. At night there was nothing left to throw off and their bedding grew sticky. Fighter pilots flying the noon CAP with open cockpits and 150 knots of wind to cool them returned parched and dehydrated, for the wind itself was like a volcano's breath. Search pilots welcomed the tropic showers and turned off their courses to fly through them, canopies wide and heads out, blowing like porpoises. The fire- and engine rooms of the ships were hell itself.

On the eighteenth Halsey's force took up a patrol on an east-west line a hundred miles north of the Samoan Islands and *Enterprise* threw out her long searches to the north-west in the direction of the enemy. The fighters buzzed protectively overhead and the Marines and their equipment began to unload at Pago Pago.

Then the force moved in closer to the islands. From her deck the men of *Enterprise* could see the distant blue-green cloud of Suvaii, British Samoa. Here were the South Sea Islands of books and dreams, of *Treasure Island, Robinson Crusoe* and the *Bounty* mutiny, where Captain Cook and the frigate *Essex* had sailed and fought, where in some lush and savage valley lived Herman Melville's lovely Fayaway. Men found time to stare wistfully across the sea. They envied the Marines ashore. They missed their homes and loved their wives, but they were men and mostly young and they dreamed of the bare-breasted Polynesian girls with gardenias in their long black hair and names like the jungle waterfalls.

For eight days the Big E was on patrol; then, with the Marines safely unloaded, Halsey joined up his two carrier task forces and swung off to the northwest.

The plan of attack was announced.

In order to blunt the point of the enemy drive on the U. S.—Australia life-line, the admiral's mission was to de-stroy Japanese forces and installations in the Gilbert and Marshall Islands from which such a drive would most logi-cally be launched. The *Yorktown* group, under Rear Ad-miral Frank Jack Fletcher, was assigned Jaluit and Mili in the southern Marshalls and Makin in the northern Gilberts. Halsey reserved for himself the older and therefore stronger bases on Wotje and Maloelap in the northeastern Marshalls. And when the U. S. submarine *Dolphin* reported after a careful reconnaissance that the Marshalls were more lightly defended than had been thought, he added Kwajalein and Roi, in the center of the archipelago, to his list of targets.

For five days the combined forces steamed steadily north-west. Every hour took them deeper into waters controlled by Japan (under a pledge not to fortify them) since the First World War. During that time all non-Japanese shipping had been excluded, and no adequate charts were available.

On the first day out of Samoa, Lieutenant (j.g.) "Misty" Fogg of Scouting Six encountered a four-engine flying boat on his regular search. Enemy planes of that type were known to be in the area, but this one did not have enemy markings. Fogg flew alongside but the stranger refused to answer his recognition signals. A warning burst of tracers was also ignored and Fogg opened fire in earnest. The first bullet had hardly entered the big plane's fuselage when a hatch flew open and out streamed the flag of New Zealand. From other ports and hatches appeared anxious, definitely occidental faces and hands extended in the V for Victory sign. The friendly crew had acted just in time; Halsey's ships could not afford to be sighted now.

The twenty-eighth of January was refueling day. From first light until far into the night the gray ships slid up alongside the tanker *Platte*, hoses were rigged, pumps started, and the black "Navy Special" oil splashed into the empty tanks. Since their need was more urgent, the smaller ships had priority. When the Big E's turn came it was 8:00 P.M. and dark, and in enemy waters no light could be shown. No heavy ship had ever fueled at night in the open sea. But *Enterprise* had to have oil to run in fast for the attack, to maneuver during flight operations and to retire in a hurry when the strike was over.

Replenishment of combatant ships under way at sea is an exact and demanding science. The two vessels are required to steam on exactly parallel courses at identical speeds within twenty to seventy feet of one another for hours while all the material to be transferred is passed across the fast and narrow river between them. Quick, skilled hands and precise judgment are necessary, especially on the receiving ship. The captain in most cases assumes control himself, his best helmsman is at the wheel, his most efficient talker at his side to relay his commands. In the engine rooms picked men are at the throttles, and out on deck chief boatswains mates direct the men that handle the heavy lines and hoses. Line handlers must wear life jackets because they work along the extreme edges of the deck and the sea has a way of boiling up between the steep sides. The dynamic forces involved when a 25,000-ton carrier and a 15,000-ton oiler are maneuvering at eight to twelve knots within fifty feet of each other are difficult to compute or imagine. Where one ship happens to brush the other, as sometimes happens, at the points of contact the steel structure is torn and mangled as though a head-on collision had occurred. A parting manila hawser can snap back and kill a man.

On this January night in the hostile South Pacific, Captain George Murray brought his carrier alongside the *Platte* as though it were a summer noon in Long Island Sound. Smoothly and steadily he eased her up until the two ships were close abreast and from his bridge he could look down on the tanker's decks. Then he held her there for five and a half hours.

The seamen and engineers of the Big E did the rest. Heaving lines, messengers, receiving lines and the hoses in their saddles were passed and secured and the oil poured across the frothing gap between the ships. Below decks the "oil king" and his helpers directed the flow of oil to one tank after another, maintaining the balance and stability of the carrier. Constantly the lines were tended to keep a steady tension as the distance between the vessels changed. Men with axes and sharp knives stood by to cut everything away in the event of enemy attack or other emergency.

At one thirty in the morning the Big E's tanks were full and she went back to her place in formation.

On the evening of the twenty-ninth, *Enterprise* and *Yorktown* parted, heading for their respective targets. That night the two carrier task forces, in line abreast but far out of sight of one another, swept westward across the date line into the thirty-first. This was the last day before battle.

During this final day of inaction, Lieutenant Roger W. Mehle, the engineering officer of Fighting Six, and his leading chief, acting under orders issued by Wade McClusky at the urging of Lieutenant Jim Gray, supervised the installation of cockpit armor, ingeniously fabricated out of boiler plate, behind the seat of every Wildcat in the squadron.

The admiral ordered every ship of his force to rig for towing and being towed, a fairly long and complex job of breaking out and coiling down the heavy towing hawsers free to run and clear of all other gear, of readying windlasses and assuring that special tools and hardware are at hand. This would save valuable time in getting a wounded ship clear of the area.

Late in the afternoon radar detected an enemy patrol plane. The weather was clear, calm and sunny, visibility

unlimited. A sighting now, instead of destroying enemy
bases, could turn the entire carefully planned and badly
needed operation into a dangerous defensive action with
the carriers fighting off a horde of land-based bombers.

The admiral was called. In *Enterprise*'s tiny radar room
he watched the little blip of light move across the scope. In
the dim cubby hole, hot with the glowing tubes of its equipment, no one spoke except the radar operator reporting
ranges and bearings to the plotter. Steadily the range
closed. Forty miles. Thirty-seven. Thirty-five. Thirty-four.
The enemy plane was now dead astern and in Air Plot they
thought of the long wakes that trailed back across the sea.
Radio receivers were tuned to Japanese frequencies, waiting to pick up the contact report. Then the range began
slowly to open. The radar blip moved straight along its
course and in a few minutes disappeared from the scope.

Somehow the enemy pilot had missed the task force. It
seemed impossible. In sheer relief Halsey called up an intelligence officer who was trained in Japanese and dictated
a letter to the enemy admiral in the Marshalls expressing
thanks for the scout's failure to sight the U. S. ships. The
letter was reproduced and dropped on the islands the next
day.

On his darkened bridge, Captain Murray, with the wind
of her passage in his face, felt his ship strong and eager under his feet, sensed around him the tense alertness of the
watch, listened to the sea hiss down the side and the occasional whine of electric motors moving the guns. Coolly,
he went over in his head the capabilities and limitations of
his *Enterprise* as she ran full tilt into her first battle. Heavily in her favor was her slow and careful construction at
Newport News, Virginia. No reasonable expense had been
spared, no substitute materials used to make the Big E the
ready ship she was this night. Only two United States vessels before her had been designed and built as aircraft carriers, and Uncle Sam had taken no chances. Even more
comforting to her skipper was the magnificent state of
training that existed in both the ship's own crew and her air
group. U. S. Navy pilots were generally conceded to be the
best trained in the world, and this group had been addition-
ally sharpened by long weeks of operations and harshly
realistic war games. The captain knew that no more proficient team of aviators flew from any carrier. Within the
ship's company was a strong nucleus of experienced old

hands in each department whose knowledge and example had spread and joined until it was felt by every sailor aboard. These men were the products of the years between the wars when there was not the incentive of self-preservation to force a man to learn, when the Navy carefully selected the men permitted to enlist and screened them again for re-enlistment, when those that lasted had a quiet pride in work professionally done and an unspoken but contagious loyalty to ship and service. Their commanding officer knew that in *Enterprise* these men wore both the gold of rank and the eagles of rate and that they had a hundred names, that they had stood on her deck in their creased and spotless whites when the ship was commissioned in May of 1938 and that with luck and courage many would stand there again when the enemy had been destroyed, and the *Enterprise* retired by bigger, stronger sisters. A ship is only what her people are.

Bill Halsey, whose determined spirit filled the ship, smoked and drank coffee in his sea cabin, unable to sleep. His was the responsibility for the first United States offensive action of the new war. His two invaluable forces tore westward through poorly charted waters sown with low coral islands and infested with the enemy. Two hours before launch time, a staff officer reported sand blowing in his face. The admiral, with a steady voice and a dry mouth, ordered an immediate double check on the ship's position, discovered in a moment that the "sand" was blowing down from the radar platform where a lookout stirred sugar into a cup of coffee.

At 3:00 A.M. on February 1 all hands were called. A full moon was still high in the west. There was no wind and the calm sea seemed to sweep eastward between the dark shapes of the warships. The crew went to breakfast. Some ate well but there were many closed throats and full plates when the silent meal was over.

By 4:30 the pilots had been briefed and filed up out of their ready rooms to the flight deck. There the Big E's Sunday punch was cocked and ready. Every available aircraft was gassed and loaded with its assigned assortment of bombs and ammunition. Plane captains stood by in the dark to settle the pilots in their seats and to report the exact condition of their planes. The men picked their way through a hardware jungle of props and tails and folded wings, indistinct and distorted in the moonlight.

The loudspeaker blasted across the crowded deck: "Start engines!" and it was the last voice command that could be heard until every plane had left the deck. Starter motors whirred reluctantly; the big props swung, caught, slowed again and spun into disks; exhausts flamed red, then white, and the blue smoke swirled among the parked planes and streamed out astern.

Enterprise surged up to 30 knots to give her loaded planes a wind for take-off at 4:43 A.M. the first Dauntless thundered past the island and rose slowly into the night sky. A recurrently roaring stream quickly emptied the deck. Scouting Six and Bombing Six led off with thirty-six SBDs for Roi at the northern end of the long Kwajalein Atoll, 155 miles away. Nine Devastators of Torpedo Six followed, bound for the anchorage at the south end of the same atoll. The squadron's other nine planes were loaded with torpedoes and held aboard as a reserve force to be thrown against any major shipping targets which might develop. The combined force was designated the Kwajalein Attack Group, and Commander Howard Young in a thirty-seventh Dauntless was in command. As soon as the attack group was off, six Wildcats scrambled into the air above the ships to guard against a counterattack.

But it was not as simple as that. Each pilot had to steer his heavy plane down the narrow, darkened deck, craning his neck to catch the dim lights hooded at its edges and at the end lift the dead weight of bombs and fuel into the air. Then he had to locate in the three dimensional darkness the tiny white light on the tail of the plane ahead, assure himself by the blue exhaust flames on either side that it was not a star, and join up. He could not ram the throttle forward as he would have liked and close as rapidly as possible because another pilot was attempting to follow the white light on his own tail and the cumulative effect would spoil the rendezvous.

So the laden planes circled, climbing in the dark, forming for the flight to the target. Only well-trained and practiced airmen could have effected that night rendezvous of two and a half squadrons without mishap. And even they needed luck. Once the swinging circles of the two Dauntless squadrons intersected and the stepped-down formations sliced through one another horizontally, two bombers sliding above and below a scout or a single bomber passing between two scouts. Somehow there was no accident.

But at 6:10 when Gray led six fighters off for Maloelap, Ensign D. W. Criswell became disoriented in the dark and spun into the sea. Fighting Six had lost a pilot with the enemy still asleep.

The Big E's first strike was scheduled to hit all targets at 6:58, exactly fifteen minutes before sunrise. At that time it would be light enough for the pilots to find their targets and early enough to find the enemy asleep.

Young's Kwajalein Attack Group had the farthest to go. It climbed steadily out to the westward into the setting moon, the Dauntlesses stacked together in stepped-down Vs and the Vs themselves forming other Vs and echelons. With open canopies the gunners faced aft over the slanting twin barrels of their guns; the pilots looked out across their wings at each other and around at the brightening sky. Below, the late moon lighted a few puffs of cumulus, and the surf broke in delicate rings on the coral.

At 14,000 feet the group leveled off and their speed increased as they neared the target. In the windless dawn, the flat irregular oval of coral islands that makes up Kwajalein Atoll was half hidden in sea mist. One of those islands three miles down was the enemy base at Roi.

The time was 6:53. Five minutes to go.

Hallsted Hopping leading his scouts, and William Hollingsworth at the head of the bombers, compared their ancient charts with the half-dark, mist-obscured scattering of islets below and shook their heads. They glanced toward the single Dauntless of Brig Young, the strike leader.

Young thought he knew which blob of brightening green was Roi. He also knew that, whichever one it was, his SBDs were plainly visible, and that the sound of their thirty-seven engines was a clear call to enemy battle stations. But he could not waste his bombs on a wrong target and under the present conditions it was impossible for him positively to identify the correct one. At his signal the formation swung off in a wide circle to the northward. Halfway through the turn a nervous trigger finger sprayed tracers among the planes of Scouting Six. There were no casualties but the nerves of the pilots were not improved.

As the strike group turned back toward Kwajalein, Roi was clear of mist and easily discernible in the increasing light.

With Hal Hopping in the lead, the first six Dauntlesses of Scouting Six slanted abruptly down, beginning their glide-bombing runs. Earl Gallaher followed with his second division of six, and Dickinson was right behind him with six more.

The enemy was wide-awake. His antiaircraft guns opened up at once; and as the SBDs came down, fighters were rising from the coral strip.

The number of gun flashes increased as the scouts swooped in and black puffs sprouted briefly around them, jostling the pilots and gunners. Hopping bored straight in, in a long flat glide. He crossed the beach at a thousand feet and released his bombs over the airfield. The enemy gunners concentrated on this lead plane, an easy target in its nearly level run, and a Japanese fighter, just taking off, came right up on its tail. For two or three furious seconds the red tracer lines intersected in Hopping's Dauntless as ground and fighter bullets poured in and pilot and gunner returned the fire. Then the SBD sliced into the Pacific on the other side of Roi and sank at once. Commander Hallsted Hopping had dropped the first bomb of the Second World War to land on Japanese soil.

Most of the pilots of Scouting Six had watched their skipper go down. They made a shambles of Roi. Dickinson laid his 200-pound bombs on a big building and Norman West hit an ammunition dump, which went off with a flash and a roar and leveled every structure around the field.

Having dropped their two light bombs and finding no targets worthy of the 500-pounder each still carried, the scouts came back to strafe. They swept in low over the enemy base with their fixed guns hammering straight at parked planes, vehicles and personnel which grew enormously in the pilots' sights until the pull-up and the swing-around to let the gunner bring his free guns to bear. The sun was not yet up and the tracers formed a thousand angles as they ricocheted back into the sky.

Two enemy fighters attacked a wedge of three Dauntlesses but were driven off by combined fire from the free guns. Then, out of range, the enemy pilots put on an air show: loops, slow rolls and barrel rolls, all beautifully executed in formation but with very little effect on the dive bombers that were wrecking their base.

Shortly after seven o'clock, just as the sun was beginning to rise, the authoritative voice of the group commander cut through the confusion of battle at Roi. "Targets suitable for heavy bombs," it said. "Targets suitable for heavy bombs at Kwajalein anchorage."

Bombing Six was detached immediately and headed south with all intact planes of Scouting Six which still carried the big bomb. They left forever behind at Roi four SBDs and their crews. But in the heartless account books of war, the United States was in the black, for lost to the Japanese were three fighters shot down, seven bombers destroyed on the ground, an ammunition dump, two big hangars, a fuel depot and a radio station.

Young's voice was also heard aboard the *Enterprise* and the nine remaining torpedo planes were made ready to launch.

Lieutenant Gene Lindsey, skipper of Torpedo Six, arriving with his nine bomb-loaded Devastators at Kwajalein anchorage, had uncovered a nest of enemy shipping. Fortunately for the big slow TBDs there was no fighter opposition, and, after calling for more planes, he took his boys in at masthead height. The low-level surprise attack panicked the enemy gunners, and, although the flak was heavy, it was poorly directed and ineffective. The low angles of their fire and the confusion caused considerable damage to the enemy's own ships and installations.

When the Dauntlesses from Roi, climbing all the way with throttles jammed forward against the stops, arrived over Kwajalein they found a light cruiser and five submarines, plus two big merchant ships and three tankers among scores of other smaller vessels. Many were reported smoking, listing or aground as a result of Lindsey's attacks.

Hollingsworth shifted his planes into echelon and ordered the attack. One by one the SBDs pulled up to slow, split their dive flaps and rolled into their 70-degree dives. Down out of the dawn sky they poured and the frantic enemy elevated his guns and fired everything that would shoot. The flak streamed wildly upward, but hurriedly aimed and with fuses set for nothing in particular. The Big E's Dauntlesses plunged through and released, and fountains rose around the enemy ships, explosions shook them and men dove for cover as machine-gun bullets swept their decks.

Kwajalein had only fifty minutes to make repairs, dispose of the dead, tend the wounded and get more ammunition to the guns before Lem Massey arrived with the reserve force of nine torpedo-carrying Devastators. He attacked from 700 feet in a right echelon of echelons, his planes jinking and weaving to dodge the flak, and filling the air with such exuberances as, "Get away from that cruiser, Jack! She's mine!" "Bingo!" and "Look at that big bastard burn!"

Massey's torpedoes found two of the tankers and one of the big merchantmen, which turned out on closer inspection to be a converted liner, all three of which had already been hit by at least one 500-pound bomb. Lieutenant (j.g.) Pablo Riley was diverted with his section of three when the cruiser was seen to be making for the entrance to the lagoon. She was hit by two torpedoes and stopped, listing heavily, the storm of fire from her guns sputtering down to an occasional rattle. Six hits were reported of the nine torpedoes dropped; then all the lumbering, vulnerable TBDs returned safely to the *Enterprise*.

While the longer-legged squadrons were attacking Roi and the Kwajalein anchorage, McClusky's Wildcats were working closer to the ship. Jim Gray took his five fighters south to Maloelap. Like Young at Kwajalein, he had map and navigation troubles, and each plane wasted one of its pair of 100-pounders on the nearly deserted and completely unfortified island of Tjan in the Maloelap Atoll. On the pull-up they quickly discovered the enemy field at Taroa, their assigned target.

At Taroa they had expected to find a coral strip, a hangar and half a dozen planes. What they saw below them was a firstclass base, comparable to their own Ford Island. Two brand-new mile-long concrete runways gleamed in the early sunlight, and parked between them were thirty to forty twin-engine bombers. Close by was a small navy yard, a beautiful stone administration building and a radio station. And enemy fighters were overhead.

Gray's F4Fs hurtled in to put their remaining bombs on the navy yard and strafe the parked bombers in repeated runs. Here was the real danger. The fighter pilots knew what would happen to the *Enterprise* if those planes were armed and launched. Their guns punched lots of holes in the enemy bombers but they had no incendiary ammunition and only Ralph Rich was able to set one on fire. Then, with Japanese fighters beginning to engage, the Big E pilots ran into gun trouble. Since early November, Fighting Six had been trying to solve the problem of gun-jamming which occurred with dangerous frequency whenever the wing ammunition cans were fully loaded. By flying and fixing and flying again, the frequency had been reduced, but on this day, one after another, each gun jammed and stayed jammed.

Nevertheless, Rawie, pulling up from his second strafing run, flew into a section of enemy fighters, and, when one attempted a head-on approach, held so solidly to his course that he scuffed his propeller on the enemy plane as its pilot lost his nerve and pulled up.

Gray failed to realize the presence of the Japanese fighters until after his third strafing attack when one climbed out just in front of him. With his one still-operating gun, Gray got in a good burst, and saw the enemy try a downwind landing, then crash and smear the field with a quarter of a mile of flame and smoke. By this time Rich, Rawie, Heisel and Holt, bombs gone and guns jammed, had departed for home, and Gray was left alone over Taroa with the enemy and four observation planes from the heavy cruiser *Chester,* which was just beginning her bombardment.

His position was critical. The single Wildcat was the target for about twelve enemy fighters and, directly below, the cruiser's eight-inch salvos were throwing shrapnel and debris into the crowded sky. He somehow found a cloud and escaped, but with no rudder control, and all the gasoline in one tank drained out through a bullet hole.

When he landed aboard, the plane handlers counted thirty to forty holes in his plane, including one through the propeller. They had to push it out of the arresting gear because the brakes had been shot away and it was out of fuel. There were fifteen dents in the homemade armor protecting the pilot. Charlie Fox remarked that the plane "looked like the moths had been at it in the attic all summer."

Wade McClusky took six of his fighters to Wotje. He barely had time to crank up the wheels of his Wildcat before he was over his target. The stubby, square-winged Grummans dived in steep and fast on the enemy field and harbor, bombing and strafing whatever seemed most worthy of their attention. From the deck of the *Enterprise* the crew could see smoke rising from their hits. Twice the Big E's Wildcats dived across the base, and, when every enemy gun and eye was turned warily upward, the first full salvos from *Northampton* and *Salt Lake City* rumbled in from the sea and hurled concrete and coral high into the morning air.

When reports had come in from all the strikes, Admiral

Halsey saw that the threat to his forces lay in the dozens of bombers on the big new field at Taroa. While the *Chester* and her accompanying destroyers pinned down the enemy there, the first dive bombers to return from Roi were re-serviced and rearmed for Taroa.

Bill Hollingsworth took them in, seven of his own bomb-ers and two scouts. He climbed all the way to his target and came down out of the sun like a stream of meteors. With his three bombs, Holly blew up seven parked bombers and his wingman hit a hangar that flared so viciously that it seemed to have been filled with gasoline. The third plane hit another hangar and smashed three parked fighters. The others did as well, concentrating on the rows of planes and the hangars that might contain still more.

On its way back to the ship Hollingsworth's group passed nine more SBDs headed for the same target. They were led by Lieutenant Richard Best. At Taroa they flew into a swarm of enemy fighters and a storm of antiaircraft fire stirred up by the previous attack. The Dauntlesses dived stubbornly on the parked aircraft with their gunners fight-ing off the enemy interceptors all the way.

Perry Teaff in his SBD acquitted himself miraculously by surviving a long-sustained single combat with a Nakajima fighter. Ed Kroeger shot down one enemy plane and got a bullet in his foot from a second which his gunner, Achilles Georgiou, destroyed. Bucky Walters, who had landed among the concrete mixers and bulldozers at Kaneohe, with his three bombs knocked down a radio tower, blew up a fuel dump and finished off the new administration build-ing. Only Ensign Jack Doherty, who, at the tail of the for-mation, had fought and flown desperately to keep the fight-ers off the other planes, and then pressed home his own at-tack, failed to return. His last words as his Dauntless twisted and swirled among three Nakajimas were: "These goddam Japs will never get me."

When the last strike returned to the *Enterprise* it was one o'clock in the afternoon. For nine hours the carrier task force had been maneuvering in a five-by-twenty-five-mile rectangle within sight of Wotje and within easy range of half a dozen enemy air and surface bases. During those hours she had launched and recovered twenty-one times. Sweat poured from the engineers who swung the throttle wheels and worked the valves among the steam lines down below. It darkened the blue chambray shirts of the me-

chanics and gunner's mates toiling over the damaged planes
on the hangar deck, spreading in blotches from the armpits
and the middle of the back where the material pulled tight
against the flesh. Under the open sun of the flight deck the
bright jerseys of the plane handlers were simply sodden,
grimed too with oil and dirt from prop blast and deck and
cowl. In the gun tubs and five-inch mounts the sweat
trickled from under the gray helmets and smarted in the
eyes, dripping annoyingly from the ends of noses.

And the Big E had stood back and forth in her little
rectangle of the great sea, launching her warplanes slow
and heavy and recovering them light, hurried and holed by
the guns of the enemy. Her people heard over the loudspeakers the voices of the senior pilots assigning targets,
the orders to attack and to withdraw and the shouts, curses
and sobs of men delivering death in the face of death. They
gaped at the perforated planes and their wounded crews
and on the horizon watched the fires and the firing on
Wotje. Returning pilots hurried to their squadron ready
rooms to be sure their friends had survived the latest strike,
or to learn that they had not. The officer whose responsibility it was to interview plane crews and assess the damage
to the enemy was continuously surrounded by excited
young aviators in their sweaty khakis, showing him with
precisely maneuvering hands exactly the way it had happened.

When Bill Hollingsworth made his report to Admiral
Halsey and Captain Murray on the bridge, he had a sug-
gestion.

"Admiral," he said, "don't you think it's about time we
got the hell out of here?"

Halsey had been wondering how much longer his luck
would hold. A periscope had lately been reported and it
was optimistic to think that his planes had destroyed all the
hostile aircraft in the area. He told Hollingsworth: "My
boy, I've been thinking the same thing myself," and the Big
E was shortly making 30 knots in the direction of Pearl
Harbor.

Now the tension relaxed a little as, with all her planes
aboard except the usual Combat Air Patrol, the Big E leveled out on the course for home.

At about twenty minutes of two, five twin-engine Japanese bombers in an open V broke out of the low clouds on
the carrier's starboard bow and attacked in a shallow glide.

In a few seconds every gun in the force was firing at them, but in the excitement of firing on their first live target, the gunners aimed straight at the attackers instead of leading them. "Our AA guns," Admiral Halsey later wrote, "might as well have been water pistols."

The enemy formation sailed straight in across the ship. From the deck of the Big E her men could see the bomb-bay doors swing open and the bombs fall away. The ship leaped and shuddered as the heavy bombs detonated in the sea around her, throwing up spouts of dirty water.

In the machinery spaces below the water line where the engineers listened and looked up as they went about their duties, the bomb bursts sounded like the blows of a gigantic hammer on the hull. Fifteen bombs were dropped and all went over the ship, landing to port. One burst about thirty feet off the port quarter. Fragments tore into the ship, cutting a gasoline line, igniting the spilled fuel, and shattering the leg of a second class boatswain's mate, George H. Smith, who was manning a machine gun in the port catwalk. Smith continued to fire until the action was over and his shipmates hauled him off to sick bay. He died there two hours later, the first combat casualty in the *Enterprise*. Damage control crews quickly put out the fire.

The last enemy bomber over the ship, already damaged by the guns of the CAP, dropped suddenly out of formation and dived steeply to the left, sweeping around in a full circle in an obvious attempt to crash on the carrier's deck. Captain Murray saw what was coming and ordered full right rudder. Every gun that would bear concentrated on the single fanatical attacker. He was hit repeatedly but kept coming, guns winking along the edges of his wings, maneuvering desperately toward the ship. If it had not been for George Murray's hard right turn and Bruno Peter Gaido, aviation machinist's mate second class, he might have been successful. As the Big E swung out from under him, he attempted to turn his aircraft sharply enough to hit the flight deck. Bruno Gaido, from his catwalk battle station, saw the enemy pilot attempting to smash the *Enterprise*. Halsey on the flag bridge watched Bruno's helmeted, tightly jerseyed figure dart across the open deck and scramble into the rear seat of the sternmost Dauntless. Then from the parked dive bomber poured the tracers of its free gun as Gaido opened up right in the face of the enemy. It almost seemed as though the action had become a personal

duel between the oriental at the plane's controls and the
bony, Mediterranean face over the twin 30s of the Dauntless. In a final right turn the enemy pilot tried for a deck
crash. His right wing tip sliced through Gaido's SBD,
shearing its tail off three feet from where the mechanic
furiously kept up his fire. The right wing of the enemy
plane separated from the fuselage and skidded into the port
catwalk, the fuel from its ruptured tanks drenching the ship
forward to the island and up into the superstructure. The
broken Dauntless was knocked far over to port on the extreme aft edge of the flight deck. In its rear seat Gaido
stood to depress his guns, hammering their tracers into the
wreckage of the Jap bomber as it settled into the sea astern.
That afternoon Bruno Peter Gaido became an aviation machinist's mate, first class.

In the next two hours Halsey's task force put sixty more
miles of sea and sky between itself and the enemy.

Then at four o'clock two more enemy planes were
sighted. They were fast and clever, coming in high from up
sun and dodging McClusky's fighters in the clouds. The
Wildcats of the CAP closed on them with painful slowness.
When McClusky saw he could not catch them before they
made their drops, he began to coach the AA gunners below.

"Your bursts are low," he reported. "Get them up. That's
better. Now you're a little high. Just a little lower now.
Now you're on! You're on! You've got him!"

One plane was hit but stayed on course. They both
dropped two heavy bombs which missed badly. By now the
fighters had closed in and their skipper's voice came down
out of the sky again.

"Knock off AA fire. We'll take 'em."

The ships' guns went silent and McClusky, Daniels and
Mehle swooped in from both sides to knock one plane into
the sea in sight of the task force. The other escaped, smoking, because the F4Fs were too short of fuel to chase it.

Just before sunset, Mehle found a twin-float seaplane
snooping. He made two runs, twisting down in high side attacks, guns blinking, to flash past underneath and pull up
sharply, hands and arms suddenly heavy and blood draining
downward, to position himself for another attack. On the
first run he killed the rear-seat gunner, and on the next
shot the snooper down.

At dusk all the Wildcats were called in. Night fighters did not exist.

The moon rose in a clear sky and the long thirty-knot wakes were signposts for the enemy. With no fighters and ineffective guns, still well within range of land-based aircraft, the Big E was in serious danger. Further, the enemy would certainly know that the force was heading northeast for Pearl Harbor and search that track with diligence.

As soon as his ships were clear of the atolls of the Marshalls, Halsey turned them to the northwest. Shortly thereafter radar picked up a group of air targets that proceeded steadily out that northeast course toward Pearl and disappeared from the scope.

Luck was with the *Enterprise* that night. Lieutenant William H. Ashford of the admiral's staff made out a cloud system in the distance which turned out to be a beautiful weather front with such low ceilings and bad visibility in rain and fog that even the ships in the force could not make each other out. The men of *Enterprise* secured from battle stations, and under the protecting weather front Halsey turned back for Honolulu.

Just before noon the next day, R. J. Hoyle of Fighting Six made out the shape of a submerged submarine 3,000 yards, broad on the Big E's starboard beam. As he climbed into attack position and broadcast the alarm, he saw the periscope break the surface, trailing its tiny feather. His bomb landed just forward of the scope. The sub crash-dived, its propellers spinning wetly in the sunlight, and Hoyle, banking violently back, poured 600 rounds of .50-caliber bullets into the stern. A destroyer arrived and laid a pattern of shallow-set depth charges which hammered on the hulls of the ships and erupted in solid columns of water. A large oil slick spread upward and out across the surface and air bubbles arose at intervals. Contact was never regained and the submarine was listed as "probably destroyed."

It was the fifth of February when *Enterprise*, flying her big battle flags, steamed back up the channel into Pearl. At Fort Kamehameha and at Hickam, where two months before she had been so bluntly warned that she would be "nailed," the khaki-uniformed troops gathered on the shore to cheer her. At Hospital Point the nurses, doctors, orderlies and patients waved and shouted. The crew of each warship in the big harbor manned the rails and cheered in repeated bursts of male voices. From the far corners of the base other ships blew their sirens and whistles in congratulation. The men of the Big E, standing at quarters in their whites, answered cheer for cheer until they were hoarse and their voices caught.

On the bridge of his flagship, grim, salty old Bill Halsey's eyes shone. It made little difference that postwar evidence would show much less damage done in the Marshalls than Young's pilots thought. He and *Enterprise* had brought the war's first victory back to Pearl.

5 BACK TO WAKE

There were eight days in port.

Every afternoon one quarter of the men were granted liberty which expired at 5:30 p.m. After two months at sea the young sailors made such heroic efforts to waste no minute of their two hours ashore that the Shore Patrol longed for the day *Enterprise* would sail again.

Every pilot had a few days of "rehabilitation" at the Royal Hawaiian where now a Navy band had replaced the guitars and where the USO supplied girls to dance with instead of the old, expensive, random quest. Enlisted men manned the desk, and the guests carried their own baggage. Rations from the Navy general mess were served by mess attendants in the dining rooms. Juke boxes and pinball machines appeared in the vaulted lobby. But the elaborately furnished rooms with views of Waikiki and Diamond Head, with the soft sea air ballooning the drapes and the sound of the surf to sleep by, had not changed. Despite themselves, the nervous, wound-up pilots and submariners back from war patrols felt the frown-wrinkles smoothing out and the quick angry words coming less frequently to the tongue.

In Honolulu good whisky either did not exist or was prohibitively expensive. The armed services, to conserve and apportion the supply, rationed it at the rate of a bottle a week per customer. The Big E's pilots chafed under the restriction, resenting both the principle and its practical application as it affected their few days of freedom. They promptly determined that the type of training most necessary to carrier-based aviators during this period was cross-country flying and the gaining of familiarity with airfields other than their own. Accordingly, the Dauntlesses, Wildcats and Devastators of the *Enterprise* air group became known at all the island airports. They visited Ewa, Wheeler, Kaneohe and Hickam; they investigated the isolated strips at Mokuleia, Haleiwa and Bellows Field. And at each station they drew their weekly ration.

Factory-made armor arrived at last and was installed in the fighters. Some of the planes got self-sealing tanks. Eight *Enterprise* Wildcats were assigned to the Army and placed on ready duty at Wheeler Field.

On February 10, Admiral Halsey received orders for his next operation and sent them back to headquarters. He welcomed the mission, but he balked at having his ships designated Task Force 13 and sailing on Friday the thirteenth. The force's number was changed to 16 and the sailing date to the fourteenth, Valentine's Day.

The early afternoon of the fourteenth found *Enterprise* at sea again, and from her decks the gray ships around her had the comfortably familiar look of old and trusted friends. *Northampton* and *Salt Lake City* steamed close by behind the semicircle of screening destroyers, *Maury, Balch, Dunlap, Blue, Ralph Talbot* and *Craven*. Only *Craven* was new, only the cruiser *Chester* was missing from the force that had raided the Marshalls and Gilberts. The tanker *Sabine* replaced the *Platte*.

For a week Halsey steamed in a generally northwesterly direction while the exec drilled the ship's company for action and the air group fired at target sleeves and rehearsed tactics.

Throughout the crew was an awareness of the necessity for staying "manned and ready." The successful strike against the Marshalls had raised their spirits, but they knew it had been only a raid, a prick at the flank of the enemy, an attempt to hinder and divert him from his steady sweep to the south.

Even in Europe things continued to go badly. On the eleventh the *Scharnhorst, Gneisenau, Lutzow* and *Prince Eugen* had run the English Channel from Brest to Wilhelmshaven shooting down forty-two attacking aircraft in the face of all the guns, ships, planes and radar the British could muster in their own front yard.

And on the fifteenth, Singapore was overrun. Clearly the victory in the Marshalls had not altered the course of the war.

Three days later, two PBY Catalinas came in low from the northeast, and one dropped a package on the Big E's flight deck. It was delivered at once to the admiral.

On the same day Lieutenant (j.g.) Thomas Eversole of Torpedo Six, returning from an afternoon search, became disoriented in the shifting winds and poor visibility of a cold front, and was forced to ditch, nearly out of fuel, some sixty miles from the ship. The next morning a search was launched and Tom was quickly found in his bright yellow life raft, steering carefully for Midway, 250 miles to the eastward, and keeping time for the steady aluminum oars of his two crewmen. After he was safely back aboard he was subjected to an unmerciful ribbing, and amateur cartoons appeared on the ship's bulletin boards depicting "Eversole's first command."

On the fourteenth, Admiral Halsey announced that the Big E's mission was a strike against Wake Island. The men cheered when they heard the name. Wake had become somehow personal to the men of the *Enterprise*. It was not a hitherto unheard-of speck on the chart of the Pacific like Maloelap or Kwajalein, but a real place, a United States possession to which they had only recently delivered men they knew. They remembered the day the Marines had taken off in their F4Fs from the Big E's deck for Wake. They had followed the fighting with tense interest as those same Marines repelled the initial enemy attacks and sank his ships, and they had been sad and bitter when the island fell. Now Halsey was taking them in to strike the Japanese that had overwhelmed it. There was no target short of Tokyo to which they would rather have been assigned.

The plan was for the two heavy cruisers under the command of Rear Admiral Raymond A. Spruance, with *Maury* and *Balch,* to circle out and approach Wake from the west, the least suspected direction. *Enterprise,* with the remaining destroyers, would run in on a southerly course and launch from a position a hundred miles north. The cruisers and their escorts would open up with their guns at dawn on the twenty-fourth, the "open fire" signal, like that for the blowing of the bridge in *For Whom the Bell Tolls,* to be the crump and flash of the first bombs on the target. The package dropped on deck by the Marine Catalina had been recent photographs of Wake.

Enterprise reached her assigned position in the full dark of 5:00 A.M. and turned into the wet east wind to launch. There was no moon and a low, solid overcast shut out the light of the stars. Along the sides the night sea sloshed in a high, confused chop.

The bull horn blasted its mechanical voice across the waiting mass of aircraft; propellers swung and caught. Each prop as it began to spin condensed the moisture in the laden air and spiraled it back in concentric rings from the blade tips to envelop its own plane. Each droplet in the whirling rings reflected the steady flame of the exhausts. Every aircraft as its engine started was cocooned in electric blue light out of which the pilot could not see.

In time of peace the launch would have been postponed. But a hundred miles to the south *Salt Lake* and *Northampton* were in gun range of Wake awaiting the signal to commence firing and expecting the air support they had been promised. On the island itself the enemy could be expected to have his scouts up at dawn.

The air group was ordered to take off.

Scouting Six was first. Blindly and erratically the SBDs roared down the deck, still enveloped in their eerie hoops of light. A few got off and at once disappeared into the low clouds. Then Perry Teaff missed. His Dauntless angled to port, the left wheel dropped into the catwalk, the left wing struck a five-inch gun mount and he plunged off into the sea.

Flight operations were suspended. *Blue* raced up and was granted permission to use her searchlights. In a few minutes she located Teaff bobbing in the breaking chop, his head bloody. His radioman/gunner, E. P. Jinks, was heard briefly, calling in the darkness, then vanished and was not recovered. Perry Teaff lost his left eye.

As the light slowly increased, the pilots were able to see better where they were going but rendezvous was difficult in the dimness and the layers of clouds and it was 6:50 A.M. before the strike was formed up and inbound for the target.

Fifty-two planes and 106 men made up the Big E's surprise party for the enemy occupation forces on Wake Island. Earl Gallaher led all eighteen SBDs of his Scouting Six and Bill Hollingsworth another eighteen of Bombing Six. Gene Lindsey brought nine Devastators and left the other half of his squadron behind in reserve, as at the Marshalls, in the event any good torpedo targets turned up. Wade McClusky with six Wildcats flew cover for the bombers, and the Air Group Commander Howard Young directed the four squadrons from his SBD.

En route to the target the planes climbed through the lightening sky to attack altitudes, the dive bombers and fighters to 18,000 feet and the horizontal bombers (TBDs) to 12,000. The trip took one hour.

The rough and broken arrowhead of Wake, with its green scrub growth and its white sand, lay pointing to the southeast. At its broadest part, just behind the tip, were the runways of the airfield which gave the island its principal value. Northwest of the field where the head was notched to receive the shaft lay the lagoon with the long barbs protecting it on both sides. The tip of each barb was broken and slightly separated from the head by a narrow channel, thus forming two separate additional islands. The one on the north was Peale, where Pan-American had had seaplane facilities and a new hotel, and the one to the south was Wilkes. It was at the Pan-American hotel on Peale that Ambassador Saburo Kurusu had stayed on his way to Washington to "negotiate" while the Japanese striking force was steaming toward Pearl Harbor.

Wilkes was important because of the gasoline storage tanks just across the channel and the shore batteries and antiaircraft emplacements along its seaward shore. It was at Wilkes a little over two months before that Marine Captain H. M. Platt, a casual South Carolinian, with sixty assorted artillerymen, had wiped out some hundred enemy Special Landing Force troops and held the mile-long strip of sand until the fall of the main island made it untenable.

In the seconds before he ordered the attack, Howard Young could see on the south coast, close to the airfield, an enemy destroyer and a destroyer-leader beached and broken, holed by the Marines and run ashore to keep from sinking. He glanced at the tents of the contractors' camp across the channel from Peale and wondered if any of the defeated Marines and civilian volunteers were still held prisoner there. His orders were to leave it intact in case. Then he picked up his mike, and back in the Big E they heard his words: "Attack. Attack."

Hollingsworth took his division of six down first, the Dauntlesses nearly vertical in their dives, their perforated dive flaps split at the trailing edges of the wings, pilots leaning forward tensely, feeling the pull of their seat belts as they picked their targets and the island grew enormously beneath them. The gunners were merely lying on their backs, the twin barrels of their guns pointing at the sky.

All six planes in staggered tandem were well into their dives before the leader released his bomb and began the pullout. On the ground the antiaircraft fire sputtered back, and black dots formed above the island.

With the flash of Hollingsworth's big bomb, Gallaher pushed over with six more SBDs, and thus the Scouts and the Bombers followed each other in coordinated split attacks by divisions. There was no air opposition, and McClusky's fighters had a ringside seat while the bombing squadrons professionally worked over their targets.

In a well-executed attack the group commander and the three photo planes joined up with a section of Devastators to lay a close pattern on the gasoline storage tanks across from Wilkes. Seven of the ten tanks went up in a boiling, rolling flare of orange flame and black smoke.

Another section of horizontal bombers wiped out a four-engined seaplane moored just south of Pan American's pier on Peale, and Lieutenant L. A. Smith of Bombing Six in a glide attack destroyed another one on a barge in the same vicinity.

Ensign Delbert W. Halsey (unrelated to his admiral), having dropped his big bomb and strafed enemy gun positions, looked for targets worthy of his two smaller ones. He found instead another four-engine seaplane in the air off the island's eastern shore and was able to make one attack from behind and below before the enemy pilot opened his throttles and left the SBD behind. Remembering the Wildcats circling overhead, Halsey opened up on his radio: "This is Halsey. This is Halsey. I got a Kawanishi five miles east of the island heading straight east and can't catch him."

Wade McClusky had been patrolling at 15,000 feet for thirty minutes by this time while the other three squadrons were in action. While Ensign Halsey's voice was still on the air the fighters were plunging, spiraling toward the surface. Their initial turn was toward two cruisers which were bombarding the island, and the ships' antiaircraft batteries opened up. McClusky turned away and continued the descent. The fighters pulled out at a thousand feet and found themselves behind and to the right of the enemy flying boat in perfect attack position. The skipper made the first run, silencing the enemy gunners and smoking the left outboard engine. B. H. Bayers was next, his tracers raking the fuselage and starting a second engine burning. Then skinny, aggressive Roger Mehle bored in, firing in long, repeated bursts. Before his eyes the big plane blew apart. Ducking under the debris, Mehle saw the enemy pilot tumbling toward the sea. Later a piece of hinge fitting was found embedded in the leading edge of Mehle's right wing. On it in very unJapanese characters was stamped "1938."

By 9:45, fifty-one of the fifty-two-plane attack group were back over their carrier under the watchful eye of her CAP.

That night the men of the *Enterprise* added up the score. Jinks was lost at sea; Foreman and Winchester, if they lived, were prisoners of the enemy; Teaff faced life with only his right eye. The enemy had lost a flying boat and a patrol craft with their crews and two other four-engine planes destroyed on the ground plus an unknown number of ground defense personnel, several hundred thousand gallons of gasoline and the use of Wake Island as an effective base for a period of months.

On the evening of the twenty-fifth of February, as the Big E, with *Ralph Talbot, Craven, Dunlap* and *Blue,* steamed northeastward for her rendezvous with Admiral Spruance's cruisers and the tanker *Sabine,* Bill Halsey received an urgent dispatch from the commander-in-chief, Pacific Fleet: "Desirable to strike Marcus if you think it feasible."

Marcus is a tiny triangular island 650 miles west of Wake. It is a thousand miles east of Tokyo and, in 1942, six or seven hundred miles from big Japanese bases in the Bonins and Marianas.

Halsey reassembled his forces off Midway and headed west.

Rough weather was forecast all the way to Marcus and high speed was necessary to avoid detection. Halsey left the destroyers behind to protect the tanker and with his single carrier and two heavy cruisers stood off to the westward at twenty knots. The little force of three gray ships raiding deep into enemy-controlled waters was an indication both of Bill Halsey's bold leadership and the thinned-out condition of the U. S. Navy. On the evening of the twenty-seventh came news that the Japanese had landed in force on Java and that the cruiser *Houston* and the old *Langley*, the Navy's first carrier, had been sunk.

On the second of March radio silence was broken to recover the morning search planes and during the day two submarines were sighted and driven down with bombs. There began to be some doubt about achieving surprise at Marcus.

All day the third the ship was at full alert, buttoned up tight, guns manned and pilots in their planes with engines warm. After sunset each man felt the now-familiar trembling of the deck beneath his feet as turbines and propellers came up to speed for the run-in. *Enterprise* came down fast in a long diagonal from the northeast straight for Marcus.

At 4:35 A.M. the insistent, nerve-shaking clang of the general alarm filled the ship. Eleven minutes later the first Dauntless of Bombing Six clawed up into the night sky. By four minutes after five the thirty-eight-plane attack group was air-borne and the carrier slowed to await its return. It was another night take-off and rendezvous for the air group, an evolution that soon became known as a "group grope."

A heavy layer of cumulus clouds extended from four to eight thousand feet and in the dark below it the Big E's squadrons circled with dimmed running lights, joining up. For his one-punch, hit-and-run smash at Marcus, Howard Young had seventeen Bombers, fourteen Scouts and six fighters. His own SBD made the thirty-eighth plane.

It took twenty minutes to complete the rendezvous and during the climb through the thick, turbulent clouds, many sections and divisions became separated. It is only surprising that the attack force did not become more scattered. To climb a single-engine aircraft in formation at night through the churning, bouncing fog of a cumulus cloud, knowing that in that same cloud are some thirty or forty other planes flying at more than a hundred miles an hour with the same lack of visibility, is a stern test of nerves and skill in time of peace. To do so with the dry mouth and tightened stomach that come to most men in the hour before combat, over a hostile ocean two or three thousand miles from the nearest friendly base, requires in addition the highest degree of courage and concentration. Trying to close his mind to the coming action and the nearby planes he cannot see, a pilot must stay in close enough to the gray shape of the adjacent plane so as not to lose sight of it in the fog that pours between them in the darkness, and yet not so close that a collision will result. He must also monitor his instrument panel to assure himself of engine performance, air speed, heading, attitude and altitude.

On the Big E's radar, the air group was a cluster of little blobs of light, some merging and overlapping, others, like Gray's fighter, separate from the cluster. Each time the bright rotating line swept around the scope, the blobs which were the strike force changed position slightly as they moved toward their target.

Lieutenant John Baumeister, the radar officer, could not share in the demanding formation climb through the cumulus, nor see the moonlight that shone above the clouds, but he knew that in the predawn darkness the *Enterprise* air group had to find a few acres of earth and rock 128 miles away and although it had never been tried before, he thought he knew how he could help. On his scope he had drawn a line which was the track to Marcus. Young's planes showed up a few miles to the left of that line. Out over the coded, high-frequency radio, guarded by all planes, went a series of staccato dots and dashes. In the rear seat of the group commander's Dauntless his radioman/gunner jotted the letters and numerals down on a knee pad and read them over the intercom. They told Howard Young the course correction to stay on the track to his objective, and exactly the distances he had covered toward it. In this way the long, invisible beam of the Big E's radar pointed the way to the target, and the pilots in their darkened, laden planes could stay high in the clear moonlight, climbing to attack altitude, with the comforting knowledge of their exact position. And in the hands of the men of *Enterprise* the new, not quite believable phenomenon of radar was growing toward maturity.

At 6:30 a break in the clouds dimly showed the solitary triangle of Marcus Island. It was simply a small airfield surrounded by water. The attacking aviators could see the three gleaming coral runways paralleling the short coastlines, a white triangle inscribed in the solid black one.

Young led the attack group down from 16,000 feet, a camera-equipped plane of Scouting Six on either wing. While the three SBDs were in their dives, a cloud drifted in, momentarily obscuring the target. The group commander's section released at 6,000 feet above the cloud, and pulled up steeply for another run. But the drop was lucky. The characteristic orange flare of a gasoline fire boiled up out of the semidarkness where the bombs hit.

The rest of the group was close behind. From 6:30 to 6:45 they poured down onto the enemy-held island out of the clouds and the dark sky.

Lieutenant Jack Blitch of Bombing Six made his run on an L-shaped building near a pair of radio towers. On the ship, the men in the radio shack heard an alarmed Japanese voice come suddenly on the air and then as suddenly go off in mid-phrase as Blitch's bombs wrecked the transmitter.

Pulling away, Howard Young thought he saw fighters on the runway, and the chilling order went out to the Wildcats: "Get those fighters taking off!" Young's radio was acting up and only Gray heard the order. He swept in over the field, his finger curled around the trigger on his stick but found nothing.

After the first few planes had made their drops, the enemy came awake. From emplacements scattered around the perimeter of the field between runways and beach he opened up with heavy-machine-gun fire which was of greater volume and more accurate than any the Big E's pilots had seen in the Marshalls or at Wake. The long streams of tracers followed them, uncomfortably close, far out to sea on their retirement. Several planes were holed. Dale Hilton of the Scouts reported that his plane was on fire and he was going to ditch. Dickinson saw him slide by underneath, his engine and one wing wrapped in flame. Dick Best saw the water landing and circled while Hilton and J. Leaming, his gunner, climbed into their rubber raft and waved, giving the thumbs up signal that both were O.K. Then they settled to their oars, pulling strongly away from Marcus. They were taken prisoner by the enemy.

All planes were back aboard by 8:45. Except Gray. Gray's radio, like Young's, was off frequency (which was the reason that only he had heard the order to get the fighters taking off) and he was unable to receive the Big E's homing signals. He navigated back with the best data available and he was close. John Baumeister's radar picked up a single stranger going by and *Enterprise* ducked into a rain squall to avoid being sighted.

Baumeister guessed the lone plane was Gray's, remembered that the evening before, handsome hot-shot Gray had mentioned his faulty radio. Baumeister detuned the homing device to a frequency on which he thought an out-of-kilter radio would be. All the guessing, thinking and remembering worked. Gray received the new frequency and landed aboard after four and a half hours in the air, with only nine gallons of gasoline left.

All that day Fighting Six kept a double CAP of eight Wildcats aloft as the Big E "hauled out with Halsey."

The damage done to Marcus was difficult to assess. Ironically radar's help had so expedited the flight to the target that the strike had been made in semidarkness rather than at dawn as planned and thus no photographs could be taken. The clouds and heavy antiaircraft fire had made poststrike reconnaissance too costly. But as the last fighters left Marcus for the *Enterprise*, two large and several smaller fires were burning brightly, still visible at thirty miles. Young's gasoline storage and Blitch's radio building were known to have been destroyed, besides hangars, other storage tanks and small buildings in the center and on the south shore. In addition the coral runways had been made unusable and an AA emplacement silenced. Most important in the long run was the blackout that the raid caused in Tokyo itself and the doubt that entered the Japanese mind as to the infallibility of the defense provided by the Imperial Navy.

On the tenth of March, 1942, *Enterprise* was back at her berth in Pearl Harbor and her pilots were unwinding at the Royal Hawaiian.

While in port, in an impressive ceremony in whites on the flight deck, Admiral William F. Halsey was awarded the Distinguished Service Medal. That evening the crew gathered on the hangar deck for the nightly movie. Just before starting time Bill Halsey entered, and with a scraping of chairs and benches and a clumping of feet, the men quieted and stood. "Carry on," he said, and the crew reseated and settled themselves and the buzz of conversation began to pick up again. Then it died out because the admiral was standing, facing the front row under the screen. For a few seconds his eyes ran over the rows of faces all turned toward him. And for a few seconds the men of *Enterprise* looked hard and expectantly at their admiral whose decisions so vitally affected them. They saw a solid, square man in his late fifties, with a wide face and mouth and a stubborn jut of jaw, whose straight back and look told the habit of command. Halsey was not yet a hero who wanted to ride Hirohito's white horse through Tokyo. He was simply a vice admiral of the Navy with thirty years of experience and a reputation for boldness and integrity.

After the quiet seconds of looking, Halsey spoke and his voice was clear and strong, carrying easily to the back row of sailors craning their necks to see. He held out the medal he had received that morning. "Men," he said, "this medal belongs to you. I am honored to wear it for you." He paused as if gathering his thoughts for a short speech, and then said quickly, "I am so damned proud of you I could cry." He turned and sat down.

There was an instant of silence while the words and the voice went home. Somehow they shattered the tension and control of the weeks of combat and suddenly those boys who had so recently become men and those men who had so lately come of age were standing on their chairs and stools and mess benches and cheering, cheering to tear their throats out, glancing at each other and cheering again. It was a full five minutes before the long cavern of the hangar deck was quiet enough for the movie to begin.

6 COLONEL DOOLITTLE GOES TO TOKYO

In the predawn hours of the eighth of April the last bitter acres of Bataan Peninsula were occupied by the enemy.

At noon, *Enterprise, Salt Lake City* and *Northampton,* with four destroyers and the tanker *Sabine,* issued in single file through the torpedo nets of Pearl Harbor and shortly turned northwest. Two hours after departure the air group had flown aboard, and the force was armed and complete.

The fighters were flying a new breed of Wildcat, the F4F-4, equipped with self-sealing tanks, cockpit armor and folding wings for improved stowage and shipboard handling. Everyone except the pilots loved the folding wings. They made the pilots uneasy. It was like sailing in a ship with a removable bottom or driving a car with collapsible wheels.

The topside look of *Enterprise* herself was changed. In her catwalks and gun tubs the new 20-millimeter Oerlikon machine gun had replaced the old water-cooled .50-caliber Brownings. The heavy coiled springs around their barrels and the size of the projectiles in their snail-shaped magazines were impressive and a new confidence in antiaircraft gunnery spread through the mess halls and berthing spaces.

For three and a half days the gray ships steamed steadily northwestward. Each day brought colder, damper weather. The Big E's men shivered in their light khakis and gooseflesh erupted under the tan of the tropics.

Just before 6:00 A.M. on the twelfth, *Enterprise* was steaming slowly in huge circles at a point in the North Pacific as close to the Kamchatkan Peninsula of Siberia as to Oahu, halfway between Midway and the Western Aleutians, latitude 39 north, longitude 180 degrees. A chilled *Enterprise* lookout, dark-jowled and red-eyed in the early light, reported a carrier to starboard. She carried a deckload of large aircraft which he could not identify.

Captain Murray and Admiral Halsey were notified at once. When they arrived on the wings of the bridge, several other ships were visible under the low gray clouds.

The carrier was the new *Hornet* under Captain Marc Mitscher fresh from the West Coast, and with her, drab and businesslike, were the heavy cruiser *Vincennes,* the light cruiser *Nashville,* the tanker *Cimarron* low in the water with her seven million gallons of oil, and the destroyers *Gwin, Grayson, Meredith* and *Monssen.*

Smoothly the two groups combined and turned their bows west, the strongest United States naval force to sail these waters since the seventh of December.

On the topside of the Big E all available binoculars and long glasses were trained on *Hornet.* A row of eight planes was parked along each side of her flight deck, the noses angled in toward the center line. Inboard wing tips overlapped. Tails and outboard wing tips overhung the sea. By the twin rudders and two engines the recognition experts soon identified them as Army B-25 Mitchell medium bombers. Speculation swept the ship. Obviously, planes of that type could not take off loaded from a carrier, and, in the event they did, they certainly could not land since no tailhooks were visible. The mission must then be to reinforce a land base. But what base? Was there a new one in the Aleutians? The plausible guess was a delivery to a Soviet field in Kamchatka for future operations against Japan.

The fact that no one seriously considered as a possibility the real mission of the B-25s and of the combined task force is the best indication of the aggressive imaginations of those who planned it and the courage and ability of those who executed it.

Halsey was to take his ships to within five hundred miles of Tokyo and there launch Lieutenant Colonel James H. Doolittle and his sixteen Mitchells on a raid against the enemy capital and other large cities. Their attacks completed, the Army pilots were to continue for 1,400 miles across the Japanese islands and the Yellow Sea to the friendly Chinese field of Chuchow. Doolittle himself would take off three hours early at 2:00 P.M. with a load of incendiaries and act as pathfinder, striking at dusk and starting big fires on which the other aircraft could home. In this way the enemy homeland would be crossed at night when detection was most difficult and the landing at the strange and distant field accomplished in daylight.

It was a beautifully direct and simple plan. As modified, the planes were capable of flying about two thousand miles with a full load of fuel and an adequate supply of bombs. Therefore, if they were launched 500 miles east of Tokyo, they could overfly the city, drop their bombs and proceed for another 1,500 miles. There was even a one-hundred-mile or forty-minute reserve. They would approach from the sea and almost certainly have the advantage of surprise. But the plan depended on maximum performance of every man and every machine involved. First Bill Halsey had to take the *Hornet* undetected deep into waters where superior enemy forces could be encountered at any time, and then get his ships back out again, because they were far too valuable to lose at this critical point in the war. The Mitchells, exposed to the weather for more than a week, had to be kept in mechanically perfect condition for the demanding take-off and the long flight. Then the Army pilots, accustomed to take off a B-25 at 90 knots in 3,000 feet, had to get them in the air at 60 knots in less than 800 feet. Once air-borne, the navigators, used to overland flights, had to traverse 500 miles of open sea and, with no groping or circling which could alert the enemy defenses, come in on a predetermined course to a hostile city. Bombs should be dropped accurately on defense installations, avoiding adjacent civilian areas which, if hit, would carry screams of "atrocity" to the ears of remaining neutrals. With bombs unloaded, the air crews faced a flight of several hours over an aroused and well-armed enemy homeland where fighters and antiaircraft fire could be expected in quantity and where capture was considered tantamount to death. Before the flight would be completed there was another sea to navigate across and, with fuel running low, a strange field to find in an alien country where large areas were occupied by the enemy.

The mission was tersely announced by signal:

THIS FORCE IS BOUND FOR TOKYO

When the word was passed in *Enterprise*, a shout went up that rang through her steel compartments like the stroke of a great bell. High on his flag bridge Halsey heard it and smiled from the warmth in his heart.

Bill Halsey could well smile, even now, committed to as daring an action as had yet been undertaken in the young war. The men of the Big E were proud of their ship and its skipper, of their reputation as veterans, of their admiral who had the guts to take them in and the skill to get them out. Bataan had just fallen and here was something they could do about it.

For three days the task force steamed straight west, covering three to four hundred miles a day. With *Hornet's* deck unusable, *Enterprise* search planes scouted 200 miles ahead and on both flanks, and her fighters patrolled above.

On the cold, rough morning of the fourth day, about a thousand miles east of Tokyo, the carriers and cruisers fueled and then, as at Marcus, left the tankers and destroyers behind for the dash to the launch point. Through the afternoon and night they rolled and pounded at 23 knots in the heavy seas, kicked up by a gale wind from the south, barely able to make each other out through the drizzle. Then, at 3:15 A.M. on the eighteenth, for the first time in six weeks, the insistent electrical clammering of the general alarm sounded in earnest throughout the ship. The Big E's radar had two surface contacts ten miles ahead. On Halsey's order the force turned north to avoid detection and when the contacts faded from the scope it swung back to the westward.

The predawn radar contacts indicated the presence of enemy patrol vessels, but every mile on a westerly course meant a gallon of gasoline to the Army pilots, and Halsey was going to take them in until the risk to his irreplaceable ships became unacceptable.

At 7:15 a Bombing Six SBD flew in low and slow over the deck, flaps down but wheels and hook tucked up, the pilot's gloved hand extended and dropped a beanbag with a scribbled message attached chunked down. A lean, yellow-jerseyed man coming out of the port catwalk scooped it up on the dead run the way a good infielder fields a grounder, and in ten seconds it was on the bridge.

The Dauntless pilot had spotted an enemy patrol vessel fifty miles ahead and, more important, he was sure he had been sighted.

For another thirty minutes Halsey stood westward—eleven more miles that the Mitchells would not have to fly—while shutters clattered on the signal searchlights and in the gray superstructures the Morse characters showed round and bright. Then the Big E's own lookouts made out the two masts and low black hull of a small ship off the port bow. There was no longer any doubt that the alarm had been sounded. *Nashville* was ordered to destroy the enemy picket, and the carriers turned into the wind to launch.

Aboard the *Hornet,* Jimmy Doolittle swung down the steep ladder from the bridge. In his pocket was an official dispatch just received. It read:

LAUNCH PLANES. TO COL. DOOLITTLE AND HIS GALLANT
COMMAND GOOD LUCK AND GOD BLESS YOU—HALSEY

He thrust his head and upper body into the Army ready room. "Come on, fellas," he said. "Let's go."

Overhead, Roger Mehle, circling with eight fighters at 5,000 feet and observing radio silence, was startled to see the *Nashville* open fire with all her guns while the other ships turned away. In the rough seas and the early light he could not make out her target until it was pointed out by the splashes of her shells—a black, two-masted patrol boat about 125 feet long with a high bow and stern and a light gray deckhouse aft. The fighters charged their guns and slanted straight into the attack, but on the way down, Rawie, leading the second division of CAP, spotted another boat closer in and the eight F4Fs turned to get it first. In a minute it was stopped and settling in a smother of tiny splashes from the .50-calibers, and Mehle moved back to the first target. *Nashville* had it heavily under fire but it was a difficult target, half the time hidden in the deep troughs. The fighters carried their attacks so low and close that the white fountains of *Nashville*'s salvos rose above them. Each of the eight planes, firing in long bursts, poured in his fire and pulled up and, as it did so, the pilots could hear the *whomp!* of the cruiser's shells striking the sea.

From the Big E's decks those of her men who could spare a moment watched the only surface action they were to see during the whole first year of the war. Off near the horizon to port the white splashes of *Nashville*'s shells rose and fell back in groups of three and long afterward came the thudding report of the guns, ragged and distorted in the wind. Above, and then among the flashes swarmed the distant specks of the fighters, lost to sight at the bottom of their runs then reappearing in steep climbs. After twenty minutes of continuous attack, Mehle, out of ammunition, called his pilots off. The enemy vessel was low and heavy in the water with no sign of life aboard and *Nashville* had closed to point-blank range.

In the cockpits of the B-25s on *Hornet's* crowded deck, pilots, copilots and engineers ran through their final checks, eyes on the tiny needles of the engine instruments as the tall levers on the throttle quadrants moved back and forth and the big props spun. The rows of bombs hanging in their bays carried unprintable messages for Tojo and Hirohito from the sailors who had helped to maintain the planes. On the nose of one bomb was wired a bunch of prewar Japanese medals, affixed in a little ceremony by Captain Mitscher and Lieutenant Colonel Doolittle.

North of Formosa, the Japanese carriers *Akagi, Hiryu* and *Soryu,* homeward bound in triumph with their escorting battleships and cruisers from a sweep of the South China Sea, the Bay of Bengal and the Indian Ocean, received new orders. Brown smoke chuffed in their stacks and their turbines whined as they increased speed and turned northeastward.

"Find and destroy American carriers."

From bases on Honshu and Hokkaido and in the Kuriles patrol bombers climbed out to seaward, heavy with gas and bombs.

Enemy submarines at sea changed course abruptly and ran surfaced at high speed, converging.

"Find and destroy American carriers."

At 8:20, 668 miles from downtown Tokyo, with the ship

pitching so violently that solid water came over her bow, Doolittle led his men into the air. *Hornet* plane directors so timed their "go" signals that the straining bombers left the bow just as it rose on a wave crest, thus gaining a few more feet of altitude and a little upward thrust when they were most needed. Because of the island structure the Mitchells could not use the exact center of the deck, but *Hornet*'s crew had painted a broad white line for them to steer by. As they roared down the short, unsteady strip their left wing tips overhung the sea.

Every man in the task force whose duty permitted watched and sweated out those sixteen take-offs. Each was a new crisis. The second plane, for instance, pulled up too steeply, and with engines roaring at maximum power, hung for half a mile on the edge of a stall, with the cresting seas reaching for its tail.

In an hour the twin-tailed Mitchells were all air-borne and stretched out between the gray sea and the overcast sky in a ragged single file along the track to Tokyo. In another minute or two the combined task force had executed what PT boat skipper John D. Bulkley referred to as "that well-known tactical maneuver called 'turn around and get the hell out.' "

Halsey, having accomplished half of his mission, was now concentrating on its completion—the safe return of his priceless force to Pearl. Course was due east, speed 25 knots.

While *Hornet*'s aircraft, at last released from confinement in the hangar deck, buzzed into the air to help, the Big E's squadrons scoured the hostile ocean for signs of enemy interception.

Sixteen Japanese picket boats were sighted and attacked that day. Several were sunk and more damaged but the small ships wallowing the heavy seas made poor targets for bomb and bullet and the misses far exceeded the hits. The most effective weapons were the cruisers' six-inch rifles and the six .50-calibers of the F4Fs. The *Nashville* and the pilots of Fighting Six got in a great deal of gunnery practice.

Shortly after 2:00 P.M. came the first news of the Army bombers. Charlie Fox's coding room watch had Radio Tokyo's English language broadcast tuned in. The enemy commentator in his musically inflected Oxford English was describing the peace and serenity of Japan in April as opposed to conditions in the occupied countries for which he blamed those who resisted Japanese forces. He was interrupted in mid-sentence by a torrent of Japanese and with a click Radio Tokyo went off the air. Jimmy Doolittle was overhead.

Enterprise had accomplished her mission. Now she had only to get home to reload for the next one.

Radar picked up an enemy search plane thirty-five miles to the northeast and he closed to thirty-two miles under the concentrated gaze of the radar officer, the skipper and the task force commander before opening out to the northwest and fading from the scope.

By 5:30 p.m. the last plane had been recovered and in the fading light under the friendly clouds the gray ships drove eastward. Every hour of the night put twenty miles of sea between them and the groping, vengeful enemy. At daylight on the nineteenth of April the destroyers joined up out of the sea ahead, and the threat of submarines was lessened.

With the decreasing danger of enemy interception the crew began to relax. They listened with delight to the endless speculation of world news media on the starting point for the bombers which hit Tokyo, and to the confusion of enemy reports and explanations. In this mood an anonymous sailor wrote a "business" letter to Mr. Tojo of Japan.

AMERICANS INCORPORATED

UNITED STATES OF AMERICA
20 APRIL, 1942

Dishonorable Sir:

It gives me great pleasure to inform you, in case it has not been brought to your attention, that, in accordance with the terms of your contract, accepted by us on 7 December 1941, the first consignment of scrap metal has been delivered to your city.

You understand, of course, that shipping conditions being what they are it is necessary for us to effect delivery via air. While we are cognizant of the fact that this method of delivery is not to your liking, nevertheless we are required to take full advantage of the terms of the contract and will continue to effect deliveries by any means at our disposal of all scrap metal contracted for. As a concession, however, we will not ask for payment until such time as you inform us that you have received sufficient material to suit your needs. In this connection I wish to remind you that we are in a position to continue deliveries for years to come.

Inasmuch as you did not stipulate the point you wished delivery to be accomplished, we will in future deliveries endeavor to spread same over as wide an area as possible in order that you may receive the full benefit of this superior material.

In order to allay any misgivings that you may have, let me again assure you that our concern fulfills its obligations at no matter what cost and if necessary the coming generations will abide by the terms of any contract which we of this generation may have entered into.

For your information we have noted your unethical business conduct of endeavoring to induce personnel serving on board our warships to return home. Such conduct cannot and will not be condoned. You entered into this contract of your own volition and must pay the price of same in full.

Further details can be worked out to the satisfaction of my concern when we meet in your city in the near future.

> *John Q. Citizen,*
> *Representative,*
> AMERICANS INCORPORATED,
> UNITED STATES OF AMERICA

7 CORAL SEA CRUISE

For nearly five months now, Japan, in a series of small but well planned, timed and executed amphibious attacks, had been advancing through the jungle islands of the southwest Pacific toward Australia. In December she was in the Philippines. During January and February she captured Borneo, Sumatra, Celebes and Timor in the rich Netherlands East Indies and landed strong forces at Rabaul, New Britain, 1,700 miles to the eastward. In March it was Java and the eastern end of New Guinea. During April, Japanese troops spread southeastward down the chain of the Solomon Islands from the new base at Rabaul. They were approaching the absolutely vital air and sea routes between Australia and North America, and planning invasions of New Caledonia, Fiji and Samoa to cut those routes completely. Another enemy move was expected in early May and *Lexington* and *Yorktown* were in the Coral Sea to oppose it.

On April 30, with *Hornet* and Raymond Spruance's four cruisers, the Big E again stood straight out of Pearl Harbor to the southwest. It was the same task force that twelve days earlier had loosed the Mitchell bombers against Japan, built around exactly half the carrier strength available to the United States in the Pacific.

The ships strained southwestward. The sea was flat and the heat of the sun increased. Below decks the men cursed and sweated.

On May 4 the Big E got word of a surprise strike by *Yorktown* against enemy troops landed the previous day at Tulagi in the Solomons. The crew could feel the approach of action. Strong Japanese forces were now known to be operating in the Coral Sea in support of the Tulagi landings. Another Japanese assault force was at sea, bound for Port Moresby, on the eastern tip of New Guinea. It could not be much longer before Rear Admiral Frank Jack Fletcher, commanding the U. S. Carrier Group, and the enemy commander would find each other.

Halsey's ships had been under way a week when Corregidor fell. When Fletcher made contact with the enemy on May 7 and the Battle of the Coral Sea began, *Enterprise* was still two full days away, plowing up the glassy calm just south of the Phoenix Islands.

The Big E's radiomen intercepted enough messages to tell how the action developed. Aboard the ships of Halsey's force the men asked each other for the latest news. The radio shack was crowded, the chiefs in charge ordering the curious away so that the men on watch could work. The carrier sailors knew that a few hundred miles ahead American and Japanese carrier forces were meeting for the first time. What happened when they met would be the first real indication of how the war at sea might go—of victory or defeat, life or death.

In the Coral Sea, two carriers were in action; *Yorktown*, sister ship to *Enterprise*, and *Lexington*. In the years just ended, the crews of all these ships and their embarked squadrons had worked and played together. The Navy was small in peacetime and all the old-timers knew each other. Nearly all the Big E's pilots had classmates from college, the Academy, or Pensacola flying from *Lexington* and *Yorktown.*

The first news came by early afternoon. Ninety-three of Fletcher's planes had found the enemy light carrier *Shoho* and twenty minutes later Lieutenant Commander Robert E. Dixon of Scouting Two made his immortal report— "Scratch one flattop!"

There could hardly have been better news. For months Japanese task forces had swept the Pacific and the southern seas destroying whatever they had encountered. Until this day the biggest combatant ship lost had been a destroyer. At last a carrier had been sunk by the bombs and torpedoes of the Big E's sister ships and squadrons, and the propaganda myth of enemy invincibility was dead with *Shoho.*

The afternoon and evening of the seventh brought only garbled reports of heavy air attacks on Fletcher's fueling group, the tanker *Neosho* and the destroyer *Sims.*

Every hour Halsey drew twenty miles closer to the battle. A day and a half to go.

During the morning of the eighth the news came fast. The big enemy carriers, *Shokako* and *Zuikaku,* were engaged. Like *Enterprise* and *Yorktown* they were first-class, prewar ships, manned by first-string pilots. Both had launched against Pearl Harbor. To the men of *Enterprise* the *"Sho"* and the *"Zui"* were the Imperial Navy itself. They were the treachery, the skill, the fanaticism and the courage of a not quite comprehensible Japan.

Their presence told at once. *Lexington* took two torpedoes. *Yorktown* was afire from a bomb hit. There were serious losses in the American air groups.

If Bill Halsey's long and selfless service to his country could have earned him the fulfillment of a single wish, he would have asked to be in range of *Sho* and *Zui* that day in May. But he was still twenty-four hours to the northeast when news came that *Shokaku* was badly hit and the battle of the Coral Sea was over. The Port Moresby assault force was recalled. The Japanese advance down the Solomons faltered until their sunk and smashed-up carriers could be replaced.

Late at night came word of the loss of *Lexington,* destroyed by internal explosions many hours after the enemy aircraft had returned to their ships.

The Big E's men were stunned into silence at the loss of
the *Lex*. They remembered her solid bulk, her blocklike island, and it seemed impossible that bombs and torpedoes
could wreck her. They lost a little of the feeling of immortality that young men (and young carriers) take into
action. If the *Lex*, which had seemed so invulnerable, could
be sunk, so could their own *Enterprise*. Many of them
faced the thought for the first time and their palms went
moist.

In Washington, in Pearl Harbor and at sea in the South
Pacific that night, a lot of heads were pondering a problem
in simple arithmetic. Five carriers minus *Lexington* equals
four. Four carriers minus *Saratoga* (now under repair at
Bremerton) equals three—*Enterprise, Hornet, Yorktown*.
No one wanted to solve the next problem—three minus
one. No one off the *Yorktown* knew how badly she was
hurt or how long repairs would take. Two carriers to hold
the Pacific against Japan?

Although she had missed the first carrier duel of the war,
Enterprise still had a mission to accomplish. Aboard was a
Marine fighter squadron for delivery to Efate in New
Hebrides. She continued on course.

A few days later Commander McClusky flew to Efate to
inspect the Marines' new field. He found it unsatisfactory
for F4Fs despite its merits, which included two French girls
in shorts loitering near by, and in the afternoon the Marine
fighters flew off for Noumea on the southeast tip of New
Caledonia.

With the Marines delivered, Halsey fueled the carriers
and destroyers and turned northward up the 170th meridian. His Dauntlesses searched the sea for 200 miles to east
and west hoping to catch the enemy carriers in an attempted detour around Fletcher.

The enemy was withdrawing northwestward with his
broken ships and could not be found, but the jinx which
had followed *Enterprise* into southern waters on the Marshalls and Gilberts raid had joined up with her again on the
thirtieth.

Two SBDs failed to return from the afternoon flight, Ensign T. F. Durkin of Scouting Three and Walters of Bombing Six. Durkin reported ditching. Nothing was heard from
Walters. Every available search plane was launched at daylight on the first of May. They found nothing, but much

later Durkin and his gunner were returned by friendly islanders. Irrepressible Bucky Walters, who had landed among the cranes and bulldozers at blacked-out Kaneohe, knocked over the radio tower at Taroa and pulled his full weight in every raid, search, liberty party and acey-deucy game available, simply did not return. Ever. Nor did P. S. Johnson, his gunner.

Just after dark, the *Benham* picked up a sonar contact and laid a shallow pattern of depth charges. In the clear night sea the exploding cans of TNT formed bubbles of fire which burst and hammered metallically on the moving hulls.

On May 16 the *Enterprise-Hornet* task force was ordered back to Oahu. A two-word message came in on the seventeeth: EXPEDITE RETURN.

The word got around. There was an atmosphere of expectancy aboard. The sailors guessed and theorized to each other across the mess tables and the open cowlings of aircraft engines and the narrow aisles between the tiers of bunks. In the lines before the shaving mirrors, at the clothing and small stores counter, and at quarters for muster they wondered aloud. Full admirals do not order vice admirals commanding major task forces to "expedite" so that bluejackets can arrive at home base sooner for rest and recreation. The engineers knew well the extra thousands of gallons of fuel oil it costs a single ship to maintain a few additional knots on a long voyage. Something big had to be in the wind, and the wind north of Oahu blows from Japan.

One day out of Pearl the persistent jinx of the southern seas killed Lieutenant (j.g.) Gayle Herman. Herman of Fighting Six, who had had the skill and coolness to spiral down onto the Ford Island runway out of the fire-swept night sky on December 7, and had been in on every action and every dull, demanding routine detail since that day, confident and at home in his cockpit, banked just a touch too steeply while still slow after take-off, stalled and spun. He floated clear of the wrecked Wildcat and was sloshing unconscious in the gentle chop when the plane-guard destroyer came up. As the ensign in charge of the rescue party dived for him, he rolled free of the parachute which held him up and sank. Fighting Six and *Enterprise* were changed and weakened by Gayle Herman's death. And it cost the enemy nothing.

The Big E was in port only one full day and it had to be a busy one. The all-important job was, of course, replenishment after the long and futile cruise to the south, but even while the dungaree-clad working parties sweated stores of all kinds aboard, the air group formed up in whites on the flight deck, the band played ruffles, the Marine guard presented arms, the bosun's call shrilled, and four stars snapped at the truck as Admiral Chester W. Nimitz came aboard to award decorations to the airmen. Of all the medals that were in the next years to be pinned on the chests of *Enterprise* aviators, the first three—Distinguished Flying Crosses—went to Wade McClusky, Roger Mehle and James Daniels of Fighting Six. As Chester Nimitz attached the weighted ribbon to Mehle's blouse, his blue eyes held Roger's brown ones for a moment and he said quietly, "I think you'll have a chance to do it again in a couple of days."

But if Mehle were going to have that chance, it would not be under the command of William F. Halsey.

Enterprise sailors had felt without thinking that when Admiral Halsey came to leave his flagship he would be carried off, burned or blown-up in action, or would step off her deck as it sank from under him somewhere on the approaches to Japan. They knew the bold, aggressive, senior admiral afloat in the Pacific, veteran of the Marshalls, Wake, Marcus and the Tokyo raid, would command in any major action. And they were more certain each day that a major action was coming.

But Bill Halsey, thin and irritable, walked off the quarterdeck and down the gangway to the shrilling of the bosuns' calls and the left-handed salutes and was driven to the Naval Hospital. There, cursing, scratching and seriously ill with the "general dermatitis" of complete exhaustion, he watched the Big E sail for Midway with the two stars of Rear Admiral Raymond A. Spruance at her truck.

8 ACTION OFF MIDWAY

In late May of 1942, the Japanese naval general staff knew that all the U. S. Pacific Fleet battleships had been put out of commission by shallow-running torpedoes on the seventh of December. Two American carriers had been reported sunk in the Coral Sea, and two others had been sighted in that area. Japanese intelligence knew of no more in the Pacific. The Americans, it was concluded, were "paying singular attention to the Australian area: the time is ripe to strike at Midway and the Aleutians."

Admiral Isoroko Yamamoto, commander-in-chief of the Combined Fleet, was an exceptionally intelligent officer. He knew that he must destroy what was left of the Pacific Fleet in 1942, before the huge industrial weight of the United States was brought to bear, or lose the war. He knew also that Admiral Nimitz in Pearl Harbor would never accept Japanese occupation of Midway. By seizing the island in an overwhelming attack and quickly consolidating and developing it, he would be in a position to annihilate the counterattacking U. S. forces.

Surprise was necessary and nearly certain. The United States was on the defensive. Japan could strike anywhere from Alaska to the Solomons with sufficient strength to overwhelm anything less than the entire effective Pacific Fleet. It was highly improbable that the Americans could detect an attack in time to assemble their scattered ships and intercept. It was so ordered.

In five major groups most of the Imperial Navy sailed from Guam, Saipan, Ominado and the Inland Sea. Two groups were bound for the Aleutians. A carrier striking force composed of four of Japan's best carriers, *Akagi, Kaga, Soryu, Hiryu,* the first three veterans of Pearl Harbor, all with experienced, combat-seasoned air groups, sortied first to clear the way to Midway. Two fast battleships, two heavy cruisers and twelve destroyers were in company. Following the carrier striking force came Yamamoto's Main Body with three fast battleships, a light carrier and twelve more destroyers. Behind them was the Midway Occupation Force: twelve loaded transports and assorted seaplane carriers, repair ships, minesweepers, oilers and patrol craft, escorted by two battleships, a light carrier, eight heavy cruisers, a light cruiser and some twenty destroyers. Sixteen submarines fanned out ahead and across the eastern approaches to Midway.

To oppose the armada converging on Midway, Nimitz could scrape together, at best, only *Hornet,* whose air group had never been in action; *Yorktown,* with her insides

ripped apart by a Coral Sea bomb; and *Enterprise*, intact
and flying a veteran air group. Some half-dozen heavy
cruisers, one light cruiser, a few destroyers and submarines
were available to support the carriers and confront the enemy's carrier-and-destroyer-escorted fast battleships. Midway itself was an unsinkable carrier capable of operating
large, long-range aircraft and heavily defended by Marines.
And Nimitz had available another weapon, invisible and
unknown to the enemy, and as potent as an additional carrier task force. Army cryptanalysts, under retired Lieutenant Colonel William F. Friedman, had broken the enemy
code even before the war. By means of deciphered messages and conventional intelligence methods, Nimitz knew
the essental elements of Yamamoto's plan of attack, including the all-important where and when.

At Pearl, *Enterprise* and *Hornet*, by sunlight and flood-
light, refueled, reprovisioned and made ready for sea and
action. Across the narrow harbor, *Yorktown* was in dry
dock under swarms of workmen attempting to repair her
bomb damage in two days instead of the ninety which had
been estimated.

On Thursday, the twenty-eighth of May, in midafternoon, the Big E sailed for Midway. At four o'clock, with
the task force well at sea and in cruising disposition, six
cruisers and nine destroyers in a circle around *Enterprise*
and *Hornet*, McClusky brought his planes aboard.

First to make an approach was Lieutenant Commander
Gene Lindsey, skipper of Torpedo Six. Lindsey was an old
hand at carrier landings and he answered the paddles of the
landing signal officer with routine precision. But over the
stern of the carrier something went wrong, a sudden loss
of power, a bad airspeed indicator, a swirl of stack gas, a
control failure—something. The TBD stalled, spun to the
deck and skidded, broken, over the port side. *Monaghan*,
the plane-guard destroyer, pulled the three-man crew out
of the sea. Chief Schafer, the bombardier, and C. T. Gre-
nat, the radioman, were just shaken. Gene Lindsey was
painfully cut and bruised about the face and chest. They
were returned to their ship next day.

While the task force stood steadily up to the northwest
to intercept and the enemy formations moved eastward,
the men of the Big E covertly inspected and openly con-
jectured about their new admiral. Raymond Spruance was
a short, wiry, energetic man who loved to walk up and

down the flight deck for hours each day. The sailors quickly saw that those walks were not just for exercise. Always another officer walked with the admiral and the two talked earnestly. When the talking lapsed, the other officer would be replaced by a new walker and the talk would begin again. Mostly, the admiral listened, questioned, listened. He was not, like Halsey, an aviator, but he had inherited Halsey's capable staff intact. Walking and talking, he became acquainted with his staff and the critical professional problems ahead.

By the last day of May, *Enterprise* and *Hornet* were well to the northeast of Midway, in position to strike from an unexpected quarter at the flank of any enemy force moving down on the island from the northwest. There they met *Cimarron* and *Platte* and topped off with fuel. Word got around that according to submarine reports the enemy was on the way as expected. The weather was favoring the Japanese, low clouds and poor visibility making it hard for the defending forces to locate and attack the oncoming ships.

On the first of June came news of an old shipmate. A doctor, newly reported aboard from the naval hospital at San Diego, related in the daily bulletin how a young officer with only one eye had demanded to be returned to duty, saying that given a chance he could pull more than his weight. A letter from the same officer to the CO of Scouting Six was published also.

"I thought I wanted a rest," it said, "but now I know that a month off is long enough. . . . I am truly sorry I am not still with you. . . . I considered fighting purely a professional duty, but now I know it is much more than that. Everything we have back here is worth any sacrifice that is necessary to keep it. . . . I know it is easy for me to shout fighting enthusiasm from a nice safe hospital . . . but I am sincere. I wish I could come back."

The letter was from Perry Teaff whose eye had been lost when, dazzled and disoriented in a propeller-spun cocoon of reflected light, he had crashed during the predawn launch against Wake Island.

The same day brought word of another war, far away. Twelve hundred and fifty Royal Air Force bombers had struck Cologne in the war's biggest aerial attack to date.

Admiral Spruance signaled his force on the first day of June to expect an enemy attack on Midway by "all combatant types, including four or five carriers," and explained his battle plan of "surprise flank attacks on enemy carriers from positions northeast of Midway." "The successful conclusion of the operation now commencing," he conservatively stated, "will be of great value to our country."

The second of June was cold and wet with the same low ceilings and with visibility occasionally down to a hundred feet. *Yorktown,* now miraculously repaired and ready for duty, joined up and added her task force under Admiral Fletcher to Spruance's ambuscade.

Admiral Fletcher, as the senior of the two task force commanders, had by the second of June almost every effective unit of the Pacific Fleet that could make the rendezvous. Practically, this *was* the United States Pacific Fleet six months after Pearl Harbor: three carriers (one green and one patched up), seven heavy cruisers, one light cruiser and fifteen destroyers.

All day the second and third of June, Fletcher and Spruance lay in wait with their hurriedly scraped-up forces. During the long hours of daylight they steamed slowly to the northeast and at night doubled back at increased speed to be at the same point each morning, some 350 miles northeast of Midway. The idea was to be within range of the enemy carriers and undetected when they launched their dawn attack against Midway.

Early in the afternoon of the third, news came in of a diversionary attack by carrier planes on Dutch Harbor in the Aleutians and a PBY sighted a large force of transports, cruisers and destroyers 700 miles southwest of Midway and inbound. Since the transports would not approach Midway without a preliminary air strike, it was evident that the carriers were closer, probably under the weather belt that lay north of the island.

Clearly the fourth of June was to be the day.

The Big E's ready rooms were noisier than usual. The torpedo pilots, with the day at hand toward which all their training had been pointed, found it ironic that they should have to attack in their obsolete Devastators when delivery of the new and doubly effective Avengers was scheduled in one week.

The pilots stayed up late and talked about the coming action because the excitement would not let them sleep anyway. They knew they were in for trouble and that it was they who would win or lose the battle.

From stem to stern, from flight deck to bridge, in all departments, at all levels, the big carrier prepared for action.

Charlie Fox made a last inspection of the Supply Department to assure its readiness. All the storerooms below would be dogged down and inaccessible while in action in order to insure the maximum degree of watertight integrity, so that whatever supplies he would need to care for 2,700 men had to be broken out and made readily available. The same went for airplane parts, gun parts, soap, lubricating oil and coffee.

Commander Fox planned to serve breakfast before morning General Quarters and supper after General Quarters had been secured, thus requiring only one meal to be served to the men at their battle stations. This meal would be sandwiches which the cooks were now preparing, fresh fruit, and coffee carried in three-gallon cans and served in paper cups.

Similarly, the air officer, the engineer, the first lieutenant and the gunnery officer made a check on their men and equipment during the final hours of the third of June. Planes, bombs, torpedoes, ammunition for planes and ship's guns, damage-control equipment, machinery, emergency pumps, arresting gear, elevators, guns of all calibers, were as ready as they would ever be. The feeling throughout the ship was one of confidence. Pearl Harbor was beginning to fade from memory and the *Enterprise* sailors, who had not actually seen the *Lex* go down, remembered best the recent successful strikes against the enemy bases when attacks on the Big E herself had been rare and always unsuccessful.

For all hands on the Big E, reveille came at 3:30 A.M. and Thursday, the fourth of June, began.

At one of the long tables in the wardroom, Charlie Fox, Gene Lindsey and Pablo Riley ate their early breakfast of one-eyed sandwiches with the others. Lindsey's bandages had recently been removed. Fox, across the table, could see the healing gash across his forehead and the blue-blackness of his left eye and cheek. He moved stiffly with the heavy tape still on his ribs and under his tan he was pale from loss of blood.

Looking at him, Fox was startled to hear that a spare torpedo plane had been broken out for him to fly that morning.

Pablo Riley felt the same way. "You look pretty beat up,

skipper," he said. "You really feel well enough to fly today?"

Lindsey, a loaded fork just in front of his mouth, turned his head to look at Riley. "This is the real thing today, Pablo, the thing we've been been training for. I'll take the squadron in."

After breakfast, Lindsey's Exec, Lenn Massey, and his Operations Officer, Art Ely, conferred with Jim Gray. It was agreed that Gray would keep his Wildcats high to preserve the altitude advantage he needed against the agile Zeros, and, at the same time, provide protection for the dive bombers. Ely's radio call, "Come on down, Jim," would be the signal that the torpedo planes needed help and Gray's fighters would dive to the attack.

By 4:30 A.M. the pilots were all in their respective ready rooms, had noted wind and weather data, discussed tactics and were lacking only two things—the location of the enemy carriers and the order to go.

Sunrise came three minutes before seven o'clock. It was a clear, balmy day with a strong breeze from the southeast and a few small white clouds beginning to form at four to five thousand feet.

Enterprise was 290 miles north and slightly east of Midway. The most important ambush in the history of war at sea was ready. On its outcome depended the control of the Pacific Ocean, a third of the surface of the earth.

A Catalina out of Midway first found the striking force. At 7:34 a Big E radioman intercepted the PBY's simple message back to base: "ENEMY CARRIERS."

Where? How many? What doing? The pilots crowded around the teletype machines that relayed essential messages to the squadrons.

"That P-boat pilot must be nuts."

"That's a hell of a contact report."

"He's probably got Zeros all over him and can't transmit any more."

Eleven minutes later the PBY was more specific, and the teletypes clattered under their invisible fingers: "MANY PLANES HEADED MIDWAY, BEARING 320 DISTANCE 150."

Quickly the pilots plotted that bearing and distance. It put the enemy planes about 230 miles southwest of *Enterprise*. But where were the carriers?

Finally at three minutes past eight came the news they were waiting for: "TWO CARRIERS AND BATTLESHIPS, BEARING 320, DISTANCE 180, COURSE 135, SPEED 25."

Within four minutes orders came from Fletcher to Spruance: "PROCEED SOUTHWESTERLY AND ATTACK ENEMY CARRIERS WHEN DEFINITELY LOCATED." The big bows swung toward the enemy, and astern the wakes boiled white.

A few minutes before nine the loudspeakers rasped in the ready rooms and throughout the ship: "Pilots, man your planes." This was the third time the order had come since 4:00 A.M. and twice it had been rescinded. This time, the aviators knew, was it. In at least one squadron they shook hands all around before crowding out the narrow door and up the ladder to the deck.

Gene Lindsey's plane captain had to help him into the front seat of his venerable Devastator. Below its fuselage the big torpedo was snugged up tight.

As the flight deck began to come alive under the starting engines, the task force divided. *Enterprise*, the flagship, continued on course, keeping with her heavy cruisers *Vincennes, Northampton* and *Pensacola* and five destroyers. *Hornet* sheered out of formation, forming a small separate group with *Minneapolis, New Orleans,* the new light antiaircraft cruiser *Atlanta* and three destroyers.

The first Wildcat hopped into the air at six minutes past nine. *Hornet* started launching at the same time. It took forty minutes to get all the strike planes from flight and hangar decks into the air. Admiral Spruance had ordered up every aircraft that would fly except a few fighters for CAP.

At 9:45 the stacked blue squadrons began to pull out of their loud circles around the force and set course for the enemy.

Gene Lindsey with his fourteen TBDs stayed at 1,500 feet to conserve fuel and be in attack position.

Jim Gray took a ten-Wildcat escort for the strike group in a long climb to 20,000 feet over the torpedo planes.

Wade McClusky led the thirty-two Dauntlesses of Bombing Six under Dick Best and Scouting Six under Earl Gallaher. With their heavy loads they also climbed, but slowly, to 20,000 feet.

Hornet's squadrons departed at the same time.

It was a long flight, launched at nearly maximum range in an attempt to catch the enemy reloading and refueling his Midway attack groups. Lindsey's Devastators flew under the white cumulus clouds that now covered nearly half the sky. Occasionally he looked up between the clouds, trying to catch a glimpse of his fighter escort.

At 11:10, Jim Gray caught sight of the enemy carriers. He looked below him for the torpedo planes and saw the tiny, wide-winged wedges disappear into a cloud, headed for the target. This tactic, he remembered, had been used at Coral Sea, where the Devastators of the *Yorktown* and *Lexington* had successfully used cloud cover in making their approaches.

The flight of fighters armed their guns and flew on toward the enemy, awaiting Art Ely's call to action.

It never came.

The planes Gray was watching almost four miles below belonged to *Hornet*'s Torpedo Eight. Somehow, in the long flight, with the clouds between, the fighters had picked up the wrong squadron.

At 11:30 Gene Lindsey made out through the light oil film on his canopy the pagoda masts of Japanese battleships protruding like small screw points on the horizon thirty miles ahead. He checked his fuel gauges and searched the sky above in all directions for his fighter escort and the rest of the group. Nothing was in sight except his own two seven-plane divisions of TBDs and the enemy ships, now hull-down through his prop disk to the northwest. Lindsey knew that the tactical plan called for coordinated attacks by dive bombers and torpedo planes with fighter protection. He knew what his chances were in an unsupported strike and his palms were wet with the knowledge. But he had been out nearly two hours and it was doubtful even now if his squadron could make it home. He hoped Gray's fighters and McClusky's bombers would show up, but he could not wait.

By now the carriers were in sight. Lindsey shoved throttle and mixture up against the stops and nosed over in a shallow power glide to attack altitude, just as the last of Torpedo Eight's fifteen planes went down under the Zeros and the guns ahead.

The ancient Devastators spread out and headed in, a hundred feet above the calm sea, torpedoes tucked up between the protruding tires, the long canopies open at either end for pilot and gunner, closed over the empty bombardier's seat between.

At fifteen miles, Lindsey could see the high bow waves of 25 knots or better, and the circling specks of the enemy CAP. The ships were going west, away from the TBDs coming in on a northwesterly course. He ordered a beam attack on the nearest carrier but before he could call Gray's Wildcats down, the enemy fighters had found Torpedo Six.

There were no more orders, no more formation. For Lindsey, Ely, Eversole, Riley and the others there was only the growing low shape of the enemy carrier which turned maddeningly away to starboard keeping the Devastators always astern and to port, denying them the beam attack they had to have. The range closed with agonizing slowness, a mile and a half each minute, and the enemy tracers smoked by, holing wings, slowing engines, wounding, killing.

For the gunners, facing aft over their twin .30-calibers, there was a sky full of olive-drab fighters with orange disks on wings and fuselage which dived in fast from behind, guns winking along the wings, and flashed by close up, banking sharply for reattacks.

At eight miles black puffs of antiaircraft fire began to appear in the clear air around Lindsey's harried squadron, and the planes jarred and shook with the bursting shells. The pilots twisted and wove, climbing and diving under the fire of planes and ships, but always pressing in.

The carrier was the *Kaga*. Steadily she turned away, the stern sliding to port leaving a slick swipe with a border of white, her guns hammering and smoking. The TBDs, flat on the water among the antiaircraft bursts and splashes and under the swooping fighters, circled doggedly for a shot at her port beam.

There were two Zeros to each Devastator and a Zero could outfight a Wildcat. The TBDs at full throttle were making 120 knots, the Zeros flashed in and out at two and three times that speed during all the long minutes of the approach. As the range closed, medium and light antiaircraft machine guns from escorting battleships, cruisers and destroyers opened up. The tracers laced horizontally across the surface, shifting and intersecting around the planes.

It could only go one way.

One after another the Devastators slid, cartwheeled, dived into the sea as fighter bullets found the engines or the controls or the gas tanks or the pilots. Splotches of skidding orange flame and black smoke, long, tearing splashes and an occasional slowly tumbling wing tip with a white star, appeared on the approaches to the port side of the stillturning *Kaga*.

Gene Lindsey and his gunner died under the bullets of the fighters or in the resulting stone-wall collision with the sea. Pablo Riley and his crewman, Ely and Eversole with theirs, went down.

When half of the fourteen planes had been destroyed, no one would have blamed the remaining pilots for jettisoning their torpedoes in the unequal fight and attempting to shoot their way out and home.

Not one did so. No one even dropped at long or middle range and turned away. Every pilot of Torpedo Six either made his drop close aboard or was killed before he could do so.

In nineteen minutes it was over.

Four of the fourteen Devastators made it back to their ship. The crew of one other, Machinist A. W. Winchell and his gunner, were later rescued.

There were no hits.

While the two torpedo squadrons were being slaughtered by the Zeros and the AA down among the enemy ships, Jim Gray circled with ten fighters four miles overhead. Between the broken clouds he could see the curling wakes and flashing guns of a fleet under air attack. Some, at least, of the frantic radio transmissions made by the torpedo pilots must have filtered into his radio, which was tuned to Ely's frequency. But he did not receive the prearranged distress signal—and he had a dual responsibility. In a decision which has been a matter of bitter controversy within naval aviation ever since, Gray elected to keep his fighters high, preserving their altitude advantage, in order to cover McClusky's dive bombers in their approach.

When the Dauntless squadrons reached the point where the enemy was predicted to be, nearly 8,000 square miles of Pacific Ocean was visible from 20,000 feet and there was not a ship in sight.

Thinking that the enemy might have turned southwestward to lend protection to his other forces approaching from that direction, the group commander continued straight ahead for another thirty-five miles.

Nothing.

The SBDs had been air-borne for nearly two and a half hours and were at the limit of their combat radius. Even if he were to order an immediate return he knew he might not get them back before their fuel ran out. But out here somewhere was the heart of the enemy's naval strength and

in the echelons of Dauntlesses at McClusky's back was the
power to destroy it. He had to find the enemy if he put
every plane in the ocean. But he could lose them all for
nothing by searching in the wrong direction.

Would the Japanese commander continue on toward
Midway to launch a second strike or would he retire northward out of range of Midway-based planes? McClusky
guessed the latter. By now the enemy would know that carrier planes were after him and would steam away from
Midway to face the more serious threat.

The dive bombers banked together and headed down the
reverse of the enemy's approach course.

The long minutes droned by and the fuel gauges moved
down toward empty. McClusky, Gallaher, Best, and their
division and section leaders squinted behind their goggles
trying to see over the horizon and through the puffs of cumulus near the surface. Under the bellies of the Dauntlesses the big bombs hung useless, dragging, costing fuel.

In Scouting Six several pilots signaled that they were having trouble with their oxygen supply. Without oxygen a man
does not last long four miles high. Earl Gallaher ripped off
his own mask so that he would have the same sensations as
the pilots in trouble and took the squadron down to 15,000,
directly under Bombing Six.

At ten minutes to noon a white featherlike streak appeared on the blue sea below, and at its tip was the needle
shape of a destroyer throwing tiny curls of spray as it sped
off to the northeast. McClusky guessed it was an enemy
ship hurrying to rejoin the task force, and once again the
thirty-two wings dipped and took the destroyer's course.

The minutes dragged. The enemy destroyer fell astern
and was forgotten. The gas receded in the tanks. Anyone
who got home now would need a talent for saving fuel and
a lot of luck in addition.

At five minutes past noon McClusky found the enemy.

At first near the far horizon there were only the curved
white brush strokes of the wakes, then the ships themselves,
in tight turns as they dodged the stubborn Devastators.

Gunners took up the slack in their belts, armed the .30-
calibers and searched the sky expectantly for fighters. The
Dauntlesses tightened up their wedges and headed in, diving slightly to pick up speed as Gray's Wildcats, low on
fuel, headed back for base. Thirty miles, twenty, ten and
still no Zeros. The pilots forgot about the warning hands of

the fuel gauges and the three hours they had already flown, in the unbelievable spectacle below them.

Down there, sliding across the blue sea, once in a while disappearing for a minute under a puff of cloud, were the narrow yellow flight decks of four Japanese carriers. Arranged haphazardly around the carriers were other big ships, two battlewagons with red disks painted on their forward turrets, several cruisers and smaller ships. But it was the carriers that fascinated the Dauntless pilots and made their hearts beat and their breath come short. Here were the yellow decks that had launched against Pearl Harbor on that quiet Sunday morning when the Pacific lay at peace. Here were the ships that had swept the southern seas in a series of impressive victories and returned without a scratch. Here was Japan's elite force, the crack ships and pilots that had given her the confidence to attack America. Here they were under the wings of the Big E's bombers, wide open in the clear and open sea—and still no fighters.

Wade McClusky's voice came crisply through the earphones:

"Gallaher, take the right-hand carrier. Best, you take the one on the left. Earl, follow me down."

From the high leading edge of the stepped-down echelons of SBDs, the group commander's plane pulled up and banked sharply to the right and as the flight passed under it, rolled into the 70-degree dive they all knew. His two wingmen followed rapidly.

In a few seconds both squadrons were spaced out in their dives. It was like a textbook illustration, far better than any practice attack they had ever made. In a dive bomber's dream of perfection, the clean blue Dauntlesses—with their perforated dive flaps open at the trailing edges of their wings and their big bombs tucked close and pointing home, the pilots straining forward, rudder-feet and stick-hands light and delicate, getting it just right as the yellow decks came up, left hands that would reach down and forward to release now resting on the cockpit edge, gunners lying on their backs behind the cocked twin barrels searching for the fighters that did not come—carved a moment out of eternity for man to remember forever.

Then McClusky released and pulled out and the Zeros which had been sucked down by the Devastators went after him as his bomb fountained the sea ten yards from *Kaga*, rattling her to her bilges.

Gallaher's 500-pounder hit flush in the middle of the flight deck 200 feet from the stern where a deckload of planes was being rearmed and refueled.

Nothing could stop it now. The *Enterprise* Dauntlesses came down in a precise series of smashing blows that no structure made by man to sail the seas could possibly withstand.

Two more of the big bombs walked down *Kaga*'s deck and Gene Lindsey's target was caught for good. In seconds she was out of sight in the black smoke and boiling flame.

Akagi, the left-hand carrier, was also servicing her planes on deck. She took one near miss, then one among the parked planes and a third went through to the hangar deck to detonate the stored torpedoes.

While McClusky's pilots were hanging in their seat belts over the growing yellow rectangles of *Kaga* and *Akagi,* *Yorktown* Dauntlesses found the *Soryu.* They caught her, like the others, with a deckload of fueled and armed aircraft ready for launching and with more being serviced below. With merciless accuracy the long 1,000-pounders plunged through her wooden deck and blew the ship apart.

If the ghosts of December 7 were watching those two minutes north of Midway, they were well content.

But now the dive bombers were down out of the cool and empty sky among the angry Zeros and under the guns of the ships. With dive brakes closed and throttles bent forward past the stops, the pilots hugged the surface, denying the fighters any but flat attacks, weaving and dodging, while the gunners twisted, swinging the .30-calibers from side to side to meet the closest enemy.

McClusky had two Zeros with him for ten minutes until W. G. Chochalousek in the rear seat fired one Japanese's engine, skidding him into the sea; the other lost his enthusiasm before the searching tracers and turned back.

Dickinson came under heavy fire from a destroyer but the enemy gunners were foiled when in the excitement of the moment he extended his wheels and flaps which slowed him to 95 knots and drew the AA fire well ahead. With his aircraft properly configured a few moments later he shot down an enemy fighter angling in ahead of him for an attack on a group of friendly planes.

Stuart Mason, a gunner in Bombing Six, was hit in the face by antiaircraft fragments in the dive and again in the legs by machine-gun fire during the retirement. Wiping the blood out of his eyes and placing his wounded legs with his hands, he fought off the enemy fighters successfully and later repaired the plane's shot-up radio so that it could receive the Big E's homing signals and guide the aircraft back to base.

In Scouting Six, Floyd Adkins, manning the guns in Ensign William R. Pittman's SBD, discovered during the dive they had broken free of their mount. The twin 30s are clumsily shaped and weigh 175 pounds. Adkins held them in his lap until the pull-out and then manhandled them so effectively that he shot down a Messerschmitt-type fighter which jumped the Dauntless right after release. (Back aboard ship, after two of his shipmates had hoisted them out of the cockpit and placed them on the deck, Adkins was unable to lift them.)

But the storm of fire over the Japanese ships, the slashing Zeros and the long flight home cost fourteen SBDs of McClusky's original thirty-two. Some of the fourteen were hit directly by AA and blown apart in the air, others, the pilots wounded or dead, dived out of control into the sea. Several, hit but controllable, made good water landings and their crews were seen in their yellow life rafts after the planes had sunk. Two or three, like Dickinson and McCarthy of Scouting Six, ran out of fuel when *Enterprise* was not where they had been told she would be. They ditched and were rescued promptly.

The group commander himself, wounded in the shoulder, landed with two gallons in his tanks after a long search for the ship.

By early afternoon all of the Big E's planes that would ever return were in.

Three of Japan's carriers were now either sunk or sinking, and the U. S. task force remained intact. Aboard the *Enterprise* there was unaccustomed space on the hangar deck. The squadron ready rooms were no longer crowded.

As the last SBDs of the strike group were buzzing around the landing pattern, wheels down and tanks empty, radar picked up enemy aircraft inbound. *Enterprise* braced for action. The men knew it was their turn to take it and with tightened stomachs and sweaty palms turned to their various tasks. The young lookouts searched the sky, straining their eyes into the binoculars to find the black specks that would be the enemy. Damage-control parties stood by their pumps and tools and waited. The guns trained out to the northwest as radar reported about twenty planes bearing 310 degrees, approaching. Overhead, the eight-plane CAP under Roger Mehle circled impatiently. Mehle was anxious to get at the enemy and had several times requested a vector to intercept the inbound bombers. But he was held overhead to protect the *Enterprise*. The ship was taut, expectant. Men spoke in low voices as though they feared the enemy might overhear.

Yorktown, operating independently, was several miles closer to the last enemy carrier than *Enterprise*. The Japanese dive bombers found her first and had no punch left for the Big E.

In *Enterprise* the men worked and waited. Messages filtered down from the radio shack, crackled in over the speakers, and news came back with landing pilots about *Yorktown*'s fight for life.

Mehle, stretching his protective circles (and his orders) swung over *Yorktown* at the last possible moment for a good shot at the incoming bombers. His gun solenoid failed and he could not fire, but Provost and Halford shot one down after its drop.

Hit three times on the first attack, stopped and burning, the *York* put out her fires, relined her boilers, cleared and repaired her flight deck and in two hours was under way again at 20 knots, refueling her combat air patrol, when the enemy hit her again, this time with coordinated high-level bombers and torpedo planes. The high bombers missed. Machinist Reid and Radio Electrician Bayers of Fighting Six got three of the torpedo planes and Ralph Rich a fourth, but four torpedoes entered the water and two hit. *Yorktown* stopped and began listing to port.

During the afternoon the Big E's squadrons replaced parts, patched, cannibalized and invented in an attempt to put another major strike in the air against the remaining enemy carrier. On the bridge Admiral Spruance waited for word on its position in order to make that strike count.

Southwest of Midway, Vice Admiral Nobutake Kondo, commanding the Japanese occupation force, was startled by word of the disastrous attack on his carriers. At four o'clock he detached two battleships, three heavy cruisers, a light carrier and a squadron of destroyers from escort duty and headed northeast at 30 knots to the rescue. At that speed he would arrive after dark and be in a position with his fast, heavily gunned ships, well trained in night operations, to surprise and destroy American forces pursuing the battered carriers.

From the northwest, Admiral Yamamoto, with his main body bored in toward the fight, hoping for a fleet action in which the big guns of his battlewagons could massacre the U. S. cruisers and carriers.

At about the time of the second attack on the *York,* one of her searching pilots found the *Hiryu.*

The fourth of June was not yet over.

At 5:30, *Enterprise* turned up wind and, with McClusky out of action, Earl Gallaher led off another strike. Twenty-four Dauntlesses, eleven with 1,000-pounders, the rest with 500s, formed up and climbed out to avenge the *Yorktown.* Included in the 24 were 14 *York* refugees, plus 6 from Earl's own squadron and 4 under Dick Best, all that were flyable of Bombing Six and Scouting Six which had launched 32 SBDs that morning.

All but one of the Big E's dive bombers were manned by crews that had made the deadly noon attack. They had seen the yellow decks and the rising tracers and dodged the Zeros. They had watched the friends of their youth skitter and cartwheel and remembered the quick splashes and the slow falling of the spray. They had waited in the empty ready rooms and tried not to consider the vacant chairs. There was no longer any illusion of immortality. There was now simply a difficult, exhausting job to be done, to be completed, and beyond that the hope of getting home.

They flew at 13,000, straight into the afternoon sun, which, even in June, was halfway down the western sky. The death of many men, the sinking of great ships and the beginning of the end of an empire's hope for glory had not changed the mid-Pacific day. There were still the clouds down close to the endless sea and, over it all, the pale sky with its interlocking wedges of black specks droning westward.

Across the slightly shifting wings, pilots and gunners in their oxygen masks looked to each other like the pictures they remembered of World War I soldiers under gas attack in France.

There was time, while they flew 150 miles, to think and not to think. To think of fuel supply, formation, navigation, the arming of the guns and bombs, to review tactics and plan for evading the fighters and flak. Not to think of what had already happened that day to squadron mates, of what it was like to hit the water at 200 knots or to feel the little stabs of the Zero's 7.7-millimeter bullets. To think and not to think. On this depended the battle. By this the hero or the coward was made.

On this fourth of June there were no cowards flying from any carriers.

At 6:50 the enemy was in sight thirty miles ahead.

What had been the Japanese striking force was now scattered all over the ocean. *Hiryu,* the battleship and both the cruisers were steaming independently, separated from the other heavy ships by several miles. With each big ship the pilots could make out the narrow shape of a destroyer. The straight white wakes meant 20 knots and all the bows were pointed west.

Earl Gallaher tightened the wedges of his Dauntlesses, pulled up his nose, pushed throttle forward and commenced a climb, circling to the left to put the sun behind him and in the eyes of the enemy lookouts and gunners.

As the SBDs climbed slowly under the weight of their bombs, engines roaring with full throttle, the gunners faced aft and searched the sky for fighters. They knew that twice in one day they could not expect the luck of an unopposed attack. The torpedo squadrons which had been slaughtered at noon were not here to draw the Zeros down, and the enemy pilots would be furious and desperate at this threat to the only deck left to land on.

One of the gunners, looking south, signaled to the men in the other planes. In the middle distance, tiny slim shapes on the sea, were three destroyers at high speed headed for the main force of the enemy. Beyond them on the horizon were three tall columns of black smoke from the hulks of *Kaga, Akagi* and *Soryu.*

At three minutes past seven, from up sun at 19,000 feet, Gallaher gave the order to attack. The Dauntlesses nosed over, the rush of air increased and the air-speed indicators moved up as they slanted in toward the push-over point. The pilots, leaning forward, concentrating on formation and the narrow yellow rectangle below, felt their planes shake and heard the windbroken hammering of the 30s as the gunners opened up. Six Zeros were climbing to intercept, guns winking, the late sun bright on the brown-green wings with their red disks. The SBDs held formation and the tiered gunners poured in their defending fire, but Ensign F. T. Weber of Bombing Six with E. L. Hilbert in the rear seat spun suddenly out of line and fell away, smoking.

Directly over *Hiryu,* Gallaher gave the signal and peeled off, and it all began again. As it was at noon, so it was at evening: the SBDs precisely plunging out of the pale sky, below the yellow deck slicing the Pacific, its wake like a curling tail while the AA blossomed and the tracers climbed with incredible swiftness to meet the planes.

Parallel to the attackers, unable to slow down enough to engage, the Zeros dived also, ready to open fire again after pull-out.

One after another, as they reached their points, the American pilots reached forward with their left hands and pulled back on the release handles. The handles moved only an inch or two and there was no click, no jar. But as regularly timed and as relentless as though dispensed from some cosmic machine, the big bombs left the wings and dropped off toward the enemy.

Hiryu turned sharp and fast to starboard, heeling away from the turn, and the first bombs raised white spouts in the sea higher than her masthead. Falling back, the water poured onto her decks. As the bombers corrected for her turn, they began to hit her. Two bombs plunged into the deck just forward of the island, opening a hole yards across and slamming the forward elevator back against the bridge in a hit identical to that which the *Yorktown* group had made on *Soryu.* Through their shattered ports, helmsmen and officers of the deck could see only the scorched lumber of the elevator a few feet away. Two more bombs ignited the remaining planes and blew out the fires under the boilers. *Hiryu* slowed, stopped, and began to list. Her fighters, with no carrier left to land on, angrily raked the retiring Dauntlesses and two of the *Yorktown*'s bombers fell under their guns.

A torn and smoking derelict, the forward third of her deck blown open to show the charred wreckage below, *Hiryu* drifted before the trades all night, and sank at eight the next morning.

Singly and in groups of two and three as they happened to burst out of the chaos over the ships, Gallaher's pilots leveled off and headed home into the darkening east. They flew at first from cloud to cloud, avoiding the Zeros, and then pulled up and settled down to navigate.

It had been a long day for the surviving airmen who had been called at 3:30 in the morning to fly six to eight hours of formation and fight two major battles. At dark they found the task force and wearily thumped onto the Big E's deck. By 8:34 P.M. all that were coming were back aboard.

In the ready rooms they sprawled for a moment with coffee cups and sandwiches and made their reports. They knew only that they had hit four carriers hard. Beyond that, their minds blurred with fatigue, they neither knew nor cared. They stumbled off to their bunks. Around them as they slept *Enterprise* hummed with the air in her ventilating systems and rolled gently to the easy swell. The hangar deck was busy with the repair of damaged planes for whatever the next day would bring. Overhead twenty of Gray's Wildcats still circled on patrol. His twenty-eight pilots had flown eighty-nine patrols that day. The last one came aboard in full dark at twenty minutes past ten, and for those that remained of the *Enterprise* air group, the fourth of June was finished.

But although their attack carriers were out of action, the Japanese still had in the vicinity of Midway 10 battleships, 15 cruisers, and 45 destroyers, all intact and combat ready.

From northwest and southwest Yamamoto and Kondo stood in toward the battle, the bulging hulls of their battleships plowing the sea at 30 knots and the biggest naval guns in the world manned and trained out under the quarter moon. Either enemy force was capable of brushing aside the U. S. cruisers, and against them the puny five-inch guns and thin sides of the carriers were a ghastly joke.

Admiral Spruance had no knowledge of either force and with the last plane aboard from the *Hiryu* strike he had to make a decision. He could steam westward toward the mangled striking force and be in position at dawn to complete the rout of the enemy by heavy, short-range strikes, or he could stay where he was and see with the dawn search how the situation stood.

To an aggressive, confident commander, whose forces had achieved at least a partial victory against heavy odds, the first choice was terribly tempting. But there was much he did not know about the location of the enemy or his intentions.

"I did not feel justified," runs his report, "in risking a night encounter with possibly superior enemy forces, but on the other hand, I did not want to be too far away from Midway the next morning. I wished to have a position from which either to follow up retreating enemy forces or to break up a landing attack on Midway."

He ordered the task force east, reversing course at midnight.

Had he turned west, at midnight he would have collided with Konodo's battleships.

Not that night, nor for long afterward, were the men of *Enterprise* aware of all they had done that day. What they had done, with *Yorktown* and *Hornet*, was to begin the defeat of the Empire of Japan. What they had done, although its future course was long, bloody, and then uncharted, was to commence the winning of the war in the Pacific. Four of Japan's best carriers had been destroyed with all their planes and most of their pilots, and the enemy would never recover from these losses.

Of the four Japanese carriers destroyed, *Enterprise* alone was responsible for *Kaga* and *Akagi*, and shared with *Yorktown*'s homeless Bombing Three the death of *Hiryu*.

If one man can be said to win a battle and change the course of a war, Wade McClusky, by deciding to search beyond the range of his aircraft and correctly calculating the direction of that search, won the Battle of Midway and turned the war against Japan. He led against the enemy air power the force that in three minutes destroyed half of it and changed the odds in America's favor for the first time. Behind him was the superb planning of Raymond Spruance and Captain Miles Browning which caught the enemy fatally vulnerable; and never again would the dive bombers of the U. S. Navy be as deadly, as implacably unerring, as on that day; nor ever again would the need be as great.

The air department worked all night repairing shot-up aircraft from *Enterprise* and *Yorktown* and readying the remaining spares. By daylight on the fifth the Big E, if she did not quite have her Sunday punch, had at least a very solid left hook available.

All morning and most of the afternoon Gray's Wildcats prowled overhead, while Admiral Spruance moved cautiously westward attempting to evaluate the various contact reports from submarines and patrol planes.

By midmorning it was evident that the enemy had abandoned any offensive intentions against Midway and was retiring. At this point, Spruance's problem was reduced to a selection of targets. He headed boldly west in pursuit.

At five o'clock in the afternoon *Enterprise* began launching, and in thirty minutes had thirty-two SBDs in the air—nine from Scouting Six, six from Bombing Six and the rest refugees from the *Yorktown*. Led by Lieutenant D. W. Shumway of Bombing Three, the group divided, half staying low to form a scouting line thirty miles across, the other half climbing to 18,000 to be in position to attack. The objective was a damaged carrier (*Hiryu* which had gone down shortly after being sighted), two battleships and three cruisers calculated on the basis of an early contact report to be some 250 miles to the northwest. Haze reduced the visibility that afternoon, and a heavy overcast darkened the sea. It was 8:30 and dusk when Shumway made his only contact, a large enemy destroyer heading northwest.

The high group pushed over at once while the low scouts climbed to attack altitude and the Japanese skipper went to full speed and began to maneuver violently. At times the ship was completely hidden among the towering bomb splashes but threw up a vicious defensive fire and zigzagged so successfully that no hits were made.

It was ten o'clock and dark under the high clouds when the strike group came in to land. In the last months, Bert Harden had moved up to be assistant air officer and now the landing signal officer was Lieutenant (j.g.) Robin M. Lindsey (no relation to Gene Lindsey of Torpedo Six).

Robin Lindsey had never brought planes in at night.

In the returning flight, many pilots were making their first night carrier landings.

At regular intervals Robin slashed his right paddle down across his body to the left and another SBD flopped onto the blacked-out deck. It was as if they had been doing this for years, but each landing was a new risk, a new threat, a new strain on Lindsey. It seemed to him that he had landed a hundred planes. He yelled over to his helper who was counting them in.

"For God's sake, how many more?"

"Dunno . . . we already have a couple more than we launched."

Lindsey had a thought that froze him motionless for a second.

"Call the bridge," he yelled over his shoulder into the wind. "Have 'em check all planes for meatballs."

The bridge was inspected. There were no Japanese planes aboard, just five from the *Hornet* whose group was returning at the same time.

On the sixth of June, the SBDs were out again.

The dawn search reported a carrier and five destroyers 150 miles west.

Hornet attacked first. There was no carrier. But *Hornet*'s planes found two heavy cruisers and two destroyers.

At 12:45 the Big E began to launch. Bombing Six got five planes up, Scouting Six put six in the air and the squadrons from *Yorktown* another twenty. Twelve fighters completed the strike group. They climbed away at 1:15 headed for an up-sun position at maximum altitude above the cruisers. The sea was calm with a hot sun and just a few low clouds hanging in the clear air. It took less than an hour to find the enemy ships, making 28 knots straight west.

Once more the deadly ritual of the Dauntlesses began. From the close, stepped-down formations, at regular intervals, they pulled up sharply in the direction of the target, split their flaps and rolled into their dives.

All the Zeros had died with their carriers. The Wildcats went down to strafe.

The cruisers turned hard to starboard and opened fire, *Mikuma* in the lead and *Mogami* following, but the inexorable process had begun and would not be stopped. Five 1,000-pounders caught the *Mikuma* and two more landed very close aboard. One bomb got *Mogami*. As the Dauntlesses pulled up the fighters dived in, six to each ship, their .50-calibers hammering in long, angry bursts, zooming only to clear the twisted structure of the enemy. Under their guns, pieces of metal were blown into the air and fires followed small explosions on deck and in the gun areas.

As the last planes headed home, *Mikuma* was dead in the water and burning with dense, copious black smoke. *Mogami* was steaming very slowly, also burning and trailing oil, with two destroyers escorting her.

At ten minutes of six Lieutenant (j.g.) Ed Kroeger of Bombing Six led off the last combat mission of the battle —a photographic flight of two SBDs to record the damage inflicted by the day's strikes.

He found only one cruiser to photograph but the Dauntlesses went over her at masthead height and the pictures they brought back of *Mikuma* in her last hour on the surface say all there is to say of the combat capability of carrier-based dive bombers. Deserted by her sister cruiser and escorting destroyers, she lay dead in the water, listing to port, smoke and steam pouring up over her starboard side and drifting down wind. Her big guns, their turrets blasted into wreckage like a tin can in which a fire cracker has exploded, pointed in all directions. One muzzle was dragging in the sea. Her decks were a smoking shambles of ripped and twisted metal and over her up-wind side hung the lines by which part of her crew had taken to the sea.

On *Mikuma* and the destroyer loaded with survivors which a *Hornet* Dauntless hit, the Japanese lost 1,000 men.

But the losses at sea near Midway were not all on one side. During the nights and days after the decisive fourth of June, word of the struggle to save the *Yorktown* had traveled through the *Enterprise*. After the second attack on that first afternoon of the battle, she had taken a dangerous list and been abandoned. A destroyer stood by to sink her if there was danger of capture by the enemy. On the morning of the fifth she was still afloat, her fires out, her list stabilized at 25 degrees to port.

The destroyer sent a salvage party aboard and notified Admiral Fletcher who ordered ships in to tow and screen her. A large, properly equipped salvage party led by the *Yorktown's* skipper was assembled and headed for the ship. On the afternoon of the fifth a little minesweeper arrived and took the carrier in tow. It was a mouse pulling an elephant. In the teeth of a rising wind they made good one knot.

By dawn of the sixth the salvage party arrived, the destroyer *Hammann* tied up alongside to furnish power, and the job of saving the *Yorktown* began in earnest. By midafternoon she was on an even keel and it looked as if she would "live to fight again and to strike another blow." At 3:30 a *Hammann* lookout reported torpedo wakes. An enemy sub had found the *York*. She took two of the big Japanese torpedoes in her damaged port side. Another sent *Hammann* to the bottom.

It was too much. At daybreak on the seventh the Big E's sister ship, still carrying the half-healed scars of Coral Sea, capsized and sank. The bottom was two and a half miles down.

When Kroeger landed aboard the *Enterprise* from his photo mission over the *Mikuma* the battle of Midway was over. Now, 400 miles west of the island, low on fuel, aircraft and pilots, Spruance turned east to meet the tankers.

Yamamoto, his untouched battleships and loaded transports useless with control of the air above them lost, steamed west to his fueling rendezvous.

Midway was the first battle of the war in which heavy losses occurred in the carrier air groups. To the young ensigns and "jagees," and the sailors who rode the rear seats, this was the first taste of the irrevocable finality of death —and it was a massive dose. For them the war before Midway had been a great global adventure, dangerous, urgent, the implications of defeat and death intellectually recognized, but essentially an adventure. Although real and painful enough, the good-bys long ago on the West Coast and at Pearl had held the ancient excitement of the warrior departing for the wars. Since then, and to some extent before, they had transferred their normal daily affection for their families to the companions in adventure who shared their meals and staterooms and bull sessions and ready rooms, their acey-deucey games and knowledge of their planes, the sky over the sea, the pride in the neat and deadly formations and the unspoken imminence of death.

Then at the end of a certain day half had died or were lost, and to each one of the other half perhaps none or one of his close friends was left. It was sudden, unexpected and devastating.

For some it was years before they could again give the wholehearted friendship of their youth. Others lost the ability forever. Every carrier airman who survived Midway is a far different man for those days in early June when they turned the war against Japan.

Let there be no doubt. To the carrier-based squadrons under Fletcher and Spruance goes full and sole credit for the victory at Midway.

Shore-based aviation, whether Army, Navy or Marine, except for some timely scouting by the PBYs, had only a minor effect on the battle. Midway-based Navy and Marine pilots thrown into the fight failed through lack of training and experience in their aircraft.

Army Air Force Flying Fortresses, although they tried hard and dropped nearly half of the total weight of bombs, made no hits. Theirs was a fault of tactics. High-level horizontal bombing, although useful against large land targets, was at Midway and throughout the war totally ineffective against ships at sea. Victory can be summed up in a sentence. On the fourth of June, when all the land-based attacks had been completed, Fletcher's pilots found four carriers untouched and left them sinking.

BOOK TWO

BOOK TWO

9 PEARL AND A MISSION TO THE SOUTH

On the way back to Pearl the radio was busy. Among some dozen congratulatory messages from United States and allied commands and officials throughout the world was a report from Radio Tokyo obviously translated into English by a German assistant.

> Japan's forces outcarried fierce attacks on Midway Island inflicting heavy damage on fleet reinforcement in that area, also damaging heavily naval and air installations. . . . Japanese sank carriers *Enterprise* and *Hornet* while 120 enemy aircraft were downshot. . . .

It was the second time the enemy had reported the sinking of *Enterprise* and, as after the Marshalls raid, her men stamped her solid decks and grinned. It was getting to be a good omen.

On June 8, Commander T. P. Jeter, after two years as executive officer, was transferred by high line and breeches buoy to the oiler *Cimarron*. All hands off duty lined up on the flight deck and cheered him off, the thousand voices loud even under the windy evening sky as the commander swayed and dangled across the moving water between the ships.

A change in executive officers is important to a crew. It is he who most directly affects their lives. The skipper decides how the ship is to be organized and run, but it is the "exec" that runs it that way. His signature appears on the Plan of the Day, the detailed schedule by which each day's events are ordered. He is the final authority on leave, liberty and pay, which, with the quality and abundance of food, most directly affect shipboard morale. It is the exec who creates or fails to create an efficient organization to handle all aspects of life aboard ship, from cleanliness through combat.

It is thus an event of personal importance to each officer and man when executive officers are changed. Commander Jeter had run a taut, effective ship, and the men were sorry to see him go.

On the afternoon of June 13, 1942, when *Enterprise* secured her main engines and doubled up her lines at Pearl Harbor, December 7 was six months and a week ago. Now there seemed to be a lull in the war. When the thug in his first rush from behind fails to overpower his victim, there is a moment of sizing up, of shedding coats and wiping palms on trouser legs before the fight goes on. It was that kind of moment for the Big E in late June and early July of 1942.

U. S. strength was growing. Back in the States new ships were being built, new squadrons forming, new men being trained. Combat-experienced officers and men were needed to form the nuclei of new units, to command new ships.

During the month after Midway, other important changes took place in the Big E's crew and air group. *Enterprise* had not been long in port before the crew learned that Captain George Murray would be promoted to rear admiral. This meant a change of skippers since only under very unusual circumstances does an admiral command a single ship.

On the thirtieth of June, George Murray stood on his flight deck in his ribboned, braided whites and turned over the command of the *Enterprise* to Captain Arthur C. Davis.

"Seldom has it been the privilege of a carrier captain," he said, "to have had such a command as this. . . . Our goal has been, is and will be the destruction of the enemy . . . the successes we have achieved and those which lie ahead could not be realized without the teamwork and mutual good will which signify so essentially the *Enterprise* spirit . . .

"Captain Davis, I relinquish this command with regret. I am confident you will find the ship one of the great ships of our time—and the ship's company the finest."

Soon after the Big E came back to Pearl, all the torpedo squadrons were equipped with the new TBF Avengers. What were left of the outmoded Devastators after Midway lined up in a short row at Ford Island awaiting disposition. There were five planes, one from *Yorktown*'s VT-3, three from the Big E's VT-6 and one from *Hornet*'s Torpedo Eight. The five battered old planes, deserted in an unused corner of the field, told the story of the torpedo squadrons at Midway at a glance—but it was the numbers on their sides that interested the carrier airmen.

Parked wing tip to wing tip were 6-T-7, 8-T-7, and 3-T-7. The number seven plane of each squadron either had not been launched or had survived the slaughter.

During that quietly critical month, which began so auspiciously on arrival at Kaneohe with bands playing and cold beer served at the cockpit sides, there were even more drastic changes in the *Enterprise* air group, the striking force for which she existed. Most of the old hands were ordered home to season fresh squadrons or transferred to strengthen decimated ones. Gray, Mehle, Hoyle, Quady, Heisel, Rawie, Bayers, Provost, Hiebert and Rich received orders to new outfits in the States, including thirty-day leaves before reporting.

Ralph Rich, who had shot down an enemy torpedo plane at Midway and shared in every action of the six-month-old war, was one of the fighter veterans ordered home. But he never got there. On the eighteenth of June, in a routine gunnery dive at 5,000 feet over Kaneohe, the right wing of his Wildcat tore off and Ralph was killed.

And there was another, and worse, tragedy. Two days before Rich's death, Ensign Carl Pieffer of Scouting Six was scheduled for a regular training flight, including a visit to Kaneohe across the island. The start of his take-off run across the mat at Ford Island looked normal but before he could gain flying speed he inexplicably lost directional control. The SBD swerved violently left, then right, and as the crash sirens began to howl, tore off its entire tail section on a parked crane, became briefly air-borne, skimmed across the perimeter road barely clearing a loaded station bus and crashed, flaming, to a stop a hundred feet away. Neither Carl nor his rear-seatman made any move to escape the burning wreck and the busload of startled sailors ran to pull them out. Jim Gray was a passenger on that bus. He leaped out with the others and started for the crumpled Dauntless. Suddenly, he remembered that all SBDs were required to carry a live 500-pound bomb on every flight. In the flaring, gasoline-fed fire it would have to go up any second and rescue was impossible. Yelling a warning, Gray dived for the roadside ditch just as the bomb detonated with a flash and a roar. When he lifted his face from the dirt he found a steward thrown sprawling into the ditch by the blast, the dark flesh of his stomach laid open and the redness from inside slowly blotting his tattered whites. Both airmen and five rescuers died in the bomb blast and seventeen more were injured, some critically.

Most significant of all changes in personnel was the arrival of Commander John Crommelin to take over as air officer.

Crommelin was sandy-haired and enthusiastic, with a southern accent and an unqualified belief in the ability of carrier aviation to sweep the enemy right back into the Inland Sea. He was a highly skilled veteran fighter pilot and a born leader. His presence was immediately and continuously felt aboard the Big E. Bert Harden, up from landing signal officer, was his assistant.

To complete the month of transition, Rear Admiral Spruance was ordered to the staff of commander-in-chief, Pacific Fleet, and Rear Admiral Thomas C. Kinkaid came aboard to command the new task unit built around the Big E.

The new unit contained the pride of the fleet, fresh from her shakedown cruise, the fast battleship *North Carolina*, with nine 16-inch guns and bristling antiaircraft batteries. She was the first U. S. battlewagon able to steam with the fast carriers and cruisers and a welcome sight to the men of *Enterprise*. The remainder of Admiral Kinkaid's unit consisted of the heavy cruiser *Portland*, the new light antiaircraft cruiser *Atlanta*, and destroyers with familiar names —*Balch, Maury, Gwin, Benham* and *Grayson*.

In those first months of the war Oahu was no longer a tropical vacationland but a rapidly growing, heavily armed base for operations to the westward. The cooling trades still poured across the island under the soaking sun, and neither the voice of the surf nor the hot, sweet smell of the land was changed. But the famous beaches were destroyed by double barricades of barbed wire and patrolled by suspicious sentries. In Honolulu, two out of every three men on the street wore the uniform of the United States or her allies, and men outnumbered women by three or four to one. Carrier men on evening liberty after weeks at sea groped along the nearly empty streets between the blacked-out buildings and were almost glad to be back aboard before the 10:00 P.M. curfew closed down the city.

The young carrier pilots, who had looked death in the teeth and lost the friends of their youth, who knew now for the first time that they too could die, went about the business of living with incredible energy. The immediate possibility of death combined with the joy of their recent escape from it served to release them from accepted standards of behavior. Defiantly they plunged into whatever pleasures were available. They took rooms at the Navy-managed rest hotels, the Moana and the Royal Hawaiian, supplemented their liquor rations ingeniously and unscrupulously, and pooled them in bathtubs full of ice where they became available to all.

On the first night ashore after the fleet's return from Midway, the dining room of the Royal Hawaiian was jammed with officers of all services. Six or seven pilots of Scouting Six, including Pittman, Jaccard and White, were drinking toasts to their absent squadron mates. At the next table a group of Army Air Corps B-17 pilots were loudly describing to each other the manner in which the Flying Forts had won the battle. "Nig" White was a tall, muscular, sentimental Southerner and the moment came when liquor, sorrow, pride, anger and a final Army boast brought him to his feet.

"By God," he yelled, "that's a damned lie!" and his big fist smashed into the face above the khaki shirt. In a second the men at both tables were up and swinging and in ten more the spacious dining room held a full-scale riot—a cursing, flashing tangle of white and khaki that grounded many a pilot and took the Shore Patrol twenty minutes to subdue. Even with their cuts and bruises, everyone felt better the next day.

A few men, whose wives were employed in the islands, maintained apartments in town, and they were the lucky ones. Even they were half smothered under the heavy curtains in the black-out. Lieutenant and Mrs. Harvey Lanham of Bombing Six shared such an apartment, and one war evening after Midway were talking quietly in their blacked-out living room when there was a heavy knock at the door.

With some reluctance Harvey opened it in his undershorts. It was a Honolulu policeman, ticket book in hand.

"You know you've got a light showin' from that window, Bud?"

"No, of course not, or I would have fixed it."

"Well, yuh have, about two miles wide. A dive bomber pilot could see that light from twenty thousand feet and drop a bomb right in yer lap!"

"That would be a damn sight better night bombing than I've ever heard of," Harvey said, "and I've been a dive bomber pilot for the last five years!"

"I guess I shouldn't have said that," Harvey admitted later, "because right then was when he started writing the ticket."

For two weeks *Enterprise* was in the Navy Yard for up-keep and repair. She was dirty with chipped paint and soot and littered with air and gas lines and power cables so that it seemed to the crew that she would never be clean and shipshape again. Day and night the pneumatic hammers clattered against the steel, the cutting torches hissed, and the blue welding arcs flashed and sputtered their hot electric smell throughout the ship.

There was a lot to be done. It is hard to maintain so complex a piece of machinery at sea under the constant threat of action. Most of the maintenance and repair for the past few months and several yet to come had to be done in the yard at Pearl. The crew knew it well and in their urgent pride painted a large sign which appeared at her gangway to greet yard workmen:

THIS IS NO. 1 SHIP, A VETERAN OF THE MARSHALLS,
WAKE, MARCUS AND MIDWAY—EXPEDITE HER WORK.

Just after lunch on Bastille Day, the fourteenth of July, a few of Bombing Six's pilots were walking down the gangway for a last shore leave in Honolulu. Along the sun-drenched dock came an Aussie soldier, unmistakable in his broad-brimmed hat, high shoes, shorts and short-sleeved, open-collared shirt. Not one of the young pilots knew any Aussie soldiers, yet there was something familiar about this man, his walk, his manner. He waved, they waved back politely, hesitantly, and then, as he faced them coming up the gangway, they howled and threw themselves on him, pumping his hand, slapping his back, feeling his arms and legs. It was Durkin, lost two months ago on the trip to the Coral Sea—returned from the unknown reaches of the sea —long given up for dead, his effects inventoried and sent home. Durkin was a tanned and healthy ghost returned to the living, after two weeks in a rubber boat which killed his gunner, rescued by an Australia-bound ship from an island beach, a fine month down under and the long trip back. That evening there was a great celebration at the Royal.

On the morning of July 15, *Enterprise*, with her new men and planes and guns, sailed against the enemy again.

Outside the harbor the trim new *North Carolina* and *Atlanta* and familiar, reliable *Portland* joined up behind the semicircle of destroyers and stood south.

With the swelling line of cumulus over the Koolau Range still visible astern, the air group came aboard from Kaneohe. It was a different group from the decimated veterans of Midway who had landed on Oahu to the music of the bands a month ago.

The ready rooms were full of eager, determined new faces, and *Enterprise* pilots, who a month before had been "boots," now found themselves filling the veteran shoes of the departed Grays, Mehles, Gallahers, Bests, Dickinsons and Rileys.

While Admiral Kinkaid's ships steadily decreased their latitude to zero and then steadily built it up again on their southward progress, John Crommelin worked out his pilots. Every day the 200-mile searches went out ahead and, on both flanks, the antisub Avengers made their horizon sweeps and maintained inner and intermediate patrols and the Wildcat CAP was constantly overhead. Every day also all available planes were up for training—the fighters in enthusiastic dogfights, the new torpedo planes in flat, fast, simulated attacks and the bombers stooping vertically down the sky to drop on towed targets.

Ten days after leaving Pearl Harbor the watch on deck began to smell the sweet green odor of tropical vegetation and see the towering white clouds that build up over the islands of the southern seas.

Up to this point most of the Big E's men were prepared for another strike on enemy installations, and it seemed logical that, after smashing the Japanese attempt at Midway, such a strike should be in the south, at the other end of the enemy's long line of conquered islands. But in Tonga's crowded harbor was evidence that the present operation was no hit-and-run attack, but a sustained offensive campaign. Departing from Nukualofa just ahead of the carriers was a group of high-sided gray transports, their decks green with Marine fatigue uniforms and ringed with small landing craft hanging from their davits. It was evident that a landing was to be made, but where? The sailors hardly knew the islands of the Pacific well enough to guess. But wherever it was, the Big E was to have a radically new job, the covering and protection of landing forces.

In the past, at the Marshalls, Wake, Marcus and on the

Tokyo raid, *Enterprise* had learned to strike and get out.
Even at Midway in three major strikes the battle had been
over and the ship had returned to port. Now, with a landing of troops in prospect, the Big E and her sister carriers
might have to remain within easy fighter range of the assault area in order to protect the Marines from enemy aircraft and provide necessary offensive air support. This
would mean staying in a relatively small area which could
be easily calculated by the enemy, until land-based aviation
could arrive in sufficient strength to relieve the carriers. It
could mean, in short, the voluntary self-denial of the aircraft carriers' most valuable advantage, mobility—the ability to appear out of the limitless sea, strike and disappear
again to seaward to strike again next day a thousand miles
away.

At noon on the twenty-sixth of July, 400 miles southeast
of the Fiji Islands, the *Wasp* and *Enterprise* task units and
the transports with their escorts met *Saratoga*, *Minneapolis*, *New Orleans* and five destroyers, and other groups of
cruisers and destroyers including *Vincennes*, *Quincy*, *Astoria*, *San Juan* and the Australian cruisers *Australia*, *Canberra*, and *Hobart*, to form the most powerful naval force
the Allies had yet assembled in the seven-month-old war.

Admiral Kinkaid was transferred by high line to the
Saratoga to confer with Admirals Fletcher, Turner, Noyes,
McCain, Callaghan, and General Vandegrift of the Ma-
rines.

The sight of an ocean filled with warships was a welcome
one to the *Enterprise* sailors who very well remembered
the lonely run-ins toward enemy installations of unknown
strength with just two cruisers in support. Their spirits rose.
It didn't seem that anything could stop the force spread out
before them with its three big carriers, the new battlewagon, eleven heavy and three light cruisers and innumerable
destroyers, plus the twenty-odd transports full of heavily
armed Marines.

When the conference was over the force moved off to
the northwest under its circling CAP and behind the long
searches of its Dauntlesses and Avengers.

From the twentieth to the thirty-first of July there was a
dress rehearsal off the island of Koro in the Fijis. The Marines climbed down cargo nets into the bobbing landing
craft while cruisers and destroyers trained their guns on
the beaches and the Big E's planes made bombing and

strafing runs on targets ashore. It was a good lesson in co-
ordination, but a coral reef prevented all but a few Marines from getting ashore.

From the Fijis, the invasion force steamed slowly west
for several days, limited to the speed of the slowest transports, and then turned north. Crommelin and Harden kept
the searching pilots briefed on friendly shipping in the area.
Everything not mentioned at briefing was suspect.

On August 7 reveille in the Big E was an hour and a half
before daylight. As the men came out onto her blacked-out
decks, they could sense the land from the flat calm of the
sea, the stealthy, silent movement of the ship as she eased
along at ten to twelve knots, and the rank, wet, rotten
smell of the jungle. They went below for breakfast and before dawn the general alarm sent all hands to battle stations.

As the first light grayed the black sea, the men topside
could make out a dark mass ahead and over the loudspeakers Captain Davis read a message from Admiral Turner:

> "On August seventh this force will recapture Tulagi
> and Guadalcanal islands which are now in the hands
> of the enemy. . . ."

10 FIRST VISIT TO AN UGLY ISLAND

The Solomon Islands lie in the sea a thousand miles
northeast of Australia. The line of their long dimensions
runs northwest to New Britain and New Ireland and southeast to the New Hebrides. Northward is the open Pacific,
southward the Coral Sea. Guadalcanal is the plumpest, except for Bougainville at the northern end of the chain.

If the 10th parallel of south latitude and the 160th meridian east were the crosshairs of a telescope sight, the weapon would be aimed just a hair below Guadalcanal but
otherwise nicely centered. Like the other islands, it is
mountainous and rank with equatorial jungle but on the
north coast are open, level places suitable for airfield construction.

In early May of 1942, supported by *Shokaku* and *Zui-*

kaku and despite a vigorous counterattack by *Yorktown's* air group, the enemy had succeeded in establishing a seaplane base at Tulagi on Florida Island twenty miles north across the sound. The action in the Coral Sea which followed prevented any further conquests in that area for the time, and in late June, after the loss of four carriers at Midway had indicated the wisdom of consolidation rather than invasion, the Japanese commenced construction of an airfield at Guadalcanal.

Since Allied strategy in the South Pacific called for a step-by-step advance up the chain of the Solomons to the main enemy base of Rabaul, New Britain, from which Australia was being threatened, the creation of a strong enemy air base in the southern Solomons could not be accepted.

Thus, with the assignment of a few labor troops to scrape out an airstrip on an unheard-of island, the enemy unwittingly selected the fetid lump of Guadalcanal as the point at which the United States and her allies must begin the long bloody amphibious march on Tokyo.

On the *Enterprise*, the order was given to start engines at quarter past five, the props swung, caught, spun briefly, stopped and swung again, while the engines coughed blue smoke. As each engine cleared itself and began to idle smoothly, warming up, it developed a blue halo of light which circled the cowling at the exhaust manifold. To the night-adapted men on deck and on the bridge it seemed that the bright series of blue rings would give away the ship's position as she eased in toward the islands. They remembered the predawn launch against Wake Island when the blue cocoons blinded the pilots, lost Perry Teaff his eye and spoiled the careful timing of the attack.

One hour before sunrise, *Enterprise, Wasp* and *Saratoga* began launching. As Lou Bauer in the first of eight Wildcats left the Big E's bow it was 5:35 A.M. Except for the dim light of a quarter moon, it was full dark, the sky half covered with low cumulus clouds, and a faint horizon. Three minutes later Lieutenant (j.g.) T. S. Gay led off another eight fighters, and, at 5:40, Lieutenant Turner Caldwell took off with nine SBDs of Scouting Five, carrying 1,000-pound bombs. All the *Enterprise* pilots, thanks to John Crommelin, Bert Harden and Army aerial photos picked up in Efate, were thoroughly and accurately briefed, knew exactly what their targets were and where to find them.

In the black sky thirty miles west of Guadalcanal the planes of three carriers circled, joining up. Until five miles from the ship each plane was allowed to show only one dim white light at the tail for his mates to follow. In the rendezvous area, navigation lights could be turned on.

The predawn rendezvous on August 7 was a dangerous and haphazard affair. Blacked-out planes narrowly missed each other. Fighters joined up with bombers, and bombers from one carrier found themselves flying with squadrons from another. At a critical moment there was a brilliant explosion in the rendezvous area and the nervous pilots, most with recent experience of near misses, scattered, thinking it was a collision. They learned later that a Dauntless pilot from another carrier had inadvertently dropped his bomb, which, with its instantaneous fuse, had detonated on contact with the water. But it took more long, anxious minutes in the crowded darkness over the sea to get them together again.

Despite the inadvertent bomb exploded offshore, the enemy was sound asleep and not even dreaming of the presence of United States ships and planes when the USS *Quincy* opened up with her eight-inch guns at thirteen minutes past six. Other carriers and destroyers joined the firing as the light increased and the carrier planes arrived overhead. The loaded transports slid in toward the landing areas, labeled in the Operation Order as "Beach Red" on Guadalcanal and "Beach Blue" across the sound at Tulagi.

While the fire-support ships steamed slowly back and forth, parallel to the shore, guns trained out abeam and firing at gun emplacements, warehouses and small craft, the carrier-based F4Fs swept in just above the coconut palms, raking the wooden buildings, boats, tents, trucks and anything that moved with tracer and incendiary bullets. The fighters at Tulagi were followed in a few minutes by Turner Caldwell's nine SBDs which slammed their big bombs into the southwest coast of the little island and then went down to strafe.

There was very little opposition. Occasionally an antiaircraft gun would sputter into action and be quickly silenced by the searching fighters, the crew running for the woods.

By seven o'clock the carrier pilots could see the stubby landing craft jammed with green-uniformed Marines beginning to move shoreward from the transports.

Shortly after seven, Ray Davis arrived over Tulagi with eighteen SBDs of Bombing Six armed with 1,000-pounders, which were promptly delivered according to the desires of the *Wasp*'s air group commander, Lieutenant Commander Wallace M. Beakley. Beakley, in a TBF, controlled and co-ordinated the supporting aircraft over Tulagi and was in indirect communication with the ground forces as soon as they got ashore.

On the Guadalcanal side, Lieutenant Commander Maxwell F. Leslie, the Big E's new group commander, with two fighters as escort, performed the same task from 9:00 A.M. until 6:20 P.M. His contact, the transport group fighters director officer, was Slim Townsend.

All morning, although the Marines at Tulagi ran into trouble, the carrier planes had no opposition, suffered no losses. The fighters, in addition to their strafing duties, flew uneventful CAPs over the carriers and over the cruisers and destroyers that steamed between the unloading transports and the enemy bases to the northwest. The dive bombers made repeated deliveries of their heavy bombs and returned, unmolested, for more. The torpedo squadron remained aboard the *Enterprise* in reserve—ready to meet the inevitable enemy reaction.

Each undisturbed hour meant additional Marines and their equipment delivered ashore. *Enterprise* sailors, munching their luncheon sandwiches at battle stations that morning, could see the dark green hills of Guadalcanal to the east and northeast and the columns of black smoke that rose from across the island where the ships and planes were at work.

The north coast of Guadalcanal and the south coast of Florida Island form a rough V of water which lies on its side with the large open end to the northwest. Beach Red on Guadalcanal is halfway along the lower arm of the re-clining V, and Beach Blue at Tulagi on Florida Island is directly across on the upper arm. The body of water between in the months after early August became known, with good reason, as "Iron Bottom Sound." Directly in the center of the open end of the V is the high, volcanic bulk of Savo Island.

The most direct course for an enemy force attempting to oppose the Guadalcanal-Tulagi landings would be into the open V past Savo. Thus it was on either side of Savo Island, in the mouth of the V, that the United States and Australian cruisers patrolled against an enemy surface counterattack and it was over these ships that the Big E kept a combat air patrol.

But thirty minutes past noon, the period of unchallenged U. S. control of the air over Guadalcanal ended.

Lou Bauer, flying CAP over the screening force with Reid, Halford and Hartmann, was notified of a large bogey (unidentified aircraft) approaching, and the F4Fs were vectored out to the northwest. In the immediate vicinity of Savo Island they received another vector which, if obeyed, would take them back to the carriers some fifty miles southeast. Bauer immediately requested confirmation of the vector and when it was repeated led his fighters home. Over the carrier task force they orbited uselessly while the first Japanese air attack struck the ships off Guadalcanal.

A fighter-director officer had read the wrong side of the azimuth ring on a radar scope, ordered Bauer's Wildcats on a bearing reciprocal to the right one and stuck to his error. And while Bauer was being inadvertently withdrawn from the danger area, Gay, DePoix, Sumrall and Achten, on patrol over the carriers, were being ordered to Tulagi as protection against the incoming enemy planes.

As the four *Enterprise* Wildcats crossed the western tip of Guadalcanal at 16,000 feet, they could make out the black dots of antiaircraft bursts over the screening cruisers east of Savo and over the transports unloading off Beach Red. They continued on course for Tulagi, 1,000 feet above the bursts of flak, their heads turning from side to side and up and down, as though they were doing neck exercises, while they searched the sky for the enemy they knew was still close by.

Lieutenant Vincent DePoix saw them first, a swarm of black specks like disciplined flies heading northwest at 12,000 feet over the south end of Florida Island, where the apex of the V was broken. He turned at once to intercept and the others followed, guns charged and throttles open. Over the center of Florida Island on the opposite coast from Tulagi they made the interception. There were thirty twin-engine bombers in a flat, tight V of Vs escorted by Zero fighters and making a steady 180 knots.

The four Wildcats attacked at once.

DePoix came in from above and ahead, closing the enemy with a relative speed of nearly 500 knots, fired a single long burst during the seconds he was in range and on target, then pulled up hard underneath and behind and attacked from astern. Sumrall saw DePoix's first target smoke as the tracers stitched into it, and on the stern attack, with a chance to watch, Vince saw the second enemy plane roll out of formation and crash in the sea north of Florida.

Sumrall and Gay attacked simultaneously from high on opposite sides of the brown-winged bombers, crossed under the formation to exchange sides and reattack. Both watched their tracers hit. Gay was momentarily distracted at the beginning of his run by the sight of two Zero fighters slightly below and behind the formation, but his attack was good and his target smoked and lost speed.

Achten attacked behind DePoix and was immediately engaged by the two Zeros lurking astern. He singled one out, managed to get on its tail and fired a good, accurate burst. The Zero left the fight in a vertical dive but did not smoke and Achten was prevented from observing any further by the tracers which burned past him and the 20-millimeter holes which began appearing in his right wing. Damaged and unable to shake the enemy pilot, he dived for a cumulus cloud and eluded him in its cool, gray interior.

After their second attacks the other three pilots were smothered by the escorting Zeros and, like Achten, with their planes full of holes, escaped into the towering cumulus clouds over Florida Island.

It was the beginning of a busy afternoon for Fighting Six.

Firebaugh, Stephenson, Warden, Disque, Rhodes and Mankin were launched at 1:00 P.M. as CAP for the cruiser screening force. En route to station, they were warned of the presence of enemy bombers and, while in a wide circle to the northwest of Savo Island, sighted the same formation that DePoix's flight had just attacked. By now the flat brown-winged wedges were thirty-five miles northwest of Savo, over the southeast tip of Santa Isabel, the next island up the Solomon chain. They were still headed for home at 12,000 feet and 180 knots.

Firebaugh at 16,000 "fire-walled" his throttle and took up the chase. The Wildcats gained rapidly on the Mitsubishi 97s and five miles astern Firebaugh divided his forces. With Stephenson and Warden he pulled off to the right and sent Disque, Rhodes and Mankin to the left so the Americans could strike from both flanks simultaneously. At three miles the pilots first saw the escorting Zeros. There were three behind and below the bombers and seven more in a stepped-up right echelon below and ahead. With a starting agility that the heavier, more rugged F4Fs could not match, the enemy fighters ahead entered a steep, climbing right turn and bored in, firing. At the same moment the three Zeros astern climbed straight ahead at an unbelievable 45-degree angle to join the assault on Firebaugh's division.

Unmolested, Disque, Mankin and Rhodes came down out of the sun in high side runs on the bombers. Disque and Mankin, seeing no results from their first runs, pulled up and reattacked. Two of the bombers, smoking, fell behind the formation and Disque immediately jumped the nearest one and sent it on a long flaming slant into the sea.

During the tail chase and the series of attacks the bombers had been flying steadily northwest at better than three miles a minute. By the time Disque and Mankin had driven off the Zero they were 150 miles from *Enterprise*. The high-speed pursuit and attacks had brought their fuel supply to a dangerously low level and it was time to go home.

Lieutenant (j.g.) Raleigh E. Rhodes, after his first attack, continued to the other side of the enemy formation to lend Firebaugh and his two wingmen a hand. He found no Wildcats but four Zeros instead, and in a swirling melee of brown-bodied, yellow-winged fighters, with the horizon usually vertical, the sea frequently above and vision restricted to dead ahead by the Gs which leadened his guts and dragged down the blood from his head, he shot one down and escaped riddled with 7.7 holes into a friendly cloud and home.

Neither Firebaugh, Stephenson nor Warden returned from this flight.

By midafternoon of this first day at Guadalcanal, the enemy had changed his tactics from high-level to dive bombing. At 2:30 P.M. Lieutenant A. O. Vorse of Fighting Six, on patrol with four F4Fs over the screening ships near Savo, sighted three dive bombers halfway between Guadalcanal and Tulagi at the same altitude as the CAP. Since they were approaching the anchored transports, there was not time to climb or maneuver for position and Vorse headed straight in with a flat side approach which developed into a tail chase of the third plane. When Vorse opened fire the enemy bomber pushed over in his dive with the F4F on his tail shooting steadily. Momentarily Vorse expected to

have to break off the attack as the bomber opened his dive
flaps and slowed far below the minimum speed the clean
and heavy Wildcat could maintain in a nearly vertical descent. But the enemy failed to open his flaps, perhaps in the
hope that he could outrun or surprise the fighter with the
increased speed. It was a fatal mistake. Vorse kept on his
tail as though the lines of his tracers were tow ropes between the aircraft. At 2,000 feet, with the dive bomber
smoking heavily, he pulled out and watched the enemy dive
straight into Iron Bottom Sound, leaving a flaring patch
of burning gasoline on the surface of the sea.

The other three planes of Vorse's flight lost sight of the
bombers when they began their dives.

At two o'clock six F4Fs—Runyon, Packard, Cook, Shoemaker, Nagle and March, just returned from an uneventful
patrol—were launched again to reinforce the CAP over
the screening group. As they were approaching their station, they were warned that enemy aircraft were in the
area and at the same time noticed the multiple black puff-
balls of antiaircraft fire appearing in the sky over the
screen. Reasoning that the anchored transports were the
enemy's primary target, Donald Runyon evaded the AA
bursts and headed for Beach Red at Guadalcanal. Over
Lunga Point was a single enemy dive bomber, looking de-
ceptively obsolete with its fixed landing gear. Runyon and
Packard went after it, twisting down in high side attacks.
Runyon's fire had no noticeable effect on the fish-tailing
enemy plane but under Packard's guns it exploded into
flame and black smoke and arched down into the sound.

After the first attack Runyon leveled off and looked
around. Approaching from ahead and above was another
dive bomber, evidently a wingman separated from the first
one. Runyon pulled up firing just as Shoemaker flashed in
from the side. Caught in a cross fire of twelve .50-calibers
the enemy flared suddenly, rolled over and dove into the
sea, brushing the blue sky with a black crescent of smoke.

Down close to the water, making for home, were two
more of the enemy. The Wildcats dove in for the kill. Runyon skidded one into the sea from 500 feet. Shoemaker and
March took the other, March from astern and Shoemaker
from the right side. March fired it as Shoemaker was starting his run and the sky over "Guadal" was, at least for a
time, clear of enemy planes. Runyon, March and Packard
returned to the *Enterprise*. Nagle, Cook and Shoemaker

made precautionary landings aboard *Saratoga*.

While her fighters were slashing at the Japanese counter-attacks, the Big E's bombers were methodically working over enemy positions and installations ashore, and the torpedo squadron, while holding a strike in reserve, searched the sea lanes by which the enemy would have to approach the combat area.

Eight SBDs under Lieutenant Carl Horenburger of Bombing Six were at 8,000 feet looking for targets at Tulagi when the enemy's 1:00 P.M. high-level bombing attack came in. Two Zeros of the escort came down to investigate them. One attacked from astern and ran into the concentrated fire of 16 heavy machine guns so well handled by the rear-seatmen that the Zero crashed into the sea off Tulagi. His companion made a half-hearted, long-range attack and, possibly remembering that his primary mission after all was bomber escort, withdrew. His 7.7s distorted the vane on Ensign Gibson's 500-pounder and holed the elevator of Ensign R. C. Shaw's Dauntless. All eight SBDs completed their bombing mission and returned safely aboard.

All day the eighth the Big E's flight deck was busy. Operating off the southeast end of Guadalcanal and nearly as close to San Cristobal, the next island down the Solomon chain, she provided CAP for the carriers and the cruiser screen off Savo while the SBDs continued to hammer away at the enemy wherever he was still holding out on Guadal and Tulagi.

Runyon, Shoemaker and Rouse were on patrol over the screening cruisers at 17,000 feet late in the hot, sunny morning. The three Wildcats circled easily in a loose V, throttled back to conserve fuel, the pilots' faces distorted by their oxygen masks and helmets, the black doughnuts of the wheels tucked up tight into the fuselages below the leading edges of the wings.

It was nearly noon when the screen fighter director officer announced the approach of low-flying enemy torpedo planes from the northward across the eastern tip of Florida Island. The three F4Fs dove steeply down the three miles of sky with the needles of their air-speed indicators steady on the red lines of limit speed. Strung out irregularly across the surface of the narrow channel between Florida and Guadalcanal, they found the torpedo bombers, so low on the calm sea that the blast from their props made wind streaks in the sound.

Runyon made a flat beam attack on the nearest enemy, missed, turned sharply to meet a second head on and hammer it into the sea. Rouse right behind him killed the first plane in a point-blank stern attack, veered off onto the tail of another and in a single long burst set it blazing. Rouse looked around for another target and found a Zero on his tail with Shoemaker in close pursuit, firing. The Zero veered sharply to the left to escape Shoemaker's .50-calibers and ran head on into Runyon's six guns coming in the opposite direction. He cartwheeled into the sea. With the Zero down, Shoemaker banked into a beam attack on a fifth enemy and watched its long splash and the slow fall of the spray.

The enemy torpedo attack made only one hit, on the destroyer *Jarvis*, for the loss of nearly all of twenty-six attacking planes.

At the close of flight operations on the evening of the eighth of August, Admiral Fletcher considered that his three carriers had stayed so long in the same waters that the whole Japanese Empire was aware of their location. He decided to withdraw, and the task force moved southeastward along the dark coast of San Cristobal Island.

The Big E's pilots, landing signal officers, mechanics, ordnancemen and flight-deck personnel were in need of rest. During the two-day period there had been 372 take-offs and 366 landings, 236 take-offs and 229 landings on the single day of the seventh to establish a new record for flight operations in combat. Ninety-one pilots had flown a total of 1,000 hours.

Shortly after midnight the radios began to announce some kind of surface action taking place off Savo Island. The reports were confused and conflicting but the men of *Enterprise* were confident of the ability of the sturdy, big-gunned cruisers to take care of themselves and the defenseless transports. Most of them slept well that night.

Lieutenant Commander Slim Townsend in the anchored transport *McCauley* off Beach Red at Guadalcanal was closer and saw the action, but knew no more than his *Enterprise* shipmates 160 miles to the southeast. Slim could see the flash of the big guns and long seconds later, coming across the sound from Savo, hear their thunder and the freight-car rumble of the shells. Occasionally he could make out the flight of the white- or red-hot projectiles and see the flare and bright scatter of explosions lighting the whole sky like lightning when they hit. He knew that the lives of the Marines ashore in the Solomons and the sailors in the thin-skinned transports depended on who was winning that night battle a few miles to the northwest and yet it was not until morning that he and everyone else found out.

What Slim Townsend learned, and the Big E heard minutes later, was about as bad as it could be. A Japanese column of heavy cruisers and destroyers had slipped past our destroyer patrol, caught our screening cruisers with guns trained fore and aft and most of the men asleep, and hammered them to pieces. *Quincy, Vincennes, Astoria* and *Canberra* were on the bottom of the sound near Savo and *Chicago* was so badly damaged that her survival was in doubt. The surface of Iron Bottom Sound was sprinkled with thousands of bloody and burned American seamen alive and dead. Under the black oil and the wreckage the sharks prowled hungrily. None of the wreckage and none of the seamen were Japanese.

Only confusion and the fear of carrier-based retaliation at daybreak had kept the undamaged enemy cruisers from annihilating the transports and shooting up the loaded beaches. Now, with no surface screening force above water and the carriers rapidly withdrawing, they could return at any time and finish the job.

At daylight the half-unloaded transports began picking up their boats and moving out. Enemy-controlled waters are no place for transports and, with the Battle of Savo Island, control of the sea around Tulagi and Guadalcanal had gone to the Japanese.

11 THE EASTERN SOLOMONS

For two weeks Enterprise, Wasp *and* Saratoga *cov*ered the southern approaches to the Solomons. Small fast destroyer-transports slipped into Iron Bottom Sound with men, ammunition and supplies and got out again fast. Every night Japanese destroyers and light cruisers ran down the long "slot" from Rabaul to shoot up the U. S. beachhead, appearing with such unwelcome regularity that they became known among the Marines as the "Tokyo Express." Planes from the three carriers flew daily sub patrols and search flights while the ships themselves stayed out of range of enemy aerial reconnaissance and well beyond the reach of his surface forces. With practical control of the waters around Guadalcanal, the Japanese were certain to make a major effort to drive out the Marines—and Admiral Fletcher wanted his carriers ready to meet it.

In the days after the initial landings, good news dribbled in. Lieutenant Firebaugh was safe on Santa Isabel. Machinist Warden was in the hands of an Allied coast watcher at Biarro Bay, Guadalcanal, after six days in his rubber boat. And on the nineteenth, Machinist Achten came back aboard by high line from the *San Juan,* having ditched off Tulagi.

On the same high-line transfer operation came a group of newly commissioned ensigns ordered to the Big E and her squadrons. Captain Davis shook his head and John Crommelin cursed unbelievingly as the first young officer swung across the churning gap between the ships. Over his right shoulder was a golf bag, in his left hand a tennis racquet.

While *Enterprise* and her sister carriers patrolled and dodged submarines south of the Solomons, the Japanese assembled their forces for the reconquest of Guadalcanal. Battleships, carriers, cruisers, destroyers, and land-based air squadrons converged from all corners of the stolen empire until, on the twenty-first of August, 3 carriers, 3 battleships, 18 cruisers, 25 destroyers, 100 land-based aircraft and transports loaded with 1,500 picked troops awaited Admiral Yamamoto's attack signal.

At Pearl Harbor Admiral Nimitz as usual knew his enemy's intentions. *Hornet* sailed for the Solomons on the seventeenth. Two new battleships and a new antiaircraft light cruiser left their Atlantic ports for the South Pacific.

Nearly a million tons of the world's best warships pointed their gray bows for Guadalcanal to determine whether a few thousand United States Marines who hated the place would stay or go.

On the twentieth, nineteen Marine Wildcats and twelve Dauntlesses landed at Henderson Field, Guadalcanal, and the malodorous island became an American air base that the Japanese must destroy or be forced to retreat for the first time. And on that day, Yamamoto pushed the button.

Escorted by destroyers, the transports sailed from Rabaul and stood out to the eastward in order to approach Guadal from the north. Southward from their mysterious and reputedly impregnable base at Truk came *Enterprise's* old archenemies, the big carriers *Shokaku* and *Zuikaku,* with light carrier *Ryujo* operating separately, and out ahead of everything a line of scouting submarines.

It was Yamamoto's plan to expose the *Ryujo* and, while the American air groups were attacking her, to smash our carriers with surprise strikes from *Sho* and *Zui.* With the U. S. carriers out of action, his cruisers and battlewagons could wreck Henderson Field and drive the Marines to cover until the transports arrived to mop up. Submarines and long-range patrol planes were ordered to track the American carriers.

At 10:45 on the morning of August 22, three four-plane divisions of Wildcats were on high patrol over *Enterprise* as she steamed eastward some sixty miles south of San Cristobal, the last island in the chain of the Solomons. At 10:48 the white blob of an unidentified aircraft began to show on the ship's radar fifty-five miles southwest. The fighter director officer let the bright sweep of the antenna flick over once more to be sure. Then he picked up the mike and ordered a division of fighters out to intercept. Communications were bad. The FDO's voice cracked and garbled in the static. It was seven minutes before Lieutenant Vorse's division was on its way. Watching his scope carefully, the FDO directed his fighters west then south. Twenty-five miles out they found it—a bulky four-engine Kawanishi flying boat, poking along at 8,000 feet on an easterly heading. The fighters were at the same altitude as the Kawanishi and Vorse split his division, sending two planes in from ahead and below and two from behind and above. Vorse was first in position and came down with his wingman, steep and fast on the big seaplane. It made no effort to evade and, although it was well armed with tail and side guns, did not shoot back. Vorse fired one short burst and a flame sprang out of the fuselage at the wing roots and flared immediately out into the wings. In seconds the weakened wing structure collapsed, both wings folded upward and tore off and the long tubular fuselage tilted downward toward the sea. Halfway down a man leaped from the torching fuselage, his small dark shape separating suddenly from the larger one. He wore no parachute.

By the evening of the twenty-second, Admiral Fletcher knew that the enemy was at sea in force and he turned his three carriers north.

At ten the next morning, well on the hostile north side of the Solomons, Captain Davis got word that enemy transports had been sighted headed for Guadalcanal. The news tied in with the two submarines that the Big E's pilots had already sighted that morning running south at high speed. Turner Caldwell found the first one at 7:25, but it crash-dived before he could make a good drop. Strong and Richey sighted the second one forty minutes later, blew it to the surface, and strafed until it submerged.

By 2:45 Fletcher's task forces were in range of the enemy transports and the *Saratoga* was ordered to launch. Thirty-one SBDs and six Avengers formed up and went after the enemy.

At 3:30, Maul and Estes found another sub, also surfaced and running south. The Dauntlesses attacked at once as the sub crash-dived. Both bombs hit close aboard and a minute and a half after she had disappeared, oil began flowing to the surface and spreading out over the calm sea.

That evening, Admiral Fletcher, on the basis of an intelligence estimate that all the enemy carriers were north of Truk, sent the *Wasp* and her task group south to fuel. *Enterprise* and *Saratoga*, with their supporting ships, were left to turn back Yamamoto.

Sara's strike group did not find the enemy transports, nor did twenty-three Marine planes from Henderson. Both groups returned to Guadalcanal for an uneasy night under the guns of the Tokyo Express and the *Sara*'s pilots landed back aboard at 11:00 A.M. on the twenty-fourth.

August 24 was the day designated by Admiral Yamamoto for the recapture of Guadalcanal.

Enterprise was assigned the dawn search. Twenty-three SBDs fanned out at 6:30 A.M. on 200-mile legs from west through north to east. Their long and lonely flights were over empty seas. But the enemy was out there somewhere and had to be found and destroyed before his greatly superior strength could get a grip on Guadal.

By ten o'clock reports began to come in from scouting PBYs of an enemy carrier with a cruiser and destroyers about 200 miles northwest. It was *Ryujo*. *Saratoga* fighters killed another four-engine snooper only twenty miles from the ship. A little after 1:00 P.M., Machinist Barnes of

Fighting Six knocked a twin-float, single-engine seaplane out of the sky within sight of the task force. Not only was the enemy out there, but by now he knew the location of our carriers.

After the PBY contact, Admiral Fletcher tried hard to close the range. It was difficult to do. The Japanese were somewhere to the northwest. A stiff breeze blew from the southeast, and each time planes were launched or recovered, the ships had to turn into the wind, away from the enemy. But shortly after 1:00 P.M. *Enterprise* was ordered to launch another search, this time to 250 miles. At 1:15 P.M. sixteen SBDs and seven TBFs spread out, singly and in pairs, over the hostile ocean to the north on what was probably the most eventful scouting flight in history.

At 1:45 Fletcher took Yamamoto's bait, and *Saratoga* launched thirty bombers and eight torpedo planes against the *Ryujo* on the basis of the PBY reports. *Shokaku* and *Zuikaku,* as yet unseen by any American eyes, and alerted by recent reports of *Sara* and *Enterprise* positions, stood eagerly southward.

Feeling half blind and wholly exposed, Admiral Fletcher doubled his Wildcat CAP and all remaining flyable fighters were armed, gassed and warmed up. *Enterprise* prepared to launch a strike on receipt of the first reliable contact report.

Under the bright sun the scattered groups of armed ships drew together north of Guadalcanal, and over the white-capped Pacific the carrier aircraft skimmed in neat geometrical patterns as the opposing forces groped for each other. It was something like the early moments of the first round when boxers feel each other out with long left leads, holding the loaded rights in constant readiness.

Then all the Big E's search planes seemed to make contact at once. It was incredible that after the painstaking morning sweeps had found nothing, the sea should suddenly be alive with the enemy.

Lieutenant Stockton B. Strong and Ensign John F. Richey, who had worked over a submarine together the previous day, found *Ryujo* making 16 knots to the south. They approached to five miles and for six full minutes broadcast her position, course, speed and the composition of her group (a small carrier, a heavy cruiser a few miles away, and two destroyers).

At about the same time, Ensign Bingaman in a TBF and

Ensign Jorgenson in a Dauntless located the same group. The mismatched section went down to 500 feet and, like Strong and Richey, closed to five miles and opened up on the radio. At quarter past three they saw bomb splashes rise white close astern of the carrier and, looking up, saw the tiny, dark blue shapes of two Avengers in a horizontal bombing run at 12,000 feet. In another minute angry Zeros jumped the two scouts and they headed home.

The horizontal bombers were Lieutenant Commander C. M. Jett, the torpedo squadron skipper, and Ensign R. J. Bye. Yamamoto had wisely chosen the position of his bait and it was thoroughly located. The TBFs made their runs down sun and were undetected until just before the drop when the guns below began to flash. Sharp, oriental eyes with binoculars must have watched the four bombs leave their racks, because at that instant *Ryujo* began to come hard right. Her fantail skidded out of the way as the bombs fell, and they landed in a single cluster 150 feet astern.

Again, just after 3:00 P.M., Lieutenant Myers and Machinist Corl, zigzagging between the cumulus buildups in two Avengers of VT-3, ran across an enemy heavy cruiser. Shoving their throttles forward and alerting their crews they circled for altitude as the cruiser twisted and opened fire, her midship guns flashing and smoking. At 10,000 feet the two TBFs lined up for a bombing run, but from their port quarter a Zero flashed in, rolled over on his back, and opened fire, diving away below the two Avengers. The tracers went wild, and the Torpedo Three pilots dived and twisted to avoid two more fighters, one with a wide red stripe around its fuselage, which dived in firing from the starboard. It was not until the enemy fighters attacked that Myers first saw a carrier ten miles behind the target cruiser and realized that he too had found the well-advertised *Ryujo*. In the face of the Zero attack, Myers and Corl broke off their bombing run and headed for some friendly clouds and home. Corl was last seen diving into a thunderhead with a Zero on his tail. He did not return to the ship.

It was three o'clock also when Lieutenant J. T. "Jiga" Lowe, the exec of Bombing Six and his wingman Ensign R. D. Gibson, assigned to a more northerly sector, located Yamamoto's vanguard group of heavy cruisers and destroyers. There were other groups of escorted cruisers 10 miles west, all headed south at 20 knots through the dark blue, white-capped Pacific. The prospect of facing the com-

bined fire power of three cruisers and their destroyer screen
caused not the slightest hesitation, and Lowe and Gibson
circled eastward, climbing to attack position. They pushed
over from 11,000, plunging steeply for the biggest cruiser
as the tracers rose to meet them and lethal black puffs ma-
terialized ahead. The big cruiser turned hard to starboard,
nearly reversing course as the SBDs hurtled down. Lowe's
bomb was twenty yards off her starboard quarter. Gibson's
was twenty feet from her port bow and its column of white
water sluiced down on her decks. As low on the water as
they could get, the Dauntlesses shoved throttle against the
stops and set course for home.

It was half an hour later that Lieutenant Ray Davis, CO
of the Big E's own Bombing Six, searching at 1,500 feet,
made the real find of the day. With Ensign Shaw on his
wing, he first sighted a couple of light cruisers and had begun a climb to attack when he saw *Shokaku* behind them,
unmistakable with her narrow yellow deck and her button-
like island well forward. The flight deck was busy with
planes and men and she was slicing southward at nearly 30
knots. Ray Davis found himself tense, breathing fast as he
pulled up the SBD's round nose and began the long, circling
climb to attack position. From that sliding rectangle of yellow below his right wing had come the end of peace on
December 7, a thousand years of strikes and searches ago.
Only *Shokaku* and *Zuikaku* were left of the six carriers who
committed the Sunday murders. Battered by *Lexington* and
Yorktown planes in the Coral Sea, they had been unfit for
battle at the time of Midway. Now big, smart, blooded *Sho*
and *Zui* were the heart of Japanese naval strength.

Climbing at full power, Davis broadcast the alarm, repeating and repeating, wishing violently that he had his
squadron at his back. J. W. Trott and H. L. Jones in the
two rear seats rechecked the free guns and craned their
necks around the sky. The Japanese would protect *Shokaku*
with every fighter and every gun available, and the Dauntlesses were taking a long time to climb.

Looking down from attack altitude the Big E's pilots
saw *Zuikaku* five miles astern, looking smaller than *Shokaku*, the flight deck seeming to have beveled edges. It too
was busy with men and aircraft.

Davis and Shaw very well knew that theirs was a search
mission, that instead of the long 1,000-pounders that sink
big ships they carried only a general-purpose 500 apiece;

that *Shokaku* alone was a target worthy of a full air group. But they took her on, down sun and up wind from 14,000 feet at 3:45 that August afternoon. Davis dived first, Shaw following, smoothly, precisely, ignoring the tracers reaching up like broomstraws and the heavy flak bursts that jarred the Dauntlesses, with stick and rudders lining up the growing yellow deck beginning to slide around to starboard. At 5,000 feet they put their eyes to the tube of the bombsight and centered the crosshairs with light pressures of hand and feet. At 2,000 feet left hands went from the throttle quadrant forward to the release handle and pulled sharply—then stick back in the pull-out, dive flaps closed, throttle forward—fast and flat on the water, and away with the tracers crisscrossing around them and heavy splashes in the sea. Pulling out, the two Dauntlesses flashed through seven or eight planes circling the carrier. A Zero came in on a wide sweep to attack them and the rear-seatman shrieked in delight as a burst of tracers from one of the light cruisers skidded it into the ocean. The two bombs were heartbreakingly close to the carrier's starboard side, Davis' not more than five feet, Shaw's not over twenty. There was no splash but a thin column of smoke from the shaken ship.

With bad radio conditions and cluttered frequencies, Ray Davis' contact report was not received on the Big E. But it was heard and relayed by other planes and ships, and when Admiral Fletcher got it he saw the trap and tried to divert *Saratoga*'s strike. It was too late. The *Sara*'s planes already had their target in sight and were expertly driving her, with most of her aircraft, to the bottom. Now from *Shokaku* and *Zuikaku*, heavily escorted by Zeros, thirty-six Val dive bombers and a dozen Kate torpedo planes were on their way to *Enterprise*.

While the scouts were straggling home after their brushes with the enemy, half the planes of Fighting Six were in the air over the task force ready to meet the inevitable attack. The *Sara* had up a dozen more. On both ships all remaining fighters were spotted for immediate take-off, gassed and armed to capacity. All were under the control of two fighter director officers hunched over the Big E's air search radarscope. Slowly the big bedspring antenna rotating at the masthead swept the skies, searching for the enemy, while the two FDOs, Lieutenant Commanders Leonard Dow and Henry Rowe, identified the "pips" of friendly fighters and tried to differentiate between enemy raiders and returning friendly scouts. The radio air was noisy with fighter orders and acknowledgments, reports of antisub patrols, and the queries of returning scouts, all on the same frequency.

The weather was beautiful but dangerous. Between the blue sky and the blue, white-capped sea towered the afternoon cumulus. Visibility was unlimited. Drenched in the tropic sunshine the gray ships drew long white lines across the South Pacific. An enemy could see the force from forty miles, approach behind the swelling towers of cloud. On all the ships men stood at their battle stations, waiting. Big, solid, heavily gunned *North Carolina* moved in astern of *Enterprise,* her barrels pointing out and up. Overhead and off in the direction of the enemy, the Wildcats swung in buzzing circles. The *Saratoga* task group steamed ten miles to starboard.

At 4:32 the big air-search antenna stopped, facing northwest. It turned a little right, then back a little left and stopped again. Below, in the tiny radar room Dow and Rowe had found the enemy; many "bogies" bearing 320 degrees true, eighty-eight miles. The radio crackled with *Saratoga* announcing the same target. At that long range, the radar echo was on the scope only a few seconds. The FDOs consulted their graphs. A target fading at 85 miles should be at about 12,000 feet. *Saratoga* agreed. The two carriers, ten miles apart in the center of their circular task group formations, came around into the wind and the waiting Wildcats at ten-second intervals snarled down the decks, hopped into the air, pointed their noses sharply up and clawed for altitude. Fifty-four F4Fs, in four-plane sections high and low over the force and well out to the northwest, awaited the coming of the enemy.

At 4:49 Dow jabbed his finger at the radarscope. The "many bogeys" were back. They had halved the distance and were coming straight in. Bearing still 320 degrees true, distance forty-four miles. Four sections of Wildcats slung out of their patient orbiting, flew to intercept. Lieutenant A. O. Vorse's section of four was circling *Enterprise* at 2,000 feet when he received his radioed orders from the FDO:

VECTOR THREE TWO ZERO, ANGELS
TWELVE, DISTANCE THREE FIVE.

Vorse's four planes tilted steeply up, climbing, and at 8,000 feet they were the first to see the enemy. Off to the right and still 10,000 feet higher than his F4Fs, Vorse could see two formations of enemy planes. Across the miles of sky the Japanese strike group was only an ordered assembly of black dots, but Vorse could count eighteen dive bombers in each group with fighters above and below. His "Tallyho!" went on the air at five minutes of five and it was the last loud, clear message of the afternoon.

Hanging on their props at full throttle, the four Wildcats strained up the sky toward the incoming Vals. At 12,000 feet, four Zeros of the escort peeled down on them but, in the swirling dogfights that followed, the F4Fs continued to gain altitude until at 20,000 the Zeros dived away and Vorse's fighters could get after the Vals. The dive bombers had glided down to 12,000 nearly over the task force and Vorse's section dove after them, the wind noise high around the cockpits and the controls taut under hands and feet.

At 12,000 feet the Wildcats were jumped by the Zeros again but this time the Big E's pilots had the altitude advantage. In a low, fast, side attack, Vorse burst a Zero into flames. The fire flared suddenly behind the cockpit, nearly died out, and then as the plane began to fall off toward the sea, blazed up again and was still bright at the end of its long arc of smoke an instant before the salt water put it out. In two steep, wing-over turns, with the G forces tugging the blood down out of his head, Ensign Register shot down a Zero and a Messerschmitt 109. The German-made plane fell in flames behind the spinning Zero. At low altitude the Zero pilot jumped. Like his late contemporary in Vorse's Kawanishi of the twenty-second, he wore no parachute. Machinist Sumrall raked another Zero in a flashing stern attack and it fell in a long inverted dive, its pilot dead. Out of ammunition and low on fuel, the section headed for *Saratoga*. Three made it. Vorse used his last fuel in final approach, but landed smoothly in the *Sara*'s wake. A destroyer picked him up. The loaded Vals kept coming.

While most of the defending fighters stayed high concentrating on the rapidly approaching dive bombers, nine more Japanese bombers and two torpedo bombers bored in flat on the water, hoping to evade the Big E's probing radars. But a faint echo, which worried the fighter director, kept showing up and, just to be sure, he vectored out a section of CAP under Ensign G. W. Brooks. Brooks found them still sixty miles out, unescorted, and cut down a dive bomber in a high side run, pulled up, turned into the tail of one of the torpedo planes and sent it cartwheeling into the sea. Ensign March got the other torpedo plane with a long-range stern attack. Mankin came straight down on the tail of the last Val in the formation and his six 50s ripped it to pieces. He swung his nose onto the next ahead but had not yet commenced firing when the shaken enemy pilot collided with the water. Rhodes killed another Val. The five remaining dive bombers, twisting and weaving at high speed, their free guns firing desperately over their tails, changed their destinations and headed back for *Sho* and *Zui*. There was no damage to any of Brooks' four Wildcats.

The fight for the Big E's life went on two miles up and nearly over the task force. Rowe and Dow, attempting to direct the fighters, were nearly helpless in the excited babble of radio conversation which blocked their transmissions and cut out the answers they had to have. The young pilots, alone in their planes in the desperate whirl of action around the advancing bombers, could not control the urge to talk to someone, to assure one another of mutual support. Hardly any of the talk was technically necessary. It was technically childish and dangerous. But it was of such emotional necessity that it continued, nevertheless.

"Shift to high blower."

"Look at that one go down."

"Bill, where are you?"

"Let's get that son-of-a-bitch with the double red stripe."

"Dusty, is that you?"

Determinedly, the Zeros engaged the attacking Wildcats while the Vals continued on their deadly way. Or most of them.

Machinist Donald Runyon knew the tactical value of the blinding tropic sun and used it well. His first attack was a high side-run straight out of the sun, just five miles from the Big E. It seemed as if every bullet from his six .50-calibers made a hit. The target Val exploded and collapsed into a flaming rag doll of an airplane as it fell the three miles to the Pacific. Runyon used his speed to pull back up into the sun's eye and came down again on the loose wedges of dark-winged Vals. The second plane did not explode. It flared like a struck match and, wrapped in flame and with a big plume of black smoke, fell off in a steepening glide to the sea. Climbing back for a third run Runyon found tracers passing him and evaded a Zero coming in from high astern. The faster Zero overshot Runyon and slid past just below him. Runyon pushed the Wildcat's nose sharply down and opened fire. The Zero blew up and tumbled burning to the surface. The diving attack on the Zero brought Runyon below the dive bombers with plenty of speed. He pulled up hard and the six converging lines of his tracers smoked into the belly of a third Val which ignited and fell off in a diving left turn as a second Zero dived for the deadly Wildcat. Runyon pulled up to meet him, the hot 50s hammering again, and the Zero, trailing smoke, headed for home.

The Wildcats slashed at the enemy formation, dodging and shooting their way through the Zeros, but the bombers had *Enterprise* in sight and held steadily on course for their attack position.

On the blue surface of the Pacific, at the bottom of the ocean of air in which the high planes fought, *Enterprise* was making 27 knots into the southeast wind. A tall wave curled at her bow and her wake writhed behind full swings of the rudder. On deck the five-inch guns, the "one-point-ones" and the new 20-millimeters were loaded and swung out. Radar had followed the enemy bombers in mile by mile until the range was zero. Throughout the beloved ship her men stood at their battle stations and felt her tremble under their feet, heard the whirr of electric motors as the guns trained around.

At eight minutes after five in the afternoon, Max Leslie in the last Avenger of a twelve-SBD, seven-TBF attack group, left the Big E's deck on a maximum range strike on *Ryujo*, by then a slowly sinking derelict. *Enterprise* had still not received Ray Davis' hour-and-a-half-old report of *Shokaku* and *Zuikaku*.

Now with all her fighters up and all her guns manned and loaded, with her flight deck bare and her crew ready at battle stations, *Enterprise* awaited what the enemy could do.

It is not possible in war to be consistently the striker. Always a time comes to be struck. For *Enterprise* that time had now come. As the Japanese carrier men must have done at Midway, the men of the Big E squinted into the clear sky and felt their pulses rise at the sun glints on the wings of hostile dive bombers directly overhead.

After long minutes of looking, of knowing but not seeing, a 20-millimeter pointer caught the flash of sun-on-wing as the first Val pushed over. He pointed it out to the whole task force with a soaring stream of tracers, knowing well that it was far outside his range. At gun and control stations on all the ships, man after man picked up the target and their guns opened up. From close astern of *Enterprise*, *North Carolina*'s antiaircraft batteries blended into a steady drum roll as she spread a steel umbrella over the carrier.

It was 5:12 P.M.

Three miles overhead the Wildcats had not given up. They attacked at the push-over point and followed the Vals down through the five-mile bursts and the tracer patterns, firing, until their heavier, cleaner planes overran the enemy.

Enterprise needed all her fighters and all her guns. Thirty dive bombers arrived in attack position and they attacked at intervals of seven seconds for nearly four minutes. Plane after plane came diving in, steep and determined, turning always to approach from the port quarter. The Big E's gunners watched the Vals grow rapidly larger in their sights, saw the fat bombs detach from between the faired "pants" of the Vals' fixed landing gear and steepen toward them, out of the corners of their eyes watched the planes pull out fast and close to the water as the guns swung onto the next target.

With the gunners stood three photographers, attempting to record the action for later study and evaluation. Robert Read was in the starboard gun gallery, Ralph Baker and Marion Riley in the island structure. As coolly and methodically as though they were photographing a horse race or a prizefight, the three men adjusted and swung their cameras, reloading and rewinding while looking for the next thing to shoot.

By 5:13 the bright Pacific afternoon had become like a painting of the Inferno. At its center the Big E twisted at the end of her tortured wake, her guns pouring their converging fire on each bomber in succession. The bombs fountained the sea and shook the ships with the heavy thudding of their explosive. Patches of burning gasoline on the surface drawing rapidly aft were what was left of enemy aircraft. Long trails of greasy black smoke drew rapidly down across the sky as shells and bullets went home. Mixed with the attacking and retreating Vals were Lou Bauer's square-winged Wildcats, their engines whining high under full throttle, ignoring the shipboard guns, intent on the death of the dive bombers. Among the falling, fighting planes and over the churning ships the *Enterprise* attack group circled, attempting to rendezvous, and, around the fringes of the action, returning search planes orbited, low on fuel, hoping for a deck to land on. Overhead the summer sky was dirtied by the myriad black puffs of five-inch bursts. And still the deadly chain of shining Vals unwound from overhead, lashing at the *Enterprise*.

It was too much. Neither the skill of her skipper, the aggressiveness of her fighters nor the accuracy of her gunners could save the Big E from such a sustained and well-executed attack. At 5:14 the first enemy bomb ever to violate her crashed through the forward starboard corner of the after elevator, and penetrated forty-two feet through elevator well, gun gallery and three decks before its thousand pounds of TNT went off.

The long, narrow carrier whipped like a musical saw under the hammer blow at her stern. Forward in Charlie Fox's coding room the men were flung from their seats as the giant oscillations shook the ship. It was like a sixty-mile-an-hour truck ride over a rutted country road. On every level men were thrown out of position by the vertical motion and then flung sideways by the lateral. For an instant the Big E's guns paused as gunners were knocked out of position, but they picked up again more furiously as the angry sailors found their sights and triggers again. Back on the port quarter, across the deck from the bomb hit, a 20-millimeter gunner scrambling back to his weapon found another man already there, was informed that he had the wrong gun and, apologizing politely, returned to his own fifteen feet away. Robin Lindsey, flushed and scowling, picked himself out of the port catwalk by the after 20-millimeter battery and, sighting carefully, emptied the seven rounds of his .45-caliber automatic at a strafing Val.

Below decks in the shambles of what had been the battle stations of a repair party, an ammunition handling crew and an elevator pump-room detail, thirty-five of the Big E's men were dead. Twenty-four-foot craters were torn in the steel decks, the flight deck itself had a two-foot bulge, the afterelevator would need a navy yard to put it back in commission, and at the water line six-foot holes let the sea into the big storerooms. The ship listed slightly to starboard. In the mattresses and clothing of wrecked berthing spaces fire grew. The choking smoke spread. Several electrical cables shorted out and the blasted compartments went dark. Fire-main pressure spouted uselessly from a ruptured line and the hoses would not fill.

Then, thirty seconds later, the second bomb hit. Unbelievably, out of the chaos of twisting ships and plunging planes, of gunfire and aerial combat, it struck within fifteen feet of the first one.

Again the violent whipping that knocked men from their feet, that popped rivets, started leaks, sprung doors and hatches. Again fire as the five-inch powder bags flashed with the bomb's TNT. And again death. Thirty-nine men instantly dead, blown into such small parts that of some only a piece of skull in a scorched helmet was left, or stripped and roasted in the second's flare of the powder. On the starboard quarter all the guns were destroyed. Thick black smoke spiraled heavily through the ruptured gun deck from burning aviation stores below. Listing and on fire, a quarter of her guns silenced, hundreds of her men out of action, *Enterprise* maintained her 27 knots and her fierce defensive firing while damage control and medical details went to work.

Lieutenant (j.g.) E. E. DeGarmo, battery officer of two mounts of 1.1s, looked down to see a piece of bomb fragment lodged deeply in his right foot. He considered pulling it out but was afraid he might pass out with the loss of blood. He continued to direct his guns until the attack was over, damage to his mounts assessed, all possible repairs made and his wounded men attended to.

In action there is nothing for a damage controlman to do until the ship has been hit. Spread out in small subdivisions of repair parties throughout the ship, surrounded by their equipment, blind, unoccupied, totally dependent on the good judgment of the captain and the competence of fighter pilots and gun crews, they can only wait. Distributed along a darkened, unventilated passageway or crowded into a gear locker far below decks with gas masks, rescue breather apparatus, portable gasoline "handy-billy" pumps like outboard motors on their sides in steel frames, electric submersible pumps, axes, conical wooden plugs of all sizes, lanterns, explosimeters for testing the gases in wrecked compartments, coils of fire hose, coils of emergency power cable, coils of phone wire, wedges, sledges and fire extinguishers, they sit silent in the dim red glow of the battle lights listening to the guns, feeling the heavy thudding of the bombs in the sea and the heel of the ship as the rudder is put hard over. In each isolated cluster of men they watch the one with the oversized helmet which accommodates the sound-powered battle telephone headset. He is their contact with Central Station where Lieutenant Commander Herschel A. Smith, the ship's damage control officer, sits like a helmeted spider at the center of a web of phone circuits which go out to all repair parties. Through a talker on the bridge, Central Station hears how the action is going and, as long as there is no damage, passes this information along. It is fragmentary and unsatisfactory. The bridge talker repeats things as he hears them. He is no commentator.

"Dive bombers directly overhead."

"Commence firing."

"Right full rudder."

The repair parties can tell more by the guns. First is the slow, repeated booming of the five-inch which shakes the steel structure of the ship, then the rapid pom-pom-pom-pom of the 1.1s. When the 20s begin to rattle too, the men below draw in their breath and tense, looking at the steel overhead as though to see the plane or bomb come through it. When the 20s open up, the enemy is close and any second can be it. A near miss lifts the ship bodily and sounds and feels as though she had been hit by an underwater hammer.

When the first bomb hit the *Enterprise* at 5:14, it plunged through five decks to detonate its 1,000 pounds in the chief petty officers' quarters. The small repair party stationed there was wiped out. But after all the years of drills and inspections and lectures, of equipment checks and examinations, Herschel Smith's damage control organization went into action. An investigation team from the nearest surviving repair party arrived before the yellow bomb smoke had cleared away. They reported the general extent of the damage and then, with the Vals still streaming down, bombing and strafing, and the ship's guns following them down and across the deck, the Big E's men began to control and repair the damage. The second bomb added more fire and more dead and wounded. To fight the fires, hoses were run aft from the undamaged forward section of the fire main. Emergency power cables were plugged in forward and run aft. Sailors with gas masks and flashlights entered the wrecked compartments, stepping across the jagged steel and slipping in blood and in the oil of shattered machinery. Pharmacist's mates converged to tend the ninety-five wounded on the spot and prepare them to be moved to sick bay. Men and equipment arrived promptly and went to work. But *Enterprise* was severely hurt and the battle was not over.

A few seconds before 5:16, she took a third bomb.

Like the second, this one carried an instantaneous fuse. It went off on impact with the flight deck, just aft of the island, at the starboard after corner of the Number Two elevator. This time the Big E was lucky. The bomb was a 500-pounder and defective. The detonation was low order with large pieces of the casing left intact. Even so, a ten-foot hole was blown in the flight deck and Number Two elevator put out of commission.

By 5:17 it was over. The last Val had dropped and skimmed off to the northward, low on the water with the Wildcat CAP on his tail. It had only lasted five minutes but in the history of war at sea few ships had survived such a concentrated attack. And the Big E's survival was yet far from certain. From the bridges of *North Carolina*, *Portland* and the screening destroyers binoculars and long glasses focused on her anxiously. Her flight deck had a noticeable list and two gaping holes, and from its after section poured bright flame and heavy, rolling smoke. But the deck swarmed with busy men and the carrier continued at high speed and announced that she required no assistance.

The attack was over, but for the air-borne aviators of both sides and for the Big E's sweating repair crews the battle still went on.

Prevented by the melee around the task force from making a good rendezvous, Max Leslie, the air group commander, Turner Caldwell with eleven SBDs, and six TBFs of Torpedo Three under Konig, in three separate groups were on a maximum-range strike on the already sinking *Ryujo*, flying parallel to the Solomon chain but well out over the open sea. Leslie's plane had been hit by a salvo from the *North Carolina* as he circled the force after take-off, and the TBFs had had to shoot a Val out of their formation before the last plane could join up. For the pilots of the strike group, the future was not encouraging. Their last backward glance at their carrier had showed her burning fiercely, with

Japanese dive bombers still overhead. The sky was beginning to darken. If they survived the attack on the ships they would face the choice of a night search for the wounded, possibly nonexistent carrier, or a night landing on the unlighted, unfamiliar, enemy-ringed grass field at Guadalcanal.

The sixteen Dauntlesses and seven Avengers of the eventful afternoon search had been in the air for four hours when the attack on the Big E ended. With no advance knowledge that the ship was under attack, they had begun to arrive home just as the Vals came down on her. Low on fuel, some shot up, they put in a bad few minutes. A few made those minutes count.

Ensign R. J. Bye of the torpedo squadron attacked two enemy dive bombers retiring from the action over the carrier. With the single, forward-firing .50-caliber of the TBF he made hits on both Japanese planes, but when three more enemy planes came to the assistance of the first two, Bye broke off the action. The high-power settings of the fight at the end of the long search used up the last of his fuel, and he had to ditch the Avenger.

Ensign Howard Burnett of Scouting Five had been launched from the *Saratoga* on antisub patrol and was returning to the *Enterprise* when the attack came in. Circling at a comfortable distance he discovered the direction in which the enemy dive bombers were retiring, lay in wait, and shot down a Val as it pulled away from the attack on the Big E.

For forty minutes, while radar saw the enemy approaching, *Enterprise* had depended for her life on her intercepting Wildcats. For the next five minutes under the noses of the diving Vals, survival was in the sweating hands of Orlin Livdahl's gunners. Now, holed and afire, with another strike inbound, the responsibility shifted to Herschel Smith's damage control organization.

Robin Lindsey holstered his .45 and led a hose across the deck from his station in the port gun gallery to attack the flames. Slim Townsend, back aboard now, his temporary duty completed, and Chief Prather, having stationed their flight-deck crew so well that not one was injured, led a rescue and fire-fighting party to the damaged area and at once began repairs to the ripped, holed and bulged flight deck so the Big E could land her planes.

From all parts of the ship men whose duty it was ran to help. Some were too fast.

William K. Powell, gunner's mate first class, was stationed as a trouble shooter and, in effect, technical expert for the two groups of five-inch guns on either side, aft. It was his duty to assure continuous operation of his guns. When the first bomb hit and went through the starboard gun gallery to explode four decks below, Powell was in the port gallery. Knowing the starboard guns would be damaged, he ran straight across the deck and dropped into the starboard gallery, arriving at the same moment as the second bomb. It killed him, and every other man of the thirty-seven on the gallery deck.

With the fire from the bomb hit and the resultant flashings of the five-inch powder cans still burning viciously, Ensign Jim Wyrick arrived on the run to see what could be done. The gun gallery, like a large veranda projecting out from under the edge of the flight deck, was blasted into a jumble of hot metal on which the paint and the rubber deck matting burned brightly. It was strewn with the charred and naked bodies of thirty-eight men, some still in the attitudes in which the bomb burst had found them, hands out passing a shell ahead, or back, reaching for one. Seaman Wilburt Pulaski, Carpenter's Mate Ed Clapp and Shipfitter Doug Botts were already in the flaming gallery working with the furious energy of madmen, heaving burning material over the side, spraying the fire with water and chemicals. From beside Wyrick, someone played a hose on Pulaski or he would have burned. Jim Wyrick jumped down into the inferno, quickly found a locker of unexploded powder and ammunition. In seconds he had selected and organized a working party of fifteen men, seamen, aviation machinist's mates and bosun's mates, into a human chain which passed the hot powder and ammunition out of the gallery and over the side.

Less than a minute after the last bomb had smashed into the Big E's stern, before hoses could be rigged and the broken mains or emergency lighting connected, Seaman Henry Dunn, in an asbestos suit, walked into the flaming shambles of the aviation metal shop and pulled out the injured men. Then, without pausing, he walked down two decks to the chief's quarters where the first 1,000-pounder had gone off and made sure that no life existed in the smoldering, smoke-choked darkness there.

One deck below, Chief Reuben Fisher, with a good hose led from forward, opened the door of a storeroom at the other end of which he knew was an ammunition hoist loaded with a chain of five-inch powder cases, leading directly into the fire in the gun gallery topside. Smoke and flame belched out of the open door but the chief beat it back with the high-velocity fog of his fire hose and stepped inside. Keeping low where the smoke was thinnest and moving the conical jet of high-velocity water particles from side to side, he crossed the big storeroom between smoldering racks of dry provisions, found the ammunition hoist and soaked it down, cooling the hot powder cans, as far up and down as his stream would reach. A chain explosion, flashing down the hoist from topside fire to below-decks magazine, was avoided.

But such individual actions could only strike at the fringes of the Big E's trouble. Deeply wounded, she had to have a careful and thorough cure if she were to survive. Herschel A. Smith, her damage control officer, was also her doctor, and from Central Station, ringed with deck plans and diagrams of fuel oil, gasoline, fresh and salt water, ventilation, steam and electrical systems, a battery of telephone talkers relaying his orders to repair- and fire-fighting parties throughout the ship, he provided the overall direction, the cool thinking that *Enterprise* had to have.

First the fires had to be controlled. In a warship, especially a carrier, a fire cannot burn long without coming into contact with some highly flammable or explosive substance —aviation gasoline, lubricating oil, hydraulic oil, paint, gunpowder and ammunition, bombs, torpedoes. Individual initiative and good training had already accounted for some of the more serious dangers. Machinist W. E. Fluitt, just before the first Val struck, had completed draining and venting the Big E's gasoline system and flooding the lines with carbon dioxide. A minute or two later, when hot bomb fragments tore through pipes normally full of gasoline or its more dangerous fumes, there were no additional fires.

Chief Shipfitter Jim Brewer very strongly felt his responsibility as one of the leading petty officers in the Construction and Repair Department. Smoke and fire were a threat to his ship and a challenge to him personally. As though it were a quiet Sunday noon and the Big E secured to her pier at Pearl, Brewer entered each of the wrecked, flaming, smoke-filled compartments and coolly searched out the source of the fire. Returning, he directed the fire-fighting teams and moved on to the next area. He continued this process until, being fallible and able to inhale only so much smoke, endure just so much heat, his body failed him and, completely exhausted, he had to be ordered by the executive officer to stay topside and rest.

Shipfitter First-Class Larry Wyffels was a man like Brewer. He moved swiftly and efficiently when the aft section of the fire main was disabled, helped to re-establish water pressure for fire fighting and then, like Brewer, as though he were not made of flesh, searched the damaged areas, hauling out the wounded and directing the fire parties.

Ray Owens picked himself up after the first bomb hit, saw the large jettisonable tank of low-octane gasoline close to the fires beginning in the starboard gun gallery and at once tripped the releasing mechanism which dumped it overboard. Flames from the second hit swept the area seconds later.

Jessie B. Crowder, a storekeeper, was dazed, deafened and thrown to the deck when the first 1,000-pound bomb exploded in the compartment adjacent to his battle station, ripping the steel bulkhead and filling both compartments with the yellow smoke of the detonation. As he had been trained to do, Crowder made his way at once through the torn and darkened ship to the paint and pyrotechnic storerooms and operated the CO_2 smothering systems installed there.

At Lieutenant Commander Smith's direction, hoses were led aft, foam generators and CO_2 extinguishers were brought up and a hundred men in separate parties attacked the fires on all levels and from all directions. Differing techniques had to be applied to the various kinds of fire. Burning oil had to be smothered with foam or cooled and beaten down by high-velocity fog. Water was dangerous to use on electrical fires where the current could short up the stream and injure the fire fighters, but a solid stream was the only means to penetrate the persistent fires in bedding and clothing. CO_2 pouring hoarsely from long cones was used on electrical fires. A fire among the chutes in the parachute loft was extinguished by a party organized and led by Gunner F. G. Young. The adjacent compartment was a live torpedo magazine.

Fighting the fires below decks, the men worked by the

light of flashlights in gas masks and breathing apparatus because of the thick, choking smoke. Oil from ruptured tanks, blood, foam and water made footing precarious. Slowly, as ventilation was improved by opening doors into undamaged and ventilated areas and by the use of portable ventilation blowers, the smoke was cleared away and the restricting facial masks were no longer necessary.

As the fires came under control repair-party electricians rigged temporary cables to provide lighting and power in the wrecked compartments, shipfitters like Mike Turpinseed worked to isolate and repair the fire mains and risers so that water pressure would be available for the next attack.

But even with the fires out and the injured men under treatment, the Big E was not an effective warship. There were gaping holes in her flight deck and a three-degree list to starboard. She still had planes in the air and up in the radar room there were indications of another strike from *Sho* and *Zui* coming in.

On the flight deck a repair party under Boatswain Edward Hatchell trimmed splintered timbers around the holes and hammered over them large square steel sheets of boiler plate. They cleared bomb fragments and debris, replaced torn planking, marked off the weakened areas and prepared for the recovery of aircraft.

Far below in the compartments along the water line on the starboard side aft, men worked at the much more complex task of getting the Big E back on an even keel. Three portside ballast tanks were flooded and the symmetrical tanks to starboard pumped out. Then some 245 tons of water had to be removed from the big flooded storerooms below the detonation point of the first bomb. There were several holes in the ship's side, just above and below the water line. The largest was a gash six feet long and two feet wide.

To plug these holes Herschel Smith's men under Carpenter W. L. Reames, with Leon Brown and Helmuth Bentz, working often armpit-deep in sea water and by emergency lighting, built a cofferdam of two-by-six planking placed vertically a foot or so from the skin of the ship. They covered the holes from the inside with heavy wire meshing and then packed mattresses, pillows and similar material between the mesh and the cofferdam. The next step was to wedge the cofferdam tight against the packing and start the emergency pumps.

One hour after the third bomb had hit her, *Enterprise* turned into the wind at 24 knots to recover her aircraft.

At 6:50, the twenty-fifth plane had just landed. The sun was low off the starboard quarter. Planes and men cast long shadows across the deck. The southeast breeze and the Big E's 24 knots flapped the shirts of the bridge watch and blew the brown haze from the stack flat out astern. Captain Davis leaned on the high bulwark of the bridge, watching the circling planes and the straight wake, proud of his ship, so deeply wounded and yet steaming fast and straight, her planes buzzing up her wake, catching the wires, taxiing up her deck. He caught the beginning of a twist in the white wake, turned back toward the control station, heard the young officer of the deck speak sharply to the quartermaster at the wheel:

"Mind your helm!"

"Aye, aye, sir," and the sailor spun the solid wheel to starboard while the rudder moved steadily left until the white rudder angle indicator showed full left rudder.

"Lost steering control, sir," reported the helmsman, and a siren howled far below over the rudder in the small steering motor control room where it meant, "Return steering control to the bridge."

For a second the rudder held at full left and the Big E began to swing to port. A plane right over the stern was waved off and roared across the deck, hook dangling, wheels folding upward. Then, with the bridge watch powerless, the rudder angle pointer began to move again steadily down the arc of the instrument to amidships and up again to full right. There it stopped for a second and *Enterprise* heeled away from the sharp turn. To starboard the watch on the destroyer *Balch* reported the carrier bearing down on a collision course. Slowly the runaway rudder came around to 20 degrees right rudder and there jammed.

Captain Davis took control of his ship. "All engines back emergency. Sound the danger signal."

On the flight deck and gun galleries, men with nerves raw from recent action jumped with the first deafening *whoop* of the whistle, heard the four short blasts repeated and repeated and looked up anxiously at the blue and yellow five flag which blossomed magically at the high truck. Its meaning was simple—"Breakdown."

Bells jangled in the engine rooms and the engineers, sensing the danger, spun their big valve wheels, cutting the steam to the cruising turbines, pouring it into the astern turbines. *Enterprise* trembled and shuddered as the backing screws bit the water. A puff of black smoke chuffed from *Balch*'s stack as she went ahead at flank speed. With her wake boiling above her stern, the slim "tin can" slid under the Big E's bow, clearing by barely fifty yards, while the carrier turned out of control, her screws racing in reverse.

With the *Balch* clear, Captain Davis tried to offset the right rudder by going ahead on the starboard engine and back on the port. It was no good. She could only go in one direction—to starboard. If she would not answer to the differential power of her engines, she would be impossible to tow.

There was only one thing to do. Fix the rudder. Captain Davis slowed to ten knots. Planes still in the air were ordered to *Saratoga*. The Big E circled slowly, helpless. *North Carolina* and *Portland* stood by anxiously. The destroyers chased tails around the big ships, worried about submarines. As repair and relief parties converged on the steering gear, the big air-search antenna stopped, hunted, stopped again. In a moment came radar's report to the bridge: "LARGE BOGEY, TWO SEVEN ZERO, FIFTY MILES." *Sho* and *Zui*'s second strike. Another thirty Vals.

The steering engine room is a steel box deep in the stern section of the ship just forward of the rudder. Its top is at the water line. In it is a control panel and two large electric motors which, on remote signal from the bridge, pump hydraulic oil against the long, shining plungers which control the rudder. Only one motor is used at a time to steer the ship. There are two in case one fails. Also in the steering engine room is a wheel and a compass so that if the long and vulnerable control system from the bridge were to break down, the ship could be steered from below in accordance with telephoned instructions from topside. The big motors are cooled and the steel box ventilated by air sucked down a long vent shaft from the starboard after gun gallery. Part of this air goes directly into cooling jackets around the motors. Normal access is from forward, through the elevator machinery room or directly down a vertical tunnel from the chief's quarters. To operate, maintain and repair this equipment at General Quarters, seven men were assigned on the Big E, machinist mates for mechanical problems, electrician's mates to handle the electrical duties and a quartermaster to steer if necessary.

At routine General Quarters, when for short periods the ventilation is shut down, the normal temperature in the steering engine room is 120 degrees.

As the first bomb smashed through the starboard after gun gallery it tore apart the vent shaft leading below and left it open at deck level, then angled through three more decks to explode and demolish the compartments forward of and above the steering engine room, including the elevator machinery room and the chief's quarters.

Almost at once, black smoke swirled out of the cooling jackets around the steering motors, filling the small compartment. From the starboard cooling jacket, hot water sprayed out on the steel deck. The men, moving fast, shut down the fans which sucked the air down from above and clamped down covers over the ends of the vent shaft. They were sealed in with their machinery, four levels below the hangar deck surrounded by fire and wreckage. They felt the ship jar to the second bomb. With no ventilation, fires burning forward and above, and the big starboard motor laboring to swing the rudder back and forth as the skipper dodged the Vals, the heat built up to 140, 150 degrees. At 160 degrees they stopped sweating and began to dry out. They were literally being cooked. Two or three lost consciousness.

Above the seven men, the attack had ceased. They no longer felt the water hammer blows of near misses and the starboard motor held the rudder steady. Fire-fighting crews were attacking the blazing compartments around them.

Then, from somewhere above, a remote control unit reopened the ventilation system to renew air to the steering engine room. A flood of hot water and foam from the gun gallery deluged the starboard motor and the control panel. The motor stopped, reversed, started and stopped again and the rudder went into the stops both ways and jammed at twenty right. The temperature was 170. When the steering alarm siren shrieked in the steel box, only one man, William Marcoux, had strength enough to attempt the switchover to the port motor. There was a valve to turn, a clutch to engage, a couple of switches to throw. Hanging on with both hands, his knees rubbery, he got the valve open, worked hard at the stubborn clutch, the metal burning his fingers, engaged it, reached for the first switch—

and passed out. The Big E grazed past the *Balch* and went into her helpless circling.

Aboard the *Enterprise* many men could competently operate, maintain and repair the steering machinery. Several men were exceptionally familiar with the equipment. One man was the expert. He owned it. It was his. That man was Chief Machinist William Arnold Smith.

As soon after the attack as communications with the steering engine room could be restored, Smith called to tell the seven how, by removing certain screws from a vent shaft which passed through their compartment and took its supply from a location other than the demolished gun gallery, they could get fresh air. Alex Tyrmofiew managed to get one screw out before his legs gave way.

Smith knew that the Big E was feebly circling, and the enemy threatening again. If he could get to his familiar steering engines he could save her. He had to get into the steering engine room. In thirty years of naval service he had not seen the smoke or flame or wreckage that could stop him. He buckled on an RBA (Rescue Breather Apparatus), a vestlike equipment with pockets for cans of chemicals and a face mask. By passing a man's breath through the chemicals and back into the mask with the carbon dioxide removed, it provided a closed system for breathing which made no use of the surrounding air—for a while. The one Smith used was modified by a shipmate, Chief M. D. Twibell, to provide additional endurance. Attached to the RBA was a safety line tended by a couple of men who could haul the wearer back to safety if he got in trouble.

Equipped with the Twibell-modified RBA, and with selected wrenches and other tools sticking out of his back pockets, Smith waded into the smoking oven full of rubble that had been the elevator machinery room. The heat seared his exposed flesh and baked through his clothing to dry his sweat as water dries in a hot skillet. The RBA mask fogged with the sudden heat and his eyes acquired large and haphazard formations of black spots. Halfway to the steering engine room hatch Smith toppled to the hot deck and was unceremoniously dragged back and lifted out. With the mask off and fresh air in his lungs he came to at once. He got his feet under him, walked to the nearest supply ventilator, breathed deeply a few times, buckled the RBA back on, and charged back into the furnace. This time he had a helper, Cecil S. Robinson, a first-class machinist's mate who also knew the steering machinery.

While the two machinists were assaulting the isolated steering compartment horizontally by way of the elevator machinery room just forward, a rescue party was attacking from above, vertically down the trunk from the wreckage of the chief petty officers' quarters. A big third-class fireman of Swedish descent, Ernest Richard Visto, volunteered to lead the way. The smoke-filled trunk was too small for both Visto and an RBA so he slipped on a gas mask, secured a safety line around his waist and went down. Visto was not an expert on the steering gear. In fact, he hardly recognized the machinery. But he knew when a man was in trouble and he urged, hoisted and wrestled all seven parched and half-conscious men up the trunk to the rescue party that had followed him. Visto was the last man out, up the trunk and through the smoldering wreckage to the hangar deck. There, having completed in 180 degrees of heat a job that would have been difficult at 70 degrees, he apologetically collapsed.

Breathing heavily, slipping and stumbling in the charred and sodden debris, Smith and Robinson got their hands on the hatch before the heat brought them down again. Once more they were revived, rested a few seconds and again stormed the hot gates. Now they knew the obstacles in the way. Rapidly they banged back the heavy dogs that sealed the watertight door at its four corners and stumbled into the steering engine room. One glance showed Smith the drowned starboard motor, the half-completed shift to the port. With rapid, careful movements he completed the operation. Hydraulic oil hit the long rams and the rudder moved again.

On the bridge the helmsman reported: "Steering control regained, sir." It was just thirty-eight minutes since he had reported it lost. *Enterprise* straightened out on a southerly course. Down came the breakdown flag. *North Carolina* and *Portland* assumed their stations and the relieved destroyer skippers formed the bent line of their screen.

Of the seven baked men, six survived. Williams, dazed and weakened, became separated from the rescue party on the way out and inhaled a massive quantity of smoke. All efforts to revive him failed.

After the fighters and gunners had had their turn, Herschel and William A. Smith had saved the Big E.

Sho and *Zui's* second strike had missed. While *Enterprise* lay vulnerable, the bomb-heavy Vals flew by fifty miles away going southeast. Then radar watched them reverse course and disappear. Had they turned north instead of northwest, ten-minutes' flight would have put them overhead.

Smith and Robinson stayed on in the steering engine room. Even machinery cannot operate long at temperatures close to the boiling point of water. They ripped away the vents so that the foam and water could drain into the bilges and allow the air to come through. They replaced the grease that had melted off the long plungers that controlled the rudder. Lovingly, in the slowly cooling room, they repaired, adjusted, checked, lubricated, making certain *Enterprise* would continue to answer her helm. Smith was still there the following afternoon. He was going to be sure.

While the Big E's men fought to save her from the fires caused by the Japanese bombs, her scattered strike groped for the enemy carriers over the darkening sea.

Turner Caldwell, leading eleven Dauntlesses, was so high that for several minutes the sinking sun reddened the wings of his planes and flushed his pilots' faces while below Lieutenant R. H. Konig's six TBFs bored through a deepening twilight. Somewhere between the two groups flew the Big E's Air Group Commander Max Leslie in a single Avenger, vainly trying to establish radio or visual contact with either one.

For two hours the attack group flew northwestward. Turner Caldwell watched the red light of the sun fade from the sky ahead and over his shoulder saw the first curve of the full moon break the eastern horizon. Leslie, lower, saw it too and counted on the moonlight to illuminate the Japanese for his searching pilots. But the low, broken clouds increased, shadowing the sea's surface until his task seemed hopeless.

At 7:05 Leslie's faulty radio came to life. Konig reported his Avengers over the enemy force. Leslie's reply was instant: "Attack."

Flying at a thousand feet, Konig's pilots had suddenly picked up through the twilight the long phosphorus trails of high-speed ships. They needed no order to attack. Konig, with Jay and Stablein on his wings, pulled off to the left. Herriman, Baker and Holley turned right, slanting for the surface. They would attack from either bow so that whichever way the ships turned to parallel one set of torpedo wakes, they would expose their beams to the other. Ed Holley was blind with prop oil on his windshield. He stayed on Fred Herriman's right wing as though welded there, planning to drop when he did. The six TBFs circled and headed in, low and fast, engines wide open, torpedoes ready. In their ball turrets the gunners sat tensed, straining their eyes into the semidarkness for fighters. None came. The range closed. The pilots leaned forward, goggles pushed up, searching for the targets. The big wakes foamed white across the empty sea. Where were the ships? At three and a half miles every minute, the Avengers bored in and were suddenly overhead.

There were no ships. As they flashed over the shipless wakes at fifty feet the TBF crews could see the curl and fall of breakers. The Big E's torpedo planes had found Roncador Reef, a hundred miles off the northwest tip of Santa Isabel.

Feeling discouraged and ridiculous, the six planes rejoined and for five minutes more flew out to the northeast. Below the clouds and with the rapidly increasing darkness it became apparent they would find nothing that night. Konig checked his fuel quantity and his plotting board and then ordered the heavy, expensive torpedoes jettisoned. Three thousand pounds lighter, the TBFs angled up to 2,500 feet and began the long flight back to base. Behind them, Leslie found the same reef and took the same action.

High overhead Turner Caldwell's SBDs also turned back. But the Dauntlesses were shorter-legged than the Avengers, and, since Guadalcanal was fifty miles closer than *Enterprise*, Caldwell took his squadron there.

It was not easy. The field at Guadal was unpaved, unlighted, unfamiliar, with no radio communications and periodically shelled by the enemy. Low, broken clouds half hid the island coast. Caldwell led his flight in from a friendly direction and established his identity by signal light. The Marines set out a thin, dim line of kerosene lights to indicate the runway and the SBDs came in, roaring low over the palm tops and dropping onto the dirt.

The TBFs flew back toward *Enterprise*. It was nearly 10:00 P.M. when they reached the position at which she should have been. She was not there. The Avengers were low on fuel, having been in the air nearly five hours, and Konig was not even sure the Big E was still afloat. She had been burning and under attack when he last saw her. He led his planes up to 8,000 feet in order to be able to receive the Big E's high frequency, line-of-sight homing signals and turned south, guessing that, if she were afloat and wounded, she would head down for Espiritu or Noumea. At altitude there was only the night sky and below the black and empty sea. The radios were silent. The needles on the gas gauges were approaching zero.

Finally a radioman with better ears than the rest picked up a faint signal. It showed Konig to be right. The ship was south of them but nearly a hundred miles. The pilots pulled back the mixture controls until the engines began to lose power, leaning out for every mile they could get, angling down to be ready for landing and to get into denser air where the engines operated more economically. When the dark bulk of *Enterprise* appeared the gas gauges were on zero. Baker landed first with no difficulty. Ed Holley was next, hindered by the oily windshield he had flown behind all day. Sailing high and fast over the fantail and the arresting gear, Holley flew straight into the Big E's island structure without ever touching her deck. Miraculously there was no fire and Holley and his two crewmen crawled uninjured from their demolished plane. But the heavy Avenger blocked the deck and disarranged the boiler plate patches so that for a while further landings were impossible.

Up in the primary flight control station ("Pri-fly") Bert Harden ordered the remaining four planes to the *Saratoga*, fifteen miles to starboard.

Flying on the fumes from their damp tanks, the TBFs skimmed the black sea to the *Sara* and eagerly came aboard. Herriman was third to land. When the cable stopped him there was another plane in the landing area dead ahead, and, looking over his shoulder, he saw the last plane receive a cut just behind him. The *Sara*'s deck was jammed with her own and *Enterprise* planes which she had been taking aboard all day while the Big E had been damaged and under attack. Even the barriers, which normally prevent landing accidents from damaging parked planes, were down and planes were parked on top of them.

Konig, Herriman, Jay and Stablein remained aboard the *Sara*. Their gear came over by destroyer the next day.

There was no sleeping aboard the *Enterprise* the night of August 24. Repair crews worked straight through for twenty-four hours after the action, isolating and repairing damage to the complex systems that the ship had to have to operate, constructing supports for weakened decks, repairing or replacing damaged machinery. It was dirty, unpleasant, tiring work, under the glare of temporary lighting, but, with red-rimmed eyes and in sweat-soaked dungarees, the men stayed at it, occasionally stimulated by the coffee that Charlie Fox's men distributed. Finally, even the coffee had to be rationed. The first bomb hit had flooded the storeroom containing the main supply. Doctors and pharmacist's mates worked continuously on the burns, lacerations, fractures and smoke-filled lungs of the injured men, and they did their job well. Of the ninety-five wounded, four died, and they were the result of multiple and extreme injuries.

At midnight a stubborn fire reignited in the damaged living spaces, and was put out only after more hours of crouching through the smoke, and more dragging of heavy hoses.

With daylight on the twenty-fifth, *Enterprise* was clear of the combat area, and the *Wasp* with her task group, fresh from refueling, was on station. Admiral Fletcher was ready to renew the action, but the enemy was not. *Ryujo* was down and so were some seventy planes from *Shokaku* and *Zuikaku*. As at Midway, the Japanese heavy ships were nearly untouched, but without control of the air they could not risk continuing the action.

Early in the sunny afternoon of the twenty-fifth of August, *Enterprise* buried her dead. Each of the seventy-four bodies, carefully sewn into a clean mattress cover and weighted appropriately with a five-inch projectile, was tipped overboard to the thoughtful, prayerful words of the chaplain.

On the twenty-sixth, *Enterprise* was ordered back to Pearl with a stop at Tongatabu for temporary repairs. *North Carolina, Atlanta* and three destroyers were detached and the Big E went her way with *Portland* and four destroyers to screen. Six fighters and six bombers stayed aboard as CAP and antisub patrol. The rest of the air group was scattered among *Saratoga, Wasp,* Henderson Field and Espiritu.

But Captain Davis knew his ship could not be spared for long. The Japanese would be back to try again for Guadalcanal, and when they came *Enterprise* would be there to meet them.

12 ORDEAL OFF SANTA CRUZ

Enterprise *left the war in the South Pacific to her* sister carriers for two months while she made the passage up to Pearl and the Navy Yard undid the damage of the three bombs.

First, however, she anchored in Nukualofu, Tongatabu, and pumped fuel and ballast to port to bring the wound in her starboard quarter out of the sea. Then in the full daylight of the peaceful harbor, Carpenter Reames' battle-installed patches of wire mesh, mattresses and pillows were removed, rough edges cut away and steel plates welded over the hole from inboard and outboard, braced and reinforced for the twenty-seven-hundred-mile voyage to Oahu.

On the first day of September a dispatch was received by Admiral Kinkaid, Commander, Task Force 16. It was from Admiral Nimitz, Commander-in-Chief, Pacific Fleet. With the traditional understatement of the naval service, it bestowed an accolade:

DELIVER WELL DONE TO ENTERPRISE

While the work went forward at Tonga, the Big E's men heard with disgust that *Saratoga* had picked up her second torpedo of the year and was likewise departing for repairs. That left only *Wasp* and *Hornet* to cover Guadalcanal.

The voyage to Pearl was long and peaceful. The men still went to General Quarters at morning and evening twilight and a third of the gun crews were on station at all times, but a man could take off his clothes at night, and turn in after a shower to sleep until called for his watch. There was time to think of home, and to write letters for mailing in Hawaii, and to wonder what the incoming mail would hold on arrival. With only twelve planes aboard in place of eighty-seven, the ready rooms and the hangar deck were empty. The ship's officers planned the repairs the Navy Yard would make, but many men had little to do and thoroughly enjoyed the change. But one thing they all did. At one time or another on the long Pacific passage every officer and man made a pilgrimage to what had once been the starboard after gun gallery. They didn't think of it as a pilgrimage. They just walked aft to look, and stood, silent or talking quietly, before the cavern three decks deep of blackened, twisted metal where their shipmates had been blasted out of their young lives. Despite the sweep of the sea wind and the wash of salt water from the cleansing hoses, a sweet, blood-and-oil odor of death still permeated the Big E's starboard quarter.

In Pearl the Navy Yard worked around the clock, and each day one third of the crew went ashore from ten to five. *Enterprise* was not only repaired but modernized. The delicate, water-cooled 1.1-inch, intermediate-range antiaircraft batteries were removed and replaced by 40-millimeter Bofors "quad" mounts, probably the most effective antiaircraft gun in use during the war. Improvements were made in the damage control systems.

While the Big E lay at Pearl, the pilots she had left in the Solomons fought to hold off the Japanese.

Ray Davis, with what was left of Bombing Six, was ordered to Efate, halfway down the chain of the New Hebrides from Espiritu, to operate with the Marine fighter squadron already there. He had twelve pilots total and, when a call came for a four-plane division to go aboard the *Wasp*, they held a drawing. Dick Jaccard, the tall, lean, humorous Kansan, who with Bill Pittman had flown wing on Wade McClusky at Midway, drew one of the short straws.

Five days after the Big E entered the yard at Pearl, an enemy submarine caught *Wasp* with three big 24-inch torpedoes. They laid her starboard side open and ignited uncontrollable gasoline and ammunition fires that progressively tore her to pieces. Jaccard was asleep in his bunk after a patrol when one of the enemy warheads obliterated the officers' quarters. A dozen pilots that the Zeros and the AA in as many actions had failed to touch died in their bunks that afternoon of a shot fired from beneath the sea. *Wasp*'s crew was forced overboard in a little more than an hour and in the evening, the most recent U. S. carrier to arrive in the Pacific was a burning derelict that a friendly destroyer had to sink with a second torpedo salvo.

Turner Caldwell and his pilots and gunners of Scouting Five and Bombing Six had in effect become a small, land-based dive bomber squadron. They were known, from their listing on the *Enterprise* flight schedule of August 24, as Flight 300.

Flying from the alternate mud and dust of Henderson, dodging the wrecks and pulling up for the palm trees was greatly different from operating off the clean, wind-swept deck of the *Enterprise*. The jungle tents of Guadalcanal were not the shined and sheeted staterooms of the Big E, nor a can of K rations and a handful of Japanese rice in a forest clearing the linened, silvered wardrooms or the food-heaped mess trays of the carrier. The similarity lay in action. Once air-borne, from field or deck, it was the same. Always there were the enemy ships, with their curling wakes and climbing tracers, always the Zeros to dodge.

They lasted for over a month of strikes and air raids and night bombardments, eating wormy Japanese rice or sharing the slim Marine rations in foxholes and tank parks, bathing hurriedly in a muddy creek with one eye cocked at the sky, bewhiskered, red-eyed and skinny. With the ten Dauntlesses all expended in one way or another, the last man was evacuated by DC-3 on the twenty-seventh of September.

On October 14, as the Big E was beginning to clean up the shipyard mess and load for sea, Ray Davis brought eight more *Enterprise* pilots of Bombing Six with their gunners into Henderson Field. For over a month they too flew troop support missions for the Marines, strafed landing barges, beached and at sea, searched the surrounding waters for submarines, scouted long pie-shaped sectors for approaching surface forces, and once in a while were able to roll down in the long precision dives they were trained for, to plant their big bombs on the decks of warships. Between flights, they ate with any outfit that had food to spare. During the twice-daily high-level air raids, they either scrambled into their planes and flew them out of danger or raced on foot for the beach and out of the bull's-eye of the field itself. Once the amused Marines saw two pilots running through a palm glade as the bombs began to march across the field. Red-headed Bill Pittman, trailing, had breath to yell ahead: "Hey, Richey, wait for me! I don't want to get killed and not have anyone *see* it."

Often the Navy pilots flew with Marine gunners. When Duncan's eardrums were ruptured in a vertical, no-flap dive to avoid a Zero, Pittman went searching for a replacement. His first volunteer was a big Marine baker who inadvertently released his chute in the SBD's rear seat and was nearly smothered in the sliding yards of white nylon. Finally, he settled on a wiry little tank gunner who knew nothing about planes but much about guns and was not bothered by rough engine or holed wing so long as he could bring his .30-calibers to bear on the enemy.

The Big E's pilots on Guadalcanal were only a portion of the land-based Navy and Marine Corps squadrons that operated out of Henderson Field during those critical months in late 1942 when no one knew who would finally own it. Marine scouting, bombing and fighter squadrons were the major force, assisted by a squadron of Army P-400 low-altitude fighters; *Saratoga*'s Scouting Three and Fighting Five and *Wasp*'s VS-7 were also there, and the Navy pilots with recent carrier battles behind them were a seasoned, veteran group who could pass their knowledge to the newly blooded Marines.

In mid-October the Japanese had large numbers of troops on Guadalcanal and were pressing heavily against the Marine lines protecting Henderson Field.

Hornet, supported by only one new battleship, the *Washington,* was now left as the only carrier in the South Pacific. From Truk, the home islands, and the East Indies, enemy task forces, including *Shokaku* and *Zuikaku,* were gathering for another attempt on Guadalcanal.

Repairs to *Enterprise* were rushed, and on the sixteenth she cast off her last line and once more stood out the narrow channel past Hospital Point and Fort Kamehameha. When Diamond Head had settled into the sea on her port quarter, she headed back for the Solomons.

John Crommelin went to work on his new Air Group Ten commanded by Commander Richard K. Gaines. Crommelin had a feeling that this brand-new air group was going to see action very soon and if they could be made ready he would do it. Other department heads felt the same way and the ten-day run down across the equator was a time of hard work for all the men of the Big E. The flight deck roared with action from dawn General Quarters until after evening General Quarters had been secured.

At daylight on the twenty-third of October *Enterprise* and her supporting ships met the tanker *Sabine* some 850 miles southeast of Guadalcanal and went alongside two at a time to splash all their tanks full of the black Navy Special fuel oil. Later that day the *Hornet* task group edged up over the calm horizon and, except for one battleship and three cruisers, the U. S. Navy's effective strength in the Pacific was gathered under the tactical command of Rear Admiral Thomas C. Kinkaid. Bareheaded, he walked the Big E's flag bridge with binoculars around his neck.

At 3:00 P.M. on the twenty-third, the combined task force began a sweep to the northwest to interpose between Guadalcanal and the threatening enemy fleet to the northward.

By destroyers and barges at night and an occasional daylight landing, the Japanese had slowly built up their forces on Guadalcanal. Their strongest naval forces since Midway were at sea: four carriers—*Shokaku, Zuikaku, Zuiho, Junyo*—eight heavy cruisers, two light cruisers and twenty-eight destroyers. The goal of the Japanese Army on Guadalcanal and the Navy a few hundred miles to the north was Henderson Field. The Army was to capture the field. Carrier planes would fly in at once. Caught between the carriers and Henderson, U. S. naval forces would be sunk or forced away and the U. S. Marines, cut off, could be mopped up. The evil-smelling, worthless, priceless island would be back in Japanese hands, the threat of an American counterattack up the Solomon chain ended, and the march to cut the U. S.—Australian life-line could be resumed. But first it was necessary to capture Henderson Field.

October 22 was selected as the date on which the all-important airport would change hands. The Marines upset the schedule by driving back tank and infantry attacks. They upset it again around midnight of the twenty-third. By this time the Big E had arrived from Pearl to double U. S. naval strength in the Solomons.

By the twenty-fourth the big enemy sea forces had been circling between Truk and Guadalcanal for nearly two weeks. Oil and patience were running low. Admiral Yamamoto in Truk radioed the Army commander on Guadal that unless Henderson Field could be delivered quickly, naval forces could be counted out. Fuel would be too low to risk battle.

In the small hours of the twenty-fifth, the Army announced Henderson in Japanese hands and Yamamoto's fleet turned southeast. At daylight the enemy soldiers were no longer so sure about Henderson, and Kinkaid was approaching head-on at 20 knots with *Enterprise* and *Hornet*

SBDs fanning out ahead. Unless the Japanese retreated hurriedly, they were committed to action, Henderson or no Henderson.

At ten minutes of one on the afternoon of the twenty-fifth Admiral Kinkaid, then some 250 miles east and a little north of the Santa Cruz Islands, learned the whereabouts of his enemy. A PBY out of Espiritu had found two carriers 360 miles ahead steaming southeast at 25 knots. With the range closing at nearly fifty miles each hour, 12 armed SBDs left *Enterprise* at 2:30 P.M. covering from west through north out to 200 miles. An hour later the air group commander led off an attack group of 12 more Dauntlesses and 7 Avengers escorted by 16 fighters. The search extended beyond the Santa Cruz Islands and well to the northward over the darkening Pacific. It found nothing. It was an hour after sunset when the planes got back over the carrier. Many of the younger pilots had never made a night carrier landing. Lieutenant Frank Miller flew his Wildcat into the sea forty miles from the ship and was killed, probably as a result of insufficient oxygen during the long, high-altitude flight. Three TBFs and three SBDs used the last of their fuel in the landing pattern and ditched. Destroyers picked up all the crews. The moon was just clearing the horizon as the last plane caught a wire and was snubbed to a stop on the Big E's blacked-out deck.

All night Admiral Kinkaid's ships zigzagged northwest toward the enemy at 20 knots.

Every man in *Enterprise* knew the next day would bring action with the enemy. The brand-new, eager air group was just ten days away from the classrooms and training flights of Kaneohe. Throughout the ship new men wondered how they would act under the bombs or guns of the Japanese and the old hands went carefully about their duties assuring themselves that their particular equipments were ready for the morning and, to the best of their ability, closing their minds to the coming battle.

Commander John Crommelin called his pilots together in the wardroom. While they sat in their open-collared khaki along the green-covered tables with coffee cups before them and the smoke flattening out among the trunks and cables on the overhead, he gave them the straight, true, vigorous words they needed to hear. They had all been carefully and thoroughly trained, he told them; they knew how to drop a bomb and have it hit. And he damned well

expected them to do just that. The safety and success of
the Marines in their long, miserable struggle for Guadalcanal now depended 100 per cent on how well the Big E's
pilots did their duty. There was no room for waste, no excuse for misses. If they were going to get out there and
miss, it would have been better if they had stayed back in
the States and given *good* pilots their bunks and a crack at
the enemy. Crommelin's Alabama accent thickened as he
made his last point and the lights on the low wardroom
overhead glittered on his sandy, graying hair. He hoped no
one had any illusions about being overworked. The men in
that room were a major part of all that stood between the
Japanese and Guadalcanal. And on Guadalcanal depended
the war in the South Pacific. He would use them however
and whenever necessary and the better they were the better
their chances. He would use them over and over and over
again. Now they were to rest and knock those sons-of-
bitches off the face of the earth in the morning.

All the *Enterprise* pilots knew Crommelin's combat record, had seen him slow roll across Kaneohe at a hundred
feet to give them confidence in their planes, knew he was
requiring nothing of them he was not well able to perform
himself and they went to their bunks and fell asleep with
his words stringing across behind their eyes—". . . over
and over and over and over again."

Before daylight on the twenty-sixth—while early breakfast was being served to sailors with faces still creased from
their bedding, while aircraft were being armed and rechecked and pilots briefed—a message was received from
the headquarters of the commander, South Pacific Force,
at Noumea. It was in a familiar style. Three words:

ATTACK. REPEAT, ATTACK

Only one man could have sent it and the Big E's men knew
him well. Bill Halsey was back in the war.

Halsey had taken over as commander, South Pacific Area
and South Pacific Force, on the eighteenth and it was by his
order that Kinkaid's task force was engaged in the northwestward sweep which had found the enemy. A new confidence stirred through the *Enterprise*.

At 6:00 A.M., twenty-three minutes before sunrise, sixteen Dauntlesses left the Big E's deck and fanned out in
pairs to search the morning sea from southwest through

north to a distance of 200 miles. A few moments later eight Wildcats clawed steeply up to establish a Combat Air Patrol and six more SBDs circled out on the watch for subs.

The battlefield had been chosen. It was a thousand square miles of the South Pacific lying just to the northward of the fiercely malarial Santa Cruz islands. The sea was calm except for the long ground swell that is never still and the friendly ripples of a six- to ten-knot breeze. From 1,500 to 2,000 feet drifted white and gold cumulus clouds covering nearly half the dawn sky. Above them there was no ceiling and below visibility was unlimited.

Like exploring fingers the Big E's scouting sections probed westward across the sea that had to hold the enemy. Eighty-five miles out, Welch and McGraw of Bombing Ten passed a single-float enemy scout on the opposite course, and twenty minutes later they made the first contact, the strange pagoda-like superstructure of a *Kongo*-class battleship breaking the clean line of the horizon ahead. The two SBDs pulled up into the bases of the low clouds and circled the enemy force at ten miles, alternately in the bright sunlight and the gray turbulent insides of the cumulus. At 7:30 A.M. the "dits" and "dahs" of Welch's contact report beeped loudly into the Big E's code room with the unhurried clarity of a communications drill:

TWO BATTLESHIPS, ONE HEAVY CRUISER, SEVEN DE-STROYERS. LATITUDE 8 DEGREES 10 MINUTES SOUTH, LONGITUDE 163 DEGREES, 55 MINUTES EAST. COURSE NORTH, SPEED TWENTY KNOTS

Bareheaded and short-sleeved among the Big E's helmeted and life-jacketed bridge crew, Admiral Kinkaid paced and fretted. The admiral stopped for a minute to watch the big bedspring antenna of the air-search radar slowly sweeping the sky, then walked to the rail and looked for the twentieth time at the loaded SBDs and TBFs crowded together on the flight deck. Ducking through the crowded pilothouse to the starboard wing of the bridge, he lifted the binoculars hanging around his neck and saw a bigger deck load of planes ready on the *Hornet* ten miles away. This was the Big E's day to search and follow with a small strike. The real punch was on the *Hornet*.

At ten minutes of eight Kinkaid heard what he had been waiting to hear. The radios in the coding room came alive again and the watch could recognize the firm clear hand of Chief I. A. Sanders, flying with Lieutenant Commander J. R. "Bucky" Lee, skipper of Scouting Ten:

TWO CARRIERS AND ACCOMPANYING VESSELS, LATITUDE 7 DEGREES 5 MINUTES SOUTH, 163 DEGREES 38 MINUTES EAST

The admiral stepped into Flag Plot and looked closely at the chart. Two hundred miles to the northwest. The bright flags soared out of their bags to the yardarms and the shutter clattered on the 36-inch signal searchlight trained on the *Hornet*. Force speed went up to 27 knots and the bows swung into the northwest.

Fifteen miles east of the Japanese carriers, Lee and his wingman, W. E. Johnson, noses up and throttles forward, struggled for attack altitude. In Lee's rear seat Chief Sanders hammered out his contact report three more times to be sure it was received and then dropped his key and swung his guns up to the ready. Below them the enemy ships, as though in terror of the two thin-tailed SBDs, turned westward at high speed and fouled themselves with thick clouds of black smoke. From high overhead two four-plane sections of the Zero CAP spiraled down to attack. Lee and Johnson turned their Dauntlesses into fighters with guns at both ends, and in a wrapped-up, heavy-gutted, low-altitude swirl of wings and props and stringing tracers, with the horizon usually vertical and the ocean frequently overhead, shot down three of the overconfident Zeros before ducking into the friendly cumulus. In the desperate aerial game of hide and seek that followed, Lee and Johnson became separated. There was no chance of approaching the enemy ships again, alone, and, their mission completed, they returned singly to the ship.

Lieutenant Birney Strong, with Ensign Charles Irvine on his wing, were at the tip of the third of the Big E's probing fingers to the northward, a hundred miles from the two carriers reported by Chief Sanders. They had believed John Crommelin's words and absorbed the aggressive, determined spirit in which they were spoken. Garlow and Williams in their two rear seats had copied Welch's contact report on the battlewagons. Obviously the action was all to the south. Here the 500-pound bomb they each carried was wasted, the two loads of fuel and ammunition lugged around the sky for nothing. Strong could hear John Crommelin's confident voice loud in the wardroom: "There is no room for waste, no excuse for misses!" Working fast, he plotted the Japanese battleship position on his board, drew the course line, figured briefly in pencil off to the side, glanced at his fuel gauges and motioned to Irvine, close on his wing. The right wings of the two Dauntlesses tipped up sharply as they turned south. Both pilots as they started climbing on the new course, eased back their mixture controls, watching the RPM and listening intently to the engines. They would need every yard they could get out of the gas left in their tanks now that they had added to their long search a climb to attack altitude, an extra hundred miles, and a fight if they could find it.

When Lee's report on the carriers came in a few minutes later they had to alter heading only a few degrees.

Lieutenant Stockton Birney Strong had no illusions about the two-plane attack on a task force that he was planning. He had been on carriers since the war began. The Gilbert Island strikes, Coral Sea and the August battle off the Eastern Solomons were all behind him, plus raids on Tulagi and the Lae Salamaua area off New Guinea. At Eastern Solomons he and Ensign Richey had located the *Ryujo,* carefully and accurately reported her position, course, speed and the composition of her force but had not attacked through the fighters and the flak. Strong had been thinking about that since the twenty-fourth of August and every time he thought about it, he thought it had been a mistake. He would not repeat it.

In the bright sunlight at 14,000 feet the four men in the two slim Dauntlesses stalked the heart of the enemy's naval strength.

The carriers that Lee and Johnson had found were *Shokaku* and *Zuikaku.* Their CAP was up, their guns loaded and trained out. A heavy cruiser and seven destroyers surrounded them.

Although they had been navigating only between careful visual searches and checks of engine instruments and fuel gauges, guessing at wind drift, Lee's contact report and Strong's interception were exactly accurate. At 8:30 A.M. Strong picked up two narrow yellow decks sliding toward him far below. They were *Shokaku* and the light carrier *Zuiho. Zuikaku,* a few miles away, was out of sight under a cloud.

Chuck Irvine saw them at the same time and moved in
close. Both pilots charged their guns. Garlow and Williams
clicked the safeties off their twin 30s. Strong led the section
in a left turn, heading for an up-sun attack position. Below,
the small yellow rectangles disappeared occasionally under
puffs of cloud. The Zeros and the AA were overdue. Strong
knew that luck alone was providing him with these moments and he was not a man to question the gift. Directly
up-sun from *Zuiho,* the nearest carrier, he patted his head
to Irvine, pulled up, split his flaps and rolled into the long
dive that since December had become the purpose of his
life. A thousand feet behind, Irvine followed down. Still
there were no Zeros. Unruffled by any flak the dive was as
smooth as a training exercise. The gunners lay on their
backs wondering at the empty sky, waiting for the bouncing of the AA while the two pilots leaned forward, sweating with pure concentration, an eye pressed to the tubular
scope where every pressure of right hands and toes moved
the crosshairs on the expanding deck. There was time to
notice that both decks were empty, that the enemy air
groups had been launched. In succession at 1,500 feet their
left hands went down and forward, found the release handles and pulled. It was done. And as the bombs fell away
the AA came up and the Zeros closed from all directions.
But it was too late. Both bombs plunged into the enemy
flight deck near the stern and opened it wide with two
splintering blasts rapidly followed by a pouring of black
smoke.

Then the SBDs were flat down on the white caps, slipping, jerking, twisting under the lash of AA fire from the
ships and repeated runs by the Zeros. With mixtures, throttles and prop controls all pushed forward over the end of
the control quadrant, bombs gone, the pilots dodged and
weaved and tried to cover each other. But Garlow and Williams, with their swinging, hammering .30-calibers, held the
only real hope of getting the section back to base. Occasionally a Zero got careless. One of the first to attack
ceased firing too soon and banked away, showing the
plane's defenseless belly. Garlow stitched it thoroughly with
lead during the instant it was exposed, and the fighter exploded into flame and rolled inverted into the sea. A few
moments later Williams got one too and after that the attacks were not pressed home so closely. But the Zeros still
came on, banking in from astern, all prop disk and wings

with the guns blinking along the leading edges. And they could not all miss. Holes appeared in Irvine's right wing and tail, slowing him. Strong, seeing the holes and remembering his depleted fuel supply, doubted that they would make it home. But it was important that Admiral Kinkaid (and Commander Crommelin) know of the damage to the carrier. So with the Zeros still attacking, and Garlow doggedly giving them burst for burst, he opened up on his radio and announced the two hits, giving position, course and speed of the enemy force. Then he repeated it. The task force commander had to have the tactical information and John Crommelin had to know that with two SBDs they had put two 500-pound bombs on the target—two out of two. No waste of bombs or planes or gas or training. You couldn't do any better—unless you could get home too.

The two Dauntlesses took to the scattering clouds and at nine o'clock after a forty-five-mile chase, the last of the Zeros turned back. Now it was only a problem of flying home. But home was a hunted carrier, maneuvering on unknown courses at unknown speeds and maintaining radio silence some 150 salt-water miles away. With nearly empty tanks and shot-up airplanes only a direct and perfect course would provide a chance of success. At 10:26 A.M., Robin Lindsey's paddles waved Strong and Irvine aboard the *Enterprise* on the first pass, and with insufficient fuel for another had it been necessary.

Every SBD of the sixteen-plane dawn search returned safely to the ship. Half had made contact with the enemy. They had shot down seven Zeros attempting interception and left a carrier and a cruiser burning.

Now it was time for Thomas Kinkaid to strike his enemy. It was, in fact, past time.

A *Hornet* strike of 29 planes went off first. *Enterprise* followed with every flyable plane aboard except for 20 fighters of the CAP, and another *Hornet* group of 25 fell in behind. Loaded with bombs and torpedoes and with the target 200 miles away, the various formations could not wait to join up, but departed immediately and separately in the direction of the enemy.

The *Enterprise* strike consisted of eight Avengers, heavy with the long torpedoes in their bomb bays, three SBDs with 1,000-pound bombs and an escort of eight Wildcats. Behind and above, Commander Gaines, the air group commander, controlled the flight from a ninth TBF. With six

Dauntlesses at the bottom of the sea after last evening's long search, six more on antisub patrol for the task force and sixteen straggling back from the morning scouting flight, the Big E was desperately short of dive bombers.

The attack group, conserving fuel, climbed slowly out on course. To the right and left, ahead and a thousand feet above, the two four-plane divisions of Wildcats weaved gently back and forth, throttled back to avoid outdistancing the slower Dauntlesses and Avengers. Navy Cross winner Lieutenant Commander James Flatley, the skipper of the "Grim Reapers" of Fighting Ten, led the right-hand division, Lieutenant John Leppla the left. Lep had been handpicked by Flatley out of a Dauntless squadron on the old *Lexington* where he and his gunner John Liska had also won a Navy Cross at Coral Sea.

Twenty minutes after take-off and about forty-five miles from the ship, the fighter pilots, at 6,000 feet, were getting around to charging their guns, wondering what lay ahead of them and how they would conduct themselves. Below and behind them, at 4,000, some of the Avengers had not yet turned on their radio transmitters. The earphones of all the pilots crackled gently. Nothing was on the air. Jim Flatley led his division in another shallow turn to starboard and held it for about a minute. Then slowly he turned back and glanced over his left shoulder at the formation. The TBF piloted by Lieutenant Commander John A. Collet, the CO of Torpedo Ten, was spinning, with flame and smoke pouring from the engine and back over the cockpit. A second Avenger was slanting toward the sea, the canopy shattered and the pilot slumped in his seat. Behind and below, the four Wildcats of the other division were locked in a series of tight turns and climbs with a dozen Zeros. Two Zeros were falling away from the action in black ribbons of smoke. Ahead another was turning toward the TBFs for a second run. Flatley attacked in a diving left turn; the Zero turned right and pulled up but Flatley recovered above him and attacked again with a long burst at maximum range. The Zero began to smoke but continued straight ahead; on his next attack the fighter skipper hammered it into the sea.

When the seemingly endless string of Zeros flashed down out of the sun and through the torpedo plane formation, Ensign Dusty Rhodes reacted like the others in his Wildcat division, with shocked disbelief for about two seconds and then with a hard right turn toward what was left of the other group, shucking his drop tank, charging guns, jamming throttle, RPM and mixture into the stops in an attempt to close the dangerous speed advantage the diving Zeros held and to keep them off the remaining bombers.

The heavy, rugged F4F required an altitude advantage, which its weight could quickly convert to speed, in order to match the maneuverability of the Zero. Here the Zeros had caught the Wildcats slow and committed to the altitude of the bombers they were escorting, so they could not even dive away to gain speed and fight it out at low altitude. While Leppla's division closed up under full power and turned in to the enemy, the Japanese fighters literally looped around and through their formation, making run after run until the blue wings were pocked with holes from the 20-millimeters and 7.7s, canopies were smashed, pilots wounded.

Rhodes and Reding had opposite kinds of trouble, both bad. Rhodes' drop tank would not release and enemy tracers set it flaming like a huge blow torch under his wing. Reding's tank released and fell away but when it did his engine stopped, leaving him helplessly spiraling down trying to restart while Rhodes circled over him with his built-in fire, covering and receiving repeated runs by the Zeros.

In this sudden nightmare of looping, swirling fighters, of flame and tracers and engines screaming under wide-open throttle, with the G forces of wrapped-up turns tugging at his abdomen and the horizon everywhere except horizontal, Dusty Rhodes had his canopy riddled, his pushed-up goggles shot off the top of his head and his instrument panel so completely shattered by gunfire that his electric gunsight swung by its wiring before the empty space where it had been. And somehow in the midst of the holocaust his mind had time to remember how impressed he had been with the bullet hole in Machinist Runyan's instrument panel which he had seen on first reporting to the Big E, and to hope he could get this one back to show the guys.

Dusty did not see Al Mead after leaving the formation to cover Reding, and the last he saw of John Leppla was Lep in a head-on run against one Zero and with another on his tail. Later he caught a glimpse of a half-opened, streaming chute dropping seaward and thought it must be Lep. Then Chip Reding got his engine going on the internal tanks, and Dusty's fire burned itself out with the last of the fuel in his drop tank, and the two F4Fs joined up against the cloud of Zeros.

Rhodes' radio was shot to pieces along with his instrument panel and Reding's whole electrical system was out, including radio, but, by hand signal and an understanding developed out of long hours of flying together, they joined to execute a defensive, scissoring maneuver worked out by Jimmy Flatley and his friend Jimmy Thach which was beginning to be known as the Thach weave. Neither pilot could see his own tail but each could see the other's. Rhodes started out to Reding's left. Reding saw a Zero begin a run on Rhodes' tail and at once turned left toward Dusty to bring his guns onto the enemy. Rhodes, seeing Chip's turn and knowing its meaning, turned right toward Chip to draw the Zero into Chip's line of fire. The Zero turned away and the two F4Fs leveled out again, having reversed position, with Rhodes now on the right, ready to execute the same maneuver again. They worked the weave together for minutes that passed like hours and the Zeros usually turned off when the Wildcat noses began to bear on them. But there were too many. While Dusty and Chip were weaving against a couple behind, several more were making runs from ahead or the flanks. Then, at about 2,500 feet, Rhodes' engine stopped, its bearings burned out and fused together, the prop not even windmilling—just stationary before him. He nosed over to keep his speed and started a turn upwind to ditch, but the Zeros were not finished. Another one came in from behind and Dusty felt both his rudder pedals go slack as the control cables parted. He thought he might be able to set it down on ailerons and elevator and he remembered an old chief in flight training who had said never bail out below a thousand feet, but well below five hundred. Dusty Rhodes, in nearly a single explosive motion, hurled back the shattered canopy, stood up in the cockpit, booted the stick full forward into where the instrument panel had once been and pulled the ripcord of his chute. The riddled Wildcat with its dead engine shot under him, the parachute opened and snatched him erect, and as he swung down under it he hit the water.

He hit hard and went deep but going down he released the snap hooks that held his chute and when he broke the surface again he was clear of it. Overhead, he could see Chip Reding's F4F headed south with three Zeros behind it and in the sudden watery silence he could hear the whine of the four engines under full power. He noticed that one of the Zeros was smoking.

When he rejoined the Big E's strike group, Flatley found it halved. The enemy ambush, diving straight out of the sun so close to friendly forces, had destroyed outright two Avengers, including the squadron commander's, forced a third to ditch and sent a fourth back to *Enterprise* with a damaged engine. Three of Leppla's four fighters had gone down, and the survivor, Chip Reding, dazed and shaken at the sudden overwhelming attack and heavy losses, outran three Zeros and gentled his riddled Wildcat back toward the Big E.

The Big E's best punch was now reduced to four Avengers and three Dauntlesses with a four-Wildcat escort. Commander Gaines, unnoticed or disregarded by the enemy, made a radio report of the action and continued with the reduced attack group.

At 10:30 A.M. the enemy battleships and cruisers came in sight, ploughing northward between the spreading shadows of the cumulus. For ten minutes the planes circled, searching behind the building clouds for the carriers. Then Lieutenant Thompson, leading the Avengers after the loss of his skipper, asked Flatley if he had enough fuel to go another ninety miles in search of the carriers. Flatley's fighters decidedly did not. Having shucked off their wing tanks to counter the Zero ambush, they had barely enough to return. Accordingly, the Big E's strike took on the enemy battleship force instead.

The three SBDs (Bombing Ten planes flown by Scouting Ten crews) lined up on a *Kongo*-class battleship. Richey put his big bomb in the water close aboard the starboard bow, Henry Ervin got a hit flush on the top of number two turret and Estes planted his amidships on the starboard side. The big battlewagon shook and smoked but plowed ahead on her mission.

While Jim Flatley's fighters kept the gunners busy with repeated strafing runs, the Avengers circled in low to attack a heavy cruiser. They bored in close and dropped the big fish straight but the enemy skipper was able to evade them all.

On the way home a single Zero pilot made the last attack of his life into the combined fire of the three SBD gunners, and two thirds of the way back, the Big E's eleven planes passed directly over shouting, whistling, waving

Dusty Rhodes, seated uneasily in a half-inflated, half-swamped one-man raft some 165 miles north of Santa Cruz and east of the Stewart Islands, nursing a bullet nick in his left leg, and full of salt water and a feeling of amazed gratitude that he was still alive. They did not see him.

The dive bombers of *Hornet*'s first strike did much better. They avoided contact with the enemy air until nine Zeros tangled with the escort Wildcats over the battleships. None got through to the SBDs, and at 10:30 they found *Shokaku* and *Zuiho*. Even from 12,000 feet they could see smoke coming from two holes in light carrier *Zuiho*'s flight deck. With *Zuikaku* under a cloud at the moment of attack, it was *Zuiho* that Strong and Irvine had hit. The *Hornet*'s bombers fought through the enemy CAP and put several 1,000-pounders into *Shokaku*. They left her burning from stem to stern and barely making steerage way.

The torpedo planes of that first strike, and her entire second wave, like the Big E's battered attack force, never found the carriers but made some hits on a cruiser.

Admiral Kinkaid's morning attack was over. *Shokaku* and *Zuiho* were out of the battle, a battleship and a cruiser badly battered. But *Zuikaku* and *Junyo* were untouched and, worse, unlocated and now launching strikes.

The Zeros that surprised and shot up the Big E's strike only forty-five miles from her deck were part of a sixty-five-plane attack group from *Shokaku*, *Zuikaku* and *Zuiho*, which fifteen minutes later had the United States task force in sight. The fighting ships of Kinkaid's Task Force 16 were formed into two tight, gray circles ten miles apart. Each circle, with the flat rectangle of a carrier at the center, raked the morning sea with parallel white lines at 27 knots. High overhead and westward in the enemy direction thirty-eight Wildcats circled, controlled through the eye of radar and the voice of radio by the *Enterprise* fighter director officer.

As close around the Big E's priceless deck as high speed and full rudder would allow were a new battleship, and an antiaircraft light cruiser. Eight destroyers formed an outer ring around the heavy ships. One of them was the *Shaw*, a ship that had had experience with Vals flown from *Shokaku* and *Zuikaku*. They had caught her helpless in dry dock and blown off her bow in Pearl Harbor on the seventh of December. The same skipper and some sixty of the same men were aboard.

Hornet, flying the two-star flag of Rear Admiral George

Murray, the Big E's old skipper, was protected by two anti-aircraft cruisers, two heavy cruisers and six destroyers.

Shortly after ten o'clock, her deck empty and every flyable plane in the air, *Enterprise,* at the center of her armored circle, was passing under the base of one of the big cumuli that covered more than half the sky. Warm rain rattled in her gun tubs and on the helmets of her sailors. Radar had enemy aircraft on the scope close in and several divisions of Wildcats were ordered to intercept.

It was too late and most of the fighters were out of position.

The enemy strike group missed *Enterprise* in the shadow of her rain squall and spread out, diving, to attack the *Hornet. Enterprise* and *Hornet* Wildcats scrambled desperately after the enemy planes, following them down through the thickening five-inch bursts and the shifting tracer streams. Lieutenant Stanley W. Vejtasa, climbing steeply, was able to slow one down with a long burst from his six guns just before the enemy pilot reached his push-over point. Lieutenant Albert D. Pollock, carefully conserving his ammunition and firing only two of his outboard guns, silenced the gunner of an enemy dive bomber with his first burst, then, with the Japanese well into his dive on the *Hornet,* he turned on all six guns and burned the belly out of the enemy plane. He had to pull up hard to avoid the wreckage. Ensign Steve Kona of Pollock's flight got one in the same dive. Ensign Donald Gordon on his second attack blew up a torpedo plane ten feet off the crests of the swells and just a few hundred yards from the force. "Flash" Gordon was ten days out of Kaneohe and this was his first action.

But most of the bombers got through. Over George Murray's task group the automatic weapons of the new antiaircraft cruisers and the five-inch guns of those and the other ships poured tons of hot steel and high explosive into the sky. Many of the Japanese planes, still unmistakable with their obsolete fixed landing gear, suddenly caught fire in their dives and twisted out of control. Others, hit by the five-inch, disintegrated in a flash and a ball of yellow flame and black smoke from which large and small pieces fell. But there were too many, and they dived in close and made their drops courageously and well. The commanding officer of an enemy bombing squadron, already badly hit, drove through the *Hornet's* flight deck with two big bombs. Four more bombs and two torpedoes stopped her and set her afire and a torpedo plane flew into her port bow.

At 10:25, when *Enterprise* turned eastward into the
wind to recover her search planes, the men topside could
see *Hornet* off to the southwest dead in the water at the
base of a slanting column of black smoke. *Hornet*'s four
big bronze screws had made their last revolution, and the
deck from which Colonel Doolittle's B-25s had flown to
Tokyo would rest that night on the dark mud of the abyss
three miles below the Big E's keel.

Enterprise was now the only effective United States aircraft carrier west of Oahu.

The Japanese may not have known that, but they knew
very well she was the only one left to cover Guadalcanal.
And Nagumo still had two untouched carriers, with their
strikes on the way.

At eleven o'clock *Enterprise* radar reported large groups
of hostile planes at twenty-three miles, closing. Again the
Wildcats flew to intercept, and again they were mostly below and behind when they finally saw the bombers. Frequently the leader of a four-plane division of F4Fs would
be told to "look on the port quarter" or "look on the starboard bow." To a pilot miles away and frequently out of
sight of his task force, such directions based on the ships'
heading at the moment meant nothing, and the division
leaders would have done better had they simply been stationed high above the force and out in the enemy direction,
provided with radar data on enemy aircraft and permitted
to act according to their own judgment. The radar performed well, but poor use was made of the information it
supplied.

Some two minutes after radar's warning, Dave Pollock,
orbiting over the task force with three F4Fs of his CAP
division, noticed one of the destroyers dead in the water
beside the bright yellow oval of a rubber life raft. A pilot
was being rescued and Dave hoped he was one of the Big
E's fliers, missing on the morning strike. As he watched
there was some sort of activity in the bright blue sea a few
hundred yards off the destroyer's beam. Something was
circling erratically just under the surface and leaving a
wake. A torpedo. From a mile up Dave could make it out
well enough, but he knew that from the low deck of the
destroyer, or even from her thirty-five-foot bridge it would
be hard to see. He had to warn the ship but he had radio
contact only with the FDO and there was no time on that

already too-busy circuit to relay. He decided to go down and explode the tin fish with his guns. He knew the jittery shipboard gunners would fire on him but at least he could call attention to the torpedo. He turned over the lead and dived his Wildcat for the water. As expected, the destroyer opened fire at once, and her sisters joined in viciously. Pollock, cursing, tried to ignore the tracers and made repeated strafing runs on the circling torpedo, his bullets churning the sea around it. After the second run, the surface gunners saw his friendly markings and ceased fire. The destroyer simultaneously recognized his warning, and her screws began to churn just as the torpedo exploded amidships in a towering burst of white water and tumbling debris. Pollock sadly pulled up and rejoined his division.

The destroyer was the *Porter*. She completed the rescue of Lieutenant R. K. Batten and his gunner R. S. Holgrim. Batten had ditched his Avenger after the morning ambush of the Big E's strike. The *Porter* could not be salvaged with the enemy so close. Batten and Holgrim jumped across to the *Shaw* when she came alongside to take off survivors, and watched from her deck as she sank the wounded *Porter* with her five-inch guns.

While the badly positioned, poorly directed Wildcats were struggling for a shot and Pollock was trying in vain to save the *Porter*, the Big E's fire controlmen were working hard to bring the new fire-control radar onto the approaching enemy. Theoretically and in controlled tests, the five-inch guns firing under the direction of this equipment could knock down targets at long ranges and invisible from the ship in clouds or darkness. Now its scopes would not pick up the incoming planes. At 11:15, as at Eastern Solomons, the men of *Enterprise* could see the shining dive bombers of the Imperial Navy plunging out of the clear sky directly overhead. They were flashes of silver that made small popping noises. At first they seemed ridiculously small and unmoving, but they looked unmoving only because they were moving straight toward the eye of the looker. Then swiftly they began to grow, and on all the waiting ships the gunners opened fire. One of Flatley's Reapers, glancing down at that moment, thought the *San Juan* had been hit and exploded, but she had simply commenced firing with all her guns. On *South Dakota* a hundred muzzles flamed in steady mechanical unison and the dark brown powder smoke sprang from her decks and superstructure and drifted out astern. The *Portland* and every destroyer in the screen hammered steel into the sky. But in *Enterprise* Orlin Livdahl's gunners had the easiest shooting. For them there was no deflection. Each plane was pointed down the barrels of her guns. She was the bull's-eye of the task force target.

On the bridge Captain Osborne B. Hardison held his helmet on with his left hand as he looked straight up at the chain of dive bombers twisting down on his ship, and maneuvered with full rudder to spoil their aim. A scant thousand yards away 45,000 tons of battleship matched his every turn, remaining at the Big E's side like the wingman in a flight section.

Enterprise staggered through a storm of bombs and falling planes. The sea spouted into columns around her and her hull jarred and rang with the water hammers of submerged explosions. For four minutes she fought it out with the seasoned, determined Japanese airmen who were less than two hours off the decks of her old enemies, *Shokaku* and *Zuikaku*. Half of them were caught and dismembered in the shifting web of tracers and became momentary flares of gasoline on the broad surface of the Pacific. Others were harrassed by the rising metal into dropping early and turning away, often into the guns of Flatley's frustrated Wildcats. Through the measured booming of the five-inch and the steady hammering of the smaller guns the men topside could hear the mounting roar of enemy engines which faded suddenly as they pulled out across the deck. Below, men braced their feet wide on the oily gratings of the engine and firerooms as the Big E heeled to full rudder, first one way, then back. The men of the repair parties had checked and rechecked that the 662 watertight compartments were buttoned up tight, with every hatch and door and scuttle not used to fight dogged down solidly. Now they sat on the steel decks of passageways and small compartments with their tools and apparatus around them in the dim red battle light, and waited for the clang and the blast that would give them something to do.

It came at 11:17. John Crommelin, standing life-jacketed and helmeted on the open bridge and watching the incoming dive bombers with professional detachment, suddenly announced, "I think that son-of-a-bitch is going to get us." The 550-pound bomb ripped through the forward overhang of the flight deck just to port of the center line, was in the clear again for some fifteen feet, went through the fo'c'sle deck and then left the ship again through her port side. Its delayed-action fuse, intended to fire in the vitals of the ship, detonated it in the open air just above the ocean surface and close to the port bow. Fragments sprayed the side of the ship, leaving jagged holes of all sizes from a quarter of an inch to a foot. A Dauntless parked on the starboard bow was blown overboard. With it to his death went Sam Davis Presley, a first-class aviation machinist's mate, manning the twin 30s in the rear seat.

Another man was killed and several wounded in the Radio Direction Finder Room. A tank was flooded with salt water. A small fire licked the edges of the hole in the flight deck and others burned below in the holds. Another SBD caught fire and gasoline ran from its pierced wing tanks to feed the flames. Machinist Bill Fluitt, the gasoline officer, charged forward on the flight deck, yelling and getting help as he ran. He took down the guard rails and, as the attack went on and enemy gunners swept the deck with machine-gun fire, pushed the burning plane and its rapidly baking 500-pound bomb overboard.

Ralph Baker, a first-class photographer's mate, calmly taking pictures of the action on the forward edge of the flight deck, had his left index finger severed and his camera deeply dented by a bomb fragment as he held it a few inches from his head.

In the same minute, another bomb hit just aft of the forward elevator in the middle of the flight deck and broke in half. Part exploded in the hangar deck, destroying two spare planes lashed to the overhead and five more below them. The nose half went through two more decks and detonated in the officers' quarters where Repair Party Number Two was stationed. Repair Two was wiped out. So was the medical party which had been manning the battle dressing station there. Forty men were blown apart or fatally seared by the blast. Stubborn fires flared up in bedding, clothing and the personal effects of the officers whose quarters had been demolished. Light, power and communication lines were cut. The fire mains were damaged. Salt water from the ruptured mains mixed with blood and oil. Pieces of men, internal and external, slid back and forth as the ship heeled, and the choking smoke poured into the hangar deck and out through the small neat hole above. From forward and aft Herschel Smith's damage control parties closed in on the flaming shambles.

Of the six men in the handling room crew adjacent to Repair Two, four were killed. The other two were knocked out by the blast and came to in the dark, smoke-filled wreckage littered with the torn bodies of their shipmates. Jim Bagwell, a third-class gunner's mate, groped his way, only half alive, through the flames to where a shattered hatch let in light from the hangar deck above. As he started painfully up the short vertical ladder, William Pinckney, a third-class officers' cook and the only other survivor, found the same hatch. In the first seconds after the bomb, the burnt area was worse than any imaginable inferno. Flames towered out of the smoke that burned the eyes and lungs. There were dark holes where the steel deck had been. Even a half-conscious man could smell gasoline enough to blow the whole deck again any second.

Carefully, little colored Bill Pinckney helped Bagwell up the ladder, but when the gunner's mate got his hands on the hatch combing at the top he yelled sharply with pain and fell back to the deck unconscious. With fires above and below, the hangar deck hatch was hot enough to sear the flesh. Nearly blind with smoke and barely able to breathe, still in shock and his ears ringing from the bomb blast a few feet away a few seconds ago, Pinckney picked Bagwell up and lifted him through the hatch to safety before he climbed the ladder himself.

The battle did not stop to let *Enterprise* dress her wounds. The chain of Vals still unwound down the sky, each link lashing viciously as it flashed overhead. *Sho* and *Zui*'s pilots could see the holes and the smoke and they were eager to complete the kill. Their bombs threw tons of water on the Big E's deck, knocking her men from their feet, throwing the guns out of position. The bullets of their gunners searched her decks and gun positions. On their five-inch, 40s, 1.1s and 20s the Big E's men steadily and angrily returned the fire. And *South Dakota* supported them with a beautiful seamanship which kept her close, and a constant, effective fire from a hundred guns.

Japanese aircraft fell out of the sky at the rate of one to every two bombs dropped. At a single instant three were visible from the Big E's bridge, bright flares streaking black smoke down toward the sea. The cost was high, but just one bomb might finish the only carrier the Americans had left and give Guadalcanal back to the Emperor.

At nineteen minutes after eleven there was a muffled explosion aft of the island on the starboard side and almost every man standing on his feet aboard the *Enterprise* was knocked to her deck. The wounded, driven ship shook the full length of her eight hundred feet so violently that any given point whipped up and down through a foot and a half, every second for several seconds. Machinery and equipment were flicked from their foundations. With the carrier turning hard to port, the flight deck slanted to starboard, and each time it whipped, the parked planes rose in the air and banged down nearer the starboard side. The farthest SBD forward and to starboard went overboard; a little farther aft another landed in the gun gallery. Tools and equipment secured to the overhead crashed down onto the hangar deck. Mercury spilled from the big master gyros. The entire foremast rotated one-half inch in its socket, throwing out of alignment all the complex antennas mounted on it. The after-bearing pedestal on one of the high-pressure steam turbines which drive the ship was cracked. A fuel tank was opened to the sea and *Enterprise* began to leave a broad trail of oil for the enemy to follow. Two empty fuel tanks were flooded and she listed a little to starboard. At 11:20 the attack appeared to be over.

Loading crews cleared the hot piles of empty casings from around the guns. Some of the 40-millimeter crews, working fast, changed barrels; the used barrels hissed briefly in the cooling tanks.

On the bridge Captain Hardison stood close to his talker, receiving reports of damage and corrective action being taken from Herschel Smith and George Over in Central Station. He quickly granted permission to counterflood as necessary to take the list off the ship and frowned at news of the heavy casualties in Repair Two.

Admiral Kinkaid hunched over his chart in Flag Plot with his staff and listened to radio reports of the attempts being made to save the *Hornet*. Admiral George Murray was shifting his flag to the cruiser *Pensacola* since radio communications no longer existed in *Hornet*. *Northampton* was attempting to take her in tow.

Enterprise was showing less smoke as the fire-fighting crews from forward and aft converged on the fires around Number One elevator. Her propulsion machinery, except for the cracked bearing pedestal, was undamaged and she maintained a steady 27 knots. But in the battle dressing stations, Commander John Owsley, the senior medical officer, Chief Pharmacist's Mate Adair and other medical personnel worked steadily against pain and loss of blood and death, injecting drugs, applying tourniquets and splints, dressing burns, suturing wounds, amputating shredded limbs.

And down on the first platform deck ten men were trapped in the five-inch ammunition handling rooms for the forward guns. The only way out was through the access trunk directly above which now was eight feet deep with salt water from the hoses which battled the fires overhead. One of the men trapped was little twenty-year-old Vicente Sablan of Guam, who at Pearl Harbor had known the Japanese to be "very bad and tricky. But we Americans too smart. We catch him and give him hell." Sablan had grown much older in the ten months since those words were spoken and most of his aging had been to the sound of the remote hammering of the guns on deck and the huge booming of near misses in the deep handling room where he was now sealed with nine other men, three Caucasian, four Negro and two Filipino.

At 11:27 a lookout reported a periscope off the starboard beam, and the Big E leaned hard to put her stern to it before it was identified as a porpoise.

At 11:44 another periscope was reported in the same position but there was no time to maneuver. Fifteen torpedo planes were boring in from both bows to catch the *Enterprise* as they had done the *Hornet,* whichever way she turned.

Admiral Nagumo had launched these torpedo planes with his dive bombers from *Sho* and *Zui.* They were to attack at the same time, dividing the fire of defending guns and complicating almost hopelessly the problem of evasion. But they had arrived half an hour after the bombers, and now it was the guns of the task force against the shining Kates, flat on the water, holding their torpedoes for close-in drops.

The regularly spaced black five-inch bursts building neat rows close to the surface flamed one plane five miles out. Briefly the spray rose above the greasy smoke where he went in. Captain Hardison held his ship on course, waiting for the AA to take effect, waiting to see which group of planes dropped their torpedoes first. On either bow the destroyers increased speed with chuffs of smoke to take position between the carrier and her enemy and take the torpedoes themselves if necessary. The guns were trained horizontally and there was no problem of loading at high-elevation angles or squinting into the bright sky. The tracers skimmed straight and flat to meet the planes. Three miles out a Kate on the port bow pulled up suddenly, rolled inverted and crashed. Two more came apart and skidded in as the 20-millimeters opened up at two miles. Then, in quick succession the five remaining Kates on the starboard bow made their drops and turned away. Captain Hardison looked quickly to port; four more were coming in but had not yet released. To starboard and a little ahead now he could see the parallel wakes of three torpedoes close together and moving fast, the middle one slightly ahead. It was a beautiful drop and if the Big E continued on course they would hit her amidships and rip out her insides. For a second the bridge watch was silent, poised. The quartermaster at the helm, the seaman at the engine order telegraph, the officer of the deck, waited for the skipper's command. At the end of that long second it came.

"Right full rudder."

"Right full rudder, sir!"

The helmsman spun his wheel, pulling over the top and down hard with his right hand, letting it carry around to the bottom, then reaching up for another hold, getting his back into it, bending his knees a little with each downward pull. The gray pointer slid down the right side of the rudder angle indicator mounted by the wheel until it stopped at 35 degrees right. Back in the steering engine room the starboard ram was all the way aft, the full gleaming length of the port ram exposed. The three-story rudder with its top ten feet below the hull was angled far out to starboard and the wash of the starboard screws poured onto it, increasing its effect. The Big E's stern began to slide across the sea to the left, and slowly the bow came right toward the bubbling echelon of the torpedo tracks, as though to meet them. The flight deck with its smoldering holes leaned down to port and, having done all that could be done, Captain Hardison stood on the port wing of the bridge to witness its success or failure. Admiral Kinkaid came silently to stand beside him.

Now there were only a few hundred yards separating *Enterprise* and the three bubbling lines on the sea's surface. They seemed to increase speed as the bow swung onto them

and then from the bridge they were out of sight under the
port overhang of the turning deck as the captain ordered:
"Rudder amidships" and the quartermaster spun the wheel
down to port. The Big E straightened up from her turn and
the three torpedoes, running straight and true, passed ten
yards down her portside, parallel, at 40 knots.

Enterprise, safe for the moment from the most threatening of the torpedoes launched against her, was now headed straight for the destroyer *Smith,* which already had
enough trouble without being run down by a carrier. An
enemy torpedo plane, smoking and barely under control after tangling with a pair of Wildcats, had flown straight into
her forward gun mount. Flames shot up higher than her
mast, engulfing her bridge and superstructure, and as they
were beginning to recede the Kate's torpedo had baked off
with a roar, making everything forward of the stack untenable. Somehow, the destroyer had stayed on course and
at fleet speed, and her after guns continued to hammer
away protectingly at the planes attacking *Enterprise.*

Captain Hardison came left again and cleared the *Smith,*
which dropped back and then moved up astern of *South
Dakota* and buried her burning bow in the high wake of the
battlewagon. In another few minutes her fires were out and
her skipper returned to the bridge and resumed his duties
in the screen.

But *Enterprise* was still in trouble. Another torpedo was
sighted on the starboard bow. There was no room this time
to turn inside it. It was too close and too fast. The bow was
already across the torpedo course. Once again Captain
Hardison came hard right, and the Big E's stern skidded
clear to port as the "fish" passed thirty yards to starboard.
A half-mile farther up the fading torpedo wake, *Enterprise*
plunged past the wreckage of the Kate that had dropped it.
From the debris two half-drowned oriental faces looked up
in hatred.

From dead astern now five more Kates, fast and low on
the water, maneuvered for attack position. Like Gene Lindsey attacking the *Kaga* at Midway, but with far faster aircraft, the Japanese pilots swung wide for a shot at the Big
E's port beam. Like the *Kaga's* late commanding officer,
Osborne Hardison kept swinging to starboard, presenting
only his narrow stern as a target while the task force guns
blasted steadily at the circling torpedo planes. And, as it
had been at Midway, the tactic was successful. Within a

mile of *Enterprise,* three were shot down in rapid succession by the storm of 20-millimeter fire from every gun in the force that would bear. The fourth, nearly at dropping point, pulled up sharply, releasing his torpedo in a climbing turn, then continued in a diving left bank to the sea. The fifth made a good drop from nearly dead astern and Captain Hardison paralleled the torpedo attack and watched it pass his ship to port.

There would have been eleven more to deal with if it had not been for Lieutenant Vejtasa.

Swede Vejtasa was the leader of a division of four F4Fs launched at 9:00 A.M. to augment the twelve Wildcats already on Combat Air Patrol and to intercept the enemy dive bombers. With him were Lieutenants Harris and Ruehlow and Ensign Leder. Although caught underneath the incoming raid, Vejtasa, by climbing hard and shooting well, was able to knock down a Val before it could begin its dive on the *Hornet.* Since he was too late and too low to intercept the other bombers, he led his division in an attack on two which had completed their drops and were retiring. Both flamed and fell off into the sea. For a long time, under orders from the FDO, Vejtasa's flight circled at 10,000 feet searching the sea for torpedo planes, while more dive bombers came in overhead to attack *Enterprise.*

Shortly before noon, Swede heard the FDO order another flight of fighters out to the northwest and led his own in the same direction. Just as the FDO warned that the incoming aircraft might be friendly search planes returning, he made out eleven dark-green, shiny Kates below in a stepped-up column of three-plane Vs with a two-plane section at the rear. Ruehlow and Leder, after a brush with a pair of Zeros, had spotted the Kates and were already attacking. With Harris close on his wing, Vejtasa pushed over in a steep, fast, high side attack. The enemy torpedo planes were already close and slanting in at 250 knots to make their runs on *Enterprise.* On their first pass Vejtasa and Harris each set a Kate explosively afire, then used their speed to overtake one of the three-plane Vs just as it entered a large cumulus. In the turbulent gray belly of the cloud Harris and Vejtasa became separated but Swede did not lose the enemy. He was angry at the misdirection of the FDO and the chances lost all morning but he was clear and cold in his head. The Wildcat in his hands felt like the smooth stock and grip and trigger of a familiar rifle. And he was careful and absolutely accurate. He began with the left-hand plane of the V. He flew in close, directly astern and blew him up with two short bursts of his six guns. Methodically, Vejtasa kicked rudder and slid his Wildcat to the right in behind the leader. His first burst brought the Kate's rudder soaring up and over his head, his second as the enemy began to yaw set him on fire and he fell away in a spiral to the left. In the cloud the tracers glowed like accelerated Roman candles. Still in the gray damp of the cloud, Vejtasa eased over behind the remaining enemy who began a shallow right turn. Swede's six guns raked it from engine back to tail in a single long rattle of bullets and it flamed violently and nosed abruptly downward.

In the shredding fog above him and to the left, Vejtasa saw the shadow of another Kate and he pulled up hard in a low side run but failed to knock him down. He followed him out of the cloud where the task force AA at once took over. Swede could see the enemy was too high and too fast for an effective drop and let the AA have him. It was this plane that crashed the *Smith*.

Vejtasa circled at 3,000 feet outside the ring of destroyers and with the last of his ammunition shot down a fifth torpedo plane as it was attempting to retire low on the water after its run.

Thus did Swede Vejtasa, on a single combat flight, shoot down two enemy dive bombers and five torpedo planes with one more probable. Out of the eleven Kates which he discovered deploying for an attack on his ship, he personally destroyed five and led his wingman on a run that accounted for a sixth. Three others jettisoned their torpedoes and fled and it was the opinion of Vejtasa's commanding officer, Jim Flatley, that "the other two were so demoralized that they were ineffective."

Captain Hardison, by clear, fast thinking and flawless timing, had evaded nine torpedoes dropped with the same determined skill as those which had just reduced *Hornet* to a drifting hulk. It is improbable that without Swede Vejtasa's help he could have evaded eleven more.

At noon, under the low broken clouds, *Enterprise* was making 27 knots at the center of her bristling task group. *South Dakota*, still on her starboard quarter, could see she was down by the bow. Black smoke streamed aft from the holes in her flight deck. Within a radius of twenty miles, almost her entire air group circled in small formations or singly, low on fuel and ammunition, waiting to come aboard. *Hornet*'s successful strike, having laid *Shokaku* open like a sardine can, had only the Big E's damaged deck on which to land. But *Enterprise* could receive no planes on her holed and smoldering deck, with the raw ulcer of bomb damage below and bogies still showing on her scopes. With her guns trained out and ready, her radars and binoculars searching the sea and the sky, she concentrated on repairing her damage and saving the lives of her men.

The second bomb had ruptured three decks just aft of Number One elevator on the Big E's center line. A tangle of broken planes was burning in the hangar deck and flaming gasoline had run down into the forward elevator pit. On two decks staterooms, washrooms, dressing stations, gear lockers and ammunition handling-rooms were demolished. Flames licked at severed electrical cables, wrecked equipment and steel rubble in the smoking darkness. Doors and hatches were blown open, decks and bulkheads blasted out of shape, piping slashed, machinery scored and riddled. And below the worst of the damage, in the ammunition handling-room for the forward five-inch guns, were Sablan and his nine mates. Aft of them were the five-inch powder magazines, on both sides narrow void spaces separating them from fuel tanks and, on the other side of a solid, watertight bulkhead forward of them, workshops and elevator machinery. Below them was aviation gasoline and above were smoldering storerooms directly under the bomb explosion point. There was only one access to them, a vertical trunk leading up through the storerooms to the wrecked living quarters. There was a firmly closed watertight hatch in the trunk on the overhead of their compartment. A similar hatch directly above in the deck of the demolished living space had been blown off by the bomb. The trunk was eight feet deep in salt water and chemical foam from the fire fighting above and clogged with wreckage and parts of bodies. There was no light and dangerously little air. The battle telephone was dead. Paul Petersen, electrician's mate second class, was senior petty officer in charge. With him were Carl Johnson (another electrician's mate), five officers' cooks—Bagsby, Richardson, Cordon, Taijeron and Sablan—two mess attendants—Ramentas and Howard—and Schwarb, a seaman. There was no panic, or hysteria. Petersen conserved the batteries in his battle lanterns and told his men to remain quiet in order to use a

minimum of the valuable air. One man kept on the headset
of the silent phones, hoping that they would come alive
again. Overhead they could hear the encouraging sounds of
the fire fighting. The two electricians knew how the ship
was organized for damage control and that if she survived
the action they would be rescued. The ten men waited in
the dark.

In Central Station, Herschel Smith and George Over
marked the damaged area on their big schematics and received reports from fire-fighting and repair parties. A few
minutes after the explosion scores of men were at work to
minimize its effect.

The combined labor of the repair parties began to show
below decks. The fires went out under salt water and
foamite, and blowers were rigged to suck out the smoke
and provide fresh air. The wounded were taken out and
emergency lighting strung. The battle telephone connections
were repaired and Chief Forrest got in touch with Petersen
below.

"For Christ's sake," he told him, "don't open that hatch.
There's eight feet of water on top of it. Just relax and we'll
get you out, but it's going to take a little while."

At a quarter past twelve John Crommelin began to take
aboard his planes, holes or no holes, damaged or not. Back
on the port corner of the deck Robin Lindsey signaled them
in with his eloquent paddles. No LSO ever had more difficult conditions. Many planes were damaged and not under
full control. Number Two elevator was temporarily stuck
in the down position, leaving a huge square hole in the deck
less than three hundred feet from the stern. With continuous reports of bogies and periscopes coming in, *Enterprise*
twisted under the low clouds, her deck heeling each time
the rudder was put over. To the incoming pilots the narrow, smoking, shifting deck with a yawning pit in the landing area looked impossible. But they remembered Lindsey's
competence and their empty tanks and grimly came on in.
One after another, answering Lindsey's signals, they snarled
in over the wake and dropped onto the extreme stern. The
arresting cables pulled out reluctantly and stopped each
plane aft of the stuck elevator. Then with a roar of throttle
they taxied around the hole and forward out of the way.

Only a few pilots got aboard before a third attack came
in. The others rolled up their wheels and banked away as
the task force guns opened up at 12:21.

Twenty more of Nagumo's dive bombers slashed at the Big E, dropping suddenly out of the cloud bases in 45-degree dives. The fat clouds sheltered them at first from the searching gunfire but, when they broke out, their shallow dives were terribly vulnerable. The Big E's seasoned, angry gunners chopped down eight and riddled others so that they dropped short and turned away. Robin Lindsey threw down his paddles and jumped into the rear seat of an SBD he had just landed to empty its remaining ammunition into the attackers. Near misses threw up their familiar waterspouts around the ship. With *Enterprise* leaning hard to port in a tight starboard turn, one bomb glanced off her exposed starboard side below the water line and detonated eight feet away and fifteen feet below the surface, dishing in her side and flooding two void spaces through breaks in the skin. The ship lashed throughout her length, her decks again whipping a full foot for several seconds. Number One elevator jammed in the up position. The damage control-men sweating under jury lights on the third deck were knocked sprawling into the blood and oil and torn metal underfoot. Petersen, Sablan and the others tensed in their dark hole where water, leaking down through broken vent trunks, was by now nearly up to their waists.

Some two hundred feet above the sealed-off, slowly flooding handling-room, the whiplashing near misses and enemy strafing had so damaged the Big E's main antenna that her search radar was blinded. Without her radar, *Enterprise* could see only as far as the eyes of her lookouts, which were thwarted by clouds, haze, dazzling sunlight and shadow. She was helpless to control her fighters. Lieutenant Brad Williams was the radar officer, in fact the first in the U. S. Navy, to be so designated. More even than his admiral or his skipper, Williams knew the capabilities of his equipment and the odds against the survival of a radar-blinded ship under those enemy-infested skies. He climbed the mast with a loaded toolbox and went to work at the highest and most exposed point on the ship while Captain Hardison and his gunners fought off the enemy planes. The painted metal under his hands was granular with salt and sooty with stack gas and he had to hold strongly to it with one hand while trying to repair the antenna and its drive motor with the other. It was not a singlehanded job and Williams finally had to lash himself to the antenna and work with both. If he noticed the continued strafing or the near misses or the violent swinging of the radar platform as the Big E leaned into her turns, no one below could tell it. He could almost look down into the five-inch muzzles that were answering the strafing of the Vals and feel the heat when they fired. The 40s and 20s along the deck edge barked steadily and their tracers soared past him to meet the enemy. The bomb that glanced off the Big E's starboard side missed him so closely that for a moment, as he looked up, its blunt torpedo shape was foreshortened to a ball. The bomb's blast destroyed his hearing for weeks and would have knocked him off the mast but for his lashings. Working hard and fast, hampered by bolts jammed with paint and salt corrosion, Williams finished the job. In the radar room below it was evident that *Enterprise* would see again. Eager to get back into operation, a technician switched on the antenna training motor and Brad Williams revolved a dozen times at the masthead, his angry shouts swamped by the voices of the guns, until an officer on the bridge noticed that his majestic sweeps around the horizon were apparently unintentional.

There were perhaps three minutes of tense and busy silence for the men topside and of relative relief for the sailors trapped in the darkness below before the repaired radar picked up another strike inbound. Coached on by radar, the high-power telescopes of the forward range-finder found it seventeen and a half miles away at 17,000 feet. There were fifteen Vals in two groups with an escort of nine Zeros above. After nearly two and a half hours of attack and the threat of attack, the defending Wildcats were out of ammunition and low on fuel. Now it was up to Orlin Livdahl's gunners and their determined supporters on *South Dakota* and the other ships of the force.

At eleven miles, still only high flecks of sunlight in the sky, the enemy raid disappeared behind a rain cloud. For two minutes the many barrels swung silently and the thousands of young eyes stared upward, trying to penetrate the clouds and outstare the glaring sun. Then the Vals were overhead, steep in their dives, and the guns blasted into action again. By this hour of the early afternoon, the kids who gripped the wide handle bars of the 20-millimeters and peered through cartwheel sights to follow the tracer flight, and the ones who sat in the farm-tractor seats of the 40s rotating with their humming mounts, were true veterans. They had seen that their weapons could kill the enemy before he could kill them, and seen too the bloody damage of the bombs. Now they were cool and steady and Orlin Livdahl's careful training was paying off. Glancing up, most of them could see him high in the island at Sky Control—exposed, calm, deliberate, completely competent. As the Vals strung down for the third time that day, Livdahl's tracers rose to meet them, shifting and converging steadily with no breaks as the loading crews worked smoothly and the well-kept guns had few jams or failures. Battery officers shifted targets to take the most threatening enemy under the heaviest fire. Chief Turret Captain Willson alone probably saved the Big E from serious damage when he directed his five-inch mount against a dive bomber which had already missed but was turning back to crash on board.

In *South Dakota* a bomb detonated on top of the forward turret, which was so well armored that most of the gun crew didn't know of the hit, but a fragment seriously wounded the battlewagon's skipper and steering control was shifted to the executive officer aft, who for a moment had no communication with the helm. Big, fast, heavy *South Dakota,* so magnificently handled throughout the battle, headed straight for *Enterprise,* and Captain Hardison turned away just in time.

San Juan took a heavy bomb that went through all her light decking and out through her bottom before it exploded. The blast shook the fast but fragile cruiser so fiercely that circuit breakers protecting her steering mechanism popped and she too lost control of her rudder in a high-speed starboard turn. The ships of the task group saved themselves by scattering until she regained control.

At 12:45 P.M. radar finally showed a sky clear of the enemy and *Enterprise* began again to take aboard her planes. Fighters and dive bombers were given precedence over the longer-legged Avengers but even so there were many ditchings. The pilots who survived the skips and dragging splashes had plenty of time to get out their rafts while the planes floated nose down, held up for a while by the empty fuel cells in the wings. The destroyers were kept busy with rescue work.

Number One elevator, the farthest forward, seemed permanently jammed. With planes landing over the other two, it was impossible to strike any below, and by four o'clock the Big E's long deck was so jammed with *Enter-*

prise and *Hornet* aircraft that Robin Lindsey could bring no more aboard. Slim Townsend's flight-deck crew, after the long morning of work and action, fell to again. By lowering planes on the after elevators, and launching thirteen Dauntlesses for Espiritu, they made enough room to get the last air-borne Avenger aboard.

It seemed that the enemy had made his last attack. Probably he had little left to launch. He had lost 100 planes in the attacks on *Enterprise* and *Hornet* and in the defense of his own ships. Two of his carriers were out of action. More planes must have gone down from fuel exhaustion and accidents.

Admiral Yamamoto ordered his carriers to retire to the northwest and sent fast surface forces in for a night attack. But Kinkaid, with ten months of experience with the Japanese, outguessed him and pulled off to the south. The enemy destroyers found only the burning, listing derelict that had been the *Hornet* and quickly sent her on her long tumble to the bottom.

The battle was over and Guadalcanal was safe for a while. There would be at least a few more days to reinforce and prepare for the inevitable next assault. Only one other warship in history had survived such a sustained air attack—the HMS *Illustrious* in her battle with the Luftwaffe in the Mediterranean. And it too was delivered by obsolescent prewar dive bombers (Stukas) with fixed landing gear. Now it was the Big E's duty to rescue her men, repair her damage and be ready for action as soon as possible.

While the flight-deck crew was jamming on board the desperate, empty planes, Herschel Smith's repair parties were pumping and bailing, splicing and shoring below. It was after 5:00 P.M. when the narrow escape trunk over Petersen's trapped handling-room crew was empty enough to get them out. On a hatch cover two decks above, Chief Forrest had a neat pile of human bones and limbs removed from the flooded trunk. He called Petersen on the battle phones:

"You guys can open that hatch now but there's still some water and crap on top of it. Open it fast and come out fast and you'll be OK."

Petersen's boys did just that. They came up out of the trunk soaked and blinking under the emergency lights, but with the alacrity of Olympic rope climbers.

At three minutes before eight, after thirteen hours and forty-seven minutes, the men of *Enterprise* left their battle stations. For most there was a hot meal, but battle damage had reduced the supply of fresh water so that a quick wipe and a pat had to do for a bath. For the Construction and Repair Department there was no rest that night or the next day. Throughout the ship they worked to restore lights, power, water pressure and all the services essential to running a carrier.

And 250 miles northwest Ensign Dusty Rhodes sloshed in the dark sea in his limp life raft, with most of the enemy fleet between him and *Enterprise,* and paddled spasmodically in a direction which he hoped was toward Santa Cruz. As soon as he had broken the surface after his plunge of the morning, Dusty had pulled the toggles on his Mae West. One side did nothing, the other puffed up briefly and then went flat. Treading water, Dusty laboriously blew up the jacket by lung power. Fortunately, husky, deep-chested Dusty had plenty of that. Then for the first time he had noticed his leg wound and could see his blood ribboning into the water below him. Blood, he knew very well, was a powerful attractor of sharks and he was most anxious not to have anything hanging down into the sea to tempt them. He reached around, zipped the pararaft out of its package and jerked the inflation toggle. It whuffed out beautifully into shape and then, like the Mae West, went slowly flat again. He grabbed for the attached hand pump and it pulled off in his hand. Close to panic but aware of it and holding himself under tight control, he found the raft's oral inflation tube and blew with desperate energy for several minutes before he noticed a bullet hole in the yellow rubber and realized there must be several more.

When a bullet is fired through a packaged pararaft, it is like punching a hole in a folded piece of paper. When the paper or the raft is unfolded, there are many holes. Dusty had six. But he had to get that bleeding leg up out of the water. Attached to the pararaft was a kit for such emergencies, containing what amounted to blow-out patches and two small rubber plugs.

Supported only by his Mae West, hundreds of miles out in the South Pacific, Dusty was working with his knife and the patching kit, when the three Zeros which had been chasing Chip Reding came back into sight. The one which

had been smoking was now smoking badly and, while
Rhodes watched, it went into a long glide and ripped a line
of spray up out of the sea several miles away. Dusty prepared to slip out of his Mae West and surface dive to avoid
being strafed by the other two, but they continued on and
disappeared to the northward.

When he had patched all the holes as best he could,
Dusty orally blew the raft up again and it held enough air
for him to struggle aboard, flopping in on his stomach over
the low end and then rolling over to half sit, half lie, face
up. At best he could only inflate the raft to about three-
quarters of its designed capacity and there was always several inches of water where he sat, but he got his arms and
his bleeding leg up out of the sea.

Every twenty minutes it was necessary to blow some
more air into the raft to replace that which continually
leaked out around his patches and to do so meant reaching
down over the side for the inflation tube. Rhodes' equipment consisted of his hunting knife in its sheath sewn to the
lower leg of his flight suit and a .45-caliber automatic pis-
tol in a holster on a web belt around his waist. The .45 was
at all times under water and by noon had already acquired
a thin coat of rust, but Dusty test-fired it and it worked,
surprising him so that he nearly rolled out of the raft.

He was sitting there taking stock of his resources and
wondering how long it would be before he was picked up,
when he heard and then saw the TBFs, SBDs and F4Fs of
the strike group he had been escorting as they returned to
the *Enterprise*. While he waved and shouted and whistled
in his anxiety to attract their attention, he counted them
and noted they were all present, none had been lost over
the target. When the sound of their engines had died out to
the south, Dusty was much more alone on that empty sea
than he had been before.

He stayed alone all that long, hot afternoon while *Enterprise* was fighting for her life, splashing water on his fair
skin to cool it and three times every hour blowing up the
raft. Occasionally, for a minute or two, a white puff of
cloud sliding northwest on the light breeze threw its shadow over the tiny human figure drifting in its faulty pneumatic doughnut on the empty face of the sea. For those
few minutes it was cool and the air felt soft and pleasant.
Then the equatorial sun came back to sear the flesh and
the breeze could not be felt. By nightfall Dusty's mouth

was sore from the inflation tube and his left leg stiff from the knick of the bullet, and he had had a lot of time to think. He thought especially of John Leppla, hoping he had somehow survived and remembering that Lep had had a hunch about this battle. He had heard Lep say that he felt he had used up his quota of luck and didn't really expect to come back this time. Lep had even written a last note home.

The tropic night after the Battle of Santa Cruz was endless. Dusty could not just sit any longer and, although he was unsure of direction and half waiting for the dawn to show in the east, with the small paddles strapped to his wrists he rowed in a direction he hoped was south, for Santa Cruz, stopping every twenty minutes to blow into the inflation tube.

When the sun finally broke the horizon, it was an angry red ball that flushed the cumulus puffs with pink and was already hot on Rhodes' salt-caked face and the exposed flesh at wrists and ankles which the shrinking flight suit had exposed. Early in the day he made out formations of planes far away which he thought were F4Fs of the task force CAP. Then nothing. Nothing but sea and sky and sun and an occasional blessed cloud.

In midafternoon the breeze died out to a few random breaths and the sea was silent except for a soft sloshing in and around the raft. It was nearly time to blow it up again. Dusty heard a small noise behind him, like the tentative squeak of a frog, just enough sound to attract his attention, and, turning, he found that the sharks had come. There were three, lying just beneath the surface, parallel, their dorsal fins exposed, like three torpedoes in an invisible triple mount, ready for launching. The nearest was so close Dusty could have touched its nose. His mouth dry, he was afraid to move. His mind kept shouting that only a couple of layers of rubber-coated fabric separated his flesh from the jaws he couldn't see but could imagine too well. Desperately he ignored the shouting. Moving slowly and steadily, his eye on the long gray shapes so close aboard, he got out his knife and laid it ready on his lap, then reached into the warm water he sat in for the .45, cocked it and held it sighted on the head of the nearest shark. The ugly devils might get him, but not easily.

As he sat with knife and gun motionless except for the rocking of the raft in the gentle sea, he could feel its increasing limpness as the air continued to escape, but to inflate it required reaching into the sea two feet from the nearest shark for the inflation tube. The minutes grated by and Dusty's nerves stretched under the malevolent patience of the three unmoving shapes. Five, ten, fifteen minutes. He had to prop his elbows on his knees as the .45 grew heavy and he sagged deeper in the sea and more and more water spilled over inside the raft. Then, as though stupidly giving up the game, the far shark turned and swam away, and the others followed, their dorsals cutting the sea in zigzags and then disappearing completely. Limp and sweating heavily, Rhodes reached overboard, found the tube and with rapid breaths reinflated the raft and scooped the excess water out.

Late in the afternoon a line of tiny masts appeared and drew slowly northward along the eastern horizon. Dusty fired the rusty .45 into the air, took off his white T shirt and waved it with a methodical careful rhythm so as to continue a long time. The distant sticks moved steadily along the rim of Dusty's watery world. After a time one seemed to have stopped its lateral movement and to be approaching. A stack and then a superstructure appeared above the horizon, then a gun mount. It was a destroyer coming bows on and fast. Rhodes could see the white water slide up her thin bow, curl over and fall back. Vigorously Dusty paddled to put himself as close as possible to her course. Finally, there was no doubt that the destroyermen had seen him and rescue was only minutes away. The ship slowed, reversing, the water boiling at her stern, but she overshot and had to back down. Dusty paddled up to the sheer, steel wall, rising and falling on the swell at its foot, and a rope was flung down to him. He grabbed it solidly with both hands and tried to heave himself up, but he was too weak and the ship's wet metal side too slick. The raft was carried away by the crew current and he fell back into the sea. Holding to the rope Dusty for the first time looked up at the men on deck, his mouth open to shout for a net to climb or a sling to get into. Far above, the rail was lined with faces, and they were all Japanese.

On the thirtieth of October, three days after Dusty Rhodes' "rescue," the Big E let go her anchor in the hill-rimmed tropical harbor of Noumea, New Caledonia, with the small white replica of Notre Dame de Paris at its head. The sweet warm earth smell blew softly over her, clearing the fuel fumes out of the hangar deck, and was picked up by the blowers and distributed below.

13 THE SLOT

In November of 1942, Japan and the United States were irrevocably committed by their basic strategies and by the lives and equipment already expended to the conquest of the island of Guadalcanal. After the bloody draw of Santa Cruz which had been a U. S. victory only because it had for the moment thwarted a Japanese attempt at recapture, both sides made plans to build up their own forces and cut off reinforcements to the enemy. The Japanese had seen the inadequacy of landing small contingents of troops by night which could be chewed up by the Marines before an effective force was assembled. This time some 13,000 soldiers in eleven transports awaited Yamamoto's order to head down the Slot. While they waited the small nightly landings continued.

Bill Halsey was not a man to tolerate a tie. As he saw it, he had three jobs to do:

(1) Get enough supplies and reinforcements to Guadalcanal to assure conquest of the island.

(2) Prevent the Japanese from landing reinforcements.

(3) Destroy as many enemy ships and kill as many Japanese as possible in the process.

On November 7 a destroyer unloaded ninety tons of ammunition for the Marines. Seven transports with 6,000 troops aboard were loaded at Espiritu and Noumea, and by the ninth all were under way for Guadalcanal.

The enemy was slower. His eleven transports escorted by eleven destroyers sailed the evening of the twelfth from Faisi in the Shortlands.

The thin-skinned transports of both nations needed protection. The soldiers and Marines jamming their decks would be potent and deadly once they were deployed ashore with their equipment, but at sea they were only defenseless and fragile cargoes of flesh and blood.

From U. S. bases in the islands to the southeast, and from enemy harbors in the Carolines and the Shortlands, the armed and armored men of war moved in to furnish

that protection. Available to Halsey were two fast battleships and eight cruisers with sufficient destroyers to screen
and escort them. His only carrier, *Enterprise*, lay at anchor
in Noumea desperately trying to repair the bomb damage
of Santa Cruz. Yamamoto was in better shape. At his command were two light carriers, five battleships and ten cruisers with their supporting destroyers.

Submarines from both sides prowled along the approach
and retirement courses of their enemies and land-based aircraft from Espiritu overlapped others from Rabaul. Henderson Field itself, the objective, buzzed with Army, Navy
and Marine Corps planes and was, in effect, a fixed but
unsinkable carrier.

After Santa Cruz the Big E returned to her anchorage
in the harbor of Noumea. The soft wind blew down from
the double row of mountains protecting the bay, and the
town at its head dozed in the tropic sun as though there
had never been a war. But aboard the carrier lights burned
all night and there was no respite from the chatter of pneumatic hammers and the spark and sputter of the welders'
arcs. Some sixty officers and men from the repair ship
Vulcan and a battalion of Sea Bees labored with Herschel
Smith's Construction and Repair Department around the
clock.

The air group lived ashore at the grass field of Tontouta.
The men bathed in a river a mile down a dirt road and if
a truck or a jeep went by as they were returning, they arrived at the field as dirty as when they left. During the day
the Dauntlesses bounced over the uneven grass strip and
into the air, checking out the pilots of a Marine bombing
squadron en route to Guadalcanal. In the evenings the men
of the air group hiked, hitched and jeeped into Noumea.
Some of them made friends among the French and there
were evenings in their pleasant homes, with music and conversation and tasty French food and wine which left the
American airmen sad and uneasy for the years wasted in
war. They tried to look ahead but could see no end. It had
been nearly a year since Pearl Harbor and despite his losses
the enemy seemed as strong as ever. On the blacked-out
road to the airfield after an evening with the happy family
of another man, the war in the Solomons became the ugly
mess it really was and the feeling of loss was heavy.

The *Vulcan*'s repair officer estimated that it would take
three weeks to put the Big E back in operating condition,

but after eleven days Halsey ordered her back into this new war and she sailed for Guadalcanal with Sea Bees and the *Vulcan's* repair crew still hard at work below. With the green coast of New Caledonia stretching away to the northwest, the air group came back aboard and each man had a new appreciation of his clean bunk and the heads and showers of the Big E.

No one knew better than Bill Halsey the value of the Big E to the campaign in the Solomons, and he intended to take care of her, exposing her as little and protecting her as much as possible. She headed for a position southwest of Guadalcanal from which her planes could attack the traffic in the Slot at long range, using Henderson Field as a staging and refuge base. Since SBDs, TBFs and F4Fs were already flying out of Henderson, her aircraft would not give away her presence. On either side of the *Enterprise* steamed the fast new sister battleships, *Washington* and *South Dakota,* with the destroyers forming a semicircle ahead.

The day *Enterprise* sailed for the Canal, three U. S. transports anchored there and unloaded Marine reinforcements. They were attacked by carrier-based Vals. On the twelfth, while Kinkaid's task force was coming up across the Coral Sea, four more transports successfully put Marine and Army troops ashore on Guadalcanal. On the same day the enemy's eleven troopships got under way, and his battleships and cruisers moved in to soften up the island defenses for their arrival. Intelligence reported two enemy carriers operating to the north.

It looked like another Santa Cruz.

Enterprise was not fully recovered from that battle. So far as anyone could tell, the Number One elevator was fixed, but Captain Hardison refused permission to test it. Suppose it were to jam in the down position? The Big E could not fly off a single plane with that deep, square hole across the forward end of her flight deck. That flight deck was the only one left in the Solomons. This meant a slowdown in flight operations. Planes could not be taken below for storage, maintenance or repairs while others were landing. Once landings began, all planes had to remain on deck until the last one was aboard and the two after elevators could be used. There was still a disconcerting bulge in the starboard side of the flight deck at the landing area. Down below, seventy sets of officers' quarters had been destroyed

and the "refugees" were jammed into the tiny staterooms
of the more fortunate. In the blast area of that second
Santa Cruz bomb, watertight integrity did not exist. Flooding in one compartment could spread rapidly through torn
bulkheads and decks and ruptured fittings to half-a-dozen
more. Burning oil or gasoline would act the same way.

At 8:00 A.M. on the morning of Friday the thirteenth,
Enterprise was some 280 miles south of Henderson Field
on Guadalcanal. The dawn search of ten Dauntlesses scouting ten sectors to 200 miles was at maximum range and
turning back with no contacts reported.

At 8:22 the first of nine fully loaded torpedo planes and
six fighters left her deck with orders to report to the commanding general at Henderson for duty. Commander
Crommelin directed the flight to approach Henderson Field
from the west in case there might be some enemy ships in
that direction.

John Crommelin was uneasy about this mission. Reports
coming in to the admiral showed heavy forces, including
carriers, coming down the Slot. The Japanese were obviously throwing everything they had in the South Pacific into a
major effort to retake Guadalcanal. The Big E's fifteen
planes seemed a formation of sparrows sent to kill a tiger.
There was not even any certainty that Henderson Field
would be in U. S. hands when the flight arrived, and if it
were not, neither the carrier's deck nor any other field
would be in range. Crommelin was personally concerned
about every man in each squadron of his air group. Some
thought his eyes were wet when he briefed Torpedo Ten
that morning.

Lieutenant Al Coffin, the CO of Torpedo Ten after Col-
lett's death in the ambush at Santa Cruz, led the TBFs.
Lieutenant John Sutherland commanded the escorting
Wildcats.

The torpedo planes flew at 500 feet, below the bases of
the cumulus, with the fighters a few thousand feet above
on either side. By 10:30 the jungles of Guadal's southern
coast were in sight and the flight swung west. Thirty minutes later, still low on the water, they approached Savo Island and Cape Esperance from that direction, and encountered a Japanese battleship and four destroyers. The enemy
ships were incredibly only ten miles north of Savo and
headed at a dignified pace straight in toward Henderson
Field in broad daylight.

"Scoofer" Coffin's Avengers banked steeply away under full throttle and climbed hard behind the screening cumulus. Sutherland took his six Wildcats up at a near 45-degree angle to search for the Zeros that must be covering one of their battlewagons. Above the fluffs of cumulus he found them but when the F4Fs headed in they turned away. Sutherland's fighters circled warily, staying between the cautious Zeros and the torpedo planes, now nearing attack position.

The TBFs spiraled up to 5,000 feet behind the clouds and then split. At 11:20 Torpedo Ten attacked. From both bows the big Avengers spread out and slanted in at *Hiei*, keeping behind the thick white clouds as long as possible while the air speed built up and the altimeters unwound. Two or three miles out, the eight planes broke out of the bases of the clouds at better than 250 knots, still losing altitude and headed straight in on either bow. The battleship and her escorts opened fire. Black puffs appeared around the planes and the tracers licked out at them. But the big ship's fire was split by the two-pronged attack and weaker than Coffin's pilots had expected. At a mile and a half they were at dropping altitude, 150 feet above the sea, but too fast. If the torpedoes were released at more than 180 knots there was a chance they would break up on impact or fail to arm or to run straight. In all the Avenger cockpits, with the tracers soaring past and the flak clouds blossoming ahead, throttles came back and the engines quieted as the planes slowed but were held flat and straight with stick and rudder. At a thousand yards and 170 knots they began to put the long torpedoes in the water. In desperation *Hiei* let go a main battery broadside of her 14-inch rifles at Coffin's four planes attacking from the port. The heavy shells rumbled overhead and the TBF turret gunners saw them fountain the sea in an even row several miles astern.

With all their "fish" away less than half a mile out, the torpedo pilots jammed throttle back on and dropped flat down on the sea. One after another they flew close down *Hiei*'s sides below deck level where her guns could not bear and then fanned out, swooping and skidding to avoid the AA as they pulled away astern. As the American pilots at full throttle swept past the battleship with their square Grumman wing tips nearly scraping her sides, they saw why her defensive fire had been weak. Her topsides were scorched and holed, the metal rent and twisted, an occasional gun barrel warped and blackened. The big ship had been in a hell of a fight.

It took about a minute for the torpedoes to make their half-mile run and then there were three nearly simultaneous explosions on the *Hiei*, one to port, one to starboard and one on the stern. The wounded battleship slowed and turned north to starboard, her rudder destroyed and her machinery spaces flooding.

Not one of "Scoofer" Coffin's planes was lost and the eight high Zeros would not engage Sutherland's Wildcats. At 11:45 all fifteen planes landed at Henderson. The United States still owned it.

From the Marines on Guadal the *Enterprise* pilots learned that the *Hiei* was the battered survivor of a flashing, thundering surface battle fought the previous night around Savo. On their way in they had seen another equally battered survivor, the cruiser *Portland*, surrounded by tugs and small craft at the opposite end of Iron Bottom Sound from *Hiei*. *Portland* had sailed with *Enterprise* in every action since the start of the Guadalcanal operation and her shape was familiar to all the airmen. *Hiei* had been steering in her direction when Coffin hit her. VT-10 liked to think they had saved *Portland* from the big guns of the battlewagon.

Two hours and forty-five minutes after landing, two-thirds of Coffin's Avengers were back in the air with eight Marine SBDs and an escort of eight fighters. Again they climbed, circling behind the clouds to 5,000 feet, and slanted in from both sides of the big ship, now nearly dead in the water. They repeated their tactics of the morning, dropping their torpedoes at half a mile, 150 feet above the surface and slamming throttles forward to skim out under the weakened but still dangerous fire of the battlewagon's guns. Coffin and Welles both hit, one amidships and one astern and *Hiei* stopped and stayed stopped as more of the Pacific entered her hull and the black smoke curled up from her wounds. Norton's torpedo made an erratic run and missed. All three of the portside "fish" hit *Hiei* but only one exploded. The other two either failed to arm or had damaged exploder mechanisms from the rough and primitive handling facilities at Henderson. Again VT-10 came out unscathed and flew back to spend the night on Guadalcanal.

The torpedo pilots and their crews were fortunate in their quarters at Henderson, crowded with Army, Marine and Navy pilots and hundreds of survivors of the cruiser and destroyers sunk in the preceding night's battle in Iron Bottom Sound. The Sea Bees took them in. They had clean, well-set-up tents with good cots. Instead of the dreaded powdered eggs and Spam, the Sea Bees had Australian bully beef and hot cakes. And there was grapefruit juice for mixing with torpedo alcohol to toast their safe arrival at Henderson Field and a quick death to the Emperor. This last was so pleasant after the long anxious flight from the carrier and the two attacks on *Hiei* that it was 11:30 before they wandered, singing happily, off to their tents and to bed.

As the Big E drew closer to Guadal and the Slot on the thirteenth, she was joined by the heavy cruiser *Pensacola* and two destroyers at 9:00 A.M. At 10:45 she maneuvered with flank speed and full rudder to evade a submarine attack. An hour later one of the destroyers that had joined the force with *Pensacola* eased up alongside the Big E's starboard quarter and several sacks of mail acquired at Noumea slid dangling across the high line to her deck. The carrier sailors watched a dozen hands convoy the precious mail off to be sorted and they knew that in an hour every cubbyhole and corner on the little ship would hold a man deep and apart in the priceless words from home. Only the man at the wheel and the officer of the deck and the fireman actually on the throttles would not be reading the small papers that were the only reminders that a world other than that of the balmy and treacherous South Pacific existed. An occasional man would go below to lie in his bunk stolidly, staring, having received no mail. And for a while the other men would avoid him in embarrassment, as though he had had a death in his family and there was nothing they could say.

Eight minutes after noon Swede Vejtasa's section of CAP shot down a Japanese patrol plane, a four-engine Kawanishi flying boat, forty miles north of the ship. It had to be assumed that Kinkaid's position had been reported.

All day the ship stayed buttoned up and at General Quarters. Sandwiches and coffee were served at battle stations. A full CAP and an Inner Air Patrol against subs were continuously overhead.

At 7:15 P.M. the two battlewagons and their escorts

pulled away and disappeared into the darkening sea ahead. *Enterprise* secured from General Quarters. Her men went below to a bath and a hot meal and, except for the watch standers, a night's sleep before the battle. At 11:00 P.M. Admiral Kinkaid ordered 25 knots and the task force ran in in the darkness toward Guadalcanal.

The second and third decks amidships sparkled and flashed all night with cutting and welding as Sea Bees, Vestal's repairmen and the Big E's C and R Department restored the watertightness of more decks and bulkheads, steadily reducing the vulnerable damaged area.

Dawn of the fourteenth came with a series of blustery squalls, low, fast clouds and heavy bursts of warm rain that delayed the morning search until after seven. But by six o'clock *Enterprise* was ready for battle with her men at their stations and her hull dogged down against damage. Then in rapid succession ten SBDs and eight F4Fs ran down the Big E's rain-puddled deck and lifted into the air. The Wildcats climbed sharply, forming into two sections of CAP and the Dauntlesses fanned out on their assigned search sections. Like the search before Santa Cruz, this was first a search and then a strike. Crommelin's orders were to make careful, accurate contact reports and then attack. Each SBD carried a 500-pound bomb.

As the searching Dauntlesses disappeared to the west and north, very little was known in *Enterprise* of the strategic and tactical picture in the Solomons. Captain Hardison described it best:

> The situation at dawn on the 14th was obscure. No further contact reports on enemy carriers had been received, the presence or absence of other enemy forces within striking distance was not known, and no information as to the situation at Guadalcanal or the availability of the field was at hand.

Under these circumstances the best that could be done was to send out the minimum search necessary to provide good coverage, retain a heavy CAP overhead and keep the strongest possible strike ready for instant take-off.

It did not take long for the search to produce results. At 8:08 Lieutenant W. I. Martin, flying with Ensign Chuck Irvine in the most northerly search sector, reported a group of ten planes, 140 miles out, approaching the task force at 2,500 feet. *Northampton, San Diego* and *Pensa-*

cola pulled in close to the Big E's irreplaceable deck and the six destroyers closed a moving steel ring around the bigger ships. Radars swept the morning sky and guns trained out and elevated, their muzzles snuffing for the enemy. Twelve more Wildcats clawed up to reinforce the CAP and 17 SBDs with 1,000-pound bombs and an escort of 10 fighters were right behind them. Kinkaid had decided to launch his strike. They could be given targets by radio or they could find their own.

With her deck bare, her guns ready and 20 of her fighters overhead, *Enterprise,* at 25 knots, awaited the coming of the Japanese.

At 9:15 Lieutenant (j.g.) Robert D. "Hoot" Gibson made the first contact report. He had nine ships in sight a few miles south of the New Georgia group and some 270 miles northwest of *Enterprise.* At 9:21 he reported ". . . weather conditions favorable for dive bombing," and at 9:35 he identified the enemy ships: "Two battleships, two cruisers, one possible converted carrier, four destroyers. . . ." Because of the clouds and the distance and the gunfire, he had misidentified the force, but he had located the Japanese bombardment group of four heavy and two light cruisers with their screen which had worked over Henderson the previous night and was now retiring, while the assault force of transports for which they had been preparing the way advanced down the Slot. The two Dauntlesses had first sighted the enemy from low altitude at 8:50 A.M. They circled, climbing, and followed by black bursts of long range AA until 9:15 when they had enough data to send the first contact report. For one more full hour they climbed and circled in the clouds, reporting every move of the enemy task group and getting in position to attack. In the course of that hour they noticed that the Japanese ships were steaming more slowly than could be expected and then they saw why. One of the heavy cruisers was trailing a wide oil slick and listing to starboard. When all their reports had been acknowledged by *Enterprise,* it was the wounded cruiser they decided to attack. Yamamoto had every fighter he could spare covering his transports, and the cruisers heading home on the other side of New Georgia were on their own. So that at 10:15, when Gibson and Buchanan sent their last report and came down on the crippled cruiser from 17,500 feet, they had only the ship's guns to oppose them. Those guns were good, their fire heavy and accurate, and the two light planes jounced and bucked in their dives as it burst around and below them and the tracers skimmed by in long, shifting strings. At 2,000 feet the 500-pounders separated and nosed down, increasing speed. At 1,000 feet the SBDs pulled out, retracted dive brakes, opened throttles and departed flat on the friendly sea. Gibson's bomb landed on the starboard side of the cruiser's forward deck, Buchanan's hit amidships a little to port. The big ship slowed and the black smoke poured out of her. Both planes landed at Henderson at 12:20. Buchanan's Dauntless had an eight-inch hole in the fuselage, a direct hit by a major caliber gun of a heavy cruiser.

Between Gibson's last two reports *Enterprise* had some immediate excitement of her own. The attack group reported by Bill Martin had evidently missed her. Nothing was seen of it by radar or visually. But Yamamoto was keeping track of Kinkaid. At 9:20 radar picked up a snooper and Lieutenant MacGregor Kilpatrick's section of Wildcats was vectored out to intercept. Five minutes later Kilpatrick and his wingman dropped out of the sky in simultaneous high side runs with all guns firing, and a big four-engine Kawanishi flying boat caught fire in its fat belly and sloped down into the sea. It had been scouting the task force from low altitude and was thirty miles north when Kilpatrick found it. From the Big E's deck her men could see the smoke of its burning.

Each section of scouts that made contact with the enemy did exactly as John Crommelin had directed. They circled out of range, carefully reporting disposition, course and speed, and then they attacked.

Ensigns Hoogerwerf and Halloran arrived over the cruiser force just after Gibson's and Buchanan's departure. The enemy ships which had so effectively shot up Guadalcanal a few hours before were now disorganized, their formation breaking up. The main body was standing off to the northwest at 25 knots. The cruiser, which Gibson had hit, was low and dead in the water, burning badly, with two destroyers standing by. A light cruiser and a destroyer were ten miles west of the sinking ship, paralleling the main body, and a heavy cruiser and a destroyer were headed west about twelve miles southwest of the derelict. The two ensigns circled the main body twice and picked their targets. Hoogerwerf took a heavy cruiser and Halloran a light cruiser. They attacked down wind and down sun from the east, and like Gibson and Buchanan, pushed over from 17,500 feet and met no air opposition. The ship's gunners did not sight the two Dauntlesses in the dazzle of the sun until they were plunging through 12,000 feet. Red Hoogerwerf came down on the heavy cruiser from astern and his bomb was fifteen feet behind her in the wide white water of her wake. He turned south, low on the sea, and called to Halloran to join up. There was no answer except for a beautiful direct hit on the light cruiser which left her smoking heavily. There was never any answer from Ensign Halloran or his gunner, nor were they ever seen again.

Lieutenant Commander "Bucky" Lee, with sixteen 1,000-pound bombs slung under his Dauntlesses and ten fighters overhead, was approaching the Japanese bombardment cruisers while the two search sections were attacking. If his planes could do as well as the scouts had done—three hits for four bombs dropped—few cruisers would survive to anchor in Tokyo Bay.

The sixteen engines droned strongly and the dark blue planes with their open cockpits and slender tails shifted gently in relation to each other. A few pilots grimaced and made hand signals to each other across the wings. Some sent messages in code: the closed fist on top of the hand was a dot, the open hand a dash. Most flew, kept formation, navigated and thought their own thoughts. Gunners checked their weapons a dozen times, searched the sky and sea and had occasional brief conversations via intercom with their pilots. Clusters of friendly fighters were reassuringly in sight on either bow ahead.

As the strike group approached Guadalcanal, Lee ordered a course change of 30 degrees to the left. Because of the time required to change coils in their radios, the fighters were not on the "search and attack" frequency used by the bombers, but still on the frequency used for CAP operations. Flatley and all but two of his Wildcats missed the turn, continuing ahead on a course of 330 degrees. They flew far to the northwest to the north coast of Santa Isabel, searched briefly to the westward and, with fuel running low, returned to the ship and landed at 1:00 P.M. All Flatley could think of on the long, futile flight was Jim Gray's tragic mistake at Midway, and he had to force his imagination not to picture a horde of Zeros chopping Lee's Dauntlesses to pieces while the armed fighters droned on through the high and empty sky.

Lieutenant Stan Ruehlow and his wingman remained with the bombers until 11:30 when their fuel gauges forced them to turn back for Henderson. And at 11:30, when he had been two hours and forty-five minutes in the air, Lee located the six remaining cruisers and four destroyers of the bombardment force's main body withdrawing at 25 knots. The cruisers were in two parallel three-ship columns. As Lee's bombers pulled up behind them there was a decision to be made. Was this really, as the day's contact reports so far indicated, the main enemy force in the area and as such the right target for the heaviest strike *Enterprise* could launch that day? Or was this bait, a surface force deliberately placed between *Enterprise* and the enemy carriers to absorb her blows while the Vals and Kates came down on her, as they had done at Santa Cruz? With the white cumulus covering nearly half the surface, there could easily be a carrier around, her strike ready or already off and her CAP prepared to decimate the unescorted Dauntlesses. At the attack point Lee decided on a compromise. He ordered Thomas and his five planes of Bombing Ten to get the heavy cruisers. He sent the five planes of his own squadron under Birney Strong after the light cruisers, and with the five SBDs of his first section he dove under the bases of the cumulus in a wide sweep for the carrier that could be there. But there was only the blue empty surface of the Pacific blotched by cloud shadows and Lee turned back for the cruisers, climbing.

Thomas, Wakeham, Stevens, Welch, and Carroum went straight down through the heavy flak to near-miss a heavy cruiser, the first ship in the right column.

Birney Strong led his division down on the lead light cruiser of the left column. The fast, tender-ruddered vessel twisted violently under the striking chain of dive bombers, and the guns of all the ships ripped and blackened the sky around them. But Finrow and Burnett hit her solidly and she slowed, turning and listing to port, while the black smoke poured out of her hull and drifted along beside her, shadowing the sea.

Bucky Lee, with five SBDs at his back, settled for 7,500 feet in his climb to regain attack altitude and pushed over on the second light cruiser. Four bombs ripped into the Pacific so close to the turning, speeding ship that for a few seconds she was hidden by the suspended white columns of their splashes. The other two bombs failed to release.

Out of gun range east of the retreating cruiser force, Lee reformed his scattered groups. The blue-star-painted Dauntlesses, with their open cockpits and slender tails, angled together from all the corners of the sky, some climbing at full throttle, some gliding down, throttled back. Singly and in pairs and Vs, they slid together, crossing over and under section and division leaders until each was in its place and headed for Henderson. Five minutes east they watched a heavy cruiser of the Imperial Navy roll over and go down messily, her shiny bottom exposed and the sea around her littered with her broken gear and greasily iridescent with spilled oil. Minutes after she had disappeared the homing SBDs could see small splashes as buoyant pieces broke away from the settling hulk, shot through the surface and fell back.

But at 9:49 Lieutenant (j.g.) Doan Carmody had found the transports. All eleven were there on the well-worn course line down the Slot, halfway between New Georgia and Santa Isabel, and escorted by what looked like six destroyers, three light and two heavy cruisers. They were only 120 miles from Guadalcanal and making 14 knots. Unless they were stopped, slowed, or turned back, they would begin unloading at 7:00 P.M. and on the morning of the fifteenth General Vandegrift's Marines would have 13,000 new enemies in the stinking, shot-up jungles around Henderson Field.

Carmody and Lieutenant (j.g.) W. E. Johnson took on the twenty-two enemy ships at ten o'clock, immediately after their final report had been received on *Enterprise*. From two miles high, each picked a transport. For a second their eyes met across the two wings before Carmody pulled up and rolled over into his dive. Johnson followed him down as the black AA began to blossom around them. The transports grew rapidly and the decks they had thought to be painted brown were seen at half a mile above to be crowded with troops, shoulder to shoulder, thigh to thigh. At a quarter-mile they dropped and pulled out fast and flat as the gunners went to work. Carmody's bomb missed ten feet astern, Johnson's hit well aft. Then there were seven Zeros to fight off as the two SBDs headed for the clouds. Carmody and Liska in his rear seat had a moment to strafe a destroyer that loomed up ahead, firing, on their way out. Johnson did not make it to the clouds. Liska saw a plane skid into the waters of the Slot and Carmody turned back white-faced and suddenly sick to see two Zeros strafing the surface where it landed. Carmody and Liska landed aboard *Enterprise* at 12:33 after five hours and twenty-one minutes. There were five gallons of fuel in the SBD.

On Henderson Field it was apparent that the manner in which the precious daylight hours of this fourteenth of November were used would be decisive in the campaign for Guadalcanal.

The first strike had left Henderson at 7:15 A.M., forty-five minutes after the morning search had left the *Enterprise* and an hour and a half before Lee's attack group was launched. There were six torpedo planes, seven dive bombers and seven fighters. Three of the torpedo planes were from VT-10: McConnaughhay, Boudreaux and Oscar. The other three TBFs were flown by Marine crews. One hundred and seventy miles out they had sighted the withdrawing cruiser force and attacked at once. In the clear, stable morning air under the bases of broken clouds the Big E's pilots were cool and deadly. They came in fast and flat, disregarding the jouncing, splashing flak, slowed for their drops, sighting occasionally across the drum-shaped torpedo sight mounted above their instrument panels, opened bomb bays and let their fish go close in. The three torpedoes nosed into the sea with small splashes for such a weight of steel, plunging deeply but quickly leveling off at their preset depth. Then, while the TBFs poured on throttle and skimmed down the cruiser's side to safety, they bored in straight, the two small propellers at their tails whirling in opposite directions and the compressed air bubbles of their exhausts rising steadily behind them. With the Avengers not half a mile out and under heavy fire, in short succession the three stubby warheads smashed into the cruiser's starboard side and fired with heavy slamming booms that threw stained pillars of water into the air. The TNT, explosively expanding, found the sea water incompressible and expanded deeply into the hull of the enemy cruiser. A moment later a Marine-dropped torpedo opened her portside. The big ship slowed and settled, smoking heavily. Half an hour later Gibson and Buchanan found her and added their two bombs and two and a half hours later Lee's retiring attack group watched her sink.

While the TBFs were making their attack the Dauntlesses had hit a light cruiser twice and left her, like the heavy one, slow and burning. No Zeros challenged the seven Wildcats, and all twenty planes landed back at Henderson at 10:15 A.M.

Doan Carmody's position report on the transports was in. Henderson Field was a kicked-open hill of flying ants. In the sweltering, unmoving air there was a sense of urgency that kept every soldier, sailor and Marine involved in any way with flight operations moving at a trot. All hands were aware of the overpowering enemy forces moving steadily down the Slot and only a few hours away. The hospital tents were jammed with wounded from the cruiser battle off Savo. Hundreds of uninjured survivors of those ships clogged the bivouac areas. The enemy had to be stopped short of the island and everyone at Henderson knew that the field was its own most effective defender.

Sweating and straining, covered with dust and grease under the noon sun that rode their shoulders like a tangible weight, the sailors and Marines of the ground crews had a second major strike ready for launching in two hours. As the dozen fighters angled up over the shattered palms to cover eighteen Marine SBDs and seven of Torpedo Ten's Avengers, soldiers and Marines dug in along Bloody Ridge and across the jungle trails around the field, looked, heard and blessed them in whatever prayers or thoughts or short obscenities were their personal ways. Sweating and itching under their bandages, beclouded with morphine over the dull edge of pain, the wounded from air and ship and jungle heard the roar of the engines and opened their eyes on the underside of sunlit canvas or the slowly drifting cumulus between the palm tops and thought: "Get 'em! For Christ's sake, get 'em!" For a while after the droning of the rendezvous circle had faded as the formations headed west, some who had never flown in combat tried to imagine what it would be like to fight in the swift, deep sky rather than from an iron deck or in the rank closeness of the jungle. Then they drifted back into sleep or semisleep while at the field itself there was time for neither imagining nor sleep in the shoving and hoisting of bombs and torpedoes and the stiff coiling of belted bullets in their cans, the gassing, the oiling, the changing of damaged parts, in the noise of engines and blown dust and the sharp smell of high-octane fuel.

It was amazingly only thirty minutes before Scoofer Coffin at the head of the Henderson-based TBFs made out the enemy convoy. The high, clumsy transports were boring

southwestward in three columns with destroyers guarding
their flanks like collies herding cattle. Coffin watched the
Marine SBDs start down, and then selected two transports
not yet under attack. He led four Avengers against one,
while Thompson took three in on the other. Six Zeros appeared, driving fast, and the Wildcats came down to meet
them. In the low-altitude whirl of planes among the tracers
and black puffs of AA the Zeros were driven off and Coffin's four planes made two hits on their ship. Thompson's
three got one. The Marine SBDs made more. Several of
the weirdly painted transports dropped out of formation
listing and burning. The rest moved steadily ahead. It was
obvious that to stop the eleven ships it would be necessary
to sink or cripple each one. So long as one remained afloat
with way on and under steering control it would keep going for Guadalcanal. The Japanese also recognized the importance of this day.

When Coffin took off with this first major Henderson
strike on the transport group at 12:20 P.M., Gibson and
Buchanan were circling waiting to land after their five-hour
morning search and their attack on the cruiser force.
Thirty-five minutes later Hoot Gibson was back in the air
headed for the transports as part of a seventeen-Dauntless
attack group. On his wing flew Ensign Len Robinson, and
Marine Sergeant Beneke was the third SBD in the section.
As they approached the advancing troopships a Zero
curved in behind and under Robinson firing steadily and
pulling up. The blade antenna mast mounted just in front
of Robinson's face between cockpit and engine was chopped
off and flew up and back over his head. Gibson could see
holes in the bottom of Robinson's wings. Schindele in Gibson's rear seat drove the Zero off with his twin 30s just before the section pushed over.

The orange-, pink- and white-painted transports were still
in three columns and Gibson picked the second ship in the
center column figuring that the enemy would place his most
valuable ships near the center of the formation protected
from ahead, astern and both sides by other ships. From
6,000 feet down the AA was heavy and accurate, the tracers whipping past close aboard and the heavy bursts jarring
the crosshairs off the target. Gibson and Robinson in reply
strafed with their two fixed guns and Gibson did as well in
the afternoon with his 1,000-pounder as he had in the
morning with his 500. He planted it dead amidships. Rob-

inson five seconds later put his in nearly the same hole. Sergeant Beneke, as he dropped his close in, watched the big transport crack in half, her back broken, men and equipment spilling from the edges of the break. All three planes strafed the wreck as they pulled away close to the surface of the sea.

The long noon hours passed with the almost constant drone of aircraft shuttling between Henderson and the doggedly approaching enemy. The Big E stood in, closing the range, and at 2:10 P.M., she launched everything aboard that could fly and carry a bomb except eighteen fighters for her own protection. Eight dive bombers of VB-10 and VS-10 were covered by an even dozen F4Fs again under "Reaper Leader" Flatley. It was two hours and twenty minutes to the transports.

Enterprise, her men at battle stations, her CAP up and her decks bare of planes, turned south toward a friendly band of heavy clouds.

As the afternoon began to wane two dozen twin-engine Bettys took off from Rabaul on the basis of a report from a Kawanishi shadowing Kinkaid's task force. With all her scouts heavily engaged over the Slot, the Big E could see only as far as her constantly searching radar and the eyes of her fighter pilots overhead, and had no knowledge of the inbound raid. By 2:30 P.M., 300 miles south of Henderson and rapidly approaching the bad weather belt, Captain Hardison secured his men from their battle stations. With the Rabaul Bettys closing at nearly three miles every minute, *Enterprise* turned into the wind at 3:00 P.M. and recovered the eight Wildcats of her CAP. She was as nearly defenseless as she had ever been before the enemy, with no planes aloft, only half her guns manned and many of her watertight doors and hatches standing open. The Bettys, bunched specks high over the southern ocean, drew closer, their bomb bays stacked full, their crews searching the surface for the carrier they were sent to get. At eight minutes past three the first curtain of rain rattled down on the flat metal surfaces of Kinkaid's warships, visibility was reduced to half a mile and the Big E was safe from any attack by air. The loaded Bettys, armed with an erroneous position report, crisscrossed the empty sea some sixty miles to the westward and carried their bombs back to Rabaul. The decks of Kinkaid's ships steamed as the warm rain evaporated on the sun-heated steel. Having delivered the

Big E's air group into battle there was nothing now that the task force could do except to assure the survival of the empty flight deck at its center.

But Jimmy Flatley with his twenty planes was still en route to the marine battlefield in the Slot, and the hurried attacks out of Henderson continued.

All the human energy and skill available at that broiled and battered jungle airstrip on a forgotten island in a remote corner of the Pacific were concentrated on the fastest possible reservicing, rearming and relaunching of aircraft. The urgency was so great that it was often impossible to organize strikes by squadrons, or even services. The enemy ships were there and closing with each hour. The job was to deliver bombs and torpedoes to them at the maximum rate.

At 2:45 P.M. three separate attack groups took off. The smallest was composed of four SBDs. Three were Marines, the fourth, Ensign John Richey of Scouting Ten, the leader. The second group had nine Dauntlesses, seven Marine and two Navy, Bucky Lee and Glen Estes. Lee and Richey smashed their 1,000-pounders into two transports.

The third strike was made up of eight VS-10 Dauntlesses led by Lieutenant Bill Martin. The worrisome possibility that an enemy carrier was in the vicinity still made the Henderson command uneasy, and Bill Martin's mission was to make a sweep to the northwest in search of her, and, if he found nothing, to put his bombs on the transports. From 16,000 feet, northwest of the Russell Islands, Martin could see that the waters between New Georgia and Santa Isabel contained no carrier, and he swung back south for the transports. The eight Dauntlesses and their fighter cover came straight down the Slot over the route of the Tokyo Express and along the trail of broken ships left by the day's attacks. At the end of that trail was a loose formation of seven, with destroyers along the flanks. Martin's SBDs broke from their neat echelons into three-mile dives that put four more 1,000-pounders into the packed transports. There were explosions and fires; ships listed, slowed, trailed oil; but when Martin headed back for Henderson they were still on course for Guadal. It was four o'clock.

At 4:10 the harried enemy gunners were surprised to see a single Dauntless break away from the glinting Zeros high overhead and dive on their leading ship. Relieved of the usual necessity to divide their fire, every gun in the force concentrated on the lone SBD. He came down straight and fast, untouched by the pouring AA, seeming to fly between the black puffs of heavy caliber shells until the sweating soldiers on deck could make out the perforated dive flaps behind his wings and see the long bomb come loose and nose down toward them. For very many that was their last sight. Chuck Irvine's bomb was a direct hit and by 4:45 he was back on the ground at Henderson.

At 4:15 Jim Flatley arrived over the target with the Big E's second strike. There were only two hours of daylight left, and seven transports, although most were limping and burning, were still under way and headed for Guadalcanal. Flatley's twenty pilots now over the enemy force held the best hope for stopping it. All were veterans of the intense carrier air group training program and the Battle of Santa Cruz; each section was led by a pilot with combat experience which covered the full year of the war; each aircraft was armed and serviced by well-trained men aboard ship where equipment and facilities were vastly superior to the gallant jury rigs of Henderson.

No one was more aware of the importance of this strike than Jim Flatley. With the transports spread out below him in two lines of ships abreast, now only sixty miles northwest of Savo Island, he designated a ship for each bomber, holding the extra Dauntless to repair a miss. In the distance a formation of Zeros circled but did not attack at once. The SBDs spread out to hit their assigned targets. Edwards, Carmody and Edmundson of Scouting Ten circled around astern of the ships to take the ones on the left flank. Goddard, Wiggins, West, McGraw and Frissell attacked the right side of the formation. But before the three VS-10 planes could reach their push-over points, five Zeros which had evaded Flatley's fighters swept in on them. Bobby Edwards' gunner, W. C. Colley, angrily returned their fire, and fired two in quick succession, watching them fall away burning all the three miles to the sea. Ed Edmundson's rear-seatman R. E. Reames, also got one, and then it was time to dive. The Zeros with no dive flaps could not follow. The Dauntlesses went down from 16,000 feet, steady and familiar in their dives, confident with the dozen Reapers covering their tails and with only the guns of transports and destroyers to worry about below. At 9,000 feet they began to meet the tracers. There were plenty of them but poorly aimed by the tired and battered Japanese gunners. On the left flank the three VS-10 planes released in succession and pulled out. Each of their three 1,000-pound bombs was a direct hit on a separate transport. On the right Goddard missed. Wiggins missed but hit much closer and then West, diving last and seeing the right flank ship still untouched, hit her cleanly amidships. Frissell and Mc-Graw attacked the center. Frissell's bomb hit the well deck near the portside and passed through to detonate in the sea. McGraw hit his ship amidships to port and blew out her side, stopping her dead with a heavy list but no fire.

Jim Flatley, circling at 18,000 feet, still had twelve fighters with six guns in each and 400 rounds of .50-caliber ammunition per gun. Leaving four planes under Lieutenant Fritz Faulkner at 10,000 to act as cover, Flatley and Dave Pollock took their four-plane sections down to strafe. Each section picked a large and apparently undamaged transport and attacked in 60-degree dives, opening fire with all six guns at about 4,000 feet and releasing their triggers at about a thousand to pull up for reattacks. One after another the stubby, square-winged Wildcats slanted down, the gray gunsmoke streaming behind and the converging tracers ahead raking the packed decks of the enemy ships from stern to bow. Small pieces of bulkheads and decks flew up and fires began. From 1,000 feet and at 300 miles an hour the Grim Reapers could not see the blood and human debris that must have made the transports' decks unspeakable.

Ensign Ed Coalson was the last plane in Dave Pollock's strafing section and, in the course of his run, fell several hundred yards behind. Immediately he was attacked by four Zeros, all coming up from below, two from ahead and two from behind. Coalson used his diving speed to loop up and over, avoiding the pair ahead and coming down on the tails of the pair astern. One of them he promptly shot down and the other fled.

All twenty of Flatley's planes were on the ground at Henderson by 5:30 P.M.

Five transports still steamed stubbornly southeast.

At the moment when the Big E's second strike arrived over the enemy ships, three of Torpedo Ten's Avengers were lumbering into the air from Henderson Field as part of a seventeen-plane attack. The three Avengers glided in on two transports which were dead in the water but crowded with troops available for transfer to destroyers for run-in after dark. Coffin and Thompson dropped two 500s each, each got a hit and a near miss.

At 4:30 P.M., a quarter of an hour behind Scoofer Coffin's Avengers and while the second *Enterprise* attack group was in action over the transports, Lieutenant Commander J. A. Thomas' Bombing Ten mounted a strike of its own out of Henderson. Fighter cover had been arranged but, in the frantic shuttle between field and ships, fighters and bombers missed each other and Thomas took his squadron in bare. He had seven Dauntlesses in two sections. Lieutenant V. W. Welch, his exec, led the second section and Jeff Carroum was on his right wing.

Welch was an old *Enterprise* hand from Bombing Six. In the air his SBD was as solid and steady as though it were on tracks. Little Jeff Carroum, with the coast of Guadalcanal drawing astern, noticed again what a pleasure it was to fly wing on a pilot like Welch.

It no longer required much flying to find the transports and before 5:00 P.M. the VB-10 pilots at 12,000 feet had them in sight. The five big ships were still under way and pushing for Guadalcanal. Astern of them others lay dead in the water or burning and one or two seemed to be headed west. As Thomas picked up his mike to assign targets, the seven Dauntlesses were suddenly smothered by Zeros.

A dozen of the clean, low-winged fighters dived in on the portside of the bomber formation. Some were dark green and shiny, some were bright aluminum as though unpainted except for the large red disks of the rising sun on their wings. They all had in common the 7.7s that winked along the leading edges of their wings and the twin 20s that flashed steadily through the prop. Hoot Gibson on the extreme left was the first target of the Japanese and Schindele in his rear seat swung his twin 30s out to port to meet them. Two of the enemy concentrated on Gibson; Schindele hit one and he slanted off, smoke trailing from his engine, but Gibson's Dauntless was badly holed and spun out of formation. With full forward stick and stiff-legged full opposite rudder, he fought the spin until the rugged little SBD came out in a swooping glide close to the water. Riddled, with leaking tanks and most of his systems out, Gibson decided he had used up his quota of luck for the fourteenth of November and concentrated on getting back to Henderson in one piece. With the free guns jammed and a Zero on his tail he hedgehopped across the Russell Islands, dodging and weaving like a tired boxer until the Zero ran out of ammunition and turned away.

With Zeros making runs on them from the port beam, ahead, astern and underneath, and free guns sweeping from side to side to meet the nearest threat, Thomas and Stevens pressed on to the push-over point and pealed off in their dives.

Unable to stay with the Dauntlesses in their braked 70-degree dives, the Zeros turned away. Fire from the guns of the scattered, discouraged ships was light and even after the sudden scuffle before push-over, both pilots put their 1,000-pounders solidly amidships into a previously untouched transport and departed, low on the water, strafing the crowded decks as long as their guns would reach.

Robinson and Wakeham were the last two planes of the seven and the enemy fighter pilots gave them special attention. Like Thomas and Stevens in the lead, the two SBDs locked themselves in tight formation, their gunners sitting only a few feet apart to present four .30-calibers to each banking, swooping Zero in succession. But the enemy fighters came in from ahead and astern at the same time. Wakeham and Robinson bored in for the push-over point, firing their fixed guns at the enemy ahead while Stanley and Teyshak handled the ones astern. Robinson watched his tracers knock pieces of cowling from a Zero making a head-on run and saw its prop falter before it flashed past below. Then he was conscious of 20-millimeters and 7.7s eating into his left wing and moving up into Wakeham's right. As Robinson skidded right, out of the line of fire, Teyshak saw the guns in the other Dauntless go silent and swing up as Stanley slumped over their breeches. Before Robinson could close in again, a 20-millimeter exploded in his engine, stopping it and sending flames licking back toward the canopy. He sideslipped violently until the lateral windstream blew out the engine fire, then pushed over in a violent dive to escape the Zeros which continued to fire all the while. With his big bomb still on and no dive flaps, the SBD headed for the sea like a dropped rock, and the rush of air whirled the dead prop and miraculously restarted the engine. A Zero followed him down, and still diving, Robinson aileron-rolled to the right and then back to the left again. When he leveled off at 2,500 feet Len had 320 knots, but the Zero was still with him, its tracers clipping into his wings. He pulled up hard and flipped over in a tight Immel-

man, but in a few seconds the Zero was back on his tail, its
tracers pouring past his sick engine. Teyshak, out of ammunition after the constant attacks, could only train his
guns and hope to fool the Zero. By now the two planes
were over the Russell Islands, and Len plunged for the
palm tops. He skimmed through a coconut grove so low
that Teyshak saw the green tops go by at eye level, then,
still with 240 knots from the dive, he followed the valleys
and rising contours of the jungle-covered hills to the crest
of the island. Teyshak, looking over his cold guns at the
beautiful deadly Zero as it followed with tilting wings
around the hillsides and up the slopes, was lifted in his seat
by the sudden descents and jammed heavily into it by the
sharp climbs. At the ridge crest the Zero was still there and
Robinson, seeing a heavy white cloud ahead, dived steeply
down the reverse slope, flat on the treetops to gain speed,
and then pulled up with a jerk and full throttle for the
cloud. The Zero was still there, but, with the safety of the
cloud only 500 feet away, the enemy pilot evidently also
out of ammunition pulled up briefly alongside, rocked his
wings in congratulatory salute and broke away. As the gray
damp of the cloud closed in around him, Teyshak saw the
Zero heading back for the transports.

Robinson and Teyshak landed at Henderson Field at
5:30 P.M. and counted sixty-eight holes in the SBD. Gibson had just landed, and Thomas and Stevens came in next.
The VB-10 pilots waited in weary and desultory conversation for their exec and the other two pilots of his section,
but they did not return.

When the enemy fighters broke up Robinson's and
Wakeham's defensive formation, Welch and Carroum,
ahead, were nearing their dive points, heavily engaged by
the swarming Zeros. For another minute with fixed and
free guns, skidding, slipping, banking sharply together to
meet the constant attacks, they fought through and then
they were in position. Welch waved a thumbs-up to Carroum, flipped over and went down, diving to the south and
crosswind. Jeff Carroum, maneuvering to get his fixed guns
on a Zero coming in ahead, overshot the point, and, when
he finally dived, he had to come down on his back in a
more than vertical descent in order to get back on his target. It was an uncomfortable dive, hanging hard against the
seat belt, the negative G tending to lift feet from the rudders and pull hands from stick and throttle. But after the

lashing fighters at 12,000 feet any dive was good. With
fighters over them the ships did not dare to fire heavily at
the dive bombers, so that in the seconds of the deadly drop
toward the enemy there was actually the peace of concentration between the fight above and the inevitable one below.

The big transport in the center of the formation grew
rapidly through Jeff Carroum's prop disk and, as he put his
eye to the sight, Welch's bomb flashed directly amidships
sending large pieces soaring and tumbling up as black smoke
began to bloom in the rubble. As Jeff's Dauntless leveled
off, Hynson saw the flying debris of a second hit on the big,
crowded ship just abaft the first one and caught a glimpse
of Welch's SBD as it headed north low on the water. Staying flat and fast for a few seconds, Jeff looked around for
Welch or Wakeham. No friendly plane shapes were in sight
and there was not much time to look. A couple of destroyers nearly across his escape course were firing heavy, accurate bursts of tracers which smoked past his nose and
soared over his head. Jeff zoomed sharply and dove for
the wave tops, slipping and skidding when the tracers got
close, but a burst caught his engine some six feet forward
of the cockpit. It bucked and missed. Jeff eased back on
the throttle and it ran again but smoking and leaking oil
which quickly filmed his canopy. Well away from the enemy ships, a Zero was circling for a head-on run. Jeff re-
charged his fixed guns to be sure, pulled up adding power,
and turned into the enemy fighter firing steadily. As he
turned, climbing, the engine backfired heavily and stopped.
The Zero flashed past, firing, and there were about ten flying seconds remaining. Jeff banged down flaps and tail
hook, yelled to Hynson to brace and then, before the flaps
could extend, they were in the water. The tail hook dragged
first, giving warning, the belly banged down, skidding like a
flat stone, and the sea dragged the SBD from 90 knots to
zero in a hundred feet. Jeff lurched forward from the waist
and his head smashed the now useless instrument panel,
knocking him out.

Carroum came to with Hynson tugging at him and yelling in his ear. The silence was deafening after the long
roaring of guns and engines. The ripples of an eight-knot
easterly breeze slapped against the Dauntless as it floated
heavily nose down and tail clear. The afternoon sun was
warm on his shoulders. On the horizon the enemy ships

were hull down, the Zeros circling specks above them. Around to the left of the low sun, to the south, was the distant loom of land and Jeff Carroum knew those were the Russell Islands.

The Dauntless was settling fast and Carroum and Hynson worked hard to release the circular hatch in the left side of the fuselage between the two cockpits and tug the inflatable rubber raft out of its cylindrical stowage and out onto the wing. Jeff was dazed and weak from his battered head and the blood trickled down out of his dark hair and dried on his face and neck. If he had been a bigger man instead of just a hair over the minimum size that naval aviation would accept, Jeff, jackknifing from the waist, would have smashed his face instead of the top of his head on the instrument panel a few feet ahead of him. But, dazed as he was, he knew better than to inflate the bright yellow raft and invite the idle, angry Zeros down to strafe. As the SBD slipped out from under them Carroum and Hynson went off the wing into the warm sea, the still uninflated but buoyant rubber raft between them. Once the wings with their nearly empty tanks went under, the rest of the plane followed with a rush and the protruding tail surfaces grazed the men in the water. Some projection caught in the lashings of the raft and as it disappeared beneath the surface Jeff Carroum felt himself being dragged under also. It was as though the wrecked SBD had determined to leave no evidence of its defeat. Wriggling and groping and going deeper every second Carroum found that it was the belt holding his .38 revolver that had caught on the plane and, with his lungs bursting and the surface a rippling mirror high overhead he released the belt, jerked the CO_2 toggles on his Mae West and shot up to the air and light again. He lost consciousness again on the way up but after several minutes the breeze and slap of the wavelets on his face awakened him.

He recovered quickly after that and began to feel that he must strike out to survive. He could not bear the idea of waiting far at sea for the rescue which might never come or, if it did, might mean death under the two-handed samurai sword or years in a POW camp. So that night, while his squadron mates waited with lessening hope, Jeff and Hynson, with their shoes off and their life jackets inflated, swam toward the Russells twenty-five miles away.

The last attack of the day on the transports was led by

Glen Estes of Scouting Ten. With three Marine SBDs and fighter cover, he left Henderson fifteen minutes behind Thomas' costly strike, flew the well-known route to the target, made a direct hit with his big bomb and returned to the field as the fast tropical dusk was fading into night.

When full dark stopped air operations on the fourteenth, four damaged transports were still afloat and headed in but the Slot was aglow with a string of burning ships and others, without fires, lay listing and settling along the route from Rabaul. Seven transports loaded with troops would never sail again.

Enterprise, out of range of effective enemy aircraft, cruised easily in the rainy, gusty security of her weather front while Kinkaid awaited Halsey's orders on what to do with a carrier that carried no planes. At Henderson Field the Big E's pilots turned in early hoping for a night's rest before another day of action.

A few miles up the Slot a battleship, four cruisers and a destroyer squadron of the Imperial Navy headed for Guadalcanal to shoot up Henderson and destroy the planes that would be out again at daylight. And nine miles off the northeast coast of Guadal, swinging around toward Savo Island, came *Washington* and *South Dakota* with their four destroyers, under the command of Rear Admiral Willis A. "Ching" Lee, and with orders to prevent any Japanese bombardment.

North of the Russell Islands, Jeff Carroum and Hynson watched an enemy destroyer throb by in the darkness fifty yards away as they doggedly swam for the Southern Cross and the shore. Jeff, a strong swimmer, led, with Hynson, working hard, trailing by a few yards.

At around 11:15 P.M. the Americans around Henderson Field sat up in their cots or glanced and whispered to each other in the darkness of their jungle positions. From the north came the booming of heavy guns. Ching Lee had found the enemy and the surface forces had taken over the war for the night. Smaller guns joined in a few minutes and the shooting continued intermittently, sometimes rapid and heavy, sometimes carefully spaced, now and then a couple of rounds and then a long silence. In an hour and a half the firing died out and there was only the occasional rattle of automatic weapons when Marine and enemy patrols brushed in the jungle around the field.

At 1:00 A.M. a rain squall blotted out the Southern Cross and Jeff Carroum changed his navigational system from visual to tactile, keeping the light east breeze on his left cheek as he swam on for the Russells.

When the big guns went silent in the night sea north of Guadal, Admiral Lee, at the eventual cost of three of his destroyers and a shot-up *South Dakota,* had accomplished his mission. The enemy task force hurried off to the north to be as far away as possible when sunrise stirred the hornet's nest of Henderson. The Japanese bombardment force was short one battleship and one destroyer and two cruisers would spend some time in the yard.

At 5:00 A.M. Carroum and Hynson were still swimming. The east was beginning to gray, and when the gentle swell lifted them they could see the shadow of the islands to the south. They seemed no nearer than at sunset.

By 6:00 A.M. Henderson was noisy with aircraft engines and another day of air war was beginning. The first search flight found the four surviving enemy transports beached at Tassafaronga on the northwest corner of Guadalcanal. Two thousand men, most without weapons, equipment or rations, were coming ashore.

What followed was a day of slaughter. First, Army fighters strafed, then Marine and *Enterprise* bombers took over. Scoofer Coffin planted a 500-pound bomb on one ship at 6:45. Lieutenant Goddard of Bombing Ten lighted the biggest fire ever seen on Guadalcanal when he put his 1,000-pounder into a suspicious area at the dead end of a jungle road from the beach. Columns of boiling black smoke rose to 2,000 feet. Sixteen hours later it was still burning. *Enterprise* squadrons flew dozens of missions against the beached ships and their partially unloaded troops and equipment. The beaches around the ships were red with blood and littered with pieces of bodies.

At 10:00 A.M. Jeff Carroum thought he saw a reef a few hundred yards ahead and called to Hynson. The young gunner was nearly exhausted and shouted feebly for Jeff to go ahead and bring help. Carroum struck out strongly but when he had been swimming for an hour there was no reef, only an island ten or fifteen miles away. He turned back but Hynson, who had flown with Jeff since their training days at Kaneohe, was no longer there. Sadly, Carroum swam on, the tropic sun scorching his head and face, the salt of the sea caked on the burned flesh, tired to death, hungry, thirsty and chilled by the warm sea that was yet twenty-odd degrees cooler than his body temperature.

In the middle of the forenoon watch Halsey ordered *Enterprise* back to Noumea.

At 3:20 P.M. sixteen of Jim Flatley's Grim Reapers, led by their skipper, Stan Ruehlow and Bobby Edwards tangled with eleven Zeros high on the approaches to Henderson, shot down six and turned back the bombing raid for which the Zeros were cover. Flatley lost one Wildcat when Dave Pollock exhausted his fuel in the action and ditched off Lunga Point. A crash boat picked Dave up unhurt.

When darkness fell on the fifteenth of November the enemy threat to Guadalcanal was over. His transports were all sunk or wrecked, his heavy surface forces driven off, his air raids turned back and the few men he had landed without supplies or equipment more a detriment to his troops on Guadal than a help.

The Big E's Air Group Ten stayed at Henderson a few more days to mop up and Jeff Carroum swam until midnight before he passed out from exhaustion and thirty hours in the water without food, drink or rest. Small fish gathered under him nuzzling the flesh of his stomach as he drifted with the wind and current, sleeping, his head back on his jacket collar and the small waves breaking over it now and then.

14 ESPIRITU, NOUMEA AND CHICAGO

On the sixteenth of November, Enterprise *arrived* back in the harbor of Noumea, unhit and unattacked, and having contributed hugely to the defeat of the last major enemy effort to recapture Guadalcanal. And, for most of her airmen, the night of the sixteenth was the last on that bloody, evil-smelling island.

At 11:30 that morning, Thomas, Gibson, Goddard and

Robinson took off on a search for Carroum and any other survivors of the action in the Slot. They swept in low and slow over the Russells, scanning the beaches, bays and inlets, and looking for a white face among the black upturned ones in native villages. Hoot Gibson found one white man and dropped him dungarees and cigarettes, but he was not of Bombing Six or *Enterprise*.

When Thomas' four Dauntlesses landed back at Henderson at 2:00 P.M., Jeff Carroum was still swimming. By now the sun and the sea had so burned and swollen his face that he was nearly blind. He looked out of his scarlet, salt-caked puff of flesh through narrow slits that he kept open with difficulty, one at a time, by repeated salt-water baths. In the small hours of the morning he had bumped into a coconut and until noon he had kept it with him for added buoyancy and because, even though unattainable, under the tough, fibrous shell there was food and drink which he had not tasted for two days of swimming and drifting. All morning he had swum for the nearest island but the current had held him off and he had passed out again from weakness and exhaustion. By midafternoon he was in the middle of a big lagoon, with native huts in sight along the shore but with the current still against him, and once again, doggedly, starved, baked, half blind and tired beyond belief, he settled down to swim.

At 4:30 P.M. Russ Reiserer and Bobby Edwards flew the Grim Reapers' last combat mission in the November battle for Guadalcanal, strafing the wrecks of the grounded transports and the salvaged supplies stored on the beaches and in the nearby jungle.

Early in the evening Jeff Carroum lost consciousness again and all night he slept in the sea like a dead man while the wind and current drifted him out of the bay that he had been swimming for two and a half days to reach.

On the seventeenth, the last *Enterprise* squadrons left Henderson Field and Jeff Carroum was still in the water. But he knew this was his last day. No man can survive more than three days in the sea without food or drink and supported only by a life vest.

Jeff slept for twelve hours, drifting and rocking in the gentle sea, and only woke up when the scorching 10:00

A.M. sun burned into his upturned face and penetrated the swollen slits of his closed eyes. It took him nearly fifteen minutes of work on his eyes to get one open and then, peering through the narrow window of his own flesh, he saw an island ahead and felt the breeze at his back. If the wind held, and he could swim all day, he knew he would make it. So for the third day he forced his legs to kick and his arms to pull and like some broken water bug, inched his way downwind across the tropic sea which his shipmates had fought over and searched and left.

During the same four hours that it took Bucky Lee's retiring Dauntlesses to cover the 500-odd miles from Guadalcanal to the New Hebrides, Jeff Carroum got two miles closer to land. At 6:00 P.M. when the SBDs touched down at Bomber One, Jeff was half a mile offshore and the sun was just a few minutes out of the western sea. Now the will to survive, which had kept him moving for three days and twenty-five miles, poured its last c.c. of adrenalin into Jeff's tortured body, and he struck out strongly for the coconut palms ahead. The wind was still at his back and there was no current.

At about 7:00 P.M. Jeff kicked against a coral head and cut his bare foot. He lowered his legs and found the water only waist deep but he could not stand. Staggering and thrashing, half swimming and half walking, he got to where he could crawl the last few yards through foot-deep water. After seventy-three hours, he struggled onto the warm sand of the beach. A few feet from the tide line a pool of muddy water was left from an afternoon shower and Jeff drank with his face in it like an animal and rolled over on his back and slept all night while the warm rain spattered down and the sea broke at his feet and he knew nothing.

On the morning of November eighteenth *Enterprise* lay at anchor in the harbor at Noumea, her hull ringing with continuing repair work and the chipping hammers and wire brushes of normal maintenance. Air Group Ten was scattered through the New Hebrides in transports and carrier planes, en route back to the ship. John Crommelin, in conference with his skipper, was arranging replacements for the F4Fs and SBDs transferred to the Marines or lost in action. Bill Halsey, commander South Pacific Area and South Pacific Forces (COMSOPAC), was planning the re-

lief of the First Marine Division on Guadalcanal and the
mop-up of the now cut-off Japanese forces on the island.

On that same morning Jeff Carroum started on the way
to recovery from his ordeal by water. When the blazing
sun awakened him he found another fresh-water pool and
was standing naked washing the salt from his body and
rinsing it from his flight suit and his underwear when he
heard voices behind him and found a very black man, with
coarse bushy hair cut off straight around his head and un-
naturally red lips, accompanied by half a dozen boys, in-
specting him cautiously from a few paces away. Jeff wanted
no confusion about his nationality and, if the color of his
skin were not enough, there should be other ways to show
he was not Japanese. From a rock beside the pool he picked
up his ID card and showed it to the natives, then, holding
up his flight suit, pointed to the heavily stenciled "USN"
above the left breast pocket—saying, "Me friend." To his
relief one of the boys answered, "Me friend too" and his
identity was apparently satisfactorily established. Saying,
"You come me," and, "Him airplane come bye-m-bye," the
natives helped him to a canoe made from a hollow log and
in an hour took him to their village. There he was given
roast yam, fish and coconut, and assigned his own palm-
thatched hut where for days he slept, waking only to eat
and sleep again. In the bends of his knees and elbows where
his flight suit had rubbed the soaked, soft flesh during the
long swim, and around his neck under the hard rubber edge
of the Mae West, the skin was worn away and flies and
mosquitoes attacked the raw, open sores. Jeff was uncomfortable when he had rested enough to notice, and afraid
of infection, but like his hosts, he bathed thoroughly in the
sea each day and the clear salt water gradually healed over
the open spots.

The chief of this village of some eighty souls took a liking to Jeff. He made him presents of mosquito netting, a
suit of brand-new pajamas, a razor, toilet paper and a brok-
en piece of mirror. The chief caught fish for Jeff's meals
and in pidgin English made him understand two most important things. First, there were thirteen Japanese soldiers in
a nearby village who had missed their transport when the
enemy occupation force had been pulled out several weeks
previous. And, second, there was another American pilot

on one of the other islands. The chief made it clear that he and his people had no use for the Japanese. During the short occupation, the Imperial troops had taken the natives' livestock and stores of food and left them to starve or live as best they could. The thirteen enemy soldiers were isolated in their village and the natives took them food each day to prevent any further pillaging.

On the third day the other American arrived in Jeff's village. His name was Hurst and he was a staff sergeant and a Wildcat pilot who had been flying with VMF-121 out of Henderson when he had been shot down over the Russells.

A few days after the two Americans had joined forces (Jeff briefly considered designating himself COMUSFORI —commander, U. S. Forces, Russell Islands) the thirteen Japanese in two canoes appeared at the village asking the way out to the sea. There was plenty of warning. The enemy soldiers had been visible for miles as they approached, wearing wide straw hats which the bushy-haired natives did not use. Carroum and Hurst waited hidden in the jungle until the two canoes had left.

A week passed. Jeff regained most of his strength on a diet of yams, sugar cane, coconut, fish, chicken, rice and, in the last days, beef. There might be other foods at each meal, but there were always yams for breakfast, lunch and supper. Jeff learned that the bright red of the natives' lips and their teeth was the result of chewing the mildly narcotic gum of the betel nut tree. Only the adult natives of both sexes wore any clothes at all and they wore only a loincloth. Where the men cut off their hair straight around, as with a large bowl, the women apparently neither cut nor combed theirs from birth. All the adolescent girls of the village lived together in a large hut, all the adolescent boys in another some distance away. The children apparently only graduated from these dormitories when they married. Carroum and Hurst came to refer to the two huts as "Boystown" and "Girlstown" and the words caught. Perhaps some twenty-first-century lexicologist, studying the Russell Islands dialect of Melanesian, will stumble on those terms and remember the months when the Russells were on the outskirts of a war and Americans drifted up on the beaches and dangled down from the sky under nylon canopies.

On the twenty-sixth of November a canoe brought word from another island that a small float plane had landed looking for a Marine major ("Indian Joe" Bauer) and had designated a particular lagoon where in two days a Catalina would land to pick up Carroum and Hurst.

Jeff's hosts, taking no chances, got the two pilots to a village on a small island in the lagoon a day early. But the Japanese learned of their arrival and sent word that they would be over to pick up the Americans at 5:00 P.M.

Carroum and Hurst had no intention of being captured, and the natives supported them. From somewhere in the village came a Japanese .25-caliber carbine and three cartridges, and from everywhere came the long machetes used in the constant fight against the pressing jungle. In collaboration with his ally, the chief, COMUSFORI arranged a neat and deadly ambush along the trail from beach to village, the single carbine backed up by fifty razor-sharp machetes in strong black hands. The enemy appeared on schedule in two canoes and nosed in toward the beach. But apparently he did not like the look of the quiet village nor the lack of adult males in the vicinity. Paddles were reversed, the canoes backed off, circled the small island twice with evident distrust and departed.

The following day, in midmorning, a PBY orbited low over the lagoon and then skimmed in for a landing. Carroum and Hurst were paddled out and climbed in through the gun blisters. The canoe backed clear and the Catalina took off at once and was in Tulagi, across the sound from Henderson, in less than an hour.

When news of Jeff's survival reached the *Enterprise* at Noumea there was a delighted scramble to collect and return the minor items of his personal effects that had been dispersed among his squadron mates. It was relatively easy. His clothing was too small for anyone else anyway.

When Scouting Ten, en route back to Noumea, arrived at the Marston matting field of Bomber One on Espiritu five miles from the harbor by road, they were a worn and bedraggled bunch of young men. They had been in the same clothes, day and night, for three days of much action and little sleep. They were unshaven, unwashed, red-eyed and edgy. They had all lived at Bomber One before and it was only a little better than Henderson Field. Because U. S. forces were beginning to build up in the New Hebrides, there had to be some sort of facility around where a man could get a bath, some clean clothes, a hearty meal, a drink of good whisky and a night's sleep. Bucky Lee and Glen

" 'Tater Head" Estes appropriated a momentarily idle jeep and went out on a reconnaissance.

After two hours of haphazard driving on the narrow, dusty, jungle-bordered roads, the two dive-bomber pilots found what they wanted. Scattered through a parklike glade on a hilltop were the Butler huts, shops and tents of an Acorn, a manned, equipped and packaged repair base assembled and trained in the States and shipped out to set up business wherever directed. This one was designated "Red Two."

Through the screened sides of the Butlers, tables with white cloths and silver, and bunks with clean sheets were visible. One building was obviously a laundry, another a bathhouse. Bucky Lee in five minutes found the commanding officer and explained his squadron's needs. Commander Cooper, the Acorn skipper, and the scouting squadron commander saw eye to eye and the entire squadron was invited to be guests of Acorn Red Two for so long as their duties would permit.

"We're wearing the same suit, aren't we, Commander?" Cooper said to Lee. "Out here we've got to look out for our own—and it will be good for my troops to see someone that's been shot at. Up here you damn near can forget there's a war."

The hilltop base was thrown wide open to Scouting Ten. Each officer and man was issued two new suits of khaki and toilet gear. For three days the Big E's weary airmen ate well from the linen cloths and slept long in the clean sheets, bathed and shaved, their strength and their good humor returning. There was even good U. S. bonded whisky to loosen the tongue and unknot the nerves in the cool tropic evenings. On the third day Lee led his people down the chain of the New Hebrides and across to Noumea on the southwest corner of New Caledonia where *Enterprise* lay anchored in the bay.

By late November of 1942, life for the men of *Enterprise* had settled into its Noumea pattern. While replacement aircraft slowly arrived in pairs and fours and half dozens on the decks of transports and landing craft, the air group lived ashore along the edges of the grass field of Tontouta, working the bugs out of new planes and training on land targets and towed sleeves. In the week it had taken the Big E to steam to Guadalcanal and turn back the Japanese and return to Noumea, the Sea Bees had built wooden decking into the four-man tents and installed open-air showers made from 55-gallon oil drums. It was no longer necessary to walk the dusty mile to the river for a bath, and the things that crawl on the earth and thence into a man's cot were handicapped to some extent by the raised flooring in the tents. Over the protests of the local management, Commander Dick Gaines, the air group commander, managed to fill Tontouta's spacious meat lockers with hundreds of cases of Australian beer and the cold brew after the sweaty, dusty days earned him the affection of every airman at the field.

Aboard the carrier the repair work never stopped. With the immediate enemy threat reduced, Captain Hardison gave permission to test the forward elevator. It worked. Flight operations could now be resumed at normal speeds. Each day more of the Santa Cruz damage was undone, more compartments made watertight, systems extended and restored. The old battle of steel ships equipped with complex machinery and floating in the salt sea went on as always against rust and corrosion. The chipping hammers and wire brushes were never still and patches of red lead and the yellow of zinc chromate appeared and disappeared daily as rust spots were cleared, the primary coats applied and quickly painted over with the gray war color. Scaffolds were over the side and sailors in dungarees wearing bulky kapok life jackets and safety lines touched up the bad spots here and there. On Fridays bedding was neatly secured along the lifelines to air and "field day" was held throughout the ship; swabs, scrub brushes and bright-work polish were in use in every compartment. Every day liberty parties of sailors in whites filed down the companionway and into the wide-beamed fifty-foot motor launches, and with a clanging of the coxswain's bells moved off for Noumea. Other fifty-footers took men in dungarees to the white beach across the bay for soft ball and swimming and a few cold beers in the late afternoon.

Then, three days before the war was a year old, *Enterprise* got under way again, the air group flew aboard and she moved northwestward into the Coral Sea.

Bill Halsey had learned something of the Japanese mentality in the past year. He felt that, if it lay within their power, they would strike a major blow on this first anniversary of Pearl Harbor. If they did, they would not find his only carrier airing bedding and fighting rust in port.

On December 7, 1942, *Enterprise* was operating in the central Coral Sea, with a full veteran air group, loaded and ready for whatever the enemy might try.

He tried nothing. The Big E waited another two or three days and on the eleventh steamed into the harbor at Espiritu Santo in the New Hebrides. Air Group Ten landed back on the matting strip of Bomber One and on the palm-lined fighter strip up the coast, and took up residence in the damp Quonsets and tents at the edges of the fields.

Off and on, for nearly a month, the Big E swung with the gentle southern tides and the light breeze around her anchor in Segond Channel of Espiritu.

During the same weeks enemy carriers based 2,000 miles northwest at the mysterious and reputedly impregnable base of Truk in the Caroline Islands were working desperately to qualify pilots in carrier operations. Each time the enemy ships would put to sea, alert U. S. submarines would report the movement, and *Enterprise* would weigh anchor, take aboard her planes, and steam northward past Santa Cruz and the Solomons to patrol between Truk and Guadalcanal, her SBDs and TBFs searching to maximum range and her fighters up. Twice, early morning strikes were launched in an attempt to catch enemy submarines refueling seaplanes at Indispensable Reefs. Both strikes found only the low coral and the breaking ground swell and the empty sea. But two days after the first strike, Ensign Lewis Gaskill of the Reaper CAP shot down a Betty only fifteen miles west of the force.

These voyages to the northward were welcomed by the Big E's men. The air group vastly preferred the closer quarters of the carrier to Bomber One and the coral fighter strip up the coast, where at night the nearly naked men in the open Quonsets would be awakened by the sharp toes of rats scurrying across their chests or by teeth nibbling sharply at their fingers, and where in the morning the scorpions and spiders had to be dislodged before shoes were put on. More than this, the frequent sorties from Espiritu gave the men of *Enterprise,* both airmen and crewmen, the justification they were beginning to need for the long months away from home. If there were days and weeks to spend swinging around the hook in this remote tropic harbor or flying routine training missions out of temporary fields ashore, why could they not be spent as well in port in the States where there would be liberty in the evenings and leave to go home?

Christmas in Espiritu did not feel like Christmas. Eighty-four bags of mail containing battered packages and bundled letters arrived. It was hot and humid. The men made Christmas trees of small coconut palms. There were a few scratchy carols that were played over the public address system. Religious services were held among the parked and partially dismantled planes on the hangar deck, and ashore two oil drums, two planks and a tablecloth became an altar for the Christmas service.

In mid-December *Enterprise* operated briefly with a force built around *Saratoga*, repaired and back at work after her August torpedo hit. It was the first time that the men of the Big E had seen another carrier since they had stood with moist palms and leaden guts and watched *Hornet* burning on the horizon at Santa Cruz.

On the twenty-eighth day of January *Enterprise* sailed out of Segond Channel, Espiritu Santo, and into her first action in over nine weeks. Rear Admiral Frederick C. Sherman, who had commanded the *Lexington* when she was lost in the Battle of the Coral Sea a month before Midway, had his flag in the Big E and was under Halsey's orders to assure the safe arrival at Guadalcanal of four transports full of troops and equipment. In order to fulfill this mission, he was to "destroy any Japanese forces advancing on the southern Solomon Islands."

Under Sherman's command was Task Force 16, composed of *Enterprise, San Diego* and five destroyers.

By late January there were other United States naval forces in the waters around the Solomons. *Saratoga* had been back for a month as the flagship of Task Force 11, Rear Admiral Ching Lee with three new battleships was operating in the Coral Sea, and two cruiser groups were out. All five task forces were deployed in the seas off northeastern Australia, moving northward. Their mission was the same. When and if the transports departed Guadal for the return trip, they would have on board the last of the Marines to leave the odorous island—Marines who had been there since the preceding August when *Enterprise* had covered their landing, and were leaving now for home, and not POW camp in Japan, because of their own fighting ability

and the help provided by the USS *Enterprise* at Eastern
Solomons, Santa Cruz and the south end of the Slot.

In the Bougainville Strait between the high, dark green
islands of Espiritu Santo and Malekula the seventy-four
planes of Air Group Ten came aboard from Bomber One,
and *Enterprise* turned west for the central Coral Sea.

On the evening of the twenty-ninth things looked quiet
enough for Halsey to order Task Forces 16 and 11 to rendezvous the next morning and conduct combined training
exercises. Accordingly, *Enterprise* turned southwest for the
rendezvous point. But shortly after midnight Admiral Sherman sent a message to his ships that at once changed their
course and speed, and the whole of the easy, peaceful
cruise:

INFORMATION X TASK FORCE 18 ATTACKED BY ENEMY
BOMBERS AND TORPEDO PLANES SOUTH OF GUADAL-
CANAL DURING NIGHT 29–30 JANUARY X CHICAGO
DAMAGED AND UNDER TOW OF LOUISVILLE IN POSITION
LATITUDE 10–33 LONGITUDE 160–07 AT 2115 29TH
COURSE 150 X THIS FORCE WILL SEARCH FOR AND PRO-
VIDE AIR COVERAGE AT DAYLIGHT FOR TASK FORCE 18 X
ENTERPRISE ASSIGN 18 VF TASK AIR COVERAGE FOR TASK
FORCE 18 X MAINTAIN 6 VF OVER TASK FORCE 18 DUR-
ING DAYLIGHT X LAUNCH 4 SEARCH PLANES AND FIRST
SECTION OF VF AT EARLIEST DAWN X MAINTAIN INNER
AND INTERMEDIATE PATROLS OVER TASK FORCE 16 AND
COMBAT PATROL IN READINESS ON DECK X OPERATION
ORDER 2–43

When Sherman's Operation Order 2-43 went into effect,
Enterprise was some 350 miles south and slightly west of
the crippled heavy cruiser *Chicago*. Task Force 16 turned
north at 28 knots.

In the predawn dark just before 6:00 A.M. the first planes
left the Big E's deck. Hoot Gibson and Red Hoogerwerf,
Buell and Frissel, in two search sections of SBDs, fanned
out to locate *Chicago*. Gibson located the damaged heavy
cruiser at 7:15, some thirty-five miles north of the eastern
tip of Rennell. She was down by the stern and trailing a
broad, iridescent river of oil. *Louisville*, at the other end of
a long catenary of anchor chain and towing cable, was easing her southeastward toward Espiritu at about four knots.

Wichita steamed slowly to starboard of the other two heavy cruisers, and the three light cruisers patrolled back and forth to port. The eight destroyers chased tails around the heavy ships and a fleet tug with her high bow and low stern was approaching *Louisville* to take over the tow.

Hoot at once transmitted the force position to Flatley's fighters, then dropped dive brakes and flew slowly over *Louisville* giving his gunner a "mark" to throw down a beanbag with a message giving the Wildcat radio frequency. At eight o'clock as Hoot and Hooger left to find the escort carriers, six of VF-10's blunt-winged Wildcats swung into position overhead.

Gibson found the two stubby little carriers with their thin island structure and high sides thirty minutes away. The four men in the two Dauntlesses looked these strange craft over with interest, noting the short, wide decks, their unsteady motion, and were glad they were flying from the *Enterprise* with her 30 knots and her long deck bordered with gun barrels. Gibson dropped another message requesting the frequency of the small carriers' fighters and then circled slowly while the answer came back by flashing light from high in the island.

Sherman tried to keep his force close enough to *Chicago* to give his fighters a short flight to station and to control them by radar and radio and yet remain far enough away to prevent being sighted by any aircraft sent to finish off the cruiser. The nicest judgment was required.

At 8:30 A.M. the four-plane CAP circling high over *Enterprise* sighted the moving speck of a single Zero about twenty miles to the westward. The Wildcats headed in at full throttle but the Zero climbed away, leaving them easily behind. In the too-familiar pattern of air war at sea this incident was an indication of action to come. The single fighter, fast, light and avoiding battle could only be a recon plane, and enemy airmen at their bases up the Solomons would be launching strikes to get the carrier and finish the sick cruiser.

The morning passed, and at noon the navigator came out on the bridge with his sextant and determined the latitude to be checked with radar ranges and bearings from Rennell. The afternoon moved across the southern sea and above the thickening overcast the sun eased downward toward Australia and still there was no action. At four miles every hour, *Chicago* was creeping out of danger. She had covered thirty miles since the tug *Navajo* had taken over from *Louisville.* By morning she could be another sixty miles along and out of sight from Rennell, harder to find in the open ocean while her repair parties worked around the clock to get her own propellers turning.

In midafternoon Admiral Halsey ordered the undamaged cruisers to Efate in the New Hebrides, and they pulled away from *Chicago* leaving her with six destroyers and hard-working little *Navajo.*

At quarter of four the news came that everyone in the task force, from Admiral Sherman and Captain Hardison to the junior destroyer mess cook, had been expecting all day. The code room crackled with the dots and dashes of Radio Guadalcanal:

ELEVEN UNIDENTIFIED TWIN-ENGINE AIRCRAFT BEAR-
ING 268° x DISTANCE 130 MILES COURSE 150° x

Course 150 headed them straight for *Enterprise,* and, in the radar room where Lieutenant Stan Ruehlow was advising and assisting the fighter director officer, they estimated the enemy planes would be overhead in fifty-five minutes.

At 4:10 P.M. the CAP over *Chicago,* led by Lieutenant Commander William R. "Killer" Kane, exec of the Reapers, made out the unmistakable silhouette of a twin-engine land-based Japanese bomber approaching high and alone from north of Rennell Island. Kane detached Wickendoll, Boren, Leder and Donahoe and they peeled off in pursuit. The enemy plane, a Mitsubishi Type 1, or Betty, swung south and then southwest around the eastern end of Rennell getting a good look at *Chicago,* the withdrawing cruisers and probably *Enterprise* and her task force. The four ensigns in their F4Fs shoved throttles into the stops and pulled up the charging handles of their guns, three to the right of the seat and three to the left. The Betty increased speed and turned away. The Wildcats closed very slowly from astern. At maximum range with their engines roaring under full power, each of the fighter pilots pulled his nose up a little and tried a long shot. The tracers smoked out, in long, shallow trajectories, converging gradually and then separating slightly again. Some seemed to be hitting. Again each pilot tried a burst with the range very slightly shorter. A piece of metal broke off the Betty and tumbled back and down but the bomber kept going and fast. Once again.

This time the starboard engine trailed a wisp of smoke which quickly became a pouring, and from astern they could see the prop falter and the bomber swerve and slow as it lost power on that side. The Wildcats came up fast now, firing in short careful bursts and the enemy tail gunner returned the fire with the slow Roman candle balls of a 20-millimeter. Hank Leder was ahead and he ignored the 20-millimeter and bored in, his six .50-calibers chewing into the wings and fuselage of the Betty. Gasoline in a white ribbon sprayed from punctured wing tanks and then a flame flickered across the wing behind the smoking engine and caught the fuel. In another second the Betty was a ball of orange fire tumbling for the sea two miles below. The four ensigns reduced power, leaned out mixture and reversed course to return to *Chicago*. They were forty miles southwest.

At 4:24 P.M. *Enterprise* radar picked up the incoming torpedo attack at sixty-seven miles, bearing 300 degrees. It was headed straight in and moving fast. Each time the thin pencil of the radar swept around the scope the clustered blobs of the attack showed closer to the center—the center was the bedspring antenna rotating at the Big E's masthead.

Enterprise went to General Quarters, the electric clanging of the general alarm blended with the stamp and scrape of feet as the crew ran to their battle stations. When the captain's talker clamped on his phones and plugged in, the reports were already coming in.

"Sky Control manned and ready."

"After steering manned and ready."

"Group One five-inch manned and ready."

"All repair parties manned and ready, condition Able set."

"All machinery spaces manned and ready."

Below decks the whine of the turbines rose an octave as speed went up to 27 knots. A young engineer lieutenant who had been caught in the shower by the general alarm stood determinedly at his post on the hot gratings below wearing only a few soapsuds. Ten more fighters clawed up into the sky and headed for station and, as they had done before, the men of *Enterprise* settled down at their battle stations to await the coming of the enemy.

John Crommelin, now executive officer, made a quick tour topside. He put a hand on a gun captain's shoulder and asked how many of the twelve he thought his gun would get, passed a couple of sentences with the first-class shipfitter in charge of a repair party gathered at a hatch at the base of the island, climbed to the high director to see how Orlin Livdahl felt about his new five-inch proximity fuses and called down to the chief engineer to see that all was well below.

While *Enterprise* braced for battle and *San Diego*'s sixteen five-inch guns moved in closer to her at the center of the destroyer circle, the twelve torpedo planes closed at 160 knots, two and two-thirds miles every minute. The bearing never changed but the range closed steadily—60 miles, 55, 50, 45—straight for *Enterprise*. Each glob of yellow-white light on the radarscope was a Japanese torpedo warhead of the variety that had ripped out *Yorktown*'s bottom at Midway, broken the *Lexington* at Coral Sea and finished *Hornet* at Santa Cruz. The Big E's guns trained out to the northwest and dozens of pairs of 7/50 binoculars searched the cloudy sky in that direction.

At 4:35 the FDO called Lieutenant MacGregor Kilpatrick, circling with his six Wildcats over *Chicago*.

"Vector 190, 20 miles."

Kilpatrick's six fighters turned south with open throttles and at 4:40 there they were. An even dozen of the dark, twin-engine Bettys spread out wing tip to wing tip in line abreast in a fast power glide for the Big E. They were just east of Rennell Island and slanting down through 6,000 feet.

Kilpatrick had a 4,000-foot altitude advantage and his heavy Wildcats picked up speed in a rush as they dived in to attack position. The flight leader knew he had to get as many as possible of the twelve with his six fighters. As calmly and coolly as if it were a training exercise, he sent "Flash" Gordon, Rip Slagle, Steve Kona and Whitey Feightner high on the enemy right flank and with Bob Porter took the left, ready for a series of crisscrossing highside runs that could, if competently executed, slash the enemy formation into scorched aluminum ten miles short of the Big E's tender sides.

Below, the enemy leader, with *Chicago* already a few miles away behind his left wing, saw clearly what was happening and abruptly changed targets. Seventeen miles from *Enterprise* the dozen Bettys broke sharply left, at over 200 knots, nearly reversing course to get at the wounded cruiser.

Enterprise was safe, but *Chicago,* creeping under tow at four knots, was in serious trouble. The four fighters that had been ready to attack from ahead and to the right of the Japanese formation were now badly behind and committed to a tail chase. But wiry, florid little MacGregor Kilpatrick, with Bob Porter on his wing, was well ahead and in attack position. The two Wildcats flipped up and over into high side runs. In fast, diving turns they swept down on the shiny, olive-drab Bettys, catching them expanding in the etched dots and ladders of their gunsights, pulling the blunt noses ahead and squeezing out the tracers. The .50-calibers walked the Betty wings and stitched into the fuselages and two flamed and fell. Aboard the *Enterprise* a lookout stopped the steady sweep of his binoculars on northwest and reported to the Officer of the Deck: "Black smoke bearing 348 degrees, sir, looks like a plane going down." With the Gs of the recovery pulling at their bellies, Kilpatrick and Porter passed under the bomber formation from left to right, rammed on full throttle and climbed back into position high and ahead on the enemy's starboard bow. Down they came again, the white gunsmoke streaming behind them. Kilpatrick's target flipped over on its back and dived into the sea. Porter's smoked and fell back.

There were eight healthy Bettys and a cripple when they passed over the circle of destroyers around *Chicago* and splashed their torpedoes into the sea. Black bursts of five-inch and long squirts of tracers rose from all the ships, smoking and crisscrossing close to the ocean surface. Kilpatrick's six fighters at full throttle roared in right behind, slashing at the Bettys in shallow stern attacks. Jimmy Flatley with Russ Reiserer, Cliff Witte and Pete Shonk whistled in, firing, over the destroyer masts at the end of a long max power glide, ignoring the "friendly" antiaircraft fire to rip at the bombers. One skidded into the sea well short of its target. Three more crashed close aboard the cruiser leaving brief bonfires on the surface. The gunfire shifted across *Chicago* to follow the dark brown torpedo planes with ten Wildcats angrily on their tails, and three more of them, shot down ten feet from the surface, tumbled and cartwheeled in sheets of spray. Another faltered, streaming fuel. One Betty, apparently untouched, scurried off to the northward skimming the flat crests of the ground swell.

As the action moved out of the destroyer screen, and the snarl of aircraft engines and the hammering of gunfire died down, torpedoes, released by Japanese pilots already dead, began to hit *Chicago.* Four times the sailors of the task force felt the decks thump against their feet with the concussion of the warheads and saw the fatal spouts rise from the cruiser's starboard side. Aboard *Chicago,* bosun's calls shrilled and the word was passed— "Abandon ship!" A destroyer ahead and to starboard of *Chicago* stopped a fifth torpedo and went dead in the water. Twenty minutes after the attack *Chicago* rolled over to starboard and started stern first on her two-mile voyage to the bottom. More than 1,000 officers and men scaled cargo nets and ladders and climbed into the whaleboats of other ships. The wounded destroyer skillfully repaired herself sufficiently to get under way, and clear the waters off Rennell Island, now littered with oil and debris from *Chicago* and the bodies of Hirohito's aviators.

While *Enterprise* aircraft were engaging the Japanese torpedo planes over *Chicago,* the four transports were unloading at Guadalcanal. The following day they took the last of General Vandegrift's Marines off the bloody island where they had been for six months.

The Battle of Rennell Island was over. *Enterprise* went back on the Espiritu-Noumea patrol-train-and-wait routine.

Early in February a message went from the Army general in command of the troops on Guadalcanal, to Halsey:

ORGANIZED RESISTANCE ON GUADALCANAL HAS CEASED

The long, touch-and-go campaign on the festering island was over—and *Enterprise,* which had covered the original landings, and at Eastern Solomons, Santa Cruz and the Slot battered back the inevitable enemy counterattacks, was still on guard. The birthdays of Abraham Lincoln and George Washington and the feast of St. Patrick found her there still.

"There" was mostly Espiritu, with the ship swinging around her anchor to the light tropical breeze or the seas around the Solomons which she patrolled.

On the morning of February 8, Radio Guadalcanal received a report from a searching B-17 of a Japanese carrier task force 250 miles northeast. Air Group Ten, then at sea in *Enterprise* well to the south, was ordered at once into Henderson. In three and a half hours the echelons of fighters, dive bombers and torpedo planes were dropping onto the scarred dirt field they knew so well, and taxiing through the dust to their fueling areas. While they were gassing and the squadron commanders were planning the strike, the B-17 search planes returned. None had seen any Japanese forces, none had sent the contact report. The only enemy around was the clever enemy communicator who had sent the message and achieved one of the most successful deceptions of the war.

In the early evening of February 13, Lieutenant Commander James H. Flatley was detached from duty as the commanding officer of Fighting Squadron Ten and left the *Enterprise* to return to the United States. Slight, dedicated Jimmy Flatley, known proudly in the air as "Reaper Leader" was the father of Fighting Ten. He had formed it, trained it, infused it with his thorough, aggressive spirit and led it with deadly success in action. Lieutenant Commander W. R. "Killer" Kane took over the squadron and ran and fought it in every way as competently as had Flatley. And down the years there would be other skippers. But despite time and many complete turnovers of officers and men, Fighting Ten remained Jimmy Flatley's child and has inherited his character. To Flatley, as much as to each pilot who squeezed out the tracers and had never seen him or heard his voice, goes the credit for each of the hundreds of enemy planes shot down, each enemy ship and installation smashed by strafing, each American life and ship saved by the Grim Reapers.

In March, actor Joe E. Brown's warm heart led him into that remote corner of the Pacific and John Crommelin walked him, swinging his pith helmet, through the seated sailors on the hangar deck, in their sweat-darkened dungarees to the partially raised elevator which formed a stage. The officers and men in khaki and dungarees and the stewards and mess cooks in their whites all forgot the war and how long it had been since home and love, and laughed with him until their stomachs and facial muscles were tired.

A few days later, in a quasi-formal but deeply serious little ritual of order reading which took place in the squadron's crowded Quonset while the rain rattled on the metal roof, Bucky Lee turned over command of Scouting Ten to Bill Martin, his executive officer. The bond between Lee and the officers and men of his squadron, a mixture of pride and loyalty and love, was too real to be stated and might have been spoiled in the stating. Bill Martin only

said that it could not be said—and opened the bar. Bucky
Lee left for the States to command an air group and Martin took over as skipper of the Scouts. In his report of the
actions of his squadron in the Slot, under Recommendations, Bucky Lee had written this paragraph:

> . . . that Lieutenant W. I. Martin, U. S. Navy, be
> given command of a squadron, having clearly demon-
> strated his ability, leadership, resourcefulness, and
> aggressiveness in action against the enemy.

Now Martin had a squadron, the one he liked best, his
own. *Enterprise* would see more of him.

On the seventeenth of March while the Big E was at sea
requalifying her pilots in night landings and conducting other training, she lost six Dauntlesses. The six were assigned
to intermediate air patrol and at the end of their patrol
were to rendezvous with Martin and fly back to Bomber
One. Somehow they missed the rendezvous, using an hour's
fuel in the attempt, and then found the route to Espiritu
blocked by a black, turbulent storm which they were unable to penetrate or circumnavigate. Lieutenant Tom Ramsey was in command of the flight and Glen Estes had the
second section. Without enough gasoline to return to the
ship and unable to get through the storm to Bomber One,
Ramsey went on the air advising his pilots to ditch while
they still had control of their planes. One SBD landed neatly beside the U. S. destroyer *Coney* which appeared as if
dispatched for the purpose. The others flew down the southwest coast of Malekula, the next island south of Espiritu
Santo, watching the needles of their fuel gauges and looking
for a rumored French hospital with rumored French
nurses. If they had to ditch, and clearly they did, it should
be made as pleasant as possible. They never found it. Estes,
Lucier and Bloch skidded their SBDs into the calm waters
of the lagoon at Hambi, one of the many small islands off
the coast of Malekula. Ramsey and his wingman got a few
miles farther along and also ditched. Espiritu Radio had
heard Ramsey's intentions (along with some conjecturing
about the hospital) and within a few days all pilots and
crewmen were back aboard ship.

Swede Vejtasa flew aboard during a training cruise with
a new fighter—a long-nosed, gull-winged, pointed-tailed
plane with a huge three-bladed propeller that barely cleared

the deck. It was the Chance-Vought Corsair—the first the men of *Enterprise* had seen. Jimmy Daniels waved him aboard for five practice landings.

On Monday, the twelfth of April, with the casual familiarity that comes in wartime of the constant handling of lethal weapons, a couple of sailors dragged a 100-pound bomb to the movies at Bomber One for a seat. The movie was scheduled to start at 7:00 P.M. but, there being little else to do, the officers and men gathered early to get good seats. At 6:35 an ordnanceman noticed the bomb smoking. Someone grabbed it and threw it against a bank of earth behind the screen where it detonated. Shrapnel sprayed out into the early-bird audience. Sixteen men were killed, over thirty badly wounded with many losses of arms and legs and shattered faces which had been turned toward the blast. Bud Lucier and Bobby Edwards of Scouting Ten were sitting together. Lucier received a chunk of shrapnel which lodged near a kidney, Edwards an eight-inch gash in the side of his head. Both survived. Many crewmen of *Enterprise* squadrons were wounded, among them J. E. Crisswell, Bud Lucier's rear-seatman.

Three days later a Scouting Ten SBD crashed on a predawn take-off at Bomber One when the wing hit a crash truck. The plane burned so fiercely for an hour that Glen Estes and others who attempted to rescue the pilot and crewman could not even approach. The dead pilot was Ensign Tom Kelly, newly reported to the squadron, and burned to death in the rear seat was J. E. Crisswell, sufficiently recovered from his shrapnel wounds to fly again, although his regular pilot was still out of commission.

When Captain Samuel P. Ginder took over command of the *Enterprise* on April 16, he announced that the "men may soon be rewarded with a yard period." This in all probability meant several months in the States, and from the straight military white lines came a spontaneous cheer that turned heads on small craft in the harbor half a mile away. Here at last was the partial confirmation of rumors that had been flickering through the ship since Rennell Island when it became common knowledge that *Enterprise* was no longer holding the line alone; *Sara* and the "jeep" carriers were around and a British carrier was reputedly on the way. The rumors had increased and persisted with the final conquest of Guadalcanal and each man had bitten hungrily on each rumor since it bore directly on his dear

and continuous desire to go home, now that he had survived
to a new appreciation of life.

Captain Ginder's word was good. A few days later, lighters came alongside and all hands turned to unloading bombs
and ammunition, spare parts and supplies that should remain in the combat area. Barge after barge of the bombs
in their rolling rings and ammunition in heavy cans was
tugged ashore and *Enterprise* rose slightly as the tons came
off before she was ballasted back to a seaworthy depth.

On the first of May at 10:00 A.M. in a holiday mood, her
band playing "California, Here We Come," *Enterprise*
sailed from Espiritu for Pearl Harbor. Several destroyers
formed a bent line ahead and the Dauntlesses and Avengers
of Air Group Ten prowled the nearby waters to look for
subs. Until well clear of any possible enemy aircraft, Kane's
Grim Reapers kept a CAP overhead.

Enterprise was a happy ship. All hands counted the days
to Pearl, calculated a few days only there to report, refuel,
load and pull out for home. Five days to San Francisco and
under the bridge. Leave and liberty and a chance to brag a
little, appropriately, and at the right times and places. But
first a parade of the ship's company of the world's greatest
warship up Market Street in whites while the citizens
cheered and waited to buy drinks and the women cheered
and waited.

John Crommelin formed the crew into companies and
each day they marched on the flight deck, sailors who had
not done a column left or a squads right since boot camp,
sailors whose time had been spent watching boiler gauges
or repairing fire-control equipment, or signaling or receiving the dot-dash of light or radio, relearned to step off
smartly on the left foot—to dress and cover, to keep in step
with the music of the band. They looked ragged and straggled badly at first but a day out of Pearl they were shipshape and respectable—a potential asset to a parade in
any city.

On the morning of the eighth of May, Air Group Ten
flew off the Big E for the last time that cruise, and hours
later the big signal searchlight at the Harbor Entrance Control Post at Pearl was talking to *Enterprise*.

The message which flickered in blue-white dots and
dashes was in technical naval phraseology and spoke of the
dissolution of one task force and the organization of a new
one but what it really said in effect was: "You will remain

at Pearl Harbor training a new air group for about six weeks. Air Group Ten will be detached from *Enterprise* on arrival."

The signalman showed the message to Captain Ginder who called Crommelin over. John Crommelin's flushed face grew redder and his words were neither proper nor restrained, but in a few minutes he was on the public address system passing the word to his crew. He gave them the facts, told them they were not to be downhearted; the Golden Gate was now only 2,000 miles away and they would get there yet; that it had been a couple of years, could a month or two more of training duty make any serious difference to men that had seen the action they had seen?

It made a difference, a big difference, even to the men of the air group who were going back to the States anyway but who had wanted to go home in triumph with the Big E, but only a few said so and the crew received the sad news well. Over the soda fountain a large sign almost instantly appeared:

ALL HANDS LAY BACK TO SICK BAY FOR A PROPHYLAXIS

When *Enterprise* slipped through the narrow channel past Fort Kamehameha and Hospital Point and into bustling rebuilding Pearl, it had been over nine months since she left. Nine months ago no one had ever heard of an island called Guadalcanal.

On the twenty-seventh of May, 1943, at a point on the flight deck a few feet aft of the patch marking the impact point of the bomb that wiped out Repair II at Santa Cruz, and a few feet forward of the new deck section on the starboard quarter covering the replaced five-inch guns where thirty-nine men had died instantly at Eastern Solomons, Admiral C. W. Nimitz, commander-in-chief United States Pacific Fleet, who had engineered the victory at Midway and guided his fleet from near-defeat to defense to offense, stood at the center of a white-clad square and read a paper for the President of the United States. Afterward he presented the paper to Captain Ginder who later had it copied word for word in six-inch letters on the island for all hands to see as often as they liked. It was the first Presidential Unit Citation ever to be awarded to an aircraft carrier. It read:

> For consistently outstanding performance and distinguished achievement during repeated action against enemy Japanese forces in the Pacific war area, December 7, 1941, to November 15, 1942. Participating in nearly every major carrier engagement in the first year of the war, the *Enterprise* and her air group, exclusive of far-flung destruction of hostile shore installations throughout the battle area, did sink or damage on her own a total of 35 Japanese vessels and shoot down a total of 185 Japanese aircraft. Her aggressive spirit and superb combat efficiency are fitting tribute to the officers and men who so gallantly established her as an ahead bulwark in defense of the American nation.

And then it listed the actions which the men of *Enterprise* remembered well enough:

Gilbert and Marshall Islands Raid	February 1, 1942
Wake Island Raid	February 25, 1942
Marcus Island Raid	March 4, 1942
Battle of Midway	June 4-6, 1942
Occupation of Guadalcanal	August 28, 1942
Battle of Steward Islands (Eastern Solomons)	August 24, 1942
Battle of Santa Cruz Islands	October 26, 1942
Battle of Solomon Islands (The Slot)	November 14-15, 1942

The Tokyo raid was not mentioned because it was possible that the enemy had still not figured out where Doolittle's B-25s had come from.

When Admiral Nimitz had gone ashore, *Enterprise* went back to work. There was a new air group to train for combat.

BOOK THREE

15 INTERMISSION

Enterprise *spent May, June and half of July, 1943,*
at Pearl Harbor.

While the ship worked and trained and rested, and was
even inspected for combat readiness, Air Group Ten shrank
under the constant pressure of the demand for experienced
pilots and crewmen. Old hands who had been with the
group for the full cruise aboard *Enterprise* were ordered to
training commands, staffs or embryonic groups and squadrons. The others, most of whom had come as replacements
during the preceding winter, went to Sand Point Naval Air
Station at Seattle to form the nucleus of a new Air Group
Ten which would operate from the Big E when her repairs
and modernization had been completed. The separation of
ship and air group carried the shock of major surgery.

During those ten weeks the men of the Big E came to
remember that their ship was a carrier of aircraft, that
those aircraft were organized into air groups and that no
one air group could be assigned permanently to one carrier.
Enterprise had become identified with Air Group Ten.
Many of the dividing lines between air group and ship's
company had been dissolved away by the heat and pressure of action and by days and hours of talk in the sultry
months around Espiritu and Noumea.

Then, nearly two months after her air group, on the anniversary of the day that Paris mobs released Louis XVI's
dazed prisoners from the Bastille, *Enterprise* was released
from her ordeal at Pearl and started home.

The whole feeling of the passage was different from any
that even the old hands remembered. It was strange and
wonderful for the navigator, Commander Oscar Pederson,
and his quartermasters to lay off a course to the northeast
out of Pearl instead of southwest or west, and to study recent, up-to-date U. S. Hydrographic Office charts of the
continental United States instead of ancient British Admi-
rality or other foreign charts of unheard-of islands with un-
pronounceable names. For the flight-deck crew there were
hours of idleness with only the few SBDs of the antisub

patrol to launch and recover. In the engine and firerooms no bells rang as the revolution indicators and the pitometer log remained steady on 20 knots.

On the morning of Tuesday, the twentieth of July, the sunrise was obscured by a dripping gray barrier of fog lying across the entrance to the Straits of Juan de Fuca which separate the State of Washington from the Province of British Columbia. In the first hours of the morning watch, *Enterprise* and her escorts groped toward the mouth of the straits on radar and radio direction finder bearings at ten knots, their whistles blaring into the grayness every two minutes, their lookouts staring across the narrow strip of dim and greasy sea that was all they could make out before the fog closed off their vision. The fog formed in droplets on the hair and eyebrows of the men topside and the first men across the flight deck left footprints in the wet.

When the watch changed at eight o'clock, the sun and the breeze had thinned and shredded the fog so that Oscar Pederson could make out Cape Flattery light abeam to starboard at eight minutes past the hour. As the Big E slid farther into the Sound and the weather continued to clear, her speed went up again; her men tumbled up on deck to see the low, heavily wooded green hills to starboard which were their first glimpse of home since the half-forgotten days of peace so long ago.

All morning *Enterprise* steamed eastward through the straits, and by early afternoon she was far enough into protected waters for Captain Ginder to turn his escorts loose. The Big E slid on alone with the land closing on both sides as the straits narrowed, and her quartermasters calling bearings on points and landmarks as they plotted her along the channel. In the afternoon she rounded Point Wilson and entered Puget Sound, and four hours and twenty minutes later she had left Restoration Point abeam to starboard and entered Rich Passage, only thirty miles from her destination.

The lights were beginning to come on along the Seattle waterfront as *Enterprise* coasted by like a tired gray ghost and angled westward into Bremerton across the bay. It was ten minutes after nine on the evening of July 20, 1943, when her chain rattled out of the hawse, her anchor splashed, and came to rest fifteen fathoms down on American bottom for the first time since September of 1939. From her berth in Sinclair Inlet, off Bremerton, the men of the Big E could see barrage balloons tugging gently at their cables above the cranes of the Navy Yard and the lights of Seattle glinting through the evening haze some twelve miles across the water to the east.

No one waited ashore for any man aboard the *Enterprise*. Wartime security had kept knowledge of her arrival from everyone who did not have an official need to know. Sailors in dress whites with their leave papers in their hands paced impatiently or stared out across the dark bay at the lights ashore. The wardroom was full of officers in khaki, with heavy suitcases stacked near by, smoking and drinking coffee and waiting for the word that would send them ashore and thence to every corner of the United States where there would be doors and eager arms open to them.

Enterprise was scheduled to be slightly over three months in the yard and John Crommelin had divided the officers and men who wanted leave into three groups, and assigned each group a thirty-day-leave period. Men who had slept soundly on the eve of battle had been restless for the past two nights. In the darkened berthing spaces and staterooms they had dreamed of missed connections and wasted time or that they were already home and heavy with some terrible disappointment and then waked with relief to find it was not so.

Some men planned surprises—to walk in unannounced at dinnertime, in midafternoon or morning, or to arrive at midnight in their parents' homes and simply be there when the households awakened. Other men considered asking wives or parents to meet them halfway and share the trip home. All knew it would be good; most thought it would be beautiful; all wanted very badly to go home.

At 10:30 that evening the word was passed, "Now the first leave party lay up to the starboard gangway!" and the big fifty-footers began ferrying 630 men and 50 officers ashore. Included were Lieutenant (j.g.) Jim Wyrick, who had helped get the hot powder overboard at Eastern Solomons, Chief Shipfitter Jim Brewer, who had explored the shattered and burning compartments during the same battle, Boatswain Hatchell, who had repaired the flight deck, Lieutenant Brad Williams, who had fixed the radar under fire at Santa Cruz.

Who, except each man himself who has not forgotten, knows how it really was? For two men it was like this.

A young officer hitched rides by military air across the continent to New England in two days, taxied at phenomenal cost the last forty miles and arrived before the spacious frame house of his in-laws at 10:00 P.M. when the last light was fading and the little town was quieting between the hills. There was a light in the living room but no sound or movement, and he stopped on the wooden porch with his hand on the door which had never been locked, to let his heart slow from the heavy thumping which sounded in his ears so that he thought it would rouse the house. When he entered the dim hall he could see his mother-in-law's white head under the standing lamp and her face as she looked toward the door. Her eyes flew wide and her mouth opened to speak before a second thought made her point in silence to a shadowed couch at the other end of the long room where the officer's dark-haired young wife slept lightly on her back with one arm thrown up on the cushion above her head, beside a baby carriage which contained a son he had never seen.

A seaman, whose wife wore red to set off her black hair and startling blue eyes, was to meet her at a railroad station in the Midwest. His train was early and he leapt from it knowing she was close and with his vision so tuned that a glimpse of red anywhere in the 180 degrees ahead would send him to General Quarters. On his second pass through the crowded station he saw it—a red dress at a lunch counter behind a revolving glass door to his left. As he entered, the RPM increased so abruptly on the revolving door that an elderly gentleman was expelled in a shambling run in the opposite direction. Conversation at the lunch counter stopped as he caught the red dress off the stool and her hat fell to the floor, and for two people for a little while the war did not exist.

All over the country, on hilltop farms in Maryland, in the suburbs of Houston and Minneapolis, on the wide side streets of small corn towns in Iowa, men who had been boys came home and were stuffed by their mothers, had the family car which had been so hard to get pressed on them by their fathers, were listened to and affectionately caressed by girls they had considered unapproachable, and generally began to feel that the war was not so bad after all. And the feats of *Enterprise* and her men increased in drama and magnitude everywhere.

For the men who did not go on leave there was liberty

in Bremerton and Seattle and plenty of work to do aboard ship. For the gunners, there was a six-day period of gunsmoke, gun grease and gun oil, and noise and the smell of powder of the Anti-Aircraft Training Center at Pacific Beach, Washington.

The morning after arrival, *Enterprise* began unloading ammunition so that she could safely enter dry dock. The off-loading of ammunition is an all-hands operation. No matter what a man's normal duties or what his department or division are, unless he is actually on watch or sick or a cook in the galley preparing sandwiches for the workers, he takes his place in the long lines of men that carefully pass the shells and powder and cans of ammunition from the tops of hoists to the barges secured alongside. While the red Baker flag flies from the truck there is no smoking in the ship. Officers and chiefs patrol and supervise and expedite and caution. With her magazines open and her explosives all exposed, a carrier or any ship is terribly vulnerable to an accidental spark or a carelessly dropped shell or even a flicked match or butt.

The job was not finished until 2:00 A.M. and by that time 3,700 rounds of five-inch ammunition, each with its can of powder, 1,725 boxes of 40-millimeter, 30 1,000-pound bombs, 32 1,500-pound bombs, 36 torpedoes and 62 depth charges had been manhandled out of the magazines and barged ashore.

At eleven the same morning the Big E got up her hook and went alongside the dock to await the right tide for drydocking and at 8:00 P.M. she entered Dry Dock Number 5 at Bremerton, the big doors closed behind her, the water began to recede and her long hull settled on the keel blocks like a patient into a hospital bed, for a good long rest and lots of beneficial minor surgery.

For the men who stayed in Bremerton, reunion was first by telephone and then, if they were lucky and could manage it, a room at the Enetai Inn. One young wife, installed in her room at the Enetai when the husband she had not seen for two years knocked loudly on the door, in half fright and love and confusion, would not open until she had on her new hat to show him.

On the first night in, John Crommelin took ten officers ashore in one of the first boats. One knelt to kiss the ground as his first act on the mainland. All made for the local office of the telephone company since they had heard this was the fastest way to get a call through. On the way they passed a corner phone booth and Lieutenant John Munro, the Big E's assistant damage control officer, popped in and tried his nickel. In less than a minute he was talking to his wife in Boston for the first time in a year, and $25 later he returned to the ship a much happier man. It took the others two hours to get through.

As families began to arrive at Bremerton, Crommelin arranged temporary custody of the small new wooden houses with coal stoves just across the inlet from the Navy Yard at East Port Orchard known as "Splinter Center." He also put an officer in charge, assigned a medical officer, arranged drivers and vehicles and set up a bus schedule. *Enterprise* shipfitters, electricians and machinists were assigned to assist the families at Splinter Center when it did not interfere with their normal duties. Officers and men lived together in a new and un-Navylike relationship in the rows of little wooden boxes with their wives and children. Since the Big E was out of commission and, in effect, temporarily no longer a man-of-war at all, her men had three out of four nights to be ashore, standing duty on the fourth night. But they had to be aboard at 8:00 A.M., and the Navy ferry left Port Orchard at seven, which necessitated early reveille in the little houses on the shores of Puget Sound.

The men and the officers learned more about each other in the weeks at East Port Orchard—reasons now for what they had already learned in the months at sea. And they rediscovered that babies are more than cute snapshots, that they cry at late and inopportune hours, that they demand considerable and not always pleasant personal attention, that they eat almost continually and rise very early in the morning with no regard whatever for what has occurred the previous night.

For the officers and men of the Big E who were unattached either legally and technically, or by virtue of distance, circumstances and inclination, life was vastly different from that at Splinter Center. Both family and nonfamily men shared the eight to ten daily hours of work aboard ship and the necessary watches, but where one group knew the Navy ferry to Port Orchard, the other came to know the names of *Kalakala* and *Chippewa* and the other big steam ferries that made nearly hourly trips between Bremerton and Seattle. Bachelors of all ranks and rates lived close to the knowledge that the last ferry left Seattle at

11:30 P.M., that there were certain hazards to be overcome in making it, like the frequent freight trains which blocked the only auto road to the slip; that there were further hazards once the voyage began, such as becoming fouled in the torpedo nets that stretched across the channel at Bainbridge Island; that in the event of this sort of delay, there was a beer bar aboard which provided a certain amount of comfort during the untangling process. The bachelors were also aware of the alternatives which faced them were they to miss the last boat—that they could—

(1) drive around the 114 miles if one had custody of an automobile;

(2) return to the nearest bar for solace, and then, when it closed, find a place to wait until the next ferry at 6:00 A.M.—as a last resort the wooden benches of the waiting shed would do;

(3) if one were an officer, have a more comfortable variation of (2), which was another drink at the "O" Club and then a nap in the bunk room which the club thoughtfully provided to meet just this type of emergency.

Seattle and Bremerton were cities friendly to the Navy. Both had seen the big prewar battlewagons steam out of the sound for Hawaii, and after Pearl Harbor had seen one limp back in with a composite crew. Long before the war Seattle was known throughout the Navy for Fleet Week in August, when the gray ships anchored in Elliot Bay, full-dressed in their colors and displaying their searchlights at night, and the people of the city could look down from their hills and see the backbone of their country's seapower in one anchorage. In those days the children of Seattle who visited the ships were given sailor hats and large slabs of freshly baked pie, and the citizens took the men of the fleet into their homes.

While the men of the Big E put in their eight hours aboard ship and went ashore to their families and their friends, as was their right and their reward, the workmen of the Bremerton Navy Yard, working around the clock, almost literally took the *Enterprise* apart and put her back together again. Under the organized confusion of air hoses, power cables, water lines, oxygen-and-acetylene tubes, pneumatic chipping hammers, the flash and sputter of welders' arcs, dirt, dust, floodlights, portable blowers, paint, oil, and scaffolding, *Enterprise* was becoming a more modern, more powerful warship.

The most noticeable change was a long steel blister being welded on both sides and extending for three-quarters of the ship's length and well below and above the water line. Inside the blisters were tanks for fuel oil but their main purpose was torpedo protection. A warhead detonation on the blister would still be several feet from the real hull of the ship, and the steel blister and the space behind it would absorb a large part of the force of the explosion, sharply decreasing damage.

There were many other major alterations being performed. The spaces in the island that had been known as Flag Radio and Flag Plot were combined with the tiny Radar Room to make a Combat Information Center (CIC) where radar, radio and visual information could be received, evaluated and then distributed to the officers who needed it to make combat decisions. Two new 1,000-gallon-a-minute Diesel fire pumps were installed, complete with fuel tanks and necessary piping, providing completely independent major sources of fire-fighting water, even in the event of loss of all steam and electrical power. Two complete additional ready rooms were constructed. Bunks and living accommodations were provided for fifty-seven additional officers. A new meat room and a new vegetable room were built, giving the supply officer another 5,000 cubic feet of cold-storage space. Eight new five-inch dual purpose guns, with their supporting structure, power supply, ammunition supply facilities and directors were installed, four forward and four aft. Seven 40-millimeter twin mounts were added. Two more 40-millimeter quad mounts were also installed. Fourteen additional 20-millimeters were bolted to the ship's structure for a total of fifty. For all the guns, except the 20-millimeters, improved radar-controlled directors were installed, enabling them to open fire at night or in bad weather on targets that only the eye of radar could make out. New and better radars replaced the old equipment and remote scopes were added in the pilothouse for the officer of the deck, in the Chart House for the navigator, in Air Plot and in Sky Control.

Not only was all this new equipment provided and new spaces built, but most of the Big E's old systems were modernized and improved. The fire main, probably the most important single factor in damage control on a carrier, was extended fore and aft and given greater versatility and resistance to damage by new cross-connections, sectionalizing and group cutout valves, riser cutouts and overhead loops. The old salt-water system for flooding the ship's magazines was removed and a sprinkling system installed in its place and extended to include all bomb and torpedo storage rooms, the torpedo workshop and all 40- and 20-millimeter and .50-caliber belting and clipping rooms. The casualty power system was similarly extended, the sound-powered telephone and battle announcing circuits expanded and increased, steam heat and ventilation extended and improved. All the ready rooms and medical spaces, the steering engine room, CIC and the Damage Control Room (old Central Station) were air-conditioned. The barriers and arresting cables and equipment were removed, overhauled and replaced. The catapults were removed and replaced with new, improved versions, six feet longer and capable of launching heavier aircraft at higher end speeds. As important to the crew as any of these improvements was the installation of more and better ice cream equipment in the galley.

All of this the Bremerton Navy Yard was rapidly accomplishing and at the same time repairing bomb damage from Eastern Solomons and Santa Cruz. And yard management was in sympathy with the Big E's crew, willing to do extra work where it seemed desirable without formal approval from Washington which was technically necessary. It was this type of semiofficial "cumshaw" work which earned the yard the lasting gratitude of the damage control organization. At the ship's request, sound-powered phone outlets were installed in protected locations along the hangar deck, enabling the repair parties to move their battle station up out of the confined spaces on the third deck where so many had been killed in August and October of the previous year.

And yet, with hundreds of men working at all hours of the day with dangerous equipment, and heavy weights and great heights from which to fall or to drop equipment on others, there was not a single serious accident. And the work was well done and completed on schedule.

John Crommelin was promoted to captain, and at 1:30 A.M. on the thirtieth of September he was detached and made his final double salute to the officer of the deck whom he had trained and to the quarter-deck he had helped save in the Solomons. Driving away from Dry Dock Number 5 in a gray Navy sedan with his gear piled in the back, and looking back at *Enterprise,* floodlighted, sputtering and ringing with the work which would send her back to sea without him, in a war that was only half done and seemed much less than that, Crommelin could not have known that of all the men, great and small, whatever their talents or reputations, who sailed in her, his was the personality which most indelibly stamped itself on the entity of steel and flesh which was the *Enterprise.* As the molecules in a hammered piece of iron tend to turn within the metal and align themselves north and south, so had *Enterprise,* under the blows of Yamamoto's dive bombers around the Solomons, tended to align her own individuality with the dominant, aggressive personality of Crommelin. When men think of *Enterprise,* they most often think of Crommelin. The Big E's own special close and efficient relationship between ship's company and air group had been forged largely by Crommelin—the pilots' pilot who was also air officer and then exec. *Enterprise* would continue to be blessed with excellent executive officers, one of whom was Commander Cecil B. Gill, who took over the job early in October, but she would be another ship without John Crommelin.

While the carrier rested on the keel blocks of the dry dock at Bremerton, a new Air Group Ten was forming and training at Sand Point Naval Air Station eighteen miles northeast across the sound on the Lake Washington side of Seattle.

Commander Roscoe L. Newman was the new air group commander, replacing J. A. Thomas. The bombing squadron had absorbed the scouts and the new, nearly double-strength Bombing Ten was under the command of Lieutenant Commander Richard L. Poor. Bill Martin, with his intense interest in instrument flight and his conviction that a well-trained instrument pilot assisted by the eye of airborne radar, could do the same things at night or in bad weather that he could do in the clear, had asked for and received command of Torpedo Ten whose big Avengers were being equipped with radar. William R. "Killer" Kane, who had inherited the Grim Reapers of Fighting Ten from Flatley, still commanded the new squadron and was receiving late-model fighters, Grumman F6F Hellcats, to replace the Wildcats of pre-Bremerton days. Some of the pilots in the new group had been in the old squadrons for a few months before the Big E's return to Pearl. Some had seen action in the Solomons. Most were new.

The re-forming air group had acquired a head start on the rebuilding carrier. The new squadrons had been organized, and ground training had already begun when *Enterprise* dropped her anchor off Bremerton on the evening of July 20. Commander Newman needed all the time he could get to put his new group in fighting condition. Except for a small nucleus of trained and seasoned men, he had new aircraft being flown by green pilots and maintained by inexperienced mechanics in weather which was most often bad. But he had superb squadron commanders with combat experience and inherent ability, capable of imparting to their men the critical importance of the training they were undergoing, and of infusing those men with their own demanding, aggressive spirits. They knew that nothing less than perfection could assure success or even survival in the coming months.

The only significant difference in equipment was the new Hellcat. (VB-10 and VT-10 had improved versions of the same Dauntless and Avenger that had been operational for the past year or more.) The Hellcat's engine had 800 additional horsepower and was equipped with a supercharger for high-altitude operation; improved and larger auxiliary fuel tanks gave the plane more range; the cockpit was faired smoothly into the top of the fuselage; nearly twice the Wildcat's ammunition supply was available to the Hellcat's six .50-calibers. The landing gear could now be raised and lowered hydraulically by shoving up and down a lever, so that no longer would carrier sailors watch the fighters fly off, all bobbing slightly while their pilots turned the landing gear crank 38½ times to retract their wheels. Flaps were operated electrically with a hydraulic emergency system. Guns were charged electrically, and a built-in plotting board pulled out over the stick and the pilot's lap from under the instrument panel and could be quickly shoved back out of the way. In other words, Kane's Grim Reapers now had a plane that would climb and fly faster, higher and farther, shoot better and was more convenient to operate.

At Sand Point and Bremerton summer passed into fall. On the twentieth of August and the twentieth of September the huge leave parties returned aboard ship and others shoved off the following day.

There were times of unexpected excitement, such as a

loss of all lights and power in *Enterprise* when a dropped welding rod shorted out the main electrical board, or when the heat of welder's arcs ignited paint or oil films on the reverse sides of bulkheads. At Sand Point there were ground loops and minor accidents and remarkable experiences coming home through the weather among the mountains. Once Lieutenant Russell "Kip" Kippen, feeling out an SNJ single-engine advanced trainer after hundreds of hours in Catalinas, rolled the J-bird over on its back after cautioning his back-seat passenger to tighten his seat belt, watched a chute blossom far below and called his passenger's attention to it, only to find that it was the passenger who was dangling beneath the chute, having fallen out of the J, seat and all.

Early on the morning of September 25, water began pouring back into the dry dock, floating the accumulated debris of two months of work, covering the keel blocks and wetting the Big E's bottom. At 7:00 A.M. *Enterprise* was afloat and backing out of the dock to berth starboard side to Pier 5, where work went on as usual, and on the nineteenth of October she nosed into Dry Dock Number 4 while cranes placed large concrete weights on the edges of her deck to make her list so that yard engineers could verify and measure her stability with her new tanks and equipment.

At 8:10 A.M. on the twenty-fourth, the Big E was really under way for the first time since late July when the gates of the dry dock had closed behind her. She headed out into Puget Sound to conduct post-repair trials, to be sure the new installations and equipment were going to function properly, to see that she was safe for sea, that her crew could still operate her after the months of inactivity, to flex her cramped muscles and find out what had to be done before she saw action. For two days she made speed runs, stopped each shaft separately, proof-fired her new guns, landed one of each type of aircraft in her air group. Yard supervisors and engineers went along to assist in calibrations and adjustments and to see at firsthand what bugs had to be worked out, what discrepancies existed in the work their men had done. There were few bugs or discrepancies and those were readily put right. Bremerton had done a magnificent job on *Enterprise*. Shortly after 5:00 P.M. on the twenty-sixth she was back in the yard. Less than five days remained of the three months plus that had looked so long from July.

In those final days, while the yard performed the work that the post-repair trials had shown to be necessary, and supplies and stores of all kinds were struck below, the officers and men of Air Group Ten arrived in squadron groups and settled into their quarters. Only those were left at Sand Point who would fly aboard later.

Each of the hundreds of warships that cruised the oceans of the world in those days had at one time to sail from its home port or from some United States port that had grown familiar and even dear by association; and in the act of sailing, of backing away from a dock with a long blast of the whistle, of watching the oily harbor water widen between ship and shore and the familiar figures on the dock grow small and finally indistinguishable from all the others, had to wrench the lives of her men away from home, or what for the time had served as home, had to force the break with warmth, with affection, in one form or another. That moment had come for *Enterprise,* and she and her men endured it and turned their faces and minds and sore hearts to the job at hand.

The first of November, 1943, was the Big E's last day in U. S. waters. She was under way before eight and at 8:45 Killer Kane was overhead with twenty-nine of his new Hellcats from Sand Point. While Kane circled waiting for *Enterprise* to turn up wind, she sent him a message by flashing light. It read:

   THE BIG E WELCOMES ABOARD HER MAIN BATTERY

16 MAKIN AND THE MARSHALLS

Less that five days after the new Air Group Ten landed aboard *Enterprise* in the chill Straits of Juan de Fuca, the squadrons were relaunched for the Naval Air Station at Puunene, Maui, and on the evening of Saturday, the sixth of November, the Big E was back at her berth in Pearl Harbor.

On Sunday morning at 9:45 Captain Matthias B. Gardner took over command of *Enterprise.* At 11:45 A.M. on

Tuesday, Rear Admiral Arthur W. Radford, Commander Carrier Division Eleven and Commander Task Group 50.2, broke his two-star flag at the Big E's truck, and at 6:18 the next morning the ship was under way for secret combat operations 2,000 miles to the southwest.

In the middle of the forenoon watch, with the task group clear of the islands and on course for its destination, the carriers swung up into the wind to receive their aircraft. One of the first Hellcats to enter the *Enterprise* traffic pattern made a bad approach. The LSO waved him off, but as he roared low over the deck, nose high and under full power, his tail hook caught a wire. The F6 slammed to the deck and careened into the port catwalk flaming from a broken belly tank. One wheel and one wing dropped into the 20-millimeter batteries, the other wing tilted toward the sky and red gasoline flames boiled aft with the wind. The broken fighter had hardly come to an uneasy balance on the deck edge when Lieutenant Walt Chewning, the catapult officer, was on it. Using the flaring belly tank as a step, he scrambled over the leading edge of the up wing to the cockpit and pulled the shaken pilot out before the running fire fighters and the asbestos-suit men could reach the crash.

The planes and pilots which landed aboard *Enterprise* that day were not those of Air Group Ten. Roscoe Newman's outfit had been left at Puunene for advanced operational training before being committed against the enemy, and it was Air Group Six which flew aboard the Big E southwest of Oahu. It was commanded by Lieutenant Commander Edward H. "Butch" O'Hare, who was known throughout the Navy for the Congressional Medal of Honor he had earned in four busy minutes high over the old *Lexington* off Bougainville in February of 1942. His single F4F had been all that stood between nine twin-engine Japanese bombers and the carrier, and he had shot down five and so demoralized the other four that they dropped prematurely and turned away.

Butch was a stocky, aggressive, likable Irishman with beetling black eyebrows. He was inclined to pudginess but was unchallengeably the best shot and the best pilot in his command. His men stood in awe of him for the hero he was. They respected him for his repeatedly demonstrated professional competence and they loved him for his warmth, his enthusiasm and his courage. A popular feeling on Maui was that Butch had personally saved the island from the Japanese. On his return from the action off Bougainville, the rooftops around Puunene carried messages of welcome to him and his squadron spelled out in living flowers. Each subsequent return to Maui was an occasion for prolonged celebration.

Although Air Group Six was familiar to the old hands in the Big E as her own prewar and early-war group, this was in reality a fresh and untried organization composed of the normal salting of green and eager youngsters with a few combat-wise veterans. The squadrons had completed all prescribed training but had practically no carrier experience, and this sudden assignment to *Enterprise* and immediate departure had left no time for ship and air group to work out any of the myriad little problems that mean the difference between smooth, safe operations and difficult, more dangerous ones. And *Enterprise* had training problems of her own. Forty per cent of her men were new and freshly fitted into her department and division organizations, assigned to watches, battle stations, bunks, sections and duties. But the experienced, dedicated nucleus crew in all departments and divisions, in all spaces, on all decks, during all watches and working hours, on leave and liberty and rope-yarn Sundays, passed to the men they worked with, talked with, ate with, drank with, defecated with in the absolute nonprivacy of a man-of-war, their real, soul-deep, inexpressible and unadmittable love of the ship, the *Enterprise*.

These were not articulate men. None would ever say, "I love the *Enterprise*." They simply identified themselves with her. They cursed her as all sailors have always cursed their ships but their shipmates understood the blessings. They went ashore and got horribly drunk (or some did) but not before they had arranged to be delivered on board before the expiration of liberty, and they were on deck at their stations and duties when "turn to" was sounded or when the special sea details were called away. And this sailor's love, this pride, this will to work, this *Enterprise* spirit, spread slowly like a benign contagion so that others caught it and in turn passed it on, so that for each man of the original nucleus who was transferred to other duty (and they were few), five or ten newer men were left who knew what he knew and felt as he felt about *Enterprise*. It was this peculiar process which was going on throughout the ship as the Big E steamed back into action after Bremerton.

The men who had made the early island raids with Halsey and battered back the Japanese for nine months around Guadalcanal could see and feel that the war in the Pacific was now a different kind of war.

Pearl Harbor was filled with ships, most of them new, fast battleships with bulbous bows, new *Fletcher*-class destroyers mounting five five-inch guns, new light and heavy cruisers and new carriers bearing the names of the Big E's sisters lost in actions which *Enterprise* survived. And all those ships, new and old, were fully manned with fresh young men just out of school and training camp, officered mostly by reserve officers commissioned after some accelerated course of three or four months; the eager, green crews held together by 10 or 20 per cent of regular officers and men, and reserves with recent experience in combat.

Now as she stood down to the southwest, *Enterprise* was not the lone carrier of her task group, flanked by one or two old cruisers and four or five destroyers and embarked on a semisuicidal hit-and-run raid on a mysterious and formidable enemy-held area. In Admiral Radford's Task Group 50.2, known as the Northern Carrier Group, in addition to *Enterprise*, there were the light (cruiser-hulled) carriers *Belleau Wood* and *Monterey*, three fast battleships, *North Carolina*, *Indiana* and *Massachusetts* and six destroyers. In the various other task forces and task groups of the Fifth Fleet were five more big carriers (including the new *Yorktown* and the new *Lexington*), three more light carriers (CVLs as opposed to CVs), eight escort or "jeep carriers" (CVEs), three more fast battleships and seven old battleships raised, modernized and restored since Pearl Harbor. Also involved were several cruisers, many more destroyers, eighteen attack transports, oilers, minesweepers, tenders and amphibious craft.

The Fifth Fleet was commanded by Raymond Spruance, now a vice admiral, who had made all the right decisions aboard the Big E at Midway a year and a half ago. His mission was the capture and occupation of the Gilbert Islands, the first of the several island groups which string across the central Pacific toward Japan.

The Gilberts consist of the three atolls of Makin, Tarawa and Apemama, with Makin the farthest north, Tarawa some seventy miles south and Apemama another fifty miles to the southeast of Tarawa. If you lay off a southwesterly line from Pearl Harbor to Guadalcanal, Tarawa lies two thirds of the way along it, 2,100 miles southwest of Pearl and 1,000 miles northeast of Guadal.

Japan took the Gilberts from nearly nonexistent British garrisons early in the war, and had since been building airfields and seaplane bases from which their aircraft could raid and scout for eight or nine hundred miles forcing a wide detour in the arterial supply line from the United States and Hawaii to the Australian area.

With the Marshalls which extend off to their northwest, the Gilberts form a screen across the central Pacific behind which lay the main enemy base at Truk in the Carolines, a screen which denied to the United States the use of millions of square miles of ocean on the approaches to Japan and forced Allied supply routes far to the south.

Since the thirteenth of November, long-range planes flying from newly acquired U. S. bases in the Ellice and Phoenix Islands had been hitting the Gilbert atolls every day. Since the tenth some 25,000 troops had been at sea, 6,500 soldiers for Makin and 18,500 Marines for Tarawa. Apemama was unfortified and virtually undefended. D-Day was the twentieth of November, 1943.

Enterprise went into action on the nineteenth. With *Belleau Wood* and *Monterey*, her mission was to acquire and maintain control of the air over Makin, destroy enemy positions on the island on D-Day minus one, support the actual landings on D-Day and then stand by as a striking force in the event that Japanese naval forces cared to challenge American activity in the Gilberts.

Seventy-five miles northwest of Makin, Captain Gardner pointed the Big E's bow into the predawn trade wind and began catapulting the first of fifteen strikes scheduled for that day.

By 5:40 A.M. the 33-plane *Enterprise* first strike was on its way to Makin. It climbed easily en route to 12,000 feet in the gradually lightening sky, the Hellcats throttled back and weaving to stay with the loaded Dauntlesses. Ten miles out the island was in plain sight, lying like a dark, irregular T with its top to the southwest. The crossbar of the T and the south side of the shaft were sharply traced in the white of breaking seas, but the north side, on the lagoon, showed no breakers. Makin, sleeping in the mid-Pacific morning twilight, looked as it must have looked a thousand centuries before, when the receding sea exposed and killed the little coral animals that had built it and the palms and mangroves rooted and spread. Only from close range could the Big E's pilots make out the four stubby piers poking out into the lagoon on the north side of the T, which indicated the presence of man on the sleepy little island.

The men on Makin were in for an ungentle awakening and the Japanese lieutenant who commanded the garrison was about to begin his last and busiest days.

The Big E's Hellcats went in first, sweeping the beaches and gun positions with .50-caliber fire, and the hammer of their guns and the rising whine of their engines as they dived were reveille for Japanese and Gilbertese that morning. Nine thousand feet overhead, as the fighters completed their sweeps, the SBDs rolled over into their classic and deadly dives and the 1,000-pounders began to rock the island.

By 6:30 A.M. when the sun rose out of a dark cloud bank and cast long shadows down the shaft of Makin's T toward the crossbar, half a dozen fires were burning and clouds of brownish smoke blew down wind on the trades. There was no return fire from the Japanese who either did not get to their guns in time or preferred to take cover from the raking 50s of the Hellcats. But as the *Enterprise* SBDs joined up and flew, well out of range, around the narrow eastern end of Makin, a single major-caliber antiaircraft gun at the foot of one of the piers on the lagoon opened up long enough to be located and have five planes of the second strike assigned specifically to its extinction.

Throughout D-Day minus one, the nineteenth of November, *Enterprise* and her two smaller sisters pounded the beaches, gun positions and installations on Makin. *Enterprise* launched and recovered her scheduled fifteen strikes, depending for the first time on the improved catapults installed at Bremerton to launch enough of the heavily loaded planes so that the remainder had sufficient deck to fly off. The only air opposition was a single Dave fighter which started a run on a formation of VT-6's Avengers on their way to the target on the second strike. It was instantly smothered by Lieutenant Harris' section of four Hellcats which opened fire simultaneously from a point-blank 300 yards, ripping the enemy plane into flaming chunks. The SBDs continued to hammer at solid targets with their 1,000-pounders. VT-6's TBFs dropped 2,000-pound, instantaneously fused "daisy cutters" to flatten above-ground installations and kill troops. They also photographed beaches and fortifications and delivered the developed, printed and partially evaluated pictures to Admiral Turner in the *Pennsylvania* by message drop. VF-2 strafed everything that moved and maintained a CAP over the target and the ship all day. By sunset only an occasional sputter of light anti-aircraft fire was left to answer the U. S. planes over the island.

As the central Pacific began to lighten under the morning twilight of D-Day, silent, darkened shapes were easing in from the sea toward the western beaches of Makin. As the light increased, Japanese machine gunners peering from behind coconut log emplacements along the shore could make out the high sides of six big transports only two or three miles out, and, flanking the transports, low and heavy in the water, the bristling bulks of battleships. To seaward dozens of other blacked-out ships were moving in.

The enemy did not have much time for observation. With sunrise still twenty minutes away he flattened out behind his coconut logs under the roar of engines and slamming explosions of heavy bombs as the first strike came in from the carriers. Then he had nearly ten minutes to dig out, dust off, salvage his weapons and shift position before the 14-inch salvos of the battlewagons began to rumble in like freight trains on a short, one-way line. After that the Japanese on Makin did not see much of the action. Destroyers and cruisers joined the bombardment, carrier fighters came in to strafe and, as the boats approached the beach, their rockets rattled down in dense explosive patterns. Coral dust and smoke from oil and equipment fires obscured large areas of the island until the steady trades could clear the air.

The ships offshore could only see the near beaches and the strike groups had only glimpses of a few moments before dropping their bombs and joining up for the return flight. But one *Enterprise* pilot had an excellent view of the action and he had it nearly all day. He was Lieutenant Commander J. C. Phillips, the skipper of Torpedo Six, who was assigned a liaison mission over the island. His orders were to observe and report the activity on Makin to Rear Admiral R. Kelly Turner who directed the operation from *Pennsylvania*, to relay messages from the task force commander to the various strike groups—in short, to be Turner's eyes and ears over the target.

Phillips rolled his heavy TBF off the Big E's bow at four minutes past seven while the battlewagons and their helpers were working the island over with 14-, 8- and 5-inch high explosive projectiles. The weather was clear above and below the thick scattering of cumulus clouds which extended from about 3,500 feet to perhaps 6,000 feet. There was a steady trade-wind swell rolling the wide face of the sea and a light chop with an occasional whitecap. Behind Phillips, midway back on the wide wing under the plexiglas "greenhouse," sat Lieutenant W. H. Fitzpatrick, acting as naval observer, and behind him, Aviation Ordnanceman First Class A. B. Kernan manned the ball turret with its single 50. Below and aft of Kernan, in the "tunnel" or "hell-hole" of the Avenger, J. C. Sullivan manned the radio position, and when needed moved from his headset and transmitter key to the .30-caliber tunnel gun pointing down and astern. All Phillips' guns were fully loaded but he carried no bombs. Instead, half his bomb bay was filled with gasoline in a large, unprotected tank, intended to keep him in the air over the target all day.

A few minutes after take-off the other three men could feel their aircraft shake briefly and then smell an acrid cordite smell as Phillips test-fired his fixed guns.

At 7:22 the radio came alive under Sullivan's skilled fingers and a cryptic daylong conversation began. Rear Admiral Kelly Turner's command radio in *Pennsylvania* was "Viceroy"; Phillips was "Clipper One."

As Phillips approached the shaft of the T from the north, he and his crew could see scores of boats milling around the larger ships off the crossbar. The battleships, cruisers and destroyers were still firing, their guns flashing and smoke moving off down wind close to the surface. The island lay under a cloud of dust and smoke which spurted new smoke and new dust as each salvo landed. From the carrier task group to the northward an air group commander reported nineteen fighters, nineteen bombers and fifteen torpedo planes air-borne and ready to support the landing troops with prearranged strikes.

The boats were forming into lines and beginning to move toward the Red beaches on the cross of the T, trailing short, white wakes when Viceroy requested an investigation of the small islands of Little Makin and Mongoose, lying a few miles to the northeast. Phillips went down low and checked them over. On Little Makin he reported "no activity, no AA, no installations, very few natives." On Mongoose, where friendly troops had landed at dawn, he observed, "Soldiers walking along beach to landing boats. Seem O.K."

By the time Clipper One arrived back over the target the first irregular line of amphibious tanks, also called amtracs or LVTs or alligators, were churning and bucking the sea only a mile offshore. Farther out other lines followed, forming up between two anchored destroyers and moving out together like aquatic horses from a starting gate. The strike from the carriers swung in wide circles overhead awaiting the word to go down. There was no visible response from the enemy except for a few splashes around the advancing amtracs.

When the line of some thirty alligators was half a mile from the beach where the friendly salvos had been landing with vicious regularity, the ships ceased firing for the first time in an hour and a half. As the cloud of dust and debris began to clear away on the trades, the fighters that had been waiting overhead peeled off one at a time and swept in in single file, their guns raking the crossbar of the T parallel to it and just behind the beaches. The gray gunsmoke streamed back over their wings and the tracers slanted out ahead, kicking up the coral and ricocheting in a hundred directions.

Phillips circled just clear of the action and out of the way of the strafing Hellcats and kept Viceroy advised of developments.

At about 400 yards smoke blossomed from the leading alligators and spread along the whole line as they fired their rockets and opened up with machine guns.

At 8:32 A.M. the first amtrac grew larger as Phillips and Fitzpatrick watched and as its tracks bit into the sand and its black steel sides emerged, streaming from the sea. Up the beach it came, big and menacing, its guns flickering; and all along the shore those strange craft that rode so deep in the water, lumbered up from the edge of the sea eight feet tall from beach to deck, and headed inland.

A minute after Clipper One reported to Viceroy, "First boat lands on beach," the SBDs and TBFs started to lay their big bombs down in shallow, high-speed glides parallel to the shore and ahead of the advancing alligators. The coral dust and smoke, which had begun to clear when the ships ceased fire, boiled up again as the 2,000-pound "daisy cutters" erupted all over the island. One caught a fuel dump and thick black smoke interlaced with orange flame blossomed midway down the shaft of the T. By 8:45, with most of the bombs delivered and friendly troops well beyond the beaches, Viceroy ordered. "Cease bombing," and Clipper One relayed, "All bombing cease . . . all planes reassemble and return to base."

From 8:46, when the last bomb of the landing support strike shook the atoll, until 8:55, when the ships resumed firing, it appeared from the air that there was relative quiet on Makin Island.

The island was a desolate shambles pocked with bomb and shell craters, its trees down and fires burning at a dozen different points. No enemy was visible but an occasional black burst of AA over the beach and the sudden flopping of friendly troops under unseen and (from overhead) unheard small-arms fire indicated that he was still around.

When the ships opened up again their targets were the Yellow beaches on the north side of the T's shaft and about halfway down, where the projections of On Chong's wharf and King's wharf poked out into the light green waters of the lagoon. While their guns flashed and smoked and coconut palms ashore went down in the haze of smoke and shattered coral, a minesweeper and two destroyers groped gingerly into the lagoon followed by a long, narrow, highsided landing ship, tanks (LST) loaded with manned amtracs ready to file out of her bow door, and a landing ship, dock (LSD), with loaded tank lighters (LCMs) in her dock ready to emerge when she flooded it and opened the gates.

At 9:15 Phillips took another close look at the extreme eastern end of the island, the tail of the prone T, and reported nothing there of interest except a few dummy guns with which the Japs hoped to draw valuable bombs away from actual emplacements.

At 9:33 Phillips commented that on each circle of the island "a machine gun . . . located in Ukiangong village [at the south end of the crossbar] . . . takes pot shots at us as we go by!" Viceroy was not impressed.

"Thank God there's at least one Nip in there," he said. "Have the destroyers started firing from inside the lagoon on Yellow Beach yet?"

"Negative."

The radios were silent on that frequency for three minutes and then Clipper One inquired of *Enterprise* if the strike scheduled to support the Yellow Beach landing was air-borne yet. It was in the air and scheduled to arrive in ten minutes.

At 9:58 Clipper One reported to Viceroy:

"Salvos. falling near tank traps. Heavy fires have started at middle of island [between the two tank traps which crossed the T's narrow shaft in two places] and natives assembled on Red beaches under guard."

Viceroy was most interested in the latter.

"If you see any nice females down there," he requested, "save me one."

Clipper One kept his mind on his business: "Friendly troops have reached Ukiangong Point," and "DDs [destroyers] in the lagoon have opened up." Then he relented, "It looks like all the girls have skivvy shirts on."

By this time the *Enterprise* strike was overhead awaiting orders, 20 SBDs, two TBFs and three Hellcats. They were encouraged by an irreverent Viceroy:

"Let's put on a good show for the big shots; they are all out there with their glasses and sunbonnets."

At 10:15 Phillips and Fitzpatrick counted sixty-six landing boats in the lagoon and advancing on the Yellow beaches. Sixteen were alligators of the first wave, churning purposefully shoreward, throwing white water and leaving a short, wide wake. The others formed two other waves about half a mile apart, the bigger LCMs, each with its tank aboard behind the blunt toaster-grill bow, in the second, and the smaller personal boats in the third. At 10:30 Clipper One reported the first wave just one mile out. Just before 10:30 he went down, took a good look at the battered beach and reported that he could ". . . see no activity on the island."

When the first-wave amtracs were 500 yards from shore, the impatient fighters from *Enterprise* and one of her sister carriers went down to strafe and a minute later the lead boats fired their rockets, the signal to commence strafing.

At 10:42 Clipper One reported to Viceroy that the first alligator had reached King's wharf and two minutes later, "Boats beaching all along now." For the last few hundred yards the amtracs had been crawling over the shallow tidal flats, churning the coral mud under their heavy treads and rising farther and farther out of the lagoon. Now they had actually crossed the beach and were fanning out, firing, to clear the wharfs on either side of the landing area. Behind them the LCMs had grounded on the reef and unloaded their tanks in the shallows to splash their own way in. This was at once reported: "Boats with tanks have disembarked 300 yards from beach. They are cutting through the water." As the tanks began to waddle up the beach, the personnel boats touched bottom a few yards closer to shore than the LCMs and the assault troops came down the bow ramps and waded shoreward in the hip-deep, tepid water in long loose columns, holding their rifles high.

As soon as the fighters had completed their runs, as at Red Beach two hours earlier, the bombers and torpedo planes shook the earth behind the beaches with their 2,000-pound antipersonnel bombs in a prolonged hammering that the wading soldiers must have enjoyed watching since every thudding crash should mean fewer Japanese riflemen to hunt down later.

At 10:59 Viceroy wanted to be sure: "Have any troops landed on Yellow beaches?" Clipper One's reply was accurate: "Yes."

At 11:04 Phillips saw and reported that troops from the earlier landings on Red Beach had penetrated down the T's shaft to the western tank trap.

Phillips and Fitzpatrick saw about everything of note on Makin. At 11:05 Viceroy was informed that "a small green sedan is parked on the road down there. Maybe it has four good tires on it."

From 11:15 to 11:26 Clipper One conducted another search of the areas outside the two tank traps for any signs of enemy activity. There were none.

Then, at 11:26, the four men in the circling, snooping TBF smelled what no airman likes to smell, the heavy sweetish, penetrating odor of aviation gasoline. Phillips at once ordered the "smoking lamp out" and shut down everything he could think of that might make a spark. His last transmission before also turning off his radio was to Viceroy. "Have bad gas leak . . . request permission to return to base." As Viceroy replied, "Roger, you have done a good job, Clipper One," the three men behind the pilot could see the gasoline welling up in the bottom of the fuselage from the bomb bay and streaming aft to the .30-caliber tunnel gun. Fitzpatrick dumped his drinking water and coffee into it to cut down the fumes and eleven long minutes later, during any one of which the Avenger and its crew could have disappeared in a flash of orange flame, they landed aboard the Big E and quickly abandoned the aircraft.

The plane captain at once found that a gas line had been cut by an enemy bullet.

Shortly before 1:30 P.M. John Phillips and his crew were back in the air with a fresh TBF. Viceroy was delighted to have eyes again as his first orders clearly indicated: "Look over the island and tell me where our troops are. Locate troops from Red and Yellow beaches and report. . . . Situation ashore obscure to me."

Round and round over the smoking, crookedly T-shaped island wheeled the Big E's lone Avenger while four pairs of eyes noted the activity below and Phillips described it in short, significant sentences to the task force commander's headquarters deep in the old *Pennsylvania*.

Even to men untrained in infantry tactics the plan was clear, to land troops on the head of the T and others halfway down the shaft, unite the two groups by pinching off enemy units between them and then sweep down the remainder of the T's shaft with the merged force. But everything seemed to move with agonizing slowness. Soldiers and tanks moved a few yards and stopped for long intervals, then moved a few more yards and stopped again. From a thousand feet overhead Phillips could see no evidence of the enemy snipers and/or machine-gun nests and strong points which must have been responsible for the stops.

At 2:00 P.M. a greatly relieved Viceroy told Clipper One: "Your information is very valuable. It is the only information in two hours that I have received."

By early afternoon the TBF crew could see the flashes of friendly 105-millimeter guns at Ukiangong Point at the south end of the crossbar as they fired diagonally across to support lagoon beach troops moving down the shaft.

At 2:19 P.M., in the middle of a troop position report to Viceroy, John Phillips heard a loud bang in the fuselage below him and felt the stick in his right hand go slack as he lost elevator control. He broke off his radio message and switched to intercom.

"Stand by for crash landing." Then, back on the air to Viceroy: "My elevator controls are gone. I'm going down on Red Beach . . . I suggest you ask for a relief for me. I can't get back to base without elevators. Stand by for crash landing."

To lose elevator control in an airplane in level flight is

something like losing steering control in an automobile on a turnpike. When the wheel of the car is turned nothing happens. If the driver is quick and lucky he can brake to a stop while he is still on the road. If the pilot is the same way and has the plane properly trimmed for level flight, he can continue to fly for a while, but he has no direct control over the up-down travel of his aircraft.

For two minutes Phillips experimented gingerly and discovered that he had slight control of his elevators through the use of his elevator trim tab. There was time to alert *Enterprise:* "Blue Base, this is Eighty-five Blue. I'm making a crash landing on Red Beach."

Phillips circled wide in his approach but had time and attention left over to report the current position of the lagoon beach tanks.

Viceroy was worried about Clipper One, and informal: "Thanks, boy. You'd better get that crate on the ground, you can't play a harp. I'm half gray-headed now and I don't want to be white-headed." But he too still had time for business. "Have Red and Yellow Beach people joined up yet?"

"Not quite, but soon."

Two minutes later Fitzpatrick discovered what had happened. A chunk of shrapnel had penetrated the fuselage and severed the elevator cable. Sullivan went to work in an attempt to splice it together.

Phillips decided to hold up his crash landing since he was able to maintain level flight with his tabs and there was a chance the severed cable could be repaired. In the meantime he continued his reports.

"Tanks in 892 [a coded grid position] stopped. The road seems clear. They are just momentarily held up." Eight minutes later the tanks had still not moved. "I see no reason for halt. Tanks advanced 892 and stopped."

At 2:48 P.M. Phillips inquired about the repairs.

"Can you fix it, Sully?"

"I think so."

"There it goes again." Phillips felt the stomach-tightening looseness return to his stick.

"I let it slip," said Sullivan.

"Well, tighten it and I'll try to get aboard."

For eleven more minutes Sullivan worked at the broken cable, tying the severed ends together with additional wire and binding the connection to make it hold.

At three o'clock Sullivan reported: "That's as tight as I can get it."

Phillips felt it out tentatively and the heavy Avenger dipped and soared gently. "It's awful slack, awful slack. I'd hate to try to go aboard that way. I'll get a little altitude and see what I can do with her. Kernan, take a good look at the rudder. Sullivan, check the other wires."

While Sullivan crawled around in the fuselage tracing out the control cables, Kernan in his plexiglas turret trained back and forth examining the rudder and the vertical fin. Everything seemed normal. A few thousand feet higher, Phillips slowed to near landing speed, dropped his flaps and felt out his elevators. They felt loose but the Avenger responded well, and he decided to attempt a landing aboard and inquired of Viceroy:

"Shall I return to base or await relief?"

"Return to base and initiate own relief. Good luck to you, boy, you did a hell of a swell job."

At 3:15 the TBF was over *Enterprise* and Phillips reported in: "Blue Base, this is 85 Blue. Would like to make a deferred forced landing. My elevator controls have been shot away. I will have to make my approach a bit erratic."

The Big E's new air officer, Commander T. J. "Tom" Hamilton, was thinking of her tender and precious deck and the planes parked forward.

"Test your controls. Do you think it safe to land aboard?"

"I have tested them. I think they will hold."

"Roger. Wait."

For more than an hour and a half Phillips and his crew circled the ship while other planes were brought aboard, and the flight-deck crew struck all the aircraft below so that a bad landing could not damage them.

At 4:50, with the sun only an hour and twenty minutes above the western sea, John Phillips started his approach. Kernan was strapped tight into his ball turret. Sullivan and Fitzpatrick crouched in the fuselage holding tight to the splice in the elevator cable to take up the slack. As Phillips gentled the Avenger up the Big E's wake, nose high and hook hanging, the four white-knuckled hands on the patched-up cable eased an inch or two forward and then back and forward again as Phillips moved the stick. Then the two men crouching blind in the fuselage heard the engine cut, felt the cable slide sharply forward as the TBF stalled in and braced for the landing or the crash.

The big Avenger thumped to the deck in a perfectly normal touch-down at 4:54 and *Enterprise* turned with her task group and headed seaward for the night.

It had been a busy day for the green squadrons and the flight-deck crew. On D-Day the Big E had launched two strikes in support of the landings on Yellow Beach, two CAPs, four "support air groups" (planes available in the vicinity of the target in case of need), two photo flights and two antisubpatrols, for a total of 135 take-offs and 137 landings (one SBD made a water landing and three fighters came aboard from *Belleau Wood*). But the night of the twentieth of November was dark and quiet, and as the blacked-out carriers withdrew to seaward, evading the snoopers, their crews rested. The Big E's berthing compartments were stacked three deep with young men in rumpled skivvy shirts sleeping heavily while the ship's blowers sucked the cooling night air below and the watch on deck stood guard.

A hundred miles south of Makin, at Betio on Tarawa atoll, some 18,000 Marines of the tough, Guadalcanal-experienced 2nd Division were either dug into a few yards of coral sand at the water's edge or still afloat waiting to come ashore between the wrecks and over the bodies. The 2nd Division was committed in mortal combat against the best-fortified, best-defended atoll in the Pacific. On that first vicious day it had taken 5,000 Marines to occupy a narrow strip of beach under the muzzles of the Japanese guns and by nightfall some 1,500 of them had been killed or wounded. The "issue [was] in doubt."

At midnight the big ships turned on signal, and before dawn they were in position to launch another day of combat flights.

All that was left to do on Makin was to mop up. There were scattered stubborn nests of enemy machine gunners and snipers in the broken pilings of the docks, in the wrecks of palm-log fortifications and in the hulks of sunken ships in the shallows of the lagoon. The small-arms fire from the offshore wrecks was especially irritating since it interfered with the heavy boat traffic bringing ashore supplies and taking off wounded. The hulks were difficult to attack because of their clear field of fire in all directions and the protection their metal hulls provided to the enemy.

At the direction of Viceroy, *Enterprise* dive bombers and torpedo planes made two attacks on the hulks. The planes came in low and fast, releasing the heavy bombs close to the surface in an effort to "skip" them into the targets. But in the shallow water the bombs skipped too well. They ricocheted over the wrecks and detonated in the air or in the lagoon a thousand feet beyond. On later runs, the pilots tried other tactics. Some dropped farther from the target, attempting to make use of the 1,000-foot ricochets but at that point the lagoon was even shallower and the ricochets correspondingly longer so that the bombs were still over. Others dropped from as high as 400 feet and as slow as 160 knots. The bombs ricocheted higher but not as far. One pilot released at 400 feet in a momentary dive, but could not affect the unpredictable inaccuracies caused by the shallow water.

Finally the hulks were silenced by raking, concentrated fire from the six .50-caliber machine guns of the Big E's Hellcats.

During a morning Avenger attack on enemy strong points ashore, an *Enterprise* torpedo plane was responsible for one of the inadvertent tragedies that add to the wastefulness of war. The TBF was one of four assigned to deliver 2,000-pound "daisy cutters" in glide-bombing runs from 5,000 feet. On the first run the bomb did not release, and the pilot pulled up, closed his bomb-bay doors and circled for a reattack. When he opened the bomb bay at the start of his second glide the bomb fell out. The Avenger was over friendly troops. Three United States soldiers were killed and a dozen more wounded. On the Big E's hangar deck, squadron ordnancemen found that the shackles securing the big bomb to its rack had failed, probably from the G forces exerted in the pull-out from the first run.

After D plus 1, with no further organized enemy resistance on Makin, the mission of *Enterprise* and the Northern Carrier Group became essentially defensive: to stand by the battlewagons and transports of Admiral Turner's attack force while they unloaded and completed the occupation of the atoll, acting as a striking force in the event of Japanese counterattack.

To tether a carrier task force, even with a long leash, to any fixed geographical position, is to deprive it of one of its most effective weapons, mobility. In the Solomons, *Enterprise, Wasp* and *Hornet* had been tethered to Guadalcanal for six months and only the Big E, badly battered, had survived the campaign.

Enterprise, Belleau Wood and *Monterey* were going into their third day off Makin. The Japanese by then had had two full days to find out that Makin was being attacked with the support of carrier-based planes and to take whatever measures they could to get those carriers. Since their own carriers were without air groups (they had been poured down the rat hole of the Solomons in an attempt to stop the inexorable Allied advance in that area) and they could not risk the big new battleships anchored in Truk lagoon without adequate air support, the only weapons left to the Japanese were submarines and long-range, land-based planes.

Shortly after 5:00 P.M. on the twenty-first, *Enterprise* radar picked up a bogey at a range of forty-seven miles. The CAP lined out after him but he got away. That night several other bogies skirted the edges of the scope.

All morning on the twenty-first it was a bloody draw on Betio, but by afternoon the Marines, after heavy losses, were beginning to win.

On the twenty-second nothing happened at sea. At Tarawa, victory was now certain.

On the twenty-third the carriers retired to the eastward to fuel and then returned to Makin. That night the last Japanese on Betio was dead.

In the morning twilight of the twenty-fourth, the escort carrier *Liscome Bay* was blown up and sunk by a submarine torpedo twenty miles southwest of Makin. Six hundred and forty-four of her crew were lost. One of the survivors, recovered burned and naked from the oil-scummed sea, was a captain on the staff of the carrier division commander. His name was John Crommelin. The same day *Enterprise* torpedo planes searched fruitlessly for a sub reported in her area, and twice extra fighters were launched against radar bogies they could not find. Shortly after dark a two-engine enemy plane crossed the Big E's deck from starboard to port at an altitude of 300 to 500 feet, so low that the startled plane handlers, respotting for the dawn launch, could see the blue exhaust flames and the outline of the plane itself. Evidently the Japanese crew was asleep or occupied with other matters, because they continued straight on their course and there was no further action that night.

On the twenty-fifth, enemy activity increased. Twice

more twelve Hellcats scrambled off the Big E's deck and were vectored out by radar after bogies which at once retired out of range. But after sunset, with the F6Fs back on deck and the pilots in their ready room, the bogies came back. In the increasing darkness lookouts reported dim lights blinking in the sea. With their slowly spinning sweeps of light, radar operators tracked white blobs which were enemy aircraft approaching, turning, paralleling the task force. Gun crews, signalmen, control officers and others on topside battle stations could now and then hear the drone and buzz of enemy engines as the Japanese airmen groped for attack position. The Big E's long hull sliced through the tropic ocean, sliding the water back on top of itself with a continuous splashing, hissing sound. At reduced speed her wake bubbled white and flat astern. Her blowers hummed steadily and occasionally a 40-millimeter mount buzzed sharply as it swung to a new direction, bearing its helmeted sailors with it like an intermittent merry-go-round. The carriers' guns were ready but Admiral Radford had ordered them not to fire unless under direct and immediate attack. He knew the difficulty the enemy pilots were having and he had no desire to assist them by pointing out a target with the flashes of its guns.

Suddenly, as if a light had been switched on, a parachute flare hung in the night sky over the formation of American ships, then two more, throwing a pale, green-white light on the ships and the sea and giving the men on deck an uncomfortable feeling of exposure and vulnerability. With the flares halfway down in their maddeningly slow descent, the white blobs on the radarscopes closed in toward the center. Ahead, *North Carolina*'s guns, firing slowly and carefully on full radar control, flashed and stabbed out into the dark, angled upward only a little. A few long seconds after each flash, the sharp bark of the five-inch banged across the Big E's deck. After a few rounds something flared bright orange far out to starboard, arced downward, and went out. A minute later a red light appeared in the sky, moving low and fast from starboard to port until it disappeared. Then the battlewagon's guns ceased firing and the quiet dark returned with the quenching of enemy flares. For another thirty minutes the bogies appeared hesitantly and indecisively on radar and then the scopes were clear. Captain Gardner kept his ship well buttoned up but secured his crew from their battle stations to get some rest. The next night was liable to be worse.

It was. By now Admiral Radford's carriers had been tethered to Makin for one full week. The sun had hardly set on the twenty-sixth of November before the bogies began to appear around the edges of the scopes, many more of them than the radar operators remembered having seen before.

But young, aggressive Arthur Radford had no desire to skulk passively in the darkness hoping that the enemy could not find him, or see him well enough to make a hit, depending on last-minute defensive gunnery to protect his ships. He wanted to hit the raiders before they were ready to hit him—and he had men in *Enterprise* who convinced him they had a way to do it.

Up to this time, night carrier operations had been limited to recovering strikes and searches which for one reason or another had been forced to return to the ship after dark and to launching strikes, searches and CAP in the hours just before dawn. Little, if any, actual combat operations had been attempted during the hours of darkness and for a very good reason: a pilot had to see his target before he could hit it and he could not see far or well enough in the dark to do so. But late in 1943 there were a few clear and imaginative heads in naval aviation which saw that radar might be made to provide, at least partially, the visibility a pilot needed to find and hit his target. Bill Martin had been thinking and experimenting along these lines for months, and while *Enterprise* was cruising off Makin he was leading his newly formed squadron on solely radar-guided flights and simulated radar bombing and torpedo attacks around the Hawaiian Islands, training for future night strikes against the Japanese. Aboard the Big E, Butch O'Hare, Tom Hamilton and others had been working with the idea that the ship's radar could guide a TBF close enough to an enemy plane so that the Avengers' own radar could pick it up and bring the pilot in close enough on a clear night to shoot him down. But the TBF, although it had the great advantage of radar, lacked speed, fire power and maneuverability, all three of which were built into the Hellcat. Therefore, they reasoned, let's send an Avenger out to find the enemy and give him a Hellcat on either wing to help out when the shooting starts.

On the evening of the twenty-sixth, while the enemy was

gathering his forces for a massive night torpedo strike against Radford's carriers, five men left the Big E's deck to counterattack. It was an elite group. Tall, precise John Phillips, commanding officer of Torpedo Six, with 1,000 hours of instrument time, who had been Clipper One over Makin on D-Day, flew the radar-equipped Avenger; Butch O'Hare, the air group commander, and wearer of the Congressional Medal of Honor, piloted one Hellcat, and his wingman, Ensign Warren A. Skon, the other. Riding behind Phillips and operating the TBF's radar was Lieutenant (j.g.) Hazen B. Rand, a graduate in radar studies of the Massachusetts Institute of Technology and the Navy's Airborne Radar School, with additional months of operational training at Pearl Harbor. Behind Rand, covering the Avenger's tail in his ball turret, was Aviation Ordnanceman First Class A. B. Kernan.

The Hellcats were catapulted first and made a slight right turn when air-borne to get their prop wash away from the deck. Skon joined on O'Hare in a climbing left turn as the fighter director officer gave them a heading to the nearest bogey. It was 6:00 P.M. and there was still enough light in the evening sky to kill the enemy if they could find him. The Avenger took off two minutes after the fighters and was given the same vector. The three planes droned out over the rapidly darkening sea into the nearly black sky to the east where the enemy bombers were lurking, waiting for full night. The pilots were in continuous contact with the *Enterprise* FDO who watched their progress on his big scope in the ship's new Combat Information Center. But the enemy planes were elusive in the dusk, and at the limit of radar range they appeared and disappeared erratically on the scope. Several times the FDO told O'Hare he was within a mile of a bogey but neither he nor Skon could see anything but dark sea and dark sky.

Phillips followed, staying in the general vicinity of the fighters, but he could not see them nor they him. Rand, seated close behind Phillips in the big TBF, was better off. Occasionally the small green scope before his face showed the passage of an enemy plane but he would lose it before the TBF could be maneuvered within sight.

When, at the end of an hour, the *Enterprise* FDO had reported O'Hare's two fighters "in the midst of many bogies" and he had had to report "no contact," the group commander realized that his only hope of success lay in joining with Phillips. Accordingly, the FDO coached the Hellcats around and to within a few miles of the Avenger.

But Phillips was busy. Rand had finally locked his radar on a bogey given him by the FDO, and flying entirely on instruments, with the smoothness of long experience and confidence, John Phillips was closing on the enemy. The enemy target on Rand's scope moved down from the top and crossed the range circle that marked two miles, a mile and a half, one mile. At a mile Phillips took his eyes from his dimly red-lighted gauges and searched the darkness ahead. He could make out the flickering blue points of the exhaust stacks and he added a little throttle, closing on them, his eyes going back and forth between his instruments and the enemy engines ahead while Rand switched to a larger scale and kept reading him ranges over the intercom. A thousand yards, eight hundred, six hundred, four hundred. Phillips could make out the dark shape of the Betty now and his palms on stick and throttle were sweating and his mouth dry. He wanted to be sure. His altitude was O.K., 1,200 feet. He was in nearly level flight at 190 knots. His two fixed .50-calibers were charged. Two hundred yards. Phillips squeezed the trigger and the red tracers poured in two long streams out of the TBF's wings reaching for the enemy. He held the trigger down while the plane shook and chattered and the range closed to fifty yards. The Betty answered from tail and top and side blisters, the small white tracers skimming by over Phillips' head and under his feet as he bored in until he saw fires begin along the dark wings growing in his sight. Then he pulled up and left and leveled off while Kernan in the ball turret fired down over the starboard side into the burning enemy plane. To Phillips' amazement, as he took his eye from the gunsight and looked around, he could see tracers lancing through the sky at several points on both sides ahead, none of them directed at him. In their surprise and confusion the enemy bombers were shooting at each other.

Three miles off to the northwest, O'Hare and Skon saw a burning object fall into the sea and spread a pool of red flame which burned on for nearly half an hour. They turned toward it and the TBF, still trying to join up.

Phillips reported: "Got that one. Any more around?"

The FDO had another a few miles south and Phillips turned smoothly after him at an altitude of 500 feet. This time, perhaps because his eyes had adapted to the flash of his tracers and the light of the burning Betty had reduced his night vision, Phillips did not see the enemy until he was in to three quarters of a mile. Then, looking up from his panel he found two Bettys ahead in a gentle right turn at the same altitude. As Phillips checked his guns and Rand read the decreasing ranges, the familiar voice of Butch O'Hare drowned out the intercom:

"Phil, I figure we're about a mile to starboard of you. Can you turn on recognition light to help us join up?"

Phillips picked up his mike with his throttle hand, his eye still on the enemy shapes ahead: "I've got another one of the bastards in sight, Butch. Don't like to use lights. I'll flash them a couple of times for you."

The Avenger recognition lights flashed and the Betty abruptly banked left and then right again with Phillips following like the second plane of a stunt team while the range continued to close. At 200 yards, again in a gentle right turn, Phillips opened fire and held his guns open for nearly a minute until the Betty began to burn with small, licking orange flames along the wings and then dropped toward the sea. It must have hit nearly flat because it left a narrow streak of fire on the surface 300 yards long which continued to burn for a long time with bright red flames like the first Betty. A minute or two later, Kernan fired a few rounds at a blacked-out enemy plane crossing under the Avenger's tail.

O'Hare and Skon were close enough this time to see the long burst of tracers before the Betty flamed and fell and they closed in at once to help out with the next one. With no targets in sight for the moment, Phillips turned on his navigation lights and, on orders from the FDO, went into a left-hand orbit at 1,200 feet to facilitate the rendezvous. The Hellcats also lighted up (although nervously because of the possibility of enemy planes nearby) and slid in toward the Avenger. Skon was on O'Hare's left wing and the torpedo plane was to the left and ahead of the fighter section, so Skon elected to take Phillips' left wing and O'Hare his right. Skon slid under the TBF's tail, taking up his position about a hundred feet to its left and slightly below. O'Hare moved in toward his right-wing position. With O'Hare still some three hundred feet out of position something went wrong. Kernan in the TBF's ball turret opened fire. Skon thought the tracers passed between his plane and O'Hare's. Kernan reports that he fired at another unlighted plane which appeared near Skon and then crossed over near O'Hare. Whatever happened, Butch O'Hare was killed.

Five to ten seconds after Kernan ceased firing, Skon saw O'Hare's plane with its lights still on slide down and to the left. He thought Butch was making a run on an enemy below in the vicinity of the burning wreckage of Phillips' two Bettys, and tried to follow him down. But O'Hare's Hellcat lost altitude too fast and Skon did not see it after the first seconds. Kernan thought he saw a chute blossom in the night. Reluctantly, and with difficulty, Skon rejoined the TBF and the two planes circled the area for forty-five minutes calling O'Hare by radio and assuring a good navigational fix on the position for rescue purposes. Admiral Radford dispatched a destroyer which searched the area all night and on the twenty-seventh six planes from *Enterprise* and a rescue PBY crisscrossed the calm, clear sea and found nothing.

No one knows what happened to Butch O'Hare. Probably he was killed by Kernan's .50-caliber. But, lighted up in the midst of the enemy, he could conceivably have been caught by nontracer fire from a darkened Betty or his head cold could have pushed him into vertigo at the moment of rendezvous. However he died, his death was a great boon to the enemy and an immeasurable tragedy for the Navy of the United States.

The men of *Enterprise*, some twenty miles southeast of the scene of O'Hare's death, spent a tense and eerie evening. The ships steamed slowly and in silence with crews at battle stations and guns trained out as they had done the previous night. In the Big E's Combat Information Center (CIC) the FDO sat at his scope with earphones on his head, a microphone in one hand and a grease pencil in the other, marking the positions of friendly and enemy aircraft each time the sweep of the antenna seemed to move and relight the little blobs which stood for aluminum and high explosive and high-octane fuel and flesh and blood rushing through the night sky twenty miles away at 200 miles an hour. The speakers overhead amplified his words to Phillips and O'Hare and their replies to him. Tom Hamilton had wedged his big body into CIC to keep track of his night fighters, and the two other squadron commanders, unable to sit still in their ready rooms, had come up to watch and listen. They clapped each other on the back and swore when Phillips reported shooting down two Bettys, and stood tense and silent, listening with every nerve while the futile calls were broadcast to Butch O'Hare.

On deck the men watched in anxious silence while twenty to thirty parachute flares strung down the starboard side of the formation, three to five miles away. Occasionally, a lookout high in the island reported a red, white or green light blinking in the sea as the enemy tried to give his formations a visual reference point for rendezvous.

The enemy did not attack. Or if he attacked it was by individual planes which scored no hits or known near misses. Confused, disorganized and knocked off balance by the *Enterprise* counterattack, the Japanese pilots milled around in the dark for another half hour, occasionally shooting at one another, and then returned piecemeal to their bases.

When Phillips and Skon landed aboard the Big E at 9:00 P.M., the parachute flares had hissed out in the sea, the enemy had gone home and the tropic ocean seemed at peace. They did not know then that Butch O'Hare was dead. They did not know that they and he had taken part in the first successful night interception ever flown from a carrier, an interception which he had skillfully planned and fearlessly executed.

In the final days of November the fast carriers were at last untethered from Makin. *Enterprise* moved to seaward out of range of enemy patrol planes and lost herself in the vastness of the Pacific from which she could strike wherever she was needed.

On December 4, after a week of relative rest, she was needed to strike Kwajalein in the Marshalls.

Enterprise went to work at 6:30 A.M., under a brightening dawn sky some hundred and fifty miles north of target. When the sun broke the horizon a few minutes before seven o'clock, she had 56 planes in the air, 22 fighters, 20 bombers and 14 torpedo planes. The pilot of one of the Avengers was John Phillips, the new air group commander.

Half a mile to starboard, *Essex* had launched at the same time, and, astern of the big carriers, *Belleau Wood* was providing CAP for the task group. Just out of sight over the curve of the earth, the new *Yorktown* and the new *Lexington* had also launched and by quarter past seven about 250 planes were on the way to Kwajalein.

Enterprise old hands, who remembered February of 1942 when Halsey had taken the Big E in alone to hit Kwajalein with Gene Lindsey's old Devastators and Wade

McClusky's F4Fs, in the very first U. S. offensive action of the war, while a different *Yorktown* attacked the Gilberts and a different *Lexington* was operating the South Pacific, stood on her empty deck in the sunrise and looked up in awe at the Vs and echelons that roared across the sky.

Kwajalein is the largest atoll in the world. Air Group Six's target was the main island of Kwajalein itself at the extreme southern end.

As the air groups of the four big carriers droned in from the north, those from *Enterprise* and *Essex* split off to the left to follow the long reef south, while the *Yorktown* and *Lexington* squadrons continued straight in for Roi-Namur at the lagoon's northern tip.

Lieutenant Commander William A. Dean's fighter pilots at 22,000 feet picked up the big atoll first but in a few more minutes Hampton's SBDs at 13,500 and Phillips' torpedo planes at 11,500 also had it in sight. The usual scattering of white cumulus covered the face of the sea but under it, visible in the large gaps between the clouds, pilots could see the irregular outline of the reef, greenish white where the myriad coral animals had pushed within a few feet of the surface, dark green with vegetation where they had pushed out above the tide and made islands and died. It was the dark green blotches along the reef and the protected waters inside it that interested the Big E's airmen.

The broken, distorted ring of Kwajalein had points and corners and it seemed that it was in those places that the coral had been most active and the islands were larger. Roi and Namur at the north tip were flat and squarish and connected by double man-made causeways. On Roi was a good airfield, and across the causeways on Namur were the barracks and living areas for the troops. South along the reef the islands become smaller and spaced farther apart, until, near Kwajalein itself, they begin to be larger again.

As Air Group Six passed east of Roi-Namur it was already under attack. Bomb splashes fountained and boiled around ships in the anchorage and smoke bloomed in the airfield and barracks areas. A large cargo ship was burning so furiously that even from their altitude and distance the Big E's aviators could see the flame boil out of her. The unmistakable low, bristling silhouette of a warship lay among the high-sided freighters and, as the pilots watched, a bomb flashed on her stern and a moment later a torpedo fountained against her side and the black smoke began to boil and bend in the trades.

Past Roi-Namur there had still been no fighter opposition and the air groups attacking those islands reported none. John Phillips, flying with two other TBFs equipped with cameras, pulled away from them and his air group in a long, high-speed glide to get an advance look at his target. The big Avenger slanted down, the wind noise increasing in pitch and volume, and Phillips with his left hand, not looking, retrimmed it for the power glide and occasionally pulled the throttle back slightly to keep the manifold pressure from building up.

The reef stretched out ahead from under his right wing. He was still well above the layer of scattered cumulus but in the distance over his nose he could make out the short, wide crescent of Kwajalein Island and the smaller, round-ish blobs of lesser islands closer along the whitish line of the coral. One of the largest of those blobs, Ebeye, he was especially interested in because his briefing folder showed a seaplane base located there. As he passed over Ebeye, slanting down toward Kwajalein, he looked it over closely. He was still high but he could make out aircraft drawn up on a coral apron near the lagoon beach and others in the shallow water just offshore. Without altering course or changing the shallow angle of his glide, Phillips picked up his mike and spoke tersely to Bill Dean, three miles above him and ten miles behind. Twelve F6Fs with Dean in the lead dove away out of the high covering position at 22,000 feet and three minutes after Phillips' call, their .50-caliber tracers were ripping into the grounded enemy planes and ricocheting off the concrete structures at Ebeye. In repeated dives, Dean's Hellcats got their stubby noses on target, and as the six guns clattered heavily and the smoke poured back over wings and canopies, the noses would come up and the bullets walk a row of planes, knocking pieces of aluminum into the air and spouting flame and black smoke from enemy gas tanks. Island antiaircraft batteries answered back, weakly at first and then more strongly as the surprised gun crews got to their stations, but they were heavy guns, slow to move and ineffective against the F6Fs flashing down across the base and back up and down again.

When Dean called his pilots off and climbed back out for another mission—five float planes were burning and sinking offshore and six more were afire on the ramp. Others which did not burn were riddled and unusable. Fires burned in several buildings around the base.

Phillips continued his descent and as he approached the big island itself he began to see ships. There were twelve to sixteen large freighters moored in the blunted triangle with Kwajalein as its south tip which made up the atoll's main anchorage. The air group commander picked up his mike again and the SBDs of Bombing Six with their 1,000-pound bombs and the TBFs of his own Torpedo Six with four 500-pounders each, turned slightly right and began high-speed glides to attack position over the anchorage.

With his air group assigned to the best targets, John Phillips cut across the apex of the triangle and over to its western leg to inspect another island on which an airfield had been reported. He found none, reversed course to come back over Kwajalein and then north to join his planes in their attacks on the freighters in the anchorage.

The Dauntlesses of Hampton's Bombing Six attacked first, sloping down from 13,500 to 9,000 for a fast run-in over the final twenty miles, and then broke and dived in three-plane sections on the frantically firing ships below. As the first planes began their pull-outs just below 2,000 feet, the first of the 1,000-pounders hit. The shallow lagoon water erupted into towers and huge white bubbles that broke and spread. Bombs flashed deep in the thin freighter hulls and men and debris soared outward and dropped back into the sea. Seven ships were hit, some twice, and while the squadron watched, three of them sank, one of them burning briefly and then exploding into nothingness.

With their bombs away several of the SBDs stayed down to strafe small craft in the lagoon before joining up in close defensive formation for the flight back to the ship.

While the dive bombers were attacking, the torpedo planes, armed this time with bombs, circled to the northward awaiting their turn and dodging the heavy methodical flak that reached up after them in carpets of black bursts but could never quite get on. Then, with the bombers clear, the TBFs began their runs. They dived steeply along the fore-and-aft axis of the anchored ships, down wind and fast, pushing over at 7,000 feet, and releasing the first bomb at 3,000 and the last of the four at 2,000 before beginning the pull-out. The heavy Avengers were used in effect as dive bombers but with no dive brakes their speed went up to

350 to 360 knots, well beyond the manufacturers' "red line" design speed. Desperate enemy gunners poured up erratic streams of tracers but, when the last TBF had flattened out over the lagoon and headed for the rendezvous point, four more of the anchored freighters had been hit.

John Phillips, joining the fight, picked the largest of the ships in the north sector of the anchorage but missed her in two down-wind runs.

With the attack delivered and the bombers and torpedo planes en route home, the photo planes took over. Two TBFs and two SBDs had been especially equipped with cameras for photographs of the Kwajalein installations, both to record the damage done by this strike and to provide up-to-date information for a possible amphibious assault. The Avengers were to take vertical and the Dauntlesses oblique views.

While sixteen covering Hellcats circled in the vicinity, the two TBFs crisscrossed the big island and the neighboring small ones snapping pictures, then turned north and flew forty miles up the reef to Roi-Namur where they did the same thing.

The two photo SBDs, in order to obtain the desired oblique views, had to separate and fly well out on either side of the islands being photographed. In so doing they lost contact with each other and with their fighter cover. But both VB-6 lieutenants assigned the photo mission carried it out alone and unprotected. Both photographed the southern islands around Kwajalein, dodging the AA, and then flew north up the reef to Roi-Namur at low altitude. Over Roi one of the Dauntlesses encountered two Zekes (the new designation for Zeros) still climbing after takeoff. One made a head-on attack but broke off when the Dauntless turned into him and opened fire, and neither Zeke attacked again. The other photo SBD was able to avoid a Betty which attacked him, and both returned safely to the Big E with their pictures.

The photographic planes might have had more trouble over Roi without the help of a division of Hellcats led by Lieutenant R. J. Griffin and assigned as cover for one of the TBFs. They were flying at 2,000 feet when four light brown Zekes with the familiar red disk of Japan on their wings climbed steeply up out of the airfield. Griffin left Redmond up as cover for the TBF and, with Carlson and LeForge, dived on the enemy. The Japanese pilots, caught slow at low altitude, could only make violent turns from side to side to avoid the plunging Hellcats. Within thirty seconds, three of the four Zekes were headed for the lagoon wrapped in flame around engines and cockpits and the fourth was flat on the water in retreat, at full throttle.

By 10:30 A.M. all the Big E's planes were back aboard except Ensign Redmond's F6F which ditched from fuel exhaustion near the destroyer *Kidd*. Redmond was returned to *Enterprise* that same day. His was the only plane lost by Air Group Six in the Kwajalein strike.

A second launch had been planned for noon but despite the groans of every squadron and air group commander concerned, it was called off, and the task groups retired to the eastward at 25 knots.

Rear Admiral Charles A. Pownall, an ex-skipper of *Enterprise*, in overall command, had decided that the risk to his carriers in the middle of the complex of enemy bases was too much to justify staying around for another strike. But the pilots who had seen thirty or forty untouched Bettys on the field at Roi knew the kind of a night they would be in for, and would have much preferred the second attack.

The task force did not have to wait for night. Just before 1:00 P.M. while *Yorktown*, in the other group a few miles away, was launching a strike against Wotje, 145 miles northeast of Kwajalein, four of the vicious Kates that *Enterprise* gunners had learned to hate in the Solomons came in fast and low, under the radar, to lay their torpedoes at the carriers. The ships erupted into gunfire. The sea was ripped and splashed around the dark Kates, and five-inch bursts layered the air below flight-deck level. A cruiser and two destroyers got two of them but, in crashing, one nearly hit the *Yorktown*. A third turned off and the fourth, wounded, frightened or confused, flew across the center of the force where every gun could bear until a final descending right turn cartwheeled him into the sea.

There was an uneasy peace during the long, tropic afternoon while the trade wind increased, and the blue sea was so heavy with whitecaps under a clear sky that formation speed had to be reduced for the battered destroyers. A slower speed meant remaining closer to enemy bases that night and that much longer that enemy planes could stay over the task group.

It began at quarter of eight. The new men in *Enterprise*

would never forget the next six hours.

Around sunset, after the CAP had landed, snoopers began to appear on the radarscope, tracking the force. General Quarters was sounded and the Big E rang to the familiar sound of running, climbing, jumping sailors en route to their battle stations. Within a few minutes every gun and watch station was manned and ready. *Enterprise* slid along into the choppy sea at 18 knots, tense and expectant, while the moon, on her port quarter, grew brighter as the sun's light decreased. The center of attention became the radarscopes in CIC and their repeaters, where glowing blobs, regularly relighted by the sweeping pencil line of the antenna, showed the positions of the enemy.

With full dark there were scores of bogies on the scopes —and the strike pilots of that morning knew what they were—the Bettys they had left intact at Roi.

The moon, which in other places and at other dimly remembered times had been a thing of beauty, was painfully and dangerously bright. Each ship was plainly visible to her sisters, and to the enemy pilots sitting out there in the dark above their torpedoes. High-flying planes laid flares above the force which increased the illumination and the danger. The bogies collected in murderous little gangs of two, three and four and rushed the ships. Admiral Radford took personal tactical command of the Big E's task group. He ordered his carriers not to open fire under any circumstances and, standing over the repeater scope on the flag bridge, he maneuvered his ships in simultaneous turns by voice radio command in an attempt to thwart the enemy pilots.

Inside *Enterprise* the tension was like a charged gas in the air. Phone circuits relayed bogey ranges and bearings to men at battle stations and pilots in their ready rooms. The guns buzzed and hummed to cover the most threatening direction just in case. Hour after hour her men could feel the Big E heel over under full rudder first to port, then to starboard and back, as Admiral Radford matched wits with the Betty pilots in the semidark.

Around 11:30 word came that *Lexington* in the other group had been hit and was circling helplessly, her steering control lost. The men on deck could see bursts of tracers arching up from that group as they repelled raid after raid. Closer aboard they saw the flashes of destroyer guns as they took their own bogies under fire.

Enterprise remained blacked-out and silent, maneuvering

constantly as the deadly blobs moved in on her from around the edges of her scopes. In one of her engine rooms, radar reports had been piped into the loudspeaker system and the crew at their gauges and valves and control boards tensed as the ranges came in:

"Bogey dead astern, four miles."

"Bogey dead astern, three miles."

"Bogey dead astern, one mile."

Men looked upward at the gratings of the overhead as if they expected the Betty to fly through the steel itself. Knuckles turned white on wheels and levers as the next report came in: "Bogey dead astern, two miles." "Christ!" came the voice of one of the most intent listeners, "we're gaining on the bastard!" Tension broke with the burst of laughter in the engine room and the chief in charge had no further worries about his crew.

When the moon set at 1:30 A.M. and the enemy at last withdrew, and the men of *Enterprise* could go below to their bunks for a few hours before morning General Quarters, Admiral Radford's handling of his ships had been so successful that not one had been hit or had even seen a torpedo splash or a wake go by.

On Sunday, the fifth of December, *Enterprise* radar picked up a large flight of enemy bombers but they passed off the scope without finding the force.

The sixth was fueling day and on the ninth *Enterprise* steamed back into Pearl Harbor with one more campaign under her belt.

17 FIRST STEPS WEST

As Christmas of 1943 approached, many of the Big E's men grew glum and homesick with thoughts of the miles of sea and land that separated them from wives and families. But the old hands felt a cautious optimism. Christmas in Pearl Harbor was certainly not the way they would have arranged things, but it was better than last Christmas at Espiritu or the one before that, patrolling north of Midway while the Japanese, with the momentum of the Pearl strike, overran the Pacific world. The "man on the deck" of *Enterprise*, judging only from what he had seen of the war, could tell it was going well, that there would not be very many more Christmases like this one. He had covered landings in the Gilbert Islands where, a year and a half before, even a Halsey could only hit and run. He had fought around Guadalcanal until there was no longer an enemy there to fight and he knew that now that bloody island was as safe as Oahu, where this Christmas the lights burned all night in the Navy Yard for the maintenance and repair of scores of brand-new ships. He had been only a few hours away when *Lexington* was sunk and he had seen *Yorktown* and *Hornet* receive their mortal wounds. Now the new *Lexington*, the new *Yorktown*, the new *Hornet* and half a dozen other big carriers sailed the hostile seas with *Enterprise*. Clearly with this kind of progress there could not be many more lonely Christmases.

As 1943 rolled over in the soft, tropic island night and nudged 1944 into life, there were pilots and air-crewmen at Puunene and Kahului and seamen and firemen and mechs and ordnancemen and ship's officers in *Enterprise* herself for whom this New Year's Eve would be the last, whose bones a year from then would have begun to settle into the ocean bottom in some sunlit shallows or abysmal valley of the Pacific. And to some extent all hands sensed the prospect. Since it is not a prospect that a man can consider for very long, all hands to a great extent closed their minds to it. It was not difficult. The odds were heavily in each man's favor; they were in a good and lucky ship, well equipped and ably commanded; the enemy was obviously losing ground; on the mountains of Oahu the white cumulus glowed in the moonlight and it was hard to remember that war existed; and, besides, mutilation and death were things that unfortunately happened to others, not to this flesh and blood now lifting the glass in song and laughter with only a faint anxiety somewhere at the back of the brain.

Some of the very best were the first to go, and there was not an enemy within a thousand miles.

Energetic, enthusiastic Commander Slim Townsend who had bossed the flight deck for the first year of the war mostly from a dead run, and whose long legs were reputed to be able to carry him halfway up the side of the island when he was excited, had in recent months been assistant air officer under Commander Tom Hamilton. On the Big E's last day in Pearl, Slim took an SNJ out of Ford Island to keep his hand in and fly his required time for the month. An hour or two later, reports came in from ships at sea and observ-

ers ashore that a small silver monoplane had spiraled into
the sea just off the entrance to the Pearl Harbor channel.
Two of VT-10's planes went out at once on a search, and
other planes and ships followed up but no trace was ever
found of Slim or his plane. How can the loss of an experienced healthy pilot on a routine flight from a land station
on a clear day be explained? Structural failure of the aircraft from too vigorous aerobatics or for some other reason? Collision with a bird? A heart attack? Food poison-
ing? In the wide loneliness of the sky where there are no
witnesses nor helpers, death has come before and since Slim
Townsend, but seldom more tragically or to a better or
more beloved man.

During a final concentrated three days of training and
warm-up exercises at sea from the fourth to the seventh of
January, Lieutenant Warner Clark's Dauntless lost power
on take-off and flopped into the sea off the carrier's starboard bow. The plane guard destroyer, *Sullivans,* arriving
in about two minutes, found no plane and no pilot, only
the rear-seatman bobbing in his Mae West. Warner Clark
was still another victim of the inherent hazards of operating aircraft from a mobile base at sea. Ashore, he would
have simply relanded, but with shore bases only, we would
have lost the Pacific war.

At Puunene and across the saddle of Maui's mountain
ridge at Kahului, the squadrons of Air Group Ten had
known for weeks that, when *Enterprise* sailed on her next
war cruise, they would be aboard. Early the morning of
January 9 they received their orders to embark. Squadron
gear was packed and ready, and that same day the Hellcats of VF-10, and the four F4U-2(N) Corsair night
fighters of Lieutenant Commander R. E. Harmer's VF(N)-
101 from Kahului, the Dauntlesses and Avengers of Poor's
Bombing Ten and Martin's "Buzzard Brigade" from Puunene, swarmed onto the crowded concrete of Ford Island.

On the morning of the twelfth, air group pilots and key
ship's officers, in a secret briefing ashore, were given the
details of the coming operation. *Enterprise* was going back
to the Marshalls, but this time it was no strike but occupation, and she would have plenty of help.

Task Force 58—Fast Carrier Force—had been born in
those first days of 1944 and this would be its first action.

Rear Admiral Marc Mitscher, as task force commander,
had six big carriers—*Enterprise, Yorktown, Essex, Intrepid*

(Air Group Six embarked), *Saratoga* and *Bunker Hill;* six light carriers, *Belleau Wood, Cabot, Monterey, Cowpens, Princeton* and *Langley,* eight fast battleships, six cruisers and thirty-six destroyers divided into four task groups, any one of which during the months a year ago that *Enterprise* had held them alone, could have swept the Japanese clear of the seas around the Solomons.

The Big E's own Task Group 58.1 was commanded by Rear Admiral J. W. Reeves in *Enterprise* and consisted also of *Yorktown* (Admiral Mitscher's flagship) and *Belleau Wood,* the battleships *Washington* (with Rear Admiral Ching Lee still aboard), *Massachusetts* and *Indiana,* the light cruiser *Oakland* and eight destroyers. The commander of a similar task group (58.4) was Rear Admiral Samuel P. Ginder, who, two months previous, had been the skipper of the *Enterprise.*

The Big E's mission was the destruction and suppression of the enemy air base of Taroa on the atoll of Maloelap in order that planes from that field could not interfere with the occupation of Kwajalein, then prelanding strikes and landing support strikes on Kwaj itself.

On the morning of Saturday, January 22, while, half a world away, United States forces were storming ashore over the beaches of Anzio, TG 58.1 angled down across the equator. And even on the way into battle, it was necessary for the hundreds of "pollywogs" aboard, for whom this was the first crossing, to be initiated into the "solemn mysteries of the Ancient Order of the Deep" and thus become "trusty shellbacks."

It was a long, painful and undignified passage from pollywog to shellback. The initiation ceremonies only varied in degree of indignity and discomfort. And "Neptunus Rex" was no respecter of rank. Officer and enlisted pollywogs alike had their heads shaved or clipped in bizarre scalp locks and fringes and tufts. They were decorated suitably with a near-permanent blue dye, dressed in imaginative combinations of attire and set to performing ridiculous or menial tasks. One group of air group pollywogs was herded into the fireroom, lined up behind the boilers and baked at 140 degrees for twenty minutes. Others, in skivvy shorts, leggings and homemade sunbonnets, with brassieres painted on their naked chests, were stationed forward with twin-coke-bottle binoculars to keep a sharp lookout for the equator. Junior officers with clipped heads served the noon meal in the chief petty officers' mess. As a finale, all pollywogs of all ranks and rates were paraded around the flight deck in their miserable and ludicrous condition before the assembled shellbacks and under the cold stare of Neptunus Rex himself.

The King of the Sea was Chief Torpedoman Jasper Congill, with a real Hemingway white beard, an officer's cap and, over his open-collared khaki, the blue uniform coat of a j.g. liberally festooned on both breasts with wings and ribbons of every variety and bearing an assortment of chevrons and "hash-marks" on the sleeves. His chariot, from which he reviewed the nondescript parade, was a flight-deck jeep and his throne its hood.

But each hour that the ridiculous ritual of the ruler of the sea was going on, *Enterprise* was drawing closer to the enemy, and Gardner, Gill and Hamilton made sure that the ceremonies had no effect on the alertness of her watch or the readiness of her weapons.

On the evening of the twenty-eighth, radar picked up land thirty miles to the northeast, and all night as the force approached its target, the low coral atolls, all enemy held, came and went on the scope.

In their squadron ready rooms the pilots brought their chart boards up to date with last-minute data on wind and weather and intelligence guesses as to ships or other forces to be encountered. In the ready rooms, high spirits and enthusiasm had to substitute this time for experience. In Bombing Ten there were perhaps half a dozen pilots who had seen action; in VF-10 another six; but in the torpedo squadron, Bill Martin alone, the squadron commander, had seen the tracers fired with the intention of killing him.

The next day *Enterprise* was steaming fifty miles southwest of Maloelap atoll in the solid blackness just before dawn. The task force had been running through a series of squalls since midnight and the sky was low and heavy with rain. Across the curve of the earth lay the enemy base of Taroa, pocked and handicapped by the bombs of Army Liberators flying from new fields in the Gilberts, but still very much alive and dangerous. It was important to surprise the sleeping field at first light before the presence of U. S. forces was discovered and counterattacks could be mounted. But the decision to launch the planned fighter sweep in the increasing rain and under the low clouds was a difficult one and arrived at only after Admiral Reeves and his staff,

Captain Gardner and Tom Hamilton, had been able to discover no acceptable alternative.

At 5:17 A.M. Commander Roscoe Newman, the air group commander, was catapulted into the blackness in a TBF to act as a reference plane and, with his radar, assist the fighters in joining up and homing to the target. It was as though his take-off broke a dam in the sky. Rain lashed at the parked Hellcats and their props picked it up and blasted it back over cockpits and deck. The plane handlers slipped and staggered on the slick deck and shielded their eyes against the driving rain. The catapult crews had been trained to work in the dark, but the added rain trebled their difficulties. Nevertheless, five of the fighters were catapulted in rapid succession and with streaming windshields, the soaked pilots groped their way to the rendezvous point where, five miles out, a destroyer was burning her twin red truck lights. As the weather worsened, thirteen more F6Fs splashed down the deck and climbed into the darkness.

Two of the catapulted fighters were never heard of again. Lieutenant (j.g.) E. W. Tolin and Ensign B. D. Steward simply disappeared. Probably they became disoriented in the horizonless darkness, with the occasional single lights of planes and ships the only reference, and flew into the ocean. Tolin was assigned as Killer Kane's wingman, Steward as wingman for Lieutenant Edward G. Colgan. Colgan joined up on Kane in the turbulent darkness and they flew the mission together.

When eighteen fighters were in the air, there no longer was any ceiling or visibility over the carrier's deck, and further take-offs were delayed nearly an hour.

The seventeen Reapers that found Taroa through the shifting cloud layers arrived there singly or in random formations of two or more. A few found the atoll of Maloelap but could not locate the target island itself. Those that arrived over the enemy base tried to make up for their absent mates in aggressiveness and accuracy.

Lieutenant (j.g.) R. O. "Rod" Devine, with Ensign Jimmy Kay on his wing, broke out of the clouds over Taroa at 8,000 feet right on top of four shining green Zekes coming in the opposite direction at 7,000. "Sighting was simultaneous." The Zekes pulled up firing, and Devine and Kay, in a violent wing-over, swept over and behind the enemy fighters, got on the tail of one, and with the third close-range burst Devine set him afire and watched him slant into the sea while his mates ran for the clouds. Jimmy Kay shot another up so badly in engine and cockpit that he probably crashed out of sight under the cloud bank.

Flash Gordon, a veteran of Guadalcanal days with the old VF-10, had just dropped his belly tank and begun his strafing dive from 8,000 feet, when he saw seven Zekes at 1,000 feet directly below. Flash and his wingman dived in, steep and fast, for the enemy leader. Gordon gave him a long five or six seconds of his six .50-calibers before he flipped suddenly over on his back and dived into the lagoon.

Lieutenant (j.g.) J. E. "Frenchy" Reulet got a Zeke which attacked him first. Frenchy was able to turn into him and meet him head on with the awful fire power of those six heavy machine guns. He destroyed a second in an easy beam attack when his bullets raked the cockpit, shattering the canopy and killing the pilot.

With enemy fighters shot down or chased away, Kane's Hellcats went down to strafe. Taroa was little more than an airfield surrounded by water, with the two runways crossing the island from shore to shore and intersecting in the middle. Along the coast, between the runway ends, were shops, hangars, fuel storage tanks, barracks and all the installations necessary to support the base. In the angles of the runway intersection at midisland were aircraft revetments and parking areas, and on each corner of the island were antiaircraft emplacements of all calibers. Under the heavy overcast the Hellcats forced antiaircraft gun crews to cease firing and run for cover, then worked over parked aircraft, magazines, workshops, garages packed with vehicles, radar installations and the radio station. The .50-caliber tracers chewed into their targets, throwing chunks of debris into the air and starting fires.

When the fighters had done their work, the bombers and torpedo planes arrived.

Bill Martin was in the air at quarter of seven with thirteen of his eager and well-trained but combat-inexperienced Avengers. The weather was improving with the rising, warming sun and he joined up over *Enterprise* with a twelve-Hellcat escort, a formation of SBDs from *Yorktown* and other TBFs from *Belleau Wood*.

The big Avengers, each loaded with one 500- and ten 100-pound bombs, dived at steep 60-degree angles, building up to well over 300 knots. The pilots sighted carefully, and released their entire bomb loads at 5,000 feet. The maximum error was less than 200 feet. Their bombs tore their targets to pieces.

Martin, who made the first run, made the best one. His bombs whumped into a fuel and ammunition storage area which ignited with a flash a string of explosions and a blazing orange pillar of flame and smoke. Other bombs stomped with iron boots through the aircraft revetments, across the runways, shops, hangars and gun emplacements. As the TBFs circled to the westward joining up, most of the island was obscured by dust and smoke rising from the explosions of their bombs.

Bombing Ten got off an hour behind the torpedo planes and, like them, joined overhead with *Yorktown* squadrons. Dick Poor led a flight of eighteen of his own Dauntlesses in a strike group which also included eleven *Yorktown* Avengers and a twelve-Hellcat escort.

Half of Poor's eighteen planes carried the big 1,000-pound general purpose bombs, the rest were loaded with one 500- and two 100-pounders. These they laid on vehicle revetments and garages, torpedo and warhead magazines, a torpedo repair shop, miscellaneous buildings and a couple of parked Bettys. When they pulled away to the southeast to rejoin for the flight home, the whole north side of the island, which had been their target area, was burning and exploding in a very satisfactory manner.

As the *Enterprise* dive bombers retired, the *Yorktown* TBFs began their runs. And so it went all day. The three carriers of TG 58.1 so scheduled their strikes that the enemy on Taroa had no peace. "Planes from various squadrons were bombing and strafing incessantly."

Just before six o'clock the evening of that first day, all flights had returned aboard except the seven-plane CAP led by Lieutenant Bud Schumann. The sun was low on the starboard bow as the task group headed down for a circling approach to Kwajalein. At 5:50 the general alarm clanged electrically through compartments, passageways and decks. Gunners, buckling on their helmets and life jackets at their battle stations, could see the destroyers firing and the Hellcat CAP diving, and out to the west, low on the water in the sun, were nine twin-engine, twin-tailed bombers headed for the task group. They were identified as "Nells." *Enterprise* guns that would bear opened up. Schumann's CAP began firing runs and the bombers fired back.

One of them trailed smoke briefly and then skidded into the sea ten miles southwest of the force. And then the word came over the ship's loudspeakers and the radios on all units of the group: "Cease firing! Cease firing!" The guns went tensely, reluctantly silent. The Hellcats pulled up, circling. A destroyer headed for the downed plane where heads bobbed in the froth of the crash. In another minute the explanation came: "Target identified as friendlies."

The bombers were U. S. Army Air Force B-25s.

All but one of the crew of the lost plane were rescued by the destroyer *Gatling* and, on Sunday the thirtieth, transferred by high line to *Enterprise*. The Army command involved protested sharply to Admiral Mitscher. A board of investigation was held. The admiral expressed his profound regret at the loss of a United States airman but, in view of the unannounced appearance of the Army aircraft and the threatening manner of their approach, he could only concur in the defensive action taken by the forces under his command.

Aboard the Big E, her men found that the B-25s were out of Tarawa, flying low to stay under enemy radar and because their mission was low-level skip-bombing. What had looked like a torpedo approach to the task group had been intended as a circle to stay clear.

The next day Mitscher concentrated on Kwajalein.

While *Enterprise* and Task Group 58.1 had been working over Taroa, 58.4 had been hitting Wotje and 58.2 and 58.3 had been attacking the islets of the Kwajalein Atoll itself. Now, with enemy air power in the Marshalls so crippled that not a single Japanese airplane remained flyable east of Eniwetok, the fast carriers concentrated on softening up the main objectives, the big, boomerang-shaped island of Kwaj itself at the southeast corner of the biggest atoll in the world, and the well-equipped and defended twin-island air base of Roi-Namur at the northeast corner.

For five days the fighters flew CAP over the carriers and the island, strafed at the end of each flight and escorted strikes and photo flights; the bombers delivered their loads where and when requested by the landing forces; the torpedo planes bombed, flew antisub patrols and delivered unused depth bombs and machine-gun bullets ashore at the end of each flight, maintained an air coordinator and an air liaison flight over the island during the hours of daylight, and all three squadrons took photographs for intelligence purposes as the action ashore progressed.

For that five days the Big E steamed back and forth southwest of Kwajalein, close enough to give her pilots short flights and yet well out of sight of enemy eyes. Her crew was busy with the continued flight operations and increasingly uneasy at being bound for so long to the small patch of ocean in the Marshalls which by now must be known to every enemy aircraft squadron commander and submarine skipper in the Pacific, not to mention the main body of the Japanese fleet a few hundred miles west at its bristling major base of Truk in the Carolines. Almost every night a screening destroyer would report a sonar contact, torpedo defense stations would be manned and Admiral Reeves would spin his ships on their broad sterns in emergency turns away from the contact. But the enemy squadron commanders had no aircraft left in the Marshalls to fly and no fields from which to fly them; the enemy submariners were unskilled, unlucky or merely outwitted by United States opposition; and Admiral Koga, at Truk with three battleships and eleven cruisers, had lost the air groups for his eight carriers in the Solomons (as he had lost his best carriers and pilots at Midway) and "could not commit the fleet without carriers."

So the garrison on Kwajalein Atoll was left to defend itself against the pounding of the U. S. battleships, blasting of the U. S. carrier planes and the amphibious assault forces of the U. S. Army and Marine Corps, which went ashore on the islets flanking Kwaj and Roi-Namur on the thirty-first of January and on the main islands themselves on the following day.

Early on the morning watch on February 1, TG 58.1 lost the services of two of its fast battleships. *Indiana,* maneuvering in the predawn darkness into position to fuel destroyers at first light, collided with *Washington* 3,000 yards southeast of *Enterprise.* The grinding crash of the collision of twice 35,000 (probably nearer 45,000) tons of steel, carried across the still sea and caused the watch on deck throughout the force to catch their breaths and turn their heads. Men died, and heavy steel plate and expensive equipment was sliced and rent and twisted, and at dawn the two battlewagons were out of action and headed for a rear area to make repairs, while *Enterprise* torpedo planes circled them on watch for subs.

On D-Day, *Enterprise* radios carried a blow-by-blow account of the action that was a little like the broadcast of a football game except that where men were dying under steel and high explosive, and many others exposing themselves to death, it was no game. Into the Big E's speakers came the voices of the senior aviators assigning targets for bombs and guns, liaison officers describing the situation, and individual boats and planes and tanks as they went about their deadly duties.

While the land campaign went on, the Big E's air group and squadron commanders alternated as air coordinator over the target. In three-and-a-half-hour shifts they directed strike aircraft against objectives on Kwaj and the islands, directed the rescues of downed air crews, reported results and made recommendations to the commander, Support Aircraft, and when their watches were over, went down themselves with professional aggressiveness to strafe and lay their bombs on whatever targets they considered most worth-while.

Bill Martin had only one day of this and then, late on the afternoon of the thirty-first, he slipped while exercising on the fo'c'sle and, in the resultant fall, broke an elbow on the steel deck. It was a bitter piece of bad luck for Martin and his squadron, since it grounded him for weeks while the men he had worked so hard to train flew against the enemy without the benefit of his tactical leadership. But it was also a proof of the quality of the training he had given them that his men could successfully perform the demanding tasks expected of them without him.

By full daylight on the fourth of February only a few yards of shattered coral remained in the hands of the surviving Japanese garrison on Kwajalein, and, when morning General Quarters was secured, the ships' loudspeakers announced that *Enterprise* and her task group were leaving the Kwaj area to refuel and resupply in the spacious lagoon anchorage of Majuro, 200 miles southeast.

The occupation of Kwajalein, as far as *Enterprise* was concerned, was over. For the first time, prewar Japanese territory had been forcibly taken. And so overpowering and successful were the fast carriers of TF 58 that in the week's action, in the midst of enemy-held islands 2,000 miles west of Pearl, not a single United States ship had even come under attack by hostile aircraft.

Enterprise was eight days in Majuro. No one got ashore.

Six hundred miles southeast of Eniwetok, a hundred miles south of Taroa, even closer to enemy bases at Mili and Jaluit, and, within a dangerous radius of the dreaded enemy fortress at Truk, the ships in Majuro were on one-hour sailing notice.

By Monday noon *Enterprise* knew her next target. The ship buzzed with talk and it was not all happy talk. Marc Mitscher's carriers were going to raid the reputedly impregnable and mysterious heart of Japanese power in the central Pacific, dreaded Truk itself. The mission was to destroy enemy air and naval power and installations at Truk and, in so doing, prevent any interference with troop landings at Eniwetok, the westernmost atoll in the Marshalls, scheduled for February 17.

When men thought of Truk they pictured a "Gibraltar of the Pacific" bristling with guns, defended by hundreds of fighters and the superbattleships and other heavy units of the Combined Fleet. To attack an isolated atoll or defend a remote and smelly island was reasonable, but to raid a heavily armed and carefully protected fortress like Truk was a matter which required some thought. Aboard the Big E, it received a great deal.

Despite the restful days at anchor, it was apparent to the men who thought about it, that the tempo of the war was picking up. No longer could they count on training for and building up to a major strike, making it, and then devoting a month or so in a rear area for repairs, ship's work and a build-up to the next operation. Weeks and months of relative inaction like the ones at Espiritu and Noumea were no more. Things were beginning to happen fast—Kwajalein late in January, Eniwetok and Truk in mid-February and already rumors were around of other, equally serious operations to follow. And it made sense. The men had seen with their own eyes, at sea and in the Marshall lagoons, the big, powerful U. S. task forces now operating in the Pacific. The sooner and the faster this growing power was used, the sooner the enemy would be rolled back to Japan and the endless war ended.

On the evening of the fourteenth, the three task groups of the Truk raiding force joined up. Officers and men in *Enterprise* stood topside in the late afternoon sunshine and gaped at the naval power plowing along to the westward in geometric dispositions that stretched to the horizon in all directions. This was the U. S. Navy's first team, the best and strongest that it could field. And it was superbly led. Vice Admiral R. A. Spruance, who had walked the Big E's bridge at Midway, flew his three stars at the truck of the *New Jersey* as commander of Task Force 50 (Truk Striking Force). Close by, in *Yorktown,* Rear Admiral Marc Mitscher commanded Task Force 58 (Fast Carrier Force). And under those two capable gentlemen, dedicated to the destruction of Truk as a tenable, useful enemy base, were nine carriers, six new battleships and ten cruisers plus screening destroyers, by far the most potent force to steam in the same formation on the same mission since the war began.

At sunset Spruance signaled 25 knots and the big ships built up their speed for the run-in to Truk, slanting down from the northwest on the most improbable approach course to avoid detection.

On the evening of the fifteenth, Bill Martin made a desperate, last-minute attempt to get ungrounded so that he could lead his squadron against Truk, and especially so that he could lead the scheduled night bombing attack for which he had been planning and training since Guadalcanal. Long, rangy Killer Kane, the Air Group commander; big, solid, ex-All-American Tom Hamilton, the air officer; stocky, wax-mustached Cecil Gill, the exec, and VT-10's flight surgeon, John Ridley, stood beside a Torpedo Ten Avenger while Bill attempted to demonstrate that he could enter it, leave it and fly it perfectly well, broken elbow and all. The basic flight controls, stick, rudders and throttle he could handle adequately, but he had trouble with trim tabs and essential gadgets in more remote corners of the cockpit. The high-level delegation was skeptical. The doctor was unimpressed and stoutly insisted that Martin stay grounded. Martin, not without difficulty, extricated himself from the cockpit, and the five men proceeded to the bridge where Captain Gardner sat with his binoculars around his neck, squinting out over his deck and the formation. The problem was put to him. Mat Gardner turned his strong, hawk-beaked face on Martin and said no. He had made it fast but it was a hard decision. Martin had been working toward this operation for years and his squadron was all new, leaning heavily on him for leadership, especially in the air. And Gardner knew how badly he wanted to go. But the captain also knew Bill Martin and he was not going to waste him on a mission on which a man needed everything he had, and where that still might not be enough. There would be action enough for Martin when he had regained the full use of his arm.

All night *Enterprise,* surrounded by the darkened shapes of warships, closed steadily on Truk. The radar showed occasional bogies which did not approach the force.

Flight quarters sounded through the ship and across her dark flight deck at 6:00 A.M. on the sixteenth. Pilots and crewmen filed into their ready rooms with coffee mugs in their hands and "sack tracks" on their faces, wrestled into flight suits and Mae Wests and settled into their chairs with chartboards and pencils ready. The ship was some ninety miles northeast of Truk, the weather good but with rain clouds around and a light northeasterly breeze.

Mitscher's first blow at Truk was a fighter sweep to clear the fields and the skies over the target of enemy planes, so that the bombers and torpedo planes could do their work without interference, and the task force itself would not come under aerial counterattack.

At 6:30 the Hellcats began to unfold their wings and move into position in the dark, and at quarter of seven, Killer Kane made a short, noisy run between the dim, recessed deck-edge lights and climbed into the night sky. Eleven of his best were right behind him. All around the Big E the other carriers were also launching, and by shortly after seven o'clock, seventy-two fighters were in the air behind Kane, the strike leader, and headed for the target, their black wedges roaring across the ships and blinking out the stars as they departed. It was still an hour and ten minutes to sunrise.

Truk Atoll is not like Kwajalein, Majuro, Tarawa and others in the Marshall-Gilbert groups. There is, of course, the great circling coral reef (at Truk, some thirty-three miles in diameter), but, from the floor of the enclosed lagoon rise a dozen volcanic islands, not flat and narrow strips of coral sand, but lush and hilly, with peaks as high as 1,500 feet, good harbors and pleasant valleys. When Mitscher's Hellcats swung in over Truk in the morning twilight of February 16, 1944, theirs were the first non-native, non-Japanese eyes (with the exception of those belonging to the crew of an enterprising Marine recon Liberator twelve days before) to see it since Japan had taken it from Germany early in World War I—more than a quarter of a century before.

No one really knew what to expect, except trouble. At 7:14 the watch in the code shack heard Truk Radio go off the air. The incoming raid had been discovered.

As the square-wing-tipped blue fighters came in over the reef in three groups of 24, at ten, fifteen and twenty thousand feet, about fifty of the enemy—Zekes, Hamps, Rufes and Tojos—were just air-borne and climbing desperately to meet them. For the next hour the scene was like a modernized combat sequence from *Hell's Angels*. All over the sky, brown planes with red balls on their wings swirled and zoomed and swooped in hoarsely screaming tangles with the blue Hellcats. Plane after plane blazed and fell spinning or diving straight in. Against the still-dark west the flaring orange of the falling planes was lurid and terrible. For perhaps twenty minutes, no thirty-second period went by when there was not at least one burning plane torching down across the sky. The airfields teemed with taxiing fighters trying to take off, and runways and overruns and nearby woods and waters were dotted with the smoky gasoline fires of those that had been caught in the act by the F6s. Tracers from light and medium antiaircraft guns smoked up at the strafing carrier planes. In the crowded anchorage between the islands, the ships, including two cruisers, began to move, getting under way, and their guns flashed angrily when the fighters dived in to strafe the fields and whenever American planes were separated sufficiently from Japanese to make a target. But the Hellcats were interested only in planes at the moment. There would be time for ships later.

Killer and Verne Ude, his wingman, met a division of four Zekes as they approached the central islands. The Zekes were higher and to the right but they attacked sloppily so that the two F6s turned into them and both Kane and Ude shot one down. Coming out of that scuffle, Ude saw another Zeke with one wheel hanging and set him afire with one long burst. Then Kane and Ude rejoined and went down to strafe the carrier-like fighter-base island of Eten. They arrived just as two Tojos were taking off. One was about 100 feet in the air and the other so low he had not yet retracted his wheels. Kane burned both in the same continuous firing run. Five planes for Killer and his wingman in the first five minutes of action.

Lieutenant Ned Colgan, leading Kane's second division, with Ensign Phil Kirkwood on his wing, was attacked by Zekes as he was starting his strafing run. In the scramble that followed, Colgan got on a Zeke's tail and stayed there as though he were tied, firing short bursts as the Zeke tried to dive away but burned and crashed instead. Pulling out of his dive after the first Zeke, Colgan saw another zoom by in a nearly vertical climb, and pulled straight up after him, his guns chattering. The zooming Zeke was beginning to smoke when Colgan's F6 spun out of the steep climb. Phil Kirkwood lost Colgan in that violent maneuver but caught another Zeke in a flat side run, riddling his engine and fuselage so that he slanted off, smoking into the lagoon. When Kirkwood found Colgan again, Ned was "playing the part of the ham in a ham sandwich." He was on the tail of a Zeke, firing, and behind him another Zeke was doing the same thing. Kirkwood raised his nose from a thousand feet away and sprayed bullets at the enemy behind Colgan. The Japanese turned away.

Flash Gordon turned hard into four Zekes making a high side run on him, shot down the first in a blazing head-on approach and got on the tail of a second before his guns jammed and some friendly F6F finished off his enemy.

Frenchy Reulet fired a Zeke in a quick tail chase and then followed a Rufe float fighter through a loop and burned him at the top just before his Hellcat stalled out. Later he shot a Hamp off the tail of another F6 and saw the pilot bail out of the blazing plane with his clothes on fire and burn to death swinging below his chute in the morning sky. Reulet's wingman, Ensign Walker, saved him by shooting a Rufe off his tail with a long burst that chewed into the Jap's engine and set it on fire.

Lieutenant Jack Farley, flying with Ensign Linton Cox, shot down a Rufe from behind in a tight turn but the next second a 20-millimeter exploded in his cockpit, wrecking the instrument panel and lacerating his left leg and hand. He never saw the plane that hit him nor did he or anyone else see Linton Cox after that. The same Japanese that hit Farley must have killed Linton. Farley found that his plane still flew and his guns still worked, so he dived and strafed the fighter field on Eten, then flew across the harbor to Param, where he found a Zeke taking off and sent him smoking into the lagoon.

Only Kane, Gordon, Reulet and a few others in VF-10 had any real combat experience before Truk, and yet after the blessed thumps on the Big E's deck and the good grabs as the arresting cables engaged the hooks, down in the

ready room the score showed three kills each for Kane and
Reulet, two for Ude and Farley, and one apiece for Colgan, Gordon, Kirkwood and Walker—plus the "probables"
and the "damaged." And that was in the air. On the ground
five of the Reapers strafed a line of parked enemy planes
and burned three Bettys, nine Zekes and four Tojos. Kane
set a Nick afire on the field at Param.

In an hour and a half the Hellcats of Task Force 58
owned the skies over dreaded Truk. More than thirty enemy planes had been shot out of the air and another forty
burned on the ground. Four F6Fs were missing. It was still
only 9:30 A.M.

Now the bombers and torpedo planes went to work. Every two hours, beginning at 7:00 A.M., *Enterprise* launched
a strike which averaged out at seven Avengers, eleven
Dauntlesses and an escort of twelve Hellcats.

The first of these strikes came in at 8:15, while the fighter sweep was still going on and the sun had just broken into
the eastern sky. The *Enterprise* group joined up with a
similar one from *Yorktown* off the Northeast Pass into
the reef, and began their approaches. Lieutenant Russell
"Kip" Kippen's Avengers were loaded with six 100-pound
fragmentation clusters and six 100-pound incendiaries for
the planes and facilities on the fighter field at little Eten Island. He made his approach from the east, spreading out
and circling around between the two big islands of Moen
and Dublon, to dive on Eten from west to east. His target
was hard to find with thick clouds covering more than half
the sky and their bases as low as 2,500 feet, but the TBFs
dived in fast and released their twelve bombs in exploding
strings across the parking areas, service aprons and shops
and hangars of crowded, busy Eten. From the hill beside
the strip and from the ships and islets in the harbor the
guns flashed back at them, and the slow tennis balls of 20-
millimeter and the black puffs of heavier stuff whipped past
their wings but did no serious damage.

Bombing Ten's SBDs, lugging 1,000-pound bombs, arrived over their targets four minutes behind the TBFs and
dived through the obscuring clouds on the ships in Dublon
anchorage. Most of the enemy warships had left for safer
waters, but two of the big bombs hit a merchantman and
two more landed close aboard a heavy cruiser; the others
spouted the lagoon around those ships and a nearby tanker.

The eight Hellcats of that first *Enterprise* strike, under

Lieutenant (j.g.) Walter "Tommy" Harman, arrived in time to help Kane's dozen beat down Jap fighter opposition. They went in ahead of the torpedo planes to strafe Eten and reduce the antiaircraft fire, and then pulled up to fight. Harman himself shot two Zekes down at altitude, caught a Rufe float fighter trying to get off the Eten seadrome and dropped him in the water.

Richard "Tabu" Taber attacked a Zeke, at low altitude, which tried to escape by rolling over on its back and pulling through in a split S. Not even a Zeke can get away with a split S from 500 feet, and the enemy fighter crashed into the sea.

Ensign Gene Redmond had perhaps the most eventful morning of all. His section was attacked in its initial strafing run by four Zekes, of which Flash Gordon got one, and then by a Rufe which occupied the attention of the other pilots while still another Zeke came in behind them. Redmond turned into the last Zeke and it caught fire at once. On their way back to the rendezvous point off the Northeast Pass, Redmond and Gordon came under simultaneous attack from opposite directions by a Rufe and a Zeke. Redmond took the Zeke in a head-on run but it zoomed over him and split-S'd onto his tail, its 20-millimeter chewing holes in his right wing. Redmond started home at full throttle but was jumped by two more Zekes which he was able to outrun. About thirty miles from the task force he came on a Val dive bomber sneaking in at 1,500 feet. The enemy pilot was looking straight ahead for the U. S. ships, and Redmond came up behind and stitched the Val with .50-caliber holes until it flamed and winged over into the ocean. When he landed aboard after nearly an hour of wide-open operation, his abused engine was pouring smoke.

The SBDs of the day's second bombing attack blew the sides out of a large tanker in Dublon anchorage and made a third hit on the small carrier which had been hit twice by the previous strike. Both ships were left burning and settling, but when Ensign Bob Wilson pulled out of his dive to the south of the anchorage, he found four Zekes and a Rufe beginning runs on him from above. He shoved throttle into the stops and headed for the nearest cloud. The first two Zekes made high side runs but were handicapped by the SBD's 800-foot altitude which did not give them room to recover below it. They were also handicapped by H. Honea's twin .30-calibers which opened up when they were 500 yards out and followed them to the break-off point. The first Zeke flew past the Dauntless to port with his engine smoking, then pulled up, stalled and executed a "falling leaf" into the south end of the lagoon. The second Zeke made the same kind of run, received the same attentions from Honea and left the fight with his engine also smoking. Thereafter the other Japanese were more cautious in their attacks, and Wilson and Honea made it to the cloud and thence home with only one small bullet hole in the horizontal stabilizer.

In midafternoon a strike of eight of Torpedo Ten's Avengers went after the shipping in the anchorages around Truk, in company with ten bombers and twelve fighters from *Enterprise*. Each TBF carried four 500-pound general-purpose bombs. They attacked in steep dives with high releases, and all missed except Ensign Joe Jewell, whose bombs failed to release. The planes recovered to the northeast and were outside the reef on the way home when Jewell decided he could not face Bill Martin with four bombs which he had lugged at considerable trouble, expense and risk, over enemy territory and then brought back to the ship. He turned alone and headed back in to use them. But on the way he saw a destroyer with a high bow wave and a long wake, making for the North Pass through the reef. He swung north and came up astern of the enemy ship at 9,000 feet. When his position was right he opened his bomb bay and pushed over in a 50-degree dive while his speed built up to 300 knots and the thin, speeding ship expanded in his sight and threw up smoking balls of medium AA. At 3,000 feet he dropped, remembering this time to pull the emergency release also, and this time his 2,000 pounds of bombs separated and plunged away. Joe banked around as he leveled out and watched his bombs smother the destroyer. One landed in her wake. The other three walked her length, blowing gaping holes in decks and sides and blasting debris that fell back in showers of large and small splashes well out from the ship. As Jewell wheeled back around for base, the enemy "can" was dead in the water and nearly out of sight under a swelling mass of smoke and flame. Joe landed aboard last of his squadron and the only one on that strike to get a hit.

Late in the afternoon of that first day, Admirals Spruance and Mitscher took steps to safeguard their ships against night counterattacks from Truk. The Big E's part was a raid on the enemy bomber field on Moen, the northern-most of the large islands in the lagoon. Other carriers hit the other fields at the same time.

Five Hellcats with the delayed-action 1,000-pounders went in first, planting all five of the big bombs deep in the single runway. Then ten SBDs attacked in their precise, near-vertical dives, concentrating on the revetted bombers, which answered with machine-gun fire from their dorsal turrets. The strafing fighters that followed found a dozen big planes flaming with a ferocity which indicated that they had full gas loads aboard, and they burned eleven single-engine enemy planes themselves. Four TBFs came in last and every one of their forty-eight 100-pound bombs hit the battered field of Moen. As the *Enterprise* planes pulled away to rendezvous, the bombers that had been loaded and manned to strike the U. S. task force, and the interceptors which would have risen to defend against the next morn-ing's raids, crumpled in the flames of their own fuel. In the concrete of the runway, 5,000 pounds of high explosive was set to explode at random intervals during the night.

But the Japanese were not yet entirely beaten. As Tom-my Harman's four-Hellcat division pulled up from a straf-ing run, it encountered four determined Zekes in quick suc-cession. Harman fought the first one for fifteen minutes during which neither pilot could get a decisive advantage, but finally he hit the enemy cockpit and the Zeke flew straight into a mountain on Moen. Harman dove back into the fight and shot another Zeke off Larry Richardson's tail just in time.

Richardson, with only three-quarters of his rudder, two cannon holes in his left wing and one through the fuse-lage, a hit in his engine, the right side of his windshield missing and no means of lowering his wheels, gentled his Hellcat back to the task group and, at six minutes before eight, skipped it into the ocean alongside the destroyer *Dortsch*. He was rescued with nothing more than a cut forehead.

Woodie Hampton had much worse luck. After he was hit he started for the ship. But the Japanese, after a full day of continuous attacks, had figured out that Northeast Pass was a navigational check point for inbound, and a ren-dezvous point for outbound strike groups. Three of them—a Zeke, a Hamp and a Rufe—were waiting there, hoping to knock off a cripple. No friendlies were around. As soon as they saw him, the three enemy pilots started a series of attacks on Hampton's shot-up Hellcat. All he could do was shove throttle forward, head for home and wait for the enemy to get careless. He was hit again repeatedly, but then the Hamp recovered from a run too close and flew past Woodie above and to port. The Hellcat's nose came up and swung left, the .50-calibers hammered briefly, and the Hamp continued its climb, smoking, for a few seconds before it expelled a huge puff of black smoke, rolled over and went down.

In desperation, with two undamaged enemies still on his tail, Hampton turned off his electronic recognition gear (IFF) to appear as a bogey on the force radarscopes, and bring the CAP to his rescue. It worked, but too slowly. The CAP was vectored out, but while it was on the way the Zeke became overconfident. He started a run from dead astern and then changed his mind and pulled out straight ahead above the F6. Woodie pulled up his nose and gave the Zeke a long burst as he went over. The brown fighter with the red balls on its wings flamed and fell. That left only Rufe and only three of Hampton's six guns still firing. The next time the Rufe made a stern attack, Woodie cut back his throttle and, as the enemy overshot him, jammed it forward and opened fire (his plane skidding with the unbalanced recoil of the guns). Rufe climbed sharply, and departed to look for a more crippled cripple. Woodie Hampton, with no compass and marginal control of his plane, like Richardson, landed on the water beside a destroyer. The landing was rough and Woodie's head smashed forward into the gunsight, knocking him out. Swimmers from the destroyer, seeing the F6 submerging with the pilot still aboard, reached him just in time. He was returned to Fighting Ten, barely recognizable, with two very black eyes and a healing gash in his forehead.

Enterprise had been busy, and worried—worried about her airmen and the seeming certainty of aerial counterattacks. All day plane captains and handlers had leapt to the wings of returning planes to ask, "How did it go?" "What was it like?" "What have they got in there?" Twice bogies had been destroyed by the CAP inside of thirty miles, and in the evening a sub had been sighted submerging only seven miles away. But as the hours passed and the word filtered through the crew that the strike groups were getting away with their destructive attacks on this Truk that they had heard was impregnable, the worrying stopped and the men became confident and even cheerful.

At eight o'clock it was announced that the day's operations had broken the ship's record for tonnage of bombs dropped.

Around the mess tables aviators and air-crewmen discussed the day's action and explained to those who had stayed aboard how it was.

Ernie Lawton, of VT-10, who, ever since his crash two days before, had been avoiding Doc Ridley in fear of being grounded, could tell of making two hits on a heavy cruiser attempting to make it out of North Pass. Bob Jones described with great relish and eloquence how he was hit by a Zeke, "heard a poof and the cockpit filled with smoke . . . looked out on the wing and there was a yard-square hole in it with flames shooting out." Shonk, Shinneman, Kincaid and Perrault of the Reapers told of their twenty-minute dogfight with six Zekes, high over Truk, in which three of the enemy went down and three Hellcats were shot up but made it home. There were as many stories as there had been sorties and each was a vivid, firsthand account of a small part of one of the more important days of the war in the Pacific—a day when the Japanese lion had been bearded in his den and found to be only a scrappy alley cat.

It was barely dark before the inevitable bogies began showing up on the force radars. For three hours, from a few minutes past nine to quarter past twelve, small groups of enemy planes, circled, approached, were fired on by the screen, and withdrew to circle and approach again. In the darkness, the Big E's guns hummed around to each new danger bearing, but never fired. Below decks she was buttoned up tight in a "modified materiel condition Able" to provide maximum protection against torpedoes. And it was a wise precaution. About ten o'clock the men topside were startled by a bright, white flash—lasting perhaps a second —on the horizon to port. They found out the next day that it had been caused by an air-dropped torpedo detonating against the starboard quarter of the big new carrier *Intrepid*. In that flash, eleven men had died and seventeen more had been wounded. Between eleven and midnight, CIC provided direction to a night fighter from the *Yorktown* detachment commanded by Lieutenant Russ Reiserer of the old VF-10 and the *Enterprise* of Guadal days. The night fighter made contact but was unable to keep it in the swift, electronically assisted game of aerial blindman's buff over the night sea.

Two hours and a few minutes after the last bogey had faded from the task group radars, the pilots and crewmen of Torpedo Ten filed into Ready Room Number Six. The night that Bill Martin had dreamed of and planned for years, and for which his men had trained for months, had arrived. Permission had been granted by the task force commander to attempt what no carrier planes had ever done before—a minimum-altitude, night bombing attack on shipping in an enemy harbor. It was with this kind of mission in mind that Martin's TBFs had been out in all kinds of weather at Sand Point, Seattle, and logging hundreds of night hours navigating by radar around the Hawaiian Islands. It was in preparation for a mission like this that Martin had borrowed Scoofer Coffin's Avengers at Espiritu and practiced bombing rocks and reefs on radar. It was this kind of mission that had been the subject of long, technical discussions between Martin and anyone who knew anything about air-borne radar, instrument and night flight, particularly Lieutenant Henry Loomis of the Pearl Harbor Radar School.

Every pilot and air-crewman in the squadron knew how to go about this attack. It was only a matter now of relating the learned tactics to the specific area of the Truk anchorages. So, in an hour, the briefing was over and the word came down from Air Plot, "Pilots, man your planes." But Bill Martin was not quite through, and over the squawk box he asked for a couple of minutes. For those two minutes he talked to his squadron earnestly, trying to give them the confidence they would have had if he were leading the attack. His audience gained confidence from his words, but it was a confidence derived from a determination not to disappoint this man who had lived for this night's action and now would not see it. A little before four in the morning, Martin's flight crews filed out of the island and fanned out across the darkened deck to their planes. A team of six radio technicians under their chief stood by to check the Avengers' radar, on which success or failure depended, as the planes were warming up. Complete extra radar sets were ready as replacements in the event of failure on the deck.

Torpedo Ten's dozen Avengers were not launched for the

first night carrier-based bombing attack of the war with the hustling urgency of normal daylight strike launches. Tom Hamilton knew the psychological value of a careful, thorough launch and he had instructed Air Plot, flight-deck and catapult crews accordingly. Regularly and methodically, after time for warm-up and check outs, the TBFs were catapulted from the Big E's bow until twelve were in the air over the moonlit sea. Lieutenant V. Van Eason, Martin's executive officer, was the flight leader, and burned his navigation lights while the planes joined up in loose formation ahead of the ship and departed for Truk at 500 feet. It was eighty-eight miles to the southeast tip of the reef.

Although the thirty-six men in the twelve darkened torpedo planes were too preoccupied with the complex techniques of delivering 500-pound packages of high explosive onto the decks of anchored vessels in the dark to notice in any but the most professional way or to enjoy it at all, the predawn hours of February 17 in the Western Caroline Islands were full of the soft magic of the southern seas. The half moon was two thirds up the southeastern sky, lighting the trade-ruffled Pacific between the moving shadows of the clouds. The wind was warm and gentle, and near the islands it carried the sweet smell of tropical vegetation.

But to Martin's men, sweeping westward between clouds and sea at two and one-half miles every minute, the South Pacific night could mean only broken clouds with bases at 3,500 feet, visibility unlimited below and above, good radar conditions because of a low sea state, and the wind from the east-northeast at ten knots as a navigational notation. In the seats between pilots and gunners, radar operators concentrated on their small green scopes and carefully adjusted the knobs around them to bring in the best possible "picture." The radar compartments smelled of hot tubes and hot electrical insulation. In each bomb bay were four 500-pound general-purpose bombs with their fuses set for a four-second delay to allow the low-flying Avengers to escape the blast of their own bombs.

Lieutenant William B. Chace, operating Van Eason's radar, picked up the Truk reef twenty miles out, and Van led the formation north, skirting the east edge of the reef. They passed within a few miles of two ships but left them alone because of the chance that anything outside of the lagoon might be friendly.

Five miles off Northeast Pass, the formation broke up.

Eason, with five planes, began to circle there, while Kippen with three, and Robert Nelson with four, cut across the lagoon to a point five miles off the reef's northwest corner.

By 5:40 A.M. all three divisions were in position and the attack began.

At one-minute intervals, single TBFs left their circles and headed for the two main Truk anchorages. Radar operators, with the main islands showing on their scopes in a familiar pattern of lighted blobs, directed their pilots in. Eason's five planes attacked from their initial point outside Northeast Pass, southwest across the lagoon and into the anchorage east of Moen and between Moen and little Eten. Kippen and Nelson's divisions came in single file, a minute apart, from their initial point off the northwest corner of the atoll, southeasterly across the lagoon and into the big anchorage west of Moen and Dublon. As each plane headed in, it climbed to 1,000 feet to have altitude for a dive to pick up speed in the attack.

The Japanese at Truk were not asleep that morning. As the first planes angled in from opposite sides of the reef, a hospital ship in the northeastern part of the lagoon turned on her lights, her white sides and red crosses seeming to leap out of the dark sea, and seconds later a red rocket arched up across the sky from Moen, apparently an alarm signal to all enemy forces present.

As Eason's TBF approached from the northeast and Kippen's from the northwest, a searchlight stabbed out from the airfield side of Moen and searched jerkily around the sky, puddling brightly on the bottoms of the clouds. Searchlights were something the torpedo pilots had hoped would not happen, because, even with radar, the moment of the bomb release itself has to be selected by the pilot who sees the dark bulk of the target come under his nose; and a pilot whose night vision has been lost in the glare of a searchlight cannot see the target to release or a mountain to avoid. A minute or two after the light came on, Russ Kippen, still miles out on his approach, saw the flash of a big explosion light the field on Moen and the searchlight go out. It was one of VF-10's 1,000-pounders with a twelve-hour fuse, blowing up the bomber runway; the enemy must have thought his searchlight was being attacked as they had been at other places, and promptly switched it off.

Then the Avengers were among the moored and anchored ships like foxes in a henhouse. At 250 feet above

the quiet harbor, with open bomb bays, Bill Martin's men
lined up on the biggest targets by radar and bored straight
in at 180 knots until the pilots could see the black shapes
of the sleeping ships. Then, at that instant that a man can
only feel from practice and a good eye is the right one,
when the dark mass of the target has just gone under the
nose or is just ahead of it, at about the time that the radar
operator's voice says "Mark!" the right thumbs came down
on the release buttons on top of the sticks, and two bombs
at close intervals nosed down out of the bays. There was
time to swing up and away from the hills and bank around
toward position for another run before the delay fuses fired.
Every minute for seven minutes another TBF swept in between the islands to attack. Eason hit a tanker on his first
run and its flames helped show up other ships in the small,
crowded anchorage between Eten and Dublon. For thirty
minutes, as the tracers of the AA grew in volume and accuracy, the dozen Avengers skimmed back and forth across
the ships, searching visually and by radar for the best targets and deliberately and methodically attacking them.
Ship after ship exploded and burned under bombs delivered
at masthead height by the blacked-out planes that were
only loudening sounds in the night and then shadows and
then receding blue points of exhaust flames to the enemy
gun crews listening and peering on their dew-wet decks.

In the spacious, moonlit anchorage west of Dublon and
Moen, "Kip," Nelson and their divisions could see their
targets from as far as a mile away and identify them from
half a mile. There, the shore guns were on only one side of
the harbor. In that anchorage, conditions were close to the
ones they had been trained to meet. But around the corner
of Dublon, between it and the tiny, fighter-strip island of
Eten, Van Eason and his four crews ran into trouble. Because of the surrounding islands they could attack only
from one direction, northeast, cross moon rather than up
moon, with their targets silhouetted. Antiaircraft guns from
Eten, Dublon and Fefan could bring them under crossfire.
Several small islets rose out of the waters of the anchorage
and looked, on radar, like ships. Many of the biggest ships
were moored so close in that they merged on the Avengers'
scopes with the shore line. But, in the increasingly heavy
AA from ships and shore, Van and his pilots searched the
Eten anchorage until they found suitable targets and then
drove in their attacks.

Each plane, after its last run, closed doors on the empty bays and skimmed off to the rendezvous point five miles east of the most southerly point on the atoll, waited a few minutes to join up with anyone who came along and returned to base. They left behind two anchorages full of broken, burning, sinking ships. Two tankers and six freighters had been sunk and another five freighters badly damaged. Flames lighted the tropical harbor, bodies and debris drifted in its quiet waters, now covered with a stinking film of black oil in the morning twilight. As Martin's torpedo planes filed out between the enemy islands, the dawn fighter sweep was coming in over the reef.

Torpedo Ten's pioneering night bombers landed back aboard the *Enterprise* in the fresh, soft light that just precedes the sunrise. Van Eason's rudder and fuselage were perforated with holes of varying sizes, Ralph Cummings had a hole in his port fuel tank. Nick Nicholas, with Docktor and Thornton, did not come back at all. Although before Taroa and Kwajalein he had never been in action, Nick had quickly become a determined, aggressive combat pilot. His squadron mates could only guess that he had pressed in, hard and close to be sure of his target, and had been shot down by point-blank automatic weapons fire like that which had riddled Eason's plane.

The night low-level radar bombing raid, in which Lloyd Nicholas and his two crewmen were killed, proved Bill Martin's theory of night attacks by carrier planes. It showed that properly trained carrier squadrons, flying at night when a fighter escort is not required and when lack of visibility, surprise and rapidity of movement reduce the effectiveness of antiaircraft fire, can attack from such low altitudes and short ranges that they are several times as accurate as day bombers. Half the dropping runs made by Van Eason's planes that night made direct hits. In daylight, only about one-fifth of attacks make hits.

If carrier planes could search and attack effectively at night there would need be no wait for the dawn to launch a strike group or a search and no worry about getting an afternoon strike back before dark. With night-flying carrier planes at work, the enemy would get no sleep, have no chance to repair his runways, move his planes or prepare for the next day's attacks against us. If night operations from carriers were practical, the opportunity to strike the enemy would double, thus halving his ability to strike us.

In his report of this action, Bill Martin "urged that a night air group be created immediately to operate from a CV designated primarily for night operations." Killer Kane "strongly endorsed" that recommendation and added that "a night minimum altitude bombing attack has been proved to be a practicable weapon . . . that will bring the maximum pressure to bear on the enemy when he is least able to defend himself."

February 17 was mop-up day for the American carrier pilots over Truk.

The dawn fighter sweep did not find a single enemy plane in the air, and went down to strafe the wreck-covered fields and the shipping.

Enterprise launched three final strikes. Twelve of Bombing 10's SBDs with an eight-fighter escort flew through heavy antiaircraft fire from enemy batteries that at last could see something to shoot at, and dropped their 1,000-pounders on a big tanker and a freighter in the anchorage west of Dublon. Kippen and Nelson's TBF divisions had done their work so well there that those were the only two worth-while targets left.

A second strike of TBFs, SBDs and an F6F escort hit two more big freighters, and McCrary and Moore of VT-10 sank a destroyer with an attack pressed so closely that Shannon McCrary was caught in the blast of his own bomb. Some twenty-five pieces of mixed American and Japanese metal went through his plane, puncturing gas tanks, cutting hydraulic lines and damaging radio gear.

For a day and a half, Mitscher's pilots had been saving one target for the last attack. It was the oil storage and magazine area on Dublon. Ten bombers, two torpedo planes and thirteen fighters from *Enterprise* took off to get it at 11:00 A.M. The thoroughly aroused Japanese gunners put a solid blanket of heavy AA bursts over the island, and under them the tracers of small weapons streamed and intersected. But the SBDs dived through and the fighters and torpedo planes skimmed under the AA and put eleven 500s and five 1000s into the tanks and magazines. As they wheeled out over the lagoon in their recoveries, the pouring black oil smoke had already obscured the town and was rapidly covering the anchorage. The top of the smoke cloud reached 8,000 feet.

When the last strike returned to *Enterprise,* she was already steaming eastward away from Truk. Mitscher and

Spruance, with a couple of surface actions and some thirty strikes, each stronger than either of the two Japanese raids that hit Pearl Harbor, had destroyed Truk as a major naval base, called the bluff of the "Gibraltar of the Pacific," and, as a bonus, destroyed or damaged 250 to 275 aircraft, sank or damaged beyond repair 2 light cruisers, 4 destroyers, 2 submarine tenders, 27 more or less armed merchant ships and other small craft.

18 PENETRATION TO PALAU

Task Force 58 divided after the Truk raid. Enterprise, in company with antiaircraft light cruiser (CLAA) *San Diego* and four destroyers, went on to Majuro, with a raid on Jaluit on the way, while the rest of the force turned northwest for a strike and some photo runs on Guam, Rota, Saipan and Tinian in the Marianas. Much to the disgust of the aviators, Air Group Ten furnished 10 fighters, 3 bombers and 10 torpedo planes with their crews, to the various carriers making the Marianas attack. All were supposed to be returned eventually, but squadron commanders shook their heads pessimistically and doubted that they would see their boys or their aircraft again.

On the afternoon of the twentieth, a reduced *Enterprise* air group hit Jaluit twice. Killer Kane went in with 13 fighters, 17 bombers and 3 torpedo planes at 1:00 P.M. No aircraft came up to meet the Big E's pilots but the enemy AA gunners were accurate and were not trying to conserve ammunition. Five-inch and three-inch bursts followed the planes closely and the leading SBD flew through several in its dive, surviving out of luck and the inherent toughness of the SBD, with holes and gashes in tail surfaces and engine cowling. Four other SBDs were hit but all got home safely.

A second attack hit Jaluit four hours after the first. When it returned, a big fuel fire boiled and churned ashore and the radio station, powerhouse and dock area were in ruins. A building evidently used to store explosives no longer existed and one magnificent concrete structure was still intact except for the chips in its roof from direct hits by three 500-pound bombs.

By 6:00 P.M. flight operations were over for the day, and

late in the morning of the twenty-first, the Big E steamed through Calalin Pass for a rest in Majuro Lagoon.

On Monday, the twenty-eighth of February, the Marianas Attack Force returned to Majuro, and the Big E got under way for five hours to recover the planes and crews she had lent to that operation, plus a few replacement aircraft. In bunk and wardrooms that evening, the talk was about the Marianas strike, and soon most of the ship knew about the hundred enemy planes destroyed, the big new airfields smashed and the ships sunk.

Early on the morning of Tuesday, the seventh of March, *Enterprise* was on her way southward and four days later her anchor chain was shackled to the mooring buoy in a familiar berth, B-19, in Segond Channel at Espiritu Santo in the New Hebrides.

Bill Martin, Killer Kane and all the *Enterprise* men who had known Espiritu too long and too well in the winter of 1943, when the Big E kept her lonely watch over the Solomons, found it almost incredibly changed. From a Marston matting field, surrounded by tents, Espiritu had become a bustling major air and naval base, with a radio range for instrument approaches, two new bomber fields, new roads connecting warehouses, barracks, repair shops, supply depots, movie theaters and all the activities one would expect to find at Pearl Harbor or Malta. The beverage supply had so improved from the days when Scoofer Coffin and Bill Martin had had to fly 200 miles to Efate for a Christmas supply that now the Officers' Club easily handled the hundreds of parched and sweating officers from the task group ships on a strict schedule: beer from 3:00 to 4:00 P.M., rum and brandy from 4:00 to 5:00 P.M., and anything the customer desired after that.

Enterprise pulled out of Segond Channel, for the last time ever, at 6:15 A.M. on the fifteenth of March.

As Admiral Reeves' task group paralleled the long chain of the Solomons, her air group flew routine antisub and CAP missions, but no enemy challenged it in waters through which, a little over a year ago, had come the enemy carriers whose Kates and Vals had sunk the *Hornet* and twice nearly got the Big E herself.

On the eighteenth a Catalina came in low and slow over the flight deck, looking big and clumsy after the carrier planes, and dropped an operation order.

At dawn on the twentieth, Reeves' task group was off the

island of Emirau. It was D-Day, and H-Hour was 9:00 A.M.
But there were no Japanese and no military installations on
Emirau, and the natives smiled and waved at the Big E's
low-flying, sightseeing planes which brought all their bombs
and bullets back aboard. The 4th Marines waded ashore
from their tank lighters and rolled up the beaches in their
alligators, in the atmosphere of a Sunday picnic on the
lower Mississippi.

The carriers stayed off Emirau another day and then ran
back eastward to convoy the transports of the second echelon of the occupation force.

On the evening of Sunday the twenty-sixth, when the
last mail had left the ship, the men of the Big E found out
where they were going. Clearly, not only the tempo but the
confidence of Pacific strategy was increasing. When they
had been told of the Truk raid, 1,000 miles west of the
freshly captured Marshalls, they had wondered at a pene-
tration so deep into enemy-controlled waters. Now they
were going 1,100 miles west of Truk, well west of Tokyo itself, just 500 miles short of the Philippines, to strike the key
base to Japan's inner defense perimeter, the headquarters
of the Combined Fleet since Truk had become untenable—
Palau in the Western Carolines. The objective was the
destruction of enemy naval forces, merchant shipping and
shore facilities to neutralize Palau as a base from which
Japan could counter General MacArthur's planned assault
on Hollandia, New Guinea, 700 miles southeast. On the way
back east after Palau, the carrier planes were to demolish
enemy air bases on Yap and Woleai.

It sounded to the men of *Enterprise* like a big job, but
when they came on deck on the twenty-seventh of March,
they could see that Spruance and Mitscher were going in
strong, and they felt better. Three of the task groups of
Mitscher's Fast Carrier Force were there, with a supporting
group of tankers protected by their own cruisers, destroyers
and escort carriers. All together, in the striking force spread
out across the gentle ground swells of the South Pacific,
were 11 carriers (5 CVs and 6 CVLs), 6 big, new battlewagons, 15 cruisers—light, heavy and AA—and 48 destroyers.

From the rendezvous point, due north of the Solomons
and just south of the equator, the combined task groups
steamed west, well south of the target, in an attempt to
deceive the enemy and then swing north toward Palau. It

did not work. By the afternoon of the twenty-eighth, an astounded enemy search pilot had reported the dozen carriers headed straight for Palau, and for a frantic day and a half the Japanese rushed preparations to meet them. Ships that could get under way did so—and met United States submarines waiting outside the reef. Those ships that for any reason could not escape were moored close in to the jungle-covered volcanic islands and camouflaged with palm tops and branches, or simply moved to shallow water so that they could be salvaged after being sunk.

Mitscher knew he had been sighted and increased speed. K-Day was moved up two days, from April 1 to March 30.

If there had been any doubt about the loss of surprise, it was dispelled shortly after noon on the twenty-ninth. Lieutenant M. O. ("Mo" or "Easy") Marks, with a four-plane division of Hellcats, was orbiting his assigned station twenty miles north-northeast of the force at 6,000 feet with radios silent. There was nothing on the force radar scopes. But when Marks looked down over the portside of his cockpit, he saw the sandy-brown twin-engine shape of a Betty, six or seven miles away, flat on the water and headed for the task force. The four F6Fs banked over and went down at full throttle. The Betty was fast, and it took them three long minutes to catch up. Then Marks split his division, two to the Betty's left, two to its right. All four Hellcats made flat side runs, their bullets going through and tearing up the sea under the snooper. As Marks began his second run, a ball of fire appeared under the Betty's starboard engine, expanded until the wing root and fuselage were afire and the plane skimmed into the sea, burning and breaking up. While the CAP circled, a man in a red life vest emerged from the flaming wreckage and floated clear, holding on to a tire. He waved as the Hellcats buzzed him, and dropped one dye marker.

Easy Marks' Betty was the first casualty in the destruction of Japan's Palau base. From then on, as Mitscher's deadly gray ships surged up from the south toward their targets, as irresistible as a tidal wave and with the same certainty of devastation, the frequency and intensity of hostilities increased. At quarter of seven, with several bogies on the radars, the Big E's bugles sounded Torpedo Defense and an hour later the general alarm sent her men to battle stations. In the dusk of 8:00 P.M., lookouts reported a column of black smoke on the western horizon and in a few minutes the loudspeakers announced that another Betty had gone down, this time killed by the CAP from *Hornet*.

By 9:00 P.M. it was dark. As many as twenty bogies were showing on force radars. The moon was not up yet but the enemy had provided his own illumination with parallel strings of red, green and white flares which seemed to hang in the sky forever and drop suddenly into the sea for the last few hundred feet. Colored float lights bobbed and flashed in the sea astern of the formations. The carriers did not fire, but the men with topside battle stations and the aviators who had come out of their ready rooms in un-accustomed steel helmets to watch the show could see the flashing of the cruiser and destroyer guns out to the horizon on all sides and the sudden red and white streams of tracers as a bogey came into 40 and 20 range. When the battle-wagons opened up, it was as though they erupted, the five-inch flashing, and the hundreds of barrels of 40- and 20-millimeter fountaining their tracers into the night sky. Over the sound of the blowers, the wind and the training gun mounts, the thudding and hammering and rattling of the guns came across the water. Twice points of light seemed to form at the intersections of the tracer streams, skim low between the ships, growing brighter, and then angle down to hit the surface in flaring explosions of red flame which drew quickly aft and quickly died down. No men who watched that evening could ever again be excited by a July Fourth fireworks exhibition, no matter how extrava-gant or expensive.

But tough, eager TF 58, with deckloads to launch in the morning, slapped the night torpedo attack aside as a husky rifleman moving up for a dawn assault slaps his way through a cloud of mosquitoes. By quarter past ten the scopes were clear, and fifteen minutes later Captain Gard-ner secured his men from General Quarters and stationed the regular cruising watch. There had been no damage to any ship of the force.

When March 30 was only a lighter darkness in the east-ern sky, the pattern of air warfare at sea, which had been established at Truk and which was to become as familiar to *Enterprise* aviators as their class schedules in the colleges most of them had just left, began again. In the semidark-ness of the gasoline-smelling flight deck, windy with the ship's passage and crowded with aircraft parked so close together a man had to duck under wings to get between them, the bull horn blared "Start engines," and the props of the fighters turned, caught, spun, belched a few puffs of blue smoke and then idled smoothly. At 6:47 A.M., sixty-five miles south of the target, Killer Kane led eleven other F6Fs into the predawn sky, their white turtleback lights on dim to facilitate the joinup. The other carriers launched fighters at the same time. By 7:00 A.M., seventy were in the air under Kane's command, on their way to sweep the skies and the fields of Palau clear of enemy planes so that the following bombers could do their work.

Palau is Truk with more and larger volcanic islands and with the reef squeezed in close around them. The whole atoll is long and narrow and oriented roughly north and south. Peleliu is the second island from the south end, and between it and the much larger main island of Babelthuap lies the Western Lagoon, full of small, irregular islets and anchored shipping and Palau Harbor on the east side of the lagoon. There are two airfields on the south tips of Peleliu and Babelthuap and seaplane bases in the Western Lagoon on Koror and Arakabesan.

At 7:30 the Hellcats of TF 58 were over their targets. Towering cumulus clouds, shaded dark at their bases, surrounded the islands, and off to the northwest and north they thickened into squalls with curtains of rain between clouds and sea. But over the target itself the morning sky was clear. It was still only half light when they pushed over in their first strafing runs and the converging tracers were bright in the dusk as they ripped into the parked Bettys on the field at Peleliu. The flames of the Bettys were bright orange as they crumpled in their revetments.

When Killer Kane's Hellcat swarm hit the islands of Palau, there were no enemy fighters on the ground. After the third strafing run, the F6Fs swung north over the anchorage and the field at Babelthuap, and there they encountered the first Zekes. They had been air-borne and waiting when Kane arrived but showed no desire to engage unless they could find a single, a cripple or a bomber separated from his formation. The seventy square-winged blue Hellcats swept across the fields and harbors of the Palaus, strafing everything that looked as if it needed strafing and enthusiastically engaging any enemy planes that tried to interfere.

The fighter sweep found seventeen or eighteen big ships

in the Western Lagoon and the pilots suspected there were others around. The Grim Reapers of VF-10 found the Babelthuap field not quite completed and unusable, but burned ten Bettys at Peleliu, shot down three Zekes and damaged four others.

Kane's Hellcats were still over the islands when the bombers came in. The *Enterprise* share was three dozen planes, a dozen from each of her three squadrons, all under the command of Bill Martin.

The *Enterprise* strike flew north along the western edge of the reef. Opposite the seaplane bases, six TBFs loaded with fragmentation and incendiary bombs peeled off, angled down through the tracers of light and medium AA and plastered their assigned targets.

The remainder continued north, observing the uncompleted field on Babelthuap, and looking for the warships which were their primary objectives. There were none in the lagoon, but a few miles outside and headed northwest at high speed was what appeared to both Bill Martin and Ira Hardman, leading the bombers, to be a cruiser. Martin decided on a coordinated attack. His six TBFs, carrying torpedoes, slanted down in long, fast power glides and took position three miles on either bow. On the way, Martin ordered the torpedo depth mechanism reset from eight to twelve feet for the bigger ship. The dive bombers continued straight ahead, to arrive over the cruiser at 11,000 feet. The warship below increased speed with a chuff of black smoke and headed for the protection of a squall area ahead, the white water curling at her bow.

Hardman's Dauntlesses, lugging 1,000-pound bombs, reached attack position first. Up and over they rolled, and down in the time-honored discipline of their dives, their heavier, faster escorts dropping like hunting hawks ahead of them. The torpedo planes turned and headed in, three on either bow, at 250 feet and 190 knots, bays open and torpedos ready. Already the sea around the ship was being chopped into spray by the strafing fighters and geysered far above her masthead by the bombs of the SBDs. She started a turn to port as one of the Dauntlesses hit her on the stern, giving the three TBFs on her starboard bow a beam shot. The hit seemed to lift her out of the water for a moment and slowed her from 25 to about 8 knots.

A mile and a half out, as he approached the dropping point with his deep-set torpedo, Martin could see that distance, weather and the dim morning light had fooled him, and his target was not a cruiser but an old destroyer. Hanging in his shoulder straps directly overhead, with the smoking balls of AA pouring up at him, Hardman saw the same thing. Both pressed in the attack, but Martin would have traded all his worldly goods for the chance to retract his order changing the torpedo depth. An old destroyer barely draws twelve feet of water aft where she is deepest, and the chances were that the best aimed of his "fish" would swim right under her.

In rapid succession VT-10 put their long torpedoes in the water from less than half a mile. Two broached and ran in circles like badly designed mechanical toys; a third hooked badly off to the left and a fourth to the right. The two remaining ones ran straight and true but nothing happened.

With the torpedo attack completed, the dive bombers were just finishing up. They hit again on her bow and the destroyer stopped, burning, listing and sinking slowly. But she fought back hard, and Martin and his men watched in horror as the last of the twelve SBDs, under heavy fire, continued its dive straight into the sea to port of the dying enemy vessel. The Big E's planes circled, out of bombs, but pouring bullets into the still-firing wreck. Then nine more TBFs from another carrier swept in with more torpedoes of which one hooked hard right and straightened out, broached several times and hit directly amidships. "The destroyer exploded and sank immediately," showering the sea around her with bodies and debris.

The old Japanese destroyer had been expensive. She had cost TF 58 fifteen torpedoes, twelve 1,000-pound bombs, two completely equipped, combat-ready Dauntless dive bombers and the lives of two young Americans, Lieutenant (j.g.) Charles B. "Stubby" Pearson and his gunner, T. W. "Tommy" Watterson, aviation radioman, third class.

Stubby Pearson must have been killed outright by the AA in that final dive of the destroyer action, because his professional dive never wavered. He had trimmed up his SBD for the dive and when he died it simply continued into the sea. Tommy Watterson behind him, facing up into the morning sky, probably never knew anything was wrong until the crash that wiped out his consciousness. Like all rear-seatmen, Watterson had willingly placed his life in the hands of his pilot. Pilot and rear-seatman during the hours that they are air-borne and particularly in the hurtling moments of the dive, which is their reason for being, are closer than man and wife, sharing, utterly and inseparably each time, a straight look into the face of death. Neither man can survive without the other. The gunner is most dependent. His pilot controls the wings on which both leave the narrow deck and return to it. Pearson and Watterson died as the team they had become. Their loss was keenly felt in *Enterprise*. Stubby Pearson was one of those exceptional men that simply and naturally give off an aura of greatness. Every man who knew him felt that Stub would be one of the great men of his generation. He had the quiet dignity and the earthbound idealism of the great. At Dartmouth he was captain of football and basketball, Phi Beta Kappa, and president of Paleopitus, the senior student governing body. Everyone in Hanover, New Hampshire, loved him. They could not help it. Although he was only a "j.g." in Bombing Ten, he was listened to with attention by seniors and juniors because his head was clear, his judgment sound and his standards recognizably the right ones. Japan seldom sold a ship so dear.

Enterprise launched four more strikes that day, directed primarily against the shipping in Palau Harbor, and thoroughly photographed the islands, facilities and the damage inflicted. By late afternoon the bombers could find no ships that had not been hit at least once and, like the bachelor who has failed to have his shirts laundered and must dig through his laundry bag for the least soiled, they began to attack the ones least seriously damaged. All around the lagoon, among the jungle-covered islands and islets, plumes of black smoke reached up toward the bases of the clouds from burning tankers, freighters and transports.

Lieutenant (j.g.) Jay Shinneman, escorting a photo flight, encountered a nearsighted enemy pilot in a twin-float fighter. They saw each other at the same moment. The Japanese pilot waggled his wings in greeting and Jay politely waggled back before shooting him down with a single long rattle of fire. Three other Reapers ran across an old Nate fighter and for forty-five minutes chased him around and through a cloud. Although much slower, the Nate was highly maneuverable and ably flown, evading three of Fighting Ten's best pilots until Lieutenant (j.g.) Pete Long got on his tail and finished him. The three young officers, sweaty, tired and angry after the long aerial scuffle, grudgingly admired the enemy pilot and could not help being glad when they saw him bail out. But his chute caught on the tail of his falling plane and he went in with it, streaming helplessly behind.

To the men who stayed aboard the carrier, the day was full of the windy, strenuous bustle of flight operations, but the ship was not attacked, and, except for the holes in the returning planes and an occasional wounded pilot or crewman, the war could have been far away. Two events brought it closer.

At 2:00 P.M. with a strike just launched, a *Lexington* TBF circled in overhead and requested permission to land with a badly wounded gunner. From the bridge, officers with binoculars could see the shattered ball turret. The Avenger made a good approach and landing and the Big E's plane handlers dived under its tail, disengaged the hook and it taxied quickly forward out of the arresting gear with a burst of throttle. But, when the doctor and corpsmen climbed up into the blood-spattered turret, they found the gunner already dead.

An hour after the *Lex* torpedo plane had taken off with his dead for his own carrier, the bow lookouts reported an object in the water ahead that appeared to be a floating plane. It passed close aboard down the portside. It was a scorched, brown twin-engine bomber with red disks on its wings, floating nose deep and tail high, and, close alongside, holding to a tire that must still have been secured in some way to the Betty, was a Japanese airman in a red quilted life jacket, alive but too weak to do anything but stare impassively up at the faces that lined the carrier's gun galleries to see him. A destroyer picked him up and found two dead Japanese still in the plane.

The evening of the thirtieth was like the evening of the twenty-ninth except that it was longer and the enemy pressed his attacks more vigorously. But by midnight it was over, and the only casualty was a rudder knocked off a screening destroyer. It could have been much worse. Shortly after 8:00 P.M. a Betty skimmed past the Big E's stern from port to starboard, and shortly afterward there was a solid bang on the portside amidships, which John Munro, and the engineers stationed in the vicinity, identified as a hit by a dud torpedo. Fortunately for *Enterprise*, America had no monopoly on faulty "fish."

When *Enterprise* circled northeast toward Yap on the evening of the thirtieth, the most important part of her mission in those western seas had been accomplished. The two strikes of twenty-nine and twenty-five planes against that single, large, flat island found no ship or planes. The strike leaders undid as much as possible of the work that had been done on two half-finished airfields, and destroyed oil storage tanks, docks, radio stations, warehouses and any facilities in sight which might be of use to Japan. In the late morning, a third raid on Yap was canceled and sent instead against the atoll of Ulithi, another hundred miles northeast. Bill Martin's forty-plane strike wiped out the radio and radar station there, burned some metal-roofed buildings, sank a small wooden patrol boat and thoroughly photographed the whole Majuro-like atoll.

Just before dark, *Enterprise* and her task group rejoined the rest of TF 58. Despite all-day bogies, the night of the thirty-first was as though man had never fought a war in the Pacific, and on the morning of the first of April the combined force hit the enemy base of Woleai, about halfway between Truk and Palau.

Fighting Ten's twelve Hellcats on the dawn sweep were the first to hit the field, which was the heart of enemy strength on Woleai. No enemy planes got into the air. On the first run, Killer Kane and his pilots burned three of the four parked Bettys and riddled half of the eight fighters. F6Fs from other carriers finished the job. But enemy AA gunners hit back hard. Light and medium automatic weapons, some installed in pits under the wings of parked planes, hit four of Kane's fighters, including his own. One pilot was wounded. And, in return, Kane's Hellcats concentrated on the enemy AA positions themselves, so raking them with the focused streams of .50-calibers that when the bombers arrived they reported AA opposition light.

With no air opposition and no effective antiaircraft fire, three more strikes settled down to the business of destroying all military facilities at Woleai, and by noon TF 58 was through with what was left of the enemy base.

With the destruction of Woleai, TF 58's cruise to the west of Tokyo was over, and Spruance ducked into the equatorial front for the run back east.

This time the interlude in Majuro was brief. A week after it anchored, TF 58 was under way again, on signal from Vice Admiral Mitscher in the *Lexington*.

Two thousand miles southwest, General MacArthur was bypassing 50,000 enemy troops in eastern New Guinea with a three-pronged amphibious landing in the vicinity of Hollandia on the big island's north coast, two thirds of the way to its western tip. Task Force 58 was to "destroy or contain enemy naval forces attempting to interfere with the seizure of Hollandia . . . neutralize enemy airfields by repeated strikes . . . and . . . provide air support requested." D-Day was April 22.

The task group composition was changed for this operation. Now the Big E steamed with *Lexington, Princeton, Langley* and their supporting ships.

It was a long, hot, busy week to Hollandia, full of gunnery practice, battle problems, torpedo defense drills, General Quarters and squadron and air group tactical practice, zigzagging at 18 knots all the way. There was a tense moment on John Munro's watch on the morning of the sixteenth, when *Princeton* cut sharply across the Big E's bow and it was necessary to slam the big brass handles of the engine room telegraph all the way around to the Back Full, Emergency position in order to avoid a collision.

TF 58 crossed the equator on the midwatch of the twenty-first and four hours and twenty minutes later began launching against Hollandia.

Enterprise was sixty miles north of Humboldt Bay on the mountainous, jungle coast of New Guinea. Her first launch was, as usual, a fighter sweep. It was scheduled for 5:15 A.M. but did not get off until after 6:30 because of the heavy black clouds at deck level, lashing rain and lightning.

Twelve of Bud Schumann's Grim Reapers, another dozen fighters from *Lexington* and eight more from *Langley,* following two of Bill Martin's radar-equipped TBFs as pathfinders, were to work over the three airfields in the valley just inland of the 7,000-foot coastal mountains. Martin was delayed by radio trouble, and Bob Nelson led the fighters to their targets, with Martin attempting to join up before reaching the coast. The three groups of Hellcats, with *Langley's* high, Schumann's intermediate and *Lexington's* low, bored through the tattered, rain-filled clouds of a weak tropical front and broke out into the clear morning sunlight with the sheer, green wall of the Cyclops Coastal Range dead ahead. They swept across its crest, already pushing over for the fields beyond—and found the valley full of cotton. A sea of solid white clouds 3,000 feet deep covered the airfields from the back of the mountains to narrow, irregular Lake Sentani a few miles farther inland. Some *Lex-*

ington planes let down through the cotton to strafe but found the ceiling so low that there was no time to pick targets, aim and fire. There was nothing to do but circle and wait for the clouds to break up and burn off under the tropic sun.

Bill Martin, a few minutes behind, photographed some barges and patrol boats in Tanahmerah Bay and then flew across the mountains toward the target fields to find the same conditions that had thwarted the fighter mission. But Martin saw something else. Skimming the top of the overcast below him was a brown twin-engine Japanese Sally. He moved into position for an overhead run but never got the chance to make it. A dozen F6Fs saw the Sally at the same time and scrambled after it so vigorously that there was serious danger of midair collisions between the fighters. Either the Japanese pilot never saw his enemies tumbling over each other to get at him, or he froze in terror, or he was incredibly stupid. For five to ten seconds, he could have saved his life by simply nosing over into the cloud bank a few hundred feet below him. He did not, and quickly it was too late. Both engines and both wings caught fire and he sloped down into the clouds like a thrown torch.

While the thick undercast forced the fighters to circle waiting for a break, it did not stop Martin and Nelson. Independently, at different times, Martin and Nelson let down over Lake Sentani until they were below the overcast, and then skimmed in, between clouds and terrain, half on instruments and half visual in the shreds of cloud and patches of fog, to lay their fragmentation and incendiary bombs on the parked planes at Hollandia, Sentani and Cyclops, while turret and tunnel gunners strafed. Martin strung his entire load across a concentration of eleven undamaged planes and left them all in flames. On the way out he reported a ceiling of 600 to 800 feet below the clouds and the dive bombers of the second strike began to let down with their 1,000-pounders, breaking out, releasing, and pulling quickly back up to avoid the blast of the big bombs. Five Martin-trained TBFs of the second strike used the same tactics as their skipper and laid their "frags" and incendiaries, like strings of lethal firecrackers, across the parking areas and revetments. The escorting Hellcats dived through the thinning clouds and strafed the length of the fields.

The Japanese resisted with antiaircraft fire of all sizes, mostly poorly directed; but, with such a volume, some had to hit. Lieutenant Woodie Hampton, on a strafing run, was first. A 20-millimeter shell hit the engine of his F6F and another exploded in the cockpit, spraying shrapnel into his left ankle. Woodie used the speed of his run and the power left in his smoking, rough-running engine to zoom for altitude. On his right the high green slopes of the Cyclops Range crested well above him, cutting him off from the sea. The blue-gray of the bay with open water and safety beyond was seven or eight miles ahead, across a broken, jungle-covered plain. Hampton had been well-briefed on New Guinea. As his engine popped and smoked and shook on its mount, losing power steadily, and his F6 as steadily lost altitude, he vividly remembered the several species of poisonous snakes, poisonous insects and strange tropical fevers the briefing officers had described as an introduction to the more serious dangers of elephantiasis, head-hunters and Japanese hidden by the soft-looking green of that jungle valley. With the last horsepower in his hot, oilless engine, he glided between a 5,000-foot mountain on his right and a 2,000-foot foothill to his left, skimmed across a narrow beach, leveled off, dropped his flaps and skittered onto the surface of the bay a couple of miles offshore. It was a good landing, and he was able to inflate his boat and climb aboard before the F6F lifted its tail and sank. Two hours later a float plane from *Louisville* skimmed in with an *Enterprise* night fighter on either wing as escort, landed, picked Hampton up and, after a long run, got air-borne again.

By midmorning, the sun had burned the clouds out of the valley and exposed the fields to TF 58's full strength. By afternoon, individual pilots had to search to find targets worthy of their bombs. The difficulty in finding worthwhile targets was greatly increased by recent visits of B-24s and A-20s of the Army Air Force.

April twenty-second was D-Day of the biggest amphibious landing in the Pacific war up to then. Transports and landing craft of all kinds, from big LCTs carrying several tanks, to LCVPs with a jeep or a handful of troops aboard, circled and foamed offshore. The first wave was already on the beach at Tanahmerah Bay when the Big E's first landing support strike arrived, delayed again by low clouds and heavy rain, and four Australian cruisers had just finished a prelanding bombardment and were moving off down the coast.

There was no opposition to the landing. Except for two hours in the late morning when thick clouds moved in to obscure the area, *Enterprise* kept command groups over the assault troops all day. By evening the troops were well inland and ahead of schedule.

TF 58 remained on station off Hollandia for four more days, but there was not much to do. Everything worthwhile had been bombed and strafed. There was no sign of the enemy except an occasional burst of AA. The command groups kept the troop command informed of movements of the soldiers and searched roads and trails for Japanese but found none. They were, in effect, performing the function of observers for the Army.

At 6:00 P.M. on the twenty-third, *Enterprise* came up into the wind to receive a single, wounded TBF. The plane came in sight escorted by two Hellcats from another carrier. One wheel dangled and the other was up and locked. The pilot reported that he could not use his flaps, and that his elevator control was poor, his right aileron not working and his air-speed and needle-ball indicators shot up. Lieutenant Hod Proulx brought him in but had to wave him off, and as the Avenger flew down the portside, climbing, the men on deck could see the holes in tail, fuselage and wings. Hod could see that the pilot was covered with blood. The two strange F6Fs circled anxiously. Once more Hod's paddles fluttered, crossing and uncrossing in the wave-off signal as the shot-up TBF went around again. It had been dangerously high and fast with the flaps not working. The third approach looked good except for that dangling single wheel. On the flight deck, hoses were led out, foam cans standing by, barriers up, a driver in the salvage crane, Doc Ridley and his corpsmen waiting beside the island. With a slash of his right paddle down and across his body to the left, Hod cut the Avenger, and it eased down under good control, hit on its one wheel and tail, caught the third wire, and then sagged down, dragging the wing tip and turning slightly right, the prop digging splinters out of the deck before it stopped.

Enterprise sailors, who were beginning to be complacent about the soft Hollandia operation, quickly lost their complacency at the sight of the three men being helped across the flight deck toward sick bay, soaked and spattered in their own blood, while plane handlers worked to get the riddled TBF clear of the landing area.

Big, good-looking, twenty-four-year-old Lieutenant (j.g.) Cliff Largess, of Worcester, Massachusetts, and Holy Cross, the pilot, had dozens of cuts on his face, neck, upper body and left arm from flying glass and small pieces of metal. The most serious wound was in his right forearm and he had had to apply his own tourniquet there on the way home. Jim Spates, the radioman from Arkansas, hobbled between two shipmates, with a nasty bullet wound in his right heel. Second Lieutenant Pronel, the Army observer, was luckiest with minor cuts on hands and face.

Cliff had bombed, strafed and sunk a half-concealed barge at the west bank of Lake Sentani and dropped the rest of his bombs on barracks at Hollandia Field. He was heading out, low, over the same route that Woodie Hampton had taken earlier, from Hollandia across the jungle plain to Tanahmerah Bay, when a single fighter came up fast behind him and fired two short devastating bursts from dead astern.

That same afternoon, the skipper of the fighter squadron on another TF 58 carrier was flying Target Combat Air Patrol (TCAP) over Humboldt Bay, some twenty-five miles east of Tanahmerah. He was instructed to watch carefully for enemy planes trying to slip in from the land side to attack the troops and ships of the assault force. A few minutes later, the TCAP over Tanahmerah reported a single plane flying low over the field at Hollandia, and asked the FDO, "Do we have any friends there?" The FDO said "negat," and notified the fighter skipper over Humboldt who was in a position for a dive at Hollandia. He took his Hellcat down through the haze and scattered clouds, circled once at 5,000 feet, and saw a single plane, low over the trees, headed out from Hollandia toward the ships in Tanahmerah Bay. He dived after it, coming up fast from dead astern, fired one short burst, then one more and then zoomed up with ice in his guts as he saw his target was a TBF.

Two F6Fs escorted the wounded Cliff Largess back to *Enterprise* and circled until they saw him safely aboard. That evening a message of regret and apology came to Air Group Ten and later a personal letter to Bill Martin explaining the circumstances and ending:

I feel considerably lower than a snake's belly about the thing. . . . I humbly request that all of you, and particularly the pilot and crewmen concerned, accept

my sincere apologies and regrets and assurance that
such a thing won't happen again even if we stand a
chance of losing a shot. I would like to know the
name of the pilot so that I can personally . . . apol-
ogize to him at the first opportunity.

And at Majuro in early May, in Torpedo Ten's Ready
Room Number Five that apology was made man to man,
differences in rank and authority erased by the shared near-
tragedy.

By evening of the twenty-fourth the carriers had been
tied to Hollandia long enough for the enemy to mount an
organized attack. He scraped up from his broken fields
around the South Pacific some dozen torpedo-carrying
Bettys, and detached two as pathfinders to locate and illuminate the U. S. ships for the others. But now detach-
ments of specially configured night fighters, flown by
specially trained pilots, were available in TF 58.

Before sunset, the familiar blobs of snooping bogies began to show on the *Enterprise* air-search radar. Lieutenant
Commander Richard E. Harmer and a wingman were
catapulted in their Corsair night fighters, but the Bettys
stayed out of range until dark.

Half an hour after the sun had set, Chick Harmer made
radar contact on a single Betty thirty miles astern of the
task group. At half a mile he saw the twin-engine, single-
tail enemy plane silhouetted against what light was left in
the western sky. It was in a steep left bank, the long,
straight wing tilted up and a glow of exhaust under each
nacelle. Visually and by watching the moving bug of light
on his scope, Harmer followed, closing. From the stinger
in the Betty's tail, a string of red balloons flowed down and
back at Harmer, and he returned the fire with a long burst
of his six 50s, moving off a little to the right to dodge the
20-millimeters while the snooper dived for the water. The
night fighter S-turned to drop back and then followed. At
200 yards the tail gun opened up again with its big, red, 20-
millimeter balloons. Dim, reddish-yellow tracers streamed
out of the dorsal turret also this time, and Harmer again
replied with his six 50s. A small red flare broke out behind
the left engine and a moment later there was a heavy
splash just behind the Betty, as the Japanese pilot jettisoned
his torpedo. Cool and calm, Harmer added throttle and
pulled up alongside and above the Betty to look it over. The
big plane, with its five-man crew, was skimming the night

sea, its port engine blazing now and leaving a heavy trail of smoke. The dorsal turret was still spraying its dim, rapid tracers around the sky but not touching the Corsair. Harmer dropped back, swung in astern, and fired another long burst, the converging white lines of his tracers chewing into the Betty's wings and back. Dorsal and tail turrets fired back wildly. Harmer glanced at his altimeter and was startled to see that he had less than 100 feet. He had to nose over to get his bullets into the enemy. He nosed over and let go a short burst just as the Betty skidded into the sea, making a good landing. The F4U pulled up and circled. Harmer could see the whole plane intact and floating, but at the end of his second circle only the tail remained in sight. It was the first definite kill for an *Enterprise* night fighter.

Harmer's teammate, Ensign Bob Poirer, made radar contact with the other snooper, and, although he never got within firing range, his persistence drove the enemy away.

On his next vector, Harmer found the main enemy force flying in formation, apparently waiting for the two snoopers to locate their targets for them. He joined up, carefully choosing his first victim, but his guns, which had been jamming in the last action, jammed completely after a couple of seconds of fire into the belly of the nearest bomber, and he could not clear them again. The enemy plane slanted away flashing its lights, and Harmer could only disgustedly return to the ship.

Deprived of their pathfinders, and worried and disorganized by the presence of a hostile plane in their own formation, the enemy attack group gave up and returned to base. By 8:00 P.M. the scopes were clear.

By the twenty-sixth, every enemy base in the area was working hard to get planes in the air against TF 58, still restricted to the waters just north of New Guinea. Five Bettys and a Nick (a twin-engine fighter with a crewman manning a free gun) were shot down around the force by the CAP that day, the last day off Hollandia. On the morning of the twenty-seventh, the sun rose on the Big E's starboard bow. TF 58 was bound northeast toward the Carolines and Marshalls, and among the thousands of men in the hundred ships, not one was sorry.

On *Enterprise*, the relief of being free of the hot New Guinea coast was spoiled by a freak flight-deck accident. A landing fighter caught the very last arresting gear wire with such force that the heavy cable pulled out of its socket at one end and the F6 continued into the barrier where it nosed up, ruining the prop. The pilot was not injured. But the thick arresting wire whiplashed across the deck at knee level spilling men like toy soldiers kicked by a petulant child. Five men, including ex-All-American Lieutenant Doyle Nave, were hospitalized for contusions of knees and shoulders, lacerations of the scalp and fractured frontal bones.

At 5:00 A.M. on the twenty-eighth, an *Enterprise* ensign gave some very bad moments to a great many other men, including a highly articulate command echelon of one vice admiral, one rear admiral and two senior captains. He ordered left rudder instead of right in executing the zigzag plan. For a horrible minute, *Enterprise*, flying the two-star flag of Rear Admiral J. W. "Black Jack" Reeves, commanding Task Group 58.3, and *Lexington*, with Vice Admiral Marc Mitscher, Commander Task Force 58 embarked, angled toward each other and a catastrophic collision at 18 knots. The error was discovered in seconds and collision averted, but Mat Gardner did not recover his calm good humor for two days, and it was many weeks and hours of instruction later that the ensign again stood watch on the Big E's bridge as junior officer of the deck.

Three days northeast of Hollandia, a conference was held in the *Enterprise* wardroom. *Lexington*, *Princeton* and *Langley* representatives were there, their planes parked on the Big E's deck. The conference worked out details of scheduling and coordinating the air operations of the next two days. Then in the cloudy, squally dawn of Saturday the twenty-ninth of April, Bud Schumann led a sweep of eleven Hellcats off the Big E's streaming deck. Task Force 58 had come back to Truk.

Everything except the messy weather and the geography had changed in the two and one-half months since *Enterprise* had last sailed these waters. Japan had abandoned Truk as a fleet base for the moment, but reinforced it as an air base. She had moved out the ships, but moved in more planes and more antiaircraft guns. TF 58 had become more confident and competent. And this time the mission was different—"inflict the maximum amount of damage to shore installations." Assure, in other words, the permanent destruction of Truk as an effective base of any kind.

The fighter sweep again had been delayed by the rain

and scudding low clouds, so that Schumann got off just a few minutes ahead of the first strike—nine Dauntlesses with instantly fused 1,000-pounders and eight Avengers with 500s and 100s escorted by twelve more F6s. Similar formations rose from all the carriers of TF 58, and, from the CVLs, CAP and antisub patrols roared off to protect the force.

The Big E's planes approached Truk above the overcast, at 10,000 feet, circled carefully to be sure of their targets, and dived through holes in the clouds or through the clouds themselves to attack. Schumann's eleven-Hellcat sweep hit the fighter field island of Eten; Dick Poor's SBDs made fast, shallow, no-flap dives on the AA emplacements on Moen, and the TBFs under Eason took the parked planes and hangars of the Moen bomber strip. Killer Kane split his twelve-plane escort, half to strafe ahead of the SBDs and half to work over the parked planes with the Avengers.

Antiaircraft fire was heavy and accurate and began to hammer at the planes the second they came in sight below the 5,000-foot overcast. Even above the clouds the black bursts of radar-controlled 12.7 cm reached out for the U. S. planes—and thus gave away the position of the field.

Enemy fighters were in the air, but perhaps remembering their losses in their last meeting with TF 58 aircraft, generally cautious and reluctant to engage. Four trim, fast Hamps passed Torpedo Ten's formation on an opposite heading only halfway from the ship to Truk but did not attack, two more were over the Moen field and dived away through the overcast as the TBFs approached. A Hamp and a Zeke began a run on Lieutenant C B "Cross Bow" Collins' Avenger below the clouds but broke off without firing, and two short bursts from Guthrie's ball turret were enough to discourage another Zeke and force him to break away in a violent split S. Husky, muscular little Tommy Harman, assisted by Karl Kirchwey, his wingman, hammered a low-flying Zeke into the lagoon after recovery from their strafing runs.

At about the same time that its planes were arriving over Truk, Task Group 58.3 itself came under attack. Two cleanly built but slow and vulnerable Kates eluded the CAP in the clouds and glided in to attack the *Lexington*, a mile on the Big E's beam. *Lex* opened up with everything she had. One bomb spouted the sea close aboard but did no damage, and the Kate that dropped it cartwheeled into the sea a few hundred yards off *Enterprise*'s port bow. It burned with a greasy black smoke and disappeared.

Only one *Enterprise* pilot went down that day—Lieutenant (j.g.) Bob Kanze, flying escort for Ernie Lawton's photo TBF, ran afoul of the only really aggressive Zeke of the day. Kanze attacked the Zeke head on and the enemy pilot did not give an inch, flying straight at Kanze and answering bullet for bullet until the rugged blue Hellcat and the light, agile, brown Zeke flashed past each other, both on fire and out of control, and the two pilots bailed out simultaneously as if it had been rehearsed.

Kanze landed in the south end of the lagoon but still inside the reef. It was late in the afternoon when he was finally sighted without enough daylight left to get a float plane in to pick him up. So Bob Kanze was left bobbing in his one-man raft the whole long tropic night, with the enemy islands behind him and the jagged coral reef with its cresting breakers ahead. It was an easy choice. The land with its warm earth and waving palms was not safety, but capture, imprisonment, perhaps death. The waste of the open sea was salvation because it was controlled, owned really, then and there, by the United States, her subs free to run under its surface, her destroyers and bigger ships free to use it, and her ship-based aircraft almost unopposed in the air above. Kanze paddled for the reef.

In the Grim Reapers' ready room his last position was plotted. Schumann, Kane and Hamilton made plans to find and rescue him if he could survive the night.

The thirtieth of April was like the twenty-ninth for the Truk garrison, but unpleasantly different. It began, first, for their attackers. The AA that TF 58 pilots faced that day was worse than any they had seen before.

Planes from Bombing and Torpedo Ten hit the seaplane base and the remaining buildings and facilities on the south side of Moen, despite the AA, and then fanned out to search for Kanze. They swept the blue, cloud-covered sea back and forth, inside and outside the reef south of the main islands, and a little over 10:00 A.M., Ralph Cummings, of Bill Martin's "Buzzard Brigade," sighted a man in a yellow doughnut about four miles outside the reef to the south. It was Kanze. Killer Kane, the strike leader, ordered Van Eason and Bud Schumann's division of four fighters to stand by Kanze, and alerted the rescue float planes and submarine. At 10:45, two OS2Us from the Big E's old friend *North Carolina* arrived. One landed in the choppy sea and taxied up to Kanze. He grabbed the down-wind wing float, losing his raft in the chop as he did so, and the pilots circling low overhead watched helplessly as the little float plane capsized and dumped its crew of two into the sea with Kanze.

The other *North Carolina* plane landed at once, and the three men climbed carefully to balanced positions, one on each wing and one close in to the fuselage. Cautiously, the OS2U pilot taxied to meet the rescue submarine *Tang,* which Bud Schumann had directed up from the south, and put his passengers aboard.

Air Group Ten had a lot of business for that *North Carolina* Kingfisher that day. It was fortunate for the Big E's airmen that its pilot had guts and skill. He was Lieutenant (j.g.) John A. Burns from Wynnewood, Pennsylvania.

Burns took off again after a rough run into the chop of the open sea, and flew around to the east side of the atoll. There he found a single pilot in the water with a Hellcat from *Langley* circling over him. Burns landed and picked him up. He tried three take-off runs, but the combination of rough water and extra weight was too much for the little Kingfisher. He could not get enough speed to fly and, in the long, splashing, plunging runs there was great danger of digging in a wing float and losing that plane too.

John Burns got on his radio and talked to another plane which relayed his predicament to *Tang.* The sub skipper said he was on his way and would arrive in three hours.

In those three hours, taxiing around the ocean in a two-seat scout plane which could no longer fly, Burns picked up six more men, all from *Enterprise,* all from Torpedo Ten.

On the second strike of the day, heavy, accurate, large-caliber antiaircraft picked up Martin's Avengers as they crossed the reef east of Eten, and the sparkling black puffs followed them to their target, Dublon. One of the first bursts hit Bob Nelson's TBF. He lost oil pressure and then all power, jettisoned his bombs, turned back seaward in a gliding left turn and landed nicely, four miles outside the reef and nine miles due east of Dublon. He and his crew got out their rafts and climbed aboard. The TBF floated, nose down, the sea breaking over its wings, for several minutes. It was 11:00 A.M.

Jim Moore and Charlie Farrell circled the rubber rafts. The others went on to the target and dived in from the west out of a right echelon, through the heaviest AA any of them had yet seen, to plaster buildings and the radio station on Dublon.

After the attack, Martin and Largess relieved Farrell and Moore over the survivors and they went in to unload. At noon, the crew in the water and those circling overhead watched a TBF glide in, smoking, from the west and skid into the sea half a mile southeast of Nelson's yellow rafts. It was Charlie Farrell. All three men changed from plane to rubber boats. It was noon.

At 1:00 P.M. Burns came buzzing and splashing up, picked up Nelson's crew, then Farrell's, and with the seven men draped all over its wings, taxied slowly out to meet the *Tang*. At 5:00 P.M., Burns, his rear-seatman and his passengers climbed aboard the sub and watched unhappily while she sank the bent, battered, and no longer flyable Kingfisher with machine-gun fire. *Tang* was crowded. She had picked up twenty-two aviators that day, seven of them from *Enterprise*.

It was a comforting thought for the carrier airmen that men like John Burns and Dick O'Kane, *Tang*'s skipper, were around, ready to risk their lives for a single pilot drifting in a hostile sea.

Marc Mitscher, in *Lexington*, released a message before he turned in that evening. It read, in part:

WELL DONE GOES TO TANG FOR RESCUING TWENTY-TWO AVIATORS OFF TRUK. ALL HANDS IN AIRPAC [AIR FORCE, PACIFIC FLEET] AND TASK FORCE FIFTY-EIGHT SEND GRATEFUL CONGRATULATIONS FOR THE SPLENDID RESCUE JOB.

In midafternoon, with the weather closing in and bombs and bullets running dangerously low, further strikes were canceled and the carriers withdrew from Truk. It was never of significant use to the Japanese again.

At 6:25 A.M. on the fourth of May, 1944, *Enterprise* lookouts made out the palm tops of Majuro fourteen miles to the southeast, and for a full month the Big E remained in or close to that midocean anchorage.

Then, just before noon on the sixth of June, 1944, recess was over and *Enterprise* was under way again, in the rain, on a mission 1,600 miles to the northwest to recapture the Marianas from Japan. At five o'clock that afternoon Tom

Hamilton's voice on the public address system announced that Allied forces were moving across the English Channel to recapture Western Europe from the Nazis.

19 A MONTH IN THE MARIANAS

The Big E's men read the mimeographed D-Day news releases in groups of three and four, leaning over each other's shoulders to see the block-typed words. They shouted each other into silence in order to hear each new announcement as it came over the loud speakers. They forgot their own war and their own immediate futures in the intensity of their interest in Eisenhower's assault on *Festung Europa*. They could not get enough news.

After they were well at sea and had again been briefed, this time on the details of the coming operation, including the extent and composition of the forces involved, the men of the Big E could see why they had spent a month at Majuro. It had been a month of replenishment and rest for them, but for others it had been a month of preparation, of preparing the biggest and boldest amphibious assault of the Pacific war. Five hundred and thirty-five ships and 127,000 troops were moving against Saipan, Tinian and Guam.

In the Big E's own TG 58.3 were 4 carriers, 5 new battleships and 16 destroyers, and, in all of the Fast Carrier Force, 15 carriers (7 CVs and 8 CVLs), 7 battleships, 12 cruisers and 58 destroyers.

As before, Marc Mitscher in *Lexington* commanded TF 58. Raymond Spruance in *Indianapolis* had the entire assault force as Commander Fifth Fleet. Both officers hoped and expected that at last the Imperial Navy would come out to fight. The Marianas were too valuable to be abandoned like the Gilberts, Marshalls and Eastern Carolines. And the Japanese Combined Fleet was still the second most powerful naval force in the world, with courage, good tactics and excellent gunnery, convincingly demonstrated around the Solomons.

Five days after leaving Majuro, *Enterprise* launched her first strike, a fighter sweep of sixteen Hellcats, against the airfields on Saipan. Two of Torpedo Ten's Avengers, flown by Martin and Eason, acted as pathfinders, guiding

TG 58.3's 59 fighters, led by Killer Kane, to the target. This
was not a dawn sweep. There had been enough of these by
now, Mitscher figured, for the enemy to be expecting one
and to be readying a big night torpedo attack to stave it off.
So over 200 Hellcats left TF 58, 230 miles east of the Marianas at 1:00 P.M. to surprise the enemy preparing to surprise us.

Marc Mitscher's official message to Kane as strike
leader read: "Cut their damned throats. Wish I could be
with you."

To avoid enemy radar, the fighter sweep stayed low.
Then thirty minutes from target, planes assigned to high
cover began their climb; twenty-five minutes out, intermediate cover started up and twenty minutes out, low
cover. Martin and Eason stayed down with their four-
plane escort until Saipan was in sight.

The Hellcats roared in over the big, checkerboarded,
Azoreslike island at 2:30. Despite precautions, radar had
warned the Japanese, and the Grim Reapers found ten
brown Zekes and two shining green Oscars in the air to
meet them. Kane split his F6Fs into fighting units of two
and four and attacked at once. Killer himself went after
one of the Japanese Army Oscars which dived for his home
field, with Kane's Hellcat right behind and gaining. At
3,000 feet Killer reluctantly broke off, being too close to
enemy AA and so low as to be in a hopeless situation if
more of the enemy were to attack from above. But ten
minutes later Kane and Al Taddeo knocked two Zekes off
the tails of Hellcats. The F6Fs climbed back up, ready for
more trouble, and in another five minutes they found it.
Kane and Harman dived on a Zeke low over Tinian and
Killer burned it with a single expert burst from dead astern.

Tommy Harman and Dick Mason each got a Zeke, but
it was Ensign Les Gray's day. First he set afire an Oscar
which tried to shake him with a shallow dive and a fast run
up the west coast of Saipan. Gray caught him halfway,
dropped him in the clear waters of Tanapag Harbor, and
joined up on Tommy Harman whose tail-hook assembly
had been shot up in a strafing run. Gray and Harman
headed for the rendezvous point, but between Saipan and
Tinian they saw three Zekes overhead and Gray pulled up
after them. The agile Zekes easily kept their altitude advantage, and, while Gray was circling futilely below them,
he was joined by another F6 with two Zekes on its tail. He

rolled up and over the other Hellcat and turned back into its enemies, getting a good head-on shot at the first one which pulled straight up and then spun in. In the strange Hellcat was Lieutenant Whitey Feightner, an alumnus of Fighting Ten at Guadalcanal, class of '43, now flying with VF-8 from the *Bunker Hill*.

Still en route to the rendezvous point for the return flight, Les Gray jumped another Zeke which looped, rolled, winged over, split-S'd, skidded and spun trying to lose him, then finally gave up and, like an angry little boy who doesn't want to play any more, ran for home. Gray set him on fire just before he got there and he crashed on the edge of his home field.

With the enemy fighters disposed of or very busy, the Grim Reapers went down to strafe. They concentrated on Saipan's three airfields—Marpi Point on the northern tip, Aslito on the southern, the dirt strip of Charan Kanoa on the southwest coast, and the antiaircraft gun emplacements around them. They made hits on parked planes, silenced guns and set fuel storage tanks blazing and smoking with miles-long black streamers.

The fight for the Marianas had begun.

June 12 was D-Day minus 3, and flight operations began with a launch of twelve Reapers led by Bud Schumann, in the full dark at quarter past four, while the last bogies were still fading from the force radars. Half an hour later, the first strike of ten more fighters, ten bombers and eight torpedo planes was air-borne. It was still dark. Five more strikes left the Big E's deck that day—169 launchings and 52 tons of bombs slammed into Saipan.

In the early afternoon of D minus 3 the war became again apparent to the men of *Enterprise* who could not fly to find it. TG 58.3 steamed through a patch of ocean littered with large and small pieces of broken wreckage and empty oil drums floating in a scum of oil. Three Japanese in oil-covered, white T shirts clung to drums. The life buoy watch dropped dye marker and smoke floats to mark the enemy survivors and the group steamed on. Later, a destroyer picked them up and transferred them to the Big E.

This welcome scenery had been created four hours earlier by Duke McCrary of Torpedo Ten on a singularly satisfactory five-plane strike led by the squadron skipper. McCrary had made two hits with 500-pound bombs on an enemy cargo ship with a deckload of oil barrels and she had rolled over to port at once with white-clad Japanese sailors scrambling down her exposed side and the drums spreading out over the sea.

On that same strike, VT-5 had "tallyhoed" a Betty and a Lily (smaller and faster than a Betty, with protected fuel tanks and a crew of three instead of seven), which the escorting VF-10 fighters quickly burned. They had thoroughly strafed two small ships, and made bomb hits on two more big ones which probably sank in Tanapag Harbor. All with no casualties and no damage to the TBFs.

On the last strike of the day, Martin, with seven Avengers, laid strings of incendiaries along the up-wind edges of the sugar cane fields, just inland of the landing beaches. By the next morning, there were only charred stalks of cane, incapable of providing cover for defending troops.

D minus 3 set the pattern of the prelanding strikes in the Marianas. TF 58 planes, in continuous, daylong attacks, hit first aircraft and airfields, then shipping, then antiaircraft and coastal gun emplacements, and then other defensive installations. They concentrated on Saipan where the amphibious forces would land on the fifteenth of June, but hammered at Tinian, Rota and Guam at the same time to shut off re-enforcements or counterattacks.

On the morning of D-2, TF 58's fast battleships pulled out of the various task groups with a brisk snapping of signal flags, and moved in on Saipan and Tinian to add their 16-inch rifles to the bombs and bullets of the air groups.

But the air strikes went on as usual. *Enterprise* launched a dozen fighters on a sweep at quarter of five and her first attack group of nine SBDs, seven TBFs and ten F6Fs at five o'clock from a position northwest of Saipan.

Bill Martin led the Big E's first strike. His mission was the destruction of guns and defense installations along the southwest coast of Saipan where, in two days, U. S. troops would be coming ashore.

The Big E's planes joined up in squadron circles and climbed to 10,000 feet on the way to their initial point, ten miles due north of the islands' northern cape, Marpi Point. There they met a strike group from *Lexington,* led by Commander Robert H. Isely, skipper of the *Lex's* torpedo squadron. Martin and Isely planned to coordinate their attacks so as to dilute the vicious enemy AA fire. Isely's Avengers, armed with rockets for the first time, would hit the guns at Aslito, at the same moment that Martin dived on the ones at Charan Kanoa, a couple of miles northwest. Bombers and torpedo planes of both groups would attack from different directions with fighters strafing ahead.

Riding behind Martin in Avenger T-41 that day, as they had done on almost every mission since the summer of 1942, were Aviation Radioman First Class J. T. Williams and, behind his single .50-caliber in the ball turret, Aviation Ordnanceman Second Class W. R. Hargrove. Between the three men, as in all veteran flight crews, was a mutual respect and understanding so complete that specific orders were unnecessary unless in an unusual situation. Williams and Hargrove knew what Martin wanted, and what he would do, and how and when. And he knew equally well what to expect from each of them. It was a relationship born of danger and an absorbing common professional interest, toughened by the hammer blows of combat over nearly two years, until the three men were closer than most brothers or sisters, many husbands and wives.

Each of the seven torpedo planes was assigned a specific target for its two 500-pound bombs. Bill Martin's was a heavy AA battery protecting a radio station at the northeast corner of the Charan Kanoa strip.

As leaders of their respective strikes, Martin and Isely were first to dive. Before they crossed the coast, slanting down in a shallow power glide from 12,000 to 8,000 feet, the AA began to blossom in ugly puffs around them, jarring and bouncing the blue planes. As Martin approached his target he could see it blinking, and with each blink another 12.7 soared to meet him. Bob Isely's voice came over the air:

"Are you ready, Bill?"

"I'm ready, Bob!"

"Here we go!"

The two leading Avengers rolled over and hurtled down, Martin in a steep, fast dive, Isely in a shallower, slower rocket run. The AA seemed to double, and in the next ten seconds both planes were hit and crashed in flames, Bob Isely's on Aslito Field, Bill Martin's in the lagoon off Charan Kanoa. One of VF-10's fighters, flown by Ensign M. D. Powell, entered a strafing run ahead of the bombers and was never seen again.

Martin's TBF had been indicating better than 300 knots in a near-vertical dive. Two heavy black AA bursts appeared dead ahead as Williams called "Four thousand" on the intercom, and at 3,500 Bill pushed the "pickle" on his stick and with his left hand reached forward and jerked the emergency bomb release toggle. He had the toggle in his hand when the plane jarred violently and then began to tumble end over end, throwing him heavily against his belt and forcing blood into his head so that he felt his eyes bulge and saw the red begin to squeeze off his vision. He groped for the mike to tell Williams and Hargrove to jump but could not find it. A blast of heat hit him and he knew the plane was burning and would crash. He heard his voice saying aloud, "This is it," and then, in four successive seconds, he released his belt, jerked his ripcord, felt a gentle tug on his parachute harness and hit the water of the lagoon.

So complex and marvelous is the mind of man that in those terrible seconds there was time for Bill to think of his wife and two little boys, for his brain to flicker like lightning across the lines of the Twenty-third Psalm, "The Lord is my shepherd . . . ," to think that there was not time for the chute to open, to remember a moment on the old *Hornet* at Santa Cruz when a Val smashed into the side of the island where he had been standing one second before, to further remember an article in an intelligence journal about a Marine who survived a free fall from 2,000 feet by straightening out his body and entering the water toes pointed, like a harpoon—and to arrange his body as that Marine had done. He hit at perhaps a 45-degree angle, in four to five feet of water and "bounced my tail on the soft sand" of the bottom. He bounced right up to haul in the bottom shrouds of the chute to spill the wind and then pull the nylon to him. Thirty feet up wind, the TBF blazed fiercely in the shallows, threatening to roast him in the flame and smoke. Overhead, large pieces that looked like elevators, horizontal stabilizers and the tunnel door were still floating down like falling leaves.

There were no other parachutes in sight. Williams and Hargrove had not gotten out.

Heaving in the chute, his back to the shore 200 yards away, Bill saw that two of its panels were badly ripped either by the high speed at which it had opened or by some part of the broken plane. He worked almost by reflex, feeling instinctively that he would need everything he had to survive, and at the same time dazed and incredulous that he was alive and apparently unhurt except for a bruised hip which had made contact with some cockpit projection on the way out, and minor flash burns on his back.

He became aware of something that went "zing-blup, zing-blup, zing-zing-blup-blup" and made small splashes around him. Rifle fire from the shore. Turning, he could see the Japanese riflemen. Some fired offhand, standing. Others rested their guns on palm boles. He could make out one or two, prone in the reeds at the top of the beach. Several were yelling something that sounded like "Yippee," and he realized they were cheering, as American gunners do when an enemy plane goes down.

All these things Martin noticed in a turn of his head before he ducked under the surface and finished pulling in his chute from there.

The reef was half a mile offshore and on the other side of it was the open sea—safety, life itself.

Still wearing his Mae West and parachute harness, with the life raft seat pack dangling from it, and with the gathered-up chute under his left arm, Martin began the 1,000-yard, underwater swim to the reef. In the sunlit blur below the surface, he could hear only the "blups" of the bullets.

Farther out, the water was deeper but there was a sprinkling of coral heads, from which he pushed off until he noticed the firing increase each time, and realized that his seat pack, towing along on the surface, must have been creating a noticeable swirl and providing a point of aim.

Halfway to the reef, he looked back during a breath, and saw two small boats moving out from the beach.

By this time Martin, in his heavy gear, had swum some 500 yards under water except for an occasional breath. He was a strong swimmer with a varsity letter from Annapolis, but his arms and legs ached. He had swallowed a pint or two of salt water. His heart pounded and his breath came fast. But he knew how the enemy, with an invasion obviously imminent, would like to know what he knew about it—and he knew some of the things they would gladly do to extract that information from him. As a senior squadron commander and an air coordinator, Martin had been thoroughly briefed. His knowledge in the hands of the Japanese could make Saipan another Tarawa, could easily cost a thousand lives. He turned on all the strength he had, kicking and pulling, rising for a breath and ducking under to kick and pull again, shifting the bundled chute to the right arm and pulling for a while with the left. With three quarters of the original distance covered and nearing exhaustion, Bill found the leading boat only about 200 yards away. On the next breath he expected to be killed or captured but when he surfaced, his lungs bursting, two TBFs were low overhead, searching, and the nearest boat had turned back. The other was still coming, but a quarter of a mile away. Black AA bursts bloomed around the Avengers and cracked loudly a second or so later. Bill knew the planes were searching for him, low and in close, defying the AA to find him. He wanted to shout and splash, spread dye marker, show himself, but bullets were still falling near him and the second boat was still coming. He was warmed by the courage and evident concern for him which the Avenger pilots showed, but wished they would leave, because shrapnel from the heavy AA intended for them ripped into the water around him like handfuls of hard-thrown gravel.

Long after he knew he could not possibly kick or pull again, but somehow managed to do so, Martin reached the reef. The firing from shore had stopped, and for good reason. The second strike, Strike Baker, had arrived. Bill sat on the shoreward slope of the reef, on a piece of seaweed-covered coral with just his eyes and nose above the surface, resting and watching happily as the bombs crumped down ashore, the dust and smoke rose and the sound carried out to him several seconds late. Not a bomb or a bullet entered the waters of the lagoon.

The second boat had turned back in well-grounded fear of the blue planes overhead, and Martin was temporarily out of danger. He could have used that opportunity to cross the reef and get to sea, but he did not. He had carefully studied the charts and the terrain models of the target over which he had been ordered to act as air coordinator, and he knew he was just off Beach Green One where, in less than two days, Marines of the landing force would be coming ashore.

Carefully, Martin lined up four objects which would appear on the blown-up target charts, and established cross bearings to fix his position, then made mental notes on the area.

Close to shore the remains of T-41 still burned and smoked, and his professional concentration and his vision were impaired for a minute by tears that welled up without warning out of his exhaustion and the miracle of his survival, when he realized that in that tangle of charred aluminum was all that was left of Williams and Hargrove.

As Strike Baker worked over the beach area, Martin noted the flashes of AA batteries which had not been known to the briefing officers, and mentally plotted their positions. He remembered the depth of the water, the nature of the bottom, the lack of current, the gradient of the beach, and when, in quick succession two big splashes slapped into the water very close, one short and one over, and he gathered up the wet chute again and dashed across the reef to open water, he remembered to count his steps —there were nineteen—to notice that there was a foot and a half of water over the coral, and that it felt, under his feet, like hard rubber. He dived into the breakers of the welcome sea and they shielded him from the guns ashore. Now, for the first time, he could inflate the Mae West. He jerked its toggles, heard the CO_2 swoosh into it, and felt it tighten and lift. Supported by the life vest, he swam, still with chute, harness and seat pack, down wind to seaward until it seemed safe to use the raft.

Bill let the raft drift to seaward, well out of small-caliber range, but he wanted to stay in the area off the beach where the search for him would be concentrated. So a mile or so off the reef, he rigged a sea anchor to reduce the drift. In addition to the canvas bucketlike drogue provided in the raft, he trailed his parachute, billowed wide underwater, his harness and everything he could find which would cause a drag against the drift of the light rubber boat. It worked. When he checked his bearings on land marks on Saipan and Tinian, they showed almost no movement.

With nothing to do for the first time, Bill held an inventory of his equipment and provisions, securing everything to the raft so that it would not be lost in case of capsizing.

As he was finishing the inventory, two planes roared in low from the west—a TBF and an F6F. Martin sifted enough dye marker out of its can to color several square yards of water and flashed his mirror at the planes. They caught the flash six to eight miles away, and as they approached he could see the markings of his own squadron on the Avenger. The two planes came over so low, while he waved a thumbs up to show he was okay, that he recognized Gibby Blake in the TBF and Al Taddeo of VF-10 in the F6. As they turned away, two puffs of AA cracked over Martin's head and he went overboard as the shrapnel rattled into the sea around him. Gibby Blake made one more pass and dropped a large cylindrical yellow emergency kit which floated close by and which Bill quickly paddled over to and retrieved.

The *Enterprise* planes waggled their wings and departed, and Bill knew that in an hour or so the blessed SOCs would arrive. But in the meantime he wanted to get out of range of those AA guns that could make a rescue dangerous or impossible.

He hauled in all his drogues and made a sail by holding up a couple of panels of the chute. The little craft slid rapidly along down wind and offshore. Admiral Reeves received a report that Martin was making three knots on a course of 290 degrees, not zigzagging.

As he drew away from the Saipan coast he was startled by a deafening rumble, as though a fast freight were passing a hundred feet overhead. The battlewagons, fifteen miles to seaward, and well out of sight from Bill Martin's three-foot height of eye, had begun to soften up the landing beaches. Not one shell landed in the lagoon.

Just before noon two SOC Seagulls appeared overhead, looking, with their double wings, like something from another era as they banked and circled, checking wind and sea conditions before landing. Escorting them were two of Chick Harmer's graceful, gull-winged Corsairs from *Enterprise*.

One SOC landed and taxied up to Martin, looking from the air like some winged water bug, moving in to eat another, smaller, wingless one.

The SOCs were from the fleet flagship *Indianapolis*, and the pilot of this one, an Ensign Townes, was on his first mission in which any kind of shooting was involved. He made a nice landing and approach, but he had no desire to linger in those waters. Martin climbed up on the lower wing and, in his thorough way, began to haul up all his gear, parachute, harness, boat and all.

"Come on, Commander," said Townes, "we've got to go!"

"Okay, but I want to bring these things along."

"No, goddammit! . . . Sir. Let's *go!*"

Martin saw that his benefactor was very much in earnest, and he cast off his equipment and climbed into the Seagull's rear seat. Townes emptied his .45 into the raft and the emergency kit so that they would not be sighted and cause concern to other pilots. The take-off, into the offshore wind, had to be toward the island, and brought the float plane back into AA range. The black bursts appeared in quantity, and Martin was uncomfortably sure he was going to be shot down for the second time that day. But the low speed of the old biplane saved it. For once the enemy, used to firing at fast-moving dive and glide bombers, overled the target, and the bursts all bloomed safely ahead.

Aboard *Indianapolis,* Martin received dry clothing, a couple of stiff shots of medicinal alcohol and went to the flag bridge to report to Admiral Spruance. While in *Indianapolis,* Bill also learned why the bombs of Strike Baker and the 16-inch projectiles of the bombardment group had all cleared the lagoon so nicely. The Fifth Fleet had gently moved its whole massive, explosive power a couple of hundred yards east, out of consideration for one of its own.

In the afternoon Bill dangled and swooped, in a canvas breeches buoy, across the high line from *Indianapolis* to *MacDonough,* and was in the destroyer's main director when she took under fire the AA position which had shot him down. He thought that, if the bombing hadn't destroyed it, "surely this did, and I wished that Williams and Hargrove might know of it."

That night *MacDonough* picked up a wounded enemy survivor of the oil-drum-loaded freighter sunk the day before by Martin's squadron, and at 7:30 A.M. on the fourteenth, Martin in a breeches buoy, and the enemy prisoner in a stretcher, were transferred back to *Enterprise.*

With enemy air opposition nonexistent during daylight, the big ships moved in close. *Enterprise* sailors standing on her flight deck between launches and recoveries, watched the same major-caliber explosions on Saipan that Bill Martin had seen from his raft a few yards off the reef. On the evening of the fourteenth, with flight operations over for the day, hundreds of men came up on deck to watch the fires and the spouting explosions still going on ashore.

On that same evening, at the insistence of Tom Hamilton, Bill Martin told his story over the ship's loudspeaker system, and in all her spaces the men were quiet and serious, listening. Later, they had further reason to be serious. A U. S. submarine reported the enemy fleet at sea—six carriers with their planes on deck, four battleships and eight cruisers, headed for the Marianas.

June 15 was D-Day at Saipan. The *Enterprise* air group

made the first strike of the day and the last one (except rocket-firing close-support planes from the escort carriers) before the arrival of the first wave of troops.

Killer Kane was the strike leader, commanding both *Enterprise* and *Lexington* planes—21 Dauntlesses, 19 Avengers and 28 Hellcats. It was a clear and lovely morning, with the waning moon hanging in the sky across from the rising sun. The sea to the west of Saipan was covered with ships of all sizes, with the big ones generally to seaward and the smaller ones close in. High-sided transports with rows of boats in davits along their upper decks, long flat-decked LSTs, looking like small tankers with their superstructures aft, squarish, cluttered LCIs, small landing craft of every description with their larger control boats, and in foaming circles, hundreds of LVT amtracs—all green from the air with solidly packed United States Marines. The ships and boats were lined up roughly north-south, parallel to the reef protecting the southwest corner of Saipan. Well out to seaward, battleships and cruisers were firing over the heads of the amphibious force, their shells exploding in clumps and rows of dust and smoke spouts along the shore.

Kane's sixty-eight planes circled southeast of Saipan at 11,000 feet while he reported to the air coordinator and was told to proceed with the planned attack.

As the combined air group crossed the island to hit the west coast north of the landing beaches, the naval bombardment stopped. Kane turned south and gave the order to attack. Air Group Ten went first, the Dauntlesses driving their 1,000-pounders into gun emplacements and fortifications at the south end of the landing beaches, and the torpedo planes laying their twelve 100-pounders in strings parallel to the beach. Ahead of both dived the Hellcats of VF-10, strafing down the AA. Eleven F6s added 350-pound depth bombs to the raking of their six .50-calibers. The *Lexington* planes followed in the same pattern a few seconds behind. There was no noticeable AA after the days of air and surface pounding.

Bud Schumann, assuming the duties of air coordinator at 9:00 A.M., found the first Marines ashore and moving steadily inland.

The air coordinator from 1:45 until 4:00 P.M. was Bill Martin, with Shinneman and Dahl, their closest friends, taking the places of Williams and Hargrove. Below them, Martin's own lagoon was churned white by a hundred boats, but the wreckage of T-41 was still visible. U. S. Marines had long since overrun the gun position which had shot him down. The reef that he had labored so hard to reach that his body ached with the memory, the reef that had been life itself, now seemed, from a few thousand feet above, to be pitifully close to shore, as though a few strokes would cover the distance. Bill wondered what the enemy commander would think if he knew that the single, desperate, hopeless-looking survivor, under fire in the lagoon two days ago, was now circling over his head, directing and controlling the air strikes that were losing him his island.

But Japan could not afford to lose the Marianas. They were too close to the homeland, within heavy-bomber range, and U. S. naval and air forces based there could cut off everything to the south.

The Combined Fleet, which had not been committed since Midway, was ordered to "attack the enemy in the Marianas area and annihilate the invasion force." But land-based air was ordered to destroy "at least one third of the enemy task force carrier units . . . prior to the decisive battle." On the evening of the fifteenth of June, the Japanese commander of land-based air in the Marianas attempted to carry out his orders.

"In the half light of twilight" seven twin-engine Sallys bored in on TG 58.3 from dead ahead. Radar had been watching them from 22 miles out, and at ten miles they had been visible through binoculars, black specks low on the water, approaching fast. Admiral Reeves ordered his ships into antiaircraft disposition, "Five Victor," and the concentric circles of the formation squeezed in tighter to provide mutual support, the carriers in the center, then the battleships and cruisers, and outside of them, the screening destroyers. All guns were trained out, loaded, crews tense, silent, waiting for their talkers to relay the word—"Commence firing."

The battleships opened up first, seeming to explode in the dusk, and every ship in the force joined in. Lines of red tracers formed a shifting web across the face of the sea. Smoke from the thousands of barrels of automatic weapons nearly obscured the firing ships in the dim light, and the gunners had trouble keeping sight of their targets through the brightness of the tracers, the splashes and the smoke. It seemed impossible that anything could fly through that horizontal net of fire and lead, but the Sallys

spread out and closed in, converging on the carriers from
ahead. The *Enterprise* Mark 37 director computed their
speed at 250 knots.

There were seven of the enemy planes, and they wanted
Lexington first, half a mile broad on the Big E's port bow,
with Marc Mitscher watching the action from her flag
bridge, and then *Enterprise*. They passed over the destroyer
screen, and the screen's tracers followed them in. It
seemed that the closer they came, fast, deadly, apparently
indestructible, flat down on the darkening sea, the heavier
the opposing fire became. Every barrel in the task group
flamed and spat as they approached the heavy ships, and
the hammering of the thousand guns blended to a roar, as
though the carrier task group itself had become vocal in its
anger.

One or two of the planes at last began to smoke, then
one flamed a little, dragged a wing tip in the water, and
instantly cartwheeled into a flaming, splashing ball of
wreckage which fell quickly astern of the racing ships.
Others went the same way, each with its seven-man crew,
but heavy splashes behind them showed where their torpedoes had begun their runs. From some unseen, unfired-on
plane, a bomb fountained the sea between *Lex* and *Enterprise*. Then the slim, fast, wounded aircraft were between
the big ships, in the heart of the formation, and nothing
made of aluminum and steel could penetrate the high-
velocity lead that filled the air in there. Only one, which
turned off to port after dropping, escaped. The other six
were all blazing at once among the gray, fast-moving ships.
One lay dead ahead of *Enterprise*, three on her port beam
and one off the starboard quarter. A minute after the last
plane was down, a single torpedo bubbled in on the Big E's
port bow. Captain Gardner swung his stern clear and paralleled the wake which passed down the portside so close that
the men in the overhanging 40-millimeter mounts had to
lean out over their splinter shields to watch it.

Enterprise gunners got credit for two of the six Sallys
destroyed and an "assist" on the third, but at a price. As
the enemy bombers skimmed through the formation at deck
level, the guns had followed them and inevitably made hits
on other ships. For this reason, the Big E's five-inch guns
had been silent throughout the action. But in such close
formation even the 40s and 20s were dangerous.

A 20-millimeter shell hit near the Number Two 40-

millimeter mount, all the way forward at the port edge of the flight deck, and sprayed shrapnel over the crew, knocking two men down. They bounced back up and the gun stayed in action. But at five-inch Group II, just opposite the forward elevator portside, a seaman was decapitated by a 40-millimeter projectile which hit his helmet, just a few feet short of the five-inch powder locker.

There were more bogies on the scopes for another hour and occasional firing by the screen.

At eight o'clock a sub was reported five miles ahead.

In the passageways, and at emergency first-aid stations forward, wounded men lay in stretchers for the first time since Santa Cruz, and Commander Clarence "Doc" Blew and his assistants were busy all night.

At 10:30, Tom Hamilton announced that the initial landings had been successful, and that, in the dusk torpedo attack, TF 58 had destroyed forty-two Japanese planes.

On the sixteenth, Killer Kane was, almost, added to the Big E's growing casualty list. Killer was the day's first air coordinator, with orders to be over Saipan at daylight, about 5:40 A.M. Task Group 58.3 was operating 100 miles west of Saipan in the direction of the approaching enemy fleet. At five o'clock he pressed his head back against the padding, braced his throttle hand full forward, and gave the signal to be catapulted into the darkness. A minute later, Bob Kanze, his wingman, did the same, and the two F6s, burning dim running lights, rendezvoused above the blacked-out ships and headed for shore, climbing easily to top the scattered cumulus at 3,500 feet. Once on course they turned off their lights so as not to give themselves away to any enemy planes that might be around, but both fighters checked their IFF electronic recognition equipment safety-wired "ON."

Twenty-five miles west of Saipan they began to see ships of the landing forces, and circled to the south to stay clear. But the surface was still dark and partly hidden by clouds, and they could not see all the ships that covered the seas off the Marianas that morning. The two Hellcats had just turned west again when a five-inch antiaircraft shell burst under Kane's left wing, knocking his goggles off and throwing him hard against his belt and shoulder harness. Gasoline poured out over the shot-up wing, and the engine began to smoke. More bursts flashed closely around, and big, red tracers scorched by from astern. Killer released his belt and opened his canopy to bail out, but found his engine still running and his plane not burning, and controllable. He led Kanze in a dive which took them out of the AA for a minute, but when they tried to climb on course, it opened up again from ahead and to port. Kane went on the air, calling commander, Support Aircraft ("Cherokee"), and announcing emphatically that he was friendly and being fired on by friendly forces. No answer, and now Kane's oil pressure stood at zero. He told Kanze he would attempt a water landing about five miles south, where he could see a group of transports. The black AA bursts still cracked around him as he dove for the surface but he leveled out low and stalled the F6 into the light wind, skipping once and then smashing to a stop that threw his head forward against the gunsight (he had not had time to refasten his belt and harness) but could not keep him from getting out and into his boat.

From that obscure and ignominious position, the *Enterprise* air group commander watched the sun rise over the western Pacific. But, soaked, angry, and bloody-headed, he was in no mood to enjoy it. For thirty minutes he searched his memory for something he should have done differently. He was showing proper IFF, approaching from the direction in which TF 58 was known to be, on a flight scheduled on the plans held by the ships that had shot him down.

Newcomb picked him up, transferred him to *Patterson*, and, that same afternoon, his head wrapped in bandages, he dangled across the high line to the starboard quarter of the Big E.

Gardner and Hamilton believed in keeping their men informed of the progress of at least the ugly little corner of the war which they themselves were fighting. On D-Day, an outline map of Saipan was painted on the side of the island below the stack. The area held by the enemy was colored red, that occupied by our forces, blue—and after each air coordinator mission had been debriefed, the huge map was revised. When Aslito Field was finally overrun, it had a new name on the side of the island—Isely Field—for Isely of VT-16 who had been less lucky than Bill Martin. The men of *Enterprise*, miles offshore, had a far better knowledge of the progress of the battle than the soldiers and Marines who were fighting it.

But the Japanese Mobile Fleet was steadily approaching for the showdown. On the afternoon of the sixteenth, Admiral Spruance acted to cover his rear and prevent enemy carrier planes from using the land fields in the Marianas, as *Enterprise* had used Henderson a year and a half ago, to reservice, rearm and strike again. *Enterprise* was assigned Orote Field on Guam. She hit it with nine TBFs, eleven SBDs and twelve F6Fs. At the same time, *Lexington,* with a similar group, hit Agana airdrome. Lieutenant Commander J. D. "Jig" Ramage led the *Enterprise* strike, and effectively put the field out of commission with a cratered runway and blasted hangars and fuel storage tanks. AA was close and vicious, and indestructible Cliff Largess of VT-10 made it back despite the loss of his entire port elevator, a bent starboard stabilizer and a bruised and unconscious radioman.

On the seventeenth, TG 58.3 hit Guam again, and the men of *Enterprise* learned for the first time that 58.1 and 2 had hit Iwo and Chichi Jima, 700 miles to the north, on D-Day, destroying scores of planes intended for use against American forces off Saipan. Now, those two carrier task forces, half of Mitscher's strength, were straining south to join up before the enemy arrived. Torpedo Ten, with 270-gallon droppable tanks installed in their bomb bays by eighteen men working from midnight to 7:00 A.M., flew a 325-mile search to the westward in an attempt to locate the Mobile Fleet, but found nothing in five-plus hours in the air.

At daylight on the eighteenth the Avenger search planes went out again, flying in pairs in narrow 10-degree sectors 325 miles to the westward. This time, although they did not find the Mobile Fleet, there was plenty of evidence of approaching action. "Crossbow" Collins and Bob Jones found a surfaced submarine 300 miles out which crash-dived before they could strafe, and at the limit of their leg saw a fast, high-flying, twin-engine enemy plane which they rightly assumed was scouting ahead of the Japanese main force. Charlie Henderson and Cliff Largess, on the short cross leg at the western end of their search, sighted a twin-float Jake, evidently also at the limit of his search. The two Avengers maneuvered carefully into position on the Jake's port beam and 2,500 feet above him, keeping clouds between, and then Henderson attacked through a cloud in a flat, fast run on the Jake's tail. Two short bursts blazed him and he spiraled burning into the ocean.

At 11:00 A.M. on the eighteenth, Tom Hamilton's well-known voice came over loudspeakers throughout the ship, after the usual shrilling of the bosun's call. The exec made the rumors positive and official. Submarine reports now put the enemy fleet only 400 miles away, and TF 58 was going out to meet it. *Enterprise* would share in the greatest naval battle in history, the long-sought, long-desired show-down with the Japanese fleet. "We are going to give the Japs their half of the Pacific," Tom said, "the bottom half!"

The ship went tense. Every department prepared for battle. Fighting Ten lovingly worked over its deadly F6Fs. The Gunnery Department broke out additional ammuni-tion until even the "heads" were stacked with the snail-like magazines of 20s and the tall, square steel boxes of 40s. Secretly, each man believed TF 58 would win. Each man had seen that tough, sprawling, young force in action, had seen the new battlewagons open fire like volcanoes, had seen the hundreds of planes rise from its many decks and roar in wedges and echelons overhead—and they could not believe the enemy could match it. They knew that Marc Mitscher was in tactical command of the carriers and that Ching Lee had the battle line. It was bound to be a clean-up for the U. S.—and with the enemy fleet defeated, what was left between Saipan and Japan? The war might be over in 1944.

But there were gloomier facts that only senior and staff officers had the training and experience to consider. One was the wind. On the eighteenth and nineteenth of June, the Marianas' wind blew from the east. Admiral Ozawa, commanding the Mobile Fleet, could launch and recover his planes while steaming eastward toward Saipan.

But Mitscher, between Saipan, with the vulnerable am-phibious forces lying offshore, and Jisaburo Ozawa, want-ing desperately to close his enemy, had to turn and steam away from Ozawa each time his carriers operated their aircraft. And, in addition, the Japanese carrier planes, lightly built, with no armor and no protection for their fuel tanks, had more range than the Americans. They could strike from outside the reach of a return strike. U. S. car-riers therefore had to run in, preferably under cover of darkness, and be close enough to hit at daylight. It was like a long-armed boxer fighting a husky slugger. And at Mitscher's back were always the Marianas' airfields to which Ozawa's strike groups could go after their attacks, to rearm, regas, and reattack.

On the night of the eighteenth, Martin's long-legged, radar-equipped Avengers went out again 325 miles to the west. This time Bill Martin led the flight of fifteen. Beginning at 2:18 A.M. a plane was catapulted every forty-four seconds, so expert had become Lieutenant Walt Chewning's catapult crews and VT-10's night-flying pilots. They joined up overhead and flew just south of west for 100 miles before Martin gave the signal to fan out on their individual 200-mile sectors. In the event of contact, they were to report three times and then attack with the minimum altitude radar technique they had used in the lagoon at Truk.

The fifteen planes completed their searches as ordered, despite frequent instrument weather and bad visibility, but there was only one contact, a submarine in a friendly sub area.

There was a chance that night, by steaming west at high speed from 1:30 A.M. until daylight, to be within striking distance of Ozawa's carriers at dawn—and Mitscher had proposed that it be done. Spruance, in overall command, said no. His primary responsibility was the protection of the invasion forces on Saipan and he would not be drawn so far to the west that an "end-around" sweep by the enemy he had still not located might destroy them. Spruance's decision was signaled at 12:30 A.M. and there was bitter disappointment on all the carriers. On the *Lex*, Mitscher, in silent disagreement, retired to his sea cabin. In *Enterprise*, calm, quiet Mat Gardner is said to have hurled down his hat and stomped on it.

Now on the nineteenth, all that mighty TF 58 could do was wait—wait for an enemy out of its reach to strike. But Task Force 58, even on the defensive between two enemies, could take care of itself. Spruance had arranged his task groups in a mirrored F about 100 miles west of the islands. Forming the north-south upright were three carrier task groups, 58.2 south, 58.3 middle and 58.1 north, each twelve miles from the other. Out twelve miles to the west of the top of the upright was 58.4 and south of that, opposite the middle of the upright, Ching Lee's seven new battlewagons forming 58.7.

As expected, the dawn search found nothing.

About 6:30 A.M. there was a fight over Guam between enemy aircraft taking off from patched-up Orote and TF 58 Hellcats vectored out to destroy them. Another scuffle took place from 8:30 to 10:00, when a group of enemy reinforcements flew into Guam from the southwest. Land-based air was trying again, and at the last minute, to destroy the ordered one-third of the U. S. carriers. They lost thirty-five planes for one F6F.

Just before 10:00 A.M. Ozawa's first strikes began to show on TF 58's radars 150 miles to the westward. Mitscher called his fighters back from Guam with the old battlecry of "Hey, Rube!" In all the ships, bugles and electric alarm bells sounded General Quarters. The circular task groups drew together, bristling with barrels pointing up.

At 10:07 A.M., the Big E's own radar picked up "many bogies" 130 miles west. Three minutes later the TBS crackled with the voice of Captain Arleigh Burke, Mitscher's chief of staff: "Prepare to launch all available fighters." "The force swung hard into the 14-knot trade wind, and at 10:16, Burke's voice said: "Stand by. . . . Execute, execute." If there were ever a fighter pilot's day, it was this magnificent nineteenth of June just west of the Marianas, and in ten minutes the blue sky roared and swarmed with blue-winged Hellcats, climbing hard downwind and down sun. *Enterprise* that morning catapulted her last eight Hellcats with an average interval between launches of fourteen seconds. She had still the fastest flight deck in the fleet.

At 10:36, word came of the first interceptions, and by 10:45 all the bombers and torpedo planes on deck had been launched to circle well to the eastward in radio contact but out of the way.

When all her planes had gone, *Enterprise* buttoned up and waited. To the old hands it was like the battles in the Solomons—the bare flight deck, the dogged-down doors and hatches, the ready guns, the swinging, searching radar, the helmeted, life-jacketed topside crew—the waiting, after all that can be done has been done. In CIC, aerology, the coding room, men listened tensely to the crackling, buzzing speakers that would tell the story of the battle before it broke overhead. Again the Big E had launched her planes and cleared her decks to repulse an enemy counterattack against a U. S. invasion force. But Saipan was far in distance and farther in time from Guadalcanal, and now fourteen other carriers with 400 other fighters shared the war with *Enterprise*.

All the carriers and all the fighters were needed. Brilliant, skull-faced Ozawa, with his enemy in range but unable to counterattack, pinpointed but still groping for him, launched everything he had in four massive waves. The American task groups steamed into the northeast wind ready to land, service and relaunch the Hellcats which were taking the full weight of Ozawa's attack.

From 10:35 on, the Big E's speakers spouted tumbling, overlapping orders, acknowledgments, reports, repeats:

"Vector two six five, angels twenty, buster."

"Vector two two five."

"Vector two four zero, bandits ahead eleven o'clock low."

"Tallyho! Tallyho! Many bandits, Zekes and Kates."

"Splash one Zeke!"

"Splash one Zeke!"

"Splash two Kates!"

And less technical phrases—like "Got the sonofabitch," and "Lookout, Joe! You've got one on your tail!"—came over the air all in the same thirty seconds, as TF 58 fighter director officers, working in the limitless dome of the sky from two-dimensional, 12-inch scopes in darkened, interior compartments, expertly put the Hellcats within pouncing distance of the first Japanese attack groups sixty miles out.

Enterprise radar officers and operators were afraid to believe what their scopes told them—the incredible reduction in the size of the smudge of "many bandits" within a minute or two of the "Tallyhoes." But their attention was taken at once by smaller groups of bogies scattered all over the screen. By 10:48 one group had closed to twenty-one miles, but fighters were vectored out and it vanished from the radar. At 11:10 lookouts picked up the skimming specks of enemy planes low on the water eleven miles astern, and three minutes later *Lexington* opened fire. That group never closed, but after thirty minutes more of tracking, intercepting, training guns and peering through binoculars, another one did.

Radar had warned of enemy torpedo planes approaching from the west, twenty-five miles out. Twelve minutes later, shipboard binoculars picked the first one up about three miles off the starboard quarter. It was a single-engine, midwing carrier plane diving directly at *Enterprise* from 3,000 to 4,000 feet. "Commence firing" echoed and repeated along the gun galleries and the 40-millimeter mounts to starboard, and Captain Gardner swung the Big E's bow hard right to bring all his guns to bear. Gray powder smoke

blew aft along the deck as the 40s pounded rhythmically
and the 20s joined with their slow rattling and even the
five-inch boomed a few times. At about 1,500 feet and less
than a mile away, the Judy, smoking badly, pulled level and
banked right, parallel to the Big E's course, showing its
brown belly and the red disks on its wings. Opposite the
bow, with tracers from *Enterprise, Princeton* and *Lexington* darting all around it, it began to glide toward the sea,
and splashed in a blooming of red flame and a puff of black
smoke about two miles ahead. The cheers of the gun crews
sounded enthusiastic but weak after the din of their guns.

There was very little time to cheer. Right behind the Judy
and from the same direction in quick succession came three
Jills, the latest and best Japanese carrier-based torpedo
bomber. The starboard guns opened up again, lacing the
noon sky with lines of smoke and fire, the small black
clouds of the five-inch and the myriad gray puffs of the 40s
detonating at the ends of their flights. The first two low-
winged Jills started their torpedo runs about two miles out
from 2,000 feet, but flew into a shifting web of tracers
from all three carriers and their supporting ships which
tumbled them flaming into the blue sea a mile off the Big
E's starboard beam. The third Jill belonged to the *Enterprise* Group III (starboard quarter) five-inch guns. The
enemy pilot made the mistake of coming in higher than his
two mates and on a steady course. The after five-inch director had a perfect solution on its computer, and the two-
gun battery opened fire on director control at 5,500 yards.
Three or four bursts were very close, and then one made a
direct hit, blowing the right wing off the Jill and sending
the plane whirling over and over into the sea while the wing
floated down, slipping and fluttering, much more slowly.
Not one Jill launched its torpedo. Officers and men in Plot
were exultant. In all actions, like the men in engineering
spaces, CIC and repair parties, they had stood blind in their
crowded compartment, setting up and monitoring their
complex fire-control equipment, waiting a chance to show
what it could do. But in all successful actions up to now,
the Big E's guns had always fired by eye under the local
control of the crew itself. This was the first time that an
enemy aircraft had been destroyed by *Enterprise* five-inch
guns firing in director control.

The violent flurry of action was over in six minutes. In
the midst of it, an explosion spouted the Big E's curving

wake some 750 yards astern. It could have been a torpedo, or a bomb dropped by a high plane that no one looked up to see.

The task group slid along into the east wind, leaving the oil slicks of the four planes astern, alert for the next attack.

High in the blue sky to the west the fight went on. There had never been one like it in the long history of war at sea.

Every hour on the hour for four hours, Admiral Ozawa, with the advantage of range and downwind position, launched full deckloads of the planes and pilots Japan had been hoarding in peaceful rear areas for the day they could once more face the hated Americans in fleet strength as they had at Pearl and Midway. Now that day had come and Ozawa was not going to lose through half measures.

In fifty-plane formations, the long-legged enemy strike groups droned upwind, four cloudless miles above the blue Pacific, knowing exactly where to find the American carriers—just a few miles west of friendly airfields in the Marianas—and knowing equally well that no American aviator had yet sighted the Mobile Fleet from which they came. At Coral Sea they had sunk the old *Lex* and damaged *Yorktown* with 69 planes; at Midway, 34 had been enough finally to burn the *Yorktown;* 170 had sent *Hornet* to the bottom and badly mauled the *Enterprise* in the waters north of Santa Cruz. How could TF 58 hope to withstand 320, attacking with far more tactical advantage than had been the case in any preceding battle, and with additional support from land-based air?

Task Force 58 was depending on some 450 Grumman Hellcats, manned by 450 of the world's best fighter pilots, radar, and half a dozen specially trained and thoroughly competent reserve lieutenants acting as group and force fighter director officers. And nature, having sided so heavily with Japan in the matter of wind direction, made a last-minute attempt to even the odds. In the clear, cool air at 20,000 feet, contrails began to stream their long white ribbons, visible for fifty miles, from the wing tips of the Japanese aircraft. The Hellcat pilots, climbing on the vectors of the FDOs, could look up and see the long streamers with black specks at their heads, and take over by eye from there. From planes at lower altitudes, and from the decks of picket destroyers well to the west of the force, men could make out the seeming slow-motion tangle of friendly and enemy planes as the Hellcats waded into Ozawa's formations, watch the sudden brush strokes of black smoke down the sky and hope they were witnessing the destruction of an enemy and not the death of a friend.

During the initial attacks, Bud Schumann circled with 15 of his Grim Reapers at 15,000 over the task group, under orders of the group FDO. Flash Gordon's division got the first orders: "Vector two five zero, angels one five, buster." Gordon acknowledged and added throttle, heading out, as the four F6Fs tightened their formation. Thirty miles from base Gordon gave the tallyho—four light brown, single-engine Judys, well below 5,000 feet, in position to attack Ching Lee's circular formation of battleships. Flash, with Dick Mason on his wing, went after the first Judy which was just beginning its attack run. The two Hellcats dropped like falcons through the two miles of sky, and Gordon's tracers, coming from directly overhead, set the brown fuselage afire. Mason followed, starting fires along the wings and the Judy dived straight into the sea.

Just before the noon attack on *Enterprise,* Mo Marks and Chuck Farmer intercepted a Kate making a torpedo run on another task group, the dark green plane fast and flat on the wave tops like those at Guadalcanal. Marks made the first flat side run and nothing happened. The Kate bored straight in for its release point. But Farmer swooped in and locked on the Kate's tail. He fired two long bursts, and on the second the torpedo plane exploded in his face so that he had to zoom up to avoid the debris which splashed and burned just out of range of the guns of the screen.

Other squadrons from other carriers, with more fruitful vectors at better times, destroyed scores of enemy aircraft long before they were able even to sight their targets. The enemy was long in range and numbers but fatally short in tactics. His bombers, whose only chance of success or survival lay in close, defensive formation flying, scattered under the Hellcat attacks and were slaughtered singly. His fighters were generally timid, failing to protect either the bombers or each other, separating under fire to dogfight individually, but usually satisfied to use their superior maneuverability to stay clear, or to fire at long range and retire to loop and roll harmlessly among themselves.

In this fighter-pilots' paradise, Killer Kane, bandaged and black-eyed from his ditching on the sixteenth, remained fretfully grounded.

In the early afternoon some of the enemy formations headed directly for the airfields on Guam, to gas and attack from there. Fighting Ten had two divisions of CAP air-borne overhead, one led by Rod Devine who got the first vector, 120 degrees. It brought him over Orote Field on the western tip of the island. Guam swarmed with enemy planes, approaching, landing, taking off and circling to land. The Japanese pilots, at the end of their long flight, found Orote anything but safe. *Enterprise* Dauntlesses and Avengers and squadrons from other carriers had been called out of their peaceful circling on the disengaged side of the force to crater the runways and destroy facilities at both Orote and Agana. They had done so well, although with 1,000-pound armor-piercing and 500-pound general-purpose bombs intended for ships, that most of the Japanese planes attempting to use the fields were unable to avoid the fresh pits in the runways and crashed, shearing landing gear or nosing over, and of no use to the enemy again.

Devine took one quick look at the numbers of enemy planes over Guam, hollered for additional fighters and led his division to the attack. In the next twenty minutes Devine's four Hellcats shot down twelve enemy planes.

Rod's first thought was to prevent any more take-offs until help arrived, and he dived for the down-wind end of the runway where a Zeke was in take-off position. A strafing burst chewed into the runway surface, and walked quickly up and through the Zeke, and Devine pulled out fast across the field as though he were making a low pass in an air show. Dead ahead he found a shining, new, blue-green Judy dive bomber with the bright red disks of Japan brilliant on its outer wings. Still in the pull-out from his strafing run, he opened fire again and the Judy flamed, rolled over and dove into a wooded hill just up wind of the field. Devine pulled back around to the westward, looking for the rest of his division, and found "Yehudi" Ude and Phil Kirkwood attacking two light-brown Judys and a Zeke attempting to slip into Orote from the west at 500 feet. Rod flashed in and with a single short burst sent the Zeke flaming inverted into the sea close to shore at the same time that Ude's guns hammered one of the Judys into a split S and a dive straight into the sea in the same vicinity. Kirkwood shattered the tail of his Judy, killing the rear-seatman, and white smoke puffed out of the plane's belly before the Hellcat's speed carried it over and past the enemy dive bomber. But the Judy turned left, and Phil banked in behind it firing. His second burst set the right wing blazing, and the Judy fell off in that direction and flew into the scrub trees of Orote Peninsula, exploding with a flash and mushroom of black smoke.

The skies over and around Guam were filled with swirling, smoking, flaming planes. At any one moment, two or three falling plumes of greasy smoke were visible, and as many as four or five parachutes floating, white and slow, through and below the frantic dive and whirl of planes.

Devine took his division out over water and around the south end of Guam where they found and destroyed two more of the hateful Kate torpedo planes they had been fighting for six months and which *Enterprise* had been firing at since Guadalcanal. A little farther south, two fixed-landing-gear Val dive bombers crossed ahead of Devine's Hellcats, headed for Guam. Rod got one and Kirkwood the other, after two firing runs.

The F6Fs had barely recovered from those attacks, when a Zeke and an old Nate with nonretractable landing gear like the Vals', came in from the southwest at 2,000 feet. Devine and Kirkwood took the Zeke and he caught fire and crashed on Rod's first run. Ude went around and around with the highly maneuverable Nate, but finally must have destroyed the elevator controls, because it dived, not burning, into the sea. This was the same kind of plane that had eluded three of VF-10's best for fifteen minutes at Palau.

Jimmy Kay, Devine's wingman and the fourth pilot in that division, became separated early in the action and joined up with Pete Long and Bob Kanze, who had seen the smoke of the action over Guam and entered the fight. Kay made a nearly vertical dive on a Val, killing the pilot and smashing the engine, and a few minutes later shot down a Zeke by flaming its right wing.

Pete Long got two Zekes right over Orote, one as it turned and he turned inside with a quick burst, and the other following it through two desperate loops.

Bob Kanze, completely recovered from his ordeal by water south of Truk, and his near shoot-down with Kane on D plus 1, made a clean, fast, high side run and burned a Val on his initial approach to the aerial battle over Guam. Another Val pilot, ahead and above the first, must have seen and been impressed with that performance, because the minute Kanze pointed the F6 in his direction, and, before a round had been fired, he bailed out. The Val shallow-dived into the sea.

The flight over Guam went on all day, as the Japanese tried hard to get their land-based aircraft into the action, and as survivors of the interceptions around TF 58 tried to land for fuel and rearming. The island hills and fields were spotted with smudgy fires ignited by falling planes; the airports at Agana and Orote smoked with the bombs of VT and VB squadrons and the wrecks of crashed and shot-down aircraft. To the west of Spruance's ships, returning fighter pilots flew for miles over a sea littered with the oil slicks and wreckage of what had been Ozawa's Sunday punch.

It was almost, but not entirely, one-sided.

Enterprise lost the executive officer of her fighter squadron. On a rescue escort mission near Guam, with two float planes and Chick Harmer of the night fighter detachment, Lieutenant Hank Clem pulled straight up after a Zeke which had strafed the SOC he was protecting. His F6F was unable to climb after the agile Zero and stalled. Before Clem could recover, the Zero pilot whipped back in a quick wing-over, made a head-on run, and Hank's Hellcat spun into the sea. Chick Harmer arrived from over his widely separated float plane in time to smoke the Zeke with a long-range burst as it headed for Guam.

Other carriers had losses too, and the final score was twenty pilots and seven air-crewmen of TF 58 killed. Ozawa's four maximum effort attack waves, totaling 373 planes, had made one bomb hit on *South Dakota*, which failed even to slow her, and near misses on two carriers. A Kate torpedo bomber spattered against *Indiana*'s eight-inch armor belt at the water line, causing damage roughly comparable to a scratched bumper on the family sedan.

But 243 of Ozawa's planes never got back to his carriers and 50 land-based aircraft never returned to their fields.

Japan, having worked, hoarded, trained and planned for months, had thrown everything she had at Spruance's Fifth Fleet, and that everything had been slaughtered by TF 58 Hellcats with losses so negligible that the strength and efficiency of the U. S. forces were not affected in any way. In fact, the added experience gained by TF 58 fighter pilots increased force effectiveness. The hurried and inadequate training of pilots, the vulnerability of planes, and, less importantly, nature's blessed contrails and a Japanese air co-ordinator whose orders to strike groups were intercepted and translated all day, had lost Japan the air arm of her navy. And without aviation, that Navy could only hope for success under the most special and unusual circumstances.

In a fighter ready room, on some carrier of TF 58, late the afternoon of the nineteenth of June, some young Hellcat pilot exultingly told the air intelligence officer "debriefing" him, "Why, hell, it was just like an old-time turkey shoot down home!" It was one of those phrases, like certain nicknames, that strike the precise note, the essential nature of the person or the event, and stick. The air battle on the approaches to the Fifth Fleet and over Guam has come to be known world-wide as "the great Marianas turkey shoot."

Admiral Ozawa's Mobile Fleet at the end of the day had still not been found by TF 58 planes. But astutely stationed Pacific Fleet submarines had found it, torpedoed Ozawa's own brand-new flagship, the carrier *Taiho,* out from under him, and later in the day sunk the Big E's old enemy and veteran of the treachery at Pearl Harbor, *Shokaku.* Ozawa turned north to fuel on the twentieth and attack again on the twenty-first with what planes were left in his carriers and those he thought he had available on Guam.

On the night of the nineteenth, TF 58 steamed westward at 24 knots, hoping to close the range enough so that the dawn search would find Ozawa. It did not, but Killer Kane, who had missed the turkey shoot, almost defiantly ungrounded himself to escort two of Martin's searching TBFs. His head still wrapped in bandages, he shot down two float search planes from the Mobile Fleet within a forty-minute period, one 110 miles and one only 50 miles from the task force. The close-in enemy was a Jill with a belly tank to extend its range and Kane set the belly tank afire with a burst from behind and level. The long flames spread to the plane's tail and it climbed steeply to about 700 feet, then dived as the flames destroyed the elevators. At 200 feet the pilot jumped. His chute did not open. Bill Balden, circling low in his TBF, could see the brown-clad body a few feet below the surface with a pool of blood spreading above it.

Mitscher continued west except during air operations, when he still had to steam away from his enemy, and launched another search in early afternoon.

Four search teams of two Avengers and one Hellcat each fanned out from *Enterprise* at 1:45. Each team covered a 10-degree sector. The two middle searches were flown by Bob Nelson, Jim Moore and Dutch Velte in one, Bob Jones, Ed Laster and Ned Colgan in the other.

For two hours the eight TBFs and the four F6s bored out to the northwest, with the lead Avengers low at 700 feet and their squadron mates and fighter escorts above and to either side. It was a clear afternoon with scattered high and middle clouds, and at lower altitudes the scattered white cumulus of fair weather. A slight layer of haze at medium altitudes made the lower ones better for long-range visibility.

Charlie Henderson's group, flying the southernmost sector, sighted a surfaced submarine which crash-dived but they neither reported nor attacked, being under orders to use radio only to report enemy capital ships, and knowing that friendly subs were in the area.

Shortly after three o'clock Bob Nelson's team saw a Kate five miles to their port, headed in the opposite direction. They let him go.

At 3:38 Bob Nelson noticed "a ripple on the horizon" off the left side of his nose. It was nothing definite, and yet it noticeably broke the clean line of the horizon and so had to be something. A couple of minutes later, Ed Laster, in the adjacent search sector to the south, suddenly dropped a smoke light to mark his position and began to circle, reporting some ships ahead partially obscured by a rain squall. Almost simultaneously the two search teams approached the opposite ends of that large rain cloud and peered around its corners. On the other side was Ozawa's Mobile Fleet. Mitscher's search planes had finally located the enemy.

Nearest to the Big E's search planes was her tough old enemy *Zuikaku*, last survivor of the five carriers that committed the Sunday murders at Pearl Harbor, with Jisaburo Ozawa himself aboard, and cruisers and destroyers around her. To the southwest, and on a westerly course which made them hard to identify, were other carriers, cruisers, destroyers and oilers.

Nelson went on the air at once with his contact report:

ENEMY FLEET SIGHTED LATITUDE 15–00
LONGITUDE 135–24 COURSE 270 SPEED 20

Three times he reported this data on voice radio and then at four o'clock gave it to his radioman to transmit in the longer-range dash-dot of "CW," with a one-degree (sixty-mile) correction in longitude, discovered by Jim Moore in checking Nelson's figures.

At the other end of the rain squall Bob Jones sent out his CW report immediately:

MANY SHIPS ONE CARRIER 134–12E14–55 N

Jones headed home at once, working his radio steadily to be sure the vital information got to Mitscher. Nelson stayed around until 4:10, ducking in and out of the rain cloud and gathering more data. He "took departure pronto" when a couple of fighters headed in his direction.

Nelson's voice message came into the *Lexington*'s receivers badly garbled, but it was obvious that he had something, and Mitscher ordered his carriers to stand by to launch. On the blackboards at the front of all ready rooms, the orders were chalked unmistakably in six-inch block letters.

GET THE CARRIERS!

The other CW reports came in better, and at 4:10, as Nelson was leaving for home, the pilots of TF 58 were climbing into their planes.

In the fifteen minutes between 4:21 and 4:36, Mitscher's carriers turned into the wind, launched 54 torpedo planes, 77 dive bombers and 85 fighters and turned back to the west again. It was not a routine strike but a desperate, last-chance effort to destroy an enemy who for two days had remained maddeningly out of reach, and was even now at extreme range and capable of escaping entirely unless this opportunity were seized.

The strike group left at 4:45. It was a minimum of two hours out, two back and a fight between, and sunset was at seven o'clock. Two hundred and sixteen planes would have to land in full darkness with nearly empty fuel tanks, many with battle damage. But it was his only chance to strike the enemy and Marc Mitscher really had no choice.

On their return legs the two middle search teams which had made the contact passed under the outbound strike. They heard themselves being reported as bogies by the high-flying attack groups, and Ned Colgan spoke up at once for his team:

"Negative bogies! This is two turkeys and an F6!"

That cleared up the mistaken identity and a few minutes

later Colgan found a Kate, flat on the water forty miles west of the force, and shot it down with a single long rattle of fire in a small tactical operation so neat and efficient that the details are clear after seventeen years. The instant the Kate was sighted one TBF dropped a float light and circled, climbing. Colgan dove after the Kate, free to maneuver as required, and the other TBF followed him, staying between the fighter and the orbiting plane. When the Kate was blazing on the surface, the second TBF, holding both Colgan and the circler on his radar, gave him a heading back to the first where the flight rejoined and continued home, having moved not one mile off its intended track.

Charlie Henderson, en route home, chased and destroyed a Jill with the wing guns of his TBF.

Killer Kane, despite his five-hour flight of the morning, and with his head still bandaged, led the *Enterprise* strike of 28 planes—12 Hellcats, 11 Dauntlesses and 5 Avengers. For two hours he and his pilots droned into the lowering sun, hoarding gasoline as best they could for the long trip home, and looking ahead at the empty, shining sea, and across the shifting blue wings at each other's familiar faces and the well-known shapes of the other planes in other squadrons on both sides, above and below. They climbed slowly, at about 100 feet a minute, indicating only 130 knots, so that the flight seemed like what it was—a long, uphill chase. There was plenty of time to think: to think that this was what all their training and their experience had been for—a crack at the Japanese Fleet itself; to think that only they, air-borne on this strike, out of all the aviators in the U. S. Navy, would get this chance; to think of how not to muff it, to review technique and tactics and recheck arming and dropping procedures; but not to think, if they could avoid it, of the murderous barrage of AA that a first-line surface force could put up, such as they had seen their own ships put up only recently; not to think of the Zekes waiting overhead, or the long 300-odd miles from TF 58 to the scene of the battle into which they were headed, or the slim chances of rescue by friendly forces if they went down in that area. There was time to wonder about the coming night landing on darkened decks, and time to figure and refigure the fuel situation—which came out painfully close each time.

At seven o'clock, with the red sun just resting on the horizon, firing the scattered clouds below them and flushing their helmeted faces, Kane's airmen found the enemy. The first ships sighted were Ozawa's tankers, and Kane knew Mitscher was out for combatant ships, so they flew on another twenty miles until they sighted the middle group of the Mobile Fleet with the carriers *Ryujo, Junyo* and *Hiyo,* and two cruisers that *Enterprise* aviators had seen before—at Midway—*Mogami* and *Nagato,* plus a destroyer screen.

Six Dauntlesses, all five Avengers and Kane's division of four Hellcats went after *Ryujo.* Four SBDs and Harman's four fighters took *Junyo,* and the remaining two bombers, in the haste of the moment and accompanied by a stray dive bomber from another squadron, attacked *Hiyo.*

At 12,000 feet the sun was still bright on the undersides of the planes, but on the sea's surface where Japan's best warships twisted and circled with flashing guns, dusk was settling.

Scattered low clouds made it difficult to observe individual ships long enough to identify them or determine their formations. As the attack group slanted down from 15,000 to 12,000 feet, picking up speed, the AA increased to unbelievable proportions, the ugly black bursts jarring and jolting the planes every two or three seconds as they passed over intervening ships to "Get the carriers!" None of the *Enterprise* airmen had seen AA like this before. In addition to the familiar black puffs of heavy stuff, the floating tennis balls of medium and the quick red streams of light automatic weapons, the Mobile Fleet was putting up in the failing half light, blues, yellows, pinks, reds, whites and even lavenders in bursting shells and ropes of tracer. Some heavy bursts threw out light red sparks at the heads of white phosphorus streamers. It was magnificent. It was beautiful. And it was all meant to kill U. S. Navy aviators. Pilots and crewmen strained their necks and their eyes, looking at the same time for targets in the dusk below the fireworks, and Zekes in the clear sky above. Almost before they were ready, the Big E's planes were over *Ryujo* at 12,000 feet, and six Zekes which had been cruising along well off to the right, peeled off to attack. Jig Ramage split his perforated dive flaps, pulled up, winged over and gentled his SBD into its familiar 70-degree lunge, and one after the other his division followed, each Dauntless rolling into its dive just as the one ahead dropped its nose. Killer Kane took his four Hellcats down ahead of the bombers, dropping fast into the tracer-laced twilight as though, personally, with his six .50-calibers, he was going to strafe down the Mobile Fleet. At 5,000 feet he opened with all six and swept the expanding deck below from stern to bow for the four to five seconds it took to swoop through 2,500 feet. Wolf, Marks and Farmer, in quick succession, also raked the narrow deck, seeing it begin to smoke and jagged chunks fly up, and then, as they pulled off fast to the eastward through the incredible streaming and bursting of the AA, the 1,000 pounders began to fall. There were four very close misses, a hung bomb and a hit. "Ack-ack" Schaal, diving last, put his semiarmor-piercing 1,000-pounder through the aft port corner of the deck. Flame and smoke spurted from the hit. The six Zekes made timid, hesitant runs, pulling out as soon as the rear gunners opened up, but they followed and passed the SBDs in their dives and were there, waiting, on the pull-out.

Van Eason's TBFs followed the bombers down. Each one carried four 500-pound general-purpose bombs. The Avengers had no dive flaps, and, to keep from building up to dangerously high speeds, they normally started their attacks from 8,000 feet, dropping at 5,000 and pulling out at 4,000. But this time, caught at 12,000 feet over the enemy carriers the whole Navy had been out to get for years, with darkness falling, not a drop of gas to waste, the AA flashing and puffing around them, and the beautiful, deadly Zekes beginning their runs, there was nothing to do but push over and go down. And down they went—Eason, Doyle, Lawton, Collins and Cummings, in that order.

Eason's heavy TBF, even throttled way back, hurtled through 6,000 feet at 330 knots, well above the builder's recommended maximum speed, but he held its nose down in the 50-degree dive to 3,500, sighting carefully on the narrow deck which tried to skid out from under him, and let his four bombs go.

Joe Doyle reported later that "when Eason wobbled his wings and turned left, I looked down and saw we were right on top of two carriers. We were out after carriers, so without looking for details I pulled up in a wing-over to the left and went down on the nearest one. . . ." He dived more steeply than Eason, and saw Aubrey Fife's 1,000-pounder throw up its fountain close to the violently turning carrier's starboard beam, and then two smaller splashes from Eason's bombs angling in to the portside. Eason saw

the same two and both he and Doyle agreed that the other
two bombs had to have entered the ship. Doyle released at
4,500 feet and pulled out straight up the deck. Looking
back, he saw two splashes ahead of the target as his gunner
reported two hits on the bow.

Ernie Lawton followed Doyle right down the fore-and-
aft axis of the ship in a dive so steep and fast that the suddenly changing pressure blew in the glass in his canopy with
a loud report exactly like the AA hit he was expecting. The
flight deck squirmed beneath him and spat up at the
plunging Avenger. At 5,500 feet he was over 350 knots,
beyond which pieces begin to come off a TBF, and he released at 5,000 and pulled out to the east. Two of his bombs
hit close on the starboard bow, the fourth as close to port,
and the third, which would have been on the deck, failed to
leave its shackle in the bomb bay.

Crossbow Collins, before he rolled into his dive, wit-
nessed Schaal's hit on the fantail, Eason's near misses to
port and debris flying from the target's portside, evidently
from Van Eason's other bombs. Collins' bombs walked
across the ship from starboard to port just forward of the
tiny island, one in the water on each side and the two
middle ones on deck near the forward elevator.

Ralph Cummings was the last *Enterprise* plane to dive
on *Ryujo*. Halfway down he found that his bomb bay had
not opened. He pulled out momentarily, opened it, and
resumed his dive. When he released at 5,000, only three of
his bombs left the bay. Two were off to port. The third may
have hit.

Ten miles to the north, while the TBFs were finishing their
high-speed overhead runs on *Ryujo*, Lou Bangs, with
Tommy Harman's Hellcats strafing ahead, was hanging in
his seat belt over *Junyo*. Tip Mester followed closely behind
Bangs and "Hound Dog" Lewis rode Mester's tail. All
three SBDs strafed all the way down and dropped their
1,000-pounders in succession at 2,000 feet. Bangs hit on the
extreme aft end of the deck, blowing half a dozen parked
planes overboard. Mester's bomb hit just forward of
Bangs', and Lewis' landed on the starboard edge of the
deck just abaft the island. "A sheet of flame enveloped the
side of the ship."

"Grube" Grubiss and his wingman had near misses on
Hiyo, which was under torpedo attack by Avengers from
other carriers, and *Enterprise* had shot her bolt.

Now all that her airmen had to do was evade the fantastic, Fourth of July AA and the vengeful Zekes, find their way 300 miles home and land aboard in the darkness on whatever fumes might by that time be left in their tanks.

All five of Eason's Avengers encountered Zekes. Hughes, in Eason's turret, shot one down which attacked on the pull-out, with a long burst into its upturned belly as it banked away after a stern attack. Hamilton, Ernie Lawton's gunner, drove off another with a damaging series of hits in its right wing and fuselage, and Collins' turret gave him another burst when he tried a second run. The other brushes were less serious. Bangs and Mester recovered to the westward and had to fly back through the AA across the enemy force to get home. It seemed that the five-minute flight took an hour and then with the AA behind them they were jumped by a flight of Zekes. One holed Mester's wing with his 20-millimeter and peppered the engine with 7.7s but the sturdy Dauntless kept going and the combined fire of the two twin 30s held the others off.

In addition to their strafing attacks on the enemy carriers, Kane's twelve fighters, while protecting their shipmates, destroyed seven Zekes. They would have killed more if the Japanese fighters had pressed their attacks. But Kane, like Mitscher with his amphibious forces, was charged with the protection of the bombers and torpedo planes and could not press the attack. He weaved overhead, turning into each Zeke attack which then immediately broke off.

As the *Enterprise* strike pulled away, intact except for Bangs and Mester who went home independently, and John Turner, who was shot down by two Zekes in an overhead pass and ditched, they could see smoke rising from half a dozen ships, thick and black over the tankers to the south, thinner and grayer over the still-wriggling capital ships to the north and west. All around them, other groups at various altitudes were also heading into the darkening eastern sky, and the air was full of anxious voices discussing battle damage, headings and especially fuel quantity remaining.

Three hundred miles to the eastward TF 58 steamed to meet the strike groups at 20 knots, its radars probing the darkening sky ahead, not for enemies this time, but for the familiar shapes of friendly aircraft bearing faces and voices known to the men who watched the scopes.

In *Enterprise*, Tom Hamilton, Dick Poor, Bud Schumann and Bill Martin congregated in Air Plot to listen to the speakers and receive the radar reports. Mat Gardner sat in his tall chair on the portside of the bridge, his binoculars around his neck, staring out ahead and waiting, his beaked and angular profile looking from the interior gloom of the bridge like a plucked hawk. Stern, stocky Black Jack Reeves walked the flag bridge one level above Gardner, pausing at the forward edge to look into the still dimly lighted sky to the westward.

In CIC, ready rooms, wardrooms, chief's quarters, berthing spaces, in aerology, the radio shack, on the hangar deck, all through the ship the men waited.

The first news was good—hits on four carriers. But that didn't get the strike group home.

By eight o'clock it was dark, and the only contact with the attack group was an occasional and not very encouraging radio transmission from one pilot to another.

At 8:24 radar made initial contact with the first returning planes 124 miles northwest. *Enterprise* and other carriers launched fully fueled night fighters to guide them in.

But the shipboard radars were far better than anything even a torpedo plane could bring into the air. The bunched and blacked-out planes, radios tuned for maximum reception, volume full up and earphones pressed against the operator's heads, heard nothing yet—not even the directionally coded ZB which would give them a homeward heading. In the radar-equipped TBFs, each radarman hunched over his gear, tuning and retuning, searching the scope behind the sweeping strobe for the first blob of light that would mean the task force and the deck and the ready room and coffee and a shower and a clean bunk and oblivion. They had been flying in solid darkness for the past half hour and their gas gauges were close to empty on their last tanks.

After the long flight, after the AA and the Zekes, now in the darkness, nearly out of fuel above the empty mid-Pacific, many of the pilots became desperate, and the air was full of calls to anyone for help. "Can anyone tell me where I am?" "Give me a vector. Can anyone give me a vector?" Others were calmer.

"Hey, Joe, how much gas you got left?"

"About a gill."

"I've got about two gills. How about you, Tom?"

"It reads five gallons less than empty."

"Let's put 'em down together while we still have power."

And the planes began to go down. The pilots realized that their chances of ditching successfully at night were far better if they still had power with which to control their planes, and, when the fuel gauges read zero and no ships were yet in sight, they began to land. One group of SB2C Helldivers ditched in formation and lashed their rafts together.

Most continued eastward.

At around forty-five miles, VT-10's Avengers began to receive the Big E's radar beacon, and at thirty-five, her homing signals began to beep faintly in their earphones.

At about 8:45, what looked to the men on deck like moving stars before they heard the high engines, were the leaders of the returning strike. The carriers swung into the wind and called the planes down, but in the moonless night one ship looked like another on the black face of the sea, and the first planes circled, groping, while others droned in, in sections and divisions from the westward. Only a few lucky or exceptionally skillful ones were getting aboard. The sky overhead filled up. Engines coughed, cut out, ran again and stopped and minutes later splashes tore the sea around the force.

The biggest disaster in the history of aviation was in the making. The pilots needed lights. But there was a war on in the Pacific. Enemy snoopers were in the air. Enemy subs had to be around. There were between 300 and 400 men total, in the circling 200 aircraft overhead and inbound. One torpedo spread could sink a carrier with 50 planes and 2,500 men aboard. Logic demanded that the ships stay darkened and the airmen land as best they could. Destroyers could pick most of them up in the morning.

Aboard the *Lexington,* slim, taut, wrinkled Pete Mitscher slipped down from his chair where he had been facing aft, watching and listening, and walked through the blackout curtains into Flag Plot, blinking at the sudden light. He perched on the extreme end of the long, brown leather couch, lit a cigarette, squinted up at Captain Arleigh Burke, and said four words: "Turn on the lights."

Mitscher, who had been flying planes since the early powered kites whose ailerons he had had to work with his shoulders, could not let his pilots down. He took the chance that no Russian, no Chinese or Japanese or German admiral would have taken.

Task Force 58 sprang out of the darkness as though a

ceremonial master switch had illuminated a World's Fair.
Thirty-six-inch and twenty-four-inch searchlights poked
bright vertical fingers into the sky. Red truck lights glowed
in pairs at the mastheads. The carriers turned on their deck-
edge lights, and destroyers fired star shells which broke and
drifted down, lighting up the sea for a mile in all directions.

Seldom have four words made a man so beloved by so
many.

The urgent, empty planes began to land, but the lights
could not make it day, nor put fuel back into empty tanks,
nor even show which carrier was which, nor certainly dis-
tinguish a carrier from a battleship or from a destroyer in
the tired eyes of a young pilot.

Confusion still ruled the night sky over TF 58. Planes
cut each other out, crowding in to land on any empty deck.
There were looming, rushing near collisions that left both
pilots angry and shaken. Planes made approaches to battleships and destroyers. In the hurry and fatigue there were
bad landings which fouled the desperately needed decks so
that planes, which could otherwise have landed, ran out of
fuel and ditched.

Larry Stevens' flight-deck crew worked like grimy de-
mons, disengaging planes and rushing them forward so
that the two or three in the groove would have a chance to
land. Larry needed all the strength and endurance and determination that had made him an All-American tackle at
USC to carry him through that incredible evening. Dick
Poor's voice on the bull horn was never satisfied. "Bear a
hand with that F6!" "For Christ's sake, get that turkey
forward!" "Tell that hook man to get the lead out!" Dick
had been pilot and squadron commander long enough to
know exactly what went on in those darkened cockpits
droning up the Big E's wake.

Hod Proulx, who had flown SBDs aboard *Enterprise*
himself as a pilot in Bombing Six, picked up each plane
with his paddles and brought him in hopefully until, at the
last minute, if the deck was clear, he could cut him or, if
it was foul, wave him off. Hod forgave a lot of bad approaches that night, giving cuts whenever it seemed halfway safe for the pilot and the ship. Once on that frantic
evening, two planes flopped down out of the lonely dark
onto the Big E's deck within fifteen seconds of each other.
Hod had cut Tommy Harman's F6 and it had caught the
fifth and next to the last wire, well up the deck. Tommy,

indescribably glad to be home (and that night *Enterprise*
was as truly home to her returning airmen as anywhere on
earth would ever be), realized the necessity of clearing the
deck for the next plane and taxied forward with a burst of
throttle. But his hook caught and the F6 stopped, still in
the landing area. Walt Chewning, responsible for arresting
gear as well as catapults, sprang out of the catwalk and
dived under the Hellcat's tail to help the plane director un-
hook it. Close behind Harman was Tip Mester's SBD,
burning its last fluid ounces of fuel after Lou Bangs, the
flight leader, had already run out and ditched. Hod either
thought his deck was clear, as it would have been without
the unexpected delay, or decided that Harman was far
enough up on the deck, and Mester low and slow enough
to land short without a collision. He cut Mester, and the
Dauntless caught the third wire. Chewning, working under
the Hellcat's tail in the darkness, the slip stream and the
engine noise, glanced back in time to see Mester's spinning
prop rushing up behind him. He leapt clear. Hod Proulx
and all concerned had somehow survived the famous
"double cut."

The first plane to land on *Enterprise,* an SB2C, fired its
fixed guns on touch-down, the startling red tracers lighting
up the deck on which, in the same second, every man lay
flat. There were no casualties. The first four TBFs to come
aboard were from *Hornet, Yorktown* and *Bunker Hill.*
Then a *Lexington* SBD missed the last wire, bounced off
the barrier and into the island. In a nearly miraculous ten
minutes, during which more of the circling planes overhead
used the last of their fuel and landed in the sea, the flight-
deck crew untangled the wreckage and shoved it overboard. The pilot and gunner were uninjured. After another
frantic twenty minutes of landings, with the lookouts almost continuously reporting planes and life rafts and lights
and whistles in the water on both sides, Joe Doyle brought
his heavy Avenger in for a perfect landing—and his
wheels folded on touch-down. It took another ten minutes
to push T-49 over the side, and more planes which could
have come aboard were forced into the sea.

And if there were confused U. S. pilots in the air that
night, there was one Japanese who personified confusion in
its ultimate degree. *San Jacinto,* at the peak of the evening,
reported that an enemy plane had flown through the vertical beam of her searchlight. Minutes later Hod Proulx

picked up a plane with his paddles which answered all his signals in reverse—going higher on a "high" signal, faster on a "fast" and so on—standard Japanese procedure. After the third wave-off, Hod flashed a light on him to assure that his hook was down and gasped to see the red "meatballs" on the wings. Walt Chewning, farther up the deck, had the same startling view. Lou Bangs, after a wave-off and just before he ditched, flashed past the stranger close enough to recognize an enemy.

At quarter past ten, Hod Proulx cut the last of twenty-three planes to land on the Big E that night. Only six were her own, out of a strike of twenty-eight.

All night, in the silent syllables of hooded, amber flashing lights, some direct, some relayed half a dozen times, the news came in of the others. Ernie Lawton and his crew were aboard the *Princeton*, the last plane she was able to take, after being cut out over *Lexington* and finding a foul deck on *Enterprise*. Five of the bombers were aboard the *Wasp*, two on *Yorktown* and one on *Bunker Hill*. Jerry Wolf, Mo Marks, Chuck Farmer and Jay Shinneman had found their way aboard the *San Jacinto*. Flash Gordon and Dick Mason were in *Lexington*.

There was no word on Eason, Collins, Cummings, Bangs or Killer Kane. It was known that John Turner was down near the scene of the strike.

By morning more messages were in. Lou Bangs and his gunner were aboard the *Cogswell* after being waved off because of a foul deck and running out of gas. Bangs had split his forehead on the sight in the water landing. Van Eason, after a near-collision, had run out of gas in the groove and he and his crew were also aboard the *Cogswell*. Crossbow Collins, after a pass at a destroyer and a foul-deck wave-off from *Enterprise*, had landed alongside the *Dortsch*. She had picked up all three men after they had watched their familiar Avenger sink out of sight far down in the clear sea with its white turtleback light still burning. When Crossbow returned, he said there had been minor difficulties after the ditching:

"My gunner opened the life raft compartment from the portside and I opened it from the starboard. He pulled the life raft out and I pulled the emergency kit out. We had a line connecting the two, and a tug of war took place until I finally gave in and pushed the emergency kit back through the compartment."

Ralph Cummings was waved off the Big E, and headed for what he thought was another carrier, but turned out to be the cruiser *Baltimore*. He ran out of gas alongside, landed nicely, and *Baltimore* rescued him and his crew.

There was still no news of Killer Kane.

All night the destroyers, released from screening duties by Mitscher in another "to hell with the Japs, let's take care of our own" order, fished sodden aviators out of the Pacific, and then, near dawn, TF 58 left any remaining rescue work to seaplanes, and headed west again to finish the Mobile Fleet.

Bill Martin had not taken part in the *Enterprise* strike because he was scheduled to lead every available TBF in his squadron on a night attack on the Mobile Fleet.

At thirty minutes past midnight on the twenty-first, Torpedo Ten gathered in Ready Room Number Six for the final briefing. Pilots and crewmen entered the latest data on their chartboards and Martin ran over the planned tactics once more. Truk lagoon had proved the value of minimum-altitude night radar bombing of ships—but that had been against moored or anchored merchantmen in harbor. Here, now, was a chance to hit the Japanese Fleet itself with this new weapon—with the eye of radar to pierce the darkness and the clouds, and with trained and proficient instrument pilots to skim in out of the darkness at masthead height and smash the unexpected enemy warships. With luck, as much damage could be done by one skillful and determined squadron, sheltered by darkness, unopposed by fighters and with the advantage of surprise, as had been done by the massive daylight strike of late afternoon.

The original plan had been to launch two snoopers at 10:00 P.M. and follow in four hours with the night attack group. But the chaos of recovering the afternoon strike forced a delay and at about 1:00 A.M., with the first two Avengers spotted on the catapults, Mitscher canceled the strike.

Though the cancellation saved VT-10 a long and hazardous flight, and probably saved the lives of several crews, there was genuine, heartfelt disappointment in the squadron ready room. Bill Martin was silent, and as near to tears as a grown man and a combat squadron commander can permit himself to get.

At 2:30, Bob Nelson and Jim Moore, who had found the

Mobile Fleet in the first place, were catapulted to find it again after the maneuvers of the night. They located it by radar at 5:30, and by 6:00 A.M. they were over the center of a huge diamond formed by the four enemy task groups, dodging in and out of clouds and steadily broadcasting position, course, speed, composition, disposition and anything else of interest that six pairs of sharp eyes could see in the early morning light. They stayed there for an hour and landed back aboard eight full hours after takeoff.

Nelson and Moore's report showed the enemy force 360 miles from TF 58, beyond effective strike range, and Admiral Spruance ordered his ships west to close the distance. But they were delayed by the necessity to fuel destroyers, and by the air operations required to re-establish the various air groups on their home carriers, and Ozawa drew steadily away. Two search strikes, including one of 29 planes from the Big E, failed to find any Japanese cripples, and at sunset on the twenty-first, TF 58 turned back east, and the Battle of the Philippine Sea was over.

Although the enemy had been turned back with heavy losses from his attempt to disrupt the occupation of the Marianas, there was a feeling of sadness and disappointment in *Enterprise*. The Japanese fleet had at last come out of hiding to fight and it had escaped the destruction which would have cleared the way to Japan. Six of the nine carriers and all the big battleships and the cruisers would have to be taken on somewhere else, at some later date, because the fast carriers of TF 58 had been tethered, committed to the defense of the invasion forces on Saipan, unable to run free and to close and strike.

And the Big E's air group commander, big, aggressive Killer Kane was still missing and hope was beginning to weaken.

All day the twenty-first, *Enterprise* was a floating dormitory. Throughout the ship, dirty, bearded, exhausted men slept on the deck, in corners, in gun tubs, on top of ready ammunition lockers, in the catwalks. For two full days they had worked around the clock, fighting off the enemy attack and then launching and recovering their own, eating battle rations at their stations, and now, with the action over, they simply slept, as tired young men can do, wherever they happened to find room.

On the twenty-second, a sweep of 17 SBDs of Bombing Ten found dozens of yellow Mae Wests and life rafts, all empty, abandoned by their owners at the time of rescue.

In the afternoon *Enterprise* fueled from *Lackawanna,* and when carrier and tanker had separated, a destroyer came slicing up over the horizon, her signal searchlight blinking as soon as it was readable from the Big E. One by one, the Morse characters flashed in and "B. J." Oglesby, the Big E's leading signalman, opened his shutter after each word and repeated it aloud to the striker recording at his side.

"How . . . much . . . ice cream . . ." he read slowly, ". . . is . . . Killer"—and he held his light open, knowing what would come—"Kane . . . worth?"

The rough, penciled message was rushed to the officer of the deck, who called Tom Hamilton, and when the loudspeakers repeated it all through the big, tough, veteran ship, a yell of joy and relief and pride went up. Within the hour, Killer, grinning at the noisy welcome, his head rebandaged and his eyes reblacked, came dipping across on the high line and scrambled out of the breeches buoy onto the Big E's fantail. He had returned direct to *Enterprise* after the evening strike, made an approach, been waved off because of a foul deck, and, exhausted, after ten hours of flight that day, and not fully recovered from his head injuries, had simply flown into the water off the port bow of *Enterprise,* slamming his wounded head once more into the gunsight. "Everyone else," he told Tom Hamilton, "was running out of gas. I just ran out of altitude."

On the evening of the twenty-third, John Turner was returned aboard after twenty-four hours in his raft at the strike scene. He was the last. The score was in. *Enterprise* claimed ten direct hits on two carriers and twelve Japanese planes shot down. She had lost five planes (only one in action) and not a single man. She also, of the fifteen carriers in TF 58, had located the enemy fleet, enabling Mitscher to launch his strike at the only time it was in range, and then relocated and tracked it the next morning.

The force as a whole had not done as well: 100 of the 216-plane strike were lost, 20 in combat and 80 from fuel exhaustion and landing accidents. But of the 209 men in those 100 planes, all but 49 survived. Total U. S. killed on the second, the offensive day of this greatest carrier battle of the war, was 55, including two officers and four men of the flight-deck crews lost in deck crashes during the night recovery.

Rescue efforts were so successful that Bill Martin recommended in his action report that task group commanders consider the deliberate use of formation ditchings in situations where the enemy can be reached in no other way.

Admiral Ozawa made port at Okinawa with three carriers, two fleet tankers, 426 planes and about 445 aviators fewer than he had when he sortied against Spruance and Mitscher.

Task Force 58, the threat of serious interference over, went back to complete the job in the Marianas.

For two more weeks, *Enterprise* cruised off the islands, fighting off occasional light attacks by small groups of Sallys, Kates and Bettys, and launching daily "milk runs" to keep the airfields on Guam neutralized.

Chick Harmer's night fighting F4Us shot down four bombers on two busy nights, two of the enemy planes falling in bright orange balls of flame in plain sight of the Big E's cheering topside watchstanders and spectators.

On one of the milk runs, Benny Sablan, who had lived to see his Pearl Harbor prediction that "we catch him [the Japanese] and give him hell" come true many times, flew over his native Guam, circling his home at low altitude after the years of war and separation. But the landings on Guam were not scheduled until mid-July.

On the fifth of July, Air Group Ten flew its last combat mission from the *Enterprise,* burning the town of Agat on Guam, evacuated by the Guamanians and occupied only by Japanese military installations. When the strike returned overhead, nothing could restrain the pilots who had faced so many grim days and survived so much AA, so many fighters, such difficult operating conditions, from expressing their delight in their survival and the almost incredible prospect of a quick return to the States. F6Fs, SBDs and TBFs rolled and looped and tumbled and flew inverted overhead, and radio discipline was lost completely for several minutes until Admiral Reeves himself called off the air show. *Enterprise* tied up at Ford Island at 5:00 P.M. on the fifteenth of July, 1944.

In the six months between the sailing of *Enterprise* from Pearl Harbor and her return, the Empire of Japan had lost, to her alone, 19 ships, 300 aircraft, and shore installations impossible to estimate, but such as could be smashed with 1,000 tons of well-placed bombs across the whole blue curve of the Pacific.

"Enterprise" *had one summer month in Pearl. It was* no holiday; it was not even peaceful. But it was a recess from action and the imminence of action. It was a month of transition.

On July 16, 1944, the first morning in port, the carrier and the air group she had carried for six months were separated again—this time for good. The Big E and Air Group Ten would not meet again. But they had done well enough together. In the six months that the old Air Group Ten was embarked, *Enterprise,* frequently alone, had been the key to the successful defense of Guadalcanal and the Solomons. When she arrived off Santa Cruz in October of 1943, the Japanese were vigorously on the offensive and in at least partial control of the seas around the Solomons. When she steamed back to Oahu in the spring they had evacuated Guadalcanal and were withdrawing under fire up the island chain they had just come down.

When the second Air Group Ten came aboard in December of the same year, Japan held the whole central Pacific as far east as the Marshalls. Now there was no effective enemy force in those latitudes east of Palau. The perimeter of the Japanese Empire had been shoved westward as far as Pearl Harbor is west of San Francisco.

When the Hellcats, Dauntlesses, Avengers and night-flying Corsairs of Air Group Ten flew off for the last time, and the remaining pilots and gunners and radiomen and mechanics filed down the gangway with their gear, it was as though the sixteen-inch triple turrets of a battlewagon had been hoisted out and taken away and all the gunner's mates, fire controlmen, turret officers, pointers, trainers and ammunition handlers had followed them ashore. *Enterprise* was once more without her main battery, an incomplete warship.

Air Group Ten, after a few hectically happy days ashore, boarded an escort carrier and cruised to San Francisco, loafing happily, eating steaks two and three times a day and congratulating each other on having been assigned to the Big E with her long, stable deck instead of the bobbing postage stamp of the CVE. At the Alameda Naval Air Station, across the bay from San Francisco, the torpedo and bombing pilots gave a "beer bust" in honor of the fighters in grateful recognition of the fact that not a single *Enterprise* aircraft had been lost to enemy fighters while under the protection of the Grim Reapers of Fighting Ten.

In Pearl the ship acquired a new paint job—a dazzling, scientifically random patchwork of black, dark gray and light gray, designed to confuse the observer as to her direction and identity.

On the sixteenth of August the long and familiar ritual of preparation for sea was repeated—boilers lighted off, gyros started, radars turned on and checked out, shore connections servered. Again, following the shrilling bosun's pipe, came the order, "Now go to your stations all the special sea details." Bridge, fo'c'sle, fantail, engine and firerooms, CIC, directors, line-handling stations all along the side were manned and reported in by sound-powered phone. The officer of the deck moved to the bridge. Rudder and engine order telegraphs were tested. Each department head reported his department ready for getting under way. Small gray tugs with low stems and high "puddined" bows stood by, and at two minutes after 7:00 A.M. the jack at the bow and the ensign at the stern dropped, the small steaming colors soared to the truck and *Enterprise* was under way, headed back to the war for which she had been created.

It was 2,400 miles and eight days to the mid-ocean anchorage of Eniwetok in the Western Marshalls. They were eight days of hard work, with nearly continuous drills beginning with morning and ending with evening General Quarters. Commander Daniel Fletcher Smith worked out the 32 fighters, 20 bombers (SB2C Helldivers this time in place of the familiar Dauntlesses) and 16 torpedo planes of his Air Group Twenty with simulated attacks on the little task group, bombing and strafing towed sleds, while aboard ship search and fire-control radars tracked the mock attackers, CIC vectored fighters out to meet them, guns followed their movements according to automatic signals received from the computers below, and the new captain, Cato D. Glover, maneuvered his ship to spoil the pilots' aim.

Eniwetok was a circular fringe of coral reef and islets, protecting a huge lagoon from the Pacific ground swell. It was also the shallow crater of a mid-Pacific volcano around the rim of which the myriad little coral animals had built islands with their limey skeletons. More importantly to the U. S. Navy, it was a calm and spacious anchorage, 2,400 miles closer to the enemy than Pearl, where fleets could rest and reprovision and make repairs. Under the equatorial sun the wind was steady, the sky and the sea clear blue. On Eniwetok itself and the other tiny islands, the stripped and battered palms made a sparse irregular fence around the anchorage.

Enterprise was there four days, and sailed on the twenty-eighth of August with the newest Pacific Fleet carrier *Franklin*, the CVL *San Jacinto*, two cruisers and a destroyer screen, for the Bonin Islands, 500 miles south and slightly east of Tokyo.

On the afternoon of the thirty-first of August, just fifteen days out of Pearl Harbor, *Enterprise* launched 28 fighters and 12 bombers against Chichi Jima in the Bonins, and Air Group Twenty was in action for the first time.

The Bonins are not atolls but small, irregular volcanic lumps poking rocky cliffs up out of the Pacific. There are few beaches and harbors, and the islands have a barren, inhospitable look even in the bright sunlight of a summer afternoon. Since *"jima"* is Japanese for "island," that is the second part of each island's name. Chichi, Ani and Ototo lie in a single group and farther to the south is Haha. Close by to the southward are the Volcanos, with Iwo, for which the lives of 5,000 U. S. Marines would soon buy immortality.

The Big E's forty aircraft, plus a couple of cruiser float planes for rescue work, came straight into the Bonins from their launching position 138 miles southeast. The craggy little islands were dark on the horizon at twenty-five miles, and the SB2Cs of Bombing Twenty added power and began their climb to attack altitude.

Most of the civilization on Chichi Jima borders the harbor of Futami Ko, which looks as if it had been formed by bending down a long northern peninsula into a short hook to the west and south. The harbor opens to the west, with the end of the hook and a small westerly cape on either side of the entrance. At the base of the small cape was Susaki, the island's only airfield. Across the harbor entrance to the north was a seaplane base, and up in the northeast corner of Futami Ko, a small naval base.

At three o'clock on that Thursday afternoon in August, Commander Fred Bakutis' twenty-eight Hellcats angled down out of the summer sky and turned loose the big rockets under their wings. When the rockets had streaked out ahead, leaving the blue fighters halfway down a double track of smoke, they opened up with the .50-calibers, raking and ripping at the three targets on the shores of Futami Ko.

While enemy AA gunners ran, or ducked out of the diagonally pelting bullets and the hiss and boom of the rockets, Commander Emmett Riera's "raggedy-ass raiders," of Bombing Twenty, followed vertically down on the same targets in their heavy SB2Cs with 500-pound bombs and new "package" .50-caliber guns in wing racks.

It was all over in one pass. Chichi was not much of a threat to U. S. plans in the Pacific. There were no aircraft on Susaki field and no shipping of any importance in Futami Ko. The bombs, bullets and rockets chewed into hangars, repair shops, runways and warehouses, drastically reducing the ability of those installations to support any planes or ships which might later arrive. Enemy gunners got back into action when the strafers had passed over, and hit several planes in the pull-out. One SB2C was hit in the engine and ditched to seaward. Two OS2Us from *New Orleans*, with fighter escort circling protectively, landed and rescued both pilot and gunner. They were back aboard *Enterprise* before dark.

The Air Group Twenty planes, with the white triangles on their tails, rendezvoused to the westward, and hit Haha Jima on the way home. Just north of Haha, the Hellcats worked over a Japanese subchaser with their machine guns and left her burning and settling in a white patch of foam from the .50-calibers.

Again on the first and the second of September the Big E's task group hit the Bonins with Chichi as the primary target and Haha to the south and Ani to the north as secondary. On each of the days *Enterprise* launched four strikes, several photo flights, provided antisub patrols and flew CAP over *New Orleans* and *Biloxi*, which had moved in close to add their flat-trajectory eight-inch and six-inch projectiles to the bombs and rockets of the planes.

Each night enemy snoopers probed the perimeter of the force but were never bold or skillful enough to penetrate and attack.

Old hands in *Enterprise* and her air group growled, during those days, that they were playing in the "minor leagues," hitting unimportant installations far away from the main action; because while they were striking the Bonins, the rest of the fast carriers were sweeping the Philippines, and radio reports said they had destroyed some 500 enemy planes in a single day.

But the decision to send *Enterprise* and *Franklin* and *San Jacinto* on a diversionary sweep against the Bonins was a good one. Those islands were closer to the Japanese home islands than anything that had been attacked before. A strike there, coupled with others in widely separated areas, tended to alarm the Japanese people and confuse their leadership. And both carriers needed the practice, needed their new air groups blooded against relatively light opposition so that that part would be over and so that they could settle down confidently to the more dangerous and important tasks which they would be assigned.

Early on Monday the fourth, *Enterprise* went once more through the familiar routine of fueling at sea, and, with her tanks topped off, anchored in the late afternoon in the newly captured harbor of Saipan in the Marianas.

The practice was just about over.

During the one night that *Enterprise* paused at Saipan, the watch could see the flare of lights and hear the irregular roaring of trucks and bulldozers, working without a minute's pause to prepare the captured airfields for the B-29 Superforts that would soon be making round trips to Japan on a schedule as solid and reliable as a well-run railroad.

Then the Big E had a schedule of her own to keep. The Palaus, 550 miles to the southwest, had been designated for amputation from the Japanese Empire. A-Day ("A" signifying an assault, not just a raid) was the fifteenth of September, and there was a lot of work to do, before, during and after the Marines hit the beaches of Peleliu.

On the way down to Palau, *Enterprise, Franklin* and *San Jacinto* worked over the already-battered island of Yap and the atolls of Ulithi and Ngulu to be certain that no support of any kind could come from them to the garrison at Palau.

They hit Yap first, early on the afternoon of September 6, with thirty-five Hellcats carrying rockets, fragmentation clusters and plenty of .50-caliber bullets. The island had been well plastered by the high-flying, long-range bombers of the Army Air Force but there were still a few buildings standing in Yap Town, including a radio and cable station, some intact gun positions and a few native huts, suspiciously isolated, which turned out to be made of concrete with apertures for machine guns.

Enterprise launched her fighters 170 miles northeast of the target and they circled the island to attack from the southwest out of the sun. "Dog" Smith led one four-plane division, Fred Bakutis another and Joe Lawler followed with three planes. Behind them were two two-plane sections. It was a routine neutralization strike. The airfields had long been out of commission. No fighter opposition, very little AA. A milk run.

Bakutis pushed over from 8,000 feet, his three planes spread out a little but close behind him. The next minute Dog Smith, already in his dive, noticed something wrong with the last plane in Bakutis' division. Lieutenant (j.g.) Harry Brown's F6 was in a fast but shallow dive, with heavy black smoke pouring out behind it. It stayed in that unnatural maneuver until it hit the barren terrain just west of Yap Town and exploded, scattering flaming wreckage for half a mile.

Lawler's three-plane division hit the push-over point right behind Smith and Bakutis. On his right wing was Joe Cox, on his left, Howard Holding. The three Hellcats nosed down and picked up speed, the altimeters unwinding, the wind noise increasing past their canopies. The pilots retrimmed with their left hands for the dive. Then Cox's plane suddenly turned left under Lawler's tail, toward Holding. For a minute Lawler lost sight of Cox. Then Cox and Holding were both in sight, both in tight, nose-down spirals from which neither recovered and neither bailed out. Either both had been hit by the same AA burst, or Cox had been hit and collided with Holding. The Yap milk run was only thirty seconds along.

On the morning of the seventh, in clear weather, with a few light puffs at 1,500 feet, eight bombers and six torpedo planes with 500-pound bombs joined six of VF-20's fighters for an attack on the guns that had been so deadly on the sixth. The rocketing fighters pressed their attacks low and close and no guns fired at the bombers that followed them in. The only incident of the flight was the loss of the whole right half of his tail section by Lieutenant Commander Sam Prickett, the skipper of the torpedo squadron. But Sam was cool and competent enough and the old Avenger sufficiently rugged to return and land aboard with no further damage.

The same day *Biloxi* and *New Orleans* moved in and slammed their six-inch and eight-inch projectiles flat across the sea and into the shore defenses around Yap Town.

Dog Smith experimented on Yap with a new weapon—a droppable belly tank filled with a clinging, penetrating, incendiary jelly called napalm, and equipped with an igniter to spread persistent fire over a wide area around the impact point. He found it to be effective for burning over a given area, but inaccurate because of the imprecise release mechanism of the tank, and unreliable. Only some 50 per cent of the tanks dropped and ignited.

By the afternoon of the eighth "all worth-while targets were considered to have been well covered," and the Big E's task group 38.4 fueled again on the ninth and steamed southeastward to attack Palau.

Enterprise had been to Palau before. Her men remembered the improbable name of the main island of Babelthuap, and Kossol Passage where Stubby Pearson died, and the airfields on Peleliu where Killer Kane's planes had burned the rows of Bettys, and over which they had won control of the island air.

The Japanese had never regained that control. For a solid week the Big E steamed in the neat geometric formations of her task group and hurled her aircraft at Palau. They bombed, strafed, rocketed and napalmed at will. Her fighters were not fighters but strafers, rocketers and light bombers, because there was nothing in the air to fight. Not a single Japanese aircraft was left. The enemy soldiers could see no farther than the top of the tallest tree on the highest of the island's low ridges, could strike no farther than the range of their biggest gun. They were moles, burrowing to escape the eagle sweeping at will through the wide sky above them.

But the Japanese moles were not defenseless, and the eagle far from invulnerable, and when the exterminators landed to dig out the moles it was hard and bloody work.

The enemy knew that the favorite prey of the blue planes was ships, ships which could reinforce, resupply or evacuate. So he set airplane traps baited with ships.

The eight bombers, eight fighters, seven torpedo planes of the Big E's first strike, operating with twelve fighters from *Franklin,* were briefed that enemy shipping in the Koror-Malakal harbor area, just south of Babelthuap, was the primary target. They swept in their echelons over the wide, green islands at daylight on the tenth, and through the clear, dawn air below the cumulus bases, found a destroyer and an armed cargo ship lying close in to the wooded shores. The fighters with their rockets, the bombers with 1,000-pounders, and the TBFs with 500s peeled off for a coordinated attack. As soon as the first aircraft was well committed in its dive, the ships and the woods on all the surrounding islands began to smoke and sparkle with automatic weapons fire. Lead laced back and forth across the attacking formations, licked up at wings and engines and cockpits. Dog Smith's pilots and gunners returned the fire. The big rockets hissed down trailing smoke, the .50-calibers chattered, chewing up the water, the woods and the target ships. The big bombs blasted beautifully. But nothing happened. The ships could not sink. They were already sunk, resting on the bottom in the shallows, holed and finished by previous attacks, now only machine-gun nests and AA emplacements ringed by other machine-gun nests and AA emplacements. The airplane trap had sprung, and it caught Hoot Gibson, the executive officer of Bombing 20.

Hoot's SB2C pulled up steeply after dropping its bomb, and winged over to the right with flames pouring from its belly. As the air group commander watched with a leaden stomach, one parachute blossomed and the Helldiver dived into the lagoon and disappeared. While the rest of the attack group bored in again, strafing the nearly invisible gun positions, Dog Smith and his wingman, disregarding almost continuous enemy fire, dived for the surface and swept back and forth across the scene of the crash looking for the survivor. He was not there. When Smith left, four Hellcats of another squadron continued the search. One was shot down but no survivor was found. For three days the dangerous waters were searched repeatedly without results. Lieutenant Commander George Davis Gibson and his gunner, Bernard Burbeck, were reported missing in action.

One of Bombing 20's Beasts had failed to release its bomb on the first attack, and the remaining seven planes turned back to deliver it, six of them covering the seventh by strafing the enemy gunners while the hung bomb was delivered. The attack worked well. Much of the ground firing stopped as the enemy crews left their guns or ducked behind their shielding. But Dave Hughes felt a slight jar and a small explosion behind him as he pulled his SB2C out of its strafing run. When he called his gunner to check the trouble, there was no answer and, when he joined up with the squadron, another plane signaled that the gunner appeared wounded and unconscious. Hughes flew home as straight and fast as his ungainly Beast would take him and made a single, straight-in approach and landing but it was no good. Young Wayne Waymack, right out of high school into the Navy a couple of years ago, was dead—shot through the head by a light Japanese antiaircraft gun.

On the next strike, that first bad morning for Air Group Twenty over Palau, the Big E's torpedo squadron lost three men and an Avenger to the Japanese airplane trap at Malakal Harbor.

For the next four days, *Enterprise* squadrons flew four deckload strikes a day against harbor and airfield installations, radio stations and fortifications of various kinds on Babelthuap, Peleliu and Anguar, the southernmost of the Palaus. On the twelfth, the underwater demolition teams arrived in their slim destroyer-transports, and Dog Smith's airmen, who by this time were convinced that theirs was a thoroughly hazardous occupation, re-evaluated their convictions at the sight of the near-naked swimmers working calmly in the clear water along the reefs, blasting passages in the coral, removing obstacles, detonating mines, while enemy guns of all calibers splashed in the sea around them. On that and succeeding days, the mission Air Group Twenty liked best was interfering with the guns that were interfering with the UDTs.

The battle of the eagle and the mole at Palau was different from any in which *Enterprise* had been involved before. The dug-in enemy was invisible, his weapons camouflaged, his equipment, if he had any, hidden. The only indication of his presence was the sudden, brown smoke from a hillside and the fall of shot around his targets offshore—or the flare and dark billowing of a fuel dump hit by a lucky bomb.

In order not to give away his gun positions to the ubiquitous and eager aircraft, the Japanese cut the ratio of tracer ammunition to ball, nearly to zero. Pilots reported no AA but returned aboard with holes in their planes.

On the morning of the fifteenth of September, D-Day, the Big E's first strike of twenty-six planes found the waters off the southwest coast of Peleliu crowded with transports and landing craft of every size and shape. The cruisers and destroyers that had been hammering the airfield area for three days were still at it, their projectiles roaring in over the heads of the Marines embarking for the assault. Thick clouds of dust and smoke towered over the beach from the explosions of the shells. But the bombardment had blown or burned away most of the natural and artificial camouflage ashore, and exposed targets for the first time. Air Group Twenty attacked block houses and gun positions with bombs and rockets, and the airmen felt the satisfaction of the certain knowledge that unknown numbers of U. S. Marines would be alive at the end of that day, who without their help would have died on the reef or in the shallows or on the beach.

As the long rows of amtracs began to churn in toward the beach, low, slow and heavy in the water with their loads of men and metal, the ships poured their projectiles into the ridges and woods once more and the LCI gunboats launched massed clouds of rockets over the heads of the first waves to saturate the landing area. Forty-seven planes from *Enterprise, Franklin* and *San Jacinto* dived through the brown dust cloud of the naval bombardment to put napalm rockets and bombs in the enemy-occupied woods just north of the airfield.

As the LVTs crawled up over the reef and headed ashore, the shallow protected waters of the lagoon boiled and spouted with enemy mortar, artillery and automatic weapons fire. It was incredible to the Big E's pilots that so much firepower could have survived the last four days of concentrated bombing, burning, rocketing and shelling. But the Japanese moles had dug deep into the limestone, connecting one gun position with another in a complex system of defense almost invulnerable from the air or sea, and now they wheeled out the guns they had been saving and poured fire into the lagoon and the beaches. Most of the first LVTs were hit, but succeeding waves avoided the wrecks and bored inland. Tanks were landed and more Marines, and the battle for Peleliu was on.

Enterprise flew six strikes, seven CAPs, an antisub patrol, an air coordinator mission and fueled a destroyer on D-Day. By sunset the Marines were well ashore and held most of the vital airfield which was their first objective.

The sixteenth began at 4:50 A.M., when another destroyer came alongside for fuel, and ended, after four strikes, two CAPs and another refueling, when the last night fighter of the twilight CAP landed just before 8:00 P.M.

On the seventeenth, Task Group 38.4 left support of the

troops on Peleliu to the escort carriers attached to the amphibious forces for that purpose, and headed south slowly, while the carriers and cruisers, having topped off the destroyers, now themselves fueled from the fleet tankers which appeared out of the endless Pacific to do the job.

Two days later, *Enterprise* crossed zero degrees of latitude, halfway between the poles, and slid down over the waistline of the earth into the southern hemisphere, passing in theory, at a computed instant, from late summer into late winter. Neptunus Rex, this time in the person of Chief Radioman D. C. Gensel, made his appearance, and the new carrier-load of pollywogs arduously and ridiculously became shellbacks at the hands of those who only eight months ago, en route from Pearl to the Marshalls with Air Group Ten, had undergone the same ordeal. Heads were clipped in weird designs with topknots, warlocks and miscellaneous tufts and toots. Bodies were painted with shoe polish and engine oil and dressed in bizarre imitations of female contours and costumes. Men were immersed, whacked on their bottoms, made to perform ignominious tasks and eat and drink highly unpalatable concoctions, but at last it was over, and in all of the big carrier's divisions, sections, watches and compartments, every man was a certified shellback, treasuring in his memory the things that had been done to him for later use on some future pollywog.

Early in the morning of September 21, *Enterprise* anchored with a splash and a long, heavy rattling of chain, in jungle-surrounded Seeadler Harbor at Manus in the Admiralty Islands, northwest of the Solomons. The spacious anchorage was crowded with ships, tankers, tenders, provision and ammunition ships, landing craft, minesweepers and low-silhouette destroyer-escorts fresh from the States.

It was hot and humid at Manus, barely south of the equator. It rained often and hard but the rain did not cool the heavy air.

Enterprise fueled, reprovisioned, rearmed and sent her officers and men ashore to the recreation island for up to six cans of cold beer each, softball and a swim. The recreation areas were incredibly crowded and unrelievedly hot during the day, so that khaki and chambray alike were solidly dark with sweat. There was a nearly continuous din of empty beer cans being hurled into trash cans and the shouts and curses and snatches of song of men working hard to have a good time. What little breeze came along brought with it an odor comprised of equal parts of rank tropical vegetation, beer and urine.

In the evenings at the small Officers' Club on the satellite island of Kuriat, it was better, with the night breeze and relief from the heavy sun, and the sound of the surf on the seaward beach.

Three days after her arrival, the Big E got under way again and turned her bow north in squally, rainy, overcast weather, with the other carriers, cruisers and destroyers of Task Group 38.4.

For a week the task group steamed off the Palaus, but took no part in the continuing action ashore. Ships and air groups worked out at battle problems in preparation for the more hazardous operations scheduled for the following weeks.

In the early days of October, a typhoon passed 300 miles north of the Big E's group and she operated in heavy, breaking seas under low clouds driven by winds that increased steadily, in one day, from 9 to 50 knots and then stayed over 25 knots for two more days while the typhoon churned northward toward Japan.

During that time the Big E did not seem herself to the men aboard. The normally steady or slowly rolling carrier now lurched and bucked like a wounded animal. Her long, dignified roll became a destroyer-like snap from far down to port to equally far down to starboard. Her gentle pitching turned into a sickening swoop and drop that left solid green water draining in cascades off the flight deck where no flying was even attempted. Food-heavy trays slid down the mess tables unless their users held them fast. Liquids spilled and left slick spots on the decks which caused other men to slip and spill more liquids. In the wardroom, fiddle-boards were rigged with holes for each dish and raised rims around each table, but the silver would get away and go half the length of the table, ringing and clattering as it hurdled the planted dishes. Soup was not served, but in the half-filled coffee cups, the level shifted precariously close to one edge and then the other. Men coming off watch tired and wet could only sleep on their stomachs gripping the thin mattresses with arms and feet and wedged motionless with pillows. Men who thought they were immune after months at sea found themselves weak and green with the real and unfunny misery of seasickness. It was a comfort to know, after a week, that the typhoon was over Japan, impartially causing equal discomfort to the enemy.

Just after noon on October 7, with the sea still running high in the wake of the typhoon, but with the dark clouds of the big storm's circular system spreading out and breaking up, *Enterprise* began to pick up the other groups of Task Force 38 on her radar: 38.1 (*Wasp, Hornet,* two CVLs and three cruisers) and 38.3 (*Essex, Lexington,* two CVLs, four battleships and four cruisers) to the south; 38.2 (*Intrepid, Hancock, Bunker Hill,* two CVLs, two battleships and five cruisers) to the west.

At evening twilight, when the Big E's navigator came out on the bridge with his sextant to try for the first good celestial fix in three days, Task Force 38, Fast Carriers, Pacific Fleet, was spread out across the disturbed sea west of the Marianas in one mighty and magnificent formation. It was probably the most powerful naval force that had ever sailed the oceans of the planet, and that is the way it looked. The big gray ships shouldered their way solidly through the heavy seas, the white water breaking at their bows and running aft in long scallops, the bright signal flags standing straight out in the wind, hooded lights flashing from the bridges and the evening CAP buzzing watchfully overhead. Nine big carriers and 8 light ones, 6 new battlewagons, 14 cruisers and 58 destroyers were in that formation. In tactical command was Marc Mitscher, and commanding the whole Third Fleet from the flag bridge of the *New Jersey* was an old friend of *Enterprise,* back in a sea command at last—Bill Halsey.

Such a force, commanded by such men, was capable of the boldest offensive actions that the boldest Allied planners could require. And some bold planning was well under way.

All day the eighth, the task force fueled, big ships fueling destroyers in the morning and themselves going alongside the tankers in the afternoon. *Enterprise* filled up *Swanson, McCall, Wilkes* and *Patterson* and then, in midafternoon, steamed slowly, closely parallel to *Marius* through seas that washed waist deep across the oiler's deck, knocking men down and threatening to disrupt the fuel lines, while the black Navy Special oil poured across and down into her feed and storage tanks.

Early on the ninth, the turbines on all the ships began to hum with a higher, louder note and their decks to vibrate as they worked up to 25 knots. All day and all night the thousand planes, the hundred barrels of heavy guns, the hundred thousand seamen, were moving into the heart of enemy-held waters at a hundred miles each watch.

Douglas MacArthur was coming back to the Philippines, and Halsey and Mitscher were preparing the way. Their orders were to "destroy enemy naval and air forces in or threatening the Philippine area."

The logical and systematic way to go about that job was to start with Okinawa just 500 miles south of Japan itself, then work over Formosa, between Okinawa and the northernmost Philippine island of Luzon, and move on the Philippines themselves.

At quarter of six in the morning on October 10, Task Force 38 went into action with a sweep of 130 Fighters over Okinawa. Less than 30 minutes behind the sweep came Strike Able, and reveille on Okinawa that morning was the whine of American aircraft engines, the crump of bombs, the heavy rattle of strafing and the flaring gasoline fires of burning Japanese planes and property.

Fred Bakutis brought his twelve planes in high, ready to fight the enemy CAP—but there was none. The enemy fighters had been caught on the deck. Fred dived steeply out of the low sun on the 80 to 100 planes that crowded the revetments and parking ramps at Naha Field. His Hellcats pointed their noses short of the field and then pulled them up at low altitude, shallowing their glides, but at very high speed, to rake the rows of planes with .50-caliber fire from 1,000 to 500 feet. A whole row of clean, new Tojo fighters were lined up ready for take-off when the strafing attack came in. None ever got off. Four exploded. The others flared and burned fiercely, crumpling to the concrete. On the parking ramps, twin-engine fighters and bombers were lined up wing tip to wing tip when the Hellcats found them and clawed them into smoke and flame with their converging streams of tracer. Fred Bakutis' pilots were only sorry they had no rockets for the bunched Japanese aircraft. They had expected air to air action, not air to ground.

But the fighters with Strike Able had rockets, and the SB2Cs and TBFs had bombs and torpedos for the ships anchored off Naha, and they used them well. Six out of nine torpedoes were hits, and a miss by the bombers was exceptional. With control of the air assured, they pressed their attacks in low and close through the frantic AA. On retirement, with bombs and torpedoes gone, the strike planes strafed and set other ships afire. A destroyer was reported to have rolled over smoking and gone down, hit by both bombs and torpedoes. Three big freighters burned and sank. Others blazed out of control.

All up and down the island of Okinawa and the Nansei Shoto chain, the carrier planes caught enemy air power on the ground and squashed it, then swept the bays and harbors, sinking ships, burning and blasting port facilities, warehouses and gun emplacements.

Enterprise flew three more deckload strikes that day and each had increasing difficulty finding its targets because of smoke from the fires set by its predecessors. Oil and ammunition dumps, barracks, hangars, docks, the town of Naha itself, went up in roaring explosions and clouds of smoke so dense it was difficult to assess the damage. But Dog Smith, circling the target area for two hours, found very little of military value left on Okinawa.

Not a single *Enterprise* aircraft was downed, not a single *Enterprise* airman lost or hurt over the Nansei Shoto that October 10.

On the midwatch, as the big, blacked-out ships slipped southwestward toward Formosa and the Philippines, bogies closed the force. Torpedo defense was sounded and the task groups tightened their rings and stood by their guns, zigzagging. But no attack developed, and all was quiet when the first watch was called.

All day the eleventh, TF 38 steamed slowly toward its next target, fueling and fighting off persistent Japanese snoopers. Around noon a sixty-plane strike was launched against Aparri, the most northerly airfield on Luzon, the most northerly of the Philippine Islands. *Enterprise* did not participate.

In the afternoon, three escort carriers, just visible on the eastern horizon, flew replacement planes to Mitscher's air groups to bring them to full strength for the coming action.

While TF 38 went about its routine business deep in enemy waters, the first elements of the invasion of the Philippines sortied from Manus and headed northwest for Leyte. It was A-Day minus 9.

As dusk closed in on the spread-out and battle-ready United States ships, so did the ubiquitous enemy snoopers.

Just before seven o'clock, Admiral Mitscher ordered night fighters launched, and *Enterprise* catapulted Commander Jim Gray (who had returned to the Big E with Air Group 20, commanding a detachment of four F6F-3 (N) Hellcat night fighters and the night-fighter squadron of which this detachment was a part) and his wingman, Ensign Ed Boudinot.

The two dark Hellcats, with bulbous radar housings faired into their right wings near the tips, spiraled up into the evening sky above the Big E's task group. For a few minutes they orbited, in contact with *Enterprise* CIC, awaiting instructions. In the Big E's island, radar operators and fighter director officers stood or perched on their high stools in the dark, watching the bright lines sweep around the scopes, marking each dim blob with a grease-pencil cross as the sweep re-established it, connecting the little crosses until a course line was apparent, computing speed, interception courses, marking the friendly night fighters with small circles, striving with radioed instructions to the interceptors, to bring the line of enemy crosses and the line of friendly circles together. The men in CIC played a fascinating and deadly game, and it was well that they were cool and skillful at it because the stakes were human lives —Japanese if they won, American if they lost.

A few minutes after 7:00 P.M., Jim Gray was vectored out to the eastward while Boudinot remained in reserve overhead. For Gray, this was no game played in a darkened room with scopes, grease pencils and computers. It was an endlessly spacious, three-dimensional blindman's buff in which he was always "it" and to "tag" was to kill. Failure to tag was to leave at large a well-armed enemy, determined to sink or damage U. S. ships and take as many U. S. lives as possible.

Gray headed into the black east at full throttle at 12,000 feet. Four thousand feet below him a solid overcast rippled away to an invisible horizon. Below the overcast, the precisely spaced, armored circles of TF 38 spread out across the darkening sea. Men on watch on the decks of a hundred ships could hear the thin, distant sound of his engine as he passed over, out of sight beyond the clouds. Close to a thousand friends, he was as alone as a man can be—except for the calm, objective voice of the FDO in his earphones giving him directions:

"Vector zero eight zero."

"Vector zero seven five."

"Bogey two o'clock level five miles."

Somewhere in the darkness ahead was a Japanese air crew: pilot, copilot, navigator, mechanics, radiomen, gunners; seven to nine men in a twin-engine airplane, engaged in a search mission, under orders to locate, report and attack the American ships that were destroying Japanese lives and property in the inner areas of the Empire. It was Jim Gray and, fifty miles astern, the Big E's CIC, against that air crew.

The enemy plane was fast. The FDO expertly put Gray in behind it, but it took a long five minutes, with the Hellcat still straining at full throttle, before the first dim shape came into sight through the binoculars which Gray had slung around his neck, and with which, from time to time, he searched the night sky ahead. First the Betty was only an indistinct shape, something a little blacker against the blackness; but if he looked slightly above, rather than concentrating directly on it, an impression came to his brain of the wings and nacelles of an airplane seen from dead astern.

Gray reported visual contact, and his Hellcat continued to close, but the enemy snooper was difficult to keep in sight, even with binoculars, in the increasing darkness. Then the Japanese pilot, perhaps thinking he had gone past the fleet for which he was searching, or perhaps looking for a hole in the overcast through which to let down for an approach and attack, began a gentle turn to the left. Gray, who could barely believe his good luck, turned carefully inside him, closing rapidly now, taking an aerial short cut to his enemy's tail. The Japanese continued his turn until he had reversed course and was clearly silhouetted against the afterglow to the westward. That gentle, graceful turn, the clean wings of the aircraft sharp against the pale rose of twilight, was as fatal as the trigger pull of a firing squad or the thrown switch of an electric chair.

Gray came out of the turn a couple of hundred yards behind the Betty with no more need for binoculars or radar except to give him a firing range. He closed steadily, shifting his eyes from the spreading plane in his windshield to the range indicator of his own radar, and, when it read 100 yards and the black wings of the Betty seemed to fill the whole forward sky, he opened fire and held the trigger down. Only his left outboard gun had tracers, one to each fourteen rounds, so that their light could not dazzle him and throw him off the target, but he watched those tracers disappear into the Betty's fuselage, and gently pressed rudder until they laced across the wing roots and the engines and he knew that the invisible bullets of five other guns, loaded with alternate rounds of armor-piercing and incendiary, were going where the tracers went. Four seconds were enough for the Betty. It seemed to ignite all over at the same instant, the bright flames pouring back over the wings. It took no evasive action, had no death struggle; it simply nosed over toward the overcast and the sea. As the tail came up, Gray could look through the clear plexiglas tail turret, and see red flames filling the cabin as though it were a cylindrical aluminum furnace grotesquely misplaced in the night sky. The burning plane was lost for a minute as it dived through the cloud layer for a few seconds and then a bright flash turned the translucent undercast to orange in a generous circle below the victorious fighter.

Gary flew back to *Enterprise* over the invisible ocean with its invisible task groups moving implacably toward the morning launch point. He and Boudinot remained airborne until 10:30, but no more bogies closed to interception range, and the rest of the night passed quietly.

An hour before sunrise on October 12, the *Enterprise,* at the center of her task group, and with the other groups which made up TF 38 spread out around her, was steaming into the fresh dawn breeze some 120 miles east of the Japanese-occupied island of Formosa, the only island of significant size between Luzon and Kyushu.

Bill Halsey and Pete Mitscher had planned long and carefully for October 12. On that day they both intended to disprove forever the military theory that sea-based air power must operate outside of the reach of land-based air, limiting itself to attacks on relatively isolated land targets and opposing surface forces. On Formosa was a major complex of Japanese air bases, some dozen fields on which were based between two and three hundred fighters and another hundred bombers, easily reinforceable from China, Kyushu and Luzon. For the first time in history, land-based air was being seriously challenged by planes from the decks of ships.

For the Big E's airmen, Formosa was a professionally attractive but personally highly undesirable objective. There were plenty of fat targets and a chance to hit the enemy where it would really hurt. But the chances of survival after parachuting or crash landing on that island were almost nonexistent. Intelligence officers, briefing pilots and crewmen, could only advise them, if shot down, to stay in or make for the friendly sea—for ashore the Japanese held the valleys and villages, savage head-hunters roamed the mountains, and eleven separate species of poisonous snakes made no distinction between highlander, lowlander and Yankee aviator.

Fred Bakutis shoved his throttle forward and made the familiar, short, loud run down the Big E's deck a few minutes before 6:00 A.M. He lifted off her bow, made a shallow right turn to bring his prop wash clear of the dozen fighters behind him, and straightened out, climbing. It was a clear, windy morning with a heavy scattering of clouds, and the evenly ruffled sea was just beginning to turn from black to gray. Bakutis planned a couple of circles for rendezvous, and then a long, easy climb to the southwest toward the corner of Formosa assigned to his sweep. But shortly after he was air-borne, enemy planes that had been shadowing all night began to close. CIC ordered the fighters of Bakutis' sweep, and the ten more ready on deck as escorts for the first strike, to CAP stations. The orderly sequence of sweep and strike and the tactical organization of the squadron was disrupted. When the enemy attack did not develop, and the fighters headed for the target, CAP, sweep and strike planes went together, attempting to sort themselves out on the way.

Fighting 20 had been two months out of Pearl without facing any significant air-borne opposition, and the pilots had been loud in their complaints. As the three divisions of the sweep, and Strike Able's escort of ten flew out of the rising sun toward their target, the man in each cockpit, looking across the shifting, lifting wings at the familiar faces of his friends, knew very well that this time there would be all the air-borne opposition that even Dog Smith, commanding the flight, could desire. The task force had been under surveillance for days, including this very morning. The enemy could expect that after Okinawa and the Philippines, Formosa would be attacked, and he was known to have radar in the hills to confirm his suspicions. Bakutis' pilots were glad for the chance to prove themselves, but nervous with the kind of nervousness they remembered having felt a very few years ago in the minutes before trotting out into the stadium for a big game, or climbing through the ropes for an important match. Most secretly wished they had not been quite so noisy about their desire to meet the enemy in the air. It was a long airplane ride through the lightening sky to Formosa.

Fred Bakutis' division of six angled high across the island to its southwest coast. There was a deck of cumulus far below but through big breaks, the pilots could see the deeply indented coastline of the Takao area and the big concrete airdrome of Einansho.

Bakutis circled twice, up sun of Einansho, looking for the Japanese planes he knew must be in the air. At the end of the second circle, he saw them—a long, staggered column of snub-nosed Tojos, some 7,000 feet below and climbing fast to intercept. Fred took a quick look at the clear dawn sky above him to be sure there would be no enemy on his tail, and dived to the attack. The six Hellcats dropped like falling safes, but in precise and deadly formation. The Tojos maintained their steady climb. The mottled brown, P-47-like wings, with their red meatballs, grew in the F6 gunsights. Then Bakutis squeezed his trigger and VF-20 had at last engaged the enemy in the air.

Fred took the lead plane because it could be expected to be the Japanese flight commander. A single burst from behind set both wing roots blazing, and the Tojo started a three-mile spin to the ground.

Ensign Douglas Baker, picked one of the last Tojos in the long enemy column, came in fast from behind, held his fire, and blasted it at short range. Instantly both wings flamed and the Tojo pulled up sharply. Baker pulled up also to avoid collision, and a second Tojo made a hard left turn across his nose. Baker followed to the left, firing, and watched the canopy fly off, the wings flame and the pilot bail out. As Baker circled, looking for his wingman, he saw a third Tojo, 4,000 feet below on an opposite course. He rolled into an overhead run, and the Tojo blew up under the vertical hammering of the six 50s. Baker dived through the debris. Still unable to locate his wingman, he joined up on Ensign Bob Nelson, who had also knocked down a Tojo in the initial attack, and together they trapped a Zeke in a thin layer of clouds and burned him when he popped out of the top. In the ten seconds after Bakutis opened fire, five Tojos were shot down, and fell, twirling and smoking down the morning sky. With their leader gone, and such instantaneous and heavy losses, the Japanese pilots scattered, maneuvering violently, every man for himself. In the next few minutes five more went down before the guns of Bakutis' six before the enemy became too scattered to follow.

Lieutenant John Laxton's division of four flew around the south tip of Formosa and up the west coast. Just south of Takao, a mixed formation of ten to twelve Zekes and Tojos in a column of twos, climbed out from inland to meet them. Laxton turned toward the enemy at once and the Japanese began to form a defensive "Luffberry" circle, with each plane protecting the tail of the other. Laxton dived in on the last plane, raking its fuselage, but the enemy leader, completing the circle, attacked him from behind and Laxton would have been in serious trouble if another F6 had not swept in, tangent to the disintegrating circle, and shot the Japanese leader off his tail. The enemy pilots, like those that Bakutis was fighting, broke formation and engaged singly. For a few minutes the badly outnumbered F6s had all the action they wanted. It seemed to the Fighting 20 pilots that the morning sky was full of Tojos and Zekes. Every second was used either to shake an enemy plane off one's tail or to get in position to fire. The horizon tilted violently at every angle. The gray sea and the barren Formosa mountains were as often above as below. The acrid smell of gunpowder filled their cockpits as the pilots rolled and dived, banked and climbed, heavy against belt and harness, half blacked-out, jerking their heads around to keep friend and enemy in sight.

Lieutenant Petersen, the squadron exec, with Turnbull and Hoeynck, reached Einansho without sighting a single enemy. They attacked with guns and rockets, strafing parked aircraft and making rocket hits on hangars and retired low on the water, climbing, diving and weaving hard to throw off the enemy gunners. At the rendezvous, a Zeke attacked Petersen, but, in a series of head-on runs and tight turns, Pete drove him off smoking. Laxton joined the three planes as they were heading home, and Turnbull, looking pale and grim, signaled to him that he had been hit by AA.

The four planes started south to return to base, with Turnbull flying steadily at first. However, after a few minutes, he began to wander off from time to time and finally started falling off in several steep dives, pulling out at extremely low altitudes and climbing back up. Petersen and Laxton saw that he could not possibly continue and told him to bail out, which he did, as the planes were crossing the mountains at the southern tip of Formosa. His parachute opened and he drifted southwest, landing in the water 20 yards offshore near Koshun. The circling planes dropped 2 rubber life rafts which he failed to use, and a few minutes later he was either helped or dragged out of the surf by several people, apparently civilians, who placed him on the beach. Presently the "rescuers" wrapped him in his parachute, placed him in a truck and drove off. On his last circle, Laxton saw a soldier with a gun standing on the beach and waving at him.

Shorty Turnbull, after being shot twice as he lay wrapped in his chute, threatened with a samurai sword and gently bayoneted as he tried to walk to the truck, spent the rest of the war in enemy hospitals, concentration and "interrogation" camps, but survived to return to his family in September, 1945.

While the Big E's fighters engaged the Japanese interceptors, the bombers and torpedo planes went down to work over Einansho. The Helldivers flew up Formosa's spinal mountain range past the airfield, then circled westward and attacked in near-vertical dives from 12,000 feet, releasing their heavy bombs at 2,500, and pulling out fast and low to seaward.

The TBFs attacked in high-speed glides, each plane stringing its four 500-pounders across the thin-roofed airfield installations and then heading west over water to the rendezvous point, strafing whatever shipping came in range.

Results were spectacularly satisfactory. Hangars burst open as the bombs detonated inside, and then flared with spreading sheets of flame. Hardly a bomb missed, and, when the attackers pulled out of the desperate AA, Einansho was out of business as an operating air base.

En route to the rendezvous point a lone Zeke came up fast from behind and below to attack the last Avenger in the ragged, retiring column. But Dog Smith and Tom Woodruff, his wingman, just out of a strafing run and headed in the same direction, saw the attack developing below them and dove on the enemy fighter. They opened fire on the Japanese pilot just as the first rounds left his guns for the Avenger. He ceased firing at once and dived, in a hard right turn, with the F6Fs locked onto him like leeches. The shallow water a couple of hundred yards off-shore suddenly stopped his diving turn and put out his fires.

While *Enterprise* worked over her corner of the enemy island, the other carriers of TF 38 were covering their assigned areas. Every Japanese installation the length and breadth of Formosa was almost constantly under attack.

But Air Group Twenty had its losses too. In addition to Turnbull in the morning, two SB2Cs and a TBF went down under the guns that ringed the harbor of Takao. In the early evening, Bombing 20 learned that the two Hell-diver crews were safe aboard the rescue submarine *Sailfish*, but the Avenger crew, last of the formation to dive, was hit hard on the way down, and continued straight into the debris-cluttered harbor. Murphy, Costello and Skeffington were lost.

All day, while she plowed back and forth in the sliding ring of her task group, the edges of the Big E's radar-scopes were lighted by the small white blobs of enemy snoopers. As dusk deepened, the snoopers grew bolder. At 6:51 P.M. a destroyer shot one down with her radar-controlled five-inch guns, twelve miles east of *Enterprise,* and at 7:10 P.M. Captain Glover ordered General Quarters as the enemy ceased snooping and attacked with torpedoes. For the next five hours, 38.4 dodged and twisted in the darkness to crisp TBS commands from the flag bridge of the *Franklin.* At 10:36, *Gridley* torched one of the low-flying torpedo planes fifteen miles to the west. The radio crackled with reports of others destroyed by other groups of TF 38.

The Japanese lost forty planes that night—and in the morning Mitscher's carriers resumed their launches against Formosa. Neither a carrier nor any other ship had been scratched by the all-night raids.

On the thirteenth, *Enterprise* launched a 12-Hellcat sweep and three strikes of 30, 22 and 25 planes and fu-eled a destroyer. Dog Smith's pilots returned to Einansho and Okayama, and burned planes caught on the ground, destroyed barracks and shops and generally completed the job they had nearly finished on the twelfth.

And in the evening the enemy hit back again. This time it was a vigorous, determined, dusk torpedo attack on TG-38.4.

It had been a hazy, rainy afternoon, and the Big E's men

could barely make out the more distant destroyers of the screen. A low layer of ragged stratus clouds obscured most of the sky. Bogies had cluttered the scopes all day, and finally Rear Admiral Ralph E. Davison ordered eight fighters scrambled to intercept. At quarter of five, two divisions of Fred Bakutis' Fighting 20 were in the air under John Petersen and Mel Prichard.

CIC kept Prichard's four overhead, and ordered Petersen out to the southeast after the most troublesome snooper. At the end of a long tail-chase, with the Hellcats straining under full throttle and water injection at 245 knots, and the pilots leaning forward squinting into the haze to find the enemy plane that radar kept telling them was there, Petersen and his wingman shot down a brownish-green Frances. On the way back home, the FDO vectored the division onto a Betty uncomfortably close to the Task group. The Betty, like the Frances five minutes before, crashed in a ball of flame which flared briefly and died out.

Enterprise had been at General Quarters since 4:30, and when Petersen reported the two bogies down, CIC's scopes were clear. Cato Glover secured his men from their battle stations. But at 6:10 the FDO sent Prichard north after another low flyer, which he lost in a series of rain squalls, and at 6:30, with the sun just seven minutes down, Prichard's division in the landing circle and Petersen's flying up the starboard side at 300 feet ready to join it, seven to ten twin-engine planes swept in, flat on the water, out of the haze and low clouds to the northward, crossed the screen in bursts of gunfire, and bore down on the carriers. In *Enterprise,* the ready guns swung onto the enemy coming in to port, while bosun's call, bugle, electric alarm and the sound of firing from the screen sent the men back to General Quarters with a rush and pounding of feet and the heavy clanging of those watertight doors and hatches still open above the main deck. In a minute every ship of the task group whose guns were in range and could bear was firing, and 40- and 20-millimeter tracers leapt and streamed horizontally across the evening sea between them.

Petersen's division pulled up hard, and turned right to get outside the screen and away from the pouring AA. On the other side of the destroyer circle they found a Betty retiring fast and low, and Petersen and Harry Nelson made it the third for the division that afternoon. At the same time, Bob Nelson of Pete's second section also found a Betty trying to get away and sent him flaming into the sea. Number four.

Mel Prichard was just turning into the groove when the attack came in. He pulled up his wheels and climbed away, and also found a Betty heading out from the formation center. Mel turned onto the Betty's tail, but a destroyer exploded the enemy plane before he could open fire.

Jim Darracott, Prichard's wingman, had the same experience, except that he was firing and making hits when the heavy shipboard tracers laced into his prey and knocked it down.

Ensign Ed Boudinot was only supposed to be ferrying his night fighter home after a rescue escort mission and a landing on *Franklin*, while *Enterprise* respotted her deck. He had barely left the *Franklin*'s bow when the enemy planes attacked and the ships opened fire. Like Petersen and Prichard, he quickly retired outside the screen. Eight miles to the east, he found a Frances low on the water. He waited while another fighter made a run and missed, and then closed fast and poured some 600 rounds into the enemy before it caught fire, plunged into the sea and exploded.

It was all over in a few minutes. The enemy seemed to have been concentrating on the *Franklin*. In the flat crisscross of tracers, six of the attacking planes went down, one on each side of the Big E's bow, one just to starboard of *Franklin*, between her and *Enterprise*, and one in the wake of the *Belleau Wood*. *Enterprise* machine guns fired at both the planes that crashed ahead, but she held her five-inch batteries silent because of the extreme low altitude of the targets and the danger of hitting friendly ships.

A little after 7:00 P.M. a destroyer shot down a final snooper and, except for the usual prowling blips around the edges of the scopes, enemy activity was over for the night.

The Big E's Task Group 38.4 had been lucky—and well defended—but in 38.1 a few miles away over the horizon, the heavy cruiser *Canberra* was so badly wounded by a torpedo that for a while it appeared she would have to be scuttled. Then Halsey decided to try to tow her out of range of enemy air, and more strikes were ordered for the fourteenth to keep Japanese bombers on the ground.

Nature helped. October 14 around Formosa was so overcast and swept with violent squalls and showers that the

Big E's early morning sweep of seven fighters and a photo plane saw no action. Clouds completely obscured their target and they returned home with the consoling knowledge that if they could not get through the weather to the enemy, the less well-trained Japanese would not be getting through to TF 38.

While the other three task groups covered *Canberra*, Admiral Davison's 38.4 steamed south on the fourteenth to hit the fields on Luzon, from which attacks could be launched against the crippled cruiser now and the invasion forces later. The invasion of Leyte was only six days away, all the assault forces at sea, converging toward Leyte Gulf.

Formosa, the closest enemy air complex to the Philippines, had some 600 less aircraft with which to oppose MacArthur's landing. TF 58 had, by sunset of the sixteenth, lost 76 planes and 64 airmen, two cruisers had been wounded by torpedoes, and a carrier, another cruiser and a destroyer had suffered minor damage. The carriers had won the battle with the airfields.

Air Group Twenty, all its squadrons blooded and battlewise, moved in against Manila.

Two hundred and thirty miles northeast of Manila, off the east coast of Luzon, the fifteenth of October broke over a disturbed sea covered by low, ragged clouds and swept by frequent drenching rains. But shortly before 9:00 A.M., *Enterprise* launched a full deckload against the U. S.-built, Japanese-occupied airfields around the capital of the Philippines. On this first strike, the Big E sent her first team— nine Helldivers under Riera and eight Avengers under Prickett, escorted by four divisions of Hellcats under Bakutis.

The formation crossed the east shore of Luzon with the bombers and torpedo planes at 15,000 feet and the four divisions of fighters stacked above, ahead, and on both sides, with Fred Bakutis' division flying roving high cover at 22,000. With forty miles to go to Manila Bay on the west coast, some three dozen geometrically arranged specks in the sky ahead developed rapidly into as many mottled-brown Oscars, Tonys and Zekes coming in high and fast to intercept.

Fighting 20, outnumbered two to one, closed up, charged guns and waited at 160 knots between the bombers and the enemy. The sleek and agile Japanese planes surrounded the *Enterprise* formation. Dog Smith's men held steadily on course, gunners in the open cockpits of the SB2Cs and the ball turrets of the TBFs cocked and ready, the tight formations of Hellcats waiting for the enemy's first move. Then a single Oscar high on the right flank rolled into a firing run. Bakutis' section of two instantly turned into him and he dived away, recovering far below to begin the climb back. Another on the left did the same thing and also dove away when the escort began to counter. Bakutis' eager young pilots were terribly tempted to follow, knowing their heavy F6s could easily catch and destroy the lighter enemy planes in a dive, but squadron discipline held and they maintained position. The Japanese were apparently trying to draw the Hellcats away in order to get at the bombers. When this tactic failed, they were forced to attack the American fighters which were always between them and their targets. They came in singly and haphazardly, and Bakutis' pilots met them in pairs and fours with the tight teamwork that they had been trained to, and which had worked so well over Formosa two days before.

Planes began to smoke and spiral down the sky on the eastern approaches to Manila—and they were all Japanese. Ensigns Doug Baker and Chuck Haverland, the second section of Bakutis' division, accounted for five between them in a wild, high-altitude scramble which lasted twenty minutes, and during which Baker scattered five attacking Oscars by firing his air-to-ground rockets at their formation and followed up with his guns to shoot down a sixth. Haverland fired at such short range on a diving Tony that oil from its broken engine streaked and clouded his windshield.

Lieutenant Bob Fallgatter's division got three more certainly, and probably five, when six Oscars attempted to attack the bombers as they were beginning their runs on Nielson Field.

En route to the rendezvous point, Lieutenant Leo McCuddin shot down an Oscar from below as it was beginning a run on a TBF. The enemy pilot bailed out and dangled eerily under his chute, dressed from head to toe in solid black.

Ensign Bill Herman, also on his way to the rendezvous, broke up an attack by three Oscars on another F6F, blowing the canopy off one and killing the pilot as he started to climb out. Ten of the enemy interceptors were seen to crash, and another four probably went down. In the words of Emmett Riera, who had reason to know:

Escort was superb; not one enemy fighter approached to within gun range of the bombers and torpedo bombers, either during approach or upon retirement; every plane that attempted an attack was either shot down or driven off.

Not a single VF-20 Hellcat was lost.

Clouds covered most of the Manila area, so that the bombers and torpedo planes had to spiral steeply down through a hole to break out underneath and find their targets. Then, with the bottom of the cloud deck at 2,000 feet, they were limited to high-speed, low-level passes across the field. In that shallow layer of clear air between ground and cloud, the AA was the worst the Big E's squadrons had ever seen. The blue planes seemed to be flying through a continuous curtain of smoking tracers. But they unloaded their bombs at foolproof altitudes on ramps crowded with parked planes.

With air opposition temporarily accounted for, the fighters swooped in under the overcast to slam their rockets into the rows of grounded planes, and then all three squadrons headed out across the crowded harbor to rendezvous.

On the way out, Ed Holley, flying an *Enterprise* TBF again as he had done two years before off Guadalcanal, caught a Zeke coming out of a cloud ahead and spun him in with 200 rounds from the wing guns of the big Avenger.

Fred Bakutis, rapidly losing oil from a bullet hole in his engine, went on alone as soon as Luzon was left behind, and arrived aboard to find the task group under attack and the fighters he had left behind as busy here, 200 miles at sea, as his four divisions of escorts had been over the target. Fred landed on the familiar deck, changed planes and got back in the air.

At 10:30 A.M., *Enterprise* CIC had vectored some *San Jacinto* fighters onto a Judy which they shot down twelve miles southwest of the force. At the same time, with more and more bogies showing on the scopes, eleven of VF-20's fighters, including the air group commander, were scrambled. One division of four, led by Joe Lawler, found five Zekes coming in at 17,000 feet, shot one down, damaged another and drove the others off.

The other four-plane division, led by Mel Prichard, encountered Zekes also and knocked down four.

But three enemy dive bombers and one bomb-carrying

Zeke, flying fast and high, eluded the fighters. The first warning was the shouted report of a lookout:

"Enemy dive bombers overhead!"

Task group guns opened with a roar, but three Judys released over *Franklin* and escaped. Two bombs were wide, but one landed close aboard, showering her flight deck and starting a fire on the port quarter.

While the big new carrier spouted black smoke, and repair parties converged on the blaze, a single Zeke, with a bomb under each wing, slanted in toward her starboard bow, All *Franklin*'s starboard guns and all those on other ships that would bear turned on the lone Japanese pilot. For a few seconds he flew on into the lead-filled sky, then flipped around in a 90-degree bank and headed home.

Franklin put out her fire in a few minutes and resumed operations, but the enemy attacks continued all day.

At 2:20 P.M., Fred Bakutis was launched with a CAP of twelve Hellcats, and in the next three hours destroyed at least eighteen enemy planes in the vicinity of the task group. The Big E's luck was running strong that fall afternoon. The first bogey to which CIC vectored him was a single, sleek, fast, twin-engine Dinah reconnaissance plane at 23,000 feet, fifty miles out. The F6Fs had to strain to catch it, using full throttle and water injection in a shallow climb from 20,000. But when Bakutis and his wingman, Walter Wood, flamed both its engines and started it on the fiery, four-mile drop to the Pacific, it was more of a victory than they knew. The next two dangerously large formations of dive bombers, torpedo planes and fighters engaged by Bakutis' Hellcats, were circling sixty miles out, apparently awaiting instructions from a coordinator who could now no longer instruct.

Ensign Walt Wood was the hero of the afternoon. Flying on Bakutis' wing as smoothly and reliably as though the two planes were the same weapon, he shared in the destruction of the coordinating Dinah, then made two passes with Bakutis on a formation of Jill torpedo bombers, knocking down one on each pass. Bakutis also got one on each attack. When the division went after a lone Zeke, it was Wood who shot it down and, a moment later, with his division leader out of ammunition, Wood expended his last rounds on still another Zeke which another fighter finally forced into the sea.

Fred Bakutis himself destroyed two, plus the Dinah, and damaged another.

But Fighting 20 had its losses too. Ensign Bruce Hanna pressed an attack so close to a Betty that he sheared off his right wing on the enemy plane and barely managed to escape from his violently spinning F6 before it hit the water. Cut and battered by the high-speed bail-out, he drifted for nearly three days in his rubber raft before an antisub patrol saw him and guided a destroyer in to pick him up.

Ensign Norman Snow became separated in a dogfight with a dozen Oscars, and returned to base in serious trouble with large holes in wings and elevators, his radio transmitter shot up and unable to lower his wheels. Another F6 joined up on him as he circled and, after consulting *Enterprise,* advised him to climb and bail out. But Snow was either wounded and could not get out, or had too little fuel to climb. He landed hard in a tower of spray alongside the destroyer *Mugford,* climbed out and swam toward the ship, which put four swimmers overboard to help him. Hurt and weighted down with his flight gear and parachute, he slipped through the hands of the destroyer sailors and was lost.

On the sixteenth, TG 38.4 fueled and received replacement planes and crews from the escort carrier, *Sitka Bay,* and on the seventeenth closed in to 150 miles to get on with the job of neutralizing the airfields on Luzon.

The early fighter sweep on the seventeenth found the entire Manila area buried under a thick white blanket of clouds, and circled for nearly an hour in the clear sky above, looking in vain for a hole or a way to get through to the enemy.

Strike Able—eight fighters, eight bombers and eight torpedo planes plus a similar group from *Franklin,* all under Dog Smith—had better luck. A hole opened up for them, and they let down below the overcast in the vicinity of Clark Field to find one of the bases in the Clark complex swarming with planes preparing to take off in the clearing weather. The field was Mabalacat East, ten miles north of Clark. Smith assigned it as the target for his group and dove in to the attack.

Lieutenant Jim Verdin's division went in first with rockets, and Verdin himself smoked four of them into a bunch of eighteen to twenty enemy fighters clustered around the approach end of the runway, their props turning, waiting for take-off. The blast of the rockets engulfed the Japanese planes in a roaring cloud of fire and sailing debris as Verdin's Hellcats swept overhead.

Dog Smith, with Tom Woodruff glued to his wing, followed in a rocket run and then, with rockets away, switched to a pair of Zekes just taking off. Smith put a short burst into the lead Zeke as it was pulling up its wheels and it crashed in a long smear of flame at the edge of the field. Turning hard left and pulling up, he found another Zeke just climbing out and flamed it with another single burst. Dog leveled off and continued straight ahead toward a third Zeke approaching head on. The enemy pilot turned hard right and Smith turned with him, hammering a third burst into the Zeke's upturned belly which set it afire. Three planes in less than a minute with 140 rounds total per gun. Dog Smith did not just happen to be the commander of the most aggressive air group on the most competent carrier in the Navy of the United States.

Other fighters did almost as well, strafing enemy planes still on the ground and blasting those down that were just taking off.

Bombers and torpedo planes followed the fighters in, laying bombs and incendiary clusters on the crowded aprons and hangars at Mabalacat East. The twenty-four planes of Strike Able destroyed twenty-eight enemy aircraft on the ground and in the air, with superficial wounds to one turret gunner of a TBF.

Strike Baker, the same morning, flattened every structure at Legaspi Field in southeastern Luzon, but lost Lieutenant George Wilson and the crew of his Avenger to heavy and accurate medium-caliber AA over the target.

October 18, two days before the Leyte landings, was a busy and a bad day for *Enterprise*. Three strikes and two fighter sweeps went to Manila that Wednesday in increasingly miserable weather associated with the fringes of a typhoon. On every mission but one, pilots and/or crewmen were lost. Flight operations began in the dark at 6:00 A.M. and ended in the dark at 8:00 P.M.

On the morning sweep, Fred Bakutis arrived over Manila Bay with twelve fighters at 25,000 feet, and found the bay and the city cloud-covered as usual. But, to the south, Clark Field was clear, and the Hellcats circled in that direction.

Over Clark a flight of seven greenish-brown, snub-nosed Tojos was climbing out, and two of VF-20's division dived to the attack, leaving one up for cover. In the next few moments, other enemy formations joined the fight until the clear sky over the Clark complex was full of mottled-brown and blue aircraft climbing, twisting, diving at full power, their guns clattering, the radio air full of urgent calls and orders in English and Japanese.

In the heavy-gutted, horizon-spinning, cordite-smelling swirl of combat, black-haired, white-toothed Douglas Baker and pint-sized, ex-tumbler Chuck Haverland each shot down three enemy fighters. Bakutis and Foye got two apiece and most of the others one for a total of eighteen.

Bill Foye, flying wing on Lieutenant Jack Laxton, was badly hit, his right wing tip shot off, his elevators shredded and smoke from his damaged engine pouring into the cockpit so that he had to open the canopy to see and breathe. Just before his radio and instruments went out, he was able to call to Laxton and Bakutis to say he was hit, losing oil pressure and trying to make Subic Bay for a water landing. A search that afternoon found no trace of Bill Foye or his F6. He was listed as missing.

Had it not been for Fred Bakutis, Ensign John Hoeynck would have been missing too. In a turning contest with three Oscars, one of them clipped about three feet off his left wing and then spun down out of control. The F6 would still fly, but at over 180 knots it began to vibrate as though it would come apart. Hoeynck climbed out of the fight and called his skipper. Bakutis and Gallagher found him at once, and covered him as he headed east across the mountains to the sea and home. An Oscar also found the cripple, and hung above and astern, making runs but pulling up when the two escorts went into a defensive weave. After four or five cycles, Bakutis had had enough. On the next pass, he reversed his usual turn, jammed on full throttle and water injection, and, with Gallagher on his wing, climbed back after the Oscar. The surprised enemy pilot was caught and slowed by Bakutis' first burst; the second blew off his canopy and killed him as he started out. The two Hellcats dived back to their crippled squadron mate.

Strike Able, nine bombers and eight torpedo planes with eight fighters escorting, in company with a *Franklin* group, hit Clark itself and two outlying fields, strafing, bombing and rocketing Japanese aircraft on the ground and destroying those encountered in the air. The SB2Cs used a new tactic of dropping in their dives at 4,500 feet and then strafing with 20-millimeter cannon during pull-out. The high angle and heavy caliber of this strafing, executed after the bombs were away and pilots could give full attention to gunnery, cost the enemy several planes parked in deep revetments which would have been difficult to hit by usual methods of low-angle strafing and bombing.

On the way to the rendezvous, Ensign John Crittenden intercepted two Tojos attacking one of the torpedo planes. He blew one up in a persistent and stubbornly pressed chase, but found the other on his tail and was unable to shake him with the most violent maneuvering. Dog Smith and his wingman came to the rescue, disintegrating the sticky Tojo with their combined fire.

Strike Baker was launched less than an hour after Able, with 24 more aircraft, to hit Nielson Field and photograph Manila Bay and Harbor. Bombers and torpedo planes destroyed another dozen aircraft on the ground, damaged some twenty others and obtained plenty of excellent photographs of shipping and harbor facilities. But the escorting fighters were kept constantly busy warding off vigorous assaults by enemy interceptors. Twelve Oscars attacked one division of Hellcats from a Luffberry circle above, two or three planes at a time rolling over on their backs, pulling through in split S's for their runs and climbing back to the circle on recovery. The Hellcats climbed, weaving defensively, shot down three and drove the others off. None got through to the bombers below.

The other Hellcat division was jumped by seven Oscars while on a photo run over Manila. Each man in the division killed one enemy, and, in addition, two more were damaged. But in the skirmish, Ensign Walt Wood was hit. He had been Bakutis' wingman three days before in the defense of the task group, with four planes to his credit. Now his blue F6 flipped violently over on its back and dived into the trees below. His body was recovered by friendly Filipino irregulars and buried with full military honors. Handsome, likeable young Wood was serious about flying for his country. In the seconds it took his broken Hellcat to hurtle from the open sky to his death he had scribbled on his knee pad his last words—"hit 3."

Strike Baker flew east through the valleys and under the

clouds until they were over the friendly sea, then climbed and headed home.

As a result of Strike Baker's report of a heavy concentration of shipping in Manila Bay, and the fierce fighter opposition they encountered, Strike Charlie was launched at 1:30 P.M. against those ships, preceded by a sweep of thirteen *Enterprise* fighters and twelve more from *Franklin*. In addition to the sweep, Strike Charlie's Helldivers and torpedo-carrying Avengers were escorted by twelve more Hellcats under the air group commander.

As the combined sweep and strike headed slightly south of west toward Luzon and Manila, their little clotted Vs and echelons lost and insignificant in the hugeness of the sky, the pilots could look to their left and see the weather moving northward. Masses of gray and dark gray towering cumulus clouds which the airmen knew from experience held turbulence, hail, heavy rain and violent and unpredictable winds, formed a long line to the south—and the whole front was moving north so fast that the leaders were forced to detour in that direction to stay clear.

Manila Bay was covered by a thick and solid layer of clouds. Fred Bakutis' fighter sweep continued on to Subic Bay to search for Bill Foye, missing since morning, found nothing, and returned to the Clark area, knocking off two Oscars almost casually on the way.

Strike Charlie circled Manila Bay counterclockwise to the north and west, let down over water, and swept into the crowded harbor between the dark clouds and the dark sea. The bristling, pitted whale's back of Corregidor spat obscenely at them as they passed. Rain squalls streaked their windshields and chopped visibility momentarily to half a mile. But, lying at anchor in the spacious bay and behind the long breakwaters of the south harbor, were scores of cargo ships, about twenty of which were major, ocean-going vessels.

The Hellcats spread out and went in first, as the ships and shore batteries opened up with everything they had, their rockets smoking out ahead in pairs and .50-caliber tracers following as the range closed. With rockets gone, they wheeled and attacked again with guns only, their bullets ripping up the calm harbor water on both sides of their targets, holing and firing ship after ship.

Riera's Helldivers, used to swooping down from 12,000 feet, had to settle for high-speed glides through the pouring, crisscrossing flak, releasing their big bombs at 1,000 to 500 feet on the larger ships inside the breakwater and strafing with their 20-millimeter cannon on the way out.

Sam Prickett's Avengers had the most potent weapons and the nastiest job. In order to aim the torpedos that could rip the whole bottom out of a thin-skinned merchantman with a single hit, it was necessary to fly for half a minute straight, steady and not too fast toward the target, presenting, for that time, an easy target for the guns that lined the shore and flashed and clattered on the ships. Like Gene Lindsey's pilots at Midway so long ago, every one of Prickett's TBFs laid its slim "fish" as carefully and close as though the frantic guns were silent and this was a Sunday exercise in Chesapeake Bay. But with their fish away and swimming straight and true toward their targets, the torpedo pilots jerked and skidded, dipped and weaved and fish-tailed with every trick they knew to evade the lead that laced the dusky belt between clouds and sea. There was neither time nor visibility enough to see the results of their attacks, but one of Riera's pilots nearby saw two torpedoes fountain against the side of a big tanker.

The bomber crews, who did not have to wait while a torpedo ran some 500 yards to see results, watched their bombs rip into five big ships, some of which were hit by several 1,000-pounders, enough to sink a carrier or a cruiser.

One SB2C caught a stream of explosive tracers and skidded into the bay. Ensign Les Hornbeak and Fred Swinney, his gunner, were lost.

With the ordeal in the murky bay completed, the planes with the white triangles on their tails had now to get home through the weather which had been steadily moving north across their route.

It was 5:00 P.M. and getting dark when the Big E's squadrons began their climb out of Manila across the spinal mountains of Luzon. The first casualty was handsome, competent Jack Laxton of Fighting 20. In a low-level strafing run over the grass fields south of Clark, an unlucky bullet out of the puny resistance offered by the enemy had entered his engine and severed an oil line. Smoking and losing oil, he climbed out to 9,000 feet with his division and signaled he was OK, but on the other side of the mountains, as the fighters began to let down for the trip home, his engine froze and stopped. Laxton, who had watched the same thing happen to Fred Turnbull off Formosa a few days before, glided down through a hole in the clouds, with Fred Bakutis following, and called repeatedly for Jack to bail out. Laxton vanished momentarily under the clouds and, when he came in sight again, he was at 2,000 feet in an inverted dive. His squadron mates circled the spreading oil slick for several minutes and then headed sadly home through the increasing dusk and the deteriorating weather.

By 5:30, Strike Charlie had been in the air four hours with considerable time spent in climbing to attack altitude, climbing over mountains, and at full power during combat. It was now necessary to swing wide to the northward to avoid the rolling weather front. It was apparent to Dog Smith that all of his planes would be landing after dark and that some of those landings would be well short of the Big E's waiting deck.

The same facts were apparent to Cato Glover and Tom Hamilton in *Enterprise*. They were also evident on the flagship, and Admiral Davison released *Enterprise* with an escort to steam westward to meet the returning strike. But, even at 26 knots, the Big E could only close the range by thirteen miles each half hour and that was not enough.

From some fifty miles out, the bombers and torpedo planes began to ditch. At ten minutes of seven desperately empty aircraft began to appear in the landing circle. It was almost totally dark. Fifteen planes landed before one crashed and closed the deck. Three Helldivers landed in the water close aboard and one Helldiver and four Avengers ditched farther out. One Avenger pilot in the darkness and confusion, and the urgency of his empty tanks, flew into the side of the *Belleau Wood* killing his entire crew. Two TBFs and three fighters landed on *Franklin,* and one of each made the *Wasp.* All the Hellcats landed safely, some with barely enough fuel to taxi out of the arresting gear.

With the strike group down all over the rapidly clouding sea, Admiral Davison released his destroyers from their screening duties for rescue work.

The destroyer sailors put in a long night. They eased out along the track of the returning strike, checking positions where *Enterprise* reported that planes had gone down, straining their eyes through night-tinted binoculars for the tiny point of light in the encompassing blackness of sea and sky that would be the one-cell flashlight screwed to an aviator's Mae West, straining their ears over the hum of machinery and the wash of the waves for the tiny sound of a voice in that waste of water. Sailors in swimming trunks, wearing light canvas harnesses from which long lines were led, stood all night by their rails, ready to dive into the sea to give an "airdale" a hand. Whaleboats were rigged out, ready for lowering, engines checked and crews standing by. Inflated rubber rafts with lines attached were ready to throw overboard, and men stood by to man them. Pharmacist's mates waited on deck with their canvas kits of first-aid materials. Cargo nets lay rolled up in the waterways, outboard of everything, secured at their tops and ready to drop down the side for survivors to scramble up. Clean bunks and blankets and straight shots of medicinal alcohol waited below decks.

By morning, most of Dog Smith's airmen had been rescued. At dawn twenty planes left the Big E's deck to search for the remainder. At 10:40 A.M., twelve more went out, and at 2:15 P.M., eleven more. The search planes swept the sea at low altitude in line abreast and nothing that floated escaped them. Survivors that the destroyers had been unable to locate in the darkness were found, and the "cans" moved in to pick them up. In the course of the searches, Bill Herman and Don Reeder also found a Betty which they promptly destroyed.

On the twentieth the destroyers began returning her pilots and crewmen to *Enterprise.* When it was all over, seven men were missing from Strike Charlie and its fighter sweep —Jack Laxton; Hornbeak and Swinney, shot down over the target; Ensign Don Conaway, Kelimoff and Riggs, the crew of the TBF which flew into the *Belleau Wood;* and Lieutenant Charles Bretland of Torpedo 20, who inexplicably became separated from his crew after ditching and was lost.

And on that busy and dangerous October 18, Wood, Snow and Foye had also been lost. But Bill Foye was not dead. He was lying, with a painfully wrenched neck and back, wrapped in his parachute, in a shelter formed by the roots of a mango tree, while friendly Philippine guerrillas fed him and made plans to get him to safety and eventually back to duty. Bill spent the next three and a half months in hiding and running from the Japanese in the towns and jungles of Luzon, in the care of the guerrillas and their friends, was finally picked up by a PBY, and

when Air Group Twenty pulled into Pearl on the fifteenth
of February on their way home, he was standing on the dock,
like a ghost, to greet them. On April 26, he reported for
duty at Trenton, New Jersey, and mentioned to the medical
officer that he still had a stiff neck. X rays showed that his
neck was broken, and had been since October 18, when he
bailed out low over Luzon. Any bad jolt during that six
months could have severed his spinal cord. It took fifteen
months of treatment to put him together again.

October 20, 1944, was the day that Douglas MacArthur
returned to the Philippines. *Enterprise* played no vital role
in bringing the general back, other than to hammer down
some airfields which might have provided some resistance.
On A-Day, the Big E furnished only two prelanding strikes
on the dirt field of San Pablo and the pathetic little town of
Dagami near the Leyte beaches. The assigned targets did
not seem worth the bombs and rockets used to blow them
up, and the pilots were more interested in the incredible
array of U. S. shipping which filled Leyte Gulf than in the
apparently deserted and undesirable coastline of the island
itself. But *Enterprise* was to have a major role in arranging
things so that the general could *remain* in the Philippines.

21 LEYTE IN THE FALL

On the twenty-first of October, Task Group 38.4
pulled off to the eastward of the Philippines, and fueled. The
next morning orders were received to proceed to Ulithi.
The Big E's men looked forward to a rest, a swim, a couple
of beers, a few good, full nights of sleep and perhaps some
mail while swinging around the hook in that sunny, wind-
swept lagoon. They had been at sea for a month, fighting
typhoons and Japanese, and they needed a holiday. And
Enterprise needed more provisions and more bombs and
ammunition than could be swung across from tankers under way.

All day the twenty-second the task group continued toward Ulithi and peace, but in midmorning of the twenty-
third a message came aboard from Admiral Halsey, and

carriers, cruisers and destroyers drew uniform semicircles on the calm sea and headed back westward toward the Philippines and the war at 25 knots. The Japanese Fleet was at sea to challenge the Leyte landings.

On the way back, Admiral Ching Lee, still in the *Washington,* joined the task group with *Alabama* and a division of destroyers.

By daylight of the twenty-fourth, *Enterprise* was close enough to launch a search for the approaching enemy and twenty-eight aircraft spread their wings and rolled off her bow into the morning twilight in the first thirteen minutes after 6:00 A.M.

The search/strike was made in two groups, each with six bombers and eight fighters, and the two groups went out in adjacent sectors to the southwest for a distance of 325 miles. Emmett Riera had one flight of bombers and Fred Bakutis one flight of fighters. All the bombers carried two 500-pound bombs, all the fighters four five-inch rockets and a full load of .50-caliber ammunition. Similar groups took off from *Franklin* at the same time to search adjacent sectors to the west.

By 6:15 the Big E's two formations were formed up and climbing out on their slightly divergent courses with the lightening eastern sky at their backs. They were still climbing when they crossed Leyte Gulf, jammed with friendly shipping, and the beaches of Leyte itself, now solidly under the control of the U. S. Army. For an hour and a half the *Enterprise* airmen droned uneventfully down the tropic sky, while the sun rose behind them and turned the black islands to green and the gray sea to blue—and found nothing. They crossed Bohol, Cebu and Negros, and winged out over the Sulu Sea and found only native sailing luggers—no aircraft, no warships, not even any merchantmen.

Then, a few minutes before 8:00 A.M., a pilot in the northern flight made out the thin shapes of two destroyers and a destroyer escort maneuvering together and apparently not part of any larger formation. The planes plotted their position and continued on course. They were looking for something more important, but, if they failed to find it, they could hit the smaller ships on the way home.

Dog Smith's search planes were looking for something which, as a unit, Air Group Twenty had not found before—major elements of the Japanese Fleet. The *Enterprise* squadrons by now were veterans at smashing airfields and shore installations, sinking merchant ships and, lately, engaging enemy planes in the air. But they had never come up against the first line of the enemy's naval strength. From air and surface, the airmen had seen the awful barrage of antiaircraft fire that their own task group could put up, and they knew the enemy must be able to do the same. The pilots of Air Group Twenty were at least as competent and aggressive as any in the Pacific and yet they could not help feeling slightly dry in the mouth, slightly uneasy in the stomach, not enough to affect their ability, nothing even that another man could know. But it was there.

And thirty minutes beyond the destroyers, as they neared the end of their sectors, they found what they were looking for—two broad-beamed, pagoda-masted Japanese battleships and a heavy cruiser with four destroyers forming a square around them, headed due north at a steady 15 knots.

Lieutenant Ray Moore, leading the bombers in the north sector, got off the contact report—position, course, speed, composition. With the receipt by *Enterprise* of that contact report, half the mission was accomplished. The enemy force had been located. Now came the second half.

The two search groups joined up at once, Riera commanding the bombers and Bakutis the fighters, and began a circling climb to an up-sun attack position. They were ten miles away and over two miles high as they passed to the west and then to the north and finally northeast of the enemy, but all the while they were under fire. None of the pilots had even seen such long-range antiaircraft fire. They looked for the flashes and saw the big guns, the main batteries, of the battleships and cruiser trained on them, and watched the Japanese admiral maneuver his ships to keep the planes under fire. Considering the long range and high altitude, the shooting was good—and very spectacular: purple, red, blue, yellow and white bursts, some with arcing streamers which burst again. A few of the bursts were as close as 500 feet and level, others above and behind.

As the formation climbed and circled under the technicolor harassment of the Japanese, Riera assigned targets.

"Ray, you take the lead battlewagon, I'll take the second. VF go in just ahead with rockets. . . . Stand by—here we go!"

Bakutis assigned four fighters to the cruiser to deny her the pleasure of shooting without being shot at.

While Riera and Bakutis were plunging out of the morning sun and into the increasing AA, their target's position was already being plotted by Jimmy Flatley and Arleigh Burke for Admiral Marc Mitscher on the flag bridge of the *Lexington* 150 miles east of Manila, and Bill Halsey in *New Jersey*, some seventy miles off the north cape of Samar was studying a chart which showed the same data. On both charts the contact was neatly labeled "Southern Force." Because there were others.

In the minutes before *Enterprise* had sighted the Southern Force, a search plane from 38.2 had reported three battleships and six cruisers headed eastward in the Sibuyan Sea. On the flag bridges of *New Jersey* and *Lexington*, this was labeled "Center Force." The admirals had good reason to believe that still a third force was approaching from the north, but it had not yet been located as Bakutis and Riera began their attack.

The *Enterprise* search-strike group pushed over at almost the same instant. The Hellcats went down first, opposing their light aluminum, their rockets, their .50-calibers and their flashing speed to the heavy guns and armor and clustered AA batteries of the enemy warships. They pressed in fast and close, feet solid on rudders, hands tight on the sticks and throttles, hissing the rockets off first and then opening with machine guns. The SB2Cs hurtled almost straight down from 15,000 feet, the pilots leaning forward, concentrating on the growing targets, wishing there were 1,000-pounders in their bomb bays instead of the two 500s, ignoring the flashing, streaking, smoking flak, around the edges of their vision seeing the altimeters unwind and the square-winged fighters sweep across their targets, the rocket hits sparkle and smoke against the steel, the bombs of planes ahead spouting close aboard or flashing beautifully on decks and turrets. One after the other they released at 2,500 to 2,000 feet and pulled out low, opening up with 20-millimeter cannon on the destroyers which suddenly appeared ahead.

Then they were across the screen and clear but with the AA still blooming around them for ten miles as they looked back to check results. A small fire burned on the stern of the lead battleship. On the second, large fires burned aft and amidships and she had slowed and sheered out of column. The cruiser had been hit with rockets and a destroyer heavily strafed but they showed no effect from the distance at which the persistent AA forced the groups to rendezvous.

As the Hellcats and Helldivers skimmed away, flat on the calm sea, Fred Bakutis' voice came strongly through forty pairs of earphones: "I'm hit and losing oil. Oil pressure zero. . . . Losing power. . . . Ditching."

Bakutis' F6 shucked its belly tank, which splashed and bounced and splashed again, and half a mile later the fighter slid with a long tear of spray into the Sulu Sea. The group circled, shocked and worried, and saw Fred climb out onto the left wing of the sinking Hellcat and, as it was about to go down, jump off the trailing edge, inflate his raft, and struggle in. A few rounds of the long-range AA blossomed overhead as they circled. Riera swooped in low and dropped a bigger, two-man raft slightly up wing, and Fred paddled over, after some difficulty inflated it, and transferred himself aboard, securing the small raft alongside.

When they were satisfied that the enemy ships were not coming back for him, and when they had carefully plotted his position, Bakutis' fighters and the bombers reluctantly left him for the long trip back to base.

When Riera's group landed aboard at noon, planes were being fueled and armed and crews briefed for a deckload strike on the powerful Center Force plowing eastward through the Sibuyan Sea. On the big chart in the ready room, Japanese strategy was easy to see. They were attempting to close a gigantic pincer on Leyte Gulf, with the Southern Force approaching along the north coast of Mindanao and through Surigao Straits, the Center Force through the Sibuyan Sea out into the Pacific through San Bernadino and south around Samar, and the still unlocated Northern Force (which had to be the carriers since they were not with Southern or Center) approaching directly from the north.

Enterprise airmen who had seen the thin-skinned, lightly armed merchant and amphibious craft clustered off the Leyte beaches, could imagine what the big guns of half a dozen battlewagons and a few heavy and light cruisers could do once they entered the gulf. When the massacre was over, the Army on Leyte would be in the same position as the Marines on Guadalcanal two years before, ashore with half of their equipment, support from the sea cut off and under fire from the guns of enemy warships.

The Big E's strike of 9 bombers, 8 torpedo planes and 12 fighters was off the deck at 1:15 P.M. and made a running rendezvous on course. Dog Smith was in command. Sam Prickett had his torpedo-carrying TBMs, Riera's exec, Jim Cooper, the SB2Cs, and Bakutis' exec, Joe Lawler, the fighters. The flight was carrying the heaviest possible armament, eight torpedoes and eighteen 1,000-pounders plus the five-inch rockets of the Hellcats.

They crossed Samar and Masbate high over the cumulus that lay along the green island ridges. Like the pilots of the morning strike, they were at once secretly apprehensive and grimly ready to take on the very best ships that Japan could send to sea.

Over Masbate they received a corrected position, reported by other air groups which had already found and attacked the Center Force, turned more to the northwest, and at ten minutes of three in the afternoon the enemy came in sight. The narrow seas between the islands seemed to be filled with warships. Two task groups were heading eastward, one behind the other. In the lead group were two battleships, four cruisers and six destroyers, and in the trailing, or western, group were three battleships, two of the monster *Yamato* class, four cruisers and seven or eight destroyers.

Dog Smith selected the trailing group with the huge battleship for his target and led his flight westward, some fifteen miles south of the enemy fleet, to attack position. Smith's pilots, like Riera's in the morning, were startled when the first of the big, multicolor, double-bursting shells exploded nearby, and then, for nearly fifteen minutes they could watch the heavy guns flash so far away and wait for the rainbow streamers to erupt in the sky just close enough to be annoying.

When he was well past the Japanese formation, Smith turned north to get the sun behind him, and began his approach.

As the planes turned north, the ships also began to turn. All but one of the big battlewagons and a cruiser and destroyer, which seemed to be protecting her, turned right. She and her escorts turned left and came all the way around, slowly, to a westward heading, the opposite turn separating her from the rest of the force. Dog Smith put all his bombers and all his torpedo planes on her, and assigned the fighters to the cruiser and destroyer where their rockets could do more damage. He knew that there were only two battleships of that size in the world, *Yamato* and *Musashi,* the newest, fastest and most expensive ships the emperor had left, armed with incredible 18-inch guns. If Air Group Twenty could sink one of those monstrous twins, it would, on that one mission, have justified its entire existence, the training of every pilot and crewman, the design and construction of every plane, all the losses in men and materiel it had suffered all across the Pacific.

As the group turned in, it passed behind a thin cirrus cloud. All AA fire stopped at once, and Smith quickly changed course to approach as close as possible behind the cloud. Obviously the enemy was using entirely visual and no radar control of his guns. And his gunnery discipline was excellent. Every gun in the force ceased firing at the same moment, and, when the planes came back in sight, they all opened up together.

The Big E's planes pushed over slightly to begin a high-speed approach, and all apprehension vanished from the heads and hearts of her airmen. Like an athlete on the field when play has started, each pilot was oblivious to everything but the immediate objective. The enemy task force poured up the most impressive barrage of shell and tracer that the air group had yet experienced, but it could have saved its powder. Smith's men noted and then ignored it, remembering, thinking only of the tactics and procedures at which they had trained for so long in peace and in war.

Prickett's Avengers divided and slanted away to make their flat torpedo runs. The dive bombers came in high and fast to the push-over point, and then rolled in succession into their dives. Four fighters stayed up as cover and the other two divisions went down with the bombers to work over the cruiser and destroyer with guns and rockets.

Musashi held steadily on course, her tremendous bulk shoving through the calm sea at less than ten knots, her decks ringed with fire as her guns hammered back. As a result of previous attacks, she was trailing oil, but on an even keel and with no fires.

The bomber pilots, suspended over *Musashi*'s growing deck, had never had such a target—big, fat and steady as a tidal rock. They stayed late in their dives, released both bombs low, and pulled out sharply as only the SB2C could do, retiring low and fast, and under heavy fire, to the north.

As the last Helldiver dropped and pulled out, the first Avenger put its torpedo into the quiet waters of the Sibuyan Sea. Four of Prickett's planes came in on either bow, spread out so that the torpedo wakes ran straight and parallel, as though an invisible four-tined rake had been dragged through the sea. The torpedo pilots, like the dive bombers, pressed in close and released late, knowing that in all the history of war at sea few men have had opportunities like this one, and grimly determined not to muff it. It was as though the voice of that remnant of John Crommelin's soul which he had left with *Enterprise* was saying in its vigorous Alabama accent: "There is no room for waste, no excuse for misses. If you're going to go out there and miss, you should have stayed home and let a *good* pilot have your bunk and your crack at the Japs."

There were few misses on *Musashi*. Eleven out of eighteen 1,000-pound bombs smashed into her, most along her center line and close to amidships. All eight torpedoes hit her solidly, well forward. The big battlewagon was momentarily lost under the towering fountains of near misses and torpedo hits, soaring puffs of white smoke from bomb hits and streaming black smoke from resultant fires. Then the long, dark bow slid out of the caldron, slowing. *Musashi* stopped, down by the head, and burning.

The rockets of the Hellcats hit torpedoes or depth charges aboard the destroyer and she exploded in a blast of smoke and flying debris and was left burning fiercely when the strike departed for base.

Dog Smith, circling with his wingman for thirty minutes to observe results, saw the battleship's bow go so deep that her fo'c'sle was nearly awash, and smoke from her fires increase. And four hours after the *Enterprise* attack, with all Smith's pilots safely back aboard, *Musashi* rolled over and sank in the tropic seas between the islands she had sailed to hold for slavery. It was the first time that a modern battleship, equipped with the best of antiaircraft weapons, had been sunk by aircraft alone.

When pilots of Air Group Twenty's afternoon strike straggled back into their ready rooms just before 6:00 P.M., Task Group 38.4 had joined with 38.2 and there was new data on the briefing charts. The Northern Group had been located: four carriers with battleships, cruisers and destroyers in support, some 250 miles to the northward. The combined task groups turned toward the enemy at

10:22 P.M., and, toward midnight 38.3 added another four
carriers, two battleships and four cruisers to the formation.

In Flag Plot in *New Jersey*, Halsey and his staff considered the chart and the day's events. Two hundred fifty-
nine planes had hit the Center Force. *Musashi* was down,
three other battleships and a heavy cruiser damaged, in
addition to three heavy cruisers sunk by U. S. subs the
previous day. When last seen, Center Force was heading
back to the westward. Apparently it had had enough.

The Southern Force was still approaching, but on the
Leyte Gulf end of Surigao Straits, Rear Admiral Jesse B.
Oldendorf, with six old battleships, four heavy and four
light cruisers plus plenty of destroyers, was waiting for it
—and the straits themselves were lined on both sides with
PT boats, ready to dash out from the edges of the jungle
and launch their torpedoes. Southern Force was taken
care of.

The major threat seemed to be Vice Admiral Jisaburo
Ozawa's fast carriers approaching from the north. No one
knew better than Bill Halsey the destructive capability of
carrier aircraft, or the relative weakness of surface ships
without them. This time he was determined to "get the
carriers."

Orders went out, and the three task groups operating
east of the Philippines were drawn together for the run
north to attack. The fourth group, halfway to Ulithi, was
ordered back to cover Leyte—just in case—but it had a
long way to come.

Enterprise, with *Franklin, San Jacinto* and *Belleau
Wood* in the center of their cruiser and destroyer ring, ran
north at 25 knots all night.

During that night, Jim Gray and the Big E's expert
fighter director team shot down a four-engine Mavis seaplane with its crew of eight, forty miles northwest of the
force.

At 3:00 A.M., *Enterprise* slowed with the other carriers
of the combined task groups, while Ching Lee's fast battleships and their destroyers untangled themselves and
moved out ahead to put a screen of 16-inch rifles between
the carriers and the approaching enemy force.

And Fred Bakutis, drifting with his two rafts in the Sulu
Sea, picked up a drifting coconut and slept spasmodically
under a clear sky and a first half moon.

Tom Hamilton's "Plan of the Day" for October 25

called for reveille at 3:30 A.M., breakfast for half the crew at 3:40 and the other half at 4:15, General Quarters from 5:29 (one hour before computed sunrise) until sunrise, working parties to handle fresh provisions, ship's work to be done and the ship prepared for action, presented certain half-hour and hour periods when fresh water would be available, and carried a handwritten postscript signed TJH which read: "Today may be the biggest in our Navy's history. *Enterprise* will set the pace."

A few minutes after 6:00 A.M., seven search teams of one Avenger and one Hellcat each, plus three night fighters for communications relay, left the Big E's deck and fanned out on 275-mile, 10-degree sectors to look for the Northern Force. They failed to find it because assigned *Enterprise* sectors were to the south and west, but they shot down a Frances and a Judy in the course of the flight.

At 6:30 A.M. a strike of 13 bombers and 7 torpedo planes escorted by 16 fighters was launched to circle fifty miles to the north and wait for orders to attack when the enemy was located. Aircraft from the other carriers of 38.4 joined up. Dog Smith was strike leader.

At the fifty-mile point, similar strikes from 38.2 and 38.3 were already orbiting. The clear morning sky was filled with blue planes with white stars on their wings, circling, waiting.

The contact report came in at 7:20. The enemy carriers were only about eighty miles north of where Mitscher's airmen were standing by. The search planes stayed overhead, circling the enemy force and reporting course, speed, formation and identity. Ozawa had changed course to the northward during the night and Lee's battlewagons had nothing to fight.

Mitscher ordered his strike groups in. "Get the carriers," he said.

Commander David McCampbell, commanding Air Group Fifteen on the *Essex,* led the combined strike groups and assigned targets.

At 8:10, the enemy ships were in sight twenty-five miles ahead at the ends of long, white ribbons of wake, headed north.

As the massed air power of TF 38 approached, a carrier on the right side of the enemy formation hauled out to the northeast to launch. McCampbell assigned his own *Essex* and *Lexington* planes of TG 38.3 to her. TG 38.2 was awarded a carrier near the middle of the enemy force, and Dog Smith drew one well to the north.

At fifteen miles, the multicolored fireworks began again —showers, fountains and double-bursting streamers bloomed around the planes, and, as the first dive bombers started down, the twisting carriers put up such a barrage of phosphorus shells that two layers formed like clouds, one at 6,000 and one at 12,000 feet.

A few high Zekes engaged the covering Hellcats but could not get through to bombers or torpedo planes.

As they had done on the previous day in the attack on the *Musashi*, the torpedo planes broke off early and angled down to position themselves on the carrier's bow, three to starboard and four to port.

The Helldivers came up astern of the enemy, and dove to their left from east to west, out of the sun.

Except for Joe Lawler's division of high cover, the fighters dived in with their rockets on a cruiser and a destroyer which were putting up a terrific volume of AA fire.

Every carrier pilot dreams of the moments, like those at Midway, like those of Strong and Irvine at Santa Cruz, like these off Cape Engano when, trained, armed and fully ready, he will hold an enemy carrier in his sights. Dog Smith's boys were not going to waste those moments. The dive bombers dropped straight and true and released low above the empty flight deck, with its unfamiliar markings over a clever shadow camouflage intended to make her resemble a battleship. The Avengers, skimming in over a sea torn with splashes of all sizes, the tracers smoking and the shells bursting around them, saw the big bombs punch into the target, the smoke puff out and pieces fly before they dropped their torpedoes in close and began jinking wildly down among the big, viciously spitting warships, on their way out.

As the Big E's planes pulled away to the north, followed to ten miles by the long-range AA, her airmen could see the carrier dead in the water, listing and smoking heavily.

On the way out, a torpedo plane, flown by Lieutenant Frank Savage, was jumped by a Zeke zooming in from above and astern. The TBM had been hard hit by AA, and smoke poured from a ten-inch hole in the rear of the engine, the intercom was out and the turret gun jammed. Carl Cutter, in the turret, unable to bear looking into the flickering muzzles of the Zeke's guns and do nothing, desperately grabbed the Aldis signal lamp and flashed it at the enemy pilot. The Japanese, perhaps thinking that the light was a secret weapon, a new Yankee trick, broke off his attack, and Savage's Avenger limped back to *Enterprise* where it was promptly pushed overboard, too badly damaged to repair.

Of all the pilots and air-crewmen that survived that first strike on the Northern Force, Ensign George Denby of the Big E's Fighting 20 had unchallengeably the worst time.

George was flying wing on Joe Lawler as high cover for the strike, when his division was attacked by five exceptionally skillful and determined Zekes. Two Zekes dived away with two F6s following, and Lawler and Denby were left with the other three. Despite a defensive weave which Lawler and Denby set up, the Zekes made repeated hits, finally firing Denby's plane so that he had to bail out. In the words of the official action report:

> This was only the beginning of his troubles. He clung to the side of his plane while it made several turns but was shaken loose. He pulled the rip cord immediately and when the parachute opened he was jerked over on his back and found himself dangling upside down by his right leg. Four or more risers were either loose or broken, causing the parachute to oscillate and spill violently as it dropped at excessive speed.
>
> He was able to pull himself right side up, but there being nothing for him to sit on, he had to hang by his hands.
>
> When he had dropped to approximately 3,000 feet, 4 Zekes appeared, one of which broke off and fired a long burst at him which fell short. The planes then joined up, made a half turn and disappeared in the direction of the enemy fleet.
>
> He hit the water on his back, receiving quite a jar but managed to untangle himself and get rid of his shoes and back pack. He found that his life raft had been shaken off when his parachute opened, that the front half of his life jacket had a rip in it and the back half had to be inflated orally every half hour. Since half the jacket would not support his head, partly because the straps had ripped off the bottom of the jacket, he was forced to swim the entire time he was in the water.

As he swam, his socks gradually worked off leaving his bare feet as a lure for sharks, which promptly put in an appearance. A number of them, always 4 or more, 4—5 feet long, stayed with him continuously but did not bother him unless he stopped kicking. However, whenever he stopped to rest for a moment one of them would make a pass at him and one of them actually grazed the calf of his left leg, leaving tooth marks

After he had been in the water several hours a local storm kicked up a heavy sea and Denby found himself swallowing salt water from time to time, causing his tongue and lips to swell up. He tried holding his nose to prevent water from being forced up it but found that remedy not entirely practicable.

Finally about 1530 [3:30 P.M.] after he had been in the water nearly 2 hours, he saw a destroyer approach. Fortunately it came directly toward him, and, in fact, came so close that the propeller wash forced him under twice, nearly drowning him. Before going under he yelled and heard the call "Standby to pick up survivor." The destroyer made a 180-degree turn and threw Denby 2 lines which he was too weak to grab. Finally a swimmer came to his aid and fastened a line under his arms by which he was hauled aboard at 1600, considerably the worse for wear.

Dog Smith got back aboard at 10:45 A.M. and was impatiently in the air again at noon, leading the Big E's second major strike on what was left of Ozawa's carrier force, decoy or not.

Ten Helldivers, five Avengers and six Hellcats under Smith joined with others from 38.4 to form an attack group of some 80 aircraft. This time they knew where to find the enemy, and flew directly there.

Ozawa's neat formation of the morning had been knocked apart. Two wounded carriers, a battleship and two cruisers of the main force were straggling northward while twenty miles astern a small carrier lay dead in the water, listing, with a damaged battleship, a cruiser and a destroyer leaving her behind to join the main body.

TG 38.3 planes from *Lexington*, *Essex* and *Langley* attacked the two carriers first. Smith's group, maneuvering into position, saw the chain of bombers unwind down the sky and the tall splashes go up around the ships. The big carrier, ancient and respected enemy of *Enterprise,* and the last afloat of the six sneak killers of Pearl Harbor, was *Zuikaku* of the dreaded Solomons team of *Sho* and *Zui.* A sub had killed *Shokaku* in June, en route to the Marianas, and now it was *Zuikaku*'s turn. Three torpedoes spouted against her simultaneously and several bombs blew out her deck. She stopped, burning and settling (and flying the most enormous battle flag the *Enterprise* airmen had ever seen) and never moved again except to make the three-and-a-half mile voyage to the bottom.

The other carrier, *Zuiho,* was hit and fires flared and smoked, but they quickly died out as her damage control teams went into action, and she continued at 20 knots toward the north.

The *Franklin* group attacked her next, but she kept going, and it was Dog Smith's turn.

Air Group Twenty's dive bombers moved in over the carrier from the southwest and dived straight out of the sun and behind a few scattered clouds. Not a gun spoke during approach or in the dive itself. The three torpedo planes also managed to come in behind the increasing clouds. Again the aggressive *Enterprise* pilots pressed in so close it would have been hard to miss. Some dozen bombs and two torpedoes hit *Zuiho,* stopped her and set her afire. This time the fires did not go out, nor did she gain steerageway again.

Commander Hugh Winters, commanding *Lexington*'s Air Group Nineteen, saw *Zuikaku* roll over and go down minutes after Smith and his airmen had left for home. *Zuiho* managed to stay afloat for one more strike to bomb, and then sank at 3:26 P.M.

Out of this action came one of the best combat pictures of the war: a close-up of *Zuiho* wounded and on fire but under way in an evasive turn. It was taken by Fred Rand from Lieutenant (j.g.) Tom Armour's Avenger as he banked after his torpedo run and flew close aboard down the carrier's starboard side.

Tirelessly aggressive Dog Smith returned from his second strike of the day at 3:30 P.M., and forty-five minutes later was air-borne on his third. He preferred this one to the other two. It was a quick, pre-dark smash at Ozawa's remnants with sixteen Hellcats carrying 1,000-pound bombs: out fast, strike and return. In the day's other actions, Smith and his brother fighter pilots had to watch other squadrons do the real job while they covered, or tried to beat down enemy gunners with their relatively puny rockets and .50-calibers. Now they had something with which to hit the enemy hard.

It was good not to have to wait and throttle back for the slow SB2Cs and TBMs. The fighters carried high-power settings, climbed rapidly to 14,000 feet and headed north indicating 200 knots. They overflew one group of enemy ships to hit the ones farthest north and slow them for the fast-approaching U. S. surface ships and submarines to finish.

At the point of Ozawa's retreating task force was an old battleship and a light cruiser. Smith's Hellcats swung around to an up-sun position and pushed over to gain speed for the attack. Dog ordered them to concentrate on the cruiser, since he felt crippling her was preferable to damaging the battleship.

The fighters slanted down to 9,000 and then pushed over in 45-degree dives through the smoking, flashing AA that poured up to meet them. Fred Bakutis had trained his fighter pilots in bombing back in the halcyon days of Pu-unene on Maui, and now it paid off handsomely, even though he himself, at that moment, was nearing the end of a long second day under the boiling sun of the Sulu Sea a thousand or so miles to the south. Dog Smith shoved his Hellcat over in a dive so steep that his air speed indicated 430 knots, 40 knots past the builder's red line, released and pulled out at 500 feet. The others pressed in as close. Five hits and three near misses smashed the cruiser and stopped her in the middle of a hard evasive turn.

When eight Hellcats had dropped, the air coordinator ordered the others to shift targets to the battleship, since it appeared that the cruiser, stopped and burning, had had enough. The sea spouted close around the battlewagon, and pilots reported three hits, but the tough old lady kept going.

On the way home, Bob Nelson, his engine holed by AA while flying wing on Dog Smith during the attack, was forced into the sea near friendly cruisers advancing to mop up, and was promptly rescued.

Dog Smith's fighter-bomber strike ended the two-day battle for *Enterprise* and her men began to piece together what had happened. It had been obvious all day the twenty-fifth that there was trouble around Leyte Gulf. The radios were loud with urgent plain-language calls for help in unmistakable American. There were incredible reports of gun duels between Japanese heavy cruisers and U. S. escort carriers, of broad daylight torpedo attacks on those same cruisers by 21-knot U. S. destroyer escorts mounting two five-inch guns.

The reports were all true. The Southern Force had tried the Surigao Strait approach to Leyte Gulf and been annihilated by Admiral Oldendorf's old battleships as planned. But the Center Force, wounded but still strong after the air attacks of the twenty-fourth, had turned again and slipped through San Bernadino and out around Samar. TF 38 was not present to challenge because it was chasing Ozawa's carriers to the northward, also as planned—by Admiral Toyoda, Commander-in-Chief Combined Fleet.

On the way into Leyte Gulf to decimate the shipping there, Center Force had run afoul of the escort carrier group operating off Samar to furnish air support to the landing operations. The baby carriers, with their destroyer escorts backed up by an occasional destroyer, the "B-squad" of the Navy had put up such a battle—flying off their Avengers and Wildcats down wind as they ran, exchanging shot for shot with the big, fast enemy first-line cruisers, unbelievably threatening and hitting with torpedoes and five-inch guns, their pilots making dry runs down the muzzles of enemy turrets when they ran out of bombs, bullets and torpedoes, and all the while screaming so loudly for big carriers and fast battleships to come to the rescue—that Center Force pulled back into San Bernadino and headed home just as the first long-range strikes came in from the fast carriers. The Center Force had sunk only one of the little CVEs, two destroyers and a destroyer escort, and had lost three heavy cruisers itself.

This "second team," according to Rear Admiral Samuel Eliot Morison, in Volume XII of his definitive *History of Naval Operations in World War II,* had "stopped the most powerful surface fleet which Japan had sent to sea since the Battle of Midway."

Of all the U. S. forces involved in this sprawling two-day slugging match, *Enterprise* was the only carrier to engage all three of the attacking enemy task groups.

On the night of his seventh day, Fred Bakutis had rigged a sail and was sleeping soundly in the clear moonlight when

he was awakened by the "growl of Diesel engines." At first
he thought it was an enemy gunboat and "stood by to
jump overboard." But it was a U. S. submarine, the *Hardhead,* and minutes later, Fred, with soup, sandwiches,
coffee, two pills and a shot of whisky in his stomach,
cleaned by a warm, fresh-water shower and a shave, had
returned to his interrupted sleep, safe in a white-sheeted
bunk.

Hardhead's skipper, Commander Greenup, had received
word that a pilot was down in the vicinity and had changed
course 30 degrees right to pass through the reported position. About ten minutes after course change, one of the
sub's sharp-eyed lookouts sighted Fred's sail a mile ahead.

Hardhead put Bakutis aboard another sub bound for
Perth, Australia, and from there he flew back to Pearl to
rejoin his squadron.

On the twenty-ninth, Ralph Davison's TG 38.4 operated
in cloudy, squally weather to the eastward of Leyte Gulf,
furnishing CAP over the battlefront and the vulnerable
anchored shipping, and searching for survivors of the
CVEs and destroyer types sunk in their scuffle with the
Japanese battle line on the twenty-fifth.

On the thirtieth it was still there—tethered to the Army
and the anchored transports and landing craft for the fifth
day. The enemy was neither stupid nor cowardly enough
to pass up an opportunity to attack a practically stationary
carrier task force—and shortly after 2:00 P.M. *Enterprise*
got her first look at a planned, deliberate suicide attack—
the Japanese Kamikaze assault.

Twelve fighters had just been launched as CAP for the
tanker group, then some 220 miles to the northeast, and
the destroyer *Morey* was lying to, her men lining the rail,
a cargo net rigged down her side and swimmers overboard
to rescue Jim Gray, the new skipper of Fighting 20, who
had crashed on take-off.

While Gray was still in the water, radar picked up inbound enemy planes fifty-five miles to the west and very
high. The task group went to General Quarters, drew its
circle tight. CAP was vectored out but the enemy planes
split up and attacked in long, high-speed glides. Four of
them managed to evade the intercepting Hellcats and at
2:25 the Big E's lookouts had them in sight.

The first one, a Zeke, never broke his 45-degree dive,

but continued at an incredible geometric angle straight through the flight deck of the *Franklin*, steaming 4,000 yards to port across the formation from *Enterprise*. A sickening boil of flames swelled and burst aft on the big new carrier, and a heavy column of smoke grew quickly and streamed back over her wake.

The *Franklin* was still smoking badly three minutes later when the second Zeke attacked her. He dived in steep and fast, the heavy bursts of five-inch and multiple lighter puffs of 40-millimeters following him down. *Enterprise* gunners knew that in the next second they would see the ugly welling of flame and smoke repeated and know that men were dying under it. But at the last instant the Zeke pulled up. A bomb splashed dirtily well forward of *Franklin*. The enemy zoomed, clawing for altitude, his engine whining and the black bursts of AA blooming around him, and at the top of his climb, dropped his right wing and began a turn toward *Enterprise*. The port 40-millimeter mounts opened with their rapid, overlapping pounding at the limit of their range but it was close enough for the enemy pilot. The Zeke's wings leveled with a jerk, its nose dropped and it dived straight at *Belleau Wood*, next ahead of *Franklin*. Again the AA laced and smoked in the sky around the plane, but this time he did not pull up. The Zeke hit the light carrier flush on the aft end of her flight deck and an explosion blasted white smoke down to the water's edge and high into the sky above her. Chunks of flaming debris arched in streamers out of the smoke cloud, red flame licked through the white and then the steady black began to billow up. From bridge and gun sponson and 20-millimeter gallery in *Enterprise*, her men in their heavy helmets, with sleeves rolled down, collars buttoned, and trouser legs tucked into socks, watched with horror and anger and nervously searched the sky above and aft for the next attacker.

On the flying bridge at the top of the island, Tom Hamilton, unmistakable by his bulk, and visible from almost every topside battle station, stood helmeted and with the bull-horn mike in his hand, describing the action as it happened. His big, well-known voice, calm and matter of fact, came from every speaker the length and breadth of the taut, expectant ship and the blind men below in repair parties, engineering spaces, steering engine room, handling-rooms, ready rooms and dressing stations could see with his eyes. It is a hard thing for a man below decks during action. Tom's voice removed the trapped, uncomfortable feeling, the ignorance of events, and the men of *Enterprise* loved him for it.

With two of his four carriers on fire but still making 24 knots, Admiral Davison ordered a hard turn to starboard. The task group had hardly settled down on the new, southerly heading, when two more Zekes came plunging in. One picked *San Jacinto,* on the Big E's starboard beam, but was hit by the streaming AA and splashed close to her bow. The other took *Enterprise.* He came in fast, at a shallow angle straight at her starboard side. Bill Smith, still gun boss, held his five-inch fire for fear of hitting other ships, but every 40 and 20 that would bear slammed its tracers up and out at the enemy. The Big E's gunners had seen the fire boils and the blasts on *Franklin* and *Belleau Wood,* and they knew they would have to kill this Japanese in the next seconds or destroy his plane to keep from dying in a similar eruption of flame and smoke on *Enterprise.* The men below, listening to Tom Hamilton's play-by-play, held their breath, hoping that the next words would be: "Splash on Zeke." But they were not.

At a mile and a half, the heavy 40-millimeter tracers were scorching past him feet away, and at a mile the 20s began to hit. At half a mile, the Zeke's left wing was tattered and flame was pouring from the engine past the cockpit on both sides. He made no attempt to turn or pull out. By now the head-on, burning Zeke filled the sights of the steadily firing starboard gunners. On the 40 quads and twins there was no shortage of rounds for the first loaders to drop into the loading chutes. The snail-shaped magazines of the 20s were changed in record time. Every man in every gun crew knew that his life depended on the amount of lead that could be poured into that insanely hurtling piece of winged aluminum. At a quarter of a mile, the Zeke's left wing could no longer provide its share of the lift, and the Zeke began to roll, the smoke spiraling behind him. But, rolling and aflame, its pilot probably already dead with the death he was seeking, the fighter never changed its course or angle. Had it been aimed a touch more to the right, or had *Enterprise* been making a few knots less speed, the Zeke would have smashed against the island. Instead he passed astern of it, rolling across the flight deck ten to fifteen feet above its parked and gassed aircraft, and exploded in the sea fifty yards to port. Pieces of a wing landed in the port catwalk.

It was close, and it left the men of *Enterprise* shaken in a way that bombs had not been able to do. There was something inhuman, something homicidally insane, about the Kamikaze, which violated the instincts of the American sailors.

Franklin and *Belleau Wood* put out their fires and continued in formation but their decks were ruined and their losses high. Fifty-six of *Franklin's* men were killed, 33 of her planes destroyed by fire. *Belleau Wood* lost 92 men and 12 aircraft.

Task Group 38.4 fueled and headed for the atoll anchorage of Ulithi, TF 38's new advanced base, where the Big E's men, for the three days in port, worked as hard at provisioning and rearming as they had been working at sea. But they could sleep all night and there was a cheering sprinkle of mail and a few hours for some on the sandy beach.

When the ships formed up again outside the reef, the sailors could see it was a different group from the one which had entered. *Franklin* and *Belleau Wood* had been left to make repairs and *Yorktown* had joined temporarily as the second large carrier. Three heavy cruisers and one antiaircraft light cruiser ringed the carriers. Command of TF 38, Fast Carriers, Pacific, had also changed. Vice Admiral J. S. "Slew" McCain had relieved Marc Mitscher on October 31, and the stern, brilliant, warmhearted little man with the long-billed cap and the wrinkled, sailor's face, was on his way home for a rest. The course was back to the Philippines.

All day the eighth and ninth of November, *Enterprise* lurched and climbed and fell away to plunge and shake and rise again in the high, fast-moving seas on the edge of a typhoon which lay to the southward. There was no possibility of flight operations from the careening deck in the typhoon winds until around noon on the ninth.

TG 38.4 was forced northeast and east, away from the storm center, and finally circled south and west, coming in behind the typhoon as it continued northward.

Early on the midwatch of the tenth, the men below could feel the Big E tremble, and hear the increased pitch of the turbines as she went to 26 knots. MacArthur had requested Halsey, commanding the U. S. Third Fleet, to strike an

enemy convoy bound from Manila to Ormoc Bay up the
back side of Leyte with 10,000 reinforcements. The Fast
Carriers answered the call, and three task groups headed
for Leyte, plunging through the heavy seas in the typhoon's
wake.

All day the tenth and all that night, the vast American
air base complex approached the Philippines, closing at a
hundred miles a watch. Dawn on the eleventh of November,
a day which had seen one war end, now saw another being
vigorously prosecuted.

Task Force 38 put 347 strike planes in the air that
autumn morning. Forty-nine were from Air Group Twenty,
with Dog Smith leading the flight.

By eleven, they were over the target—six fat, troop-
crowded transports, escorted by four destroyers and some
smaller craft.

The strike group of TF 38, which only a few days before had sunk four carriers, a superbattleship and three
cruisers and broken the back of the Japanese Navy,
smothered this lightly guarded convoy. So many aircraft
crowded the skies above the ships that Dog Smith had to
circle unhappily for twenty minutes, awaiting his turn. By
the time it came, all the transports but one were down, and
that one was listing and trailing oil. The *Enterprise* air
group was assigned three destroyers and the damaged
transport. Smith split his 12 torpedo planes between the
transport and a destroyer, put 5 SB2Cs on each destroyer
and divided his 22 fighters impartially over all targets.

It only took a few minutes. One destroyer, hit five times,
steamed eastward a short distance, burning from stem to
stern, and then disintegrated in a mushrooming double
explosion that pebbled the sea with falling debris over a
radius of half a mile. A second, hit six times, simply capsized and sank. The third, its bow blown off and its guns
silent, lay dead in the water in a spreading pool of oil. The
wounded transport disintegrated under seven 500-pound
bombs. Of the 10,000 troops bound for Leyte to oppose
MacArthur's soldiers, a few dozen of the best swimmers
made the shore, and half of those escaped the native
machetes and bolos to join the Leyte garrison where, exhausted and without equipment, they were a liability to
their new units.

There was a day of respite for fueling, and then the Big
E hit Manila again. She steamed 150 to 200 miles north-

northeast of the city for two days while her air group worked over the surrounding airfields and the shipping in bay and harbor, retired for rest and fuel and returned for a final day of strikes. It was an eventful three days.

As usual, a fighter sweep began the day and the action. Fifteen Hellcats under Dog Smith arrived over the city at 8:15 the first morning, promptly shot down the only two enemy planes that attempted interception, and dived across Clark and its outlying fields, blasting at grounded planes with their guns and rockets.

The enemy had put some new ideas to work since Air Group Twenty had last visited Clark. The usual banked-earth revetments, easy to spot from the air and not hard to hit, were empty, and his tan or mottled green and tan aircraft were dispersed instead in open grass fields, drained of gasoline, camouflaged with nets and liberally interspersed with dummy planes. As a result, they were hard to locate, hard to hit, except singly, and hard to burn when hit.

Strike followed sweep in the accustomed pattern, and at 9:30 a mixed group of twenty-five *Enterprise* bombers and torpedo planes, escorted by ten fighters, attacked the shipping in Manila Bay. No interceptors appeared, and in a coordinated dive and glide assault through the heavy AA, one big freighter was hit repeatedly and sunk, and four others badly damaged.

The second fighter sweep on the thirteenth sprung an enemy trap. Dog Smith took another fourteen Hellcats back to Clark. While some went down to strafe, one section attacked a single Tojo directly over the field. The Tojo dove away and ten more enemy fighters plummeted down from high altitude to jump the F6s. The Hellcats yelled for help and Dog instantly appeared with reinforcements. Several more Japanese planes charged in and for ten minutes a vigorous, all-out air battle swirled, roared, whined and stuttered over Clark Field. Out of it fell ten Japanese— and no American fighters. Young Doug Baker was in on three kills and Mel Prichard got two. At one point, according to the action report:

Commander Smith and his wingman, Lieutenant (j.g.) T. J. Woodruff, got on the tail of a Zeke which apparently had charged up later to join the fight. The Jap executed a series of spectacular maneuvers and, apparently confident that this had lost his pursuers, cruised blithely ahead. Commander Smith and Woodruff, however, had duplicated his tactic from beginning to end—in formation in fact—and followed to send the Zeke crashing in flames.

Bogies probed the perimeter of the combined task groups all day, and several were splashed by CAP a few miles out. The enemy knew exactly where TF 38 was operating and was gathering strength to attack.

Dog Smith's airmen had four full days of rest while *Enterprise*, in company with the other ships of TF 38, retired to the northeast to fuel. But on the nineteenth they went back to work.

At the end of a nightlong run-in, *Enterprise* launched sixteen Hellcats under the group commander on a sweep of the airfields around Manila. They hit Clark first but the field had been worked over so often there was little left to fire at.

Aggressive Dog Smith, disappointed at the lack of targets at Clark, led a low-level search of the area for better ones.

A few miles to the south of Clark, he discovered several well-camouflaged planes parked near Del Carmen airstrip, and led an attack on them. As the Hellcats pressed in low enough on their strafing runs to see through the camouflage, they found more and more targets until "a real treasury of Jap aircraft had been uncovered." Dog estimated 100 planes were hidden under foliage around Del Carmen, and, by the satisfactory manner in which they flamed and exploded under fire, they were fully armed and gassed.

He established a traffic circle over the target, with each fighter attacking in turn, pulling up and returning in a raceback pattern behind the other planes to attack again. AA was negligible, and Smith's pilots swept across the parking area at twenty-five feet, aiming carefully. When they finally left for home, seventeen enemy planes had burned to the ground and twenty-three more would not fly again. But there were plenty left.

The strike that morning hit shipping again and bombed hangars and parking ramps at Clark, but a second strike which had been scheduled for noon was canceled, and in its place Dog Smith took twenty-seven fighters back to Del Carmen to finish the job and photograph results. A similar group from *Hornet* joined forces with Fighting 20.

A double traffic circle was established this time, the *Hornet* planes taking the northern half of the field, making right turns, and *Enterprise* the southern half with left turns.

Dog Smith, seeing that target well handled, with four times the number of the morning sweep, all fresh and with full loads of ammunition, took his wingman in search of still another. Just north of Del Carmen, they found a lone Zeke in a clump of trees and went to the deck to investigate. Despite the fact that Smith had flown low over the same area several times before, he now discovered a cleverly camouflaged airstrip, its runway obscured by a dirt road down its middle, houses and trees sprinkled over it with planes hidden under every tree. Dog called a couple of divisions over from Del Carmen, and the destruction began again.

When VF 20 finally rejoined and headed home, some seventy enemy aircraft lay in their grassy hiding places, charred into scrap aluminum. Not a single U. S. plane had so much as a bullet nick.

When he was complimented by Tom Hamilton and Cato Glover on the day's work, Dog Smith felt required to disclaim the honor with a final paragraph in his official report:

> The Commander, Air Group Twenty, can accept no credit for discovering this field since at the time it was located he was flying along a railroad track in the hopes of satisfying an old ambition to blow up a locomotive.

The raid on Del Carmen and vicinity was the last serious offensive strike flown by Air Group Twenty from *Enterprise*. But there was still some vital defensive work to be done.

At about five o'clock, CAP from another carrier intercepted the enemy group sixty miles out, and shot down three of the fast new Frances torpedo bombers. The others split up and came in separately. Ten minutes later *Enterprise* launched two fighter divisions to reinforce the CAP. One division led by Lafe Shannon was vectored out. The other circled high over the task group in safety position.

Lafe's Hellcats were ordered to 25,000 feet, then back to 10,000, and there found a brown and dark-green Betty streaking for the carriers some 4,000 feet below them. They turned and made three quick runs in succession before the Betty's right engine flamed and she spun into the sea. At once the FDO put them on another vector, this time to the southeast, and in a few minutes they had destroyed a second Betty, also inbound, low and fast.

The sun set over TF 38 on the nineteenth of November at eight minutes past six. It was a clear and balmy evening. So clear that twenty minutes later, the Big E's lookouts could see a low flying plane approaching the starboard quarter of the formation or ten miles away. Motors whined and buzzed as the directors brought their guns around and found the target. A hundred pairs of binoculars focused on the growing, skimming speck, and at six miles the five-inch began to fire as the ships began an emergency turn away. The enemy came on, with the black bursts blooming around him. But this was no Kamikaze. At four miles he dropped his torpedo, aimed at nothing, and turned away to the left followed by the persistent puffs of black.

Some seventeen miles from the task group, as the Japanese air crew must have been sighing with relief at having escaped with their skins, they blundered into four Hellcats —Lafe Shannon's CAP division returning to base after its two recent kills. The enemy plane commander dived for the water and ordered his tail and dorsal gunners to open fire as the first Grumman came angling in fast from astern. Guns winked along the blue fighter's wings, and the Betty jarred with the hammering of the .50-caliber slugs. But Ed Boudinot watched tracers streaming past close under his plane and pulled up.

"Watch this bastard," he said into his mike, "he's shooting back and getting damned close."

But Bob Nelson, right behind Boudinot, was just starting his run. He pressed in, his guns smoking, and the Japanese gunners answered from tail and top of the desperately running Betty. The port engine was on fire, lighting the cockpit and the oriental faces of the pilots, straining to hold the wing up. The starboard engine was beginning to smoke and lose power. But Bob Nelson's F6, its left wing flaming, pulled up steeply, rolled over and dove into the water. The next second the Betty's starboard engine flared and lost all power and the plane hit, bounced and cartwheeled, burning, into the Pacific.

Enterprise recovered her fighters, stayed at General Quarters for another couple of hours while other bogies approached but did not attack, and then pointed her bow eastward away from Luzon and the Philippines.

On the twenty-second of November, the Big E entered Ulithi lagoon, and on the twenty-third, Dog Smith and his Air Group Twenty embarked with their gear in landing craft and fifty-foot motor launches, and crossed the anchorage to *Lexington,* while the *Lexington's* Air Group Nineteen transferred to *Enterprise* for transportation to Pearl Harbor.

Enterprise went home to Pearl for a few days in the Yard, necessary heavy maintenance and a rest for her crew. But Air Group Twenty, after two and a half weeks in the sun and breeze of Ulithi, went back to bloody Luzon, and, for two months after the Big E's return to action, worked with her and her new group wherever the fast carriers were needed.

Dog Smith and his men were only in *Enterprise* three months, but in planes and ships destroyed and damage inflicted on the enemy, they hold the record. Certainly no more spirited or aggressive group ever served in the most aggressive and spirited of all aircraft carriers.

22 HUNTERS IN THE DARK

When the Big E sailed again on Christmas Eve, she had a new skipper, a new exec, a new admiral, a new air group and a new designation. She was no longer the USS *Enterprise* (CV-6) but the USS *Enterprise* (CV(N)-6). The Big E was a night carrier, flying a night air group—the first big carrier to be assigned such duty.

Yet with all the changes, *Enterprise* had not changed. Like ancient China, she could, by now, absorb all changes and remain herself. And many of her "new" people were not new to her. Her "new" admiral was tall, hawk-faced Mat Gardner, who a year before had been her captain. Admiral Gardner's operations officer was Roscoe Newman who a year before had commanded her air group and later had been her assistant air officer. The "new" air group commander was Bill Martin, exec of old Scouting 10 in 1942, and skipper of Torpedo 10 six months ago. And in Martin's Night Air Group Ninety were more than a dozen names familiar to the Big E.

With all the changes and all the essential sameness, *Enterprise* took to the open sea again, and there spent Christmas and entered the New Year on her way west into the action for which she was born.

Before dawn on the fifth of January, 1945, *Enterprise* made contact with Task Force 38. The Fast Carriers were operating northeast of Luzon and southeast of Formosa, attempting to punch enough strikes through the foul weather that hung over those islands to eliminate Japanese air interference with the landings at Lingayen Gulf on the west coast of Luzon, scheduled for January 9.

By midmorning, the Big E, which had grown accustomed during the past two weeks to being the only major ship in sight, was at the center of "the most powerful naval striking force that the world had ever known." Formations of warships of every sort and size steamed on their zigzag courses below the dark clouds, covering the sea to the horizon on all sides. All four task groups of TF 38 were there, plus a formation of fast fleet oilers because the fifth was fueling day. Bill Halsey, commanding the Third Fleet, flew his four-star flag in the fast battleship *New Jersey,* and Slew McCain, in Mitscher's place as commander, Fast Carriers Pacific, had his three stars in *Lexington.*

At once a message came by flashing light from Halsey:

. . . WITH GREAT PLEASURE I WELCOME COMCAR-DIV-7 [COMMANDER CARRIER DIVISION SEVEN (ADMIRAL GARDNER)] AND HIS STAFF TO THE BIG BLUE TEAM AND I AM HAPPY TO HAVE THE ENTERPRISE BACK IN HER REGULAR POSITION. FROM PAST EXPERIENCE I KNOW WE CAN EXPECT GREAT THINGS FROM THE GALLOPING GHOST

Admiral Gardner took command of a fifth task group within Task Force 38, Task Group 38.5, the first night carrier task group in history, made up of light carrier *Independence, Enterprise* and six destroyers. *Independence* had been operating as a night carrier since summer, with Turner Caldwell, who had commanded the *Enterprise* detachment on Guadalcanal, as her air group commander. It was arranged that TG 38.5 would combine, for added protection, with 38.2 during daylight, but separate and operate independently at night when only the two night air groups would be flying.

Bill Martin had been pursuing his idea of night and bad weather round-the-clock air warfare since, as an instrument flight instructor at Corpus Christi, he had heard of air-borne radar and mentally put the two, instruments and radar, together. At Espiritu and Noumea he had borrowed the early TBFs (even though he was assigned to an SBD squadron) to try out his ideas in night navigation flights and low-level bombing runs on rocks and small islands. He had tirelessly trained Torpedo 10 in instrument and night flying, using a training manual which he himself had written, and planned and briefed the first night low-level bombing attack in the Truk Lagoon in February of 1944. He had urged the new tactics of night search and attack—and had personally demonstrated them at every opportunity. He had found able allies and converts, among them Lieutenant Commander Henry Loomis, officer in charge of the radar school at Pearl Harbor, and now, at his own request, on temporary duty as radar officer on Admiral Gardner's staff, and Lieutenant Commander Bill Chace, who had acted as radar maintenance officer for VF-10 and was now the administrative and radar operations officer of Night Air Group Ninety.

All the talking, arguing, urging and, most of all, the showing, had paid off—first in Turner Caldwell's night group aboard the CVL *Independence,* and now in his own group aboard the CV *Enterprise.*

Martin was intensely eager to make night operations work—to prove he was right. And he was on the defensive. There was a strong body of opinion in the fleet which thought "We are winning the war the way we are fighting it now. Why change?" This school of thought considered that the added weight, on enemy targets, of day air groups from a CV and a CVL now restricted t night flying, and the added defensive strength of their day CAPs, outweighed any advantage which might be gained by night operations.

Thus the success or failure of each night CAP, strike, heckle and search was of urgent personal importance to Martin. And gradually it began to be important to every pilot and crewman in his air group, and spread from them to the crew of the Big E herself.

The ship's company was, of necessity, as involved with night operations as the air group itself. A fast carrier, long accustomed to day work, is not transformed into a CV(N) instantaneously by decree. *Enterprise* was expected to do most of her work at night, but this did not mean that she had nothing to do during daylight. Her deck had to be kept open to receive "sick" planes from the day carriers, and to reinforce the CAP in the event of heavy attacks on the force. This meant that the flight deck had to be manned throughout the twenty-four hours, complete with LSOs (night and day qualified), catapult, arresting gear and crash crews. Control and supervisory stations such as Air Plot, Fly Control and CIC also had to be manned full-time with qualified officers actually in charge of each. CIC had a double job. It controlled the Big E's own planes at night, and was frequently called on by the task group commander to direct interceptions during the day when the other carriers were busy with their own planes. Key officers and enlisted men split up the day, standing twelve-hour watches —midnight until noon and noon to midnight. A fourth meal was served from 11:30 P.M. until 1:30 A.M., and the main meal of the day was changed from noon to evening to catch the overlap of the day crews and the night crews. With frequent torpedo defense alarms and General Quarters as bogies approached, sleep was in great demand in *Enterprise* and her men were permitted and encouraged to catnap whenever the work-load allowed, in order to store up the minutes of rest which made the difference between tired, inefficient and thus dangerous crews, and alert, competent ones.

As a night carrier, *Enterprise* carried an air group composed only of fighters and torpedo planes. Dive bombing cannot be done at night. And at night the flight deck must be kept clear forward of the catapults for take-offs, and clear aft of the barriers for landings. There must be room to use an elevator and room on the hangar deck for maintenance. Night operations are conducted in small groups, not mass strikes. So *Enterprise* carried only 55 planes—34 F6Fs and 21 TBMs. But each of those 55 planes now had radar, on which depended the success of its every mission, in addition to the usual radios which became far more important at night. Electronics maintenance tripled in importance.

Control and lighting systems which had been satisfactory for an occasional after-dark landing at the end of a day strike were inadequate and even unsafe for continuous night operations. New deck-edge lights, which gave the pilots some depth perception, had to be designed, built and installed and new procedures and controls devised.

Air Group Ninety's first strike was not an outstanding success. Three of the fifteen night fighters, because of faulty radar, hydraulics and just plain getting lost, never made the target. The dozen that made it, hit the Clark runways with rockets but found no planes on the ground or in the air. AA was heavy and Bob McCullough, pressing low and close on his first mission as squadron commander, was badly shot up. He attempted a no-flap, no-hydraulics, poor-throttle-control landing and went through all the barriers, damaged several planes, knocked one overboard and followed it himself. Four men of the flight-deck crew were injured and a fire flared briefly in the port gun gallery. McCullough was picked up at once, bruised and scratched, by a destroyer, and returned aboard. The rest of the returning sweep had to land on *Independence* and *Lexington* while the Big E cleared her deck and laboriously repaired her barriers. The pilots that landed on *Lexington* were cordially received by the redoubtable Dog Smith and his Air Group Twenty, back again in the fight for the Philippines.

On the evening of the ninth of January with dusk closing down on the United States Sixth Army newly ashore at Lingayen, TF 38 began a high-speed run southwest through Bashi Channel between Formosa and Luzon. It was the first time that U. S. naval forces, other than submarines, had entered the South China Sea since the beginning of hostilities four years before.

Bill Halsey had been wanting to sweep the China Sea for months, but some more urgent commitment had always interfered. Four task groups plowed through the Luzon Strait that night, covered by an *Independence* night CAP which destroyed three snoopers before they could report. By dawn of the tenth, TF 38 was well in and headed for Indo-China through a rough but following sea which was a preview of the foul weather the U. S. ships would be in for eleven days.

Halsey had reason to believe that some of the Japanese battleships which had survived the Battle for Leyte Gulf were holed up along the coast of Indo-China, especially in the area of Camranh Bay, and, early on the afternoon of the eleventh, TF 38 started its approach to that target. At the point of the attack was Mat Gardner's night-flying 38.5 —*Enterprise*, *Independence* and six destroyers.

Enterprise began launching four two-Avenger search teams in the solid, high-overcast dark of 3:00 A.M. *Independence* did the same. The blacked-out TBMs fanned out over the China coast from a hundred miles to seaward like the fingers of an exploring hand, peering through the night with radar, laying naked suspicious areas with the harsh brilliance of parachute flares, occasionally scorching a rocket or two into likely targets. And behind the probing fingers, the heavy fist of the day carriers was cocked and ready. In *Enterprise*, Bill Martin, aware of the increasing restlessness of his Avenger squadron under its relative inaction, stood by with a strike of eleven torpedo-loaded TBMs and ten F6s armed with rockets to attack anything the night searchers might flush.

The searching torpedo planes might as well have been investigating the coast of Florida. On the airfields there were no planes, no activity; in the bays and harbors no ships, certainly no battleships. They kept searching long after daylight and finally sighted an enemy convoy of tankers and merchant ships, sneaking northward close to shore with an escort of a light cruiser, destroyers and DEs.

When no heavy ships had been sighted by dawn, Martin changed the loading of his strike from torpedoes to bombs, and, when the convoy was reported, the TBMs took off with four 500-pounders each. The already poor weather grew worse all day. Ceiling and visibility closed in, and the wind and sea kicked up as a typhoon churned westward across the south end of the China Sea. *Enterprise* bombers and fighters, in company with a similar group from *Independence*, skimmed northwestward between the gray clouds and the gray sea, a few hundred feet off the water, turned into the coast and followed its dark, irregular contour north for another twenty miles before they found the 15-ship convoy, steaming due north in two parallel columns across the spacious bay south of Quinhon.

Over the target the base of the dark gray overcast was at 4,000 feet and visibility was ten miles or better. Mat

Gardner's nighthawks swarmed in for the kill, delighted and relieved to have targets they could see and a chance to inflict damage that could be observed and reported. Lieutenant Russell Kippen, CO of VT-90, led the attack and picked the strongest target, the *Katori*-class light cruiser. His TBMs followed him in, attacking at once from south to north with no circling or maneuvering for position. Kip's two bombs straddled the cruiser, close aboard on both sides, and she turned to port, heading for the beach. Joe Jennings put two of his bombs into a destroyer which also headed for shore, burning and under heavy strafing attack by the fighters. Jim Landon missed on his first run, but on his second run hit one of the merchantmen on the stern. The merchantman, already holed by two of Fighting 90's rockets, settled heavily, black smoke sloping downwind at a 45-degree angle.

When the night birds, with the forward-pointing *Enterprise* arrow outlined on their tails, joined up under the low clouds to seaward for the flight home, one merchantman was down, two were dead in the water, burning and settling, two more were wounded and heading for shore, and another two were hit and circling aimlessly.

In the afternoon, twelve of Lieutenant Commander Bob McCullough's VF-90 Hellcats strafed the airfield at Saigon and burned or demolished nine enemy planes, and in the evening four more F6Fs attacked the same target to be certain that Saigon would launch no counterstrikes on TF 38.

The next day was the worst of all the bad days in the China Sea. At 8:00 A.M. the typhoon was 200 miles south of *Enterprise*, and a 40-knot northeasterly wind whipped up heavy swells and blew dense rain squalls across the carrier's deck. Ceilings were never above 900 feet, and visibility ranged between zero in the squalls to two or three miles. Nevertheless, the Big E launched six Avengers on a search in the plunging blackness of 4:30 A.M. and followed with four Hellcats for the dawn CAP. The search found nothing, and the Japanese had the good sense to stay on the deck in typhoon weather and provided no business for the CAP.

All day the businesslike gray warships of TF 38 steamed northward through the cresting seas that occasionally broke over the sixty-foot-high flight decks of the carriers. Lashed-down planes on the hangar deck were bounced out of their

chocks and damaged their tails against the props of those
behind them. Nearly horizontal rain mixed with the driving
spindrift to make life miserable for watchstanders. The
Big E's men watched in awe as the destroyers knifed
through the seas, thrusting upward until half their dull-red
bottoms were exposed, and then plunging down while the
breakers seemed to sweep their length.

In the early afternoon, Captain Grover B. H. Hall of
Enterprise launched a strike of Avengers and Hellcats to
destroy an enemy radio and weather station on Pratas
Reef, a hundred miles southwest of the force. The first
team took the mission: Bill Martin, Kip Kippen and Bob
McCullough with Charlie Henderson, Ralph Cummings,
Ernie Lawton, Gibby Blake and C B Collins. The group
flew all the way to the target through a series of drumming
rain squalls under a continuous 700-foot overcast. Over
the tiny atoll the ceiling went clear up to 1,000 feet and the
visibility was out to three miles. In that narrow band of sky
between clouds and surface, the dozen *Enterprise* aircraft
roared and swooped and banked and came back down to
blast and strafe and rocket, until nothing was left of the
big concrete installation except the radio towers themselves and a pointed, gabled, wooden shinto shrine. Then
Martin, Kippen and McCullough went back down to the
water and led their boys home under the lowering Asiatic
sky.

The day after the Pratas Reef strike, TF 38 hit enemy
occupied Hong Kong, Canton and the island of Hainan,
sweeping the airfields around the anthill cities and smashing at the shipping in their harbors. The Big E's contribu-
tion was a dusk CAP and a night heckler mission over Hong
Kong and Canton which accounted for a Tojo in a long,
high-speed chase, destroyed a radar station with guns and
rockets, and fought an inconclusive duel with half a dozen
enemy searchlights at Tienho Field just inland of Canton.
The weather continued vile with low ceilings, scattered
showers, 30-knot winds and savage, breaking seas from the
northeast, not bad enough to justify canceling flight operations, but sufficiently bad to make those operations difficult
and dangerous. Of the eight fighters launched by VF(N)-
90 that evening, one inexplicably failed to return at all,
another flew into the water and exploded as he turned final,
two crashed the barriers and one landed wheels up.

On the night of January 20, TF 38 left the South China

Sea the same way it had entered, between Formosa and Luzon—a destroyer division running interference ahead, and a heavy night CAP buzzing watchfully overhead. Some fifteen planes fell to the CAP that night, but most of them were transports evacuating Luzon and not a single ship came under attack. By morning, TF 38 was back in the Philippine Sea having steamed almost 4,000 miles in eleven days around the enemy's back yard, sunk over 200,000 tons of shipping and struck targets which had been safe for four years, but would never be safe again under the flag of the Rising Sun.

The day strikes of the twenty-first had reported eighteen big cargo ships in the harbor of Kiirun at the extreme north tip of Formosa. Intelligence officers believed that the enemy was supplying his bases in the southern part of the island by assembling ships in usually cloud-covered Kiirun during the day, and running them south along the coast at night in order to avoid U. S. air and submarine attacks. Halsey had finished for the moment with Formosa, and TF 38 was some 400 miles east of Kiirun, preparing dawn strikes against Okinawa and the Nansei Shoto. Admiral Gardner and Captain Hall agreed with Bill Martin that a long-range night raid on Kiirun Harbor would have the double effect of disrupting supply traffic and leading the enemy to believe that the fast carriers were still close by for another day of attack on Formosa.

Seven Avengers were catapulted from the Big E's windy deck into the moonless darkness between 2:00 and 2:10 A.M., but one was forced to land again immediately with a sputtering, popping engine. Two three-plane sections departed for the target: Rus Kippen, Koop and Wood in the first, Bill Martin, Jennings and Cromley in the second. For the long flight, each plane carried gasoline in half its bomb bay, two 500-pound bombs in the other half and three five-inch rockets under each wing. Each was manned by a radar operator and a radioman in addition to the pilot.

The blacked-out TBMs, in loose formation, flew due west for 212 miles, then northwest for another 100 until their radars recognized the prominent northeast cape of Sancho Koku. Here they dropped to 500 feet and skirted the hilly north coast of Formosa until they picked up the scope pattern of Kiirun at 4:30 A.M.

Kiirun was socked in as advertised. Heavy broken clouds hung low over the harbor and extended up to 5,000 or 6,000 feet. Above that, the sky was clear and visibility good. Kippen and his first section headed immediately for the initial point, five miles north of the harbor entrance. Martin circled out on a sweep to the north and west for any shipping that might have recently left the harbor.

The plan of attack was very like the one that Kippen in old VT-10 had used at Truk half a war ago. Planes were to leave the initial point singly, at precisely timed intervals, and make individual attacks, navigating into the harbor by radar. They were to stay over water at 250 feet or below, hit ships in the outer harbor first and then penetrate through the narrow channel into the inner harbor only if there were insufficient targets outside. Ships had first priority, and then the various military installations around the harbor—a small arms factory, a magazine, warehouses and oil storage tanks. Kiirun was known to be heavily defended by AA and searchlights, and, in the event that they became a serious threat, Martin had a plan to draw off the fire by high-flying decoys while the real raid went in on the deck.

Kippen made the first attack. His calm report, "Departing initial point," came up through the darkness to Martin at 4:38 A.M. A minute later it was apparent that the harbor defenses had not been surprised, and would indeed be a serious problem. Searchlights stabbed up one after the other, blunting on the overcast and leaping through its breaks into the clear sky above. Guns flashed and tracers lined out across the harbor. Twice the blinding beams met Kip head on, whiting out the inside of his cockpit, utterly destroying his night visual adaptation. Unable even to see the instruments a yard before his eyes and, at low level among jutting capes and rocky islets, he twice circled back for another try. On his third run, Kip must have drawn in his breath, settled in his seat and bored on in. To hell with the lights, this thing had to be done.

Martin, partly seeing, partly hearing, partly sensing, half expecting Kippen's trouble, led his section at full throttle in a climb to the initial point, left the other two TBMs to circle there, and went in at 8,000 feet directly over Kip as he started his third run flat on the dark outer harbor below. The enemy radar received the two aircraft as one "blip" on one bearing, and guns and searchlights concentrated on Martin, the high and obvious target. Bill continued on the same course that Kip was flying, watching his time. Searchlights and guns, radar directed, probed and groped for him through the broken clouds. Occasionally, on command, Barnett, back in the tunnel of the TBM, would unwrap a long, squarish package of foil strips and feed them out of the hatch above the harbor, where they drifted down, making a large blip on the enemy radar. Often the searchlights left the plane and followed the "window" down.

The second hand on Martin's instrument panel moved with tiny jerks around its red-lighted rim. When it was time for Kip to have reached the inner harbor, Martin banked and peered down at the gun flashes and thick pencils of light rooted in Kiirun, half hidden by its constant clouds. The red flare of an explosion erupted in the inner harbor, lighting the clouds and hills and reflecting in the black water for a second or two before it contracted to a steady flaming that showed the shape of a big ship under the shifting fire and smoke. Rus Kippen, calm and competent as always, had placed his bombs perfectly.

Already the second plane of Kip's section was in the outer harbor, with Martin's second flying decoy 8,000 feet above him, and the two remaining aircraft had left the initial point inbound, one high and one low. Martin was turning and losing altitude, on the way to begin his own run, when a second, smaller, red flash and a brief fire bloomed against a hillside south of the harbor.

The decoy plan now called for the first section to climb and draw fire while the second section made its runs.

Martin ordered his section down, and a few minutes later announced his departure from the initial point on the fourth run of the attack. He flew at 160 knots and 250 feet, with Bill Chace on his scope directing him right and left and steady, through the entrance, across the empty outer bay and into the narrow inner harbor. At 250 feet, black shapes and objects loomed above the TBM and slid past on both sides. Shreds and tatters of cloud hung down below the overcast, and rain occasionally smeared the windshield and drummed loudly on the aluminum and bullet-proof glass of the canopy. Guns flashed and flickered ahead and on both sides but there were few tracers. Kip's burning tanker and the searchlight beams reflecting from cloud bases created an erratic red and white half light as the Avenger swept into the inner harbor and Martin slammed the bomb bay open. He released one bomb on a ship silhouetted against the tanker fire, and skimmed across it to drop the other on a warehouse which had not been ignited by the burning ship. Then there was only time to shove everything forward and pull up in as steep a climb as possible to clear the hills behind the harbor.

Jennings and Cromley also put their bombs on the wharves and warehouses inboard of Kippen's tanker, starting bright new fires.

When Martin's second section had completed their attacks and climbed back to a safe altitude, Bill tried to contact Kippen and then any plane of the first section. Repeated calls went completely unanswered. There was not even a garbled or weak transmission or the keying of a mike—nothing. For another hour the Big E's air group commander circled over the target, hoping that one or some of the other planes would join up. While he waited he made rocket runs on the small arms factory at the south end of the harbor which had been hit initially by either Koop or Wood, and ignited a spectacular pyrotechnic blaze. Jennings strafed the persistent searchlights which went out but came back to life a few minutes later.

Finally at 5:50 A.M. the three TBMs took departure for base. It was daylight when they arrived in the vicinity of the Japanese fighter strip on Miyako Shima, and with guns removed from their turrets to lighten the planes, they had to circle it to the north, flat on the sea to get under enemy radar. With fuel gauges bouncing on the "empty" peg, they arrived at the task group's planned position to find it was eighty miles farther to the east. The three survivors of Kiirun landed back on *Enterprise* at 9:00 A.M. Day strikes from the other carriers were already over Okinawa.

The torpedo squadron was shocked and numbed by the loss of its skipper, who had flown and worked and eaten and drunk with most of them since the early days of Torpedo 10 at Sand Point, Seattle, making all the routine patrols and all the hairy missions until he had begun to seem immortal—and by the loss at the same time of two other pilots and all three crews. Bill Martin remembered the flash and fire on the hillside right after the tanker explosion, and reluctantly deduced that it had been Kip, unable to climb out steeply enough after his attack. Jennings had seen an explosion on the water outside the harbor which might have been one of the other planes, hit by AA. All nine men were listed as missing and the squadron tried to hope they would turn up one day. But they did not.

When the last of four fighters returned from a heckler

mission over Naha Field, Okinawa, late on the evening of the twenty-second, TF 38 turned south for Ulithi.

On the last day before entering port, Chaplain Bennett held memorial services for the men of *Enterprise* and her air group who had been lost in the single month since she had sortied from Pearl. The forward elevator was raised some three feet above the hangar deck and on it, under a square of blue Pacific sky broken around its edge by the protruding cowls, props and wings of planes on the flight deck, was the band, the choir and the pulpit. From a line rigged across the elevator well hung the Stars and Stripes. The morning sun poured down on the chaplain in his robes and the sailors in their whites, and the clean wind of the Big E's passage tangled the colors and whipped the neckerchiefs of the band. The choir sang, the band played, the chaplain read the Scripture, said a prayer and gave a short sermon. This service was not, he said, in any sense a funeral but rather a group supplication to God in behalf of the dead, and the missing who might yet be alive. The long rows of men in dungarees, and officers and chiefs in khaki sat, serious and silent, each man thinking his own thoughts, and every few minutes a tow plane would drone in overhead and the services would pause to let the Big E's guns speak, adding their own ancient, pagan message of "kill or be killed" to the gentle Christian service below.

Enterprise entered Ulithi lagoon on the morning of January 26 and did not leave it again until nearly noon on February 10. VT(N)-90 kept six Avengers at the coral strip on Fallalop for antisub patrol and miscellaneous duties. Each pilot and crew drew one or two days there, living in the open-ended Quonsets, drinking warm, chlorinated water from canvas Lister bags hanging in trees, showering outdoors under a sticky trickle of lukewarm water and utilizing that most primitive of head facilities— the "pole and hole." They returned aboard with a new appreciation of the Big E's hot showers and soft bunks and a new respect for the soldiers and Marines, for whom Fallalop was luxury.

When the big lagoon at Ulithi emptied on the tenth of February and the hundreds of tough, gray ships joined up again in their armored circles to move in against Japan, they were no longer Task Force 38. Bill Halsey and Slew McCain were back at Pearl, planning. Raymond Spruance and Marc Mitscher were back at sea, operating, and "Fast

Carriers, Pacific" was now Task Force 58.

The Big E was a unit of Task Group 58.5, still a night group, and still under the command of Rear Admiral Mat Gardner, flying his flag in *Enterprise*. *Saratoga* had replaced *Independence*. It had been a long time since the Big E had been the most modern carrier in her group, but she was now, with the *Sara*'s massive superstructure looking like a solid old ghost out of the twenties. The battle cruiser *Alaska*, heavy cruiser *Baltimore*, antiaircraft light cruiser *Flint* and nine destroyers completed TG 58.5.

The fast carriers swung out to the northeast, around Guam and the Marianas, and headed north, working out their planes, their guns and their crews as they went, getting back in fighting shape after the relatively long weeks swinging around the hook at Ulithi.

Then an hour before sunrise on the windy, overcast morning of February 16, the Big E buttoned up with a heavy slamming of metal doors and hatches, and went to General Quarters as she had done in the darkness before so many other dawns, from the Marshalls to the Solomons to the Carolines to the Palaus to the Marianas to the Philippines to the Bonins to Formosa and the Nansei Shoto. But this morning's strikes were not launched against some atoll or volcanic outpost of the enemy empire, but against the same target that the old *Hornet*, under *Enterprise* cover, had hit in April of 1942—the main Japanese home island of Honshu, and Tokyo itself. And now, nearly three years later, it was not sixteen planes that hit Tokyo, but fifty times that number.

Since *Enterprise* was now a night carrier, her only part in the day strikes was to fly CAP over her own group, but the crew was awed, impressed and a little apprehensive to be attacking the heart of enemy power. On deck the men shivered in the cold, damp wind, bundled in several pairs of socks, plus shoes and rubbers, winter trousers over dungarees, winter jackets over knitted sweaters from home which had been jokes at Ulithi, helmets and mittens and life jackets.

Late in the afternoon of the sixteenth, Night Air Group Ninety launched its first offensive mission—twelve Hellcats on a "zipper" patrol to close up the airfields around Tokyo during the critical hours between the departure of the last day strike and darkness, when the Japanese, unless forcibly prevented, would be launching counterattacks against the carriers.

As the dozen Hellcats closed the enemy coast, the ceiling above them rose and thinned out until there were only high scattered clouds and unlimited visibility over Japan. They made their landfall at Yawata Saki, directly across the Chiba Peninsula from Tokyo Bay, with the sun just a few degrees off the horizon over Tokyo. They turned southwest and followed the green, hilly coast to the southern tip, inspected the air base at Tateyama in the failing light and found no planes in the air or on the ground and no activity at the field, so continued around Cape Nojima and straight up into the mouth of Tokyo Bay itself—twelve dark blue fighters from a factory on Long Island, twelve tense young officers from a bobbing base under the weather a hundred miles to seaward, heading straight into the lair of the wounded Japanese tiger at nightfall.

It took about eight minutes to fly from Cape Nojima through the narrow mouth of Tokyo Bay to the big air and naval base at Yokosuka. For that eight minutes the Big E's Hellcats used the Imperial air space without interference or objection. But when they broke up into three divisions east of Yokosuka, and nosed down to begin their strafing runs in the last minutes of sunlight, the Emperor's forces came to life. Guns of all calibers opened up from both sides of the narrow Yokosuka Peninsula and the hills just inland of the base. The AA was intense, accurate and continuous. All twelve planes were under heavy fire the entire time they were in range.

The first division dived in a long, high-speed slant from 10,000 feet to twenty feet, dividing into two two-plane sections on the way down. One section took the north side of the field, and ripped down the length of a long, double row of twin-engine planes, their six 50s blazing steadily. The other section took the south side and a similar double row of parked fighters. The .50-caliber slugs chewed and tore through the light aluminum and ricocheted from the concrete ramp into the next planes in line. Only one Japanese fighter and none of the bombers exploded or burned, the enemy having learned by now that it was unsafe to leave gassed or armed aircraft on his airfields, even on the shores of Tokyo Bay.

The second division followed the first in a strafing run at Yokosuka, and then stayed low over the bay to avoid the

AA and to work over four freighters in a series of low-level strafing attacks. They left one of the ships stopped and smoking, and cut eastward across the top of the flat Chiba Peninsula at treetop height to Naruto, which the day strikes seemed to have put entirely out of commission, Katori where there was no damage but no activity either, and finally Choshi, where they strafed some parked Jacks and Zekes and ran into light, but highly accurate, AA which holed the tail of one of the marauding Hellcats. On the way out to the coast they strafed a radio station, a radar sight and a factory, and stopped three trains by releasing the steam of their engines through .50-caliber holes instead of into the driving pistons.

The third division stayed up as high cover, dodged some twenty minutes of close, persistent AA, fought off a couple of Jacks and returned home.

All remaining eleven planes found the Big E in total darkness under the low, thick overcast and landed aboard. One crashed the barriers and had to be jettisoned but the pilot was not injured.

That same evening, Charlie Henderson, now the exec of VT(N)-90, with Henry Loomis and Ted Halbach operating the electronics gear in the back of his TBM, and escorted by Dallas Runion in an F6F, spent four hours off the mouth of Tokyo Bay reading the signals of Japanese radars and determining their characteristics and geographical positions. Twenty-three different radars were discovered to be operating in that one area and Loomis' report on their frequencies, pulse widths and pulse repetition frequency was a masterpiece of great value to TF 58 and all the increasing U. S. and Allied forces operating around Japan.

Two hours after Henderson and Runion sputtered in out of the darkness astern and banged down on the Big E's deck, Captain Hall began launching eleven Avengers to search the seas between TF 58 and Japan. Major units of the enemy fleet were known to be holed up in the Inland Sea a few hours steaming away, and Marc Mitscher could not afford to wake up one morning and find that vengeful Japanese battlewagons had sortied under cover of darkness and bad weather to gun down his thin-skinned carriers.

Cross Bow Collins' eleven Avengers were to cover the 60 degrees of azimuth from southwest, around to slightly north of west. If their radars found no significant shipping, they were to check the coastal airfields as far southwest as

Nagoya. Nine of the planes were to converge at the end of their patrols to bomb an airfield on Hachijo Jima, one of the little islands that seem to be falling out of the mouth of Tokyo Bay like crumbs from the jaws of some great beast.

It was a year and a day ago that Van Eason and Rus Kippen had taken Torpedo 10 into the Truk lagoon, 1,800 miles southeast of Tokyo, on the most daring night strike of the war to date. Joe Doyle and Cliff Largess had been on that one too.

Doyle and Largess hit the coast 180 miles from base to Cape Inubo due east of Tokyo, without encountering any ships at all, and followed the same course the fighters had taken the previous afternoon, around the tip of the Chiba Peninsula and up into Tokyo Bay. The sprawling cities around the bay, one of the most populous areas on earth, were totally blacked out, and Doyle and Largess followed the coast southwest and reversed course on the approaches to Nagoya. On the way home they illuminated with flares and then glided in to lay their bombs on the airfield at Nii Shima south of Tokyo Bay. But the flares illuminated the Avengers also and Cliff called Joe irritably, "Joe, will you for God's sake stop testing your guns?"

"I'm not testing guns, Cliff. I don't even have them charged."

"Well, then," said Cliff, after a surprised pause, "we aren't alone!" and the two TBMs dived away from the enemy fighters making halfhearted passes at them from dead astern.

At noon on the seventeenth, with the weather as bad as ever, Spruance and Mitscher canceled further strikes, and TF 58 moved off to the south to cover a Marine landing on an island south of the Bonins called Iwo Jima.

Except for the "zipper" mission of her fighters, and the offensive search by Night Torpedo 90, the Big E's part in the first Tokyo strikes had been small and defensive night CAP, antisub and routine patrols. No one in *Enterprise* liked the role. The crew had grown used to Dog Smith's heavy, aggressive strikes, used to the knowledge that the Big E was contributing as much or more than any other carrier to the destruction of the enemy. Bill Martin's air group fretted and griped in their ready rooms through the long hours of relative inaction while Admiral Gardner's TG 58.5 operated on the disengaged side of the force, under the shelter of the CAP in daylight and limited at night by the necessity to be back under that shelter by dawn.

To salvage something constructive out of the wasted hours, the torpedo pilots began Spanish language lessons under Lieutenant Ed Hidalgo, their Air Combat intelligence officer. The lessons caught on and others outside the squadron joined the class. Soon Bill Martin, who had already long been known from his initials as "William One," had a new title—"El Groupo."

Martin's action report understates the case in cool military language:

> This Air Group was not used to best advantage during this operation.

The theory of combining instrument pilots and air-borne radar to continue pressure on the enemy around the clock was brilliant. Putting the theory into practice in the middle of a war was difficult, discouraging and painfully slow. But Martin kept at it, grasping at every opportunity to prove his new weapon, defending its failures, pointing out its successes, hammering at obstacles at every level. And he had powerful allies in Mat Gardner, Grover Hall, Willie Kabler (the new exec) and Jack Blitch, formerly of Scouting Six, the Big E's new air officer.

Off Iwo, the defensive operations continued but at a sharply increased tempo.

By the afternoon of the nineteenth of February, *Enterprise,* fueled and replenished, was on station with *Saratoga* and the rest of TG 58, sixty miles northwest of the battered island where the Marines had been charging ashore over their own bodies since dawn. Her mission was "to prevent enemy night air attacks on amphibious units at Iwo Jima in order to aid our occupation of that island."

Between attempted interceptions, the night CAP watched fire-support cruisers and destroyers, lying close inshore, keep the ugly island illuminated all night with the wavering pale green light of descending star shells, and arc the white and red tracers of their heavy guns into threatening enemy positions.

On the morning of the twenty-first, *Saratoga* and three destroyers pulled out of Gardner's TG 58.5 and moved south to join the escort or "jeep" carriers providing air support to the heavily engaged Marines. Big, archaic old

Sara would be, the Big E's sailors said, "Queen of the Jeeps." That evening while the Big E's task group stood tensely by its guns and the screen pumped out a few rounds on radar control at bogies invisible to the bigger ships, *Saratoga* took four Kamikazes and two bombs. One of her "jeeps," the *Bismarck Sea*, took two more suiciders and went down. But tough old *Sara* put out her fires, patched up her holes, counterflooded and pumped out, and departed under her own power for Pearl. *Enterprise* was left with full night responsibility for Iwo.

The afternoon of George Washington's Birthday, *Enterprise* was requested to search the area south of Iwo for eight *Saratoga* pilots lost at the time she was under attack. Weather in the area was vile, with ceilings below a thousand feet and visibilities of a mile or less, but C B Collins, glad of the chance to give his idle torpedo pilots something to do, and hoping to save some lives, led eight planes off anyway. They fanned out for 150 miles, from 150 to 210 degrees from the island, found nothing, returned and began to rendezvous five miles east of Iwo for a second try. Four of them had found each other and were circling, awaiting the others. C B had Gordon Hinrichs and Ernie Lawton on his left wing and Joe Jewell on his right. The loose wedge of TBMs was flying at 400 feet under a 450-foot overcast, with a visibility of something over a mile. Around Iwo, the amphibious forces of the Seventh Fleet were under a "red alert" between sporadic Kamikaze attacks which had been going on all day. Suddenly one of the old battleships of the bombardment group, surrounded by dozens of smaller ships, popped out of the haze and fog ahead of C B. He swung to port, and passed well clear astern of the gray bulk bristling with manned guns of all calibers, but the turn brought the flight straight in on the beam of another battlewagon. As soon as he saw her, C B swung to port again, hard this time, turning into Hinrichs and Lawton, so that Hinrichs had to chop throttle and slide under him. A battery officer on an LST, seeing the four planes turn out of the low clouds head on, opened fire. On every other ship in sight, gunners who had been waiting tensely for a target and who had freshly learned the awful kill or be killed lesson of the Kamikaze, swung their guns onto the four Avengers and held down the triggers. The TBM formation broke up violently, each pilot acting out of instinct and the impulse of the moment, as the homing Wildcats of VF-6 had done on that incredible evening of December 7 over Ford Island.

Jewell and Lawton pulled up hard into the overcast, and disappeared from the sights of the surface gunners, who, if they had the equipment, had not had the time to shift to radar control. Joe and Ernie, angry and shaken, returned safely to *Enterprise*. Collins and Hinrichs dived for the surface at full throttle with the point-blank tracers following all the way. Hinrichs could see Collins' plane ahead and a little above him, its underside swept by flame, but apparently under full control. Then Hinrichs' own engine was hit, and smoke poured around and into his cockpit, blinding him completely. His two crewmen, Ryan in the turret and Caswell in the tunnel, reported the direction of heaviest firing and the location of the ships, and announced that they had secured themselves in their seats and were ready for ditching. Flying by pure feel, but knowing he was low, and getting lower and closer to Collins ahead of him, Hinrichs pulled up slightly and turned a little to port. The TBM skidded in the turn, and air from the side momentarily cleared the smoke away so that Gordon could see that he was some seventy-five to a hundred feet above the water, miraculously headed into the wind between two columns of small ships, all pouring lead at him with every gun they had. He banged down his flaps—and the wheels dropped too, almost certain death in a water landing. Instantly he jerked up the wheels and they spread back up into the wings on the ebbing hydraulic fluid left in the system. Gordon locked his own shoulder straps as he went blind again in the smoke and flame from engine and cockpit, but at that moment the steadily blazing surface guns blew his canopy off over his head, and the smoke cleared for good, showing him a demolished instrument panel but a clear space ahead for landing.

There were only a few seconds of flight left, but the heavy tracers from both sides continued to tear the tattered Avenger apart. One exploded the empty bomb-bay fuel tank back into the tunnel, dazing and lacerating Caswell strapped into his seat just behind it.

Hinrichs was afraid he was too fast as the waves reached up at him, but there was nothing he could do but level off, with the tracers still slamming into his engine, and land. It was a good one, so that all three men got out, and, with Gordon helping his dazed and injured crewmen, hung on to their inflated but inverted rubber raft until help arrived.

At first the help was not so helpful. A small wooden subchaser nearly ran them down, and then nearly chopped them up in her screws. On her deck the sailors held pistols and submachine guns on Hinrichs' crew until a closer look and Gordon's bitter and prolonged profanity convinced them that the men in the water were Americans. At this point and after two unsuccessful attempts to throw a line to the survivors had brought a shout from the water that "If you bastards were as handy with your lines as you are with those goddam guns, we'd be aboard by now!" the SC boat skipper dived overboard himself to lend a hand, and all three men were soon below in the tiny wardroom.

Three days later Hinrichs and Ryan were back in *Enterprise* and Caswell was recovering rapidly aboard a tender. No trace was ever found of C B Collins or his crew, Lieutenant (j.g.) Bob Gowdy and Ferris Ivory.

Lieutenant Charlie Henderson moved up to take command of Night Torpedo 90.

On the twenty-third of February, Admiral Mat Gardner's TG 58.5 began operating independently. The rest of TF 58 headed back to hit Tokyo again and shut off at its source the constant trickle of Kamikazes that continued to get through to the ships lying off the bloody island. The next morning the Big E's task group was officially detached from the Fast Carrier Force, and Admiral Gardner reported for duty with the Support Carrier Group off Iwo. Now *Enterprise* herself was "Queen of the Jeeps."

When lean, outspoken Commander Jack Blitch, perched restlessly on his stool in "Fly Control" high over the Big E's deck, gave the order to launch eight fighters for a dusk CAP over Iwo at 4:25 P.M. on the twenty-third, he began a week of operations that no carrier had ever equaled before.

Bill Martin's air group and Jack Blitch's Air Department split into shifts and settled down to continuous operations. Under Commander Kabler's "fair but no foolishness" guidance, all the veteran carrier's departments fell in behind Martin and Blitch until she cranked out flights, reeled in others, gassed, armed, repaired and maintained planes, fed, slept, briefed and debriefed pilots and crewmen, like a well-oiled perpetual motion machine.

Until 11:30 P.M. on the second of March, when a passing warm front smothered Gardner's task group in heavy

rain and zero-zero weather for forty-five minutes, there
had not been a moment, night or day, for seven days and
seven hours, that at least two *Enterprise* planes had not
been air-borne. Once there were twenty-two, most often
there were four to six. Bob McCullough's Night Fighting 90
had averaged fifty flights every twenty-four hours.

By the sixth, the three Marine divisions had burned and
blasted and dug out enough Japanese so that Army night
fighters, flying from Iwo itself, could take over the night
CAP. On the ninth, one minute after the last plane of the
evening Chichi strike had caught its wire, Harvey Burden
laid a due south course for Ulithi and, for *Enterprise,* the
Iwo Jima operation was over.

23 RETURN TO JAPAN

When the Big E slid between the nets into Ulithi, she
found the whole of Task Force 58 already there. A line of
fifteen big carriers, their decks geometrically jammed with
planes, stretched almost out of sight down the long lagoon
—"murderers row" someone called it, looking in awe at
deckload after deckload of destruction and bow after bow
heading proudly up into the brisk trades. Eight fast new
battleships backed up the carriers. Two new battle cruisers
and fourteen light and heavy cruisers were in support. And
the lagoon was crowded with the destroyers of the task
group screen—tenders, repair ships, floating dry docks, provision and headquarters ships, tankers, tugs, transports,
ammunition ships, reefers, DEs, PCs, SCs, minesweepers
and landing craft.

Enterprise had forty-six busy hours in which to fuel,
provision and take on bombs, torpedoes and ammunition,
and then back she went to sea, northward again to Japan,
to smother the airfields on Kyushu and keep the Japanese
off balance in support of new landings—this time on Okinawa.

All the way north, Mitscher, whose voice call was
"Mohawk," tried the bow of his air groups and sharpened
the long blade of his guns. On the night of March 17—18,

he fought his way past the enemy scouts and, at dawn, the big war party struck Kyushu and southern Honshu.

It was apparent very early in her second attack on the home islands of Japan that *Enterprise* was going to be busy. Admiral Mitscher must have changed his mind about the value and effectiveness of night operations. Perhaps he had had time to read the Big E's action reports covering her last visit to the Empire and agreed with Bill Martin's comment that his air group "was not used to best advantage." In any event, he used it this time.

At 5:30 A.M. eight fighters were launched for a dawn CAP.

The eighteenth of March was a perfect day for the sporadic, single-plane harassing tactics to which the Japanese had been reduced. Killer Kane's pilots off the Marianas in June had seen the last of massed enemy air groups sweeping in proudly for coordinated attacks on the U. S. carriers. Now, with those same carriers frequently in radar range of the home islands themselves, Japan could only scrape up whatever miscellaneous aircraft she could find and send them in, like the "bandits" they were called in the voice code of the fighter-directors, to slip from one cloud to the next, harried by fighters and jarred by AA, hoping to get in a lucky bomb hit before they were destroyed, or to spatter their flesh against some steel deck in the final act of desperation.

On this busy, tragic day for *Enterprise*, fat white cumulus clouds with bases as low as 2,000 feet and tops as high as 9,000, covered more than half the sky. Below the clouds visibility was twelve miles, above it was unlimited. A cold 18-knot wind blew steadily from the northeast. The men topside were bulky in their full quota of winter clothing—collars up, blue watch caps pulled down under their helmets.

The enemy took full advantage of the weather. With bogies all around and closing, Willie Kabler sent his men to General Quarters at 5:17 A.M., just one hour before sunrise. They were there for sixteen hours.

At 7:00 A.M. Glen Earl reported over the ship from his night CAP and was immediately sent out after a bogey. Ten minutes later and fifty miles south, he shot down a twin-engine Frances bomber with a crew of seven.

But the clouds around the task force were packed with bogies.

A little after 7:30 lookouts and gun crews forward reported several aircraft a mile or so dead ahead. A couple of F6Fs were easily recognizable. One of the planes broke suddenly away from the others and began a straight-in approach to *Enterprise*. In CIC the voice of a CAP pilot cut through the gabble and crackle of receivers:

"Plane diving ahead of the formation."

CIC passed the warning to the bridge. Captain Hall, Jack Blitch and Harvey Burden looked forward. The plane was approaching head on in a shallow glide from about 500 feet. It was clean and symmetrical with a radial engine and the wings midway on the circle of the fuselage. It could have been an Avenger. Gunners, director crews, lookouts held their breaths. The plane crossed the destroyer circle of the screen, flew down the side of a battlewagon. Not a shot was fired. Now he was down to 200 feet—nose to nose with *Enterprise* and nearly level with her bridge. Suddenly Burden could stand it no longer and yelled to the helmsman, "Right full rudder!"

Air Defense Forward ordered: "Commence firing," and a few 20-millimeters began to rattle.

The men on the forward guns could see doors open in the belly of the plane and, as the Big E's bow began to swing to starboard, a dark object separated and fell toward them. They ducked behind the light metal of their splinter shields, waiting for the blast in the last split second before death or maiming, as the Judy flashed overhead. There was time for Blitch and Burden to look straight into the set and goggled face of the enemy pilot—and then the bomb hit. Its full 550 pounds smashed at a shallow angle into the forward elevator and a hundred men knew they were watching their own deaths. There was a heavy thud, the deck planking splintered and flew, and then, incredibly, the ponderous lethal shape was back in the air, soaring end over end toward the island and the bridge. There had been no blast. The men on the bridge hurled themselves flat, away from the hurtling metal. It smashed up under the overhang of the navigating bridge, ripped aft through the supporting "bent-knee" structure, shearing the electrical wiring strung there. It flared hotly, like gunpowder ignited in the open, searing the side of the island and three men standing below, cracking the glass in Fly Control and then rolled and tumbled down the flight deck, spraying out the white picric acid of its explosive filler.

The bomb had been a dud, released too low and too fast to drop its snout and strike steeply enough for the inertia fuse in its tail to fire. The undetonated fuse was found on the elevator, just below the hole where the bomb first hit. The bent and ugly greenish thing was examined, photographed and then thrown overboard by brave men. John Munro's aggressive repair parties quickly smothered the fire in the island with foam and fog, replaced essential wiring with casualty power cables, and patched the six-by-ten-foot hole in the deck. The picric acid was hosed off the deck, the burned men treated and *Enterprise* continued the fight. One man died from his burns the next day. The Judy got away.

While the remnants of the fire still smoked and the deck was still littered with white chunks and grains of explosive, a Frances glided out of the clouds on the portside of the formation, headed in the Big E's direction. This time the enemy was unmistakable, and all guns took the twin-engine bomber under fire. *Enterprise* gunners got in a few rounds, but closer ships had already set the Frances afire and it flamed into the sea a mile or so on the port bow. Still, the attack inflicted casualties on *Enterprise*.

A ship forward and to starboard, firing at the enemy plane with its five-inch guns, depressed them too far. A five-inch projectile, equipped with an influence-type fuse, passed low enough over the Big E's starboard quarter to detonate. The shell burst with a sharp crack less than twenty feet above a two-gun 20-millimeter battery. Of the six men manning the guns, two were killed and four wounded by the spraying shrapnel.

Five minutes after the first, another Frances attacked out of the clouds on the starboard quarter. This one was after the *Intrepid* half a mile to starboard of *Enterprise*. "Snuffy" Smith's gunners picked him up early, and the 40-millimeters blew pieces of aluminum away before he crashed so close aboard *Intrepid* that the flame and smoke which blossomed high above her looked like a hit, and gunners in *Enterprise* were surprised to see her steaming and firing as usual minutes later.

At 8:30 two Hellcats shot down another Judy just outside the screen.

For a few hours, although there were bogies on the scopes, none attacked, and there was a lull during which the men relaxed around their guns, cleared away old brass and awaited the next target.

Right after 1:00 P.M. it began again. First CIC reported a bogey twelve miles southeast. Then, in less than five minutes, a Judy dived out of one of the enemy clouds in another attack on the *Intrepid*. His bomb was a towering near miss, and he pulled up in a left turn, circling forward of *Enterprise* and down her portside until the combined guns of the task group tore him apart and he crashed a mile on the port quarter. While his gasoline was still flaring and smoking on the sea, the CAP spun two more Judys in off to port of the formation. Their fires drew long parallel black lines down across the western sky.

At 1:18 still another of the persistent Judys dove out of the clouds ahead of *Yorktown*, fountained the sea close to her starboard side with his bomb and fell to the streaming tracers well astern of the racing ship.

A minute later the CAP got another one off to port, and again there was a lull while the next wave winged out from Kyushu.

At 3:00 P.M., while the chaplain was reading the burial service on the fantail for the two 20-millimeter gunners killed that morning, another Judy attacked the *Yorktown*, and the services were drowned in a wave of gunfire that sent the enemy plane spinning into the ocean with two white parachutes dangling down above it. It seemed a fitting funeral music for the two sailors who had died with the same sound in their ears.

Half an hour after midnight, Charlie Henderson led off five Avengers for an offensive search into the *sanctum sanctorum* of the Imperial Navy, the Inland Sea of Japan. *Enterprise* was some 200 miles south and a little east of Shikoku. Halfway to that island the five planes split up and, like the privateers of colonial days, each marauding TBM operated independently, on the lookout for targets of opportunity, seeking information for itself, damage, confusion, inconvenience and embarrassment for the enemy.

Consistently aggressive Charlie Henderson searched the surface of the Inland Sea from Shimonoseki on the west to the Kure Naval Base to the east, at 500 to 1,000 feet, skirting the coast, banking around the islands, sweeping across the stretches in the clear moonless night. A little after 4:00 A.M. he sighted four ships, hit a merchantman solidly with a 500-pound bomb and put two rockets into a destroyer escort.

An hour later, Ted Halbach, operating Charlie's radar, picked up the blip of a bogey, lost it, found it again. Charlie climbed to 8,500 feet, and for twenty minutes pursued the electronic phantom until he fell in behind a huge, four-engined Emily flying boat. Henderson hammered enough lead into the tough old seaplane to sink a destroyer, and finally, thirty feet above the Inland Sea, it flamed and crashed with its crew of nine.

Ernie Lawton searched the Kii Strait and the approaches to Kobe and Osaka. In the confined waters between those two cities and the island of Awaji, he made the discovery of the night—a carrier and the huge battleship, *Yamato,* three miles apart, headed southwest at twenty knots, scurrying between hiding places under cover of darkness. Ernie circled out on the carrier's starboard quarter and came in fast and low in the attack he had been practicing under Bill Martin for as long as he could remember. This was the chance every night torpedo pilot in VF-10 and VT(N)-90 had dreamed of and never had—a night minimum-altitude attack on major combatant ships under way at sea. He took the big Avenger down to 250 feet and headed in, coached by radar, until the carrier loomed in the blackness. Bomb bay open. Stand by. Mark. The two 500-pounders were set for a fifty-foot interval at 180 knots. Lawton's course took him diagonally across the carrier's deck. Kiser, peering out of the tunnel, reported one huge splash close aboard the starboard quarter. The other bomb had to have been a hit, but again darkness closed in between the plane and its target, and it was impossible to estimate the damage.

To prosecute his single-plane war against two capital ships, Lawton now had three rockets left. He fired all three at the battleship at a range of 600 feet. The flash of the rockets in the utter blackness blinded him, and again he was unable to report with certainty either hits or damage.

On the way home, Martin's marauders passed VF(N)-90's morning intruder flight of two Hellcats outbound.

The nineteenth was a quiet day for *Enterprise,* while the day carriers hit the big naval bases at Kure and Kobe where most of Japan's fleet had gone to hide. But it was not quiet for everyone. Shortly after 7:00 A.M. enemy dive bombers attacked *Franklin* and *Wasp* in a nearby task group. *Wasp's* damage was quickly controlled, but *Franklin* was hit so hard, in the midst of her gassed and armed aircraft, that the men of *Enterprise* could see the dirty pillar of smoke rising from the northwest horizon, and hear and feel a series of thudding explosions as her bombs and torpedoes baked off.

At noon the Big E was assigned as part of a task group to cover and escort *Franklin* back to Ulithi, but there was no high-speed retirement from the combat area. *Franklin,* so horribly burned that the sight of her sickened every carrier sailor in the fleet, bloody and malodorous with her 800 dead, but with an iron determination to survive, could make only three knots under tow by the cruiser *Pittsburgh. Enterprise* covered her with dawn, dusk and night CAPs, and, on the midwatch of the twentieth, Bill Martin took seven Avengers back to the Inland Sea. Cliff Largess, like his skipper the previous night, managed to shoot down a bogey with the two fixed 50s of his lumbering TBM.

By the forenoon watch on the twentieth, *Franklin's* propellers were turning again, and her rudders answered to the helm. A little after noon, incredibly and magnificently, she cast off her tow and assumed her station in the formation at fifteen knots. No carrier had ever before been so brutally damaged and survived. The wounded ship and her protectors began to pull out from under the threatening shadow of enemy air.

But the Japanese knew the task group was moving out of range, and threw in additional attacks while there was still time and while the ideal weather held.

Twice on the twentieth, *Enterprise* attempted to fuel destroyers, and both times they had to cast off hurriedly and sheer away, guns flashing, as the persistent, single-plane raids came in. Carrier and destroyer sailors slashed lines, stopped pumps, capped hoses, dogged down fuel trunks and hatches and scrambled for their battle stations. CIC was busy almost continually, vectoring CAP from *Enterprise* and other carriers on attempted interceptions. One Kate and two Jills were splashed by fighters well out from the force. But in the afternoon the enemy began to get through again, slipping from cloud to cloud like Delaware braves approaching a stockade.

A few minutes before 3:00 P.M. a single plane, showing friendly indications on the force radars, approached from the south. *Enterprise* lookouts reported AA fire from the *Franklin* group dead ahead, and a few minutes later a single-engine Judy dived out of the clouds on the *Hancock* on the Big E's port beam. The ships on that side of the force met the enemy with a concentrated blast of fire that set him flaming almost at once. A destroyer that had been fueling from *Hancock*'s starboard side had just cast off and was angling away when the crippled Judy missed the carrier's flight deck by a hair and crashed into her stern with a flash and a puff of black smoke. The destroyer, her steering gear jammed, turned back toward *Hancock* and crossed her bow dangerously close while slowing to about ten knots. In a few hours, the destroyer was back in formation but twelve of her men were dead and twenty-nine more wounded.

Half an hour later the enemy attempted a loosely coordinated attack by half a dozen planes converging on curving courses from the west and northwest through the low and middle clouds. The hard-pressed CAP intercepted some, but shortly after four o'clock another Judy began to stalk the *Enterprise*. He first appeared on the starboard beam some ten miles out and 10,000 feet high, headed straight in. At six and a half miles, the Big E's five-inch took him under fire and other ships joined in. He dodged to his right, in and out of the clouds, forcing the five-inch directors to shift back and forth from partial to full radar control, and then, at four miles, headed in again. At three miles the 40s and then the 20s opened up, and the Judy dove on *Enterprise*. He hurtled in at a 50- or 60-degree angle, seeming to be invulnerable to the storm of lead that scorched and smoked past him and puffed and blasted in his face. Every man on the Big E's topside willed that this particular Japanese was not a Kamikaze—and he was not. At 2,000 feet he released his bomb and pulled out across the deck from starboard to port. The ugly dark shape, so familiar to *Enterprise* sailors from its brother of the eighteenth, lowered its nose and slid in for the kill. It seemed to the men below it to hang suspended over the flight deck for several minutes, and then plunge for the port edge. It missed by less than fifty feet and detonated with a spout of dirty water alongside. In the engineering spaces far below, the sledge-hammer blow against the side had the welcome sound of a miss. There was no damage, but several five-inch bursts had come uncomfortably close to the ship, and the men topside were sensitive about that, after the accident of two days before.

Then at quarter past four CAP got a Tony only ten miles out, and by 4:23 there were six bogies inside the thirty-five miles, all closing. A minute later still another Judy came in from starboard, worked forward through the clouds, under fire all the way, and dived in on *Enterprise* from ahead. Objectively, it was a good dive-bombing run, steep and down the length of the ship, improving the chances for a hit. Again the exposed and busy gunners, the skipper, and the watch on the bridge prayed that this was only a bomber and not a suicider, and then, as if in answer, watched the bomb separate and drop, and for an eternity, while it grew bigger and dropped lower, resented having to pray for a bomb. The evil, lethal shape traveled the full length of the deck, lowering its pointed nose, seemingly trying hard to hit, but near-missed just off the starboard quarter so closely that it ruptured an oil line in the starboard steering unit, and the watch in the steering engine room quickly shifted to the port, so that steering control was never actually lost on the bridge. That should have ended the episode of the second Judy, but it did not.

At the instant the bomb detonated futilely in the sea astern, two explosions cracked in the air forward of the island. Six men were instantly killed and another died a few hours later of hemorrhage and shock. Thirty more were wounded, some seriously. One man had his right arm blown off. A parked Avenger was jolted off into the starboard catwalk and damaged the director for the Group III five-inch guns.

Both explosions were five-inch projectiles from the crossfire of other ships having to take big aiming leads on the fast-diving plane and so eager to protect the *Enterprise* that they had carried their fire too low. One proximity fuse had fired directly above the two quadruple 40-millimeter mounts just forward of the island. The other went off over the five-inch and 40-millimeter batteries on the port bow.

The first hit was the worst. The two circular gun tubs, the forward one slightly lower than the other, were crowded with men and ready ammunition. Close alongside on the flight deck, gassed and armed Hellcats were ready to be launched. The violent blast of shrapnel ripped through flesh and steel impartially. The barrel of one 40-millimeter was blown completely off, its shredded stub pointing uselessly at the sky. Repair parties and corpsmen charged into the shambles, but the hot five-inch fragments ignited the belly tanks of two F6s and in a minute the whole island and the adjacent deck were lost in the flame and billowing black smoke of a major gasoline fire. As the fire grew, 40-millimeter ammunition in the crippled mounts, and some 20,000 rounds of .50-caliber ready on the flight deck for rearming planes began to explode. Munro's fire fighters were driven back. Smoke poured over and into the island, and long tongues of flame lapped up its side. CIC, Main Radio, Primary Fly Control and the Coding Room had to be abandoned. The portside of the signal bridge caught fire, and the signal gang fought it until their hose, led up from the flight deck, burned through. All the ladders, internal and external, leading down out of the island were on, or opened on, the portside which was engulfed in the fire. Officers and men slid down hand lines on the outboard side. One ensign panicked in the smoke and flame, grabbed his life jacket and jumped overboard from the signal bridge. He was not missed in the desperate battle with the flames, and was not picked up.

The flames began to eat through the hangar deck overhead, where more gassed and armed planes were waiting. Far below, the bulkheads of a bomb elevator began to heat, and several magazines were already dangerously hot. On all the other ships of TG 58.5, men watched helplessly as the veteran carrier flamed and smoked in her agony. From the skies, other eyes peered at her around the corners of the clouds, and, 20 minutes after the one which had caused her troubles, another Judy circled and dove on the wounded ship. With CIC and the usual communications channels out of commission, *Enterprise* got range and bearing information from other ships by VHF radio, and passed it to the guns. All of them that still worked got on him at once but he released in a steep glide and his bomb plunged for the after end of the deck. It crossed diagonally from starboard to port and forward to aft and hit close aboard on the port quarter. Other bogies were around, and the flight deck forward was midnight-dark with smoke.

Below in Central Station, John Munro, the Big E's damage control officer, coolly went about his business. He knew where every fire, every hole, every casualty was, and how it was, nearly as soon as it happened. And he knew what to do. He ordered more foam brought to the flight deck to blanket and smother the flaming fuel—foam that would not have been available if he had not been foresighted enough to "requisition" at midnight several times his quota the last time in Pearl. He ordered the water curtain cut in at the after end of the hangar deck's forward bay, isolating the planes parked aft from the fire coming through the overhead. His men kept their hoses on that overhead so that the fire could not get a start below. He had the hot magazines sprinkled, the overheating bomb elevator filled with foam. He ordered the burning planes on deck dragged away and apart, and attacked separately with fog and foam.

Captain Hall brought *Enterprise* around so that the smoke blew off over the port bow, clearing the island and the deck around it.

The CIC crew set up in its secondary, emergency station. So did Radio. Topside men in smoke masks and rescue breathers, covered and cooled from behind and above by the long hook of low velocity fog applicators, lugged foam nozzles into the heart of the blaze and it began to die.

At 5:00 P.M. when another Judy attacked the *Hancock*, the Big E's port batteries promptly shot it down. The fires were under control.

At 5:10, still another, and the last of the day, dived on the *San Jacinto* ahead, crossed the Big E's bow, and the port guns got that one too.

By 5:15 all fires were out. Repair parties went to work to clear the ship of smoke and water before beginning the long job of repairing the damage.

The hit on the port bow had caused only minor damage, and started a small fire which was quickly put out.

At nightfall *Enterprise* was back on station, scarred again and sad with her dead and injured, but an operating unit of her task group. She had been saved by good damage control, men of courage on the nozzles of her hoses, and her captain's policy of keeping her at General Quarters and buttoned up tight all day long when in range of enemy air. The thousands of tons of water poured on her fires, and the flaming gasoline that gushed over her deck could not get inside to hurt her.

24 TOMI ZAI

It took ten days of hard work at Ulithi, even with the help of the repair ship *Jason's* experienced hands, to restore all the island compartments to their original condition, partly because a typhoon, passing to the south, poured heavy rain into the lagoon for several days, so that the metal work on the island had to be done under tarpaulins, which the high winds, also associated with the storm, threatened to blow away.

While in port, Bill Martin's squadrons received new pilots, crewmen and replacement planes. *Enterprise* herself received a draft of eighty new men.

Some hospital ships were anchored nearby, and binoculars and long glasses were in constant use. Men would watch happily for half an hour to see a nurse stroll out on deck for a cigarette a mile away. On the third of April, when twenty nurses from the *Mercy* came aboard to visit, every man not actually on watch or in some way incapacitated turned out to look. Twenty officers, selected at random, escorted the ladies on a tour of the carrier. It was the biggest event of the eleven days in port.

The men eagerly followed the progress of the Okinawa landings, which began on April first after a week of preparatory bombing, shelling and the capture of outlying islands. They felt they had already had a part in that campaign, and were bound to have more. And they were right.

At 9:30 A.M. on the fifth of April, after delaying for several hours to receive some badly needed spare parts that had been promised days before, *Enterprise* sailed on her last voyage into action but one. A destroyer division waited for her and escorted her to a rendezvous at sunrise the next day with TG 58.2, which consisted of the carrier *Randolph*, the light carrier *Independence*, two antiaircraft light cruisers and eight destroyers. TG 58.2 headed directly for Okinawa.

There was serious trouble there. The desperate Japanese,

realizing both the futility of their single-plane, random attacks, and the effectiveness of the Kamikaze, had scraped up nearly 400 aircraft of every type and age, manned them with fanatical, half-trained pilots and thrown them, accompanied and intermingled with 300-odd conventional bombers, against the ships off Okinawa. The enemy knew that the loss of that island and its conversion to a U. S. naval and air base meant the final severing of all his arteries to the raw materials and bypassed garrisons to the south, and the quick and inevitable loss of the war. On the seas around Okinawa was developing the biggest, bloodiest, strangest air-sea battle in human history. And into that battle, the men of *Enterprise* learned later in the day, the enemy had also thrown the last and best of his naval surface forces. Mighty and beautiful *Yamato* of the 18-inch guns, whose sister ship, *Musashi*, Dog Smith had helped to put under in the Sibuyan Sea in October, and which had suffered the ignominy of surprise attack by the rockets of Ernie Lawton's lone TBM as she slunk through the Inland Sea under cover of darkness, had sortied through the Bungo Strait with a light cruiser and eight destroyers, headed for the soft amphibious fleet around Okinawa. With Marc Mitscher's 14 fast carriers and 8 new battleships, backed up by 6 more of the old battlewagons that had annihilated a similar attempt at Leyte waiting across her track, *Yamato*, too, became a Kamikaze. Twenty-two hours after passing out of the Bungo Strait, she and all of her force except four battered destroyers were at the bottom of the East China Sea, 200 miles short of her objective and 150 miles from the nearest surface battery, put there solely by the air groups of Mitscher's carriers fresh from the destruction of 250 of the air-borne suiciders.

On the way to Okinawa, the Big E worked out as usual after the long stay in port, with battle and damage control problems, firing at sleeves, group air attacks and casualty control drills.

Also on the way, Bill Martin, as always the champion and prophet of night operations, already knowing the answers because he knew his men, formally interrogated the pilots of Night Air Group Ninety on their reactions to night aerial combat "for the purposes of . . . formulating recommendations regarding future night carrier air groups."

Martin, like most prophets, was still on the defensive.

And the result of his poll was not encouraging. Of fifty-two night fighter pilots, only four expressed a desire to continue in night carrier operations. Thirty-one did not "object to those operations as such" but preferred not to volunteer for them a second time, and seventeen "strongly disliked" night operations and had no desire to continue them "in any form." For twenty-eight night torpedo pilots, the score was six who desired to continue, 16 who did not object but wanted no more and six who "strongly disliked."

Why, after the successful pioneering of this new concept, after the pride they must have felt at completing difficult and dangerous missions under nearly impossible conditions, after being exposed to William One's contagious enthusiasm and competent tactical leadership, did the night pilots feel, although night operations were important and should be continued, that each, personally, would prefer the day work?

Most important was the lack of tangible results. On flight after flight, after long hours of navigating through the darkness, locating by radar the assigned target and attacking through searchlights and AA, they had had to report "results unobserved due to darkness." This did not add to the scoreboard on the hangar deck that was covered with the accomplishments of the day groups that had preceded them. This did not get them the medals which, although few would admit it, most coveted. This did not get their squadron or their names in the papers back home.

And that was another thing—lack of recognition. Night operations were still classified, and nothing about them could be released to the press. While the friends of Martin's pilots were reaping glory—they themselves operated in both physical and journalistic obscurity.

There were too many defensive, too few offensive missions. For the torpedo pilots especially, there were simply not enough missions. They grew bored and restless with inactivity, with "standing by to stand by."

The pilots knew about the advantages of night operations—the relative invulnerability to AA, the greater bombing accuracy because of the closer drops that this allowed, the indirect assistance to our forces of depriving the enemy of his sleep and his chance to prepare for the next day's action, but, personally, those advantages were outweighed by the increased hazards of night carrier landings and night catapult shots, the danger of collision, the heavy dependence on electrical and electronic devices for navigation, communication and recognition, the inability to avoid bad weather that could not be seen in the darkness, the relatively poor chances of rescue if forced down.

On the basis of this poll and his long previous experience, Martin recommended:

(1) painstaking screening and selection of pilots and crewmen assigned to night operations, thus increasing the proportion of exceptionally competent men.

(2) inclusion of at least two months of intensive night operations in the advanced training of all air groups.

(3) eventual qualifications of all air groups in both day and night operations.

In April of 1945 in *Enterprise*, all of the above was of great interest but academic. Having expressed their preferences and opinions, the pilots buckled on their incredible array of gear, their chart boards, knives, revolvers, flashlights, whistles, waterproof charts, flags, vitamins, first-aid kits, dye marker, shark repellant, Very pistols and flares, smoke flares, compasses, fishing kits, matches, helmets and goggles, oxygen masks, Mae Wests, parachutes and rubber rafts, and went back to flying against the enemy at night.

On the afternoon of the seventh, *Enterprise* got back in the fight when Dallas Runion shot down a snooping Frances thirty-four miles southwest of the ship.

The eighth, some 120 miles east of Okinawa, was the first of many days spent buttoned up tight in "Condition Able." with all hands at battle stations, eating K rations and "standing easy" when not actually threatened. But, after the fire of March 20, the crew did not mind so much the discomforts and inconveniences of the all-day GQ.

Everyone knew that the eleventh was going to be a bad day. The enemy had been gathering and hoarding his planes since the sixth for another mass, all-out Kamikaze attack. Intelligence reported that this was the day.

Admiral Mitscher canceled all support missions over Okinawa, ordered dive bombers and torpedo planes degassed, disarmed and stowed below, and increased the CAP to twenty-four fighters over each task group, and a dozen over each of the destroyer picket stations, fifty miles out on the enemy approach routes.

Enterprise went to General Quarters as usual at 5:00 A.M. and stayed there. All the windy, slightly hazy morning the men waited and the CAP circled and was relieved and circled some more and nothing happened—but at 1:30 P.M. it began.

CIC picked up a bogey thirty-seven miles southeast, closing. Minutes later two large groups showed on the scope spread out from forty to eighty miles to the northward. The long familiar pattern of events commenced again. The ships moved in on the radii of the circular task group closing their armed and armored circles tighter, carriers at the center. Speed went up to 25 knots. The destroyers' sterns squatted over the push of their screws, and the wakes foamed wide and white on the blue sea. CAP roared out to intercept, pushing over from altitude for added speed. From lookout stations, gun directors and bridge, binoculars and sights searched the sky on the danger bearings. At 2:05 P.M. the first shots were fired at a Zeke diving for the *Essex* on the Big E's starboard beam. *Enterprise* gunners opened on him early and well. He began to smoke and, as if in retaliation, leveled off and changed his target to *Enterprise*. The starboard guns of all calibers blazed steadily the full length of the deck, aiming carefully and firing fast as the ship turned away. The Zeke flamed and cartwheeled into the sea 500 yards on the starboard quarter. But he was only the first.

The Big E's last turn had brought her downwind, making 25 knots with a wind astern of 22, a relative wind of three knots. The yellow cordite smoke hung long over the guns, obscuring the gunners' vision, and before it could clear away a Judy appeared dead astern at two miles in a shallow head-on glide. He was in a good attack position. Most of the Big E's guns were lined along the edges of her deck, and only the after few could bear. But every barrel that could get on poured it to him as Captain Hall swung his ship to put more firepower on the enemy. At 500 yards his dive steepened abruptly, the clean lines, the big spinner and the ugly bomb right under the engine were clearly visible. Five-inch burst ahead and tracers poured into him. He began to spin, but stayed on course, spinning around it, as the stern, with nightmarish slowness, swung out from under him.

To the gunners in the two port quarter 40-millimeter mounts it seemed a personal duel. The Judy was headed directly for them, desperately trying to crush and burn the gun tubs full of sailors by his own death. They had learned that their only chance was to take his plane apart with their bullets before it reached them. They stuck to their weapons, hammering at the Judy until it filled the world before them, hit and disintegrated in a roar and blast and sudden silence like the end of the earth. A seaman was blown overboard and two more fell with broken legs and arms. The Judy's wing had hit between the two mounts. His engine dished in the hull plating, and his bomb grazed the ship's side and detonated under the turn of the bilge, shaking her as a terrier shakes a snake. Two hundred and twenty-five feet from the explosion, high on the island a few feet forward of the mast, the structural supports for the big SK air search radar were snapped, and it ground to a stop. The yardarms whipped so violently that the starboard one snapped off six feet from the end and fell, dangling by its guy wires and fouling the surface search antenna. Four pedestal mounts for the propeller shaft bearings were cracked. The after mounts of two of the four generators were fractured. Mercury was washed out of the bowl of the master gyro compass in Central Station, splashed onto electrical connections and badly overloaded the circuits. Eight fuel tanks were ruptured, and 150 tons of salt water flooded into the torpedo blister through the breaks in the skin of the ship. A few guns lost electrical power. Loose gear flew, and secured gear broke loose and fell on men below, as the massive flexural vibrations whipped through the ship.

But when it was all over, *Enterprise* was still under way at 25 knots, still firing at her enemies, still on her assigned station in formation and still capable of operating her aircraft. And lean, dark, John Munro, sitting like a beetle-browed spider at the center of his communication network at Central Station, initiated the necessary emergency repairs with the calm precision of a digital computer.

It was well for *Enterprise* that she was still capable of defending herself, because the war did not stop while she dressed her wounds.

Two minutes after the Judy had not quite missed the Big E, another Kamikaze near-missed the *Bunker Hill*, and a few minutes later another was shot down half a mile to starboard.

At 2:35 a destroyer reported rescuing the gunner knocked overboard by the Judy, and at three o'clock it was *Enterprise's* turn again.

Another Judy appeared out of the clouds high on the starboard beam. An alert 20-millimeter gunner saw him first and opened up, pointing out the target to the other guns which joined a second later. The Judy, looking identical to the one which had grazed the port quarter, pulled up slightly, dropped off on one wing and dived in at a steep 60 degrees for the Big E. It was a repetition of the attack of fifty minutes before: the plane plunged at the straining, speeding ship which answered with a steady broadside of guns and swung away. This Judy also was hit but he did not spin; he simply misjudged or could not correct. The plane arrowed into the sea some twenty-five feet from the starboard bow and exploded on impact. A pillar of mixed smoke, water, gasoline and airplane parts burst upward, seemed to hang while the ship moved through it and then fell back on her deck. The bomb went off close aboard, and again the carrier whipped and rattled, although this time not as severely as the last. A Hellcat on the starboard catapult, with its wings folded, caught fire from fragments or crossfire, and the flight-deck repair party had no pressure to their hoses. Quickly Damage Control went to work to supply water pressure from another pump, but Jack Blitch had a better idea. He ordered the catapult fired, and all of the flaming F6 but its tail, wings still folded, hurtled harmlessly off the bow. Minutes later water arrived at the flight-deck nozzles, and what was left of the fire was put out.

On the fo'c'sle three men were wounded and their gun's cooling system punctured when 20-millimeter fire from another ship detonated a clip of 40-millimeter ammunition. The wounded were taken below and the punctures patched with rags and friction tape. The fo'c'sle guns fired vigorously eight minutes later at another plane which dived at *Enterprise* from the starboard beam but, after being hit, changed course, passed ahead and down the portside and around the stern in a tight bank, trying to line up again, before he was pulled apart by AA and crashed off the starboard quarter.

Three more Kamikazes fell inside the task group's tight

defensive formation that busy afternoon, and darkness did not decrease the danger. All night the bogies circled and probed while their pale flares drifted down the sky, and the guns of the screen flashed and sparkled under radar control, but *Enterprise* went ahead with her night duties on schedule.

Night Fighting 90's dusk and night CAPs over Okinawa shot down five planes, bettering the score turned in by the day fighters.

The torpedo squadron shifted its attention to the airfields at Tokuno and Kikai in the Amami group, between Kyushu and Okinawa, and five two-plane teams kept them shut down and sleepless all night, from 7:45 P.M. until 6:00 A.M., with 120 bombs, 80 rockets and a few hundred rounds of .50-caliber. As a bonus, Waldo Cummings, who in quieter hours directed the Big E's choir, answered an urgent call from a fighter trailing a Japanese transport but out of ammunition, and obligingly shot down the enemy plane. The next night (except for Cummings' exploit) they repeated the performance, and in addition, the group commander and Gibby Blake conducted a thorough search for shipping to the northward, drove down an enemy submarine and worked over Tokuno Field with 500-pound bombs and rockets.

On the thirteenth came the news of the death of the President of the United States. Commander Kabler passed the word over the public address system, and *Enterprise* was shocked and numbed as she had never been by the loss of her own men. It was to each man a personal loss, as though some relative, say a strong, benevolent and respected uncle, had died. For boys in their late teens he had been President for as long as they could remember. Men in their middle twenties had been children not yet in their teens when he was first elected. There was a feeling of loss of security, of guidance, of leadership. His successor was either unknown, or untrusted to fill the biggest job in the world. On *Enterprise* and every ship with a chaplain aboard, memorial services were held and heavily attended. Whatever their politics or voting record, every man at sea that day felt that something important had gone out of his life.

On the fourteenth of April, the Big E headed back once more to the big lagoon of Ulithi, and the good repair ship

Jason. This time it took sixteen days for the Big E's Construction and Repair Department and the *Jason*'s crew to restore her full fighting ability. For a few days a deliberate eight-degree starboard list was put on the ship, by emptying port tanks and flooding those to starboard, so that repair crews could have access to her damaged port quarter. It was not bad topside, where a horizon existed for orientation, but below decks the effect was impressive. The decks seemed still horizontal and the bulkheads vertical. Only the men seemed all to be standing or walking at the same ridiculous angle. Hanging lines and clothes and flight gear angled impossibly out from their hooks. Soup, coffee and shaving water lurked improbably halfway up one side of their containers. In the normal course of the day the effect was strange but acceptable. After a late return from a highly convivial party at Mog Mog, it was the final straw which sent many an officer and man straight to his slanting bunk.

At quarter past seven on the morning of May 3, the big links clanked up through the hawse once more, the jack and the taffrail colors dropped, the steaming colors soared to the truck and *Enterprise* was under way, sailing against the enemy as she had done so many times before—but would not do again.

With a single destroyer, she steamed back and forth close to Ulithi all day testing her repairs while *Jason* engineers checked the success of their work. The gunners worked out against towed sleeves, and later the air group requalified in carrier landings. Late in the afternoon, two of Charlie Henderson's TBMs flew the *Jason* technicians back to the airstrip at Ulithi, returned aboard, and the Big E and her escort headed northwest at 20 knots to rejoin TF 58.

Early on the morning of the sixth, as a squally cold front swept the gray seas east of Okinawa, Captain Hall reported for duty and was assigned to TG 58.3, commanded by Rear Admiral F. C. Sherman in the *Essex*. By seven o'clock she was on station in that group which, besides *Essex*, included *Bunker Hill* (with Admiral Mitscher aboard), *Randolph*, two light carriers, two fast battleships, five cruisers and eighteen destroyers.

The Big E's mission, again, was to provide night CAP, night searches, night heckler and night intruder missions—and this time she would be allowed to show what she could do.

On the sixth, *Enterprise* fueled and replenished the ammunition she had expended in practice on the way north and on the seventh, she went back to work with an all-day General Quarters and dawn, dusk and night CAPs, over Kikai in the Amamis.

On the clear, moonless evening of Thursday, the tenth of May, Charlie Henderson's Avengers got back into action with an all-night close-down of enemy airfields on Minami, Kikai and Tokuno. At Minami the TBMs worked for twenty minutes with cruisers and destroyers which were bombarding the island installations, dropping flares and spotting the fall of shot for the ships.

The eleventh looked like another quiet day. No one in *Enterprise* knew, felt or guessed that, after her long years of combat, only three days were left.

A few snoopers closed the force during the midwatch but the night CAP drove them off. At intervals Henderson's hecklers and McCullough's night and dawn CAP returned and landed. From quarter of nine until quarter past, Blitch and Martin worked out newly arrived fighter pilots in take-offs and landings in a tight, continuous circle from the deck, down wind to port and back aboard again. A few minutes before ten, the competent day CAP knocked down a Jill seventy miles to the east. A flight of Corsairs was on the scopes, returning from a close-support mission at Okinawa. Everything over TF 58 was as normal and routine as anything ever is in war.

Then at 10:12 two Kamikazes in rapid succession dropped out of the clouds toward *Bunker Hill,* released their bombs and followed them through her gassed and manned planes and her flight deck. A third missed, knocked off course by the instantly replying storm of gunfire.

The flagship of TF 58 blazed and smoked like a fuel storage tank hit by bombs ashore. A cruiser and several destroyers moved in like fireboats, their hoses pouring long arching streams into her. An hour after she was hit, by flashing light, since all her radios were out, Admiral Mitscher passed command of the Fast Carriers to Admiral Sherman. At the same time, *Enterprise* took aboard fifteen of her homeless fighters.

The fight to save *Bunker Hill* was not won until midafternoon, when the assisting ships cast off—Admiral Mitscher and his staff transferred to a destroyer, and the big, new carrier, gutted almost as badly as *Franklin,* moved off under escort, with her 400 dead or missing and her 250 wounded, for major repairs in the States.

At 5:30 P.M. the destroyer *English* came alongside the starboard quarter, a lightly loaded bosun's chair dangled and swooped across the moving water between destroyer's bow and carrier's stern, three white stars on a blue field broke suddenly at the Big E's truck, and *Enterprise* became the new flagship of Vice Admiral Marc A. Mitscher, commander, Fast Carrier Force, Pacific Fleet.

The weathered little man dressed in khaki with a light field jacket, a long-billed fisherman's cap, and a quiet and almost humble air of absolute authority, waited for his chief staff officer, Commodore Arleigh Burke, and his operations officer, Commander Jimmy Flatley, father of the Grim Reapers of Fighting Ten, and walked forward to his flag quarters with Captain Hall, Commander Kabler and Commander Blitch. The men of *Enterprise* gawked respectfully at this man who controlled their destinies, whose name was already a legend next to Halsey's in the fleet.

That evening the fighters went back to Kikai/Tokuno, and three TBMs, the first of four planned launches, made the 360-mile flight to Kyushu. Admiral Mitscher ordered the remaining flights canceled because of weather.

Charlie Henderson, Waldo Cummings and Gibby Blake took the heckler mission to Japan. They flew in low, under enemy radar, to a point south of the island of Tanega, off Kyushu's south cape, and then climbed and headed in as though they were approaching from the U. S.-held fields on Okinawa.

Henderson, alone at 1,500 feet and 150 knots, lights out, approached Kanoya field from Tanega well aware that radar was tracking him all the way. Kanoya greeted him with open arms. All runway, taxiway and obstruction lights were at full brilliance, and, as he circled, the control tower attempted amiably to convey some message to him by flashing light. When that failed they obligingly illuminated the outline of a carrier deck on one side of the field, evidently a practice area for carrier landings, possibly with field arresting gear. Charlie circled a few more times. "They were so nice," he said, "I hated to drop my bombs." But he did, and not until they crunched and flashed among the buildings on the west side of the field did the lights go out.

The other two planes illuminated and then bombed and rocketed other fields in the area, hitting parked planes, starting fires and staying overhead, sources of alarm and consternation for more than an hour. Not a searchlight came on and not a round of AA rose against them.

At 8:00 A.M. on the cool, windy twelfth of May, Admiral Mitscher, his staff set up and functioning in *Enterprise*, reassumed tactical command of TF 58 and ordered it in to strike Kyushu on the thirteenth.

At 5:30 P.M. on the twelfth, when *Enterprise* had less than two days left to fight, an experiment finally began which Bill Martin had conceived two years before and had been trying to conduct since the Big E had first joined the fleet as a night carrier.

For the first time, during the approach of the Task Force on a major target area, night hecklers (followed by predawn VFN [night fighter] patrols) were sent out in advance to harass the enemy in his home bases, make him take cover, and keep him down, prevent him from "getting set" for the heavy sweeps and strikes to be launched by our Day Carriers in early morning, and to *impede*, as far as possible, his organizing attacks in force against our approaching Fleet.

It was an ambitious project. Martin had assigned his pilots all the fields on Kyushu south of Sasebo on the west coast and Saeki on the east, plus the sea lanes and harbors along the way, especially Sasebo and Nagasaki. For the job he had 16 TBMs, armed with ten to twelve 100-pound incendiary clusters, four rockets, full loads of .50-caliber and six flares. They took off four at a time, two hours apart, and approached singly from the same point, south of the Tanega Island radar installation, that had been used the night before, again giving the impression that they were based ashore at Okinawa, or Japanese planes returning from raids on that island. From Tanega they fanned out up both coasts of Kyushu to their various targets.

But this night the Japanese were not fooled. No friendly runway lights or blinking signals greeted them. At fields which had previously offered no resistance, they were met with angrily stabbing searchlights and vicious flashes of AA. Japanese defensive tactics had changed during the day.

This time the enemy was prepared and actively resentful.

At Kanoya where Henderson had been so graciously received the day before, Joe Doyle, the first to arrive, was met by fifteen radar-controlled searchlights which effectively destroyed his night vision, dazzling him so badly that at first he could not even make out his instrument panel in the glare, pointed him out to gunners below, and kept him feeling about as comfortable as if he were standing naked in Times Square at the height of the rush. He dodged and dived and retired but returned to rocket and strafe despite the lights.

At Miyazaki, Cliff Largess ran into eight or nine searchlights, but managed to confuse their guiding radars with the foil strips of his "window" and some electronic jamming so that he could make his dropping runs.

At Sasebo, Charlie Henderson was met by three or four lights which completely frustrated his attempted visual search of the harbor, but the aggressive skipper of VT(N)-90 merely shifted targets to the seaplane base at Omura and blew up the hangars with his bombs.

Thus it went all night, the darkened Avengers buzzing from one field to the next, forcing out the lights needed to repair cratered runways, move, arm or gas planes, starting fires, strafing parked aircraft, bombing hangars, rocketing power plants, barracks, control towers, remaining overhead three hours each and then relieving each other for the next three.

William One himself took the 1:00 to 4:00 A.M. watch over heavily defended Kanoya, Kanoya East and Kushira. Martin was not only the prophet and champion of night operations so that he desired above all else to prove its usefulness; he was also the most experienced and resourceful pilot in the air over Japan that night, and Bill Chace, on his radar, was as good as any operator in the fleet. They actually enjoyed their duel with the Kanoya searchlights. When the TBM was securely at the apex of four or five beams, Martin ordered plenty of window dropped and grinned to himself as the lights let his plane fly off into the darkness while they followed the drifting tinfoil down and then, embarrassedly, one by one blinked out. On later runs, while the lights were tracking the window, he dived out of the night to launch his rockets at them, and still later had his jamming gear turned on and watched the beams waver confusedly and again go out. At all three fields, the Big E's air group commander unloaded his guns, rockets, bomb bays on anything that moved or showed a light, bringing to a stop every kind of activity while the threat of his engine and the chill light of his flares hung overhead and the enemy below took cover, wondering where the next blow out of the night sky would fall.

The last of the Avengers did not leave the sleepless Kyushu fields until the predawn fighter patrol was on station. Then, as the first light began to change the black to gray, the Japanese, frustrated all night long, desperately tried to get their planes in the air, exactly what Bob McCullough's boys were waiting for. At Kanoya, Owen Young noticed the sparkle of exhaust low over the bay as a Tony took off, and swooped down so eagerly that he overshot and had to drop flaps and wheels to drop back for the burst that sent the enemy flaming into the water.

At Kanoya East, Young and Ken Smith saw the lights of planes taxiing for take-off but when they went down to strafe found that they could not see their targets until it was too late to fire. So they simply continued making runs until daylight, keeping the enemy aircraft on the ground until there was sufficient light for strafing, and then riddling four of them. In his last run, Smith's controls were hit by tracerless AA and he lost the use of his left aileron. He headed for home, but a few miles out he was jumped by two Tonys, one of which missed, overshot, ran under and pulled up in front of him, so that he only had to squeeze his trigger to shoot it down. With his controls out of commission, Ken had no desire to shoot it out with the other Tony, and gave his Hellcat all it had, including water injection, on the course for home. As he pulled away, he glanced back to see if he was escaping the Tony, and found that the enemy pilot had shared his feelings and was headed for his own home field at top speed.

At Kagoshima, Young caught three twin-float Jakes taking off the bay and splashed them all in ten minutes.

Two more fighters, after strafing a small lugger off Kagoshima, chased an Oscar over Kanoya, shot it down, and discovered three dark, 50-foot barrage balloons flying at 2,000 feet just to the west of the field which Martin, Doyle and others had been working over all night at well below that altitude.

The dawn CAP from *Enterprise* shot down, or destroyed on the ground, eight enemy planes that morning but they had to share the honors with Hot Shot Charlie Henderson of VT(N)-90. Coming back from Sasebo at 500 feet, Charlie sighted a George fighter above him. The TBM pulled up stealthily, and at a point-blank 50 to 100 feet, opened fire. The range was so short that the George's fuselage fitted between the barrels of the Avenger's widely separated wing guns, and the tracers missed on both sides. The fighter at once dived for the water and pulled out of range, with Charlie right behind, fighting slip stream and firing repeated bursts.

Henderson disgustedly continued his flight home, but a few minutes later he picked up a single-float Rufe fighter on his starboard beam, level. He turned in at full power on a low side run and poured in a long burst. The Rufe began to smoke but turned hard to the right and began a series of tight turns, with Henderson on his tail, firing whenever he could get on, and Ted Halbach and the gunner, also a Henderson, plastered to their seats and half-blacked-out by the G forces. Finally the Rufe turned so sharply that Charlie could no longer follow without stalling. But the enemy pilot overdid it and at 400 feet stalled and spun into the sea. He was Henderson's fourth kill. One more would make Charlie an ace—in a bomber.

Before the dawn CAP left, the first fighter sweeps from the day carriers were overhead.

All day the thirteenth, the day carriers smashed at the Kyushu fields, with some 700 sorties in clear weather, from a position within easy fighter range of Kyushu, but not a single enemy attack was made on TF 58.

Bill Martin's experiment had worked.

Again *Enterprise* dusk CAP relieved the last sweep of day fighters over the enemy airdromes, the first team of marauding Avengers relieved the CAP, and succeeding relays stayed destructively on station until the dawn CAP took over the interval before the first sweep came in. It was the Big E's last night of combat, but Admiral Mitscher had been converted. When *Enterprise* had joined TF 58 a week before, he had accepted her reluctantly, feeling that a "day group would be more valuable" but bowing to "this pressure for night operations [which] comes from Washington." Now, in a letter to Captain Hall, he said:

I was impressed with the enthusiasm, efficiency and effectiveness of your squadrons. In this comparative-

ly new art of night combat, your squadrons have
fully demonstrated the possibilities, and have my ut-
most admiration for their flying ability and their very
damaging night harass.

On Monday, the fourteenth of May, in the Philippine
Sea some 150 miles southeast of Kyushu, the sun rose at
5:15 A.M. on an ocean ruffled by a 15-knot southerly wind
and drifted over with a scattering of cumulus clouds, their
bases at 3,000 feet. The heavy warships of TF 58 plowed
through the dawn sea with their men at battle stations and
the shadows of long-range Japanese snoopers on their radar
scopes.

For twenty minutes, beginning at 5:30, Hellcats and
Avengers, their wheels, flaps and hooks dangling, buzzed
down the Big E's portside, swung in over her wake and
banged down on her deck as night CAP and hecklers returned to their base.

At 6:10 the first of several bogies showed up on the
radar screen to the southwest. In a few minutes there were
a dozen groups and singles approaching from the same
general direction on curving and zigzag courses. Three divisions of day CAP and the *Enterprise* dawn CAP, which
was in the landing circle, were vectored out to intercept.
Three Zekes went down in the next few minutes, but more
appeared on the radars. One group headed for TG 58.1.
Another converged steadily on the Big E's 58.3 under constant attack by the CAP. By 6:23 several were in to 20
miles and, in gun control and lookout stations, eyes strained
into binoculars, searching the sky, trying to probe the fat,
white clouds. Three times before 6:50, lookouts reported
columns of smoke on the southwest horizon where enemy
planes had fallen to the CAP. Then at 6:53, the starboard
five-inch guns shook the ship as they opened fire at a single
Zeke which broke out of the low clouds five or six miles
away, a little aft of the starboard beam. Search radar and
directors had been tracking him for nearly twenty minutes.
Other ships got the word and opened on him also, and the
Zeke ducked back into the clouds with the five-inch still
banging at him in full radar control and the row of black
puffs marking his flight path. A formation course change to
the left put the Zeke nearly dead astern, the worst possible
bearing for antiaircraft defense. Every few seconds he
popped into sight between clouds, dodging and banking

violently to avoid the persistent black bursts. For a short
time he paralleled the ship's course and closed in to two
miles, then doubled back in a cloud and opened out to
three.

At 6:56 the task group turned left again to the northwest
and the Big E's stern swung past the last cloud the Zeke had
entered. As though he had been waiting for that moment,
the clean, vicious little fighter came out of the cloud base
astern in a fast, shallow dive straight at *Enterprise*. The
port 40s and 20s took him under fire with more and more
opening up as the carrier swung to port, moving the target
away from the stern. The Kamikaze continued straight in,
not jinking at all, but his wings moving slightly as he
changed his point of aim to correct for the turning of the
ship. *Enterprise* heeled and trembled in her high-speed turn.
Thirty-five barrels of 20-millimeters (some firing across
the deck from starboard), sixteen of 40-millimeters and
four five-inch poured out their lead until the whole port
side was yellow with smoke.

On the flag bridge, Jimmy Flatley stepped out to take a
look and ducked right back into where the admiral stood,
yelling, "Hit the deck!" and did so.

But from the navigating bridge, as the pretty, deadly,
brown-green Zeke with the big bomb under its belly slanted
down over the port quarter, it looked as if he would over-
shoot and crash to starboard. The enemy pilot must have
thought so too, because halfway up the deck he rolled left
onto his back, pulled through and dived, inverted, down
through the forward elevator. In the next split second,
while the sounds of torn timbers and tortured metal were
still at crescendo, the bomb roared off five decks down, and
incredulous watchers on nearby ships saw the Big E's Number One elevator, the cap of a heavy pillar of gray and
white smoke, soar 400 feet into the sky, hang for a second
and fall back into the sea.

In the exposed Flag Plot, as *Enterprise* shuddered under
the blow and chunks of wood and metal banged against
overhead and bulkheads, Marc Mitscher was the only man
standing when the officers of his staff rose from the deck
and began to move out as smoke poured into the compartment.

Enterprise was badly hurt. Fire towered redly under the
black smoke that filled the hole where the forward elevator
had been. Flames filled the forward end of the hangar deck

and licked at the ammunition supply for the forward five-inch guns on both sides. The flight deck was blasted up three feet aft of the demolished elevator. Other fires smoldered in clothing and bedding in the ruined officers' quarters around the elevator pit. The gasoline system was wrecked, its pressure main crushed and three of the four tanks leaking. The forward guns were out of action. There were twenty-foot holes in her decks down to the third. Watertight integrity forward was nonexistent. With her buckled deck and gaping elevator hole she could no longer operate her planes. Worst of all, her holes and her smoke marked her as a cripple for the other Kamikazes closing the force.

Damage control went to work, intelligently and calmly directed, and bravely and skillfully executed. Hangar bay sprinklers were turned on, the demolished forward starboard section of the fire main was isolated, and hoses run from other sections to fight the fires in that area. Chief Carpenter Walter Woznick and Chief Bosun's Mate "Gabby" Gabbara led rescue and working parties into the flaming five-inch gun groups forward to bring out dead and wounded and throw overboard the hot powder cans and projectiles. Below decks, repair parties in rescue breathers attacked the flames with high- and low-velocity fog and solid streams of water. Other streams from the torn and buckled flight deck were directed into the elevator pit.

Seventeen minutes after she was hit, *Enterprise* had her fires under control and in another thirteen minutes they were out. Never, during that time, did she leave her assigned station in the formation. But she was down seven feet by the bow and up three by the stern with the 2,000 tons of water that had entered through the ruptured fire main and been poured onto her fires. Pumps of all kinds were rigged, and in thirty-six hours her trim had been restored to normal.

The Big E, with her competence, had also had luck. The enemy bomb had exploded in a storeroom full of baled rags, in the vicinity of stored sheets of heavy steel hull plate, smothering a large part of the shrapnel. The Number Two elevator had been in use at the time of the hit and the men who would normally have been forward were well aft and out of the way.

Her casualties had been light for such heavy damage, thirteen killed and sixty-eight wounded. Eight men who were blown overboard were promptly picked up by the destroyer *Waldron,* some standing, comfortably drying out, on a fifteen-foot section of the elevator.

But Chief Pilot Tomi Zai (his body, with calling cards in his pocket, was found at the bottom of the elevator well) had done what his superiors in the Imperial Navy had been unable to do in three and a half years of concerted effort. He had knocked *Enterprise* out of the war.

Defiantly she shot down two more Zekes before 8:15 while her plates were still hot from her recent fires. The next day Admiral Mitscher moved to the *Randolph,* and on the sixteenth of May the Big E was detached from TF 58 and began the long and welcome voyage to Ulithi, Pearl and Bremerton in the country of which she had always been a tiny, floating part, and the defense of which she could now leave to the ships which had been built and the men that had been trained while she and a few others held off the enemy alone.

The man who commanded Fast Carrier Force, Pacific Fleet, composed of the mightiest ships that had ever sailed the seas, sent after her a final accolade:

> The performance of duty of the officers and men of the *Enterprise* under fire, and their effective damage control measures, were outstanding, of the highest order, and the most efficient that I have seen during one year's service with the Force.

EPILOGUE

Enterprise *was a warship, a Second World War ship.* As some men seem to have been born to be at a certain place at a certain time performing a certain task, and are exactly right in that time and place and task, whatever they may have been before or will be after, so *Enterprise* had been built and crewed, shaken down and trained, for fighting the Japanese in the Pacific during World War II. When Tomi Zai knocked her out of that war he removed her from the special set of circumstances for which she seemed to have been created—and her significant life was over.

Yet there were good days left in the time that remained to *Enterprise,* worth mentioning because they complete her story and tell the way it was with her at the end, after her war, as well as in the beginning, before it.

She stopped in the lagoon at Ulithi only long enough to unload the bombs and bullets that she would not need to the eastward, and take aboard a couple of hundred passengers for Hawaii and the States.

Her entry into Pearl was triumphant. The ships in the harbor saluted. Bands blared their thin music to her across the waters that had been scummed with oil and wreckage when she had first sailed against the enemy three and a half years before. TBMs and F6Fs from Ford Island roared overhead forming a V for Victory and an E for *Enterprise.* On the dock another band played, and three busloads of Waves waved and smiled above the sweet, half-forgotten fullness of their blouses, so that the line-handlers fumbled their lines and the Big E must have had a slight list to starboard, since every man aboard was as far that way as he could get.

She was out of Pearl forty-five hours after entering, headed northeast for Bremerton at 20 knots, trailing a homewardbound pennant from her truck 578 feet long—a foot for every day she had been away from "Uncle Sugar." The pennant was so long that ten balloons were needed to keep it flying and out of the harbor water.

On the afternoon of the sixth of June, one year after D-Day in Europe, the Big E entered the Straits of Juan de Fuca. After the Philippine Sea and Leyte Gulf and the bright, windy atolls of the western Pacific, Puget Sound could have been an ocean on some other planet. The cool, damp air of early summer, with its perennial half-promise of fog, swept across her battered deck, and one after another the bell buoys slid down her side, clanging in their slow, haphazard, absolutely unique way to the rise and fall of the ground swell, rolling into the sound from seaward.

At noon on the seventh, a ferryboat named *City of Sacramento* came alongside, and Bill Martin took his air group ashore.

Again there were the calls made from lines of booths, and again in Bremerton and Seattle, and spreading from there out and down and across, there were the homecomings—and the lack of them.

For three months—while Halsey and McCain took over again from Spruance and Mitscher, and steamed back and forth off Honshu making daily strikes, sending their battle-wagons in to shell the coastal cities, while the B-29s fire-bombed and blasted, while the awful atom was released and the Soviet opportunists grabbed the last-minute, no-cost victory, and the war ended—*Enterprise* lay on her keelblocks in Bremerton being repaired, being readied for —what?

In September she went back to Pearl, touching briefly first at San Francisco, and the old hands remembered, as she slipped under the Golden Gate, John Crommelin's flight-deck drills for the parade up Market Street that never happened because there had been too much war and *Enterprise* too much a part of it.

She was only a day in Pearl, and then sailed, with Admiral F. C. Sherman back aboard, at the center of a three-carrier, four-battleship task group, for Panama and New York City.

The President of Panama and other dignitaries came aboard as she passed the Pedro Miguel locks, rode across the lake and left her at Mira Flores lock.

In October she was back in the Atlantic, for her the ocean of peace where she had first felt the sea. At dawn on the seventeenth she took aboard a pilot off the *Ambrose* lightship and picked her way between the blinking lights of the channel buoys through the narrows that churned with tugs, ferries, yachts and seagoing vessels of every size and type. At 7:20 A.M. she tied up at Pier 26 in the North River, with the towers of Manhattan looming over her, and rigged ship for visitors.

If it were possible for the people of the United States to thank a ship, they did so in the last two weeks of October, 1945. In that time some 300,000 crowded aboard *Enterprise* to walk her decks, touch her guns, talk to some of the men that had stood between them and their enemies for so long. They came in all ages, sizes, sexes, shapes and colors, and they pushed buttons, pulled levers, turned knobs, poked, prodded, scratched and gaped at the final score-board on the hangar deck: 20 battle stars, 911 aircraft destroyed, 71 ships sunk. These were the people to whom Tom Wolfe refers as the "faceless man-throng" and the "sidewalk cipher"—but it was for them that she had fought from Oahu to Kyushu, for them that she had lost, in the course of the war, such men as Hallsted Hopping, Gene Lindsey, Gayle Herman, Stubby Pearson, Slim Townsend, Butch O'Hare, Williams and Hargrove, Russ Kippen and C B Collins, who unchallengeably were better men than any who came aboard to thank her. But it is pleasant and perhaps at least partially true, to think that the spirit of big, tough, proud, scarred, veteran *Enterprise* knew that the thanks of those few thousands was really the thanks of all the millions of Americans for whom she had gone to General Quarters so many times, and who now were free to produce other men of the caliber of those lost ones, men who might now not have to die in midocean 4,000 miles from home, who instead could turn their skill and courage toward some small facet of the colossal task of making and keeping this beautiful and varied earth also a fit and decent place in which free, civilized men can live.

On Navy Day she moored between two concrete buoys off Eighty-sixth Street, part of a long line of her sister warships, and exchanged salutes with the new President as he reviewed the victorious fleet from the bridge of the destroyer *Renshaw*.

On the last day of October, the Big E moved to the Boston Navy Yard, and, when she sailed from there in mid-November, she was an aircraft carrier without aircraft. The shops along her hangar deck were silent and idle, but the long, steel cavern was full—full of tiers and jungles of pipe and wire-spring bunks. In the wells of the forward and after elevators were heads. *Enterprise* was equipped to bunk and feed 5000 passengers in addition to her crew, now down to 1250. She was a part of Operation Magic Carpet—the return of U. S. troops from Europe.

In November and December she made two round trips between New York and Southampton, arriving home from the second on Christmas Eve. The busy, gasoline-smelling flight deck that had broiled and bubbled under the sun of Guadalcanal and the Marianas, knew the ice-green, solid water of North Atlantic storms, and in port lay mute and empty under half a foot of snow.

At Southampton, on the twenty-third of November, Sir Albert Victor Alexander, First Lord of the Admiralty, was piped aboard in the first official visit any lord of the Admiralty had ever paid to a United States ship. Sir Albert presented to *Enterprise* an Admiralty pennant. When it fluttered to her truck it was the first time, since its creation at the time of the defeat of the Spanish Armada in 1588, that such a pennant had ever flown from a ship not of the Royal Navy.

On New Year's Day of her first warless year since 1940, she sailed for another load of troops at San Miguel in the Azores, and when she returned and tied up at Bayonne, New Jersey, on the afternoon of the eighteenth of January, it was for the last time. *Enterprise* never went to sea again.

In early May she entered dry dock to have her hull sealed as the first step in the process of inactivation which went on for nine months after she was undocked.

Late in 1946, Acting Pay Clerk S. W. "Nick" Carter, who had put her in commission in May of 1938, received his orders and left the ship. At a dinner in the wardroom the evening before his departure, the captain presented him with a wristwatch as the last "plankowner" to leave. He tried to make a speech—but could not.

At 1:47 P.M. on February 17, 1947, with the crew at quarters on the flight deck which had not felt a wheel for a year and a quarter, the last commanding officer of *Enterprise*, Commander Lewis F. Davis, gave the order and the commission pennant was slowly lowered from her truck. The final entry in her log reads ". . . placed out of commission in reserve, as a unit of the New York Group, Atlantic Reserve Fleet."

For ten years the Big E slept in her mothballs and cocoons alongside the South Wall at Bayonne, while her younger sisters prowled the perimeters of the cold war, steamed back into action in the strangely restricted "incident" of Korea, and the smell of carriers changed from gasoline to kerosene.

In 1956, when it had long been obvious that *Enterprise* could not be modernized to take the heavy jets with their high landing speeds which had succeeded her TBMs, F6Fs and SB2Cs, the order was reluctantly given to scrap her and thus recover at least some of her modest nineteen-million-dollar construction cost.

The voices of protest were many and loud. Men remembered that in August of 1945 Secretary Forrestal had recommended that the Big E be preserved as *Constitution* and *Constellation* had been, as the "one vessel that most nearly symbolizes the history of the Navy in this war." It was recalled that President Truman had approved a letter from Mr. Forrestal, which had ended:

*The men who fought her love this ship. It would grieve
me to put my name to the document which would consign
her to be broken up for scrap.*

I believe, Mr. President, that the Enterprise *should be
retired permanently at some proper place as a visible sym-
bol of American valor and tenacity in war, and of our will
to fight all enemies who assail us . . .*

Secretary Thomas S. Gates listened to the protests and
the appeals with sympathy and agreed to delay the scrapping order until an attempt had been made to raise the
necessary private funds to preserve and maintain her.

A gallant attempt was made. Fleet Admiral Bill Halsey,
aging but determined as ever, entered the fight to save
her—but it failed. The wealthiest nation on earth could not
afford to preserve its greatest warship.

Early in 1959, in a dreary shipyard on the Hackensack
River at Kearney, New Jersey, the torches and pneumatic
hammers bit into her and scientifically took her apart, her
island first in fifteen-ton vertically sliced chunks, while the
jackhammers ripped up her flight deck, then her elevators,
lower decks and bulkheads. The steel and aluminum and
Douglas fir that had been married to men, to a crew, and
out of that union had given birth to a ship—reverted under
the torches and hammers to ordinary matter. Starved and
stifled by the years-long coma of inaction, the great spirit
of *Enterprise* flickered and sank toward extinction.

And yet that spirit did not die.

During the months that the gondola cars at Kearney
were rumbling away to the melting pots with the chunks of
metal that had been history's most successful warship, a
colossal structure was growing in a graving dock at Newport News, Virginia, not far from the ways where the Big
E was launched twenty-three years before. In the Bureau
of Naval Personnel, overlooking the Pentagon, specialists
were searching their records for the best men in the naval
service to be ordered as a nucleus crew to a new carrier.

Early in 1961 the dock was flooded and *Enterprise,* the
first nuclear carrier in history, the biggest ship in the world,
again the pride of her country and its Navy, first felt the
touch of the sea.

The story of the Big E had begun again.

549-5919

CONTINUED ON PAGE 15

IGHT CLUBS

ney'll be playing the GALLAGHER'S uptown this
eekend, but Wednesday at the BIRCHMERE,
ashington's folksinging Smith Sisters offi-
ally celebrate the arrival of their official first
bum — produced with the help, on and off-
ike, of the official Watsons, meaning Doc and
rlie. You could always put off the McGarri-
e sisters till Thursday night (at ADAM'S).

I'll bet

NO BLUES
FOR YOUR BUDGET

Could't afford your usual weekend to the
Hamptons? No problem. We've got tunes in
town, buddy, and the price is right for the
smallest of budgets. The Charlie Byrd Trio
flies into Georgetown this Sunday for the free
Concert on the Canal series. And after Mr.
Byrd stops strumming his jazz guitar, you can
catch the Smith Sisters Songdrops singing
traditional folk songs. Show starts at 1:30 on
the Foundry Mall overlooking the C&O Canal
at 30th and Thomas Jefferson streets NW.
Call 862-1336.

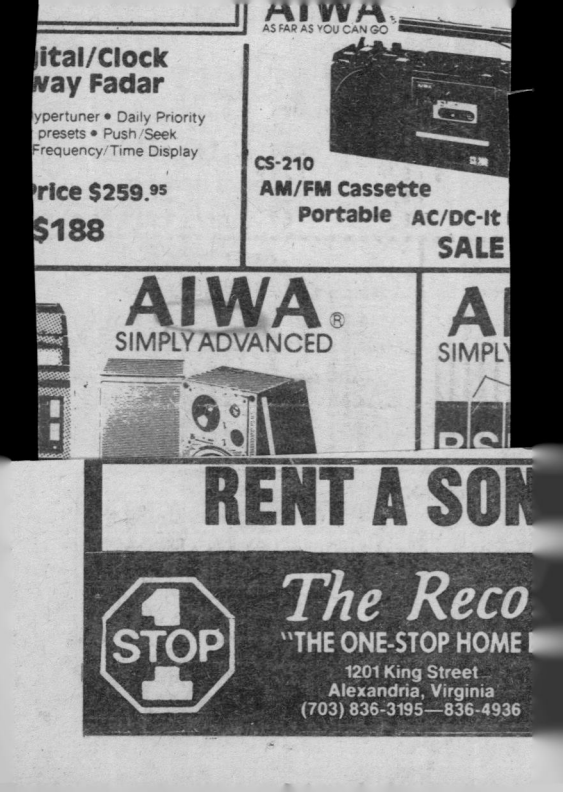

CHRONOLOGICAL ORDER OF EVENTS, USS ENTERPRISE

3 August 1933	Navy Department awarded contract for construction to Newport News Shipbuilding and Drydock Company.
16 July 1934	Keel laid.
3 October 1936	Launched.
12 May 1938	Commissioned.
Spring–Fall 1938	Conducted shakedown cruise to Rio de Janeiro, Capt. N. H. White USN commanding.
Winter 1938–39	Engaged in maneuvers in Caribbean Sea.
21 December 1938	Captain C. A. Pownall USN assumed command.
April 1939	Joined Pacific Fleet.
21 March 1941	Captain George D. Murray USN assumed command.
7 December 1941	Approaching Pearl Harbor when Japanese forces precipitated war by attack on U. S. Fleet units in Pearl Harbor.
8 December 1941	United States declared war on Japan.
1 February 1942	Gilbert and Marshall Islands raid.
24 February 1942	Wake Island raid.
18 April 1942	Escorted by *Enterprise*, *Hornet* launched U. S. Army B-25 aircraft for initial attack on Tokyo.
4–6 June 1942	Battle of Midway.
30 June 1942	Captain Arthur C. Davis USN assumed command.
7–9 August 1942	Occupation of Guadalcanal.
24 August 1942	Battle of Stewart Islands.
10 Sept.–16 Oct. 1942	Under repair in Pearl Harbor Navy Yard.

21 October 1942	Captain Osborne B. Hardison USN assumed command.
26 October 1942	Battle of Santa Cruz Islands.
14–15 November 1942	Battle of Solomon Islands.
30 January 1943	Action off Rennell Island.
7 April 1943	Captain Carlos W. Wieber USN assumed command.
16 April 1943	Captain Samuel P. Ginder USN assumed command.
8 May–14 July 1943	Under repair in Pearl Harbor Navy Yard.
20 July–31 Oct. 1943	Under repair in Puget Sound Navy Yard.
17 November 1943	Captain Matthias B. Gardner assumed command.
19–21 November 1943	Gilbert Islands occupation.
4 December 1943	Kawajalein Atoll raid.
29 Jan.–4 Feb. 1944	Marshall Islands occupation.
16–17 Feb. 1944	Truk Islands raid.
20 February 1944	Jaluit raid.
30 March–1 April 1944	Palau, Woleai and Yap Islands raid.
20–24 April 1944	Hollandia occupation.
29–30 April 1944	Truk Islands raid.
11 June–5 July 1944	Marianas Islands occupation.
19–20 June 1944	Battle of the Philippine Sea.
10 July 1944	Commander Thomas J. Hamilton USN assumed command.
16 July–4 Aug. 1944	Under repair in Pearl Harbor Navy Yard.
29 July 1944	Captain Cato D. Glover USN assumed command.
31 Aug.–3 Sept. 1944	Bonin Islands raid.
6–18 September 1944	Occupation of Palau.
10 October 1944	Nansei Shoto raid.
12–13 October 1944	Formosa raid.
14–31 October 1944	Occupation of Leyte Island.
24–25 October 1944	Second Battle of the Philippine Sea.
11–19 Nov. 1944	Philippine Islands raids.
14 December 1944	Captain Grover B. H. Hall USN assumed command.
7–8 January 1945	Operations in support of invasion of Luzon Island.

12–16 January 1945	Strikes on French Indo-China Hong Kong, Canton.
20–22 January 1945	Strikes on Formosa and Okinawa.
16–17 February 1945	First carrier strikes on Tokyo.
19 Feb.–9 March 1945	Operations in support of the occupation of Iwo Jima.
18–21 March 1945	Strikes on Kyushu and Shikoku.
7–12 April 1945	Operations in support of the occupation of Okinawa.
6–11 May 1945	Strikes on Amami Gunto and Daito Gunto.
11–14 May 1945	Strikes on Kyushu and Shikoku.
7 June–13 Sept. 1945	Under repair in Puget Sound Navy Yard.
14 August 1945	Japanese government agreed to unconditional surrender.
2 September 1945	President Truman proclaimed VJ-Day.
25 September 1945	Captain William L. Rees USN assumed command.
	Enterprise departed Pearl Harbor for Navy Day celebration in New York on October 27, 1945, and decommissioning in an East Coast port.

ACKNOWLEDGMENTS

There is, first of all, a single person, without whose sometimes tempestuous but always effective cooperation this book could never have been written—my lovely wife, 'Rie. For the four years of evenings, weekends and leaves that were required, she was in effect without a husband but not without five vigorous children and a home to run. Because of her belief in the importance of this book and of its eventual merit, she cheerfully and consistently released me from normal family responsibilities, assuming them herself, so that I could be free to get on with the job.

I owe to the Enterprise Association, and particularly to John Munro, at least a year saved in gathering and correlating material. Mr. Munro, out of his own affection for the Big E, devoted scores of hours of his own limited spare time to collecting and indexing the books, papers and pictures which provided the majority of the materials from which the book was written.

I am deeply grateful to Professor Robert W. Bolwell, who, despite temporary ill health and at a most inopportune time for him, took time to read much of the manuscript and give me the benefit of his forty years of experience in the field of literature.

Captain Roger W. Mehle also carefully read the chapters which deal with his time in *Enterprise* and made helpful marginal notes which we later discussed at some length. Captain Harvey P. Lanham assisted me in a similar manner.

Mr. Adrian O. Van Wyen, head of the Aviation History Unit in the office of the Chief of Naval Operations, by a lengthy and painstaking review of the book in its rough form, materially improved its historical accuracy and saved its author the embarrassment of many minor and some major errors.

Most of the *Enterprise* action reports and war diaries came from Mr. Dean C. Allard's Classified Archives Office of the Naval History Division. Mr. Allard and his assistants were consistently helpful and cooperative.

With a houseful of active children it was always necessary to locate a quiet place to write away from home. I am especially grateful to Commander A. P. Chartier MSC, USN, the administrative officer of the Naval Hospital at Bethesda, Maryland, for making available to me the facilities of the Medical School board room, and to our good friends and next-door neighbors in Chevy Chase, the Norman Smiths, for letting me clutter up a room in their home for weeks.

A great many people assisted in the writing of the book, including the scores of *Enterprise* men who were interviewed, and wives who foraged through old papers and pictures for me.

My editor Robert Loomis, with his constant encouragement, patient understanding and knowledgeable suggestions, has been a friend and a guide throughout.

Finally, I owe to Ernest Hemingway, who saw the first

few chapters, his example and initial encouragement which kept this book as true as I could write it.

BIBLIOGRAPHICAL NOTES

The reader should keep in mind that this book is solely the story of *Enterprise*. The point of view is exclusively that of her people. The times of day used are those kept on her clocks and the watches of her men. Only enough background information is included to relate her experiences to the general contemporary situation.

Because of the nature of this book certain basic sources were utilized throughout. Other sources applied only to specific incidents or time intervals, and they are listed below under the major divisions to which they refer.

The basic sources were the official Deck Log, Action Reports, War Diary, Plans of the Day, and miscellaneous correspondence of USS *Enterprise*. Of equal importance were the Action Reports and War Diaries of the embarked air groups and squadrons. A solid structure of facts was available in the official "Narrative History and Chronological Order of Events, USS *Enterprise* (CV-6) 12 May 1938—25 September 1945" and a supplement thereto. Three huge volumes of photographs covering the ship's whole active life, collectively entitled *"War Album USS* Enterprise" and ably captioned by Lieutenant (jg) C. J. Flynn, USNR, were of great value.

The historical board of the USS *Enterprise* Association, in the years just after World War II, drew up and mailed out some six hundred questionnaires to former *Enterprise* people. Of these approximately one hundred were returned completed and provided excellent material on specific incidents throughout the life of the ship.

Similar data, but from the other side, on particular battles and campaigns, was supplied by the U. S. Strategic Bombing Survey *Interrogations of Japanese Officers*. A semiofficial pamphlet, entitled "Saga of the USS *Enterprise*," enlarged slightly and dramatized the official narrative history, and Lieutenant (jg) C. J. Flynn did about the same thing in another pamphlet, "The Ghost Still Gallops."

In addition to the above, a number of books were helpful. The most consistently valuable was Samuel Eliot Morison's multivolume *History of Naval Operations in World War II*, followed closely by Karig, Harris, and Manson's *Battle Report*. Other excellent books, frequently consulted, were *The Navy's Air War, A Mission Completed* by the Aviation History Unit of DCNO (Air); W. F. Halsey and J. Bryan III's *Admiral Halsey's Story;* Fleet Admiral E. J. King's *U. S. Navy at War 1941—1945;* Theodore Taylor's *The Magnificent Mitscher;* Admiral F. C. Sherman's *Combat Command;* and *Le Survivant du Pacifique* by Georges Blond.

BOOK 1 (the beginnings to Guadalcanal)

The account of this critical first six months of the war as seen from *Enterprise* is based primarily on two unpublished and unofficial accounts and several interviews, backed up by the general sources listed above, plus additional specific material. The two unofficial accounts are "USS *Enterprise* Through the First Year of the War" by Commander C. W. Fox, SC, USN, and "The First Six Months," a journal kept by a pilot of Fighting Six. The officers interviewed for this section were: Captains R. W. Mehle, H. P. Lanham, W. R. Pittman, J. G. Daniels, W. K. Rawie and Commander R. Klassy, all USN. Mrs. Darlene F. Craven furnished valuable *Enterprise* orders and memoranda from the effects of her late husband, Commander Conrad W. Craven, USN, a junior officer in the Engineer Department early in the war; he was also one of the Big E's last skippers.

Two official publications relate to this period: *The Defense of Wake,* a Marine Corps monograph by Lieutenant Colonel R. D. Heinl, Jr., USMC; and *The Japanese Story of the Battle of Midway,* issued by the Office of Naval Intelligence. *U. S. Naval Institute Proceedings* in its May 1948 issue contained an excellent article by W. L. Robinson entitled *"Akagi,* famous Japanese Carrier."

John Toland's new book *But Not in Shame* treats of the first six months of World War II in the Pacific and in my opinion is the best single source for the period.

Three contemporary books were most helpful: Eugene Burns' *And Then There Was One*, R. Trumbull's *The Raft,* and C. E. Dickinson's *The Flying Guns.* Other material used specifically for the account of the action off Midway was: *Climax at Midway* by Thaddeus Tuleja, and *The Battle of Midway* by Irving Werstein.

BOOK 2 (the Guadalcanal Campaign)

Two of the sources of Book I carry over into Book II, Mr. Burns' *And Then There Was One* and the interview with Captain Pittman. The Dusty Rhodes and Jeff Carroum incidents were based on lengthy interviews with each. Brad Williams' exploit in repairing the radar antenna under fire is derived from correspondence with him. Many of the adventures of Scouting Ten people come from an unofficial squadron diary kept by Lieutenant R. P. Waters and furnished by Commander G. G. Estes, USN. Stanley Johnston's *The Grim Reapers* does a similar but more complete job for Fighting Ten. A wealth of information over several months was provided by Commander F. C. Herriman, USN, who was executive officer of a squadron in which I served while the book was being written, as well as Commander George G. Estes, with whom I was stationed in Washington; Commander Estes was most helpful in answering many impromptu questions about incidents which had occurred some fifteen years previous. Rear Admiral William I. Martin, USN, was kind enough to make available a long Saturday morning for a thorough discussion of his distinguished career in the Big E and also to provide about twenty pounds of scrapbooks, clippings and correspondence which provided invaluable detail from Guadalcanal on.

Other useful information was supplied by Mr. Francis T. Green, Mr. John Culbertson and Captain J. W. McConnaughhay, USN.

Mrs. James H. Flatley was kind enough to let me go through the mementos of her husband's brilliant service, and Captain R. E. Raeder, USN, furnished impressions of *Enterprise* from another ship in the force, the USS *North Carolina*.

BOOK 3 (from Bremerton to Tomi Zai)

This long and extremely busy period was the most difficult to relate. Here alone there was enough exciting new material for a full-length book, and the necessary cutting was arduous and painful. Most of the data for this section came from various unofficial and unpublished accounts and from interviews and correspondence. The accounts were: "Air Group Ten in Action" by Lieutenant F. J. Russell, Jr., USNR; "High Points and Low Points in the Itinerary of the Buzzard Brigade," a journal of Torpedo Ten; "Night Life," a similar journal of Night Torpedo Ninety; "Night Carrier Air Group Ninety—a History"; "History of Night Torpedo Squadron Ninety, 25 August 1944 through 31 May 1945"; "Account of Being Shot Down and Rescued at Saipan" by Commander William I. Martin, USN; and an anonymous personal diary kept by a junior gunnery officer in *Enterprise*.

Captain Edward G. Colgan, USNR, for whom I had the privilege to work during a tour of duty in DCNO (Air), acted as a ready source of answers to scores of questions which arose during the writing of this part of the book. Rear Admiral T. J. Hamilton, USN (Ret), Captains R. O. Devine and L. L. Bangs, USN, Commander R. F. Kanze, Mr. Walter Chewning and Mr. C. J. Flynn provided additional data. Mr. John Munro of Harvard University, in addition to his monumental job of indexing and organizing the data supplied by the *Enterprise* Association, supplied valuable facts from his own experiences aboard. Commander K. T. Shortall and Mrs. Jean Hunt filled me in on the general atmosphere and geographical and social details of the Bremerton-Seattle area around the time of the Big E's stay. Captain G. F. Rodgers, USNR, assisted me in understanding the brief Butch O'Hare era in *Enterprise*. Mr. Gardner Turner was kind enough to turn over to me a considerable quantity of revealing clippings, notes and miscellaneous mementos of his time aboard. Captain S. E. Ruehlow, USN, in a detailed letter, both provided helpful facts and put me in contact with Mr. Francis T. Green, already mentioned.

The most helpful published material for this section of the book came from J. A. Field, Jr.'s *The Japanese at Leyte Gulf; The Great Pacific Victory* by Gilbert Cant; B. Vogel's article, "Truk—South Sea Mystery Base," in the October, 1948, issue of *U. S. Naval Institute Proceedings;* and *The Capture of Makin* by the History Division of the U. S. War Department.

EPILOGUE

Data on the Big E's post-Tomi Zai activities was derived from her logs, the supplementary official history and other general sources mentioned earlier. The details of her scrapping I owe to an excellent article by R. F. Demplewolff in May, 1960, issue of *Popular Mechanics*.